INTELLECTUAL PROPERTY: PATENTS, TRADEMARKS, AND COPYRIGHTS

TITLES IN THE DELMAR LCP SERIES

Ransford C. Pyle, *Foundations of Law for Paralegals: Cases, Commentary, and Ethics,* 1992.

Peggy N. Kerley, Paul A. Sukys, Joanne Banker Hames, *Civil Litigation for the Paralegal,* 1992.

Jonathan Lynton, Donna Masinter, Terri Mick Lyndall, *Law Office Management for Paralegals,* 1992.

Daniel Hall, *Criminal Law and Procedure,* 1992.

Daniel Hall, *Survey of Criminal Law,* 1993.

Jonathan Lynton, Terri Mick Lyndall, *Legal Ethics and Professional Responsibility,* 1994.

Michael Kearns, *The Law of Real Property,* 1994.

Angela Schneeman, *The Law of Corporations, Partnerships, and Sole Proprietorships,* 1993.

William Buckley, *Torts and Personal Injury Law,* 1993.

Gordon W. Brown, *Administration of Wills, Trusts, and Estates,* 1993.

Richard Stim, *Intellectual Property: Patents, Copyrights, and Trademarks,* 1994.

Ransford C. Pyle, *Family Law,* 1994.

Jack Handler, *Ballentine's Law Dictionary: Legal Assistant Edition,* 1994.

Jonathan Lynton, *Ballentine's Thesaurus for Legal Research & Writing,* 1994.

Daniel Hall, *Administrative Law,* 1994.

Angela Schneeman, *Survey of American Law,* 1994.

INTELLECTUAL PROPERTY: PATENTS, TRADEMARKS, AND COPYRIGHTS

Richard Stim

Lawyers Cooperative Publishing

Delmar
Publishers Inc.

Cover design by John Orozco
Cover photo by Mike Gallitelli

Delmar Staff:

Administrative Editor: Jay Whitney
Developmental Editor: Christopher Anzalone
Project Editors: Laura Gulotty/Andrea Edwards Myers
Production Coordinator: James Zayicek
Art/Design Coordinator: Karen Kunz Kemp

For information, address:

Delmar Publishers Inc.
3 Columbia Circle
P.O. Box 15015
Albany, New York 12212-5015

Printed in the United States of America

1 2 3 4 5 6 7 8 9 10 XXX 00 99 98 97 96 95 94

Library of Congress Cataloging-in-Publication Data

Stim, Richard.
   Intellectual property: patents, trademarks, and copyrights /
Richard Stim.
      p.   cm. — (Delmar paralegal series)
   Includes bibliographical references and index.
   ISBN 0-8273-5487-8
      1. Intellectual property—United States.   2. Legal assistants—
United States—Handbooks, manuals, etc.   I. Title.   II. Series.
KF2980.S75 1993
346.7304'8—dc20
[347.30648]   93–17349
                                                            CIP

CONTENTS

CHAPTER 9   Trademarks: Selection, Evaluation, and
             Registration   294

CHAPTER 12   Patent Research, Application, and Dispute
Resolution   475

DELMAR PUBLISHERS INC.

 AND

LAWYERS COOPERATIVE PUBLISHING

ARE PLEASED TO ANNOUNCE THEIR PARTNERSHIP
TO CO-PUBLISH COLLEGE TEXTBOOKS FOR
PARALEGAL EDUCATION.

DELMAR, WITH OFFICES AT ALBANY, NEW YORK, IS A PROFESSIONAL EDUCATION PUBLISHER. DELMAR PUBLISHES QUALITY EDUCATIONAL TEXTBOOKS TO PREPARE AND SUPPORT INDIVIDUALS FOR LIFE SKILLS AND SPECIFIC OCCUPATIONS.

LAWYERS COOPERATIVE PUBLISHING (LCP), WITH OFFICES AT ROCHESTER, NEW YORK, HAS BEEN THE LEADING PUBLISHER OF ANALYTICAL LEGAL INFORMATION FOR OVER 100 YEARS. IT IS THE PUBLISHER OF SUCH RE-KNOWNED LEGAL ENCYCLOPEDIAS AS **AMERICAN LAW REPORTS, AMERICAN JURISPRUDENCE, UNITED STATES CODE SERVICE, LAWYERS EDITION,** AS WELL AS OTHER MATERIAL, AND FEDERAL- AND STATE-SPECIFIC PUBLICATIONS. THESE PUBLICATIONS HAVE BEEN DE-SIGNED TO WORK TOGETHER IN THE DAY-TO-DAY PRACTICE OF LAW AS AN INTEGRATED SYSTEM IN WHAT IS CALLED THE "TOTAL CLIENT-SERVICE LI-BRARY®" (TCSL®). EACH LCP PUBLICATION IS COMPLETE WITHIN ITSELF AS TO SUBJECT COVERAGE, YET ALL HAVE COMMON FEATURES AND EXTEN-SIVE CROSS-REFERENCING TO PROVIDE LINKAGE FOR HIGHLY EFFICIENT LEGAL RESEARCH INTO VIRTUALLY ANY MATTER AN ATTORNEY MIGHT BE CALLED UPON TO HANDLE.

INFORMATION IN ALL PUBLICATIONS IS CAREFULLY AND CONSTANTLY MON-ITORED TO KEEP PACE WITH AND REFLECT EVENTS IN THE LAW AND IN SOCIETY. UPDATING AND SUPPLEMENTAL INFORMATION IS TIMELY AND PROVIDED CONVENIENTLY.

FOR FURTHER REFERENCE, SEE:

AMERICAN JURISPRUDENCE 2D: AN ENCYCLOPEDIC TEXT COVERAGE OF THE COMPLETE BODY OF STATE AND FEDERAL LAW.

AM JUR LEGAL FORMS 2D: A COMPILATION OF BUSINESS AND LEGAL FORMS DEALING WITH A VARIETY OF SUBJECT MATTERS.

AM JUR PLEADING AND PRACTICE FORMS, REV: MODEL PRACTICE FORMS FOR EVERY STAGE OF A LEGAL PROCEEDING.

AM JUR PROOF OF FACTS: A SERIES OF ARTICLES THAT GUIDE THE READER IN DETERMINING WHICH FACTS ARE ESSENTIAL TO A CASE AND HOW TO PROVE THEM.

AM JUR TRIALS: A SERIES OF ARTICLES DISCUSSING EVERY ASPECT OF PARTICULAR SETTLEMENTS AND TRIALS WRITTEN BY 180 CONSULTING SPECIALISTS.

UNITED STATES CODE SERVICE: A COMPLETE AND AUTHORITATIVE ANNOTATED FEDERAL CODE THAT FOLLOWS THE EXACT LANGUAGE OF THE STATUTES AT LARGE AND DIRECTS YOU TO THE COURT AND AGENCY DECISIONS CONSTRUING EACH PROVISION.

ALR AND ALR FEDERAL: SERIES OF ANNOTATIONS PROVIDING IN-DEPTH ANALYSES OF ALL THE CASE LAW ON PARTICULAR LEGAL ISSUES.

U.S. SUPREME COURT REPORTS, L ED 2D: EVERY REPORTED U.S. SUPREME COURT DECISION PLUS IN-DEPTH DISCUSSIONS OF LEADING ISSUES.

FEDERAL PROCEDURE, L ED: A COMPREHENSIVE, A–Z TREATISE ON FEDERAL PROCEDURE—CIVIL, CRIMINAL, AND ADMINISTRATIVE.

FEDERAL PROCEDURAL FORMS, L ED: STEP-BY-STEP GUIDANCE FOR DRAFTING FORMS FOR FEDERAL COURT OR FEDERAL AGENCY PROCEEDINGS.

FEDERAL RULES SERVICE, 2D AND 3D: REPORTS DECISIONS FROM ALL LEVELS OF THE FEDERAL SYSTEM INTERPRETING THE FEDERAL RULES OF CIVIL PROCEDURE AND THE FEDERAL RULES OF APPELLATE PROCEDURE.

FEDERAL RULES DIGEST, 3D: ORGANIZES HEADNOTES FOR THE DECISIONS REPORTED IN FEDERAL RULES SERVICE ACCORDING TO THE NUMBERING SYSTEMS OF THE FEDERAL RULES OF CIVIL PROCEDURE AND THE FEDERAL RULES OF APPELLATE PROCEDURE.

FEDERAL RULES OF EVIDENCE SERVICE: REPORTS DECISIONS FROM ALL LEVELS OF THE FEDERAL SYSTEM INTERPRETING THE FEDERAL RULES OF EVIDENCE.

FEDERAL RULES OF EVIDENCE NEWS

FEDERAL PROCEDURE RULES SERVICE

FEDERAL TRIAL HANDBOOK, 2D

FORM DRAFTING CHECKLISTS: AM JUR PRACTICE GUIDE

GOVERNMENT CONTRACTS: PROCEDURES AND FORMS

HOW TO GO DIRECTLY INTO YOUR OWN COMPUTERIZED SOLO PRACTICE WITHOUT MISSING A MEAL (OR A BYTE)

JONES ON EVIDENCE, CIVIL AND CRIMINAL, 7TH

LITIGATION CHECKISTS: AM JUR PRACTICE GUIDE

MEDICAL LIBRARY, LAWYERS EDITION

MEDICAL MALPRACTICE — ALR CASES AND ANNOTATIONS

MODERN APPELLATE PRACTICE: FEDERAL AND STATE CIVIL APPEALS

MODERN CONSTITUTIONAL LAW

NEGOTIATION AND SETTLEMENT

PATTERN DEPOSITION CHECKLISTS, 2D

QUALITY OF LIFE DAMAGES: CRITICAL ISSUES AND PROOFS

SHEPARD'S CITATIONS FOR ALR

SUCCESSFUL TECHNIQUES FOR CIVIL TRIALS, 2D

STORIES ET CETERA — A COUNTRY LAWYER LOOKS AT LIFE AND THE LAW

SUMMARY OF AMERICAN LAW

THE TRIAL LAWYER'S BOOK: PREPARING AND WINNING CASES

TRIAL PRACTICE CHECKLISTS

2000 CLASSIC LEGAL QUOTATIONS

WILLISTON ON CONTRACTS, 3D AND 4TH

FEDERAL RULES OF EVIDENCE DIGEST: ORGANIZES HEADNOTES FOR THE DECISIONS REPORTED IN FEDERAL RULES OF EVIDENCE SERVICE ACCORDING TO THE NUMBERING SYSTEM OF THE FEDERAL RULES OF EVIDENCE.

ADMINISTRATIVE LAW: PRACTICE AND PROCEDURE

AGE DISCRIMINATION: CRITICAL ISSUES AND PROOFS

ALR CRITICAL ISSUES: DRUNK DRIVING PROSECU-
TIONS

ALR CRITICAL ISSUES: FREEDOM OF INFORMATION
ACTS

ALR CRITICAL ISSUES: TRADEMARKS

ALR CRITICAL ISSUES: WRONGFUL DEATH

AMERICANS WITH DISABILITIES: PRACTICE AND COM-
PLIANCE MANUAL

ATTORNEYS' FEES

BALLENTINE'S LAW DICTIONARY

CONSTITUTIONAL LAW DESKBOOK

CONSUMER AND BORROWER PROTECTION: AM JUR
PRACTICE GUIDE

CONSUMER CREDIT: ALR ANNOTATIONS

DAMAGES: ALR ANNOTATIONS

EMPLOYEE DISMISSAL: CRITICAL ISSUES AND
PROOFS

ENVIRONMENTAL LAW: ALR ANNOTATIONS

EXPERT WITNESS CHECKLISTS

EXPERT WITNESSES IN CIVIL TRIALS

FORFEITURES: ALR ANNOTATIONS

FEDERAL LOCAL COURT RULES

FEDERAL LOCAL COURT FORMS

FEDERAL CRIMINAL LAW AND PROCEDURE: ALR AN-
NOTATIONS

FEDERAL EVIDENCE

FEDERAL LITIGATION DESK SET: FORMS AND ANAL-
YSIS

PREFACE

At the first meeting of any new class, a student usually has two questions: (1) Will this class be interesting? (2) Will this course help me get a job? For the student taking an intellectual property course, the answer to both questions should be a strong and definite "Yes!"

It is difficult for an intellectual property course not to be interesting. The subject matter of copyrights, trademarks, and patents makes the classroom come alive as students are drawn into discussions about rights associated with Elvis Presley, J. D. Salinger, and the Coca-Cola Company. By focusing on real people and actual business problems, the student is dropped into the complex but fascinating world of inventors, writers, musicians, and artists. There are many intellectual challenges for students—for example, distinguishing between a sound recording and the underlying musical work—but these challenges are always tempered by the colorful subject matter.

Not only is the course interesting for students, but the course should also be equally interesting for instructors. In my own experience of teaching intellectual property, every class has had students who have forced me to rethink my opinions on intellectual property. Often, it is the student's *lack* of knowledge that creates a unique perspective on copyright, trademark, or patent law. For this reason, class discussion is always encouraged.

As for the second question—"Will this course help me get a job?"—the answer is as close as the nearest legal newspaper want ads. There is no doubt, within the legal profession, that the leading legal specialty currently desired by legal employers is intellectual property. A recent article in the *American Bar Association Journal* stated, "Forget the trendy law practice areas of the 1980s . . . intellectual property is where the action will be in the 1990s." As a case in point, consider one of San Francisco's largest law firms, Morrison Foerster. In 1990, it did not have an intellectual property division. In 1992, it had 75 attorneys and registered agents handling intellectual property. It is not only law firms that are adding intellectual property divisions. Many large companies have established in-house intellectual property legal departments. *Legal Assistant*

Today has acknowledged that intellectual property is one of the most desired paralegal specialties. My collection of employment ads for legal assistants includes intellectual property positions at law firms, computer companies, publishing companies, biotechnology firms, entertainment conglomerates, and even large real estate and brokerage firms. A second employment advantage for legal assistants is that intellectual property law is primarily based on federal law, making it a mobile specialty. The paralegal preparing a federal trademark or copyright application in Maryland will follow the same principles as the paralegal in Alaska.

The purpose of this text is to offer a readable, one-volume guide that can function as textbook and (it is hoped) as a resource for paralegals working in the area of copyright, trademark, trade secret, and patent law. The book is divided approximately as follows: copyright (40 percent), trademarks and unfair competition (30 percent), patents (20 percent), and trade secrets (10 percent). Although it is intended primarily as a textbook, some of its features make it useful as a desk reference as well. There is a fairly detailed explanation of preparing copyright and federal trademark applications, as well as practical guidelines for the maintenance of intellectual property rights. When possible, federal and state statutes, addresses for state and federal offices, and a listing of secondary references are provided. In addition, the text's glossary adds to the enduring value of the book.

In an effort to maintain uniformity for the paralegal student, this book incorporates features successfully applied in other Delmar paralegal texts. Each chapter starts with a "Commentary," a scenario applying the chapter principles to a "real-life" problem. These hypotheticals are often based upon actual caselaw. Legal terms appear in **boldface** and definitions are provided in the margins. Each chapter also includes learning objectives, questions for review and discussion, activities, and a chapter project. There are numerous checklists and charts, which are intended to simplify the subject matter.

Considerable emphasis is also placed upon the use of computers in the law office. Almost every employment advertisement for intellectual property legal assistants requires some form of computer literacy. Although nothing can replace hands-on experience, this book attempts to explain some of the uses and applications of computers in preparing applications, maintaining records, performing trademark and patent searches, and protecting confidential information.

Finally, the intellectual property cases of Judge Learned Hand are capsulized throughout the book. As any intellectual property practitioner will agree, Judge Hand had an unequalled influence on American intellectual property law. Judge Learned Hand's brilliant and well-written decisions formed the voice of modern intellectual property law, and his pithy interpretations make him the single most-cited intellectual property source in caselaw and treatises.

The enormity of the subject matter made this a challenging text to assemble. I hope that future revisions will enable me to devote more space to international protection of intellectual property, as well as related areas of law such as the evolving right of publicity, false advertising, and § 43(a) of the Lanham Act. I look forward to reviewing comments from students and instructors regarding this text. Please contact me with comments on CompuServe, I.D. #71614,1663. Good luck!

ACKNOWLEDGMENTS

This book exists because Jay Whitney, an editor at Delmar, recognized a need for an intellectual property text for paralegals. He removed all roadblocks, set the project on the fast track, and pleasantly cajoled me into finishing it within one year. The book is also the result of assistance and input from many other students, friends, and professionals. All the staff at Delmar were very helpful and efficient; thanks to everyone, including Chris Anzalone and Glenna Stanfield. In addition, personal thanks to the people who assisted me: Roberta Grenadier, Joseph D. Stim, Nico Sophiea, Don Ciccone, Sasha Rose Stim-Vogel, Howard Thompson, Gail Penner, S. Murphy, Matthew Polazzo, Juliana Bergman, and Lindsay Hutton.

My students and fellow instructors at San Francisco State University and the University of San Francisco were encouraging and helpful in modifying my five years of photocopied textual materials into a working textbook—special thanks to Lee Gallery, Laureen Spini, Rick Kowall, Deanna Packenger, and Diane Tucker (who started me on my course as a paralegal instructor). And, of course, a tip of the hat to Professor J. Thomas McCarthy for setting the standard by which all intellectual property writing should be measured.

In addition, the following reviewers provided extremely detailed assistance that helped me avoid errors, embarrassment, and unnecessary material.

Stuart Beck
Philadelphia Institute, PA

Julius Fisher
Montclair State College
Montclair, NJ

David Brinkman
George Washington University
Washington, DC

Steven M. Getzoff
New York University
New York, NY

Ernest Gifford
Oakland University
Rochester, MI

Louis Papa
Long Island University
CW Post Campus, NY

Mark S. Thomas
Meredith College
Raleigh, NC

The author wishes to thank all the businesses and organizations who graciously supplied copies of their marks or photographs herein displayed. Their inclusion in this text by no means implies endorsement of this text or approval of the concepts by which they are placed.

The following acknowledgments have been listed in the order that they appear within the text.

Walt Disney photo
Courtesy of The Bettman Archive

Coca-Cola logo
Courtesy of the Coca-Cola Company

Photo of semiconductor
Courtesy of NASA

Lotus logo
Lotus 1-2-3 Package Art © 1992 Lotus Development Corporation. *Used with permission of Lotus Development Corporation.* Lotus, 1-2-3 and the 1-2-3 logo are registered trademarks of Lotus Development Corporation.

WordPerfect logo
Courtesy of WordPerfect Corporation

Elvis Presley Trademark Infringement ad
"Elvis" and "Elvis Presley" are trademarks of Elvis Presley Enterprises, Inc. © 1993 Elvis Presley Enterprises, Inc. Reproduced with permission.

Saturday Night Live cast photo
Courtesy of NBC Photo

MTV logo
Courtesy of MTV Networks

CBS "eye" logo
Courtesy of CBS Inc.

ESPN logo
Courtesy of ESPN, Inc. Reproduction of the ESPN logo is strictly prohibited.

No-copy-software ad, SPA
Courtesy of Software Publishers Association

Hallmark Cards logo
Courtesy of Hallmark Cards, Inc.

Football player
Courtesy of the Miami Dolphins

CNN logo
Courtesy of Cable Network News

LEXIS logo
Courtesy Mead Data Central, Inc.

Genentech logo
Courtesy of Genentech, Inc.

Hewlett-Packard logo
Courtesy of Hewlett-Packard Company

Art Buchwald photo
Photograph distributed by the Los Angeles Times Syndicate.
Photo by Bill O'Leary

Baskin-Robbins logo
Courtesy of Baskin-Robbins Ice Cream Co.

Lotus 1-2-3 logo
Lotus 1-2-3 Package Art © 1992 Lotus Development Corporation.
Used with permission of Lotus Development Corporation. Lotus and
1-2-3 are registered trademarks of the Lotus Development Corporation.

Hilton Hotel logo
Courtesy of the Hilton Hotels Corporation, Beverly Hills, CA

AMA logo
Courtesy of the American Medical Association

Apple logo
Photo courtesy of Apple Computer, Inc.

Xerox logo
Courtesy of Xerox Corporation

Olympic Committee logo with rings
Courtesy of United States Olympic Committee

NEXIS logo
Courtesy Mead Data Central, Inc.

Compu-Mark logo
Courtesy of Thomson & Thomson

Thomson & Thomson logo
Courtesy of Thomson & Thomson

Paramount logo
Paramount Pictures logo used by permission

Nike logo
Reprinted with permission of NIKE, Inc.

Chevron logo
Courtesy of Chevron Corporation

Dow Chemical logo
Used with permission of The Dow Chemical Company

du Pont logo
Courtesy of E. I. du Pont de Nemours and Company

Kleenex logo
*KLEENEX is a registered trademark of Kimberly-Clark Corporation.
Used by permission.*

Nabisco logo
*The NABISCO CORNER TRIANGLE is a registered
trademark of Nabisco, Inc. Used by permission.*

Gallo logo
Courtesy of E. & J. Gallo Winery

Polaroid logo
Courtesy of Polaroid Corp

Johnson & Johnson logo
Courtesy of Johnson & Johnson

Band-Aid logo
Courtesy of Johnson & Johnson

John Deere logo
Courtesy of Deere & Co.

Black & Decker logo
Courtesy of the Black & Decker Corporation

Hoover logo
Courtesy of the Hoover Company

NIDR logo
Courtesy of the National Institute for Dispute Resolution

Stephen King photo
Photo by Tabitha King. Courtesy of Viking Penguin.

Working on a legal textbook can turn an academic wordsmith into a nutty professor. I would not recommend trying it alone. Fortunately, my co-pilot was able to shelter me through the process, proofreading each chapter, making comments, and, when necessary, forcing me to escape from numerous electromagnetic fields and ride my bike along the Great Highway. Considering that her musical career was in full throttle and she also was working part-time as a couture assistant, I definitely have to say (in a totally major way) thanks, Angel.

TABLE OF CASES

CHAPTER 1
Intellectual Property: An Introduction

*Because color broadcasting originated with NBC, all of
Letterman's broadcasts must be in black and white.*

*Letterman cannot use an incendiary device to blow up a GM pickup
truck because those are intellectual properties of NBC.*

Mr. Letterman cannot use the name "Letterman" because it originated with the singing group.

Jay Leno on Intellectual Property

OUTLINE

COMMENTARY

Diskco, a software company, recently purchased another company, VidGame, a video game company. VidGame owns many successful video game products, especially a series of games based upon an animated character named Gekko the Gila. *An engineer at VidGame recently developed the* Jumpstick, *which is similar to a computer joystick but hooks directly to the player's arm. Although VidGame is a successful company, the former owner was lax in protecting its legal rights. Diskco's president is concerned about protecting all of the products and properties acquired from VidGame. He asks advice from your law firm about how best to analyze and protect the properties acquired from VidGame. Your supervising attorney requests that you begin researching an appropriate course of action.*

OBJECTIVES

This chapter introduces you to the basic principles of intellectual property law. After reading this chapter, you will be able to:

- Describe the disciplines that comprise intellectual property law.
- Define a copyright, trademark, patent, and trade secret.
- List the elements of an intellectual property audit.
- Determine the ethical obligations of legal assistants regarding intellectual property.
- Explain the principles of the right of publicity.
- Contrast the various recording and registration requirements in intellectual property law.
- Identify the major tasks performed by paralegals in the intellectual property law arena.
- Differentiate between intellectual property and other forms of property.
- Know the basics of protection for fine art and semiconductor chips.
- Outline the basic requirements for patent, trademark, copyright, and trade secret protection.
- Discuss the rationale for granting artists and inventors a monopoly over their creations.

1.1 INTELLECTUAL PROPERTY LAW

Writers, inventors, and artists transform ideas into tangible property. When this **intellectual property** qualifies under law, the creator is granted certain rights. For example, the author of a book can prevent others from copying it. The owner of a patented invention can prevent others from making, using, or selling the device. After a time, these exclusive rights may be lost or taken from the owner and given to the public. For example, copyright protection has ended for books written by Mark Twain and anyone is free to copy *Huckleberry Finn* and *The Adventures of Tom Sawyer.*

Ownership of intellectual property is similar to ownership of other forms of property. For example, the owner of a home has the right to exclude others from trespassing on or converting the property. The owner of intellectual property also has the right to exclude others from infringing or taking the property. The homeowner can lease, sell, or transfer the home through a will or deed. The intellectual property owner can license, sell, or will the patent, copyright, or trademark. Like the homeowner, the owner of intellectual property is subject to rules regarding government registration, recordation, abandonment, and forfeiture.

However, not all products of the mind qualify for protection under intellectual property law. It is the function of legal counsel to recognize, preserve, and protect these intellectual property rights. Intellectual property law covers copyrights, patents, trademarks, and trade secrets. It also includes related areas of law such as the right of publicity, unfair competition, false advertising, fine arts law, and protection of semiconductor chips. All these disciplines recognize property that is created by the human mind.

Why Protect Intellectual Property?

Some people find it difficult to understand why a man named McDonald cannot open a hamburger shop called *McDonald's* or why a person who spends $600 on a computer program cannot make copies for her friends. One way to begin the study of intellectual property is to contemplate what it would be like if intellectual property were not protected. The following examples demonstrate the underlying rationale for intellectual property protection. Subsequent chapters will demonstrate the procedures and practices used by attorneys and legal assistants to offer adequate protection so that artists, inventors, and businesses can exploit and protect their respective rights.

The Doctor and the Cancer Cure.   Imagine if a doctor spent 20 years in her private laboratory inventing and perfecting a new drug to cure cancer. As soon as she finished her development, a drug company took her formula, began manufacturing the drug, refused to pay her any money, and failed to credit her for her work. The drug company made billions of dollars from the sale of the drug. Although humans may benefit from the sale of this drug, the *economic* reward of this development is diverted from the person who devoted money, creativity, and hard work to its creation. If there is no reward, then there is no incentive to continue researching. Why devote money and time to inventing new processes, drugs, or other inventions if anyone is free to take and sell these discoveries?

Every country is dependent on new inventions. That is why the drafters of the U.S. Constitution sought to promote progress by granting to inventors the exclusive right to their inventions and discoveries for a limited time. The

LEGAL TERMS

intellectual property
Any product of the human mind that is protected under law.

Constitution establishes a tradeoff. Inventors have a monopoly for a period of years. After the term expires, the invention is free for all to use. This monopoly is known as a **patent** and (assuming maintenance fees are timely paid) lasts for 17 years. Obtaining a patent depends upon several variables, as explained later in this chapter. If the doctor who invented the cancer cure obtained a patent, she could attempt to stop the drug company from manufacturing the drug without her permission and she could authorize another drug company to sell the drug and pay her royalties. After the patent expired, anyone could manufacture the drug without paying royalties.

The Writer and His History Book.   Imagine that a writer spent six years writing a history of African-American migration. A publisher obtained a copy of the manuscript, began publishing the book without permission, and refused to pay the author. Later a movie company made a film based upon the book. The movie company also failed to pay the writer. Obviously, there would be little incentive for the author to create a new work if it could be taken without his permission. The U.S. Constitution establishes the basis for federal **copyright** protection for works by authors, artists, musicians, and others. An author or artist can prevent others from copying, selling, performing, or making derivative versions of the work. The author of the history book could prevent the publisher and movie company from making and distributing their versions of his book.

The Food Company and the Tartar Sauce.   Consider a small food company, Smallco, that has perfected a new tartar sauce recipe and sells it under the name *Smarter Tartar.* A large food company, Foodco, bribes a chef at Smallco, obtains the recipe, and alters it slightly by adding preservatives, salt, and sugar. Foodco sells its product under the same name *Smarter Tartar.* There is something inherently unfair about this theft of the recipe and the product name. First, a deception is perpetrated on consumers. Purchasers who were loyal to Smallco's original *Smarter Tartar* may be confused by Foodco's version and purchase it by mistake. These consumers have been deceived. Second, this is an unethical business practice. Companies should compete fairly—the misappropriation of a successful product name and the bribery of an employee are unscrupulous acts. If the law permitted such acts, then corrupt behavior by competing companies would be encouraged and competition would be stifled.

   Smarter Tartar is a **trademark** of Smallco because it identifies and distinguishes Smallco's tartar sauce product from others. The goal of trademark law is to avoid customer confusion. The first user of a trademark in commerce may exclude others from using a confusingly similar mark on similar goods. This principle is derived from English law known as **unfair competition.**

   The tartar sauce recipe is a **trade secret** because it was developed by Smallco, was kept in confidence, and gives the business an advantage over competitors. Foodco's theft by bribery is improper and under state law it

LEGAL TERMS

patent
   The legal right, for a limited term, to exclude others from using, selling, or making an invention or discovery as described in the patent claims.

would be punished. The principles of trade secret law are to preserve ethical behavior and standards of competition and to encourage research and development by affording protection to confidential information.

An Intellectual Property Profile: Walt Disney

Another way to understand intellectual property is to examine the ways in which an artist or inventor interacts with the law. An interesting example is the empire created by Walt Disney, an American artist and entrepreneur (see figure 1-1). In the 1920s, Mr. Disney's small animation studio produced several cartoons based upon a character named *Oswald the Rabbit*. The cartoons were produced in conjunction with a larger motion picture studio, Universal. At a meeting with a Universal executive in New York in 1928, Mr. Disney was informed that Universal claimed the rights to *Oswald*. Moreover, Universal had hired away several of Disney's animators so that they could draw the character for Universal. Mr. Disney was forced to relinquish any claim to *Oswald*.

Distressed, Disney and his wife set out by train for California. On the train ride, Mr. Disney drew a new cartoon character named Mortimer Mouse. He showed the drawing to his wife, Lillian, who liked the character but suggested changing the name to Mickey Mouse. Back in California, Mr. Disney featured his new character in several shorts, including the early sound cartoon "Steamboat Willie." This time Mr. Disney was careful to acquire copyright ownership to his *Mickey Mouse* films and character.

Throughout the 1930s, Mr. Disney's company produced many successful cartoon shorts featuring characters such as *Mickey Mouse* and *Donald*

copyright
The legal right to exclude others, for a limited time, from copying, selling, performing, displaying, or making derivative versions of a work of authorship.

trademark
Any word, symbol, design, device, slogan, or combination that identifies and distinguishes goods.

unfair competition
A collection of common law precedents and statutes, that protect against unfair business practices.

trade secret
Any formula, pattern, device, or compilation of information (1) that provides a business with an opportunity to obtain an advantage over competitors who do not know or use it; and (2) is the subject of reasonable efforts to maintain its secrecy.

FIGURE 1-1
Walt Disney, entertainment and marketing mogul.
Photo courtesy of
The Bettman Archive.

Duck. He also produced award-winning shorts in which animation was mixed with famous symphonic pieces. It was in the creation of these *Silly Symphonies* that Walt Disney overcame an obstacle that had plagued animators. Because all cartoon backgrounds were one-dimensional (i.e., drawn on a flat piece of paper), the early cartoons lacked any sense of depth. If a camera moved in closer and closer to a background, it became obvious that the trees were flat. Mr. Disney wanted the cartoons to have the same depth of field as live-action movies. He hired craftsmen to build a special camera with several planes of glass at different levels. By placing different parts of the background on different pieces of glass and placing the camera above, Disney was able to create the impression of depth that is now taken for granted in high-quality animation. The first short that used the invention, "The Old Mill," received an Academy Award in 1937. The Disney invention, the multiplane camera, was granted a patent on April 23, 1940.

At the end of the 1930s Mr. Disney took a big gamble. Nobody had ever made a full-length cartoon feature. Many people felt the idea was foolish, including Mr. Disney's business partner and brother, Roy. But Walt Disney believed that the public was ready for full-length animated features, and in 1937 he borrowed heavily from the Bank of America to make the film *Snow White and the Seven Dwarfs.* The success of that film led to other classic animated features, including *Fantasia, Lady and the Tramp,* and *One Hundred and One Dalmatians.* These films are now among the most valuable copyright properties in the world and have been re-released numerous times and in different formats, such as videotape and laser videodiscs. The public never seems to tire of them.

In the 1950s Walt Disney took several new directions. His company began producing live action films such as *Treasure Island, Mary Poppins, Old Yeller,* and *The Absent-Minded Professor.* He also exploited a new medium, television, with the series "Walt Disney Presents," and sold musical recordings through his record label, *Buena Vista.* In 1953, Walt Disney hired a new assistant to sell Disney merchandise. By placing images of copyrighted Disney characters on lunchboxes and clothing, Walt Disney's company began earning $50 million a year. (See figure 1-2.) Merchandising now provides a major source of revenue for the Disney company.

But Walt Disney was eager to do something much more diverse. He often visited carnivals and zoos with his two daughters and wondered why such parks did not accommodate adults as well as children. Mr. Disney spent a great deal of money designing a character-based theme park, but was met with consistent rejection from bankers and investors. Walt's brother Roy was so opposed to the idea that for a time he refused to speak with Walt or permit use of the Disney name in association with the project. However, with great perseverance Walt Disney created the first family theme park, *Disneyland,* which opened in 1955. Theme parks like *Disneyland* and *Disney World* now seem an obvious means of generating entertainment revenue, but it required a pioneer such as Walt Disney to turn this idea into tangible property.

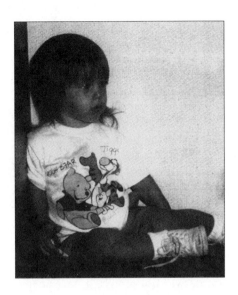

FIGURE 1-2
The shirt this child is wearing is
an example of merchandising
opportunities derived from
copyrighted products.

Today the company that Disney started is one of the largest owners of
intellectual property in the world and *Mickey Mouse,* though over 60 years
old, continues to generate revenue in films, on merchandise, and at the Disney theme parks. Copyright law protects the cartoons, characters, films, television programs, sound recordings, and books. Trademark law protects the
word *Disney* and the distinctive Disney logos and symbols. Patent law protects numerous inventions created or acquired by the Disney company. For
example, since 1990, the Disney company has acquired patent rights for the
design of an amusement ride, a film editing table, methods for creating artificial rain and artificial fog, and a computer imaging system, among numerous
other inventions. Trade secret law protects the confidential information about
the Disney company, such as unpublished plans for new theme parks, financial information, marketing strategies, and unreleased entertainment projects.

The previous sections discussed the rationale for intellectual property
and provided examples. The following sections offer an introduction to the
intellectual property disciplines discussed in this book.

Copyright Law

Copyright law protects music, architecture, writing, computer programs, plays, movies, dance, or visual arts such as graphic arts, sculptures,
photographs, or paintings. The person that creates a copyrightable work is
known as an **author**. For example, Walt Disney was the author of the original *Mickey Mouse* cartoons. Under certain circumstances, the author may be
the person or entity that commissions the work or pays for the work under an

LEGAL TERMS

author
  The person or entity
  that creates a
  copyrightable work,
  or, under certain
  circumstances, the
  person or entity that
  commissions the work
  or pays for the work
  under an employment
  agreement.

employment agreement. If an author's creation meets the standards of copyright law, it is considered a protectible **work of authorship.** Copyright protection is derived from the Constitution and therefore it is subject to federal law. The states are preempted from regulating copyright law and litigation concerning the validity and infringement of copyrights must be filed in federal courts. For a work to acquire copyright protection, it must be an original work of authorship that is fixed in a perceptible form. To be "original" under copyright law generally means that the author did not copy it from another source and that the work is more than a trivial variation on any preceding work. Originality under copyright law does *not* mean that the work possesses a high degree of creativity. For example, anyone is free to create a cartoon character based upon a mouse as long as the artist does not copy or base it on the unique features of *Mickey Mouse* (e.g., his four-fingered hands and extra-large circular ears). A work is "fixed" when it is embodied in a tangible form. For example, Walt Disney originally had an idea to draw *Mickey Mouse.* He visualized the character in his head. But *Mickey Mouse* was not fixed and therefore was not protected under copyright law until Mr. Disney put *Mickey* on a piece of paper. At that point, the character was "fixed" and perceptible by others.

It is a common misconception that copyright protection is acquired by registering a work. This is not true. Although registration is strongly recommended (because it provides certain rights and remedies), rights under the current copyright law are acquired by creating and fixing the work, not by registering the work. That is, the right to prevent others from copying, selling, displaying, performing, or making derivatives accrues once the work is finished. For example, imagine that after reading this chapter, a paralegal is inspired to write a song about intellectual property law. She strums the chords on her guitar and sings several improvised verses. Once she records this on tape or writes down the words and chords, she has fixed the work and copyright protection begins.

Initially, copyright law in America protected only books, maps, and charts, but over the centuries, the protection of copyright has been extended to architecture, music, computer programs, and movies and videos. The length of protection for copyright is longer than for patents. Generally, under the current copyright act, an individual author enjoys copyright protection for his or her life plus 50 years. In some cases, copyright protection may be 75 years from the date of first publication or 100 years from creation of the work, whichever is shorter. One reason for the difference between the patent and copyright term is that books, music, and art often take years before their value is appreciated. For example, a painting may not reach its true value until after the painter's death. Similarly, the writer of a pop song from the 1950s may earn substantial royalties (often in excess of earlier revenues) when the song is rediscovered and played decades later on "oldies" radio stations. The same is not generally true of inventions or discoveries. In addition, after a certain number of years, it would be unfair to deny the public the right to freely use inventions or discoveries such as medical or other scientific breakthroughs.

Patent Law

Congress has established the subject matter that can be protected under U.S. patent law. This subject matter includes processes, machines, articles of manufacture, and compositions of matter, all of which may, if qualified, be registered as **utility patents**. Utility patents are the most common type of patent and most patent references throughout this book are to utility patents. For example, Mr. Disney's multiplane camera qualified for a utility patent. Other examples of utility patents include the safety pin, the electron microscope, and a method for preserving human blood. A utility patent is issued for a term of 17 years, unless extended because the inventor's ability to market the invention was delayed because of requirements of U.S. government regulating agencies (e.g., the Food and Drug Administration's safety review of a new drug).

In addition to utility patents, the statutory subject matter also includes ornamental design patents and plant patents. A **design patent** is available for a new, original, and ornamental design for an article of manufacture. Unlike the utility patent (which can exist for 17 years), the design patent is issued for a term of 14 years. The design patent protects only the appearance of an article, not its structure or utilitarian features. For example, a stained glass window design could be protected by a design patent.

A **plant patent** is granted to the first person who first appreciates the distinctive qualities of a plant and reproduces it asexually (i.e., by means other than seeds). A plant patent, like a utility patent, lasts for a maximum of 17 years.

The owner of a patent may exclude others from making, using, or selling the patented subject matter (i.e., the invention, design, or plant) throughout the United States. The federal laws regarding patent rights are derived from the Constitution and litigation involving the validity or enforcement of patent rights must be brought in the federal courts.

Trade Secret Law

A *trade secret* is any formula, pattern, device, or compilation of information (1) that provides a business with an opportunity to obtain an advantage over competitors who do not know or use it and (2) is the subject of reasonable efforts to maintain its secrecy. Once the secret is made available to the public, trade secret protection ends. For example, the original plans for an exhibit at the European Disney theme park would qualify as a trade secret provided the company kept the information confidential. Once the exhibit opened, the trade secret status would end as to information that was made publicly available. Other examples of trade secrets are marketing strategies, manufacturing techniques, computer algorithms, recipes, or formulas. The trade secret has value because it *is not* published or publicly distributed. This is quite different from the value of a copyright or a patent to its owner, who makes money from the publication and distribution of copies or objects embodying the copyrighted or patented material.

LEGAL TERMS

work of authorship
Creation of intellectual or artistic effort fixed or embodied in a perceptible form and meeting the statutory standards of copyright protection.

utility patents
Legal protection granted for inventions or discoveries that are categorized as machines, processes, compositions, articles of manufacture, or new uses of any of these.

design patent
Legal protection granted for a new, original, and ornamental design for an article of manufacture. A design patent protects only the appearance of an article and not its structure or utilitarian features.

plant patent
Legal protection granted to the first person who first appreciates the distinctive qualities of a plant and reproduces it by means other than seeds.

Because of trade secret law, a business can have some security in the knowledge that the unlawful misappropriation of confidential research is punishable and damages may be recovered. Although certain federal statutes may be used to prevent the misappropriation of confidential business information, trade secrets are generally protected under state law. Most states have adopted state statutes to protect against the misappropriation of trade secrets.

Trademark Law

Subscribers to the *Disney Channel* see a familiar logo—two circular ears and the top of a head, much like the *Mouseketeer* hat worn by child actors on the Disney Television shows. This distinctive pair of "mouse ears" is a trademark because it informs consumers that they are getting goods or services from the Walt Disney Company. A trademark is any word, symbol, design, device, logo, or slogan that identifies and distinguishes one business's product from that of another. Other examples of trademarks include *Bayer* as a trademark for aspirin and *Gallo* as a trademark for wine. A mark that is used in the sale or advertising of services to identify and distinguish services performed for the benefit of others is known as a **service mark.** For example, *Super Shuttle* is a service mark for an airport shuttle service. Both service marks and trademarks are often referred to as trademarks. A trademark does not have to be words; it can be a visual image (like the *Disney* mouse ears), music, a package design, or even architectural features of a building. For example, McDonald's "golden arches" or the image of Colonel Sanders on *Kentucky Fried Chicken* take-out boxes are both trademarks.

The owner of a trademark may exclude others from using a similar trademark on similar goods or services. The underlying principle of trademark law is to protect consumers against confusion. In some cases, use of a similar trademark may be barred even if consumers are not likely to be confused. This is because a court has determined that use of the similar mark dilutes or tarnishes the trademark. Trademark rights are derived from the **common law,** a system of legal rules derived from the precedents and principles established by court decisions.

Trademark law is regulated by both the federal and state governments. Depending on various factors, lawsuits for infringement of trademarks may be brought in either federal or state court. Unlike other forms of intellectual property, trademark law does not grant rights to the person who first creates the trademark—only to the person who first uses it in commerce. Table 1.1 lists the four intellectual property disciplines and an explanation of their differences.

LEGAL TERMS

service mark
 A mark used in the sale or advertising of services to identify and distinguish services performed for the benefit of others.

common law
 A system of legal rules derived from the precedents and principles established by court decisions.

1.2 PARALEGAL TASKS IN INTELLECTUAL PROPERTY LAW

This section sets forth some of the tasks that paralegals perform when working in the intellectual property law arena.

Copyright

The copyright registration process is straightforward enough that many registration tasks can be accomplished by a paralegal. This is particularly true if the business or client is requesting periodic but similar types of registration. For example, a legal assistant working for a magazine company or music publishing company will quickly learn the basic principles for preparing and

	What Is Protected?	Examples	Length of Protection	State or Federal Law
Patent	Machines, compositions, plants, processes, articles of manufacture, ornamental designs	*Polaroid* instant camera; chemical fertilizer; Luther Burbank's hybrid peach; process of manipulating genetic traits in mice (and the resulting mice); ironing board; design of Bo Diddley's box-shaped guitar	17 years* (except 14 years for design patents)	Federal
Copyright	Books, photographs, music, recordings, fine art, graphics, videos, film, choreography, architecture, computer programs	*Gone with the Wind* (book and movie); Andy Warhol prints; Michael Jackson's *Thriller* (music recording, compact disc, artwork, choreography, and video); architectural plans for the Trump Tower; *Microsoft Windows* computer program	Life of the author plus 50 years (for works created by a single author). Other works may be protected for 100 years from date of creation or 75 years from first publication**	Federal
Trade Secret	Formula, method, device, or compilation of facts or any information that is maintained in confidence and gives a business an advantage over competitors.	*Coca-Cola* formula; survey methods used by professional pollster; buying habits of ethnic groups; new invention for which patent application has not been filed	For as long as information remains confidential and functions as a trade secret	State
Trademark	Word, symbol, logo, design, slogan, or device that identifies and distinguishes products or services	*Coca-Cola* name and distinctive "wave" logo; *Good Housekeeping* seal; *Pillsbury* doughboy character	For as long as the business continuously uses the trademark in connection with goods or services	State and federal

TABLE 1.1
Intellectual Property Disciplines

* *Some patents may be extended under certain circumstances.*
***These are general standards applied under the Copyright Act of 1976.*

processing applications. Note, though, that certain copyright applications (for example, for a computer software program) may require additional knowledge or background to adequately preserve rights. Paralegals may also be called upon to maintain copyright records. In businesses with a large copyright portfolio, this means keeping track of the registrations and any changes in ownership. Paralegals may be asked to investigate the copyright status of a work. This means that the legal assistant may have to help an attorney in determining whether a work may be used without permission. This can include searching copyright records or using a computer database. As in all intellectual property disputes, the paralegal will assist in pretrial procedures, trial preparation, and posttrial activity. These functions are similar to all federal litigation. However, some special litigation concerns may require copyright knowledge. For example, it may be necessary to expedite a copyright registration or locate an expert witness.

Patent

The tasks performed by a paralegal in patent law are not as broad as those performed in trademark or copyright law. This is because most patent law practice requires extensive knowledge of engineering and the sciences. Attorneys and agents who prepare patent applications must have a degree in engineering or science (or equivalent knowledge acquired through work experience), must pass a special examination, and must be certified by the Patent and Trademark Office in Washington, D.C. Each step of patent protection, such as determining patentability, preparing the patent, dealing with objections from government patent examiners, and litigating patent infringement lawsuits, requires an extensive technical background. If a paralegal possesses the necessary engineering or science degree or technical background, that paralegal may become a *patent agent*. A patent agent is permitted to prepare patent applications, but cannot give legal advice or represent litigants in patent disputes. However, the duties of and requirements for becoming a patent agent are beyond the scope of this book.

Paralegals often assist in patent searching. The paralegal may use computer searching services to locate information during preparation of an application or litigation. Paralegals also assist in patent litigation to the same extent that they may assist in copyright or trademark litigation (i.e., preparing a trial notebook, locating expert witnesses, etc.). A paralegal may also assist in maintenance of a patent portfolio. That is, the paralegal may manage the payment of periodic maintenance fees or may calendar payments or requirements due under a patent license agreement.

Trade Secrets

Trade secrecy requires security. The creation of a company security plan may be a task in which the paralegal is involved. Education of employees and clients as to trade secret law is also crucial, as the failure to treat material as confidential may result in loss of rights. Trade secret protection also requires execution of special confidentiality or nondisclosure agreements between employees, independent consultants, or other companies. The paralegal may be involved in the preparation of such agreements or in the maintenance of employee records. Trade secret litigation, by its nature, requires that sufficient safeguards be in place to guarantee that the secret is not lost through disclosure during litigation. For this reason, in addition to other litigation functions, the paralegal may be involved in the maintenance and drafting of special protective orders.

Trademarks

Paralegal involvement in trademark protection begins with the trademark selection process. The paralegal may be required to obtain examples of similar marks in use (i.e., the trademark search), and both the paralegal and the supervising attorney may be involved in advising the client on choice of mark. An attorney will supervise the preparation of trademark registration applications, but the process includes many tasks that can be accomplished by a paralegal. The same assistance may be required in state registration of trademarks. For example, a paralegal working for a real estate company may be required to communicate with the offices of various secretaries of state to obtain and prepare state trademark applications. Paralegals are also involved in the policing and protection of trademarks. Trademarks, like trade secrets, require ongoing attention. The paralegal may assist in the tracking of infringing and counterfeit marks and may participate in programs that preserve trademark status. In the event of infringement litigation, the paralegal will assist in the traditional pretrial and trial functions.

The Intellectual Property Audit

Intellectual property is an integrated set of disciplines. That is, there may be an overlap between copyrighted works and trademarks, patents and trade secrets. For example, *Mickey Mouse* can function as a copyrightable character and his distinctive ears and head can function as a trademark. The secret formula used in *Coca-Cola* is protected as a trade secret while the names, *Coke* and *Coca-Cola* are protected under trademark law.

When examining a new product, therefore, it is necessary to consider *all* of the areas of law discussed in this chapter. Is the design protected under copyright or patent law? Is the product a patentable invention or process? Are any names or symbols used to identify the product? Are these protectible as trademarks? Is any information regarding the product a trade secret?

One task that requires an integrated view of intellectual property is the **intellectual property audit**, which is a review and analysis of a company's copyright, trade secret, patent, and trademark portfolio. In the Commentary at the beginning of this chapter, Diskco, a software company, recently purchased a video game company and is concerned about intellectual property

protection of its video game products. The first step would be to interview the employees of the video game company and review and categorize the intellectual property. For example, the animated character *Gekko the Gila* may be protectible under copyright law. The new *Jumpstick* apparatus may be protectible under patent law. The integration of the video game company's patent, copyright, trade secret, and trademark rights becomes evident when an intellectual property audit is performed.

Intellectual property audits may occur in three different contexts. First, a company may wish to implement a plan to manage and protect its intellectual property. The audit may result in a memorandum detailing suggestions on how best to protect intellectual property rights. Second, intellectual property audits are also performed, as in the case of Diskco, when one company purchases another. The intellectual property audit may offer a valuation of the various properties as well as information regarding any potential claims of infringement. Finally, an intellectual property audit may be performed at the time of an infringement lawsuit to help a company determine the likelihood of its exposure as a defendant. A legal assistant may be involved when an attorney performs an audit, because many of the tasks require review of recordkeeping and indexing of materials. Companies that are audited may have their own legal assistants prepare for the inspection by organizing and copying all relevant documents.

Sometimes an audit occurs in two stages. First, the auditing attorneys may request information regarding the creation and protection of intellectual property. For example, in the case of the video game company, VidGame, attorneys may visit the VidGame offices, speak with VidGame engineers, and review the records of the creation of VidGame computer programs. Following this preliminary research, a more comprehensive audit may occur, involving review of all agreements, registrations, and security precautions. Figure 1-3 is an example of a letter sent to a client regarding an intellectual property audit.

**SAMPLE LETTER FOR INTELLECTUAL PROPERTY AUDIT
OF COMPUTER COMPANY**

Dear Mr. Stumpfel:

You asked our office to prepare a proposal for an intellectual property audit of your new subsidiary VidGame. Our objective is to devise a program to protect Diskco's intellectual property rights. We estimate that an audit should take between fifteen and twenty-five hours of our time. These figures are only an estimate and the amount of time actually required will depend upon the materials that must be reviewed.

To determine the policies required to protect intellectual property rights, the audit should focus on four areas of intellectual property: trade secrets, copyright, trademarks, and patents.

FIGURE 1-3
Sample intellectual
property audit letter

1. Trade Secrets. A trade secret is any business information (e.g., formulas, ideas, compilations of data, or processes) that is maintained in confidence and that gives the business an advantage over competitors who do not know or use it. A trade secret comes into existence when the party developing the secret determines to treat it with secrecy and takes all steps necessary to prevent the disclosure of the secret. We shall need to interview VidGame employees who are familiar with office security and systems and employment relationships. In addition, we will need to examine: (1) employee personnel rules and agreements; (2) consulting and third-party agreements; and (3) computer security. Following this examination, we shall prepare an outline advising as to the best means to correct any trade secrecy deficiencies. The estimated time to complete the trade secrecy aspect of the intellectual property audit will be between six and ten hours.

2. Copyright. Copyright law protects original works of authorship fixed in a tangible medium of expression, such as computer programs and video games. In addition, Congress has extended a limited form of copyright-like protection to semiconductor chip products. To audit VidGame's copyrights, our office will need to interview VidGame employees knowledgeable about the software programs that are created and owned by VidGame. In addition, we will need to examine all relevant copyright registrations, applications, licenses, assignments, and work-for-hire agreements to determine whether Diskco is acquiring full authorship of VidGame's copyrightable works. After making this review, our office will prepare an outline recommending action regarding copyright protection. The estimated time to complete the copyright portion of the intellectual property audit would be three to six hours.

3. Trademarks. A trademark is any mark that is used by a manufacturer or merchant to identify goods and distinguish them from goods manufactured by others. Our office will need to examine any relevant trademark registration applications, licenses, or assignments. Depending on the status of the marks, our office will recommend a course of action to best protect the marks. The estimated time to complete the trademark portion of the intellectual property audit would be one to three hours.

4. Patents. To acquire a patent, the object or process must be (1) a new and useful industrial or technical process, machine, article of manufacture, or composition of matter (i.e., chemical compounds) or any new and useful improvements for these items; or (2) a new, original, and ornamental design for an article of manufacture. The person creating the patentable material, process, or design must be the first to do so. Patents will not be granted for anything that is known by others in this country, already protected by patent, or described in a printed publication published more than one year ago in this or a foreign country. Further, a patent cannot be obtained for anything that is first publicly used or on sale in this country one year or more prior to the date of filing of a patent application with the U.S. Patent & Trademark Office. We have associated patent counsel to review any potentially patentable inventions, such as the *Jumpstick,* and to assist, if necessary, in the preparation and prosecution of filings before the Patent & Trademark Office. Such costs shall be included as part of the audit. In addition, we should review any technology agreements in which patentable

FIGURE 1-3
(Continued)

materials are licensed or rights are transferred. Such a review would take three to six hours, depending upon the extent of the licensing.

Please call me after you have an opportunity to review this so that we can determine a prudent course of action for VidGame to implement protective policies and procedures.

Very truly yours,
T. R. Jones
Attorney at Law

FIGURE 1-3
(Continued)

1.3 ETHICAL OBLIGATIONS OF THE PARALEGAL IN INTELLECTUAL PROPERTY LAW

The national paralegal associations have formulated rules of professional ethics for legal assistants. These guidelines are derived from the American Bar Association's Model Code of Professional Responsibility and Model Rules of Professional Conduct. Several paralegal texts, including Jonathan Lynton's *Legal Ethics and Professional Responsibility* and Ransford C. Pyle's *Foundations of Law for Paralegals* recommend placing an emphasis on the American Bar Association's ethical rules rather than the rules of the national paralegal associations. For that reason, the ethical obligations of paralegals in intellectual property are analyzed in the light of the ABA rules.

Confidentiality

One of the most important ethical concerns in intellectual property law is confidentiality. Many clients are extremely reluctant to disclose any information about their writing, inventions, or discoveries for fear that someone will exploit their concepts to their detriment, loss, or harm. To encourage the free exchange of information between an inventor or author and an attorney, a privileged relationship is created when a client retains an attorney. Generally, information that the client discloses in confidence to the attorney may be disclosed only with the consent of the client or under special circumstances (e.g., a court order). The nature of intellectual property makes it an interesting topic for conversation. For example, consider a client who invents a new device that makes people laugh when they touch it. It may be difficult for a paralegal working in that law office to avoid disclosing this incredible invention to a friend after work. Or imagine that a law firm represents a famous rock musician, and a paralegal learns that the musician will be suing a famous songwriter for copyright infringement. The paralegal may have an overwhelming desire to share this information with a friend who is a fan of the musician, but disclosure of this information could have a detrimental effect on the client. Disclosure of the invention might result in loss of trade secret or patent rights. Disclosure of the litigation might have a detrimental effect on the law firm's strategy.

The unique and extraordinary subject matter of intellectual property should not affect the paralegal's obligation to maintain the confidentiality of the client's disclosures. Perhaps more than any other field of property law, the law of intellectual property demands confidentiality. When in doubt as to the correct course of action regarding disclosure, the legal assistant should always seek advice from the supervising attorney. Although the client controls the privilege of confidentiality, the supervising attorney can best advise the paralegal as to the parameters of any disclosure.

Conflict of Interest

With some limitations, an attorney is ethically prohibited from representing a client whose interests conflict with those of another client or a former client. For example, suppose a law office formally represented an inventor who created a method of cutting grass by remote control. The law office has ceased representing the inventor and is now retained by a company that wants to sue the inventor. The law firm would have a conflict of interest, because it acquired information about the invention in confidence and such knowledge may adversely affect the interest of the inventor. It is possible (although unlikely) that the inventor and the company both could provide written waivers of any claims of conflict of interest. Under certain circumstances, such waivers may permit the attorney's representation of the company. Absent such a waiver, the law firm would be ethically prohibited from representing the company.

A paralegal, like an attorney, often moves from one law firm to another. Because knowledge can be acquired at one firm and used at another, it is important that the legal assistant fully disclose any *potential* conflicts. For example, a paralegal previously worked at a family law firm representing a writer in a divorce. At the paralegal's new job at an intellectual property law firm, a publishing client intends to sue the writer. The paralegal may believe that there is no conflict of interest. However, the prudent course of action is for the paralegal to disclose all the relevant facts to the supervising attorney and allow him or her to make the final determination as to whether any subsequent action should be taken.

Unauthorized Practice of Law

It is a violation of the ethical codes and rules for an attorney to assist in the unauthorized practice of law. State law also prohibits the unauthorized practice of law. But what is the unauthorized practice of law? The representation of a client before a court by a nonattorney, or a person not licensed to practice law in the state, generally constitutes the unauthorized practice of law, although some states or jurisdictions permit a nonattorney to appear on routine or uncontested matters.

A paralegal who has been certified by the Patent and Trademark Office as a patent agent may prepare, file, and prosecute patents within the Office. However, this certification requires an engineering or science degree and the applicant must pass an examination. The law is less clear in regard to preparing trademark and copyright applications. Some trademark and copyright filings are routine and fairly repetitive, and many paralegals quickly learn to perform these tasks. However, the most prudent course in all paralegal document preparation is to seek, and demand if necessary, that an attorney review the document or form before it is filed. It is not enough for the attorney to "trust" the paralegal. Attorney review of paralegal-prepared documentation ensures that the client is receiving the necessary analysis to preserve and protect intellectual property rights.

Finally, the paralegal should avoid giving legal advice. There is no prohibition against a paralegal providing a client with information about the law, but an ethical line is crossed when the paralegal advises the client as to the correct course of action. For example, it is permissible for a paralegal to advise a client as to the options for depositing a copy of a computer program during copyright registration. However, it would be giving legal advice to assure a client that a certain form of deposit will best protect the client's legal rights.

The paralegal also must be careful when conveying information from an attorney to a client. Clients sometimes want to be told that a certain course of action is permissible, and they pressure the attorney or paralegal to agree with the client's view. For example, a paralegal has been instructed to tell a client that a proposed trademark is likely to infringe. The client wants to use the mark and asks the paralegal whether a certain change to the mark would make it suitable. The paralegal, eager to please the client, suggests that it would probably be all right and that she will check with the attorney. The client may interpret this as permission for use of the trademark. This obviously can lead to a disastrous result. Therefore, a legal assistant should be wary of making any claims or statements regarding use of the client's property regardless of the circumstances of the statement.

JUDGE LEARNED HAND ON INTELLECTUAL PROPERTY LAW

Most of the chapters in this text include a reference to Judge Learned Hand. Judge Hand served first as a federal district judge and then as an appellate court judge in New York. He retired in the 1960s after 50 years on the bench. With the exception of Oliver Wendell Holmes, Judge Hand remains the most quoted jurist of the

20th century, and his statements about the law regularly appear in judicial opinions and treatises. One reason for Judge Hand's impact and popularity is his skill as a writer. Unlike other legal practitioners, Judge Hand avoided "legalese" and emphasized simplicity of language.

Although Judge Hand was knowledgeable in many areas of law, his handling of intellectual property cases set an unequalled standard. In copyright, patent, and trademark law, Judge Hand had an uncanny ability to weigh the facts and make a determination with timeless implications. For example, in the case of *Reiss v. National Quotation Bureau, Inc.,* 276 F. 717 (1921), a man had authored a book of meaningless phrases and nonsense words that were used to create codes. He sued a publisher who copied his work. The publisher argued that copyright could not protect the writing because it had no "meaning." Judge Hand disagreed. He pointed out that copyright law did not impose a standard of comprehensibility on works of authorship. "I see no reason why words should [not be protected] because they communicate nothing. They may have their uses for all that, aesthetic or practical, and they may be the productions of high ingenuity, or even genius." The judge pointed out that the code words were like "an empty pitcher," in that they had a prospective meaning but as yet had not received it. "Conceivably," wrote Judge Hand, "there may arise a poet who strings together without rational sequence—perhaps even coined syllables—through whose beauty, cadence, meter and rhyme he may seek to make poetry."

The *Reiss* case, decided in 1921, may appear to be only about the protection of nonsense words. But the underlying principle—that the copyrighted work does not have to be comprehensible to those who view it—has lived on as an established rule of copyright. A half-century after the decision, opponents of legal protection for computer programs argued that the software could not be protected under copyright because the computer code was incomprehensible. A national commission disagreed and used the Reiss rationale as the basis for responding to opponents.

Just as artists and inventors look to the future, Judge Hand's view of intellectual property demonstrates great legal forethought. Summaries of some of his decisions are presented throughout the book.

1.4 ANCILLARY RIGHTS AND RELATED LAW

Although space limitations prohibit a comprehensive analysis in this text, there are some peripheral areas of intellectual property law, including the right of publicity, semiconductor chip protection, and fine arts protection, all of which have become increasingly important in the past decade. A brief summary of these areas is presented in this section. Source material on where to obtain more information appears at the end of the chapter.

Right of Publicity

The *right of publicity* is the right to control the commercial exploitation of a person's name, image, or persona. Although this right is granted to all persons, it is commonly associated with celebrities because the name or image of a famous person may be used to sell products or services. For example, a vendor may use a picture of the pop singer, Madonna, on T-shirts. However, if Madonna did not authorize this use of her image, the vendor would have infringed Madonna's right of publicity. (In addition, the vendor may have infringed the copyright in the photograph.) The right of publicity extends only to commercial exploitation. The use of a name, likeness, or persona for news, information, or public-interest purposes is not a violation of the right of publicity. For example, to write about the group *New Kids on the Block*, in a celebrity magazine, or even to conduct a reader poll about the *New Kids on the Block* would not violate the group members' right of publicity.

The right of publicity is not only for celebrities. Any person whose name or image is used to sell products may claim a misappropriation of this right. For example, if a baby's photograph is used to sell watches, permission must be obtained from the child (or the child's guardian, as required by state law). It is for this reason that all models or persons used in advertisements or endorsements typically are required to sign consent or release agreements. For a payment, the model grants a right to use the image. In addition, the owner of copyright in the photograph must also authorize the reproduction of the photo.

Like other intellectual property rights, the owner of the right of publicity can exclude others from using the property. However, unlike other forms of intellectual property, the right of publicity is not always "descendible" (i.e., it does not always survive the death of the person who owns the right). For example, a copyright lasts for the life of the author plus 50 years. However, only 11 states currently recognize that the right of publicity survives death. Tennessee, the home of the late Elvis Presley, was one of the first states to recognize that the right of publicity could be passed to survivors. For this reason, the estate of Elvis Presley still controls the right to merchandise the name and images of the rock-n-roll star. Similarly, California recognizes the survivability of the right, and the estate of Marilyn Monroe acquired the right to exploit her name and likeness following her death.

Although certain claims regarding false endorsement (e.g., misappropriation of a person's name, image, or voice to falsely infer endorsement or approval of a product) may be brought under federal law, under § 43(a) of the Lanham Act, the right of publicity is primarily a matter of state law. Some states have passed statutes regulating these rights. Other states do not have right-of-publicity statutes but have established common law rights under caselaw. As Table 1.2 demonstrates, as of the writing of this book, Alaska, Arizona,

Colorado, Idaho, Louisiana, Mississippi, New Hampshire, New Mexico, North Dakota, Oregon, South Carolina, South Dakota, Vermont, and Wyoming have neither a statute nor caselaw regarding the right of publicity. However, because this area of law is evolving rapidly, the legal assistant should review the most current law when evaluating rights from state to state.

State	Statute	Common Law
Alabama	No	Yes
Alaska	No	No
Arizona	No	No
Arkansas	No	Yes
California	Cal. Civ. Code §§ 3344 & 990	Yes
Colorado	No	No
Connecticut	No	Yes
Delaware	No	Yes
District of Columbia	No	No
Florida	Fla. Stat. § 540.08	Yes
Georgia	No	Yes
Hawaii	No	Yes
Idaho	No	No
Illinois	No	Yes
Indiana	No	Yes
Iowa	No	No
Kansas	No	Yes
Kentucky	Ky. Rev. Stat. § 391.170	No
Louisiana	No	No
Maine	No	Yes
Maryland	No	Yes
Massachusetts	Mass. Gen. Laws ch. 214, §§ 3A & 1B	No
Michigan	No	Yes
Minnesota	No	Yes

TABLE 1.2
State-by-State
Review of
Right-of-Publicity Law

State	Statute	Common Law
Mississippi	No	No
Missouri	No	Yes
Montana	No	Yes
Nebraska	Neb. Rev. Stat. § 20-201 *et seq.*	No
Nevada	Nev. Rev. Stat. § 598 *et seq.*	No
New Hampshire	No	No
New Jersey	No	Yes
New Mexico	No	No
New York	N.Y. Gen. Bus. Law. § 397	No
North Carolina	No	Yes
North Dakota	No	No
Ohio	No	Yes
Oklahoma	Okla. Stat. Ann. tit. 21, § 923.1 *et seq.*	Yes
Oregon	No	No
Pennsylvania	No	Yes
Puerto Rico	No	No
Rhode Island	R.I. Gen. Laws § 9-1-28 *et seq.*	No
South Carolina	No	No
South Dakota	No	No
Tennessee	Tenn. Code Ann. § 47-25-1101	No
Texas	Tex. Prop. Code § 26.001 *et seq.*	Yes
Utah	Utah Code Ann. § 45-3-1 *et seq.*	No
Vermont	No	No
Virginia	Va. Code §§ 8.01-40 & 18.2-216.1	No
Washington	No	Yes
West Virginia	No	Yes
Wisconsin	Wis. Stat. § 895.50	Yes
Wyoming	No	No

TABLE 1.2
(Continued)

Semiconductor Chip (Mask Works) Protection

Semiconductor chips (see figure 1-4) are semiconductor materials on which are etched tiny, complex integrated circuit patterns (comprised of two or more layers of metallic or insulating substances in a predetermined pattern). These devices aid in the transmission of electronic data inside computers and other devices. Because these devices are difficult to design but easy to copy, Congress passed the Semiconductor Chip Protection Act of 1984, which protects "mask works," the integrated circuit patterns encoded on semiconductor chips. These patterns are protected for a limited time (10 years), provided that the mask work is registered within 2 years after the mask work is first "commercially exploited." The mask work is commercially exploited when the work is distributed to the public or when a written offer is made to sell it and the chip is fixed. The Copyright Office administers the Semiconductor Chip Act. Mask works are registered by using the Copyright Office's Form MW.

Fine Arts Protection

European copyright law has traditionally granted certain rights to artists based upon moral principles. For example, the creator of a work of art or the heirs of the artist could share in subsequent sales of the work and could control or prevent, to some extent, the destruction or mutilation of a work. Under these principles, known as *droit de moral,* the artist's rights over a piece of fine art continued after the sale of the art. In this way, an unknown artist who sold a work inexpensively could share in some revenues if the work later appreciated in value.

In the United States, the Copyright Amendments Act of 1990 granted a limited right to artists who create paintings, drawings, or sculptures in a limited edition of 200 copies or less (provided they are signed and consecutively numbered). Under § 106A of the Copyright Act of 1976 (as amended), an artist has the right to claim authorship, to prevent use of his or her name on works he or she did not create, and (subject to certain limitations) to prevent

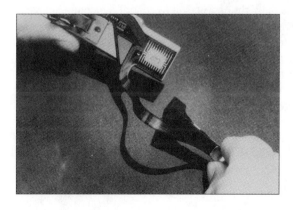

FIGURE 1-4
Semiconductors are
protected by federal law.
Photo courtesy of NASA.

intentional distortion, mutilation, or other modifications of the work of visual art. These rights complement the other rights granted to the artist under U.S. copyright law. For more information on fine art protection under federal copyright law, contact the Copyright Office, Library of Congress, Washington, D.C. 20559; (202) 707-3000.

California has passed the most comprehensive state statute regarding art preservation and resale. Under the California statute, for example, an artist may be entitled to 5 percent of the resale amount of a work of fine art. Such rights survive for 20 years after the death of the artist.[1]

SUMMARY

1.1 Intellectual property law protects the rights of people such as inventors, writers, and artists. By granting a monopoly to people who create intellectual property, the law encourages creativity. Intellectual property law includes copyright, patent, trade secret, and trademark law. Copyright law protects works of authorship, such as books, music, and art. Trademark law protects owners of names or symbols used to distinguish goods or services. Patent law protects inventions, devices, discoveries, and certain plants and designs. Trade secret law protects ownership of confidential information that gives a business an advantage over competitors.

1.2 Paralegals are involved in many aspects of the recordation, registration, transfer, and maintenance of intellectual property. To determine the extent of ownership and protection of intellectual property, a company, with legal assistance, will perform an intellectual property audit.

1.3 Ethical obligations of paralegals are analyzed in relation to the American Bar Association model rules of conduct. The attorney-client privilege binds both attorney and paralegal to a standard of confidentiality. The attorney and paralegal must avoid the conflict of interest resulting from representation of adverse interests. The paralegal also must avoid the unauthorized practice of law.

1.4 The right of publicity is the right of a person to control the commercial exploitation of his or her name, image, or persona. This right does not extend to news or editorial uses. Semiconductor chip protection is extended by Congress to "mask works," which are integrated circuit patterns embedded on silicon chips. Special protections are granted to artists who create limited-edition visual arts works. These protections may include the right to prevent destruction of the artwork and the right to receive income from subsequent resale.

NOTES

1. Cal. Civ. Code §§ 986–989.

QUESTIONS FOR REVIEW AND DISCUSSION

1. What is the rationale for granting the owner of a patent a 17-year monopoly on the invention?
2. What economic incentive is there for a country to encourage creation of patentable and copyrightable material?
3. When is artwork "fixed" under copyright law?
4. Can a work be protected under copyright if it is not registered?
5. How are patent rights acquired?
6. What elements are necessary to create a trade secret?
7. How does a company acquire rights to a trademark?
8. What are two reasons for performing an intellectual property audit?
9. What right protects a person's name or image from commercial exploitation?
10. Why is the attorney-client privilege especially crucial in the protection of intellectual property?

ACTIVITIES

1. Review the factual situation in the *Commentary* to this chapter. Identify potential trademarks, copyrights, trade secrets, and patents that Vid-Game may own.
2. Consider the career of Walt Disney as discussed in this chapter. Among the most valuable property owned by the Disney enterprises are the theme parks and full-length feature animation. Why might Walt's brother, Roy, have objected to animated features and theme parks?
3. Patent, copyright, and trademark statutes permit the owner of the intellectual property to prepare applications for registration. If the owner, who is not a lawyer, can prepare these applications, why is it considered the unauthorized practice of law for an unsupervised paralegal to perform the same services?

PROJECT

Consider the Disney theme parks, *Disneyland, Disney World,* and *EuroDisney.* These theme parks contain numerous exhibits, characters, services, and products. Prepare a chart with four columns: copyrights, trademarks, patents, and trade secrets. List as many specific elements of the theme parks as you can which would qualify in each category. For example, under copyright list all of the copyrightable characters, copyrightable merchandise, or copyrightable artwork.

FOR MORE INFORMATION

Right of Publicity
J. Thomas McCarthy, *The Rights of Publicity and Privacy* (Clark Boardman Callaghan 1987). A thorough, one-volume treatise.

Semiconductor Chip Protection Act
Information about statutory protection can be acquired from the Public Information Office, Copyright Office, Library of Congress, Washington, D.C. 20559; (202) 707-3000. Circular 100, distributed by the Copyright Office, contains information regarding mask work protection.

Fine Art Protection
Ralph E. Lerner & Judith Bresler, *Art Law* (Practising Law Institute 1989). One-volume treatise.

Toby Judith Klayman & Cobbett Steinberg, *The Artists' Survival Manual* (Charles Scribner's Sons 1984). Paperback written for artists.

Tad Crawford, *Business and Legal Forms for Fine Artists* (Allworth Press 1990). Popular one-volume paperback that includes sample contracts.

CHAPTER 2
Principles of Copyrights

The copyright law celebrates the profit motive, recognizing that the incentive to profit from the exploitation of copyrights will redound to the public benefit by resulting in the proliferation of knowledge.

Judge Pierre Leval
American Geophysical Union v. Texaco, 802 F. Supp. 1, 27 (S.D.N.Y. 1992)

OUTLINE

COMMENTARY

Your law office represents Softco, a computer company. Softco intends to distribute a promotional item, a coffee cup with three handles. Printed on the coffee cup will be a figurative drawing of Softco's president within a computer screen with the phrase, "Softco—We Offer Multiple Solutions." The company plans to produce several thousand cups for a convention. Softco's vice-president wants to make sure that no other company will distribute a cup with multiple handles. Your supervising attorney asks you to perform preliminary research to assist in determining if the cup can be protected under copyright law.

OBJECTIVES

Chapter 1 introduced you to the general principles of intellectual property law. This chapter provides a basic understanding of the principles of what can be protected under copyright and the sources of copyright law. After reading this chapter you will be able to:

- Explain the origins of federal copyright law.
- Define the concept known as federal preemption.
- Discuss the role of the U.S. Copyright Office.
- Identify the relevant U.S. Copyright Acts and Amendments.
- Know the general principle of originality used in copyright law.
- Determine whether a work meets the requirement of fixation.
- Differentiate between a work of authorship and the physical object in which it is embodied.
- List and explain the eight categories of works of authorship.
- Distinguish between a sound recording and a musical work.

- Separate a useful article from its copyrightable features.
- Describe the difference between an idea and its expression.
- Discuss the differences and similarities between compilations and derivative works.

2.1 SOURCES OF COPYRIGHT LAW

Imagine if the only way to duplicate this book was to copy it by hand. Prior to the 15th century, this was the method by which books were reproduced. It was not until the invention of the printing press that quantities of printed works could be published and distributed. Unfortunately, only publishers and booksellers profited from this invention. Authors received little compensation and their works were widely pirated. Finally, in 1710, England enacted the Statute of Anne, which granted authors an exclusive right to control the publication of their books. For the first time, authors had the legal power to stop others from copying. This grant of rights became known as *copyright.*

The drafters of the U.S. Constitution established authors' rights in Article 1, § 8, clause 8 of the Constitution. This copyright clause granted Congress the power "to promote the progress of science and useful arts, by securing for limited time to authors and inventors the exclusive right to their respective writings and discoveries." This constitutional grant became the basis for America's copyright laws.

During the past two centuries, the United States has adopted various copyright acts. The Copyright Act of 1909 governs works published between 1909 and 1978. The Copyright Act of 1976 protects works created between 1978 and the present (as well as certain works created before 1978). Though enacted in 1976, the Copyright Act of 1976 did not go into effect until January 1, 1978. Knowledge of both copyright acts is necessary for analyzing copyright issues.

Federal Preemption

Section 301 of the Copyright Act of 1976, 17 U.S.C. § 301, prohibits the states from creating any copyright laws or granting rights equivalent to copyright law. This prohibition is based upon the principle of federal **preemption**—the doctrine that the federal government has exclusive control over those powers granted to it within the Constitution and can preclude the states from exercising concurrent powers. This is derived from the supremacy clause of the U.S. Constitution, which states that "This Constitution and the laws of the United States which shall be made in pursuance . . . shall be the supreme law of the land; and the judges in every state shall be bound thereby." Title 28 of the U.S. Code, in § 1338(a), specifically provides that the federal courts shall have original jurisdiction of any civil action arising under any act of Congress relating to copyrights and that such jurisdiction shall be exclusive.

LEGAL TERMS

preemption
Authority of the federal government to preclude the states from exercising powers granted to the federal government by the Constitution.

Copyright law is regulated by the federal government in two ways: the registration of copyrighted works through the Copyright Office; and the enforcement of copyright laws in the federal court system.

The Copyright Office

The Copyright Office is a division of the Library of Congress. It is an administrative agency directed by the Register of Copyrights. Its purpose is to determine if submitted materials constitute copyrightable subject matter and then either issue a registration or explain the reason why registration is being refused. If an applicant disagrees with the decision of the Copyright Office, the Copyright Act of 1976 provides that the decision, once it is final, may be reviewed by the federal courts. The Copyright Office also issues numerous circulars and other publications, performs searches of Copyright Office information, records transfers of copyright ownership, and regulates certain compulsory licenses and royalties.

Copyright Office employees are prohibited from giving specific legal advice on the rights of authors or copyright claimants. The Copyright Office cannot advise on matters of infringement, assist in matters of publication, or enforce rights of an author under copyright law. Some rules and regulations for Copyright Office activities are established in the Copyright Act of 1976 (17 U.S.C. §§ 101 *et. seq.)* as well as in the Code of Federal Regulations (37 C.F.R. § 201 *et seq.*). The Copyright Office's rules of practice appear at 37 C.F.R. §§ 201.1–211.6.

The Federal Courts

The federal courts interpret and enforce the copyright laws. Because the federal government has exclusive jurisdiction over copyright cases, lawsuits involving the validity or infringement of a copyright can be brought *only* in the federal courts. Nevertheless, some cases involving the ownership of copyright can be brought in state court. For example, an author sells her rights to a publishing company. If a dispute arises as to the interpretation of the agreement, that litigation can be brought in state court. The most commonly litigated issue in copyright cases is whether a copyright has been infringed. **Infringement** occurs when a party violates any exclusive right granted under copyright law. The most common form of infringement is the unauthorized copying of a work.

Copyright lawsuits cannot be filed in state courts. However, if the lawsuit involves both copyright claims and state claims, the federal court is permitted to decide related claims arising under state law. This is **pendent jurisdiction**.

For instance, an employee of Diskco Company sneaks into the Softco Company's Christmas party. He copies a program for a new video game program, *Rhino's Revenge.* A few weeks later, Diskco releases *Reno's Retaliation,* which is a copy of the stolen program with some minor changes.

Softco files a federal lawsuit that includes allegations of copyright infringement and trespass. Though trespass is not a federal claim, the federal court may adjudicate the matter under the principle of pendent jurisdiction. Each party in a copyright lawsuit is guaranteed a right to appeal the district court decision. The appeal would be heard by the appropriate U.S. Court of Appeals. If either party is not satisfied with the appellate decision, that party may seek review by the U.S. Supreme Court. Such review is discretionary, and if the Supreme Court refuses to hear the case, the ruling of the appellate court is binding on the parties.

The Copyright Act of 1909

Although the Copyright Act of 1909 was later superseded by the Copyright Act of 1976, the earlier act still has significance, because works published between 1909 and 1978 are still governed by its provisions. For example, the book *The Catcher in the Rye,* by J. D. Salinger, was published in 1951. If a lawsuit arose as to the validity of the copyright in *The Catcher in the Rye,* that issue would be determined under the provisions of the Copyright Act of 1909.

The Copyright Act of 1909, like preceding U.S. copyright acts, only protects published works. Unpublished works were protected under common law, *a system of legal rules established by court decisions.* Under copyright law, a work is **published** if copies or phonorecords (in the case of sound recordings) are distributed to the public by sale or other transfer of ownership, or by rental, lease, or lending.

The Copyright Act of 1976

The Copyright Act of 1976, 17 U.S.C. §§ 101-810, is a complete revision of the Copyright Act of 1909. (Note: Many of the definitions included in this book are derived from the Copyright Act of 1976.[1]) It protects all works of authorship **created** between 1978 and the present, whether published or unpublished. It also protects unpublished works created before 1978 that are registered after January 1, 1978, and it governs the expiration of copyright in previously unpublished work created prior to 1978. Under copyright law, there is a difference between the creation and the publication of a work. A work is *created* when it is fixed in a tangible form for the first time.

Computer Software Amendments

Although the Copyright Act of 1976 was intended to encompass new technologies, disputes arose as to the issue of protectibility of computer software programs under copyright law. To clarify the protection of software, Congress amended the Copyright Act in 1980 to specifically include computer programs as protected works. A **computer program** is defined as a

LEGAL TERMS

infringement
  Violation of any exclusive right granted under copyright law; most commonly, the unauthorized copying of a protected work.

pendent jurisdiction
  Authority of the federal courts to hear a matter normally within the jurisdiction of state courts. Pendent jurisdiction exists when the state law matter is combined with a claim that is within the authority of the federal courts.

publication
  The distribution of copies or phonorecords of a work to the public by sale or other transfer of ownership, or by rental, lease, or lending; the offering to distribute copies or phonorecords to a group of persons for purposes of further distribution, public performance, or public display.

created
  When a work is fixed in a copy or phonorecord for the first time. When a work is prepared over a period of time, the portion of it that has been fixed at any particular time constitutes the work as of that time, and when the work has been prepared in different versions, each version constitutes a separate work.

computer program
  A set of statements or instructions to be used directly or indirectly in a computer to bring about a certain result.

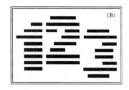

This trademark is for Lotus 1-2-3, a spreadsheet computer software.

"set of statements or instructions to be used directly or indirectly in a computer in order to bring about a certain result."

Berne Implementation Amendments

Approximately 80 nations belong to the Berne Convention for the Protection of Literary and Artistic Works. This union of countries adheres to a treaty covering categories of works. By joining the Berne Convention, the United States benefits from mutual regulations among member nations. Because various aspects of the Copyright Act of 1976 were in conflict with Berne rules, Congress amended the Copyright Act of 1976 with the Berne Implementation Amendments, which became effective on March 1, 1989. Among the modifications was the abolition of copyright notice requirements and changes regarding deposit requirements. In 1990, Congress further amended the Act to conform to Berne Convention requirements by extending copyright protection to architectural works and by granting new rights (known as *moral rights*) to the authors of works of fine art such as paintings, sculptures, and limited-edition prints.

2.2 WHAT IS PROTECTIBLE UNDER COPYRIGHT LAW?

Copyright protects the literary, musical, graphic, or other artistic form in which an author expresses intellectual concepts. An **author** is the creator of a copyrightable expression, whether literary, musical, or otherwise. However, under copyright law, this definition also may include the party that commissions a work or pays for the work under an employment agreement. Initially, the author owns the copyright but, as with other forms of property, the author of a copyrightable work may sell or transfer the ownership of copyright to a third party who thereby becomes the owner of the copyright. These concepts are explained in Chapter 4.

If the author's creation meets the standards of copyright law, it is considered a **work of authorship** protectible under copyright law. When drafting the Copyright Law of 1976, Congress specifically chose not to limit the definition of a work of authorship, realizing that authors are continually finding new ways of expression.

The Copyright Act of 1976 states that "copyright protection subsists . . . in original works of authorship fixed in any tangible medium of expression, now known or later developed, from which they can be perceived, reproduced, or otherwise communicated, either directly or with the aid of a machine or device."[2]

Originality

Originality under copyright law does not mean aesthetic worthiness, uniqueness, or novelty. It generally means that a work is original to the author and is more than a trivial variation on any preceding work. Originality requires only a modest degree of intellectual labor. For example, two photographers take pictures of a house. One uses expensive equipment and creates a magnificently composed picture, while the other uses a simple camera with a fixed lens. Each photograph would be original to its author and more than a trivial variation on preceding photos of the house. In fact, even if the photos were identical, each would be copyrightable, assuming neither photographer copied the other. Therefore, despite aesthetic issues, there would be sufficient originality to satisfy copyright for both photographs.

Unlike patent law, copyright is not based upon priority of creation. The order in which works are created does not automatically establish a superior right. All that matters is that the work be original to the author. An examiner in the Copyright Office will initially determine if a work has sufficient originality to qualify for copyright. If the applicant disagrees with the determination of the Copyright Office, the matter can be resolved by the federal courts.

Even if the Copyright Office determines that a work has sufficient originality, the issue may still arise in a copyright infringement lawsuit. If the defendant can prove to the court that the plaintiff's work lacks sufficient originality, then the plaintiff may lose copyright protection and will have no basis to vindicate a claim for copyright infringement.

Fixation

A work is **fixed** when it is embodied in a *tangible* form that is perceptible by the human senses, either directly or with the aid of a machine. The Copyright Act of 1976 requires that the work be embodied in a form that is "sufficiently permanent or stable so as to permit it to be perceived, reproduced, or otherwise communicated for a period of more than transitory duration."[3]

Under copyright law, the author's expressions must be manifested in a concrete form. Examples of works that are fixed are a song that is recorded on audiotape, a story that is printed on paper, or a visual image that is captured on photographic film. In the Commentary to this chapter, the drawing of the president of the Softco Company was affixed to a cup. This would qualify as a fixed expression. Works that are *not* fixed would include a speech that is not transcribed, a live performance of a song, or a live broadcast of a television program that is not simultaneously recorded. The requirement of fixation does not mean that a work must be manufactured or published. A handwritten diary is fixed and meets the requirement of copyrightability.

Prior to the 1976 Act, a work was protected under U.S. copyright law only if it was fixed in a form that could be directly seen or read by the human eye. This created a dilemma for songwriters in the early 20th century, because America was swept by a craze for player pianos, special pianos that were modified to play a piano roll containing perforated tracks. Millions of piano rolls were sold, but the songwriters who wrote the songs on each roll were not compensated under copyright. Why? Because the songs on the piano rolls could not be seen and read with the naked eye. Songwriters could

LEGAL TERMS

author
The creator of a copyrightable expression, whether literary, musical, or otherwise; or, under certain circumstances, the party that commissions a work or pays for the work under an employment agreement.

work of authorship
Creation of intellectual or artistic effort fixed or embodied in a perceptible form and meeting the statutory standards of copyright protection.

fixed
Embodiment of a work in a tangible medium of expression by or under the authority of the author, which is sufficiently permanent or stable to permit it to be perceived, reproduced, or otherwise communicated for a period of more than transitory duration; in the case of sounds, images, or both that are being transmitted, a work is "fixed" if a fixation of the work is being made simultaneously with its transmission.

LEGAL TERMS

copy
Tangible object (other than phonorecords) in which a work is fixed by any method now known or later developed, and from which the work can be perceived, reproduced, or otherwise communicated, either directly or with the aid of a machine or device. The term *copies* includes the material object (other than a phonorecord) in which the work is first fixed.

literary works
Works, other than audiovisual works, expressed in words, numbers, or other verbal or numerical symbols or indicia, regardless of the nature of the material objects, such as books, periodicals, manuscripts, phonorecords, film, tapes, disks, or cards, in which they are embodied.

receive compensation for printed sheet music (which could be seen and read) but not for the piano rolls. If the same rule were in effect today, the makers of motion pictures could not receive compensation for videotapes, because the viewer cannot see the work by looking directly at the videotape.

The drafters of the Copyright Act of 1976 found the requirement of visual perception to be artificial and unjustified. They extended protection to works of authorship that can be perceived directly or with the aid of a machine.

Separating the Copyrightable Work from the Physical Object

Copyright law protects fixed works of authorship. It is important to understand the difference between the protectible work and the physical forms (copies or phonorecords) in which the work may be embodied. For instance, if a photographer captures an image on photographic film, there is a distinction between the visual image and the physical or tangible object known as the photograph. The photograph is a **copy,** a tangible object that incorporates the image. The same visual image may be fixed on other items besides photographic film, such as a t-shirt, a cup, or the cover of a magazine. Each of these reproductions is a copy of the visual image. There may be many copies of a work, but only one protectible work.

2.3 THE EIGHT CATEGORIES OF WORKS OF AUTHORSHIP

The first U.S. copyright act granted protection to the creators of books, maps, and charts—all the necessary works of authorship for forging a new country. During the past two centuries, Congress has passed various copyright laws expanding the protection of copyright to include new technologies such as motion pictures, sound recordings, and computer programs. When the Copyright Act of 1976 was drafted, Congress listed seven broad categories of works. In 1990, the Copyright Act of 1976 was amended to include an eighth category, architectural works. The fact that a work does not fit into one of these categories does not disqualify it from protection. Congress intended that the act be "illustrative and not limitative." At issue in determining protectability is *not* whether a work falls into one of the categories, but whether it satisfies the requirements of § 102 of the Copyright Act of 1976.[4]

Literary Works

The textbook you are reading is a copy of a **literary work.** So is *Gone with the Wind,* the Sears catalog, a Corvette repair manual, an employee

directory, or an advertisement. The Copyright Act of 1976 defines *literary works* as works "expressed in words, numbers, or other verbal or numerical symbols or indicia, regardless of the nature of the material objects, such as books, periodicals, manuscripts, phonorecords, film, tapes, disks, or cards, in which they are embodied."

Computer software programs such as *Windows*® *and WordPerfect*® are considered literary works because they can be expressed in computer languages that use letters, words, or numbers. Certain works are not considered literary works, even though they are expressed in words. Lyrics accompanying music for a song would be part of a musical work copyright, and the script for a play would be a dramatic work.

Dramatic Works

A **dramatic work** is usually a "play" (and any accompanying music) prepared for stage, cinema, radio, or television. Although a dramatic work does not have to have dialogue or plot, it is generally a narrative presented by means of dialogue and action. *Death of a Salesman, A Streetcar Named Desire,* and *A Chorus Line* are examples of dramatic works. A dramatic work provides directions for performance. A play can be embodied either in its manuscript form or in video or another form of fixation.

Pantomimes and Choreographic Works

Choreography is the composition and arrangement of dance movement and patterns, often accompanied by music. A registrable choreographic work should be capable of being performed and usually includes direction for movement. Simple social dance steps or dances such as the "Cha-Cha" are not copyrightable. **Pantomime** or *mime* is considered a mute performance with expressive communication. Because it is a form of acting that consists mostly of gestures, there is an overlap in the categorization of pantomime and dramatic works. Traditionally pantomime and choreographic works are fixed in a system of written notation, but the Copyright Act provides that they also may be fixed in any tangible medium, including film, video, or photographs.

Pictorial, Graphic, and Sculptural Works

The Copyright Act of 1976 defines **pictorial, graphic, and sculptural works** as works that "include two-dimensional and three-dimensional works of fine, graphic, and applied art, photographs, prints and art reproductions, maps, globes, charts, diagrams, models, and technical drawings, including architectural plans." This list is not exclusive—generally a pictorial, graphic, and sculptural work is considered any visual arts work that is fixed and meets standards of copyrightability. It can range from the fine art of

dramatic works
Narrative presentations (and any accompanying music) that generally use dialogue and stage directions as the basis for a theatrical exhibition.

choreography
Composition and arrangement of dance movements.

pantomime
A form of theater expressed by gestures but without words.

pictorial, graphic, and sculptural works
Two-dimensional and three-dimensional works of fine, graphic, and applied art, photographs, prints and art reproductions, maps, globes, charts, diagrams, models, and technical drawings, including architectural plans. Such works include works of artistic craftsmanship insofar as their form but not their mechanical or utilitarian aspects are concerned. The design of a useful article is considered a pictorial, graphic, or sculptural work only if, and only to the extent that, such design incorporates pictorial, graphic, or sculptural features that can be identified separately from, and are capable of existing independently of, the utilitarian aspects of the article.

Georgia O'Keeffe, Henry Moore, or Pablo Picasso to the finger painting produced by school children.

By their nature, pictorial, graphic, and sculptural works lend themselves to reproduction on many objects. Often these objects are functional, such as a pin, a shirt, a belt buckle, or a handbag. For example, the Swatch company commissions artwork for the faces of its stylized wristwatches. Copyright law does not protect useful articles. A **useful article** is something that has some utilitarian function other than its appearance or ability to convey information. When a work is incorporated on a useful article, copyright protection only extends to the pictorial, graphic, or sculptural features that can be identified separately from, and are capable of existing independently of, the utilitarian aspects of the article. In the case of the Swatch watch, the visual image of the face may be protected, but not the mechanical or functional aspects of the watch.

LEGAL TERMS

useful article
An article having an intrinsic utilitarian function that is not merely to portray the appearance of the article or to convey information. An article that is normally a part of a useful article is considered a useful article.

audiovisual works
Works that consist of a series of related images which are intrinsically intended to be shown by the use of machines or devices, such as projectors, viewers, or electronic equipment, together with accompanying sounds, if any, regardless of the nature of the material objects, such as films or tapes, in which the works are embodied.

motion pictures
Audiovisual works consisting of a series of related images which, when shown in succession, impart an impression of motion, together with accompanying sounds, if any.

Motion Pictures and Audiovisual Works

An image of a horse embodied on a photographic slide is considered to be a pictorial work. But when that same picture is presented as part of a slide show with a series of related slides (for example, the horse in the stages of making a jump), the result is an audiovisual work. **Audiovisual works** are related images in a series, together with any accompanying sounds, which are shown by a machine or device. Protection of an audiovisual work extends to all sounds that are embodied on it, including any music, such as a motion picture soundtrack.

The Copyright Act of 1909 did not initially protect **motion pictures**. To overcome this obstacle, the early film pioneers printed each reel of images on paper and registered their works as sheets of photographs. In 1912, after the U.S. Supreme Court ruled on a case involving the film *Ben Hur,* the Copyright Act of 1909 was amended to include motion pictures.

Architectural Works

An **architectural work** is the design of a building as embodied in any tangible medium of expression, including a building, architectural plans, or drawings. The building constructed from the architectural work is a copy. If the building is located in a place that is ordinarily visible to the public, the owner of the underlying architectural work cannot prevent others from making, distributing, or publicly displaying pictures, or other pictorial representations of the building. In addition, the owners of a building embodying an architectural work do not have to obtain consent of the copyright owner of the architectural work to make alterations to the building or to authorize the destruction of the building. Note, however, if the building contains a work of visual art, such as a lobby mural, then destruction of the mural may violate state fine arts law or the moral rights provision of the U.S. Copyright Act (17 U.S.C. § 106A).

Musical Works

A **musical work** is a musical composition. For example, the song "Happy Birthday" is a musical work published in 1935. The authors receive compensation when the song is performed in plays, movies, or other works. A musical work also may be an orchestral work or music produced by traditional or electronic means. Most harmonic embellishments or rhythmic variations are considered to be in the public domain and free for all to use. One court even indicated that "originality of rhythm is a rarity if not an impossibility."[5] The predominantly protectible element of a musical composition is generally its melody.

Lyrics are words (or nonsense sounds) that accompany music and form a component of the composition. The copyright for a musical composition protects both the words and the music, and the composer can control or limit the use of either element. For example, if someone were to print the words to the rock song "Satisfaction" without permission of the songwriters, that would infringe copyright of the musical composition, even though only the lyrics were used. Certain music is not protected in the musical works category. Music that accompanies a dramatic work or an audiovisual work would be protected and registered under those respective categories.

Sound Recordings

A **sound recording** is a work resulting from the fixation of a series of musical or other sounds (including narration or spoken words). The performer, producer, or recording company usually claims copyright in the sound recording. Why is it necessary to have copyright protection for a musical work and a sound recording? Because each form of protection is different. A musical work copyright protects the musical composition. A sound recording copyright protects the way in which the composition is performed.

For example, John Lennon and Paul McCartney are the composers of the song "Yesterday." Frank Sinatra recorded the song "Yesterday." Mr. Sinatra did not write the song, so he is not entitled to claim copyright for the musical work. However, his unique arrangement and performance of "Yesterday" is entitled to sound recording copyright. Therefore, the compact disc containing Frank Sinatra's performance contains two copyrightable works: the Sinatra sound recording copyright and the underlying Lennon-McCartney musical work. As explained in Chapter 5, under certain circumstances, one copyright application may be used for both the sound recording and musical work rights.

Unlike other works of authorship, sound recordings are not embodied in copies, but are embodied in **phonorecords,** a term that can include records, cassettes, compact discs, or other recording media. Because the method of recording and selling music is constantly evolving, a phonorecord is considered to be a material object, other than a copy of an audiovisual work, in which sounds are fixed by any method, whether the method is

architectural work
The design of a building as embodied in any tangible medium of expression, including a building, architectural plans, or drawings; it includes the overall form as well as the arrangement and composition of spaces and elements in the design, but does not include individual standard features.

musical work
A composition incorporating melody, rhythm, and harmonic elements (and accompanying lyrics, if any).

sound recordings
Works that result from the fixation of a series of musical, spoken, or other sounds, but not including the sounds accompanying a motion picture or other audiovisual work, regardless of the nature of the material objects, such as disks, tapes, or other phonorecords, in which they are embodied.

phonorecords
Material objects in which sounds, other than those accompanying a motion picture or other audiovisual work, are fixed by any method now known or later developed, and from which the sounds can be perceived, reproduced, or otherwise communicated, either directly or with the aid of a machine or device. The term *phonorecords* includes the material object in which the sounds are first fixed.

now known or later developed. For instance, compact discs are considered phonorecords even though they were not available when the Copyright Act of 1976 was enacted.

Sound recordings were not protected under copyright law until 1972. Only those recordings embodied in a phonorecord on or after February 15, 1972, are eligible for protection under U.S. copyright law. If a sound recording was released on a phonorecord prior to this date, it is only protected under common law or state law. Some states, such as California, have passed specific laws regarding the protection of sound recordings fixed prior to February 15, 1972.[6]

EXAMPLES: Musical Works and Sound Recordings

In order to understand the differences between sound recordings and musical works, consider the following examples.

Example: The song "Kiss," as recorded by Prince and released on Warner Brothers Records. The song (and accompanying words) is a musical work created and owned by Prince. The recorded version of Prince's song is created by musicians, engineers, and a producer. This is a sound recording and is owned by Warner Brothers Record Company.

Example: The group *Art of Noise* wants to record a new version of "Kiss" featuring the singer Tom Jones. The group must acquire permission from Prince (see section on compulsory license in Chapter 3) to record their version of the song. However, permission is not required from Warner Brothers Record Company, because *Art of Noise* is not copying the recorded sounds of the Warner Brothers version.

Example: The rap performer, L.L. Cool J, wants to duplicate and use portions of the recording of the song "Kiss" as performed by Prince. Using a process known as sampling, the rapper intends to loop these recorded portions of the "Kiss" song as background for a new song. L.L. Cool J must acquire permission from Prince to use portions of the "Kiss" musical work. Permission *also* must be acquired from Warner Brothers Record Company because L.L. Cool J is using portions of the recorded sounds of the Warner Brothers version. (*Note:* issues as to sampling may depend upon how much of the recording is used and whether it is recognizable. If a sound recording was created prior to February 15, 1972, duplication of the sound recording may violate state law.)

2.4 DERIVATIVE WORKS AND COMPILATIONS

Derivative works and **compilations** are works that use preexisting works or materials. The author of a derivative work transforms or modifies the preexisting work, whereas the author of a compilation assembles, selects, or organizes preexisting materials. A compilation or derivative is separately copyrightable if made by or with the permission of the owner of copyright in the original work.[7]

Derivative Works

The drafters of the Copyright Act of 1976 defined a *derivative work* as a work based upon one or more preexisting works, such as a translation, musical arrangement, dramatization, fictionalization, motion picture version, sound recording, art reproduction, abridgment, condensation, or any other form in which a work may be recast, transformed, or adapted. A work consisting of editorial revisions, annotations, elaborations, or other modifications which, as a whole, represent an original work of authorship, is also a derivative work. The makers of motion pictures often create derivative works: *Rosemary's Baby* is based upon a book by Ira Levin; *The Magnificent Seven* is derived from Kurosawa's *Seven Samurai*. Bobby Gentry's song, "Ode to Billie Joe," is the basis of a motion picture. Other examples of derivative works include the English translation of a book originally written in French by Jean-Paul Sartre; Andy Warhol's paintings of Campbell's soup cans; or a new version of the *WordPerfect*® software program.

A derivative work is separately copyrightable. However, the copyright in the derivative will only protect the new material added and the compilation of the new with the old elements. That is, the new additional material must be sufficiently original to qualify for protection by itself. For example, if an artist creates a new work by painting a coat and hat on the Mona Lisa, only the new material (the hat and coat) will be protected. Any other artist may create a new derivative work with a substantially different hat and coat.

Often artists create derivatives from their own work. During the 20th century, the creation of derivative works has proved a lucrative source of income for authors. For example, Charles Addams created a series of ghoulish cartoons for *The New Yorker* magazine from the 1930s through the 1960s. Those cartoons became the basis for a television series in the 1960s and a movie in the 1990s. The television series and motion picture led to the sale of *Addams Family* imagery on merchandise. All of the works that were adapted from the original cartoons—the merchandise, the television series, and the motion picture—are derivative works (see figure 2-1). In some cases, the merchandise may be derivative from the television show or film (i.e., derivatives of derivatives).

Some derivative works are adapted from works that are not protected under copyright. For example, some of the lyrics from the song "Turn, Turn, Turn" are from the Bible. The author of the derivative may only claim copyright in the material which is original to that author. The author of "Turn Turn Turn" cannot claim copyright in the lyrics taken from the Bible.

A derivative work would be registered within one of the eight categories of works of authorship. For example, the *Addams Family* television series and film would be registered as audiovisual works, but each registration would state that the work is derived from the original illustrations by

LEGAL TERMS

derivative work
Work based upon one or more preexisting works, such as a translation, musical arrangement, dramatization, fictionalization, motion picture version, sound recording, art reproduction, abridgment, condensation, or any other form in which a work may be recast, transformed, or adapted. A work consisting of editorial revisions, annotations, elaborations, or other modifications which, as a whole, represent an original work of authorship, is also a derivative work.

FIGURE 2-1
The cereal is merchandised with the *Addams Family* similarity. The television series, movie, and cereal are all derivatives of the original Charles Addams cartoons. Each is protected under copyright laws.

Mr. Addams. If necessary, the movie may also need to acknowledge the television series if it is derived from that source as well. Table 2.1 shows more examples of derivative works.

Protection of Characters. Fictional literary or visual characters may become derivative works. For example, Walt Disney created the animated cartoon *Steamboat Willie,* in which the Mickey Mouse character first appeared. The character of Mickey Mouse is still widely recognized, while the original cartoon is remembered solely for its historical significance. Under copyright law, characters such as Mickey Mouse, Columbo, Wonder Woman, Snoopy, and Scarlett O'Hara may be protected apart from the work from which they are derived. In addition, these characters may be protected under the laws of

TABLE 2.1
Examples of
Derivative Works

Works	Derived from
WordPerfect® 5.1	*WordPerfect*® 5.0
Bart Simpson (on t-shirt)	*The Simpsons* (TV show)
Mame (movie musical)	*Auntie Mame* (book)
"Who's Afraid of the Big Bad Wolf" (song)	"Champagne Song" (song from *Die Fledermaus* by Johann Strauss)

trademark and trade dress, discussed in Chapter 8. In the case of *Nichols v. Universal Pictures Corp.,*[8] Judge Learned Hand stated that "the less developed the characters, the less they can be copyrighted; that is the penalty an author must bear for marking them too indistinctly." In other words, protection of characters is similar to the idea–expression dichotomy. A character named Joe, who is a boxer who wants to win a championship fight, is too indistinct and not capable of protection. But a poor, determined heavyweight boxer named Rocky Balboa, who speaks with a thick accent and works in a meat-packing plant in Philadelphia, is a protectible expression of a character.

Compilations and Collective Works

Often an author creates a work by selecting various components and grouping them together in a unique manner. For example, the owners of copyright in *Bartlett's Familiar Quotations* have chosen famous quotes. The manner in which the authors of *Bartlett's* have selected and arranged the quotes is protectible as a compilation. A **compilation** is a work formed by the collection and assembly of preexisting materials or of data that are selected, coordinated, or arranged in such a way that the resulting work as a whole constitutes an original work of authorship.

Not all compilations are protectible. For example, anyone may copy a short quote from *Bartlett's Familiar Quotations*. But the manner of arrangement and selection of the quotes, if it meets the standard of originality, is protectible. Similarly, a compilation will not be protected simply because an author has worked hard to gather information. In *Feist Publications, Inc. v. Rural Telephone Service Co.,*[9] the U.S. Supreme Court reviewed a case in which one telephone book company copied the "white pages" of a competing telephone book publisher. The court ruled that the names and telephone numbers in the plaintiff's directory were not protectible because they were facts. Second, the method of arranging the names and numbers did not satisfy the minimum constitutional standards for copyright protection. Justice O'Connor labeled the plaintiff's telephone directory a "garden variety white pages directory, devoid of even the slightest trace of creativity." Therefore, there was no infringement because the compilation was not protectible. Under the *Feist* ruling, the owner of a compilation must demonstrate copyrightability by selection, coordination, and arrangement of the data.

Collective Works.   The term *compilation* includes collective works. A **collective work** is a work, such as a periodical issue, anthology, or encyclopedia, in which a number of contributions, constituting separate and independent works in themselves, are assembled into a collective whole. Unlike other compilations, such as a directory or book of quotes, the underlying elements assembled into a collective work can be separately protected; for example, a collection of short stories by John Updike or a collection of "greatest hits" recordings from the 1970s. Other examples of collective

LEGAL TERMS

compilation
A work formed by the collection and assembling of preexisting materials or of data that are selected, coordinated, or arranged in such a way that the resulting work as a whole constitutes an original work of authorship. The term *compilation* includes collective works.

collective work
A work, such as a periodical issue, anthology, or encyclopedia, in which a number of contributions, constituting separate and independent works in themselves, are assembled into a collective whole.

works include a magazine or newspaper, a group of film clips, or a poetry anthology.

2.5 WHAT IS NOT PROTECTIBLE UNDER COPYRIGHT LAW?

Section 102 of the Copyright Act of 1976 defines what is copyrightable, but it also specifically excludes certain things from copyright protection. Section 102(b) states, "In no case does copyright protection for an original work of authorship extend to any idea, procedure, process, system, method of operation, concept, principle, or discovery, regardless of the form in which it is described, explained, illustrated, or embodied in such work." These exclusions are further discussed in the Code of Federal Regulations.

37 C.F.R. § 202.1   Material not subject to copyright.

The following are examples of works not subject to copyright and applications for registration of such works cannot be entertained:

(a) Words and short phrases such as names, titles, and slogans; familiar symbols or designs; mere variations of typographic ornamentation, lettering or coloring; mere listing of ingredients or contents;

(b) Ideas, plans, methods, systems, or devices, as distinguished from the particular manner in which they are expressed or described in a writing;

(c) Blank forms, such as time cards, graph paper, account books, diaries, bank checks, scorecards, address books, report forms, order forms and the like, which are designed for recording information and do not in themselves convey information;

(d) Works consisting entirely of information that is common property containing no original authorship, such as, for example: standard calendars, height and weight charts, tape measures and rulers, schedules of sporting events, and lists of tables taken from public documents or other common sources.

Ideas

Copyright law does not protect ideas; it protects only the expression of ideas. How can an idea be separated from its expression? In the case of narrative material, such as a literary, dramatic, or motion picture work, the most common standard is known as the "abstractions" test created by Judge Learned Hand.

Judge Hand's abstractions test has been used for over 60 years. For example, in the case of *Litchfield v. Spielberg*[10] a writer sued the makers of the movie *E.T.—The Extraterrestrial.* The writer claimed that the film infringed her musical play, *Lokey from Maldemar,* a social satire designed to "illustrate

JUDGE LEARNED HAND ON COPYRIGHT: THE ABSTRACTIONS TEST

In 1930, Judge Learned Hand was presented with a case in which the author of the popular play *Abie's Irish Rose* sued the producers of a movie, *The Cohens and the Kellys*.[11] Both plots involved children of Irish and Jewish families who marry secretly because their parents are prejudiced. At the end of each work, there is a reconciliation of the families, based upon the presence of a grandchild. Beyond that, the works had little in common except for some ethnic clichés. Judge Hand established a standard to separate the idea from the expression. He used the term *abstraction,* which is a process of removing or separating something. He stated: "Upon any work, and especially upon a play, a great number of patterns of increasing generality will fit equally well, as more and more of the incident is left out. The last may perhaps be no more than the most general statement of what the play is about and at times may consist only of its title; but there is a point in the series of abstractions where they are no longer protected since otherwise the playwright could prevent the use of his 'ideas' to which, apart from their expression, his property is never extended." In other words, every narrative work is based upon unique embellishments and incidents that are built around an underlying idea (in this case the basic plot summary). Copyright protection does not extend to the idea, only to each author's unique expression.

the disunity of man, divided by egotism." The district court applied the abstractions test and determined that the only similarity in both works was the basic plot line: aliens with powers of levitation who are stranded on earth, and pursued by authoritarian characters, finally bid their earthly friends farewell. These general similarities are ideas and are not protectible. The writer's expression of these ideas was not infringed by *E.T.*

This book is also an expression of an idea: to provide a text for paralegals that will assist in learning intellectual property law. The method of dividing the chapters into subject sections and the system of providing examples and questions at the end of each chapter are also ideas and are not protectible. Anyone is free to copy these ideas—but the unique textual expression of the author, the specific examples, and the system by which the information is collected and presented is protectible and may not be copied. For purposes of registration, the Copyright Office may make a preliminary determination as to whether a work is an idea but the final determination is a question of fact to be determined by the federal courts. Table 2.2 gives examples of ideas and expressions.

Idea	Expression
Players view blank spaces and guess a word or expression	*Wheel of Fortune*
The children of two feuding families fall in love and their romance ends tragically	*West Side Story; Romeo and Juliet*
An alien is stranded on earth and attempts to return to his planet	*E.T.*

TABLE 2.2
Examples of Ideas
and Expressions

Useful Articles

A *useful article* is a functional object like a lamp or a shoe. A useful article has a purpose beyond portraying an appearance or conveying information. A useful article may be protected under patent or trademark laws, but it will not be protected under copyright. However, if an "artistic expression" is included on the useful object and it is possible to conceptually separate the expression from the utility, then that copyrightable expression will be protected. For example, copyright may be granted for the motif or pattern on a hairbrush, but not for the design of the brush itself. Under copyright law, the owner of copyright would only be able to stop others from copying the exterior pattern, but not from copying the shape or design of the brush.

In the case of the three-handled cup, presented in the Commentary to this chapter, the cup, by itself, is not protectible under copyright law. It is a useful article. Similarly, the fact that it has three handles would not alter the cup's functionality. Each of the handles can function to assist the user in holding the cup. However, the copyrightable expressions printed on the cup, such as the picture of the company president, may be protectible under copyright law.

Often it is difficult to separate the functional object from the artistic expression. For instance, the *KOOSH* ball is a sphere-shaped object with floppy, wiggly, elastic filaments radiating from a central core. The Copyright Office denied copyright registration for the *KOOSH* ball, stating that the ball's function could not be separated from any artistic expression. Despite the Copyright Office's refusal to register the work, the *KOOSH* ball and its trademark are still protected under patent and trademark laws.

The jewelry designer Barry Kieselstein-Cord was involved in a copyright case when he sued a company that copied his belt-buckle designs.[12] Initially, the district court held that the belt buckles were not copyrightable because it was not possible to physically separate the sculptural work (the jewelry design) from the functional object (the belt buckle). However, the court of appeals reversed that decision and found that the artistic features of the belt buckle were *conceptually* separable. This was sufficient for protection under the Copyright Act of 1976.

Inventions, Methods, and Processes

Copyright law will not protect methods, formulas, devices, or processes. For example, Albert Einstein's equation for the theory of relativity ($e=mc^2$), Paul Newman's formula for tomato sauce, Socrates's method of investigation, or Les Paul's electric guitar amplifier would not be protected under copyright, although each person might be able to copyright the particular manner in which the method, invention, or formula was described. However, protecting the description under copyright law will not prevent a use of the underlying object or material. For example, the copyright in a book describing a system of determining personality traits would not prevent someone from practicing this system, provided they did not copy the book. Similarly, copyright law will not protect devices like slide rules, blank calendars, blank forms, scales, or other materials that are used to calculate measurements. Certain methods, systems, or inventions may be protected under patent or trade secrecy laws, however. Computer software programs generally are copyrightable because they are unique expressions in a computer language. However, certain novel algorithms, methods, or formulas used within software programs may also be patentable.

Facts

A fact, like an idea, is not protectible under copyright. For example, if the writer of a book on John Dillinger discovers certain facts about the gangster's death, that author does not obtain any exclusive rights to those facts. Even if the writer develops a theory based upon those facts, that theory is also not protectible. The producer of a television show about John Dillinger may incorporate the facts and theories without infringing the copyright. All that is protectible is the unique method by which the writer expresses the facts and theory.

Names, Titles, or Short Phrases

Phrases such as "Make my day!" or "Where's the beef?" are not protectible under copyright law. This is because short phrases, names, titles, or groups of words are considered common idioms of the English language and are free to all. Granting a copyright would, as one judge stated, "checkmate the public" and defeat the purpose of copyright—to encourage creativity. Therefore, titles of books or movies, slogans or mottoes, listings of ingredients, and names of products, services, or groups, are not protectible under copyright law. However, under appropriate conditions, names, titles, and short phrases may be protected under trademark, unfair competition, or false advertising laws. The phrase "Softco—We Offer Multiple Solutions," presented in the Commentary to this chapter, would not be protected by copyright law, although it may function as a trademark.

Typefaces

A *typeface* is a set of letters, numbers, or other symbolic characters whose forms are related by repeated design elements and whose function is use in composing text. Congress deliberately excluded typeface designs from protection under the Copyright Act of 1976. The appearance of a typeface cannot be protected. Some computer programs create digitized typefaces. The appearance of the computer-created typeface will not be protected. However, protection will be granted for the underlying computer program that creates the typeface.

The Public Domain

Material that is not protected under copyright (or other proprietary laws) is free for the public to use and is considered to be in the **public domain.** Short phrases and ideas, for example, are in the public domain. Works of authorship that are otherwise copyrightable also may be in the public domain; there are several ways by which works of authorship may become public domain material.

Expired Copyright

Copyrights expire after a limited number of years. The period of copyright depends upon who is the author, the year of creation or publication, or, in the case of multiple authors, when certain authors die. Once a copyright has expired, it falls into the public domain. Generally, anything published more than 75 years ago is now in the public domain. Exceptions to these rules are explained in Chapter 4.

Forfeited Copyright

If an author fails to follow certain copyright formalities, a court may deliberately forfeit the copyright protection and place the work in the public domain. For example, thousands of films, such as *It's a Wonderful Life* and *Night of the Living Dead,* have been placed in the public domain because of a failure to renew copyright or follow registration formalities. These films can be reproduced without paying royalties.

Dedicated Works

Sometimes an author deliberately chooses not to use copyright to protect a work. The author may dedicate the work to the public and place it in the public domain. For example, some companies sell artwork (known as *clip art*) on computer disks or in books and permit anyone to copy it freely. Some of the illustrations in this book are from public domain clip-art collections. Artists may "clip" these works and use the individual artwork, although they would not be permitted to reproduce the unique manner in which the artwork is collected in a book or on a disk.

Works Created by U.S. Government Employees

Any work created by an U.S. government employee or officer is in the public domain, provided that such work is created in that person's official capacity.[13] This rule does not apply to state or local government employees. For example, during the 1980s a songwriter used words from a speech by then-President Ronald Reagan as the basis for song lyrics. The words are in the public domain and thus no royalty was owed to Ronald Reagan. There are certain exceptions to this rule, as provided in 15 U.S.C. § 290e.

Determining Public Domain Status

Determining whether a work is in the public domain requires research. The Copyright Office does not maintain a list of public domain works. However, private companies can perform searches and furnish public domain reports. When analyzing or furnishing such reports to a client, an attorney will advise that the search is not infallible.

SUMMARY

2.1 The copyright clause of the U.S. Constitution establishes the federal power to regulate copyright law and to preempt the states from granting equivalent rights. The Copyright Office determines the registrability of works and also manages copyright records. Copyright law is under the exclusive jurisdiction of the federal courts. When a copyright lawsuit includes matters of state law, the federal court may adjudicate the state issues under the principle of pendent jurisdiction. The Copyright Act of 1909 governs works published between 1909 and 1978. The Copyright Act of 1976 governs works created between 1978 and the present, as well as certain unpublished works created before 1978. In 1989 and 1990, in order to conform to the international treaty known as the Berne Convention, the United States amended the Copyright Act of 1976.

2.2 Copyright law protects original works of authorship fixed in any tangible medium of expression. To meet the standard of originality required under copyright law, an author need only demonstrate a modest degree of intellectual labor. A work is fixed when it is embodied in a tangible form that is perceptible by the human senses, either directly or with the aid of a machine. A work of authorship, such as a literary work, is separate from the physical form in which it is embodied, such as a book or a newspaper.

2.3 Although the Copyright Act of 1976 does not define a work of authorship, eight categories of protectible works have been established: literary works; musical works, including any accompanying words; dramatic works,

LEGAL TERMS

public domain
  Material that is not protected under copyright law and is free for use by the public.

including any accompanying music; pantomimes and choreographic works; pictorial, graphic, and sculptural works; motion pictures and other audio-visual works; sound recordings; and architectural works. The primary difference between a sound recording and a musical work is that the copyright for the musical work protects the song or composition, whereas the sound recording copyright protects the way that the song is performed.

2.4 A derivative work is a work adapted from one or more preexisting works, such as a translation, musical arrangement, dramatization, or fictionalization, and is separately copyrightable, although the copyright in the derivative will only protect the new material that has been added. Fictional literary or visual characters may become derivative works. A compilation is a work formed by the collection and assembly of preexisting materials or of data that are selected, coordinated, or arranged in such a way that the resulting work as a whole constitutes an original work of authorship. A collective work is a type of compilation in which each of the contributions constitutes a separate and independent work in itself.

2.5 Copyright protection does not extend to ideas, only the manner in which the idea is expressed. Similarly, copyright does not extend to functional objects, although it may protect artistic expression included on the useful article. Copyright also does not protect names, titles, short phrases, blank forms, facts, and any works within the public domain.

NOTES

1. *See* 17 U.S.C. § 101 for copyright law definitions.
2. 17 U.S.C. § 102 (subject matter of copyright).
3. 17 U.S.C. § 101.
4. 17 U.S.C. § 102 (subject matter of copyright).
5. Northern Music Corp. v. King Record Distrib. Co., 105 F. Supp. 393, 400 (D.N.Y. 1952).
6. Cal. Civ. Code § 980 (California sound recording law).
7. 17 U.S.C. § 103 (compilations and derivative works).
8. Nichols v. Universal Pictures Corp., 45 F.2d 119, 121 (2d Cir. 1930).
9. Feist Publications, Inc. v. Rural Telephone Serv. Co., 111 S. Ct. 1282 (1991).
10. 736 F.2d 1352 (9th Cir. 1984).
11. Nichols v. Universal Pictures Corp., 45 F.2d 119, 121 (2d Cir. 1930).
12. Kieselstein-Cord v. Accessories By Pearl, Inc., 632 F.2d 989 (2d Cir. 1980).
13. 17 U.S.C. § 105 (U.S. government works).

QUESTIONS FOR REVIEW AND DISCUSSION

1. What is the purpose of copyright law?

2. Why is the Copyright Act of 1909 still applicable?
3. What is the difference between creation and publication?
4. What is originality? Non trivial.
5. What is the difference between a fixed work and a work that is not fixed?
6. What is an author?
7. What is the difference between a sound recording and a musical work?
8. Why is it important to separate a useful object from its copyrightable elements?
9. Will copyright protect the facts in a biography?
10. What is the public domain?
11. What is the difference between a collective work and other compilations?
12. Can a derivative work be created from public domain material?

ACTIVITIES

1. Examine the title pages of various books and attempt to determine which copyright law governs the literary work.
2. Examine various useful objects, such as lamps, chairs, or other furniture, and attempt to determine if there is any copyrightable expression.
3. Find the copyright law in the United States Code and locate §§ 101 and 102. Locate Title 37 of the Code of Federal Regulations.
4. Review the factual situation in the Commentary. Determine what elements of the cup, if any, are copyrightable. Would the Copyright Office register the work as a sculpture? Could the image be registered as a work separate from the cup?

PROJECT

Create a list of popular films or books and attempt to isolate the underlying (and unprotectible) idea upon which each work is based. Try to determine if another work is based upon the same idea.

FOR MORE INFORMATION

Copyright Law

The following texts may assist in researching copyright law.

Melville B. Nimmer & David Nimmer, *Nimmer on Copyright* (Matthew Bender 1978). A four-volume looseleaf treatise considered to be the leading source of copyright law.

Harry G. Henn, *Henn on Copyright Law* (3d ed., Practising Law Institute 1991). One-volume treatise.

Howard B. Abrams, *The Law of Copyright* (Clark Boardman Callaghan 1991). Two-volume looseleaf treatise.

William F. Partry, *Latman's the Copyright Law* (BNA Books 1986). One-volume bound treatise.

Steven Fishman, *The Copyright Handbook: How to Protect and Use Written Works* (Nolo Press 1991). Comprehensive, easy-to-read paperback.

U.S. Copyright Office Publications

The U.S. Copyright Office offers numerous circulars, regulations, applications, and other publications regarding copyright law. Many of these materials are grouped together as an information kit, sometimes known as an *attorney's kit,* that can be requested from the Copyright Office. Circulars and forms can also be obtained separately or in special information kits grouped by subject matter (e.g. "Books," "Cartoons," "Copyright Searches," "Sound Recordings," etc.). A good place to start is by requesting Circular 2, "Publications on Copyright."

Kits, circulars, and forms can be obtained by writing to the Copyright Office at Publications Sections, LM-455, Copyright Office, Library of Congress, Washington, DC 20559. Forms can be requested by calling the Forms Hotline number, 202-707-9100. General copyright information is available by calling 202-707-3000.

Additional documentation is available from the Government Printing Office (GPO). Among the materials sold by the GPO is *The Compendium of Copyright Office Practices,* which is the manual used by copyright examiners when reviewing applications. Information about GPO copyright publications is available in Circular 2, as previously noted, or can be obtained by writing to the Government Printing Office, Superintendent of Documents, PO Box 371954, Pittsburgh, PA 15250-7954.

Copyright Law Decisions

Reports of judicial decisions are contained in various case reporters, including the *Federal Supplement, Federal Reporter, U.S. Patent Quarterly,* (U.S.P.Q.) and *C.C.H. Copyright Law Reporter.* In addition, copyright decisions from 1986 to the present are summarized in annual Bulletins sold by the Superintendent of Documents. For Bulletins published from 1909 through 1984, contact the National Technical Information Service, U.S. Department of Commerce, 5285 Port Royal Road, Springfield, VA 22161.

Public Domain Status

The following companies may be able to provide information as to the copyright status of works.

BZ Rights & Permission, Inc., 125 West 72nd Street, New York, NY 10023

Thomson & Thomson, 500 E Street, S.W., Suite 970, Washington, DC 20024-2710

Copyright Clearance Center, 27 Congress Street, Salem, MA 01970

International Permissions Service, PO Box 33476, Detroit, MI 48232

Copyright Service Bureau Ltd., 221 West 37th Street, New York, NY 10019

CHAPTER 3
Copyrights:
Rights and Limitations

A work of art is not a utilitarian object, like a toaster; it is a creative work, like a song, a poem, or a novel. We should not pretend that all connection between the artist and the creation is severed the first time the work is sold.

Congressman Edward J. Markey

OUTLINE

COMMENTARY

Your law office represents Softco, a computer company that is planning to release a new video game, Wild Thing. *As background music, the game uses computer-generated musical arrangements of two different songs entitled "Wild Thing." One version is a rap version styled after the hit made famous by the performer Tone Lōc. The other is a version based on a song from the 1960s made famous by a British group, the Troggs. The vice president of new products at Softco wants to know if she must obtain permission. In addition, Softco is unveiling the new video game at a press conference and wants to play the recordings by Tone Lōc and the Troggs at that time. Your supervising attorney asks you to perform preliminary research as to these issues.*

OBJECTIVES

Chapter 2 provided a basic understanding of what can be protected under copyright law. In this chapter, we examine the basic rights granted to the owner of copyright and the limitations on those rights. After reading this chapter, you will be able to:

- Describe the bundle of rights granted to each author.
- Differentiate between the right to reproduce a work and the right to adapt the work and explain the extent of protection granted to a derivative work.
- Distinguish between a public performance where the public is gathered and a public performance that is transmitted.
- Describe the sources of licensing revenue for a musical work.
- Discuss the concept known as *moral rights.*
- Analyze the use of a copyrighted work under fair use principles.
- Outline limitations on rights granted for nonprofit and educational purposes.
- Describe the rights of an owner of a copy of a computer software program.

3.1 THE GRANT OF EXCLUSIVE RIGHTS

Section 106 of the Copyright Act of 1976, 17 U.S.C. § 106, provides a bundle of rights to the author of a copyrightable work. As noted in Chapter 2, under copyright law the author may be the creator of the work, the party employing the creator of the work, or the party commissioning the work. The author's bundle of rights includes the exclusive rights of reproduction, adaptation, publication, performance, and display—all the means of commercially exploiting a copyrightable work. If one of these rights is exercised without the authorization of the author of the work, an infringement has occurred. The bundle of rights is granted to authors regardless of whether copyright protection was secured under the current copyright act or the Copyright Act of 1909. For instance, the authors of the song "Heartbreak Hotel," published in 1956, can control the rights to reproduce, adapt, publish, perform, or display the song, even though protection was secured under the Copyright Act of 1909. There are some limitations to the rights granted under § 106, and these restrictions are set forth in §§ 107 through 118 of the Copyright Act of 1976. In addition to the five rights granted in § 106, under certain circumstances the owner of copyright may prohibit the importation of infringing copies or phonorecords into the United States, under the provisions of 17 U.S.C. § 602.

This section discusses the rights granted under copyright law. Certain activities may violate different rights. What difference does it make which right is violated? Different works may have different limitations. For example, under certain circumstances the owner of a computer program may reproduce the work without authorization. In some cases, a musical work may be performed without authorization. Therefore, when assessing a potential infringement, it is important to be able to characterize which rights, if any, have been violated.

Right to Reproduce the Work

A work is *reproduced* when it (or a substantial portion of it) is copied and fixed in a material form such as a copy or phonorecord. The right to reproduce a work is the most elementary power of copyright because it controls the right of duplication. A necessary element of the reproduction right is *fixation.* For example, if a speech was presented at a university and someone secretly taped the event, that taping would be a violation of the author's right to reproduce the speech. However, if the speech was broadcast live and not taped or reduced to writing, that unauthorized broadcast would not violate the author's reproduction right.

In some cases, it is not an infringement to reproduce a copyrighted work without authorization. These exemptions are discussed throughout this chapter. One specific exemption deals with the reproduction of pictorial, graphic, or sculptural works that are included on useful articles. Copyright Act § 113 (17 U.S.C. § 113) provides that the owner of copyright in the pictorial, graphic, or sculptural work cannot prevent the reproduction, distribution, or display of pictures or photographs of the useful articles in connection with advertisements or commentaries related to the articles (e.g., news reports). In other words, if an artist licenses a design for use on a backpack, the artist cannot prevent use of a photo of the backpack in an advertisement.

Right to Distribute the Work to the Public

The author controls distribution of the work to the public, whether by sale, gift, loan, lease, or rental. This is also known as the *right to publish the work* or *publication right.* Although the Copyright Act of 1976 does not specifically define "distribution of the work to the public," it is generally considered to mean dissemination to a substantial number of persons or to a substantial portion of the market for the work. The distribution right is similar and related to the reproduction right in that publication must be in the form of copies or phonorecords. The unauthorized sale of a videocassette containing the movie *Rocky* is an infringement of the distribution right. However, the unauthorized live broadcast of the same movie is not an infringement of the distribution right because a copy or phonorecord is not being disseminated to the public. The broadcast may, however, be an infringement of the public performance right, discussed later in this section. Another way of viewing the reproduction and distribution rights is that the author has the power to forbid reproduction or distribution of the work. For example, the author J. D. Salinger has created new works but has chosen not to publish them. Copyright law grants Mr. Salinger the power to prevent others from copying his unpublished works.

The First Sale Doctrine: Limitations on the Distribution Right

An important limitation on the distribution right is established in § 109 of the Copyright Act of 1976, 17 U.S.C. § 109. Once the "first sale" of a copy or phonorecord has occurred, the author's rights as to that copy are limited. This limitation is commonly known as the **first sale doctrine**. Every day, millions of consumers make use of this principle of copyright law. The rental of a videocassette, the display of a copyrighted painting, and the resale of a previously owned phonorecord are all permitted under the first sale doctrine. This principle means that the owner of a lawfully made copy or phonorecord has the right to dispose of it by sale, rental, or any other means without the authority of the author. In other words, if you buy a book, you are free, under copyright law, to rent it, sell it, or burn it if you wish. It also is the right of the owner of a lawfully made copy to display that copy publicly, either directly or by the projection of no more than one image at a time, to viewers present at the place where the copy is located, without authorization from the author.

The first sale doctrine is very narrow and applies only to a specific copy. No rights are granted as to the underlying work. For example, except as provided in the Copyright Act of 1976, the copy owner cannot reproduce, adapt, publish, or perform the work without the author's authorization. All the consumer can do is dispose of the particular copy that has been purchased. For example, in a case involving the painter Patrick Nagel, it was held that the first sale doctrine does not permit the owner of a book of copyrighted art prints to separate the prints, mount them in frames, and sell them separately. The first sale doctrine applies only to the owner of the work, not to a person who possesses the property but does not own it. For example, a store purchases a lawfully made videocassette copy of the movie *Gone with the Wind*. As the owner of that copy, the store can rent it to an individual. However, the person renting it cannot rent the copy to someone else. Only the copy owner has such rights.

Section 109 was amended in 1984 to prohibit the rental of phonorecords and amended again in 1990 to prohibit the rental of computer programs. Unless renewed, these exceptions will terminate on October 1, 1997, and are discussed later in this chapter.

Right to Adapt the Work: Right to Prepare Derivative Works

Prior to the 20th century, authors had difficulty securing adaptation rights. For instance, a novelist could not stop a playwright from adapting the novel for the stage. It was not until 1870 that Congress granted authors the right to control the dramatization or translation of their books. This was the origin of derivative rights, also known as the *right to adapt* a work. The adaptation right is particularly important to authors because it controls the making of derivative works.[1] As discussed in Chapter 2, a *derivative work* is a work based upon one or more preexisting works. The right to adapt a work

LEGAL TERMS

first sale doctrine
Right of the owner of a lawfully made copy or phonorecord to sell or otherwise dispose of possession of that copy or phonorecord, without the authority of the copyright owner. The doctrine includes the right of the owner of a lawfully made copy to display that copy publicly, either directly or by the projection of no more than one image at a time, to viewers present at the place where the copy is located without authorization from the copyright owner.

extends to all media. An image of Mickey Mouse may be adapted for use on a fabric. The song "Ode to Billie Joe" was adapted into a movie. In the case of *Rogers v. Koons*,[2] a photograph was adapted into a wood sculpture without the photographer's authorization. The photographer Art Rogers created a photograph entitled "Puppies," which features a man and a woman sitting on a bench and holding eight puppies. The artist Jeff Koons purchased two copies of the image and, without obtaining Mr. Rogers's authorization, created a wood sculpture from it. Because the sculpture was substantially similar and was prepared without the authorization of Mr. Rogers, a court determined it was an infringement of Mr. Rogers's right to adapt the work. This situation, involving a photograph and a sculpture, illustrates three important aspects of the adaptation right:

1. The author of a derivative work cannot claim a right to material that is not original to that author

2. The author of a derivative work must obtain permission from the author of the underlying copyrighted work

3. The derivative work is a separately copyrightable work.

Protection Extends Only to New Material

The author of a derivative work cannot claim copyright over the material that is not original to that author. This is true regardless of whether the material that is borrowed is protected under copyright or is in the public domain. In the case of the wood sculpture previously mentioned, Mr. Koons could make no claim to the copyrightable expressions that he borrowed from Mr. Rogers.

The same is true if the derivative is created from a public domain work. For example, the song "Love Me Tender," written by Elvis Presley and Vera Matson, is derived from a public domain song, "Aura Lee," written in 1861. The authors of "Love Me Tender" cannot claim copyright to any elements borrowed from "Aura Lee" and they cannot stop others from creating a song based upon "Aura Lee." The creation of "Love Me Tender" does not restore copyrightability to "Aura Lee"; the authors' rights extend only to the new material that was added to "Aura Lee" to create the song "Love Me Tender."

Authorization

If a derivative is based upon a work protected under copyright, the author of the derivative must obtain authorization directly from the author of the underlying work or through a clearance center representing the author. In the case of the wood sculpture, there would have been no infringement if Mr. Koons had obtained permission from Mr. Rogers. Authorization for such rights is commonly granted in return for a payment, a royalty, or a share of the profits from the derivative work. Similarly, in the case of the *Wild Thing*

DON'T JOIN ELVIS IN THE JAIL HOUSE ROCK!

TRADEMARK INFRINGEMENT IS ILLEGAL

Elvis Presley Enterprises, Inc. will pursue all remedies available against those who choose to infringe upon our trademarks. Any merchandise or advertising utilizing Elvis' name, image, or likeness must be authorized through his estate. Elvis, Elvis Presley, and Graceland are registered trademarks of Elvis Presley Enterprises, Inc. For information please contact us at the Graceland Division of Elvis Presley Enterprises, Inc., 3734 Elvis Presley Blvd., Memphis, TN 38116. Phone (901)332-3322 or (800)238-2010.

Elvis Presley Enterprises, Inc. will pursue all remedies available against those who choose to infringe upon our trademarks. Any merchandise or advertising utilizing Elvis' name, image, or likeness must be authorized through his estate. Elvis, Elvis Presley, and Graceland are registered trademarks of Elvis Presley Enterprises, Inc. For information please contact us at the Graceland Division of Elvis Presley Enterprises, Inc., 3734 Elvis Presley Blvd., Memphis, TN 38116. Phone (901) 332-3322 or (800) 238-2010.

video game presented in the Commentary, the creation of computer-generated arrangements of musical works requires the authorization of the copyright owners. If the songwriters do not authorize these derivative works, the result is an infringement.

Separate Copyright Protection

Provided that a derivative work meets the requirements of copyrightability (i.e., <u>fixation and originality</u>), it will be protected separately from the work upon which it is based. It is important to realize that copyright in a derivative work extends only to material contributed by the author of the derivative. Copyright in a derivative has no effect on the copyright status of the preexisting work. For example, the novel *The Shining* was altered substantially when it was converted into a movie. The copyright for the screenplay extends to all material that was added by the screenwriters, but does not extend to the material already created by novelist Stephen King.

As noted previously, to be separately copyrightable, the work must be fixed and must demonstrate the minimum requirements of originality. In the case of a translation, for instance, the act of translating a novel from one language to another generally satisfies the minimal standard of originality because the translator must interpret and express the novel in a manner consistent with the second language. However, simply translating a list of words from English into another language would not constitute sufficient originality to make a copyrightable derivative work.

Adaptation Right Not Limited to Fixed Copies

Unlike the reproduction right, the right to prepare derivatives is not limited simply to fixed copies. For example, a live public performance of a play based upon *The Shining* would infringe Mr. King's right to prepare an adaptation even if the performance was not fixed on videotape or film.

Right of Public Performance

To **perform** a work **publicly** has a much broader meaning than the common concept of a performance. For example, the playing of a phonorecord in a nightclub is a public performance. Other examples of a public performance include: a novelist reading aloud from her work; a dancer presenting a ballet; a motion picture company authorizing a showing of its latest film; a songwriter performing an original composition at a nightclub; a radio station playing a record of a copyrighted song; a television station broadcasting a television show; or a cable television company receiving a broadcast containing a copyrighted program and rebroadcasting it via cable transmission. The drafters of the Copyright Act of 1976 stated that "to perform a work means to recite, render, play, dance, or act it, either directly or by means of any device or process or, in the case of a motion picture or other audiovisual work, to show its images in any sequence or to make the sounds accompanying it audible." Section 101 of the Copyright Act of 1976 states that to perform or display a work "publicly" means that there is performance or display of the work where the public is gathered *or* the work is transmitted or otherwise communicated to the public. The performance right does not extend to pictorial, graphic, or sculptural works because these works, along with other works, are covered by the display right.

Public Performance: Live

Performing the work "where the public is gathered" refers to a performance at a place open to the public *or* at any place where a substantial number of persons outside of the normal circle of a family and its social acquaintances are gathered. By way of example, the song "Happy Birthday" is protected under copyright. When it is sung among a group of social acquaintances at a private party, there is no infringement of the performance right. However, when Marilyn Monroe sang it to President Kennedy at a public gathering, the work was performed publicly and was subject to the performance right.

Public Performance: Transmission

To perform a work publicly also may mean that a performance of a work is transmitted to the public by means of a device or process. For example, in the case of the *Wild Thing* video game presented in the Commentary, the playing of the copyrighted musical works at the press conference would amount to a public performance of the works. The playing of records over a public address system at a dance club also is a performance. Similarly, any transmission of a work by a radio or television station is a performance. If the performance is transmitted, it does not matter if the public receives it at the same time or place as when it was transmitted. Therefore, if one station transmits a work and another station receives the broadcast and retransmits it later, that retransmission is also a performance.

Public Performance: Playing of Videotapes

If a company provided seating, charged admission, and played a motion picture for the public, that unauthorized showing would clearly violate the right to control public performance. But what if the company rented videotapes and provided viewing rooms for the public? According to several court decisions, the showing of rented films in such private booths is public performance for which permission must be acquired from the author. In another case, however, a court held that the rental of videotapes for viewing in a hotel room is not an infringement of the public performance right. In that case, the court likened the hotel room rental to home rental of the videotape.

Public Performance: Sound Recordings and Musical Works

The performance right does not extend to sound recordings. This does not mean that radio stations may freely broadcast recordings without any authorization. As discussed in Chapter 2, an audio recording usually contains two separate copyrightable works: a *sound recording copyright* that protects the arrangement or production of a song and a *musical works copyright* that covers the underlying song being performed. By way of example, a radio station plays a recording of "Born in the U.S.A.," an original song by Bruce Springsteen. Authorization is not required from the record company that owns the sound recording. However, some form of authorization is required from Mr. Springsteen, who is the author of the musical composition. This authorization may come from performing rights societies, as discussed later. What if the radio station plays a recording of a musical composition such as the "William Tell Overture"? In that case, no authorization is required because the musical composition is in the public domain. However, if the recording was of a unique arrangement of the "William Tell Overture" (i.e., a protectible derivative work), permission might be needed.

Performing Rights Societies

It would be very impractical if the proprietors of radio stations, television stations, nightclubs, or other business establishments had to contact each songwriter for permission each time a song was publicly performed. Performing rights societies were established to facilitate the efficient licensing of such nondramatic musical works. A **performing rights society** is an association or corporation that licenses the public performance of a nondramatic musical work on behalf of the author. (A list of such organizations appears at the end of this chapter.) These nonprofit societies act as agents for songwriters and license rights to songs based upon established fees. Radio stations are surveyed on a regular basis and those samples are used as the basis for payments to songwriters. Television stations furnish logs. Separate licenses are also acquired by club owners where phonorecords are played, and by concert halls where live music is performed. Performing rights societies also license business establishments where music is played, such as clothing stores, taverns, or restaurants. Small businesses that play a radio, using home-style audio equipment, are exempt from performance rights under a limitation in § 110(5) of the Copyright Act of 1976 (this exemption is discussed in more detail later in this chapter).

Right to Display the Work Publicly

The *right to display a work publicly* refers to the public showing of a copyrighted work. For example, a painter has a right to control the public exhibition of her work prior to the sale of that work. The Copyright Act of 1976 states that to **display publicly** means to show a copy of a work, either directly or by means of a film, slide, television image, or any other device or process. The definition of *publicly* for the display right is the same as for the performance right. That is, a display to a gathering of social friends and acquaintances is not an infringement, whereas a display to the public may be an infringement. Under the first sale doctrine, a person who has purchased a copy is permitted to display that copy to viewers present at the place where the copy is located. Under copyright law, a *copy* can be the material object in which the work is first fixed (e.g., a painting or sculpture is considered a copy). Therefore, the owner of a painting or a fine art print or sculpture, for example, is permitted to display that object in a museum. This right applies only to the owner of the copy. It does not extend to a person who rented or borrowed the copy. In addition, this first sale display right only applies at the place where the copy is located. For example, the owner of the painting may display it in a museum, but may not broadcast it to persons in another room. The right to display a work does not extend to sound recordings. Although it is true that sounds can be "displayed" on computers and other devices, generally the sounds embodied on a phonorecord are performed rather than displayed.

Motion Pictures and Audiovisual Works. In the case of a motion picture or other audiovisual work, the nonsequential showing of individual images is a display. Therefore, if individual images from the film *Sleeping Beauty* were projected at a public theater, that showing would infringe the right to display the work. If the film was shown in sequence, that would infringe the performance right. In both cases, the permission of the copyright owner should be acquired.

Works of Visual Art: Moral Rights

In order to align U.S. copyright laws with the international treaty known as the Berne Convention, Congress adopted certain provisions that parallel the European theory of moral rights. **Moral rights** are rights that protect the professional honor and reputation of an artist by guaranteeing attribution and integrity. *Attribution* is the right to claim or disclaim authorship of a work. The right of *integrity* is the right to prevent, in certain cases, distortion, mutilation, or other modification of the work. Generally these rights require giving credit (or *not* giving credit) to the creators of certain works of fine art. Retention of moral rights also enables artists to profit from certain resales of their works. These rights are independent of the rights granted in § 106. In 1990, Congress amended the Copyright Act of 1976 to include these special provisions for a work of visual art.[3] A **work of visual art** is either (1) a painting, drawing, print, or sculpture, existing in a single copy, in a limited edition of 200 copies or fewer that are signed and consecutively numbered by the author, or, in the case of a sculpture, in multiple cast, carved, or fabricated sculptures of 200 or fewer that are consecutively numbered by the author and bear the signature or other identifying mark of the author; or (2) a still photographic image produced for exhibition purposes only, existing in a single copy that is signed by the author, or in a limited edition of 200 copies or fewer that are signed and consecutively numbered by the author.

3.2 FAIR USE

It was the intent of the Constitution's drafters that copyright law would encourage creativity. Creativity would be severely hampered, however, if there were no limitations on authors' rights. Imagine if a music reviewer could not quote lyrics or if the owner of a painting could not display the work in a museum. Such uses would be considered an infringement unless the bundle of rights was limited. The Copyright Act of 1976 includes several limitations in §§ 107 through 118 (17 U.S.C. §§ 107–118). Each of these limitations serves as a defense to a claim of infringement. The most commonly asserted defense is *fair use.*

Fair use is a right to use copyrighted material for limited purposes and without the consent of the author. Supreme Court Justice Blackmun wrote that the intent of fair use is "to encourage users to engage in activities the primary benefit of which accrues to others." In other words, fair use is intended to promote a benefit to the public by permitting the borrowing of portions of a work. Traditionally, this has meant the right to comment upon, criticize, or parody copyrighted works. The application of fair use principles

moral rights
Rights that protect the professional honor and reputation of an artist by guaranteeing the right to claim or disclaim authorship of a work and the right to prevent, in certain cases, distortion, mutilation, or other modification of the work.

work of visual art
Under the Copyright Act of 1976, either (1) a painting, drawing, print, or sculpture, existing in a single copy, in a limited edition of 200 copies or fewer that are signed and consecutively numbered by the author, or, in the case of a sculpture, in multiple cast, carved, or fabricated sculptures of 200 or fewer that are consecutively numbered by the author and bear the signature or other identifying mark of the author; or (2) a still photographic image produced for exhibition purposes only, existing in a single copy that is signed by the author, or in a limited edition of 200 copies or fewer that are signed and consecutively numbered by the author.

fair use
Right to use copyrighted material for limited purposes and without authorization from the author; determined by a federal court after it weighs several factors, including the nature of the copyrighted work, the purpose and character of the use, the amount and substantiality of the portion borrowed, and the effect of the use on the market for the copyrighted material.

is also meant to incorporate and balance the right of free speech granted under the U.S. Constitution.

The Copyright Act of 1976 offers several examples of fair use, such as copying for "purposes such as criticism, comment, news reporting, teaching (including multiple copies for classroom use), scholarship, or research." Other examples were presented in the legislative history of the Copyright Act of 1976, including quotation of excerpts in a review or criticism for purposes of illustration or comment; use in a parody of some of the content of the work parodied; summary of an address or article, with brief quotations in a news report; reproduction by a teacher or student of a small part of a work to illustrate a lesson; or reproduction of a work in legislative or judicial proceedings or reports.

A determination of fair use generally occurs during an infringement suit. A party accused of infringement argues that the infringement is excused under the fair use doctrine. A court faced with this argument weighs several factors; if the weight of the factors is in favor of the defendant, then the unauthorized use of the material is permitted. To guide judges in making determinations of fair use, the drafters of the Copyright Act of 1976 included four factors:

1. The purpose and character of the use, including whether such use is of a commercial nature or is for nonprofit educational purposes
2. The nature of the copyrighted work
3. The amount and substantiality of the portion used in relation to the copyrighted work as a whole
4. The effect of the use upon the potential market for or value of the copyrighted work.

Although the fourth factor—the effect of the use upon the potential market—is considered to be the most important, all four guidelines are weighed by a court. In addition, a court may consider other factors, if relevant, as to whether the defendant's use was fair. The drafters of the Copyright Act of 1976 were careful to advise that the fair use doctrine, as expressed in 17 U.S.C. § 107, was intended only as a guideline. "Beyond a very broad statutory explanation of what fair use is and some of the criteria applicable to it, the courts must be free to adapt the doctrine to particular situations on a case-by-case basis." The rest of this section is an analysis of the four fair use factors, which are summarized in Table 3.1.

Purpose and Character of the Use

The first fair use factor generally refers to the function for which the copied material is being used. Because copyright law encourages scholarship, research, education, and commentary, the defendant's position is strengthened if the copying is for noncommercial, educational, scientific, or historical. However, an educational or scientific use that is for commercial purposes

Factor	Questions
Effect of use on potential market (most important factor)	Does the use deprive the copyright owner of income? Does the use undermine a new or potential market for the work?
Purpose and character of use	Is the use for educational, scientific, historical, or other purposes that further the dissemination of knowledge?
Nature of the copyrighted work	Is the nature of the work that has been borrowed informational or entertaining? Is the work that has been borrowed published or unpublished?
Amount and substantiality of portion used	How much of the work is borrowed? How important is the portion borrowed to the work from which it was taken (i.e., is it the heart of the work)?

TABLE 3.1
Questions for
Evaluating Fair Use

may not be excused. For example, copying a scientist's statements in a cigarette advertisement or doing large-scale videotaping of educational programming is not considered fair use. Similarly, the fact that the use is not for profit will not necessarily excuse an infringment.

Certain uses of copyrighted material are automatically classified as fair use. The home videotaping of a television broadcast was determined to be a fair use by the U.S. Supreme Court, in *Universal City Studios, Inc. v. Sony Corp.*[4] However, the taping must be off-the-air and for personal use, not for commercial purposes. Similarly, the duplication of a work in a single copy or phonorecord is permitted as a service to the blind.

Nature of the Copyrighted Work

The second factor in the fair use determination is the nature of the work being copied. For example, a court will generally consider whether the work being copied is informational or entertaining in nature. As the Supreme Court stated in its *Sony* decision, "copying a news broadcast may have a stronger claim to fair use than copying a motion picture." Why? Because copying from informational works such as scholarly, scientific, or news journals encourages the free spread of ideas and encourages the creation of new scientific or educational works, all of which benefits the public.

In addition, the court will consider whether the work that is copied is published or unpublished. Often, the scope of fair use is narrower with respect to unpublished works, because of the author's right to control the first public appearance of his or her expression. For example, in the case of *Salinger v.*

Random House,[5] a biographer paraphrased portions of letters written by J. D. Salinger. Although the public could read these letters at a university library, Mr. Salinger had never authorized reproduction or publication of the letters. Despite the scholarly purpose of the proposed Salinger biography, the court would not permit the unauthorized paraphrasing of Mr. Salinger's unpublished letters as a fair use. The *Salinger* case created tremendous concern among publishers, and in October 1992, § 107 (the fair use section of the Copyright Act of 1976) was amended by the addition of the following sentence: "The fact that a work is not published shall not itself bar a finding of fair use if such finding is made upon consideration of all the above [fair use] factors."

Amount and Substantiality of Portion Used

In a case involving the late novelist Richard Wright, a court permitted a biographer to quote from 6 unpublished letters and 10 of Wright's unpublished journal entries. One factor that weighed in favor of the biographer was the amount and substantiality of the portions used. The court determined that no more than 1 percent of Mr. Wright's unpublished letters and journal was copied. When considering the amount and substantiality of the portion taken, the court considers not just the quantity of material but also the quality of material taken. For example, the copying of 1 minute and 15 seconds of a 72-minute Charlie Chaplin film was considered substantial and was not permitted as a fair use. In certain rare cases, the copying of a complete work may be considered a fair use. For example, the Supreme Court in the *Sony* case excused the off-the-air copying of complete television programs.

Effect of the Use on the Potential Market

The fourth factor in a fair use determination is the effect of the use on the potential market for the copied work. One court stated that consideration of this factor is intended to strike a balance "between the benefit that the public will derive if the use is permitted and the personal gain that the copyright owner will receive if the use is denied." A judge must consider the effect on the *potential* market for the copyrighted work. This consideration goes beyond the past intentions of the author or the means by which the author is currently exploiting the work. For example, in the case of the photograph that was adapted to a wood sculpture, the court recognized the existence of a market for new versions or new uses of the photograph and determined that the unauthorized use of the photographic image undermined its potential market. Some uses are not considered to undermine the potential market. Copying a magazine cover for purposes of a comparative advertisement is a fair use because the comparative advertisement does not undermine the sales or need for the featured magazine. Similarly, it was the lack of market damage in the *Sony* case that convinced the Supreme Court to permit off-the-air videotaping.

Effect of Acknowledgment of Source Material

It is commonly believed that the unauthorized use of a work is permitted if an acknowledgment is made. This is not true. Acknowledgment of the source material (such as citing the author or the publication) may be a consideration in a fair use determination, but it will not protect against a claim of infringement. When in doubt as to the right to use or acknowledge a source, the most prudent course may be to seek permission from the copyright owner. If permission cannot be obtained, an opinion from an attorney should be obtained before proceeding.

Fair Use Cases

The following sampling of fair use cases demonstrates courts' use of the fair use factors.

In *Harper & Row v. Nation Enterprises,*[6] *Nation* magazine was accused of infringing the rights of ex-president Gerald Ford by publishing excerpts from his then-unpublished memoirs. The publication in the *Nation* was made several weeks prior to the serialization of Mr. Ford's book in another magazine. The Supreme Court weighed the four fair use factors. The first factor weighed in favor of the *Nation;* clearly, the purpose of the use was informational and scholarly. The second factor weighed in favor of Mr. Ford, because fair use is narrowly interpreted for unpublished works. The actual portion borrowed was small, consisting of approximately 300 to 400 words. However, the determinative element was the fourth fair use factor, the effect of the use on the potential market. The fact that the *Nation*'s work was timed to "scoop" Mr. Ford's publication seriously damaged the marketability of serialization rights. The Supreme Court therefore did not excuse the *Nation*'s use of the material as a fair use.

In *Twin Peaks v. Publications International Ltd.,*[7] a company published a book entitled *Welcome to Twin Peaks—A Complete Guide to Who's Who and What's What,* which contained direct quotations and paraphrases from the television show *Twin Peaks* as well as detailed descriptions of plot, characters, and setting. The publisher argued that the use of these materials was educational and excused under the fair use doctrine. The court disagreed and determined that: (1) the purpose of the use was commercial; (2) the nature of the work taken was creative and fictional; (3) the amount of the material taken was substantial; and (4) the publication of the book adversely affected the potential market for books about the program that were authorized by the owners of copyright in *Twin Peaks.*

In *Keep Thomson Governor Committee v. Citizens for Gallen Committee,*[8] a person running for political office used 15 seconds of his opponent's copyrighted campaign song in a political ad. The court excused the copying as a fair use, taking into consideration the fact that use of the song was part of the political message of the advertisement. In *Love v. Kwitny,*[9] the defendant copied more than half of the plaintiff's unpublished manuscript. The purpose of the copying was to demonstrate that the plaintiff was involved in the overthrow of the Iranian government. The copying was held not justified as a fair use. In *Craft v. Kobler,*[10] the defendant was the author of a book on the composer Igor Stravinsky. The plaintiff had inherited the rights to Stravinsky's writings. The defendant made extensive use of Stravinsky quotations. The court determined that the defendant had taken too much of Stravinsky's protected writings and that the activity was not justified as fair use. In *Martin Luther King, Jr. Center for Social Change, Inc. v. American Heritage Products, Inc.,*[11] the defendant copied eight sentences from portions of Dr. King's speeches. The excerpts were used as part of a promotional campaign to sell commercial busts of Dr. King. This reprinting of the speech excerpts was not excused as a fair use.

Parody and Satire as Fair Use

Often portions of a copyrighted work are borrowed for purposes of satire or parody. Such uses are reviewed in terms of the fair use factors, but the parody defense has acquired some of its own characteristics. By its nature, parody demands some taking from an original work, and thus a more extensive use of a copyrighted work is permitted, in order to "conjure up" the original. At issue is often the effect on the potential market, or, as it is sometimes phrased, whether the parodist's result had the intent or the effect of fulfilling a demand for the original work.

This determination of market effect can be difficult in a parody case. For example, in the case of *Fisher v. Dees,*[12] the composers of the song "When Sunny Gets Blue" claimed that their song was infringed by "When Sonny Sniffs Glue," a 29-second parody that altered the original lyric line and borrowed 6 bars of the plaintiff's music. The plaintiff argued that the parody reflected negatively on the original song and therefore affected its marketability. The court responded that: "[T]he economic effect of a parody with which we are concerned is not its potential to destroy or diminish the market for the original—any bad review can have that effect—but whether it *fulfills the demand* for the original. Biting criticism suppresses demand; copyright infringement usurps it." The court weighed the fair use factors, determined that the balance tipped in favor of the parodist, and permitted the brief parody as a fair use. The parody of a work may also trigger similar issues under trademark, trade dress, and unfair competition law.

Parody Cases

The following parody case summaries show the range of uses courts must deal with in such suits.

Elsmere Music, Inc. v. National Broadcasting Co.[13] concerned the late-night-television comedy show *Saturday Night Live* parody of the musical

Original cast of NBC's "Saturday Night Live." Courtesy of NBC Photo.

phrase "I Love New York," using the words "I Love Sodom." Only the words "I Love" and four musical notes were taken from the plaintiff's work, yet the court recognized the musical-lyrical phrase as the "heart of the composition." However, the court determined that "the defendant's version of the jingle did not compete with or detract from the plaintiff's work." In *Original Appalachian Artworks, Inc. v. Topps Chewing Gum, Inc.,*[14] a manufacturer of novelty cards parodied the successful children's dolls, the *Cabbage Patch Kids.* The parody card series was entitled the *Garbage Pail Kids.* The court considered the parody an infringement, not a fair use because the novelty cards were meant to capitalize on demand for the successful children's toys—that is, to make money from imitating the dolls.

In *Walt Disney Productions v. Air Pirates,*[15] an underground cartoonist parodied Mickey and Minnie Mouse as free thinking, promiscuous, drug ingesting characters. The court determined that the use of the copyrighted characters exceeded the limits of fair use and infringed the rights of the author. In *Steinberg v. Columbia Pictures Industries, Inc.,*[16] the plaintiff was an artist who had created a cover for *New Yorker* magazine that presented a humorous view of geography through the eyes of a New York City resident. The defendant's movie poster advertised the film *Moscow on the Hudson* by using a similar piece of artwork with many similar elements. The court considered the movie company's commercial purpose and determined that the poster was an infringement, not an excusable parody.

3.3 MUSIC: LIMITATIONS ON MUSICAL WORKS AND SOUND RECORDINGS

MTV combines videos with music. The copyright laws have kept pace with these innovations.

Popular music has become a backdrop for 20th-century culture, as each generation marks its memories and achievements by the sound of certain songs and performers. In the 1950s, musical works were sold in sheet music, performed in concerts, played on the radio, and distributed in phonorecords. By the 1990s, the uses of musical works increased to include adaption of works for commercial endorsement, synchronization of works with videos and movies, reproduction in digital formats such as compact discs, and taking of digital samples of sound recordings to create new works. Copyright law has adapted to the changes by extending protection in certain specific manners (i.e., the 1972 amendment protecting sound recordings) and limiting protection in other ways.

In addition to the principles of fair use and the first sale doctrine, several limitations on musical works and sound recordings are specifically set forth in the Copyright Act of 1976. For example, permission is not required to play a radio broadcast of musical works in a small business establishment using home receiver equipment. (These limitations are discussed more fully later.)

Limits on Exclusive Rights in Sound Recordings

As noted in Chapter 2 and earlier in this chapter, the rights in sound recordings are limited, and are different from the rights in musical works. Section 114 of the Copyright Act, 17 U.S.C. § 114, defines the scope of exclusive rights in sound recordings. Although there is no performance or display right for sound recordings, there are limitations on the right to reproduce and adapt sound recordings. The reproduction right is limited solely to reproducing the sounds on the recording. Simulation and imitation of sound recordings is not prohibited. By way of example, it is not an infringement of the copyright in a sound recording of the Beatles to make another recording with the same arrangement and the same style of performance. However, such imitation may give rise to claims under tort, trademark, unfair competition, right of publicity, and other areas of law discussed in later chapters. The right of adaptation of sound recordings is also limited. A derivative of a sound recording can only consist of a rearrangement, remixing, or alteration in sequence or quality of the sounds. Section 114 also provides that educational television and public broadcasting entities are exempt from the reproduction, adaptation, and distribution rights in sound recordings, provided that they do not commercially distribute copies or phonorecords to the public.

No Right to Rent Phonorecords

Congress has added provisions to the Copyright Act of 1976 to curb the ability of persons to duplicate certain works. A 1984 amendment, 17 U.S.C. § 109(b), prohibits the commercial rental of phonorecords. A **phonorecord** is a material object on which sounds are fixed (e.g., audio cassette tapes, vinyl record, compact discs, and reel-to-reel tapes). A phonorecord often includes two copyrights: a sound recording copyright and an underlying musical works copyright. Unless renewed, this exception for the rental of phonorecords (as well as the prohibition on renting software) will terminate on October 1, 1997. Under the 1984 amendment, any commercial enterprise that rents phonorecords will be infringing. Nonprofit libraries, however, are permitted to rent or lend phonorecords without authorization.

Performance in Conjunction with Retail Sale of Phonorecords

The Copyright Act of 1976 exempts the performance of nondramatic musical works at businesses that sell and promote the sale of copies or phonorecords of musical works. *See* 17 U.S.C. § 110(7). In other words, it is not an infringement for a business such as Tower Records to play musical works over its loudspeaker system. Similarly, a store that sells sheet music of musical works is free to play recordings of musical works without authorization from the copyright owners. The exemption applies only if the business is open to the public, does not charge admission, and the musical performance is not transmitted outside the establishment.

Ephemeral Recordings

Radio stations often need to make copies of musical works for purposes of later transmission. These copies (or phonorecords) are referred to as **ephemeral recordings**. For example, a radio station often "carts" a new recording; that is, the employees copy a compact disc or cassette tape onto a form of cartridge audiotape that can be used more easily by the station. A broadcaster is permitted, under certain circumstances, to make ephemeral recordings. *See* 17 U.S.C. § 112. The conditions may vary, based upon the nature of the intended use, the nature of the work, and the type of broadcaster. A traditional commercial broadcaster who has complied with licensing provisions may make one phonorecord for local transmission and preserve it for archival purposes.

Recording Musical Works: Compulsory License for Phonorecords

As discussed earlier in this chapter, the right to perform a musical work is known as the *performance right*. Performance rights societies commonly grant authorization for a radio station, tavern, or television network to perform songs. The right to *reproduce* the musical work on phonorecords is commonly known as the *mechanical right*. These two rights are the primary

LEGAL TERMS

phonorecord
Material objects in which sounds, other than those accompanying a motion picture or other audiovisual work, are fixed by any method now known or later developed, and from which the sounds can be perceived, reproduced, or otherwise communicated, either directly or with the aid of a machine or device. The term *phonorecord* includes the material object in which the sounds are first fixed.

ephemeral recordings
Copies or phonorecords of works, made for purposes of later transmission.

sources of income for songwriters. The performance right is acquired by negotiating a license with the performing rights society, but the mechanical license may be acquired by a different system known as a compulsory license. A **compulsory license** is a system established by statute, that permits the use of copyrighted works under certain circumstances, provided that certain fixed fees are paid. The advantage of compulsory licensing is that the person performing the work does not have to negotiate directly with the copyright owner for permission to perform the work.

The Copyright Act of 1976 provides a very important compulsory license for singers, performers, and manufacturers of phonorecords. This is known as the *compulsory license for mechanical rights* or *compulsory mechanical license.* **Mechanical rights** are the rights to prepare and distribute phonorecords of a nondramatic musical work (e.g., a popular song) under a compulsory license.

According to the provisions of the compulsory mechanical license, a singer could record a musical work without authorization from the copyright owner. To use this compulsory license, though, there are certain conditions. First, the song must have already been distributed to the public on a phonorecord. In other words, the author may control the *first* release of the song—only after the song's initial release on phonorecords is the compulsory license available. Second, a compulsory license is available only if the primary purpose in making phonorecords is to distribute them to the public for private use. In other words, the phonorecords are manufactured for distribution through traditional retail sale outlets or for play on home audio equipment.

This license is not available for synchronizing music with movies, television, or video. This is a separate right known as the **synchronization right**. In addition, the person recording the song, cannot change the basic melody or fundamental character of the work. For example, a performer may arrange the song, but cannot alter the lyrics.

Assuming these conditions are met, the person making the recording must serve a notice of intention on the copyright owner of the musical work within 30 days of making the recording and prior to distributing it, and thereafter must make payments every month. The payments are made for each phonorecord and are based upon a rate that is periodically set. The rate varies per reproduction or per minute of playing time or fraction thereof, whichever amount is larger. Because this system, particularly the monthly recording requirement, is difficult to manage, many record companies negotiate privately with an organization that serves as an agent for copyright owners. (A list of such companies is included at the end of this chapter.) It is not a violation of copyright law for a copyright owner to negotiate a rate for mechanical licensing that is lower than the statutory right; record companies commonly negotiate such arrangements with new songwriters. In addition to the compulsory mechanical license to record a nondramatic musical work, 17 U.S.C. § 115 provides that in the case of duplication of an actual sound recording, permission must be obtained from the owner of the sound recording. For example, if a company wanted to duplicate Bruce Springsteen's version of "Born to

Run," the company would have a right to a compulsory license in the underlying musical work, but permission would still have to be obtained from the copyright owner of the sound recording, usually the record company.

Coin-Operated Phonorecord Players: Jukebox Compulsory License

When the Copyright Act of 1909 was drafted, player pianos and penny music machines were the only coin-operated machines that played music. In what was later termed a "historical accident," Congress granted a blanket exemption to all coin-operated music machines, provided that no fee was charged to enter the establishment where the machine was located. The result was that songwriters received no payment for the playing of their songs on coin-operated machines. Section 116 of the Copyright Act of 1976, 17 U.S.C. § 116, ended that exemption. The proprietors of an establishment in which a jukebox is located must pay for the right to play musical works. However, if the machine qualifies as a coin-operated phonorecord player, the proprietor does not have to negotiate licenses for use of the music; the proprietor may simply pay a compulsory license fee. A **coin-operated phonorecord player** is a machine or device that is employed solely for the performance of non-dramatic musical works by means of phonorecords and upon insertion of coins or currency (or their equivalent).

To qualify for the compulsory license, the device must be accompanied by a list of the titles of all the works, and that list must be displayed prominently. Finally, the machine must be located in an establishment that makes no direct or indirect charge for admission, and the choice of the music must be made by the patrons. For example, a jukebox kept behind a bar and operated by the owner of the tavern would not qualify for the compulsory license. In that case, the proprietor would have to negotiate performance rights either with the copyright owner or one of the performing rights societies. If the jukebox qualifies for the compulsory license, the operator of the machine must file an application with the Copyright Office, pay a fee, and affix a certificate to each licensed jukebox.

Other Limitations Regarding Musical Works and Sound Recordings

As indicated in Table 3.2, there are other limitations as to musical works and sound recordings. For example, nonprofit libraries or certain educational or fraternal organizations may perform musical or other works without payment. These limitations and compulsory licenses include many types of works, such as literary works.

LEGAL TERMS

compulsory license
System established by statute that permits the use of copyrighted works under certain circumstances and provided that certain fixed fees are paid.

mechanical rights
Rights to prepare and distribute phonorecords of a nondramatic musical work under a compulsory license.

synchronization right
The right to record music in timed relation to visual images and to reproduce, perform, and distribute the musical work in connection with an audiovisual work.

coin-operated phonorecord player
A machine or device employed solely for the performance of nondramatic musical works by means of phonorecords and upon insertion of coins or currency (or their equivalent). To qualify for compulsory license, such a device must meet the requirements of 17 U.S.C. § 116.

Use	Requirements
Playing music in a store or business	*Musical Works:* Permission required from owners of musical works if music is played to public. Permission can be obtained from performing rights societies. No permission required if a business plays a radio using home-style audio equipment. No permission required from record stores. No permission required if played via licensed jukebox. *Sound recordings:* No permission required from owner of copyright in sound recording.
Using music in a movie	*Musical works:* Permission required from owner of musical works if song is used in movie (synchronization right). Permission may be obtained from music publisher. *Sound recordings:* Permission required only if actual sound recording is being used (not if song is re-recorded).
Singer recording a song	*Musical works:* Permission required from songwriter for first publication (i.e., first release) of song. After first publication, compulsory license (mechanical license) is available. Contact permission organizations such as Harry Fox Agency. *Sound recordings:* No permission required unless using a portion of another sound recording (i.e., sampling another work).
Recording a copy of music	*Musical works:* Violation of copyright law although, if making a single copy for personal use, it may be excused under principles of fair use. *Sound recordings:* Violation of copyright law although, if making a single copy for personal use, it may be excused under principles of fair use.

TABLE 3.2
Musical Works and
Sound Recordings:
When Is Permission
Required?

3.4 BROADCASTING: LIMITATIONS ON RIGHTS

The business of broadcasting, whether radio or television, relies on copyrighted musical, dramatic, or informational works. Each broadcast may trigger performance, reproduction, adaptation, and display rights. In drafting the Copyright Act of 1976, broadcasters and other special-interest groups sought certain limitations and licensing provisions to guarantee the transmission of copyrighted works. For example, if a commercial broadcaster has complied with the licensing provisions, an ephemeral recording may be made of a work (excluding motion pictures or audiovisual works) for local transmission and preserved for archival purposes. Some of the other rights, limitations, and licenses pertaining to broadcasters are discussed in this section.

C B S

Broadcast Reception in a Public Place

It is important to remember that this exemption only protects owners of public establishments who receive transmissions on a single receiving apparatus. It is an exemption for home-style radios and televisions, but not for the use of home-style cassette or compact disc players or other apparatus that play prerecorded music or video. The playing of a CD player or a tape player in a store, or a videocassette machine in a bar, for example, is not permitted under this exemption. The exemption applies only to broadcast signals that are received and rebroadcast in a business establishment.

Transmission to Handicapped Audiences

Section 110(8), 17 U.S.C. § 110(8), is intended to aid the blind and deaf by permitting certain unauthorized performances of nondramatic literary works via transmission. To qualify, the performance must be in the course of a transmission specifically designed for blind persons (or other visually impaired persons who are unable to read as a result of their handicap) or to deaf persons (or other hearing-impaired persons who are unable to hear the aural signals accompanying a transmission of visual signals).

Section 110(9), 17 U.S.C. § 110(9), permits the performance on a single occasion of a dramatic literary work published at least 10 years before the date of the performance, by or in the course of a transmission specifically designed for and primarily directed to blind or other visually impaired persons who are unable to read normal printed material as a result of their handicap, provided that the performance is made without any purpose of direct or indirect commercial advantage and that there is only one performance of the same work by the same performers or under the auspices of the same organization.

The transmissions described in § 110(8) and (9) must occur through any of the following facilities: (1) a governmental body; (2) a noncommercial educational broadcast; (3) an authorized radio subcarrier; or (4) a cable system designed for and primarily directed to the blind or deaf.

Secondary Transmissions: Compulsory License for Cable Systems

A televised broadcast is often received and then retransmitted. For example, a cable television company receives various broadcasts and then retransmits the broadcasts to its subscribers. A hotel receives several cable channels and retransmits the broadcasts to various rooms in the hotel. The Copyright Act of 1976 breaks down this series of transmissions into primary and secondary transmissions and provides a slightly circuitous definition. A **secondary transmission** is defined as the further transmitting of a primary transmission simultaneously with the primary broadcast. The most common examples are cable television broadcasts or apartment house or hotel systems. A secondary transmission also may be a nonsimultaneous transmission of a

LEGAL TERMS

secondary transmission
The further transmitting of a primary transmission simultaneously with the primary broadcast; also, a nonsimultaneous transmission of a primary broadcast by a cable system not located within the United States.

primary broadcast by a cable system not located within the United States. A **primary transmission** is a transmission made to the public by a facility whose signals are received and further transmitted by a secondary transmission service, regardless of where or when the performance or display was first transmitted. To **transmit** a performance or display is to communicate it by any device or process whereby images or sounds are received beyond the place from which they are sent.

A **cable system** is a facility that receives televised broadcast signals and makes secondary transmissions of such signals by wires, cables, or other channels of communication to subscribing members of the public.

The regulations regarding the use and licensing of copyright works transmitted by primary and secondary transmitters are located in § 111 of the Copyright Act of 1976, 17 U.S.C. § 111. These regulations are complex. Generally, however, the relay of a transmission by a hotel or apartment house to private lodgings (where no charge is made to the guest for the broadcast) is exempt from licensing provisions. Similarly, the relay of transmissions by certain educational broadcasters in certain circumstances will be exempt. Cable systems that are not exempt must license the right to perform the work. If a nonexempt cable system meets the qualifications of § 111 of the Copyright Act of 1976, that cable system may register and pay a fee with the Copyright Office. If a nonexempt cable system does not qualify (e.g., if it creates all of its own programming and does not make secondary transmissions), then authorization and licensing must be negotiated directly with the copyright owner.

ESPN is an all-sports cable network. Cable systems have, and must comply with, special regulatory procedures.

3.5 EDUCATIONAL, RELIGIOUS, OR NONPROFIT GUIDELINES AND LIMITATIONS

In drafting the Copyright Act of 1976, Congress sought to provide benefits for certain educational, nonprofit, handicapped, religious, and charitable organizations. The guidelines and limitations examined in this section are intended to balance the interests of these groups with the rights of copyright owners.

Fair Use: Educational Copying Guidelines

When the Copyright Act of 1976 was drafted, individuals representing various groups established a set of fair use guidelines for educational copying. These guidelines were not adopted as law. These guidelines, as well as other regulations and rules regarding libraries, are available in Copyright Office Circular 21, *Reproduction of Copyrighted Works by Educators and Librarians*.

Limited Right to Reproduce for Libraries and Archives

Section 108 of the Copyright Act of 1976, 17 U.S.C. § 108, provides that nonprofit libraries or archives open to the public may, under certain conditions, prepare single copyrighted copies or phonorecords of works. All such copies and phonorecords must bear the copyright notice. For example, the preparation of a single copy for purposes of preservation or replacement is permitted. Such facilities will not be liable for copyright infringement for the unsupervised use of photocopying equipment provided that there is a notice on the photocopy machine that the making of such copies may be subject to copyright law. These rights do not extend to audiovisual works (except audiovisual works dealing with news). Furthermore, the rights may not extend to situations when the library is aware (or has reason to believe) that multiple copies are being made of a single work.

Face-to-Face Teaching Activities

It is not an infringement for any work to be displayed or performed by instructors or pupils in the course of systematic, face-to-face instruction in a nonprofit educational institution. A face-to-face teaching activity may include transmitting or amplifying the material within a place where all students are present, (as, for example, when a system hooks up several television monitors within a school). This exemption does not include broadcasting from an outside location into the classrooms. The performance must be an audience composed of pupils. A performance at a school event mixing pupils and non-students, such as a parent-student meeting, may not be exempted. There is no limitation on the types of works covered by the exemption. However, because the exemption, like the other exemptions in § 110, is for performance and display, it does not permit the reproduction of copies or phonorecords. Motion pictures are included within the teaching exemption, but the performance must be from a copy that was lawfully made, that is, produced under license of the copyright owner.

Instructional Broadcasting

Musical works or nondramatic literary works are the only works subject to the instructional broadcasting exemption. Therefore, this exemption does not include works such as motion pictures, musical comedies, or operas. Under this regulation, musical works or nondramatic literary works may be publicly broadcast, without authorization from the copyright owner, at nonprofit educational institutions or to government bodies if the broadcast is: (1) part of a regular instructional activity; (2) directly related to the teaching content of the broadcast; and (3) made primarily for reception in places of instruction (or to persons unable to attend places of instruction) or to government employees as part of their official duties. This exemption is intended to permit, for example, the performance of a song or the recitation of a literary work as part of a televised teaching program.

LEGAL TERMS

primary transmission
A transmission made to the public by a facility whose signals are received and further transmitted by a secondary transmission service, regardless of where or when the performance or display was first transmitted.

transmit
To communicate a copyrighted work by any device or process whereby images or sounds are received beyond the place from which they are sent.

cable system
A facility that receives television broadcast signals and makes secondary transmissions of such signals by wires, cables, or other channels of communication to subscribing members of the public.

Compulsory License in Connection with Noncommercial Broadcasting

A noncommercial educational broadcast station is permitted to exercise a narrow compulsory license regarding the display of pictorial, graphic, and sculptural works and nondramatic musical works. *See* 17 U.S.C. § 118. The station is permitted to display published pictorial, graphic, and sculptural works for limited periods of time (no more than three seconds) and for limited purposes such as montage. The station also may perform nondramatic musical works, but only when in conjunction with a concert or as background or theme music in a program. A noncommercial educational broadcast station can obtain this compulsory license by following a procedure that includes paying fees to the copyright owners, maintaining certain records that must be available to the owners of the copyrighted works, and, in certain situations, including a warning on reproductions of the transmission.

Certain Nonprofit Performances

The Copyright Act of 1976 provides an exemption for public nonprofit performances of musical and nondramatic literary works, which applies if the public performance is without any purpose of commercial advantage and before a live audience. *See* 17 U.S.C. § 110(4). What is the meaning of *commercial advantage?* The drafters of the Copyright Act of 1976 adopted previous judicial precedents known as "for-profit" rules. Generally, this means that the performers are not paid and that admission is not charged. If a fee is charged, the net proceeds must be used exclusively for educational, religious, or charitable purposes. To maintain the exemption, the performers may not be paid, but it is permitted to use persons who are under salary (for example, a choreographer who receives an annual salary or military performers who perform in the course of their duties). If a fee is charged, the author must be notified; however, the owner must object within seven days prior to the performance. This permits a copyright owner to object to performances for certain fund-raising activities. This exemption applies only to performance, not to the display of works. Because the exemption is intended for performance in front of a live audience, it does not apply to the transmission of a work. Therefore, under this exemption, the playing of a musical work in the presence of an audience would be exempted, but the broadcast transmission of that musical work would not.

Religious Services

As with the instructional broadcasting exemption, all musical works and nondramatic literary works are subject to a religious exemption from authorization. In addition, however, dramatico-musical works of a religious nature, such as oratorios, cantatas, musical settings of the mass, choral services, and the like, are exempted. Works such as secular operas and motion pictures, even if they have a religious theme, are not intended to be covered by this exemption. To be exempted from obtaining authorization from the copyright owner, the performance or display must be in the course of religious services at a house of worship or place of religious assembly. However, the exemption does not include performances or displays in the context of social activity at a house of worship. The exemption also does not extend to religious broadcasts, even when the broadcasts are from a place of worship.

Agricultural Fairs

Section 110(6), 17 U.S.C. § 110(6), exempts the performance of a nondramatic musical work by a governmental body or a nonprofit agricultural or horticultural organization or annual fairs or other exhibitions conducted by those bodies or organizations. It does not exempt other concessionaires at the same gatherings.

Nonprofit Veterans and Fraternal Organizations

Nonprofit veterans organizations or nonprofit fraternal organizations may perform nondramatic literary or musical works in the course of a social function, provided that the general public is not invited and that the proceeds from the performance, after deducting the reasonable costs of producing the performance, are used exclusively for charitable purposes. The social functions of any college or university fraternity or sorority are not included in this exemption unless the social function is held solely to raise funds for a specific charitable purpose.

3.6 COMPUTERS: SOFTWARE PROGRAM OWNER'S RIGHTS

Anyone who has used a personal computer is aware of the ease with which programs can be copied from disk to disk. In the 1970s, the manufacturers of computer software became concerned about the loss of revenue from unlawfully made copies. As previously noted, the first sale doctrine permitted the owner of a copy to dispose of that copy, including through rental. In the early days of the retail software business, some stores offered special trial rental agreements, which served as a means for consumers to obtain and copy software without authorization. Computer users also became concerned about copyright law because each act of copying a program, even for purposes of backup or installation, technically amounted to an infringement.

Copyright lawyers created a solution. Instead of *selling* their programs, owners would *license* these software products. The difference is that a **license** is a contract that grants rights or permission to do something under certain conditions. If the person licensing the software (the licensee) violates the terms of the grant, an infringement has occurred. Because the software has been licensed and not sold, no first sale has occurred and thus the first

LEGAL TERMS

license
A contract that grants rights or permission to do something, subject to certain conditions.

sale doctrine is not triggered. The software cannot be rented by the licensee to another. These agreements are known as **shrinkwrap agreements**, because the consumer enters into the license by breaking the shrinkwrapped plastic or envelope that seals the diskettes.

On the outside of the shrinkwrap, there is usually a warning to the effect that the consumer who breaks the wrap agrees to be bound by the terms and conditions set forth in the licensing agreement. (See figure 3-1.) The consumer is directed to these terms and conditions. The consumer is granted certain rights and warranties in exchange for the right to use the program. If the consumer does not wish to enter into the shrinkwrap agreement, a method is provided by which the program can be returned for a full refund. Sometimes the shrinkwrap agreement is triggered when the consumer signs and mails in the warranty or registration card. Because a shrinkwrap license is a combination of contract and warranty, it is governed by state law. Therefore, its enforceability may be determined by state rather than federal law.

Limited Right to Make Copies of Computer Programs

The Copyright Act of 1976 (as amended in 1984) permits the owner of a copy of a computer program to make or authorize the making of another copy or adaptation of that computer program, provided that: (1) such a new copy or adaptation is created as an essential step in the utilization of the computer program in conjunction with a machine and that it is used in no other manner, or (2) such new copy or adaptation is for archival purposes only and that all archival copies are destroyed in the event that continued possession of the computer program should cease to be rightful. Any exact copies prepared in accordance with the provisions of this section may be sold or otherwise transferred, along with the copy from which such copies were prepared, only as part of the sale or other transfer of all rights in the program. Adaptations prepared in this manner may be transferred only with the authorization of the copyright owner. Normally, the shrinkwrap agreement restates in a modified form the rights expressed in § 117 of the Copyright Act of 1976 (17 U.S.C. § 117), although instead of referring to the *owner* of the program, the term *licensee* may be substituted.

No Commercial Rental of Computer Programs

To some extent, one aspect of the shrinkwrap agreement was nullified when Congress amended the Copyright Act in 1990. An amendment to the first sale doctrine (§ 109) prohibited the commercial rental of computer programs. *See* 17 U.S.C. § 109(B). Unless renewed, this exception will terminate on October 1, 1997. Under this amendment, any commercial enterprise that rents software is infringing copyright. Nonprofit libraries, however, are permitted to rent or lend software without authorization. In addition, the rental or lending of computer programs is permitted: (1) if the program is embodied in a machine that does not permit copying (e.g., an exercise machine or handheld dictionary); or (2) if the software is intended for limited-purpose

FIGURE 3-1
This software manufacturer provides an inaccurate warning relating to return privileges. The correct statement should read "Opening this package indicates your acceptance of the terms and conditions of the attached License Agreement." The purchaser always has the right to return the disks if they are defective.

computers designed for playing video games (e.g., cartridge-style software used in Nintendo® games, but not disk-style software games used in personal computers). Finally, under a provision that went into effect December 1, 1991, the owner of a lawfully made arcade (coin-operated) video game can display or perform the game publicly without the copyright owner's consent. Despite the revision of the first sale doctrine, the shrinkwrap agreements continue to provide limitations on damages, as well as consumer warranties and notices as to rights under certain conditions such as government contracts. For these reasons, software manufacturers utilize this system of transfer of rights. Table 3.3 summarizes the various permissions required for uses of computer programs.

To protect software and to inform the public regarding copyright law, many software companies advertise or provide literature to the public regarding rights and uses of computer programs. The advertisement in figure 3-2 was sponsored by an association of software publishers.

SUMMARY

3.1 The Copyright Act of 1976 grants a bundle of rights to the author of a copyrightable work. This bundle includes the exclusive rights of reproduction, adaptation, publication, performance, and display of the work. The distribution right is limited by the first sale doctrine, which permits the owner of a lawfully made copy or phonorecord to sell or otherwise dispose of possession of that copy or phonorecord, without the authority of the copyright owner. However, the rental of phonorecords or computer programs is prohibited. The right to adapt the work (or make derivatives) has three important considerations. First, the author of a derivative cannot claim a right to material that is not original to that author. Second, the author of a derivative must obtain permission from the author of the underlying copyrighted work. Third, the

Use	Permission Requirements
Renting computer program	With some limited exceptions, a violation of copyright law, unless permission is granted by copyright owner of software program.
Making copies of computer program	Permitted to make one archival copy. May transfer the copy only when transferring ownership of the program. Any further copying is a violation of copyright law, unless permitted by license agreement. Under an amendment to 18 U.S.C. § 2319, signed in October 1992, copying of computer programs may also subject infringer to criminal penalties.
Using a program over a network	Generally a violation of copyright law, unless program is licensed for network use and the use does not exceed the permitted network license number (e.g., five users).
Adapting a program for a particular purpose	Customizing or adapting a program is permitted only to the extent such rights are granted in the license agreement. Distribution or further copying of adapted programs requires permission of copyright owner.

TABLE 3.3
Computer Programs: When Is Permission Required from Copyright Owner?

FIGURE 3-2
Sample advertisement intended to discourage software copying.

derivative work is a separately copyrightable work. The performance and display rights allow the copyright owner to control a performance or display where the public is gathered *or* the work is transmitted or otherwise communicated to the public. Congress has granted special moral rights to the copyright owner of a work of visual art.

3.2 Fair use permits the use of copyrighted material for limited purposes and without authorization from the copyright owner. A fair use determination is made by a federal court, which weighs several factors, including the purpose and character of the use, the nature of the copyrighted work, the amount and substantiality of the portion borrowed, and the effect of the use on the market for the copyright material. Parody is a form of fair use, and some borrowing from other material is permitted in order to conjure up the original.

3.3 Although the copyright owner of a sound recording acquires no performance rights, the presence of an underlying musical work requires a license of performance rights from the copyright owner of the musical work. The right to reproduce musical works on phonorecords is known as the mechanical license and may be granted under certain compulsory license provisions. There is also a compulsory license for the proprietors of jukeboxes. The rental of phonorecords is not permitted.

3.4 The owner of a commercial establishment open to the public is permitted to use a radio, television, or receiving device commonly used in private homes without acquiring a performance rights license. A compulsory license is available to cable systems for the transmission of secondary broadcasts.

3.5 Certain reproductions for educational, archival, and library purposes are noninfringing under nonprofit and educational exemptions. Performance rights for purposes such as fraternal meetings, agricultural fairs, or performance for the handicapped may be exempt from licensing requirements.

3.6 Owners of computer programs may not rent those programs, but they may make copies for purposes of installation or archival (backup) purposes. Software manufacturers use a system known as a shrinkwrap agreement to license programs to end users.

NOTES

1. 17 U.S.C. § 103 (derivative rights).
2. Rogers v. Koons, 960 F.2d 301 (2d Cir. 1992).
3. 17 U.S.C. § 106A (moral rights: fine arts attribution and integrity).
4. Universal City Studios, Inc. v. Sony Corp., 464 U.S. 417 (1984).
5. Salinger v. Random House, Inc., 811 F.2d 90 (2d Cir. 1987).
6. Harper & Row v. Nation Enters., 471 U.S. 539 (1985).
7. Twin Peaks v. Publications Int'l Ltd., 1993 U.S. App LEXIS 13454 (2d Cir. 1993), *aff'g* 778 F. Supp. 1247 (S.D.N.Y. 1991).

8. Keep Thomson Governor Comm. v. Citizens for Gallen Comm., 457 (N.H. 1978).
9. Love v. Kwitny, 772 F. Supp. 1367 (S.D.N.Y. 1989).
10. Craft v. Kobler, 667 F. Supp. 120 (S.D.N.Y. 1987).
11. Martin Luther King, Jr. Center for Social Change, Inc. v. American Heritage Prods., Inc., 508 F. Supp. 854 (N.D. Ga. 1981).
12. Fisher v. Dees, 794 F.2d 432 (9th Cir. 1986).
13. Elsmere Music, Inc. v. National Broadcasting Co., 482 F. Supp. 741 (S.D.N.Y.), *aff'd,* 632 F.2d 252 (2d Cir. 1980).
14. Original Appalachian Artworks, Inc. v. Topps Chewing Gum, Inc., 642 F. Supp. 1031 (N.D. Ga. 1986).
15. Walt Disney Prods. v. Air Pirates, 581 F.2d 751 (9th Cir. 1978).
16. Steinberg v. Columbia Pictures Indus., Inc., 663 F. Supp. 706 (S.D.N.Y. 1987).

QUESTIONS FOR REVIEW AND DISCUSSION

1. What are the five rights granted by copyright law? Are these rights granted for all copyrightable works?
2. Does it make a difference as to which right granted under copyright law has been infringed?
3. Can a derivative song based upon a public domain work be protected under copyright law?
4. When does a performance of a copyrighted work become a public performance?
5. Since the copyright owner of a sound recording is not granted a performance right, does a radio station require authorization to play a copyrighted pop song?
6. What group of authors have acquired moral rights under U.S. copyright law?
7. What copyrighted works cannot be rented after a first sale has occurred?
8. What are the four factors used for making a fair use determination?
9. What rights does the owner of a computer program have to make copies of the program?
10. Under what conditions can the maker of a phonorecord acquire a compulsory license to record a musical work?

ACTIVITIES

1. Identify a popular book, such as *The Shining,* and determine how many derivatives have been created from that work.
2. Review the factual situation in the Commentary. Based upon the information presented in this chapter, does the use of the two copyrighted

songs require permission from the copyright owner? Does this use qualify for a compulsory license? Does the performance of the music at the press release qualify under any exemption?

3. List some guidelines for a nonprofit student broadcasting station that plays nondramatic musical and nondramatic literary works.

4. Identify examples of parody from television or motion pictures and determine if such parodies qualify as a fair use or if permission should have been required.

PROJECT

Create a fictional record company and determine what rights it must acquire to release a recording. Consider the recording, the musical works, the creation of the cover artwork, and other promotional works related to the record business. Determine the ways in which the record company can maximize its income, including limiting mechanical rights or acquiring rights in musical works.

FOR MORE INFORMATION

Copyright Authorization

A claim of copyright infringement can be avoided by acquiring the copyright owner's authorization. First, the correct owner of copyright must be determined. Ownership is determined by examining the work and performing a copyright search. (Copyright search procedures are explained Chapter 5.) Sometimes a clearance service (some of which are listed here) may assist in locating the correct owner. Once the correct owner is determined, authorization can be obtained by contacting the owner directly, negotiating with the owner's agent or attorney, or using a clearance service. Clearance organizations that deal only with music are provided later in this listing.

Copyright Clearance Center, 27 Congress Street, Salem, MA, 01970. Performs clearance services.
BZ Rights & Permission, Inc., 125 West 72nd Street, New York, NY 10023.
International Permissions Service, P.O. Box 33476 Detroit, MI 48232.

Authorization to Use Musical Works

As indicated in this chapter, the duplication or performance of musical works may be authorized under a license from the owner. There are two types of licenses, a mechanical license and a performance rights license.

Mechanical licensing (i.e., the right to "cover" or make copies of the song) may be acquired through:

Harry Fox Agency, Inc., 205 East 42d Street, New York, NY 10017 or

American Mechanical Rights Association (AMRA), 333 South Tamiami Trail, #205, Venice, FL 34285.

Performance rights licensing (e.g., the right to play a song on the radio or in a tavern) may be acquired through:

Broadcast Music Incorporated (BMI), 320 West 57th Street, New York, NY 10019 or

American Society of Composers, Authors and Publishers (ASCAP), One Lincoln Plaza, New York, NY 10023.

Mechanical Royalty Rates

Currently, a business making copies of a song must pay the songwriter 6.25 cents per reproduction or 1.25 cents per minute of playing time or fraction thereof, whichever amount is larger. Therefore, if a record company released 100,000 copies of a new version of a three-minute song written by Dolly Parton, the record company would owe the songwriter or her publisher $6,250 (unless a lower rate had been negotiated between the parties). The mechanical license rate will go up in January 1994. For information on the current rate, call the Copyright Office Public Information number (1-202-707-3000) or the Copyright Office Licensing Division (1-202-707-8150).

Music Licensing

Shemel & Krasilovsky, *This Business of Music* (Billboard Publications 1985). A popular one-volume music law text used by both attorneys and nonattorneys.

Kohn & Kohn, *The Art of Music Licensing* (Prentice-Hall Law & Business 1992). A thorough one-volume treatise dealing solely with issues relating to music licensing, including sampling and other new media.

CHAPTER 4
Copyright Ownership

It terrified me to have an idea that was solely mine to be no longer
a part of my mind, but totally public.

Maya Lin, designer of the Vietnam Veterans Memorial in Washington, DC

OUTLINE

COMMENTARY

Softco, a computer company, wants to create an educational software program, Macho Math, *for students learning mathematics. The president of Softco contracts with Nancy and Lee, two programmers. Lee writes the computer program and Nancy designs the graphics for the program. They do most of their work at home on computer equipment lent to them by Softco. Twice a week Nancy and Lee use the Softco offices to test the program on various machines. Each week, the president of Softco views their progress and makes comments. Lee and Nancy receive $1,000 a week for 12 weeks. They will also receive a percentage of royalties from the sale of the program. They deliver the video game on time and receive a final bonus of $1,000. Before they commenced work, Nancy and Lee signed a piece of paper saying that the video game shall be a work made for hire. Softco registers the copyright to the video game program and sells it nationally. Nancy and Lee make copies of the video game program and sell it via a computer network bulletin board. Softco wants to stop Lee and Nancy's sale of the program.*] what can be done?

OBJECTIVES

Chapter 3 gave you a description of the bundle of rights granted to each author and the limitations on those rights. This chapter introduces you to the issues relating to ownership of copyright. After reading this chapter, you will be able to:

- Explain the difference between the rights of an author and the owner of a copy or phonorecord.
- Identify a joint work and distinguish between the rights of joint authorship and sole authorship.
- Differentiate between various types of transfers of copyright ownership.
- Distinguish between the copyright ownership of derivative and collective works.
- Explain the two methods by which works made for hire are created.
- Understand the procedures and requirements for recording transfers of copyright ownership.
- Determine the duration of protection for authors' different works.
- Understand the procedure for terminating transfer of copyright ownership.

4.1 OWNERSHIP OF COPYRIGHT

The author initially acquires all rights to a copyrightable work. This means that the author is the original owner of copyright.[1] The author may be the creator of the work, or, under certain circumstances, the party employing the creator or commissioning the work. The **owner of copyright** holds title

LEGAL TERMS

owner of copyright
Person or persons holding title to copyright; either the author or any party to whom the author has licensed or transferred a right under copyright.

to copyright or any of the rights granted under copyright law. Ownership of copyright, like ownership of real or personal property, enables the owner to transfer, license, sell, or grant rights to another person. For example, Paul McCartney purchased the copyright to songs written by Buddy Holly. Mr. McCartney, as owner of copyright, acquires most of the rights and remedies under copyright law that were originally available to Mr. Holly.

Disputes often arise as to the ownership of copyright. For example, a dispute may arise between two parties who both believe they have acquired copyright ownership. The parties may settle the matter or submit it to a court for a final determination. Proving ownership requires evidence documenting the creation of the work, the employment status of the creator, or transfer of the title of copyright. Much of the law surrounding copyright ownership is based upon court decisions. Some of the issues dealing with ownership of copyright are determined by principles of contract or state law.

Registration Does Not Prove Ownership

Registration of copyright by the Copyright Office does not prove ownership, but registration within five years of publication does create a presumption of ownership or prima facie proof of title. Like all legal presumptions, it can be overcome by a sufficient showing of proof to the contrary. For example, in the Commentary to this chapter, Softco registered the copyright to *Macho Math*. However, if Nancy and Lee can prove that they are really the owners of the program, Softco's registration would be canceled and a new registration would be issued to Nancy and Lee. Alternatively, the Copyright Office may, under certain circumstances, issue a second registration without canceling the first one and let the parties litigate the ownership issue.

Ownership of a Copy Does Not Establish Rights

Ownership of a material object, like a painting, is distinct from the ownership of copyright.[2] For example, if a person purchases original handwritten lyrics by Buddy Holly, that sale does not convey the right to reproduce or distribute copies of the lyrics. Similarly, if an individual buys a box of discarded tape recordings by famous performers, she may not authorize copying of the musical works or sound recordings embodied on those tapes. The purchaser has only acquired ownership of a material object. She has not acquired ownership of copyright.

4.2 JOINT AUTHORSHIP AND CO-OWNERSHIP

When two people create a work together, the result may be a joint work. The Copyright Act of 1976 defines a **joint work** as a work prepared by two or more authors with the intention that their contributions will be merged into inseparable or interdependent parts of a unitary whole.

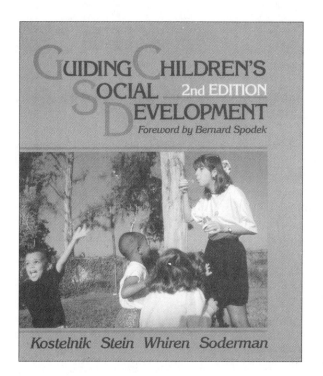

The textbook *Guiding Children's Social Development,* 2nd edition (Delmar 1993) is an example of joint work.

Some examples of joint works are a textbook on child development written by four professors; the play *You Can't Take It with You,* written by George Kaufman and Moss Hart; or the song "Satin Doll," created by lyricist Johnny Mercer and composer Billy Strayhorn. The drafters of the Copyright Act of 1976 stated that the touchstone of a joint work is the intention "at the time the writing is done, that the parts be absorbed or combined into an integrated unit." In other words, if Mick Jagger intended that the lyrics for "Satisfaction" would be consolidated with music by Keith Richards, then the resulting song would be a joint work. Most songs written by two or more people are joint works. Joint authors are co-owners of copyright. Similarly, in the case of *Macho Math,* in the Commentary, if Nancy and Lee can prove they authored the software program, they would be joint authors or co-owners of the work.

Determining the Value of Each Author's Contribution

If one person writes lyrics and one writes music, what percentage of royalties should be given to each joint author? For example, are the lyrics worth more than the music? If there is no agreement, a court will presume that each joint author had an undivided interest in relation to the total number of joint authors. For example, if three people write a song together and there is no written agreement, the presumption is that each person is entitled to one-third of the revenues. This presumption is not expressed in the Copyright

LEGAL TERMS

joint work
A work prepared by two or more authors with the intention that their contributions will be merged into inseparable or interdependent parts of a unitary whole.

Act, but is based upon common law principles, court decisions, and the writing of legal commentators.

If the authors enter into an agreement, they may divide the revenues from the work in any manner they choose, regardless of each author's contribution. The authors may also divide different sources of revenues in different fashions. For example, two software programmers may agree to one system of dividing revenues from retail sales and another system of dividing revenues from foreign licensing. When two authors set about to create a work, these proportions are set forth in a **collaboration agreement,** a contract in which joint authors specify the rights, obligations, percentage of copyright ownership, and revenues attributable to each author. Such collaboration agreements are common in the creation of works such as books (e.g., when an illustrator and a writer collaborate), songs, software programs, and screenplays.

Other Forms of Co-Ownership of Copyright

In addition to joint authorship, the co-ownership of copyright may also occur for other reasons. As discussed later in this chapter, co-ownership of copyright can result from transfer of ownership, intestate succession, or community property laws. The various methods of acquiring co-ownership are listed in the following checklist.

Checklist for Determining Co-Ownership of Copyright

- Is this work is created by two or more authors?
- Has the author of the work transferred copyright ownership jointly to several persons?
- Has the author transferred a portion of the copyright interest and retained the remaining interest?
- Has the copyright ownership passed by will or intestate succession to two or more persons?
- Is the work subject to community property laws?
- Did the renewal rights in the work vest in two or more persons?

If the answer to any of these questions is "yes," the copyright is probably subject to rules of co-ownership.

Co-Owners Are Tenants in Common

Co-owners are *tenants in common.* A **tenancy in common** is a way for co-owners to hold title so that each has an independent right to use or license the use of a work, subject to a duty of accounting to the other co-owners for any profits.

Suppose, by way of example, that Sam and Barbara jointly create the song "Love Me." Either Sam or Barbara can license the musical composition for nonexclusive uses, such as in a television commercial or movie. Either Sam or Barbara may do so without the permission of the other, provided, however, that an accounting is made for a share of the profits. If another author infringes the copyright on "Love Me," either Sam or Barbara may sue the infringer. If a judgment is awarded because of the infringement lawsuit, the parties must share in the judgment according to their percentage of ownership.

All Co-Owners Must Consent to an Exclusive License or Transfer

The only exception to rules regarding a co-owner's right to license the work is that a co-owner cannot grant an exclusive license of rights without seeking the consent of the other co-owners. An **exclusive license** is an agreement to restrict the grant of proprietary rights to one person. For example, two programmers create a software program. The Softco Company wants the exclusive license to distribute the program (i.e., Softco wants to be the *only* company that can distribute the program). The consent of both programmers must be obtained.

JUDGE LEARNED HAND ON COPYRIGHT LAW: THE BIRD ON NELLIE'S HAT

Any co-owner of the work may license the work, or, if necessary, sue infringers of the work, if the other co-owners receive a fair share of the profits or judgment. This rule of co-ownership, memorialized in the Copyright Act of 1976, was adopted from a 1944 court decision by Judge Hand.

In *Edward B. Marks Music Corp. v. Jerry Vogel Music,* 140 F.2d 268 (2d Cir. 1944), Judge Hand was faced with a case involving a song entitled, "The Bird on Nellie's Hat." The author of an infringing song was sued by one of the co-owners of "The Bird on Nellie's Hat." The defendant (the author of the infringing song) argued that *both* co-owners must sue him for the case to go forward. Judge Hand disagreed. He established the legal principle that either co-owner of copyright may bargain for, or litigate rights regarding, the copyright, provided that the other co-owner receives an equitable interest in the results of the bargain or lawsuit.

The Death of a Co-Owner

Under a tenancy in common, if a co-owner dies, his or her share goes to beneficiaries or heirs. Unlike some forms of joint property ownership, it does not matter which author survives the other. For example, John Lennon and Paul McCartney jointly created the song "Yesterday." After Mr. Lennon's death, his rights in the song passed to his estate, not to Mr. McCartney.

Table 4.1 summarizes the rights and duties of co-owners.

4.3 OWNERSHIP OF COPYRIGHT IN COLLECTIVE WORKS

A *collective work* is a form of compilation in which many separate and independent works are assembled into a collective whole. The person who selects and assembles the works is the author and copyright owner of the collective work. For example, the editor who assembles various poems for a poetry anthology is the author of the collective work (the anthology). As copyright owner, that person controls the right to duplicate the collection as a group. In addition, the owner of copyright in the collective work can revise the collection. For example, Nancy, a poet, agrees to permit the use of her poem in *Splendor,* a poetry magazine. The owner of *Splendor* only acquires the right to use the poem in the magazine (unless there is a written agreement to the contrary). The magazine acquires no right to revise the poem or to use it in a different collection.

Contribution to a Collective Work

The Copyright Act of 1976 provides that copyright in each separate contribution to a collective work is distinct from copyright in the collective

Action	Rights
Licensing	Any co-owner may bargain for, or license rights regarding, the copyright, provided that the other co-owners receive an equitable interest in the results of the bargain or contract. No co-owner may execute an exclusive license without the permission of the other co-owners.
Litigation	Any co-owner may litigate or be sued regarding the copyright. If any co-owner recovers damages in a lawsuit, that co-owner is only entitled to damages equal to its equitable interest in the copyright.
Death of a co-owner	Upon the death of a co-owner, that share in the copyright will pass to survivors of the co-owner under a legal will or the principles of intestate succession.

TABLE 4.1
Co-Ownership of Copyright

work as a whole, and vests initially in the author of the contribution. *See* 17 U.S.C. § 201(c). This makes it clear, for example, that the poet who creates the poem "Spring" maintains copyright of the poem, despite its publication in a collective work.

Distinguishing Between a Contribution to a Collective Work and Joint Authorship

What is the difference between creating a contribution for a collective work and being a joint author? By way of example, consider the following: Nancy is a poet. Her poem, "Spring," is selected for use in a poetry collection, *Great Poems About the Seasons*. Nancy has no copyright ownership or control over the book. Her ownership extends only to her poem. A musician asks Nancy to write lyrics for a song called "Winter." The resulting song is a joint work and Nancy and the musician are co-owners. Either party may license the song, provided that they share in the revenues, and provided that such a relationship does not contradict principles of state law. The difference between the book and the song is that Nancy intended, when writing "Winter," that her words would be merged with music to create a new work. She had no such intention when writing the poem "Spring."

Table 4.2 summarizes the law pertaining to collective work ownership.

4.4   WORKS MADE FOR HIRE

As explained earlier, the author, for copyright purposes, may be the employer of the person creating the work or the party commissioning the work.

Author of a collective work	Unless there is a written agreement to the contrary, the author of the collective work owns copyright in the collective work as a group and may revise the collective work or produce a new series.
Author of a contribution to a collective work	Unless there is a written agreement to the contrary, the author of a contribution to a collective work owns copyright in the individual work and only grants rights for use in the collective work. The author of an individual contribution may restrict the use in the collective work (i.e., one-time only) or may license the individual work for other uses or for other collections.
Difference between joint authorship and a contribution to a collective work	The joint author is a co-owner of copyright and acquires all rights and obligations of a co-owner. The joint author may license the work. The author of a contribituion to a collective work does not own copyright in the collective work and may not license the collective work.

TABLE 4.2
Ownership of a Collective Work

Obviously, a business that expends considerable sums to create a copyrightable work will want to claim authorship. This principle, known as the *work-made-for-hire doctrine,* shifts original ownership of the copyright from the creator of the work to the employer. Determining whether a work is made for hire is very important. Consider the following scenario: A charitable organization hires a public broadcasting crew to videotape the Mardi Gras in New Orleans. The video crew later licenses portions of the video for use in a sexy movie. The charity is unable to stop the second use because a court has determined that the video crew retained rights of ownership in the videotape and could license it freely. This result could have been avoided if the persons hiring the crew had been familiar with the concept of works made for hire.

It is important to realize that there are two separate ways that a work made for hire can occur. The Copyright Act of 1976, 17 U.S.C. § 101, defines a **work made for hire** as either: (1) a work prepared by an employee within the scope of his or her employment; or (2) a work specially ordered or commissioned for use as a contribution to a collective work, as a part of a motion picture or other audiovisual work, as a translation, as a supplementary work, as a compilation, as an instructional text, as a test, as answer material for a test, or as an atlas, if the parties expressly agree in a written instrument signed by them that the work shall be considered a work made for hire. As explained later, two parties cannot enter into a work-made-for-hire agreement to create a commissioned work that is *not* in one of these categories. For example, a work-made-for-hire agreement for a commissioned painting (not used as a part of a collective work) would not be valid.

If the work is created as a work made for hire, the hiring party (whether an individual or a business entity) is the author and should be named the author in space 2 of the application for registration.[3] The work-made-for-hire status of a work will affect the length of copyright protection and termination rights, as discussed later in this section.

Works Prepared by an Employee Within the Scope of Employment

A work made for hire can be created in two separate ways. The first method is by an employee within the scope of employment. Under this first method, the court will examine the relationship between the hired party and the person doing the hiring. If the court determines that the work was created within the scope of an employer-employee relationship, the work will be categorized as made for hire.

Scope of Employment

To qualify under the first method of creating a work made for hire, the work must be created within the scope of employment. Therefore, if a programmer creates a software program before beginning employment at a computer company, that software program will not be a work made for hire. Similarly, if a woman works as a waitress but writes a song while at work, that song is not a work made for hire, because songwriting is not within the scope of her employment.

Defining Employee-Employer Relationship: The CCNV Case

In 1989, in *Community for Creative Non-Violence v. Reid,*[4] the Supreme Court reviewed the standards for interpreting when an author is an employee for purposes of the work-for-hire doctrine. The Community for Creative Non-Violence (CCNV) is a nonprofit organization dedicated to eliminating homelessness in America. In 1985, CCNV decided to create a float for the Washington, D.C., Christmas Pageant. One director conceived of the idea of a statue as an analogy to the nativity scene with a homeless family huddled over a steam grate. They hired a sculptor named Reid. After compromising on the material to be used, Reid prepared a sketch. The CCNV requested some changes. Reid agreed to create the statue and received a $3,000 advance. The CCNV constructed the steam grate portion of the exhibit. On December 24, 1985, 12 days after the due date, Reid delivered the statue and was paid the final $15,000. After the pageant and a month on display, the CCNV wanted to take the statue to other cities. Reid, who now had possession of the sculpture, objected, claiming that the statue was too fragile. Reid wanted to take the statue on a less demanding exhibit tour. Both parties claimed copyright in the work.

The Supreme Court held that the sculpture was not a work made for hire because Reid was not an employee, as defined under law. To determine employee or independent contractor status, the Supreme stated that the following factors are weighed:

1. The skill required in the particular occupation
2. Whether the employer or the worker supplies the instrumentalities and tools of the trade
3. The location of the work
4. The length of time for which the person is employed
5. Whether the hiring party has the right to assign additional work projects to the hired party
6. The extent of the hired party's discretion over when and how long to work
7. The method of payment
8. The hired party's role in hiring and paying assistants
9. Whether the work is part of the regular business of the hiring party
10. Whether the hiring party is in business
11. The provision of employee benefits
12. The tax treatment of the hired party.

LEGAL TERMS

work made for hire
(1) a work prepared by an employee within the scope of his or her employment; or (2) a work specially ordered or commissioned for use as a contribution to a collective work, as a part of a motion picture or other audiovisual work, as a translation, as a supplementary work, as a compilation, as an instructional text, as a test, as answer material for a test, or as an atlas, if the parties expressly agree in a written instrument signed by them that the work shall be considered a work make for hire.

Other factors that the Supreme Court noted were whether the hired party is engaged in a distinct occupation; whether the work is usually done under the direction of the employer or by a specialist without supervision; and the method of payment, whether by the hour or by the job.

Reid was involved in a skilled occupation as a sculptor and supplied his own tools. He did the work at his own location and was treated as an independent contractor for purposes of payment, benefits, and taxes. The creation of sculptures was not part of the regular business of CCNV and the CCNV had little discretion over Reid's working hours or performance of further work. However, CCNV did some supervision of Reid and contributed a portion of the work (the steam grate).

Applying these factors, the Supreme Court determined that Reid was not an employee under the Copyright Act of 1976. The case was remanded to determine if CCNV and Reid were joint authors of the work. That is, did the parties have the intention that their contributions be merged into inseparable or interdependent parts of a unitary whole? The result was that the sculpture was considered a joint work and Reid and the CCNV were joint authors and co-owners of copyright.

In the case of the *Macho Math* program mentioned in the Commentary, it is necessary to consider the factors expressed by the Supreme Court in the *CCNV* case in light of Nancy and Lee's work. For example, Nancy and Lee do most of their work at home on their own machines. In addition, they are not on salary and do receive royalties from sales. All these elements would be weighed to determine if an employer-employee relationship existed.

Employment Agreement Is Not Controlling

Occasionally a hired party will be asked to sign a written agreement stating that the person is an employee and that works resulting from employment are works made for hire. Such an agreement may be a factor in a determination of ownership, and it also may be a factor in the second method of creating a work made for hire (i.e., a commissioned work in one of the categories), but a work-made-for-hire agreement does not prove that a work is made for hire. When determining if an employment relationship exists, as in the *CCNV* case, the court will examine the factors surrounding creation of the work to determine if a true employer-employee agreement exists. Therefore, when assessing whether a work is made for hire under an employer-employee relationship, an employer should not mistakenly assume that a signed agreement confirms ownership of the copyrighted work.

Effect of State Employment Law

Some states, such as California, require that employers who claim copyright ownership, through employer-employee work-for-hire relationships, must pay employee benefits, including worker's compensation, unemployment insurance, and disability insurance.[5]

Teachers and Professors: An Exception

Although there is little caselaw on the subject, some copyright practitioners believe that one exception to the employer-employee rule of works made for hire is that a university instructor or professor, not the employing educational institution, will own copyright in lectures and related works created during the scope of employment. This exception has not been extended to high-school or grade-school teachers, and may not be applicable to university administrators whose work is produced in a nonscholarly capacity.

What if an Employee Desires to Retain Control of Works?

If an employee desires to retain control of a specific work created during the scope of employment, then he or she should execute an agreement with the employer confirming that arrangement. For example, the letter agreement shown in figure 4-1 enables the Diskco company employee to retain control over a specific program.

Letter Agreement Confirming Employee's Ownership of Copyright

Emily Jones, Vice-President
Diskco Incorporated
1234 Silicon Drive
Chiptown, California

Dear Emily:

   For consideration which I acknowledge, this confirms the agreement between Diskco and myself that I shall own exclusive rights to the software program commonly known as *Macho Math* (more specifically described below). Although I created *Macho Math* within the scope of my employment at Diskco, Diskco now agrees that I shall be the owner of all rights, under copyright law, to *Macho Math,* as well as to any support documentation and manuals. You represent and warrant that you have the power to grant these rights on behalf of Diskco, and that, if required, a representative of Diskco will furnish any other necessary documents that are required to demonstrate my ownership. *Macho Math* comprises approximately 3,000 lines of source code. The program includes a means of generating formulas and equations used in instructing persons learning mathematics. It is an interactive video game and utilizes several visual icons, including a giraffe, a monkey, and

---

FIGURE 4-1
Sample letter of
agreement

other animals. You acknowledge that an object code version of *Macho Math* has been supplied to you. If this letter accurately reflects our agreement, please sign and return one copy to me.

Yours truly,
Jane L. Programmer

Acknowledged and Agreed to: Diskco Incorporated

By:_____
Emily Jones, Vice-President   Dated:_____

FIGURE 4-1
(Continued)

Commissioned Works

The second method by which a work may be characterized as made for hire is if (1) the work is specially ordered; (2) there is a written agreement signed by both parties indicating it is a work made for hire; and (3) the work is used in one of a group of specially enumerated works. To meet the standards of a commissioned work, *all* of the above criteria must be met.

Enumerated Categories

To qualify as a commissioned work made for hire, the work must be used as:

1. A contribution to a collective work
2. Part of a motion picture or other audiovisual work
3. A translation
4. A supplementary work (i.e., a work prepared for publication as a subsidiary adjunct to a work by another author for the purpose of introducing, concluding, illustrating, explaining, revising, commenting upon, or assisting in the use of the other work, such as forewords, afterwords, pictorial illustrations, maps, charts, tables, editorial notes, musical arrangements, answer material for tests, bibliographies, appendixes, and indexes)
5. A compilation
6. An instructional text (i.e., a literary, pictorial, or graphic work prepared for publication and with the purpose of use in systematic instructional activities)
7. A test or answer material for a test
8. An atlas.

If the use of the commissioned work does not fall into one of the enumerated categories, it does not matter if the parties have signed a written agreement. The result will not be a work made for hire. For example, a company commissions a sculptor to create a work to be displayed in the lobby of the company's building. The sculptor signs a work-for-hire agreement. The work will be owned by the sculptor, not the company, because the sculpture is not included among the enumerated uses. If, however, as in the case of the *Macho Math* program, presented in the Commentary, it can be argued that the program is instructional text, then Softco may be able to claim ownership under this second method of creating a work made for hire.

Signed Agreement

For a work to qualify as a commissioned work made for hire, there must be a signed agreement stating that the commissioned work is made for hire. At least one court has indicated that such an agreement will not be valid if executed *after* the work is completed. Therefore, it is recommended that such an agreement be executed prior to commencement of the work. Figure 4-2 is an example of a work-for-hire agreement.

WORK-FOR-HIRE AGREEMENT
Commissioned Work

For consideration, the sufficiency of which is acknowledged, Diskco Company, Inc. ("*Diskco*") commissions Joan Doolittle ("*Artist*") to create eight (8) illustrations (collectively referred to as the ("*Work*") as supplementary works for use in an instructional manual for the computer program *Holiday Break*. The Work consists of a series of black-and-white camera-ready pen-and-ink illustrations of the following holiday themes: New Year's, Christmas, Valentine's Day, Easter, President's Day, Independence Day, Halloween, and Thanksgiving. Artist agrees that Diskco shall acquire all rights in the Work, including but not limited to copyright in the Work as a "work made for hire" as that term is defined in the Copyright Act of 1976. Artist agrees to complete the Work according to the following schedule:

Preliminary sketches   January 10, 1993
Final Drawings   March 10, 1994

Diskco shall not be required to publish the Work, and whenever it does, Diskco, as owner of copyright, may add or delete from the Work and may or may not credit Artist as illustrator. Successors and assigns of Diskco shall have the same rights in the Work. Artist warrants that Artist is the sole creator of the work and that it is original, unpublished, and contains no plagiarized, defamatory, or otherwise unlawful materials, and will not invade the rights of privacy or publicity of any third parties.

    Artist agrees to indemnify and hold Diskco harmless from any loss or liability, including reasonable attorney's fees arising out of any breach or alleged breach of these warranties. This Agreement shall be governed by the laws of the state of _____. If any dispute arises under or relating to this Agreement, the prevailing party shall be entitled to its reasonable

---

FIGURE 4-2
Sample work-for-hire agreement

attorney's fees. This is the complete understanding between the parties and cannot be modified without an agreement in writing signed by the parties.

_____
Date

By:_____
    Diskco/Title of signer

_____
    Joan Doolittle, Artist

FIGURE 4-2
(Continued)

The following checklist will help you determine whether a work was made for hire.

Checklist: Determining if a Work Is Made for Hire

- *Method One:* Works created as an employee
  - ☐ Is the work created within the scope of employment?
  - ☐ Do the parties have an employer-employee relationship?

  Review the following:
  - ☐ What is the level of skill required in the particular occupation?
  - ☐ Does the employer or the worker supply the instrumentalities and tools of the trade?
  - ☐ What is the location of the work?
  - ☐ For what length of time is the worker employed?
  - ☐ Does the hiring party have the right to assign additional work projects to the hired party?
  - ☐ What is the extent of the hired party's discretion over when and how long to work?
  - ☐ What is the method of payment (i.e., by the job, by the hour, etc.)?
  - ☐ What is the hired party's role in hiring and paying assistants?
  - ☐ Is the work part of the regular business of the hiring party?
  - ☐ Is the hiring party in business?
  - ☐ Were employee benefits provided to the hired party?
  - ☐ What is the tax treatment of the hired party?
- *Method Two:* Commissioned works

  All three of the following questions must be answered affirmatively if the work is to qualify under this second method:
  - ☐ Is the work specially ordered or commissioned?
  - ☐ Does the work fall within one of the enumerated categories? (*See* 17 U.S.C. § 101)
  - ☐ Is there a signed agreement stating that it is work made for hire?

4.5 DURATION OF COPYRIGHT

United States copyright law changed significantly when the Copyright Act of 1976 was passed. A work that was published under the former Act of 1909 may still be protectible today, however. Thus, it is important to know which act governs a particular copyright, because the owner's rights and duties and duration of the copyright vary depending on when the copyright was acquired.

The Copyright Act of 1909

Under the Copyright Act of 1909, rights did not vest until either the author published the work or the unpublished work was registered. If a songwriter created a song and wrote it down, but never published it or registered it, it would not have been protected the U.S. copyright law, under the Copyright Act of 1909. It might have been protected under principles known as *common law copyright,* however. **Common law copyright** is a system of protection based upon the precedents and principles established by court decisions. Unlike federal copyright law, which is based upon written statutes and regulations, common law copyright is based upon precepts of law developed by judges. Common law copyright only affected certain unpublished works created before January 1, 1978.[6] Under the Copyright Act of 1909, once a work was published with the appropriate notice, the author acquired the rights granted under the federal statute.

Duration under the Copyright Act of 1909

Under the 1909 Act, protection lasted for an initial term of 28 years from the date copyright was secured. If the copyright was renewed during the last year of the term (i.e., the 28th year), protection would continue for an additional 28-year period. The second 28-year period of copyright term is known as the **renewal term**. Therefore, if renewed, the total time for protection under the Copyright Act of 1909 was 56 years. If the copyright was not renewed, protection ended after 28 years and the work passed into the public domain. Many well-known works, such as the film *It's a Wonderful Life,* fell into the public domain because the proprietors failed to renew copyright.

Effect of the Copyright Act of 1976

The Copyright Act of 1976 modified the duration of works protected under the earlier act.[7] The purpose of the modification was to extend the total length of copyright for works published under the previous act to 75 years. If a work was in its renewal term when the Copyright Act of 1976 went into effect, the renewal term was extended to 47 years. Alternatively, if a work registered under the Copyright Act of 1909 was in its first term on January 1, 1978, the work could be renewed for a period of 47 years. This 47-year period is

---

LEGAL TERMS

common law copyright
A system of protection based upon the precedents and principles established by court decisions; affected unpublished, unregistered works created before January 1, 1978; applied by state courts or federal courts interpreting state law.

renewal term
For works registered under the Copyright Act of 1909, it is a 28-year period following the initial 28-year term of copyright protection; renewal must have been made during the 28th year following first publication.

known as the **extended renewal term**. For example, if a work was created in 1940 and renewed in 1968, the duration of copyright was automatically extended to 2015 (47-year renewal term).

Works Not in Their Renewal Term as of January 1, 1978

If a work protected under the Copyright Act of 1909 was not in its renewal term on January 1, 1978 (the date the Copyright Act of 1976 went into effect), then the owner was required to renew copyright for an extended renewal term of 47 years. A failure to renew resulted in loss of copyright protection. For example, if a work was published in 1962 and the owner did not renew in 1990, the work fell into the public domain. However, because this system resulted in many unfair losses of copyright protection, Congress amended the Copyright Act in 1991 to provide for automatic renewal. Owners of copyright for works protected under the Copyright Act of 1909 no longer have to renew copyright; the protection is automatically extended for an additional 47-year period. However, certain incentives are offered to authors who voluntarily register for renewal during the 28th year.

No Provision for Restoring Protection

There is no provision under the Copyright Act of 1976 or its amendments to restore copyright protection for a work that has fallen into the public domain. In other words, if an author failed to renew, copyright protection cannot be revived. The work will never be protected under copyright law.

The Copyright Act of 1976

Prior to the Copyright Act of 1976, every copyright act in the United States provided for an initial term and a renewal term. Congress sought to avoid the confusion and unfortunate results created by the renewal process, so the Copyright Act of 1976 provides a simple system. Generally, copyright protection was granted for a period of the life of the author plus 50 years. No renewal is necessary for works registered under the Copyright Act of 1976.[8]

Date of Vesting of Copyright under the Copyright of 1976

As of January 1, 1978, an author acquires copyright at the moment when a work is created. This occurs when the work is *fixed,* e.g., when an artist places paint on a canvas, when a musician records a song on an audiotape, or when a choreographer notates the steps of a ballet. The date of creation is the date when copyright protection begins. For example, if a songwriter has a melody in her head and sings it aloud, rights are not vested until she writes it down or records it. At this point copyright protection begins, because the work has been fixed.

One Author

The term of protection under the Copyright Act of 1976 depends on the type of authorship. If a work is created by one author (i.e., a human being; *not* a work-made-for-hire author), the term of protection is for the life of the author plus 50 years. For example, a musician writes a song in 1980 and dies in 1990. Protection will extend to 2040 (50 years from the date of the author's death). This timetable will not apply if the work is published anonymously or if the work is made for hire. If a work was created before 1978, but published and registered after 1978, the author of that work also acquires protection for life plus 50 years.

Joint Authors

If a work is created by two or more authors, then protection will extend for the life of the author who lives the longest (the surviving author) plus 50 years. For example, if two songwriters collaborate and one dies in 1980 and the other dies in 1990, the work will be protected until 2040 (50 years from the date of the surviving author's death).

Works Made for Hire

Works made for hire are protected for a period of 75 years from first publication or 100 years from creation, whichever is shorter. Therefore, if a computer company created a work made for hire in 1980 but did not publish it until 1990, copyright protection would extend to 2065 (75 years from the date of publication).

Anonymous and Pseudonymous Works

An author's contribution to a work is *anonymous* if that author is not identified on the copies or phonorecords of the work. An author's contribution is *pseudonymous* if the author is identified by a fictitious name. For example, many authors, such as Mark Twain and J. D. Salinger, are pseudonymous authors. Copyright protection for anonymous and pseudonymous works is for 75 years from the date of publication or 100 years from creation, whichever is shorter. However, if the name of the author is disclosed in the records of the Copyright Office, the disclosure will convert the term to life plus 50 years. For example, if an author published a book pseudonymously in 1980 and died in 1990 without disclosing her name to the Copyright Office, the term of copyright would be until 2055 (75 years from publication). If the author's name had been disclosed, protection would extend until 2040 (50 years from her death).

LEGAL TERMS

extended renewal term
An extension of the renewal term from 28 to 47 years for works registered under the Copyrights Act of 1909 that were in their renewal term on January 1, 1978, or that were renewed after January 1, 1978.

Year-End Expiration of Copyright Terms

The term of copyright protection, regardless of when it was originally obtained, runs *through the end of the calendar year.* In other words, the last day of copyright protection for any work is December 31. For example, if an author died in March 1980, protection of her works would continue through December 31, 2030.

Presumption of Author's Length of Life

Within 75 years from the date of first publication or a period of 100 years from the creation of a work (whichever occurs first), a person may obtain a certified report from the U.S. Copyright Office indicating that there is nothing to indicate that the author is living or has been dead for at least 50 years. This amounts to a presumption that the author has been dead for at least 50 years.[9] Reliance in good faith upon this presumption is a complete defense to an action for infringement.

Table 4.3 summarizes the various copyright duration considerations.

Publication or Creation	Copyright Duration
Published between 1909 through 1921	Initial term of copyright of 28 years. If renewed during the 28th year, copyright is extended for an additional 28-year period.
Published between 1922 through 1963	Initial term of copyright of 28 years. If renewed during the 28th year, copyright is extended for an additional 47-year period.
Published between 1964 and 1978	Initial term of copyright of 28 years and automatically renewed for an additional 47-year period. Incentives exist for voluntary renewal during 28th year.
Created on or after January 1, 1978	*Sole author*—life of author plus 50 years. *Joint authors*—life of surviving author plus 50 years. *Works made for hire*—75 years from first publication or 100 years from creation, whichever is less. *Anonymous and pseudonymous works*—75 years from first publication or 100 years from creation, whichever is less. If author's name is disclosed to Copyright Office, life of author plus 50 years.
Created before 1978 but published on or after January 1, 1978	*Sole author*—life of author plus 50 years. *Joint authors*—life of surviving author plus 50 years.

TABLE 4.3
Duration of Copyright Protection

4.6   TRANSFER OF OWNERSHIP

Each right granted under copyright is separate and divisible and can be transferred, licensed, or otherwise granted to a third party, who then becomes the owner of copyright as to that specific grant. For example, Arthur Author is the author of the novel *Dead Serious*. He may transfer the rights of adaptation, reproduction, and performance of his novel to a movie company for the exclusive right to make a motion picture. He may sell reproduction and hardcover publication rights to a book publisher. That book publisher may sublicense the paperback publishing rights to a subsidiary company. Mr. Author may assign the right to translate the work (an adaptation right) to a foreign publisher. These grants may be for the full term of the copyright or for a limited time, after which the rights would revert to Mr. Author. Mr. Author may retain certain adaptation rights, in case he wishes to create a sequel, and he also may bequeath certain rights to his family in his will. All these grants flow from the initial bundle of rights acquired by Mr. Author when he created the novel. Anyone who acquires rights from Mr. Author is entitled to the protection and remedies available under copyright law. The ability to transfer rights is established in § 201 of the Copyright Act of 1976, 17 U.S.C. § 201(d).

Transfer by Written Agreement

The Copyright Act of 1976 specifies various types of transfers of copyright ownership. A **transfer of copyright ownership** is an assignment, mortgage, exclusive license, transfer by will or intestate succession, or any other change in the ownership of any or all of the exclusive rights in a copyright, whether or not limited in time or place of effect, but not including a nonexclusive license. Therefore, if an author grants an exclusive right to publish his novel, the publisher is an owner of copyright. However, if the author grants nonexclusive rights of publication to two different publishers, then neither publisher is an owner of copyright.

Generally, a transfer of rights can occur only when a copyright owner signs a written agreement transferring the rights. This rule, established in § 204(a) of the Copyright Act of 1976, 17 U.S.C. § 204(a), states that any assignment or exclusive license must be in writing and signed by the person granting the rights. Exceptions to this rule exist, as will be discussed later, for example, when a person dies without a will or when bankruptcy is declared.

Assignments and Exclusive Licenses

An *assignment* is a transfer of ownership interest. Traditionally, an assignment means that the copyright owner is transferring all of the interest in copyright to another party. If the copyright is viewed as property, then it is

LEGAL TERMS

transfer of copyright ownership
An assignment, mortgage, exclusive license, transfer by will or intestate succession or any other change in the ownership of any or all of the exclusive rights in a copyright, whether or not it is limited in time or place of effect, but not including a nonexclusive license.

the equivalent of a final sale of the property. Although the heirs of the assigning party (the *assignor*) may recapture rights (as discussed in § 4.7), the assignment is not considered limited in time. See figure 4-3.

An *exclusive license* is a grant of one or all of the rights comprising copyright in such a manner that no other party will be granted a similar right. Viewed in terms of property ownership, an exclusive license is similar to an exclusive lease. The arrangement may be limited as to time or location, and rights may eventually revert to the licensing party. Under a nonexclusive license, there is no exclusionary quality; that is, other persons may acquire similar rights. By way of example, if Diskco, a computer company, wanted to acquire all rights and become the permanent copyright owner of a computer program, it would seek an assignment. If Diskco wanted to be the only distributor and manufacturer of a game, but only sought that right for a period of years, it would acquire an exclusive license. If Diskco did not mind that other companies were distributing and manufacturing the program, Diskco would seek a nonexclusive license.

Figure 4-4 is another example of an assignment of copyright. The Copyright Act of 1976 only requires that the person transferring the rights sign the agreement. Although it is not necessary to include a provision for signature by a notary public, it is recommended because it may aid in proving the validity of the assignment. Note that this assignment provides for signature by the assigning party and the assigning party's spouse. Also included in this assignment is a provision dealing with the community or equitable property interests of the assignor's spouse. Under state laws, the owner of copyright may not have the legal ability to assign a spouse's community property or equitable property interest in the copyrightable property. Therefore, some practitioners consider it prudent to have the spouse of a copyright owner also execute the assignment.

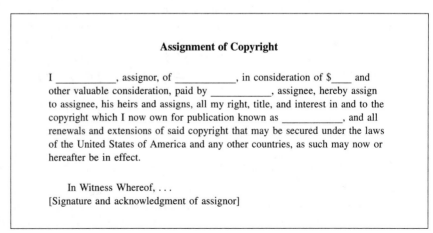

Assignment of Copyright

I _____, assignor, of _____, in consideration of $____ and other valuable consideration, paid by _____, assignee, hereby assign to assignee, his heirs and assigns, all my right, title, and interest in and to the copyright which I now own for publication known as _____, and all renewals and extensions of said copyright that may be secured under the laws of the United States of America and any other countries, as such may now or hereafter be in effect.

In Witness Whereof, . . .
[Signature and acknowledgment of assignor]

FIGURE 4-3
Form for copyright assignment

ASSIGNMENT OF COPYRIGHT

JANE DOE ("Assignor") is the owner of all copyrights in the software program tentatively titled and referred to as *Ham 'n Eggs,* a computer software game (with versions written under **MS-DOS**). The program comprises approximately 40,000 lines of source code, includes a database of simple words, and provides an interactive means of generating data so that students of the English language can learn phonetics and pronunciations while playing a game centered around a fictional cartoon cook; and

DISKCO, INCORPORATED, a California corporation ("Assignee"), desires to own the copyrights in *Ham 'n Eggs;*

THEREFORE, for valuable consideration of five thousand dollars ($5,000), the receipt and sufficiency of which are acknowledged, Assignor hereby assigns to Assignee, its successors, and assigns, all right, title, and interest in *Ham 'n Eggs,* including all copyrights and the registrations. Assignee shall have the right to register the copyright to *Ham 'n Eggs* in its own name and shall have the exclusive right to dispose of the work in any manner whatsoever. Assignor warrants that she is the legal owner of all right, title, and interest in *Ham 'n Eggs,* that the rights have not been previously licensed, pledged, assigned, or encumbered, and that this assignment does not infringe on the rights of any person. Assignor agrees to cooperate with Assignee and to execute and deliver all papers as may be necessary to vest all rights to *Ham 'n Eggs.* This includes cooperation with the recordation of the assignment in the United States Copyright Office.

_____ Dated:_____
Jane Doe (Assignor)

I am the spouse of Assignor and I acknowledge that I have read and understand this Agreement. I am aware that my spouse agrees to assign her interest in the software program *Ham 'n Eggs,* including any community property interest or other equitable property interest that I may have in it. I consent to the assignment, and agree that my interest, if any, in the program is subject to the provisions of this Agreement. I will take no action to hinder the Agreement or the underlying assignment of rights.

_____ Dated:_____
Spouse

On this _____ day of _____, 19___, before me, _____
_____, the undersigned Notary Public, personally appeared _____
_____ and proved to me based on satisfactory evidence to be the person(s) who executed this instrument.

WITNESS my hand and official seal.

_____
Notary Public

FIGURE 4-4
Sample copyright assignment

Mortgages and Security Interests

If a person owns a home, she may mortgage the home or use the home as security for a loan. Similarly, the copyright owner may mortage the copyrightable work or use it as security for repayment of a debt. For example, the author Stephen King assigned certain motion picture rights to the book *The Shining* to Warner Brothers, the motion picture company. In 1983, Warner Brothers mortgaged and assigned its copyright ownership to a bank as security for a debt that the movie company had incurred. If the company repaid the debt, the mortage would terminate and the ownership would revert to Warner Brothers. If Warner Brothers failed to pay the debt, the bank would acquire ownership of the motion picture rights.

Transfers Other Than by Written Agreement

A transfer of copyright ownership may occur other than by written agreement. The three most common examples are transfer upon death, transfer of ownership by operation of law, or involuntary transfer.

Transfer upon Death

If an owner of copyright dies with a valid will, the copyright will be transferred to a designated beneficiary. (See figure 4-5 for a sample bequest.) If an owner of copyright dies without a will, transfer of ownership will occur according to the rules of intestate succession. Each state has its own rules regarding such transfers. For example, in most states, the immediate family (spouse and children) inherit property according to a formula. Ownership of copyright is also transferred in this manner. Transfers resulting from the death of the copyright owner commonly result in co-ownership of copyright, as the author's family may divide the copyright interests.

Transfer by Operation of Law

Under certain circumstances, a court can order the transfer of an interest in copyright. For example, in a divorce proceeding, the court may order

FIGURE 4-5
Sample will provision transferring copyright ownership and rights

---

WILL PROVISION—BEQUEST OF COPYRIGHT

I give and bequeath to _____ my copyright for the publication known as _____, to _____, and direct my executor, or any successor, to assign such copyright to said beneficiary, together with all renewals and extensions of said copyright that may be secured under the laws of the United States of America and any other countries, as such laws may now or hereafter be in effect.

the copyright owner to divide the ownership interest with a spouse. In a bankruptcy proceeding, the court may order transfer of assets such as copyright ownership to a creditor.

Involuntary Transfers

The Copyright Act of 1976 also prohibits a governmental body from seizing rights from the original author of a copyrightable work. However, a transfer of rights that is the result of a bankruptcy proceeding or foreclosure on a security is not considered an involuntary transfer and is permitted.[10]

Table 4.4 summarizes the various methods of transferring copyright ownership.

Recording Transfers of Copyright Ownership

Although it is no longer a requirement of copyright law, it is prudent to record all transfers of ownership, because such recordation provides constructive notice of the transfer and because the recordation may be necessary to establish jurisdiction in a copyright infringement action. As previously noted, a transfer of ownership (transfer of exclusive rights, assignments, mortgage, etc.) must be in writing, and notarization is recommended. In addition, non-exclusive licenses, or other documents pertaining to copyright, if in writing, also may be recorded.[11] The requirements for recording documents with the Copyright Office are provided in chapter 5.

Type of Transfer	Description
Assignment or exclusive license	An assignment is a transfer of ownership interest. An exclusive license is a grant of one or all of the rights comprising copyright in such a manner that no other party will be granted a similar right. Assignments and exclusive licenses require a written agreement evidencing the transfer, signed by the party transferring rights.
Mortgage or security interest	A copyright may be mortgaged or used as security for an obligation. Mortgages and security interest transfers require a written agreement evidencing the transfer, signed by the party transferring rights.
Transfer upon death	If an owner of copyright dies with a valid will, the copyright will be transferred to the designated beneficiary. If an owner of copyright dies without a will, transfer of ownership will occur according to the rules of intestate succession.
Operation of law	Under certain circumstances (e.g., bankruptcy, mortgage foreclosure, divorce), a court can order the transfer of an interest in copyright.

TABLE 4.4
Methods of Transferring Ownership of Copyright

4.7 TERMINATING TRANSFERS

Artists and authors often enter into agreements at a time when they cannot fully appreciate the value of their works. Many rock-n-roll songwriters, for example, signed away copyright to their songs for a small amount of money. Later, those songs appreciated in value and continued to generate income far in excess of the original price paid. Both the Copyright Act of 1909 and the Copyright Act of 1976 provide a means for the author or the author's estate to recapture the copyright after a transfer.

Grants Made on or after January 1, 1978

For works registered under the Copyright Act of 1976, 17 U.S.C. § 203 provides that an author, or the author's immediate family, may, in certain circumstances, terminate a grant of rights made on or after January 1, 1978. In other words, certain types of transfers may be canceled and the author or the author's family may reclaim those rights. This right of termination cannot be waived in advance or contracted away. For example, an author licenses his book to a publisher for 70 years. After 35 years from publication, however, the author may automatically terminate that transfer and renegotiate those rights at a better price.

Only Certain Grants May Be Terminated

Section 203 only provides for termination of any exclusive or nonexclusive grant of a transfer or license of copyright or any right under copyright law executed by the author on or after January 1, 1978. This right to terminate *does not* include the following:

1. *Transfers Made Prior to 1978.* Section 203 of the Copyright Act of 1976 applies to transfers made on or after January 1, 1978. The law is not retroactive and does not permit termination of earlier grants. However, earlier grants may be terminated pursuant to § 304, discussed later.

2. *Works made for hire.* Grants or transfers of works made for hire may not be automatically terminated.

3. *Works protected under foreign copyright law.* Congress did not intend to interfere with agreements made under foreign copyright laws. Therefore, if an author licenses a foreign publisher to publish a translation of her book, the right to terminate would not extend to the foreign publication.

4. *Grants made in an author's will.* A grant made by an author in a will cannot be terminated. For example, if an author, in his will, grants a license to publish to an organization or company, that grant may not be terminated.

In addition, the right to terminate does not include related trademark and character licensing rights and ownership rights in the material object in which the work is first fixed.

Only Certain Persons May Terminate a Grant

Only the author (or, in the event the author is deceased prior to the time the right to terminate may be exercised, the surviving spouse, children, or grandchildren) may terminate a grant of copyright. The rights as to specific survivors are set forth in detail in 17 U.S.C. § 203. These termination rights can be exercised by surviving spouses, children, or grandchildren, regardless of whether such persons are owners of copyright. As for joint authors, termination of a grant may be made by a majority of the authors who executed the grant. If any such joint author is dead, that author's right to terminate may be exercised by his or her surviving spouse, children, or grandchildren, as the case may be.

Table 4.5 summarizes transfer termination considerations.

Terminating Grants for Works Registered under the Copyright Act of 1909

As noted previously, the Copyright Act of 1909 provided an initial term of 28 years and a renewal term of 28 years. The renewal term was subsequently

Termination rights do not apply to:	(1) Transfers made prior to 1978. (However, earlier grants may be terminated pursuant to the renewal procedures of § 304.) (2) Works made for hire. (3) Works protected under foreign copyright law. (4) Grants made in an author's will.
Work published before the date of a grant:	The author or heirs may terminate the transfer any time during a 5-year period that starts at the end of 35 years from execution of the grant. For example, John publishes a book in 1990. He assigns rights to the book in 1992. The grant may be terminated between January 1, 2028, and December 31, 2032.
Work has not been published prior to the grant:	The author or heirs may terminate the transfer any time during a 5-year period beginning either at the end of 35 years from the date of publication under the grant, or at the end of 40 years from the date the grant was executed, whichever term ends earlier. For example, John assigns a license for his book in 1992. The company publishes the book in 1994. The applicable 5-year period would be 35 years from the date of publication under the grant (i.e., January 1, 2028), as that is the *earlier* period.
Method of terminating transfer:	Review procedures in Code of Federal Regulations.
Office action:	At time license or grant is executed: (1) Determine if transfer is exempt from termination rights. (2) If not exempt, calendar the period when termination may occur and document termination period in copyright administration files. (3) Notify client of period of termination.

TABLE 4.5
Terminating Transfers for Works Registered under the Copyright Act of 1976

lengthened to 47 years. Two methods exist to terminate transfers for works registered under the Copyright Act of 1909.

Works in Their Initial 28-Year Term

Consider the following: An author assigns all rights to her novel to a publishing company in 1961. The assignment agreement states that the publishing company will own copyright for the initial and renewal term of copyright. The novel is published in 1962. The author dies in 1980. Will the publishing company own copyright in the book during the renewal term? Not necessarily. During the last year of the initial 28-year term of copyright, the author's heirs may renew copyright. By renewing copyright, the author's estate effectively terminates all prior grants, even if the author had promised the renewal rights to the publisher. The estate could grant rights for the renewal period to another party. However, if the author was alive at the time of renewal, she would be bound by the terms of the assignment.

Derivative Rights: The Rear Window Case

In 1990, the U.S. Supreme Court reviewed the renewal and termination rights in *Stewart v. Abend*.[12] The author Cornell Woolrich published a story *It Had to Be Murder* in 1942. He assigned the motion picture rights to a company that produced the film *Rear Window*. He also agreed to renew the copyright at the appropriate time and to assign the renewal rights to the film company. Mr. Woolrich died in 1968, before he could renew the copyright. The executor for his estate renewed the copyright in the story in 1969 and assigned the renewal rights to Mr. Abend. Mr. Abend sued to prevent any further distribution of the movie *Rear Window*, believing he owned all rights to control derivatives from the story. The Supreme Court agreed and stated that if an author dies before the renewal term has occurred, any promise to assign renewal rights is ineffective. Therefore, the movie company must renegotiate with the owner of the renewal rights. The underlying principle is the same as for the termination of all grants: the renewal term gives the author's family or estate the opportunity to renegotiate any bargains previously negotiated.

Automatic Renewal and Termination of Derivative Transfers

In 1991, the U.S. Congress amended the Copyright Act to provide automatic renewal. Owners of works that were in the last year of the renewal period no longer had to renew copyright. Protection would be automatically renewed without filing anything. However, the law provided certain incentives for authors to continue to voluntarily file for renewal of copyright during the 28th year. One incentive is that owners of derivative works cannot continue to use the underlying work if it has been affirmatively renewed. For example, an author publishes a novel in 1965. The book is adapted for a movie produced in 1970. The first renewal period for the novel ends in 1993. The owner of copyright does not have to do anything to maintain protection; the work is automatically protected for an additional 47-year period. However, if the work is voluntarily renewed by filing with the Copyright Office, the owners of copyright in the movie may not continue to distribute or perform the film without the permission of the novel's author.

Grants Made prior to 1978 (Works in Their Extended Renewal Term)

When enacting the Copyright Act of 1976, Congress added further protection for works published under the previous act. Section 304 of the Copyright Act of 1976 provides that for works in the extended renewal term (the 47-year period following the initial 28-year term), a transfer may be terminated 56 years after first publication of the work. However, there are certain limitations. The transfer must have been made before January 1, 1978, and termination will apply only to the final 19 years of the extended renewal term. The logic behind this is that the Copyright Act of 1909 originally offered protection for 56 years. The Copyright Act of 1976 extended protection 19 years longer, to 75 years. Therefore, Congress felt that authors and families should have the right to terminate grants for this final 19-year period. With a few exceptions, the rules previously discussed regarding § 203, which pertain to terminating transfers, also apply to grants for works that are in their second renewal period under the 1909 Act, even if such grants were made before January 1, 1978. One exception is that, under § 203, only grants made by the author may be terminated. Under § 304, grants may be terminated that were made by the author or the author's beneficiaries during the renewal period. In addition, grants for derivative rights may not be terminated during this second renewal period. For instance, in the *Rear Window* case, Mr. Abend could terminate the motion picture rights after the initial term, but he could not terminate the grant during the last 19 years of the copyright term. Section 201.10 of the Code of Federal Regulations provides the system by which a notice of termination for works in an extended term is accomplished.

Table 4.6 summarizes transfer termination considerations under the 1909 Act.

Failure to Give Notice of Termination

If notice of termination is not given or properly recorded with Copyright Office, there is no change in the grant of rights. For example, if an author granted a right of publication to a publisher in 1979 and the author fails to terminate the grant in a timely manner, the publisher will continue to have the right to publish the work under the original agreement.

The work is in its initial 28-year term	The work is automatically protected for an additional 47-year period. However, if the work is voluntarily renewed by filing with the Copyright Office, the author or the heirs may terminate grants, such as derivative rights, made during the initial term. For voluntary renewal procedures, see § 304 as amended in 1992.
The work is in its extended renewal term of 47 years	If the work is not (a) work made for hire; (b) a work protected under foreign copyright law; or (c) a grant made in an author's will, then the author or certain heirs may terminate a transfer during a 5-year period beginning at the end of 56 years from the date protection was first granted; or any time during a period beginning on January 1, 1978, whichever is later. For example, John published and registered his book in 1974. He assigned rights to the book in 1982. The company publishes the book in 1994. John may terminate rights any time during January 1, 2030, through December 31, 2034 (the period beginning 56 years after the date protection was secured).
Terminating a transfer	Review procedures in Code of Federal Regulations § 201.10.
Office action (at time copyright administration file is opened)	Calendar the period when termination may occur and document in files. If client is author, notify of period of termination. If client is assignee or licensee, notify of possible termination rights and period of termination.

TABLE 4.6
Terminating Transfers Made prior to January 1, 1978

Exercising Recovered Rights

Rights that are recovered by the termination process can be granted again. All persons alive on the effective date of the notice of termination are entitled to recover rights, whether they joined in signing the notice or not. That is, if three persons are entitled to terminate and two of them sign and serve the notice of termination, the third party will be bound. If there is a sole beneficiary, that person may make future grants without restriction. However, if there are multiple beneficiaries or co-owners, then the same number and proportion of owners who can terminate also may grant the new right. It does not matter if it is the same persons who terminated the grant; it only matters that the same number of persons and proportion of interest make the new grant. An agreement to transfer these rights must be executed after the date of termination, except that an agreement executed after notice is served, but before termination, will be effective if it is for the benefit of the person who will recover rights.

4.8 RESEARCHING COPYRIGHT STATUS

In the Commentary at the beginning of this chapter, a software company registered the software program *Macho Math.* Two programmers allegedly infringed the copyright. How could these programmers investigate the copyright status of the *Macho Math* program? For example, has the software company assigned rights to a third party? Did the software company list the programmers as the authors of the work? Often it is necessary to investigate the facts surrounding copyright registration. Individuals may search copyright office records at the Library of Congress, the Copyright Office may perform searches, computer databases may be accessed to find copyright information, or private search companies can be hired to perform these services. Copies of records can be ordered directly from the Copyright Office. Sometimes it is necessary to use a variety of methods to research copyright status, including an examination of a copy of the work itself.

Obtaining Copies of Copyright Office Records

Copies of registrations and records can be acquired directly from the Copyright Office if certain information is available. If the information listed here is already known, a search of Copyright Office records is not necessary to acquire copies. A request for copies should:

1. Clearly identify the type of records you wish to obtain (e.g., certificate of registration).
2. Specify whether you require certified or uncertified copies.
3. Clearly identify the specific records to be copies. Your request should include the following specific information, if possible:
   (a) type of work involved (i.e., novel, lyrics, etc.);
   (b) the registration number, including the preceding letters (e.g., TX000-000);
   (c) the year date or approximate year date of registration (e.g., 1985);
   (d) the complete title of the work;
   (e) the author(s), including any pseudonym by which the author may be known;
   (f) the claimant(s); and
   (g) if the requested copy is of an assignment, license, contract, or other recorded, document, the volume and page number of the recorded document.
4. Comply with any special requirements (as outlined in this section) for obtaining copies of certain types of documents.
5. Include the fee if the copy requested is an additional certificate of registration. The Certification and Documents Section will review requests for other copies and quote fees for each. (Payments can also be made through a deposit account with the Copyright Office, as discussed in Chapter 5.)
6. Include your telephone number and address so that the Copyright Office may contact you.

A certified copy of a public record includes a statement under the seal of the Copyright Office attesting that the document is a true copy of the record in question. Certified copies are often requested when litigation is involved, as evidence of the authenticity of documents. If all you want is an additional certificate of registration, all that is required is: (1) title; (2) registration number; (3) year date of registration or publication; (4) any other information needed to identify the registration; and (5) the $8.00 fee, which should accompany the request in the form of a check or money order payable to the Register of Copyrights. Certification of a copyright certificate requires an additional $8.00 fee. Certification of other copyright documents is charged at a rate of $20 per hour (or fraction) depending on the certification request. All requests for certified or uncertified copies of Copyright Office records or deposits should be made to the Certifications and Documents Section, LM-402, Copyright Office, Library of Congress, Washington, DC 20559. The section may be contacted by telephone at 202-707-6787. It is also possible to walk into the office, which is located on the fourth floor of the James Madison Memorial Building on Independence Avenue between First and Second Streets, S.E., between the hours of 8:30 a.m. and 5 p.m. weekdays (except holidays.) For more information, see Copyright Office Circular 6.

Obtaining Copies of Deposits

Under certain circumstances, the Copyright Office will provide certified or uncertified reproductions of published or unpublished works deposited in connection with a copyright registration. For such reproductions to be made, one of the following three items must be submitted:

1. Written authorization from the copyright claimant, his or her agent, or the owner of any exclusive right, as demonstrated by written documentation of the ownership transfer.
2. Written request from the attorney for a plaintiff or defendant in copyright litigation involving the copyrighted work. Such a request *must* include (a) the names of all parties and the nature of the controversy; (b) the name of the court where the case is pending; and (c) satisfactory assurance that reproduction will be used only in connection with the litigation.
3. A court order for a reproduction of a deposited article, facsimile, or identifying portion of a work which is the subject of litigation in the court's jurisdiction.

A fee should not be submitted unless the requesting party is certain of the amount. The Copyright Office will review each request and quote a fee. Write to the Certifications and Documents Section, LM-402, Copyright Office, Library of Congress, Washington, DC 20559.

Investigating Copyright Status

The first place to begin any copyright investigation is by examining the work at issue. Looking at a book, computer program, or phonorecord may provide certain information, such as the date of publication, the copyright claimant, and the author. There are, however, some "wild card" variables that have to be considered when performing this type of activity: Is the work known under an alternative title? Has there been a change in the name of the corporate owner of copyright? Have there been various versions of the work, such as an abridged or translated version? After acquiring this information, the person performing the investigation must plan a strategy for further investigation. What funds are available for the investigation? If money is limited, the investigating party may wish to examine the Copyright Office Catalogs at a local library, contact the Copyright Office for a search, or, if possible, search the Copyright Office records personally. If more funds are available, a private search firm may be hired or an online copyright database may be accessed.

Copyright Office Catalogs

The Copyright Office publishes a *Catalog of Copyright Entries (CCE)* that is divided according to the classes of works registered. Portions of the *CCE* are available in microfiche form. The *CCE* contains essential facts about registrations but does not include verbatim reproductions of the registration records. In addition, there is a time lag of approximately one year, so very recent registrations may not be included. Finally, the *CCE* cannot be used for researching the transfer of rights, because it does not include entries for assignments or other recorded documents. Many libraries have a copy of the *CCE*.

Personal Searches of Copyright Office

Anyone may personally inspect the Copyright Office records by visiting the Library of Congress at 101 Independence Avenue, S.E., on the fourth floor of the James Madison Memorial Building, between the hours of 8:30 a.m. and 5 p.m. weekdays (except holidays). There is an extensive card catalog in Room 459. Alternatively, a person may ask the Reference and Bibliography Section in Room 450 to conduct a search for an hourly fee. For information on the Copyright Office Card Catalog and the online files of the Copyright Office, consult Copyright Circular 23.

Searching by the Copyright Office

Upon request, the Copyright Office will search the Copyright Office records, at a fee of $20 an hour (or fraction of an hour). This search is usually initiated by submission of a search request form or by a telephone call (202-707-6850). The Copyright Office will quote a fee for such services, and this estimate should be provided to the Copyright Office prior to initiation of the search. A search may be expedited for an expedited searching fee of $30 per hour (or fraction of an hour). A Copyright Office search may not always be conclusive, because not all works are registered and recent works may not have been cataloged. For more information, see Copyright Circular 22.

SUMMARY

4.1 The owner of copyright holds title to the copyright. The owner of copyright may be the author or a successor to the author's interest. The owner may transfer rights to another party. Registration establishes a presumption of ownership. Ownership of a copy does not establish ownership of copyright.

4.2 A joint work is created when two or more authors intend that their contributions be merged. The joint authors can specify their rights in a collaboration agreement. Joint authors are co-owners of copyright. In addition to joint authorship, there are other methods by which a co-ownership can occur, such as by transfer, intestate succession, or community property laws. Co-owners share property as tenants in common. Each co-owner must account to the others and no co-owner may grant an exclusive license without the consent of all co-owners.

4.3 The owner of copyright in a collective work acquires rights to the collection but generally does not acquire rights as to the specific contributions. The author of a contribution generally retains rights to the contribution.

4.4 An employer or hiring party can acquire ownership under the principle of works made for hire. A work made for hire can be created in two separate ways. One method is a work prepared by an employee within the scope of his or her employment. The second method applies if the work is specially ordered or commissioned and if the parties expressly agree in a written agreement signed by them that the work shall be considered a work made for hire. Under this second method, the work must fall into one of several enumerated categories.

4.5 The duration of copyright depends on various factors, including the effective copyright act and type of work. Under the Copyright Act of 1976, authors receive protection for life plus 50 years. Works for hire and other works acquire protection for 75 years from first publication or 100 years from creation, whichever is shorter.

4.6 A license is a grant of rights. An assignment of copyright is a transfer of copyright ownership. An exclusive license prevents any other party from acquiring specific rights. Transfer of copyright usually occurs by written agreement, but also may occur by other methods, such by will or operation of law. Transfers may be recorded with the Copyright Office.

4.7 Under certain circumstances, an author or the author's heirs may terminate transfers of copyright. Grants for works protected under the Copyright Act of 1909 may be terminated during the renewal period. Certain transfers made under either the 1909 or 1976 Copyright Acts may be terminated by the author or the author's heirs pursuant to statutory guidelines.

4.8 For various reasons, it may be necessary to investigate the copyright status of a work. Individuals may search Copyright Office records at the Library of Congress, the Copyright Office may perform searches, computer databases may be accessed to find copyright information, or private search companies can be hired to perform these services. Copies of records can be ordered directly from the Copyright Office. Sometimes it is necessary to use more than on of these methods to research copyright status.

NOTES

1. 17 U.S.C. § 201 (ownership of copyright).
2. 17 U.S.C. § 202 (ownership of copyright distinct from ownership of object).
3. 17 U.S.C. § 201(b) (works made for hire: ownership).
4. Community for Creative Non-Violence v. Reid, 490 U.S. 730 (1989).
5. *See* Cal. Lab. Code § 3351.5; Cal. Unemp. Ins. Code §§ 621(d), 686.
6. 17 U.S.C. § 303 (duration of copyright for works created but not published before 1978).
7. 17 U.S.C. § 304 (subsisting copyrights; copyrights in first or renewal terms on January 1, 1978).
8. 17 U.S.C. § 302 (duration of copyright for works created after January 1, 1978).
9. 17 U.S.C. § 302(e) (presumption as to length of life of author).
10. 17 U.S.C. § 201(e) (involuntary transfers).
11. 17 U.S.C. § 205 (recordation of transfers).
12. Stewart v. Abend, 495 U.S. 207 (1990).

QUESTIONS FOR REVIEW AND DISCUSSION

1. What is the relationship between registration of copyright and proof of ownership?
2. What are the ways by which a copyrighted work can become jointly owned?
3. What obligation does a co-owner have to other co-owners of copyright? — *Equitable distribution*
4. How can joint authors establish the value of each contribution to the work?
5. What rights are acquired by the owner of a collective work?
6. What are the two methods by which a hiring party acquires a work made for hire? — *employee contract*
7. What are the factors in determining if an employer-employee relationship exists?
8. What is the difference between an exclusive license and an assignment of copyright? — *license only* — *transfer*
9. How long is copyright protection for a jointly created work under the Copyright Act of 1976?

10. What right does an author have to terminate an assignment made prior to January 1, 1978?

11. What advantage is there for a company to own a work made for hire instead of acquiring rights under an assignment?

ACTIVITIES

1. Review the factual situation in the Commentary. Discuss the impact of a written agreement which states that the work is "made for hire." Does such an agreement always prove that the work is owned by the hiring party?

2. Examine various copyrighted works and find examples of joint authorship in music, literature, and the visual arts. Discuss why artists and authors jointly create works.

3. Review the Supreme Court case *Community for Creative Non-Violence v. Reid.* Discuss the expectations of each party when they entered into the agreement to produce the statue.

4. Examine the date of publication for various works and determine when the copyright will expire.

5. Review the Supreme Court case *Stewart v. Abend.* Discuss the rationale for permitting the heirs or successors of the author to terminate transfers and recapture rights.

PROJECT

Create a checklist for a fictional publishing company that is preparing to pay several persons to prepare contributions to an encyclopedia of American history. Many of the writers are noted scholars and instructors. The encyclopedia will be used in high-school instruction. Discuss what issues may arise and be prepared to advise the president of the company as to the nature of the completed work and the ownership of contributions to the work. Prepare a standard work-for-hire agreement to be used with the writers. What issues will the writers be concerned about?

FOR MORE INFORMATION

Copyright Office Licensing Division

Licensing information about such things as cable television licenses, jukebox licenses, and noncommercial broadcasting licenses can be obtained from:

Licensing Division of the Copyright Office Section, LM-458, Copyright Office, Library of Congress, Washington, DC 20557.

The section may be contacted by telephone at 202-707-8150. It is also possible to walk in the office, located on the fourth floor of the James Madison Memorial Building on Independence Avenue between First and Second Streets, S.E., between the hours of 8:30 a.m. to 5 p.m. weekdays (except holidays). For more information, see Copyright Office Circular 6.

Searching Via Online Services

Certain copyright information may be acquired by computer online services. The "U.S. Copyrights" portion of the DIALOG computer database contains over 6 million Copyright Office records from January 1978 to the present. The database is designed primarily as a fast screening tool for checking the ownership and registration status of a particular work. For more information, contact:

DIALOG Information Services, Inc., 3460 Hillview Avenue, Palo Alto, CA 94304.

Private Search Companies

Many of the clearance services discussed in Chapter 3 can also perform copyright search activities. In addition to searching copyright records, companies such as the following can also provide additional information, such as tracing the copyright history of a fictional character, or provide special title reports.

Thomson & Thomson, 500 E. Street, S.W., Suite 970, Washington, DC 20024-2710.

BZ Rights & Permission, Inc., 125 West 72nd Street, New York, NY 10023.

Copyright Clearance Center, 27 Congress Street, Salem, MA 01970.

Judith Finnel Music Services, Inc., 155 West 68th Street, New York, NY 10023.

CHAPTER 5
Copyright Formalities and Registration

The ideas I stand for are not mine. I borrowed them from Socrates. I swiped them from Chesterfield. I stole them from Jesus. And I put them in a book.

Dale Carnegie

OUTLINE

COMMENTARY

The law office where you work represents Softco, a computer company. Softco is the owner and creator of a software game program, Crazy Clock, *which was created in 1988 and first published in January 1989. The company has not registered the program with the Copyright Office. Lester is a former employee of Softco who left his job after a bitter argument with the president of the company. After Lester left, the company examined Lester's computer and learned that he had copied the software code for* Crazy Clock. *Softco also learns that Lester is manufacturing and selling* Crazy Clock *through a computer club. Softco wants to file a copyright infringement lawsuit.*

OBJECTIVES

The previous chapters on copyright law have introduced you to many principles of copyright law. Most of these principles will be applied in this chapter regarding copyright formalities and registration. After reading Chapter 5, you will be able to:

- Identify the correct copyright notice for a work.
- Determine the correct placement for the copyright notice on the work.
- Discuss the ramifications of the omission of copyright notice for various works.
- Explain the advantages of registration of copyright.
- Process a request for an expedited handling of a registration.
- Choose the correct copyright application for a particular work or for a work containing mixed claims of authorship.
- Identify and list preexisting material and material added to the work.
- Outline the deposit requirements for various works.
- Prepare a supplementary registration that corrects or supplements information in a copyright registration.
- Prepare copyright applications for computer programs and automated databases.
- Outline the various methods of registering sound recordings and the underlying works.
- Record transfers of ownership or other documents pertaining to a copyright with the Copyright Office.

5.1 NOTICE OF COPYRIGHT

The most visible sign of copyright ownership is the copyright notice— the © symbol (or the word *copyright* or abbreviation *copr.*) followed by the year of first publication and the name of the copyright claimant. For two centuries of federal copyright law, Congress required that every visually perceptible published copy or phonorecord contain a notice of copyright ownership. If the notice was omitted, the law prescribed drastic penalties. Many works fell into the public domain simply because the owner failed to include the proper copyright notice. The rationale for requiring copyright notice was that it informed the public that the work was protected. The laws regarding copyright notice changed in the 1980s. To adhere to the Berne Convention, an international copyright treaty, the United States amended the Copyright Act. Works first published on or after March 1, 1989, do not have to include notice.[1] Despite this change, the voluntary use of copyright notice is recommended and certain incentives exist for its continued use. In addition, certain works published prior to March 1, 1989, may need to include notice for the remedial purposes of correcting an earlier omission.

Notice Required on Visually Perceptible Copies

Copyright notice is used on visually perceptible copies. A **visually perceptible copy** is a copy that can be visually observed when it is embodied in a material object, either directly or with the aid of a machine or device. A computer program is visually perceptible in two ways: when the program is printed out in its code format and when a user views the display screen. That is the reason a copyright notice usually appears on the first screen of a computer program. For example, if a person turned on the software program *Crazy Clock,* mentioned in the Commentary, the first screen would include a notice such as "Copyright 1989 Softco." In addition, notice should be included on the packaging for the program and on any computer chip on which the program is encoded.

Some copies of works are not visually perceptible. When a book is recorded on audiotape, the literary work is not visually perceptible. Although copyright notice is not required, it is generally good practice to include it.

Form of Copyright Notice

The copyright notice has three elements: the symbol or word *Copyright,* the year of first publication, and the name or abbreviation of the owner of copyright. Although the order is not set forth in the Copyright Act of 1976, the elements are traditionally presented as follows:

© 1989 Softco *or*
Copyright 1989 Softco Company

The only exception to this is for phonorecords of sound recordings, discussed later in this section.

The Copyright Symbol

The copyright symbol © (the letter C in a circle), the word *Copyright,* or the abbreviation *Copr.* are all acceptable for notice requirements. In addition, the Copyright Office will accept certain variations, such as "(c)." However, it is advisable to use the © symbol (instead of the word *Copyright*) because the Universal Copyright Convention, an international treaty (to which the United States adheres), has adopted the © symbol as the *only* accepted symbol of copyright protection. Therefore, to guarantee protection for works that may be placed in international commerce, it is advisable to use the © symbol. As for phonorecords of sound recordings, the symbol   should be used, as discussed in this section.

Year of First Publication

Unless there is an exception (see discussion later in this section), the copyright notice must include the year when the work is *first* **published.**

This date would be either the year copies or phonorecords (in the case of sound recordings) are distributed to the public by sale or other transfer of ownership, or by rental, lease, or lending; or the year the work is first offered to a group of persons for purposes of further distribution, public performance, or public display.

It is *not* a publication to print or reproduce copies, publicly perform a work, display a work, or send copies of the work to the U.S. Copyright Office. There is no required form for presenting the year of first publication. For example, the year 1985 may be presented as "1985," "Nineteen Eighty Five," "Nineteen Hundred & Eighty Five" or "MCMLXXXV."

Changing the date or altering the date may be treated as an error in notice and could adversely affect the rights of the copyright owner, particularly if the date is more than one year in error. However, if a new version of the work is published, the date should be changed to reflect the new publication. To qualify as a new version, there must be more than editing or correction of errors. For example, a new work is created when an author adds a new chapter to a book or additional program code is added to computer software.

Greeting Cards and Useful Articles

Certain industries successfully lobbied Congress for the right to omit the year on copyright notices. The date can be omitted on greeting cards, stationery, jewelry, toys, or useful articles on which a pictorial, graphic, or sculptural work (and accompanying text) is included. For example, in 1992 Bob Smith publishes a greeting card with an original cartoon. He may use the notice "© Bob Smith."

Name of Copyright Owner

The owner of copyright is the name that should be used in a copyright notice. An abbreviation or a generally known alternative for the owner's name also can be used. Because the author may transfer various rights to different persons, the name in the copyright notice may differ, depending on the use or the media. For example, Warner Brothers, Inc., is the exclusive owner of motion picture, television, and related derivative rights to the novel by Stephen King, *The Shining*. The name, "Warner Brothers, Inc." is the name that should be used on the copyright notice for the motion picture *The Shining*. If there is more than one owner of a work, the names of all of the copyright owners should appear on the notice. For example, if Mssrs. Gilbert and Sullivan own a work, the notice would read "© 1992 Gilbert & Sullivan."

Error in Name

If the person named in the notice is not the owner of copyright, this error can be corrected either by registering the work in the name of the true owner or owners, or recording a Form CA (Application for Supplementary

Copyright Registration) in the Copyright Office, executed by the person named in the notice that states the correct ownership. For example, if copyright notice incorrectly listed Bill Jones as the owner, instead of Tom Smith, the error could be corrected if Bill Jones recorded a Form CA with the Copyright Office, stating that Tom Smith is the author. Alternatively, Tom Smith could correct the error by registering the work in his own name.

Derivative Works

The copyright notice for derivative works should express the year of first publication of the derivative work and the owner of copyright for the derivative. For example, the novel *The Shining* was first published in 1977. The motion picture *The Shining* is a derivative work owned by Warner Brothers and was first published in 1980. The copyright notice for the motion picture should be "© 1980 Warner Brothers, Inc."

Although it is not required by law, many copyright owners indicate a range of years for a work. For example, on the introductory screen of a computer program, it is common to see a copyright notice expressed as "© 1988-1990" or "© 1988, 1991, 1992" to encompass the original and derivative versions.

It is also acceptable to specify new and preexisting copyrighted materials by separate dates. For example, Jane McLear publishes a book in 1988. In 1992, the book is published with a new introduction by Mimi Snow. The notice may read "© 1988 Jane McLear; introduction © 1992 Mimi Snow."

Collective Works and Contributions to Collective Works

Generally, the copyright notice for a collective work protects all works included within the collection. For example, if Bookco selects and groups several articles about baseball into a book called *Great Baseball Stories* and publishes the collection in 1992, the copyright notice for the book would be: "© 1992 Bookco." This notice provides the legal requirement for notice for each individual work. However, it is also advisable for the owner of each story to have a separate copyright notice.[2] This gives warning to potential infringers of the owner of the work and prevents an infringer from arguing that the copying was innocent.

Advertisements Appearing in Collective Works.   Under the Copyright Act of 1976, copyright notice for a collective work does not extend to advertisements not placed by the publisher. For example, the copyright notice in a newspaper will protect the editorial content, such as the stories and news photographs, but it will not extend to any portion of an advertisement. Therefore, if the owner of the work desires to preserve copyright, a separate notice should *always* be included.

Sound Recordings

As explained in previous chapters, there is a difference between a sound recording copyright (e.g., protection of the particular arrangement of recorded sounds) and the underlying musical work copyright (e.g., protection for a song). Sound recordings embodied on phonorecords are required to include a special notice—the letter "P" in a circle followed by the year of first publication of the sound recording and the name of the copyright holder, for example, "℗ 1993 A&R Entertainment, Inc."[3]

There is no word or substitute symbol for the sound recording symbol ℗. The notice should appear on the surface of the phonorecord label or container in such manner and location as to give reasonable notice of the claim of copyright. The symbol ℗ is used *only* for sound recordings. All other copyrightable works embodied on phonorecords (such as songs, spoken word recordings, or motion picture soundtracks) are not required to have a notice, because they are not visually perceptible. In other words, the song or literary work cannot be *seen.*

A compact disc or cassette tape will often have two notices, such as "℗ 1993 A&R Entertainment, Inc." and "© 1993 A&R Entertainment, Inc." The ℗ notice indicates protection of the sound recording. The © notice indicates protection of the artwork and accompanying text used on the cover, booklet, or label.

Works Using U.S. Government Publications

Any work published before March 1, 1989, that includes one or more works of the U.S. government must include a special notice. The notice must indicate that portions of the work consist of U.S. government publications.[4] For example, if in 1987 Bookco first publishes a book about the army that incorporates a U.S. military manual, the notice should state:

> © 1987 Bookco. Copyright is not claimed as to the U.S. Government military manual excerpted in Chapter Twelve.

This government notice requirement is optional (although still recommended) for works first published on or after March 1, 1989.

Unpublished Works

Copyright notice is never required on unpublished works. However, because issues may arise as to whether a work is published or unpublished, it is advisable to include a notice. The author may use the date of creation. For example, "Unpublished © 1990 Arthur Author."

Table 5.1 summarizes the choices of copyright notices and their proper use.

Type of Work	Notice
General rule	Apply "©" or "Copyright" or "Copr." with year of first publication and name (or abbreviation) of copyright owner on all visually perceptible copies
Derivatives	Apply © or "Copyright" or "Copr." with year of first publication of derivative and name (or abbreviation) of copyright owner of derivative on all visually perceptible copies.
Compilations	Apply © or "Copyright" or "Copr." with year of first publication of compilation or collective work and name (or abbreviation) of copyright owner of compilation or collective work on all visually perceptible copies. Although the compilation copyright notice will protect the author of a separately copyrightable contribution (except an advertisement) to a collective work, it is recommended to include a separate copyright notice for each author by his or her separately copyrightable work.
Sound recordings	Apply ℗ with year of first publication and name (or abbreviation) of copyright owner of the sound recording. Apply to phonorecord label or packaging of phonorecords.

TABLE 5.1
Determining the
Correct Copyright
Notice

Placement of Copyright Notice

The Copyright Act of 1976, 17 U.S.C. § 401(c), states that the notice shall be affixed to the copies "in such manner and location as to give reasonable notice of the claim of copyright." The Register of Copyrights has prescribed, as an example, certain regulations regarding notice placement at 37 C.F.R. § 201.20. The complete regulations may be obtained from the Copyright Office by requesting Circular 96 Section 201.20. In addition, Circular 3 explains the basics of copyright notice. The list here indicates some acceptable placements for copyright notice.

Books: Title page; or page immediately following the title page; or either side of the front cover or back cover; or first or last page of the main body of the work. (See figure 5-1.)

Single leaf (two-sided work): Front or back.

Periodicals or serials: Any location acceptable for books; or as part of or adjacent to the masthead or on the page containing the masthead; or adjacent to a prominent heading (near the front of the issue) containing the title, volume, and date of the issue.

Separate contributions to collective works: Under a title near the beginning of the contribution; or on the first page of the main body of the contribution; or immediately following the end of the contribution; or, if the contribution is less than 20 pages and the notice is prominently displayed, on any of the pages where the contribution appears.

Cover photo courtesy Collection of the Supreme Court of the United States.
Cover design by The Drawing Board.

Delmar Staff:

Administrative Editor: Jay Whitney
Editing Supervisor: Marlene McHugh Pratt
Production Supervisor: Larry Main
Design Coordinator: Karen Kunz Kemp

For information, address

Delmar Publishers Inc.
2 Computer Drive West, Box 15-015
Albany, New York 12212

COPYRIGHT © 1992 BY DELMAR PUBLISHERS INC., AND
LAWYERS COOPERATIVE PUBLISHING

All rights reserved. No part of this work covered by the copyright hereon may be reproduced or used in any form or by any means—graphic, electronic, or mechanical, including photocopying, recording, taping, or information storage and retrieval systems—without written permission of the publisher.

Printed in the United States of America

10 9 8 7 6 5 4 3 2

Library of Congress Cataloging-in-Publication Data

Pyle, Ransford Comstock, 1936–
Foundations of law for paralegals: cases, commentary, and ethics /Ransford C. Pyle
p. cm.—(Delmar paralegal series)
Includes bibliographical references and index.
ISBN 0-8273-4572-0 (textbook)
1. Legal assistants—United States—Handbooks, manuals, etc.
2. Law—United States. I. Title. II. Series.
KF320.L4P95 1991
349.73—dc20
[347.3] 91-21466
CIP

FIGURE 5-1
Copyright page for the text *Foundations of Law for Paralegals: Cases, Commentary, and Ethics,* by Ransford C. Pyle

Software programs and other machine-readable copies: Near the title on a visually perceptible printout (i.e., a printout of the code); or a notice displayed at the user's terminal at sign-on; or a notice that is continuously displayed on the user's terminal or a legible notice reproduced in a durable manner, on a gummed label securely affixed to the copies (disks or tape), box, or other permanent receptacle for the copies.

Motion pictures and other audiovisual works: Notice should be embodied on the work in a manner so that it appears when the work is performed, either: near the title; or with the cast, credits, and similar information; immediately following the beginning of the work or immediately preceding the end of the work.

If the work is 60 seconds or less, the notice may be in all of the locations specified above; and on the leader of the film or tape preceding the work.

If the work is distributed to the public for private use (e.g., videocassettes), the notice should appear on the permanent housing (e.g., the cassette shell) or container.

Pictorial, graphic and sculptural works:

For works embodied in two-dimensional copies, notice should be affixed directly and permanently to: the front or back of the copies; or on backing mounting, framing, or other material to which the copies are durably attached.

For works embodied in three-dimensional copies, notice should be affixed directly and permanently to: any visible portion of the work; or on a base, mounting, or framing or other material on which the copies are durably attached.

For works on which it is impractical to affix a notice to copies, even by a durable label (e.g., jewelry), a notice is acceptable if it appears on a tag or durable label attached to the copy so that it will remain with it as it passes through commerce.

For works reproduced in copies consisting of sheet-like or strip material bearing multiple reproductions (e.g., fabrics or wallpaper), notice may be applied: to the reproduction; to the margin selvage or reverse side of the material at frequent and regular intervals; or (if the material has no reverse side or selvage), on labels or tags attached to the copies and to any spools, reels, or containers housing the copies in such a manner that the notice is visible as it passes through commerce.

5.2 OMISSION OF COPYRIGHT NOTICE

Under certain circumstances, the omission of copyright can have a disastrous effect and may even result in the loss of copyright ownership. The effect of an omission depends upon the date of first publication of the work. As explained in this chapter, the omission of notice has little effect on works first published on or after March 1, 1989.[5] However, regardless of the date of first publication, it is important to know that an omission has occurred. For example, a client may be unaware that a copyright licensee has omitted the copyright notice in violation of a license agreement.

What is an omission of copyright notice? An omission of copyright notice can occur if:

1. Notice does not contain the copyright symbol or word *copyright* or appropriate abbreviation
2. Notice is dated more than one year later than the date of first publication
3. The location of the notice is such that it does not give reasonable notice of the claim of copyright (e.g., the notice on the back of a painting has been sealed over with backing materials and, when examined, is no longer visible)
4. Notice lacks the statement required for works consisting preponderantly of U.S. Government material
5. Notice without a name or date that could reasonably be considered part of the notice.

Works Published under the Copyright Act of 1909

Copyright protection could be secured under the Copyright Act of 1909 only if the owner had published the work with the copyright notice. If an authorized copy of a work was published without notice, the work would be placed permanently in the public domain. For example, if a computer chess game was published without notice, the author would lose all rights to the game and anyone would be free to copy it. Omission of notice was excused only if it resulted from accident or mistake. However, lack of knowledge of the law or negligence were not excuses.

The issue of omission generally arises when a copyright owner sues an infringer. The infringer attempts to locate a copy of the work published without notice. If an authorized publication without notice is found, then the work falls into the public domain and the infringement lawsuit is dismissed because the plaintiff does not own the copyright. For example, in 1970 the cartoonist Robert Crumb permitted a comic book publisher to use his drawing "Keep on Truckin' " on a business card. When authorizing the use, Mr. Crumb did not require notice on the card. Later, when Mr. Crumb sued an infringer, the district court declared the "Keep on Truckin' " cartoon to be in the public domain, because it had been published without notice on the business card.

Works Published Between January 1, 1978, and March 1, 1989

The drafters of the Copyright Act of 1976 attempted to alleviate some of the unfairness of the notice requirements of the Copyright Act of 1909.

JUDGE LEARNED HAND ON COPYRIGHT

One of Judge Hand's last decisions was in the 1960 case of *Peter Pan Fabrics, Inc. v. Martin Weiner Corp.*[6] The plaintiff manufactured fabrics. The defendant, who had copied the fabrics, claimed that the plaintiff had permitted the fabric to be sold without notice affixed. The fabric had originally included a strip containing the notice but, because of the requirements of some fabric customers, notice was removed in order to make clothing. Judge Hand refused to invalidate the copyright and delivered a decision that was contrary to the specific language of the statute. If the infringement is willful, said Judge Hand, the absence of notice could be used as a defense only if the copier could prove that placing the notice did not impair the market value of the fabric. Judge Hand stated, "literal interpretation of the words of a statute is not always a safe guide to its meaning." Judge Hand's decision predated the changes brought about by the Berne Amendments (i.e., that an infringer who was not misled by the lack of notice should not be able to profit by such copying).

Under the provisions of § 405, omission of notice is excused: (1) if the notice was omitted from no more than a relatively small number of copies or phonorecords; or (2) a reasonable effort is made to add notice to all copies or phonorecords that are distributed after the omission has been discovered and registration of the work is made before or within five years of discovery of the omissions; or (3) the notice is omitted in violation of a written agreement, for example, as a condition of licensing the work. Despite this savings clause, numerous works published under the Copyright Act of 1976 have fallen into the public domain. Therefore, copyright owners should carefully police all authorized copies to guarantee that the notice is properly affixed.

In the case of *Crazy Clock,* the software program mentioned in the Commentary, it is important to determine if notice has been omitted from any of the copies of the program distributed under Softco's authorization. If notice was omitted and that omission is not corrected, Lester will be able to argue that Softco's copyright is invalid. If Softco's copyright is invalid, Lester can copy the program freely.

Works Published on or after March 1, 1989

By the 1980s, the United States was the only country that terminated copyright ownership as a result of the omission of notice. To affiliate with the Berne Convention (a group of countries that abide by certain international copyright standards), the United States passed the Berne Implementation Act of 1988, which became effective on March 1, 1989. If copyright is omitted from works first published on or after this date, the owner will not suffer a loss of copyright protection. However, the Berne Amendments do not provide retroactive protection. In other words, if a work was published prior to that date, the notice requirements of previous copyright laws are still effective. For example, Softco, a computer company, first publishes a software program, *Macho Math,* in 1988. If copies of *Macho Math* are published without notice in 1992, that program is still subject to the notice requirements of the Copyright Act of 1976, and may lose copyright protection if the omission is not corrected. Softco also publishes *Serious Science.* The first publication is in 1990. Omission of notice will not subject Softco to loss of copyright protection in *Serious Science.*

Despite the change in the law regarding notice requirements, there are still incentives for the continued use of copyright notice for works published after March 1, 1989. The notice continues to inform the public that the work is protected and it identifies the owner. In addition, if the owner has been using the proper notice and there is an infringement, the defendant will not be able to claim that the infringement was innocent. This determination may affect the amount of damages awarded to the copyright owner. Therefore, although use of notice is optional for works published on or after March 1, 1989, it is still recommended.

Table 5.2 summarizes a copyright owner's possible actions after discovery of an omission.

Date of First Publication	Action
Before 1978	Notify copyright owner of consequences of omission (i.e., copyright invalidity) and attempt to determine if omission was accident or mistake, as interpreted under § 21 of the Copyright Act of 1909.
Between 1978 and March 1, 1989	Notify copyright owner of consequences of omission (i.e., copyright invalidity) and attempt to determine if omission can be corrected under § 405 of the Copyright Act of 1976. Consider the following questions: Is the omission from a small number of copies? Can a reasonable effort be made to add notice to copies that were distributed? Has the work been registered? Was the publication with the omitted notice done by a licensee or other transferee who was required by written agreement to include the notice as a condition of the agreement?
On or after March 1, 1989	Notify copyright owner of the change in law regarding the Berne Amendment. Is this a derivative, or has the work been published in an earlier form prior to March 1, 1989? Notify copyright owner of accepted methods of correcting omission under § 405.

TABLE 5.2
What to Do when an Omission of Copyright Notice Is Discovered

5.3 REGISTRATION OF COPYRIGHT

Registration is not necessary to obtain copyright protection. Under the Copyright Act of 1909, protection occurs once the work is published with notice. Under the Copyright Act of 1976, copyright protection begins once the work is created. Although registration is permissive and not mandatory under the current copyright act, it is strongly recommended. If a work has been registered prior to an infringement lawsuit, the copyright owner may be entitled to statutory damages and attorney fees, as explained in Chapter 6. In any case, as of the time of publication of this text, the plaintiff in a copyright infringement lawsuit must acquire a *certificate of registration* in order to file the lawsuit. For example, if the owner of a copyrighted photograph wants to sue a magazine for copying the photograph without authorization, the owner must register the work before filing the lawsuit. Note that in February 1993, legislation (S. 373 and H.R. 897) was proposed that would eliminate the copyright registration requirement for filing suit (17 U.S.C. § 411(a)) and would eliminate the registration requirement for statutory damages and attorney fees at 17 U.S.C. § 412. Although this legislation had not been enacted as of the publication of this book, the legal assistant should review the current copyright law when researching this issue.

Registration of copyright is an administrative process.[7] The applicant submits an application, a fee, and deposit materials. An examiner at the Copyright Office determines whether the material deposited constitutes copyrightable subject matter and whether the legal and formal requirements of copyright law have been met. The register of copyrights then registers the claim to copyright and issues a certificate of registration to the applicant. The certificate contains the information given in the application, together with the number and effective date of the registration. If the Copyright Office determines that the material deposited does not constitute copyrightable subject matter or that the claim is invalid for any other reason, the Register of Copyrights will refuse registration and notify the applicant in writing of the reasons for the refusal.

In the case of a refusal, the applicant can request reconsideration by the Copyright Office. If, as a result of such reconsideration, the Copyright Office still refuses to issue a registration, then a final refusal will be issued. On the basis of this final refusal, the applicant may then appeal the Copyright Office decision to the federal district court. For purposes of bringing an infringement action, the applicant, unless excluded under the Berne Amendments, must obtain either a final refusal or a registration in order to bring the action.

The Basic Registration

The Copyright Office permits one **basic registration** to be made for each version of a particular work. For example, one basic registration would be filed for the novel *The Shining,* written by Stephen King. This basic registration serves as the primary copyright record. If this registration must be corrected or amplified, a separate Form CA would be filed, as explained later in this chapter. If the ownership is transferred, a new basic registration would not be made. Instead, documents or records regarding this transfer of ownership would be filed separately.

Each version of a work is entitled to its own basic registration. For example, if the novel *The Shining* was revised, along with a new introduction and additional text, a basic registration would be made for this new version. Similarly, if a motion picture was adapted from *The Shining,* a basic registration would be made for the film.

There are two exceptions to the general rule of one basic registration per work. In the following situations, the Copyright Office will permit more than one basic registration:

Exception: Previously registered as unpublished work. If the work has been previously registered in unpublished form, a second registration can be made to cover the published version. For example, John registers an unpublished computer program. Later, he publishes the computer program (in virtually the same format as the unpublished version). Even though there are no substantial changes between the published and unpublished version, John may file a separate registration for the published version.

Exception: Someone other than author identified as copyright claimant. In cases where someone other than the author is named as the copyright claimant (i.e., the owner of copyright), the Copyright Office will accept an application from the author for basic registration in the author's name as copyright claimant. For example, John creates a computer program and assigns the copyright to Softco. Softco registers the work, lists John as the author, and lists Softco as the copyright claimant. Later, John reacquires the rights to the program. He may now register the work a second time in his own name.

Registration Creates Presumption of Ownership and Validity

The certificate of registration does not prove ownership of copyright, but registration within five years of first publication creates a rebuttable legal presumption of ownership and validity.[8] A **presumption** is an inference as to the truth or validity of an allegation. A presumption of validity shifts the burden to the defendant to disprove or show, with sufficient evidence, the falsity or invalidity of the allegation. For example, Bob registers a claim to copyright to his hand-tinted photographs. He sues Andrea for copying the photos without his permission. The court presumes that Bob is the owner of copyright and that his registration is valid. Andrea has the burden of proving that the registration is not valid and that Bob is not the owner. If she can furnish sufficient evidence as to either of these allegations, she will have overcome the presumption and the court will rule in her favor on these issues. This legal presumption is also known as *prima facie* proof (i.e., "on first appearance" or "on its face") of copyright ownership. Therefore, for purposes of evidence, the presumptions created by registration are often necessary to enforce copyright.

Registration as Prerequisite to Filing an Infringement Lawsuit

An action for infringement cannot be instituted until registration of the copyright claim has been made.[9] For example, Jane discovers that Tom has been selling unauthorized copies of her book, *Poodle Clipping Tips*. She has not registered her work. As a condition of filing a lawsuit against Tom, it is mandatory that Jane register her work (unless exempted under the Berne Amendments, as discussed later).[10] The certificate of registration will be referenced and attached to the complaint as an exhibit. There are some exceptions to this rule.

Exception: Registration Refused by Copyright Office. If registration has been refused, even though it was in the correct form, the copyright owner can still institute a lawsuit, provided that a final refusal is received from the Copyright Office and a copy of the complaint is also served on the Register of Copyrights. For example, Softco creates a video game, *Wall Banger*. The Copyright Office refuses to register the work, claiming that the game does not possess sufficient originality. Diskco illegally copies the *Wall Banger* game. Although the Copyright Office has refused to register the work, Softco can still sue for copyright infringement, provided that a copy of the infringement lawsuit is also served on the Register of Copyrights in Washington, D.C.[11] There is another basis for filing without a registration and that is if the country of origin of the work is not the United States and not a country that is part of the Berne Convention.[12]

LEGAL TERMS

basic registration
Primary copyright record made for each version of a particular work.

presumption
Inference as to the truth or validity of an allegation. A presumption shifts the burden to the other party to disprove or show, with sufficient evidence, the falsity or invalidity of the allegation.

Exception: Simultaneous Transmission. If a work is embodied in a physical object simultaneously with its transmission, the owner of that work can institute an infringement lawsuit, provided that the owner, within 10 to 30 days of embodiment on a physical object, declares an intention to register and registers the work within 3 months of first transmission.[13] For example, the National Football League broadcasts the Super Bowl football game. The NFL fixes the game on a videotape as the game is broadcast. At the time of the broadcast, Tom videotapes the game and makes copies for sale. The NFL can sue for infringement, provided that a notice is served on Tom between 10 to 30 days from the date of the game (the date when it was embodied on videotape by the NFL) and provided that the notice contains certain information, including an intent to register. The NFL must register the work within three months of the initial transmission.

Registration as Prerequisite to Recovery of Statutory Damages and Attorney Fees

Damages will be awarded if a copyright owner prevails in an infringement lawsuit. The court determines the amount of the injury suffered and awards damages that will compensate the copyright owner. By way of example, if an infringer had profits of $10,000 from the infringing activity, the copyright owner should be awarded $10,000. Often it is difficult to prove the extent of the profits or damages (when, for instance, the work was freely distributed as a sales brochure). The Copyright Act of 1976 provides that the court, in its discretion, may award damages of between $500 and $20,000

The NFL exercises strict control over the (re)broadcasting of its sporting events.

per infringement. In cases of willful infringement, an award up to $100,000 may be granted. These enumerated awards are known as **statutory damages.** The copyright statute provides for these specific sums to be awarded, and such an award does not require proof of the plaintiff's monetary loss or the defendant's profit.

However, statutory damages will be awarded in a copyright infringement lawsuit only if the work at issue was registered prior to the infringement or within three months of the first publication of the work. For example, Softco publishes a new video game, *They Came from Within,* on May 1, 1992. Diskco infringes the game on June 1, 1992. If Softco registers the work within three months of May 1, 1992, Softco will be able to obtain statutory damages. In the case of the Softco program *Crazy Clock,* discussed in the Commentary, Softco failed to register the work prior to Lester's infringement. Therefore, Softco would not be entitled to statutory damages. Note that in February 1993, legislation (S. 373 and H.R. 897) was proposed that would eliminate the copyright registration requirement for filing suit (17 U.S.C. § 411(a)) and would eliminate the registration requirement for statutory damages and attorney fees at 17 U.S.C. § 412. Although this legislation had not been enacted as of the publication of this book, the legal assistant should review the current copyright law when researching this issue.

The same rules apply to attorney fees. If a registration was made within three months of publication or prior to an infringing activity, the plaintiff may be awarded attorney fees incurred in enforcing the copyright. This award is at the discretion of the court. This means that if the court determines fees should be awarded, the infringer may have to pay its own attorney fees *and* the attorney fees for the plaintiff. This can be a substantial deterrent to a defendant who is undecided about whether to fight a copyright infringement lawsuit. There is one exception to this rule regarding statutory damages and attorney fees.

Exception: Simultaneous Transmission. If a work is embodied in a physical object simultaneously with its transmission, the owner of that work can seek statutory damages even though an infringement occurs before the work is published or registered. For example, if a news broadcast is pirated and sold by an infringer, the owner of copyright in the news broadcast can still seek attorney fees and statutory damages even if registration of the work occurred after commencement of the infringing activity.

When Registration Is Required: Correction of Notice Omission

There is one instance in which copyright registration is mandatory. It applies to any works first published on or after January 1, 1978, but before March 1, 1989.[14] If a relatively small number of copies of the work are published without the copyright notice, one of the requirements of correcting the omission of notice, according to § 405(a)(2), is to register the work within five years after the publication without a notice. In addition, a reasonable effort must be made to add notice to all copies or phonorecords that are distributed to the public after the omission is discovered.

LEGAL TERMS

statutory damages
Award of damages prescribed by statute and not contingent upon proof of the plaintiff's loss or the defendant's profits.

Expediting Registration

Because the registration process may take six weeks or longer, it may be necessary for the copyright owner to expedite the process. For a special expedited handling fee of $200 (in addition to the $20 filing fee), the Copyright Office will process an application within five working days. The Copyright Office has prepared a form for "Request for Special Handling." However, a cover letter will be sufficient if it answers the following questions:

- Why is there an urgent need for special handling? (e.g., litigation, customs matter, contractual or publishing deadline, or other reasons as specified)
- If the action is requested in order to go forward with litigation: (a) is the litigation actual or prospective? (b) Is the party requesting the expedited action the plaintiff or the defendant in the action? (c) What are the names of the parties and what is the name of the court where the action is pending or expected?

In addition, the person requesting the expedited action must certify that the statements are correct to the best of his or her knowledge. The letter and application may be hand delivered to the Public Information Office of the Library of Congress. If possible, this method is recommended, as a copyright examiner will give the application an immediate review that can enable modification of the application, if necessary. If mailed, the letter and the envelope should be addressed to Special Handling, Library of Congress, Room 100, Washington, D.C. 20540. Payment should be by money order or cashiers' check, not by personal check. If the applicant maintains a deposit account, fees can be deducted from the deposit account. An example of a sample letter for expedited handling is shown in figure 5-2. This letter requests that the Copyright Office contact the applicant (or applicant's attorney). Alternatively, the applicant may request a certain number of copies, certified copies, or that the registration be held for pickup. There is an additional fee for certification of copies.

FIGURE 5-2
Request for special handling for copyright registration.

REQUEST FOR SPECIAL HANDLING

Special Handling
Library of Congress
Room 100—Special Handling
Washington, DC 20540

To the Register of Copyrights:

Enclosed please find a cashiers' check for two hundred and twenty dollars ($220) for an expedited filing fee, a Copyright Application Form TX for the literary work, *Accordion Repair Guide,* and deposit materials.

An expedited review and registration of this work is sought because the owner, Master Music Publications, Inc., intends to prepare a claim, as plaintiff, for copyright infringement regarding this book in the United States District Court for the Northern District of California. The defendant, Anton Yonko, is a former employee who allegedly copied the book and is now selling it through various distribution channels. Because of the need for immediate injunctive relief, an expedited registration is requested. I certify that the information provided in this letter is correct to the best of my knowledge. When the expedited registration has been completed, contact me at the telephone number listed in this letter. A stamped return envelope for overnight mailing is included.

Attorney for Master Music Publication, Inc.

FIGURE 5-2
(Continued)

5.4 PREPARING THE COPYRIGHT APPLICATION

The Copyright Office receives more than half a million registrations for copyright each year. The Copyright Office examines each registration and determines its registrability. To proceed rapidly through the registration process, knowledge of registration procedures is essential. Generally, the registration process is not very difficult, and compared to form processing for litigation or tax preparation, it is quite user friendly. The copyright application was designed for use by lay persons, and additional information is often furnished with the application that can guide the applicant through the process. However, despite the simplicity of the copyright form, many of the decisions that must be made can have a serious effect on protection of the work. The person preparing the registration must be aware of many issues and nuances of copyright law, including the correct application to use, the nature of the work being registered, information about the copyright claimant, and information about the components or origin of the work. In addition, materials must be deposited with the registration. It is also important that the person assisting in preparation of the registration avoid the use of any statement or representation that may prove to be untrue or fraudulent. When in doubt, a paralegal or legal assistant should actively seek supervision in the preparation of copyright applications or other copyright forms. If additional assistance is necessary in the registration process, the Copyright Office provides guides for filling out each application, as well as Copyright Office circulars dealing with how to fill in applications for registration of particular types of works.

Choosing the Correct Application Form

Several types of application forms are used in the registration of copyrights. Examples of each are provided in the appendix D. They are:

Form TX—for published and unpublished nondramatic literary works (e.g., novels, nonfiction literary works, or short stories)

Form PA—for published and unpublished works of the performing arts (e.g., musical works, dramatic works, pantomimes, motion pictures, and audiovisual works)

Form VA—for published and unpublished works of the visual arts (e.g., pictorial, graphic, and sculptural works) and for architectural works

Form SR—For published and unpublished sound recordings

Form SE—For registration of each individual issue of a serialized publication (e.g., newspapers, journals or magazines)

Short Form SE—Simplified form for registration of collective work or issue of serialized publication

Form SE/GROUP—For registration of groups of collective works or issues published within one year

Form CA—As a supplementary registration, to correct or amplify information given in a previous registration

Form GR/CP—an adjunct application (that accompanying a Form TX, VA, or PA application) to register a group of contributions to periodicals

To choose the correct application form, the registrant must determine the nature of the work. What *is* the work? As explained in the previous chapters, the form in which the work is embodied does not determine the nature of the work. For example, the play *A Streetcar Named Desire* may be printed in a book, along with photos from the original Broadway cast presentation. The fact that the play is printed in a book form does not make *A Streetcar Named Desire* a literary work. It is a dramatic work that is intended to be performed before an audience. Similarly, the fact that the photographs are printed in the book does not change the nature of the photos. The photos are a pictorial work (i.e., a work of the visual arts). The play may be registered by the copyright owner using a Form PA and the photographs may be registered by the copyright owner with a Form VA.

Generally, the following list should assist in choosing the correct copyright form:

Form PA—Use for a work that is intended to be performed before an audience (i.e., a play, musical composition, song, choreography, opera, motion picture, or audiovisual work)

Form TX—Use for a literary work expressed in words or numbers, such as a novel, nonfiction book, short story, poetry, textbook, reference work, directory, catalog, advertising copy, or article (but not a dramatic work such as a play); a computer software program

Form VA—Use for a two-dimensional or three-dimensional visual arts work, such as an advertisement, label, artwork applied to useful articles, bumper sticker, cartoon, collage, doll, toy, drawing, painting, mural, fabric, wallpaper, greeting card, game, puzzle, hologram, computer artwork (other than audiovisual artwork that is used in a computer program), jewelry, map, logo, mask, engraving, silkscreen, sewing pattern, poster, needlework, print, sculpture, stained glass, technical drawing, weaving, tapestry, or artwork such as a record cover or book jacket; an architectural work

Form SR—Use for a sound recording such as a record, cassette recording, or compact disc (but not the audio portion of an audiovisual work such as a motion picture soundtrack or an audio cassette accompanying a filmstrip). In addition, if the author also wishes to simultaneously register the sound recording and underlying musical, dramatic, or literary work embodied on the sound recording

Form SE—Use for an individual issue of a periodical, newspaper, journal, magazine, proceeding, annual edition, or serialized publication that is intended to be issued in successive parts bearing numerical or chronological designations (but not an individual contribution to a serial publication)

Short Form SE—Use for registration of an all-new collective work or issue that is work made for hire by a citizen or domiciliary of the United States. The author and the claimant must be the same

Form SE/GROUP—Use for registration of a group of all-new collective works or issues that are works made for hire, published within a one-year period, if each issue was created no more than a year prior to publication. The author and the claimant must be the same for all issues and a complimentary subscription (two copies) must have been given to the Library of Commerce

Form GR/CP and either TX, PA, or VA Form—Use for a group of contributions to periodicals (such as a series of columns or articles) in which: all of the works are by the same author; have the same copyright claimant; and all of the works were published as contributions to periodicals within a 12-month period.

Space 1: Title of the Work; Previous or Alternate Titles

Space 1 of each application requires that the applicant provide the title and alternate or previous title of the work. Every work must be given a title to be registered. The title serves a function for indexing the work. The title should be transcribed exactly as it appears on the work. Nondescriptive titles, such as "Work Without a Title," can be registered. However, titles that are not presented in alphanumeric format cannot be registered. For example, if the title of a work is "☺," the work should be registered as "Happy Face" or a similar title. Titles in a foreign language should be presented in the Roman alphabet. The Copyright Office requests more specific information in the case of serials, discussed later in this section.

The alternate or previous title is any additional title under which someone searching for the registration might look. For example, the song "Everybody's Talkin' " is also known by an alternate title, "Theme from Midnight Cowboy." The title of a different version of the work (such as a derivative work) is not an alternate or previous title. For example, the registration for the motion picture *The Godfather III* should not list *The Godfather II* as a previous or alternate title.

Nature of Work

Space 1 of Forms VA, PA, and SR also requires information about the "nature of the work." In Form SR, the registrant must check a box indicating the nature of the material recorded (i.e., musical, dramatic, literary, etc). In Form VA, the registrant must provide a brief description such as "pen & ink drawing," "photographs," "architectural work." Similarly, for Form PA, the applicant should state whether the work is a "drama," "musical play," "choreography," "motion picture," or other performing arts work. If further assistance is needed in determining the nature of the work, consult the "Line-by-Line Instructions" provided by the Copyright Office for each particular application form. Examples are included in appendix D.

Publication as a Contribution

Certain forms, such as Form TX and Form VA, request information if the work was published as a contribution to a periodical. If the work was published as part of a serial publication or as part of a collective work, information should be presented regarding the serial publication. For example, Jane Feldman is the author of a short story, *Stereo Lovers*. The story was first printed on pages 55-60 of a magazine, *Female Trouble* (volume 21, number 2, issue date May 1, 1992). When Jane registers the short story work, she would complete Space 1 as follows:

Title of this Work: Stereo Lovers
Previous or Alternative Titles: (blank)
Publication as a Contribution/Title of Collective Work: Female Trouble
Volume 21 *Number* 2 *Issue Date* 5/1/92 *On Pages* 55-60

Space 2: Author

Space 2 of the copyright application requires that the applicant provide information about the author or authors. To fill out this space, the applicant must analyze the work to determine the manner in which the author is identified and the nature of the author's contribution. If the work being registered is a derivative work, the applicant should only provide the name of the author of the *new* material, not the author of the underlying work. For example, Joseph Heller is the author of the novel *Catch 22*. Buck Henry is the author of the derivative screenplay for the film *Catch 22*. When registering the screenplay, Buck Henry would be listed as the author.

Anonymous and Pseudonymous

An author's contribution to a work is *anonymous* if that author is not identified on the copies or phonorecords of the work. An author's contribution is *pseudonymous* if the author is identified by a fictitious name. If the author's contribution is anonymous, the Copyright Office offers three choices to the applicant: (1) leave the line blank; (2) state "Anonymous" on the line; or (3) reveal the author's identity. If the author's contribution is pseudonymous, the Copyright Office permits the author to: (1) leave the line blank; (2) give the pseudonym and identify it as such (e.g., Mark Twain, pseudonym); or (3) reveal the author's name, making it clear that which is a pseudonym and that which is the real name (e.g., Samuel Clemens whose pseudonym is Mark Twain).

Works Made for Hire

If it is unclear whether the work is made for hire, refer to the checklist, "Determining if a Work Is Made for Hire," in chapter 4. If the author's contribution is a work made for hire, the full name of the hiring party should be used.

Nature of Authorship

Provide a short statement of the nature of each author's contribution. For example, if Bob wrote both the words and the music to a song, the nature of authorship would be "words and music." If Bob wrote the music and Sally wrote the words to a song, the nature of Bob's authorship would be "music" and the nature of Sally's authorship would be "words" or "lyrics." If in doubt as to a phrase that sufficiently describes the nature of authorship, refer to the specific Line-by-Line Instructions provided by the Copyright Office for each application form. Samples of these Line-by-Line Instructions are provided in appendix D. If the work is a derivative, the nature of authorship would only describe the new material added to the work. For example, if an author writes a screenplay of a novel, the nature of authorship would be "dramatization." If the work is a compilation and all of the material in the compilation has been previously published or is in the public domain, the nature of authorship is "compilation." If the compilation contains some material being registered or published for the first time, the claim may state "additional text and compilation."

Dates of Birth and Death

If an author is deceased, the year of death should be provided. Although it is not mandatory, the date of birth of each author may be provided. In the case of a work made for hire, this section of Space 2 should remain blank. As noted in chapter 4, a presumption arises as to the length of life of the author under § 302(e) of the Copyright Act of 1976.

Nationality

The author's nationality may have an effect on the registrability of the work. An unpublished work may be registered regardless of the author's nationality; however, published works are only subject to the U. S. copyright laws if the work is published in the United States or in a foreign nation that (on the date of first publication) is a member of the Universal Copyright Convention *or* if the work is published in a nation that comes within the scope of a presidential proclamation extending copyright protection.

Space 2: Examples

EXAMPLE 1: Sole Authorship

The Joker Program. Bob Jones creates a program that causes jokes to pop up on the computer screen. Bob Jones has written the entire program, including all the jokes and computer code.

Name of Author: Bob Jones
Was this contribution to work a "work made for hire"? Check NO box
Nature of Authorship: "entire work," "entire computer code," or similar description

EXAMPLE 2: Work Made for Hire

The Bible Program. Softco creates a computer software program that helps users find verses in the Bible. The program is created entirely by Softco employees under a work-for-hire arrangement.

Name of Author: Softco Company
Was this contribution to work a "work made for hire"? Check YES box
Nature of Authorship: "entire work," "entire computer code," or similar description
The fact that portions of this work are derived from another work (the Bible) is not relevant for filling out Space 2. It will, however be relevant for Spaces 5 and 6.

EXAMPLE 3: Joint Authorship

The Will-Writing Program. Softco initiates the creation of a software program that assists a person in making a will. The program is written by two authors. One of the authors, Gina Jones, is an attorney who has written all of the "help" screens and legal text used in the program. The other author, Ed Low, is a computer programmer who has incorporated Gina's text into a complex interactive computer program. Gina is an independent contractor who has assigned all her rights to Softco. Ed is a full-time employee of Softco and his contribution to the program is a work made for hire. Softco's intent was to combine Gina and Ed's work. Therefore, the program is a joint work and Ed's contribution is a work made for hire.

Space 2a
Name of Author: Gina Jones
Was this contribution to work a "work made for hire"? Check NO box
Nature of Authorship: Legal Help Screen Text and Legal Textual Material
Space 2b
Name of Author: Softco Corporation or Softco Corporation, employer for hire of Ed Low
Was this contribution to work a "work made for hire"? Check YES box
Nature of Authorship: Entire nonlegal program text and instructions.

EXAMPLE 4: Author of a Derivative Work

The Diet Program 2.0. Softco sells a program that helps people plan a weight loss diet. The first version (1.0) was written by Jane Smith. When the first version, *Diet Program 1.0*, was registered, Jane was listed as the author. She assigned all her rights under copyright law to Softco. Softco has its employees (under a work-for-hire arrangement) revise the program to create Version 2.0.

Name of Author: Softco Company
Was this contribution to work a "work made for hire"? Check YES box
Nature of Authorship: "revised program" or "revised text"
The fact that portions of this work are derived from another author's work is not relevant for filling out Space 2. Jane's name would not be listed in Space 2. However, Jane's authorship and the previous registration of Version 1.0 would be relevant for Spaces 5 and 6.

Space 3: Creation and Publication

Space 3 of the copyright application requires that the applicant provide information about the dates of creation and first publication of the work. As indicated in previous chapters, *creation* and *publication* have two very different meanings under copyright law. A work is **created** when it is fixed in a tangible form for the first time.

LEGAL TERMS

created
When a work is fixed in a copy or phonorecord for the first time. If a work is prepared over a period of time, the portion of it that has been fixed at any particular time constitutes the work as of that time; if the work has been prepared in different versions, each version constitutes a separate work.

As a general rule, the date of completion of the particular work being registered is the date of creation. For example, if an author writes a novel and then revises it with an editor, the date of the final revisions would be the date of creation. If a computer company creates a program, tests it among users, and then revises it again before publication, the date of the final revisions would be the date of creation. If, however, an unpublished work is being registered, the date of the latest version being registered would be the date of creation.

A work is *published* if copies or phonorecords (in the case of sound recordings) are distributed to the public by sale or other transfer of ownership, or by rental, lease, or lending. A work is also published if an offer is made to distribute copies or phonorecords to a group of persons for purposes of further distribution, public performance, or public display.

The applicant must determine, first, if the work has been published. Are there multiple copies of the work? Have copies of the work been distributed to the public? A distribution of copies to a limited group of persons and for a limited purpose is not considered a publication. For example, a musician prepares demonstration recordings. She sends the tapes to record companies in the hopes that she will acquire a record contract. The limited distribution of demonstration recordings for a limited purpose is not considered a publication of the work. The Copyright Office will generally assume, when there is only one copy or phonorecord, that the work has *not* been published. However, it is possible that publication may have occurred even if there is only one copy. This is because the definition of *publication* in the Copyright Act of 1976 includes the "offering to distribute to a group . . . for further distribution, performance or display." Although public performance or display does not constitute publication, the offer to distribute to a group for further performance or display does constitute publication. Consider the following examples.

EXAMPLE 1

The News Broadcast. A television station telecasts and simultaneously videotapes a nightly newscast. The newscast is a copyrightable audiovisual work. However, it has *not* been published. Why? Because multiple copies have not been made and because the work has not been offered to a group for further distribution. All that has happened is a public performance of the work, and that, by itself, does not constitute publication under copyright law. The work may be registered as an unpublished audiovisual work.

EXAMPLE 2

The Television Commercial. An advertising agency creates a television commercial promoting Softco computer products. The agency contacts several television stations and offers to purchase time to broadcast the commercial. The work has been published because multiple copies have been offered for public performance.

EXAMPLE 3

The Portrait. A painter completes a portrait and sells it to a museum. The museum displays the work. The work has *not* been published. The painter has not published multiple copies and has not offered the work to a group of persons for further distribution, performance, or display.

Date and Nation of First Publication.   The applicant should always give the full date (i.e., month, day, and year) when the work is published. If the applicant is unsure, it is acceptable to state "approximately" (i.e., approximately June 4, 1991). If the work is first published in the United States, the initials *U.S.A.* may be used. If the work is simultaneously published (i.e., within 30 days) in two countries, for example, the United States and Canada, it is acceptable to state "U.S.A." If the work is first published in a foreign country, the foreign edition constitutes this first publication.

Space 4: The Copyright Claimant

Space 4 requires that the applicant provide information about the copyright claimant. The claimant is either the author of the work or a person or organization to whom the copyright has been transferred. In the case of a work for hire, the copyright claimant is the hiring party. For example, Jim, an employee of Softco, creates a computer program within the scope of his employment at Softco. The program is a work made for hire and the copyright claimant would be Softco. Generally, the person who owns all rights to the work is the claimant. However, if the applicant has acquired one of the exclusive rights granted under copyright law, that person may be listed as the copyright claimant.

Limited Ownership

In certain instances, a claimant may own the rights to the work for a limited period of time. For example, the computer company, Diskco, may exclusively license a work for a period of five years. Diskco may state in Space 4, "Diskco, Inc., by written agreement for a period of five years" or "Diskco, Inc., by written agreement terminating April 15, 1995."

Claimant Must Be Living

The applicant should not name a deceased person as the copyright claimant. For example, Arthur Author dies. His estate wishes to register copyright in a book that is to be published posthumously. The executor or administrator of Arthur's estate should be named as claimant, or, if known, the party who has inherited the ownership of Arthur's copyright.

Name and Address

The copyright claimant should be clearly identified. The full legal name of the claimant is preferred, although an abbreviation is acceptable if it identifies the claimant. The address for the claimant should also be included.

Transfer

If the person named as claimant is not the same as the person in Space 2 (the "author"), the applicant must provide a brief statement of how the claimant acquired copyright. For example, the following statements are acceptable: "By written contract," "Transfer of all rights by author," "By operation of state community property law," "Assignment," "By will." The applicant should *not* attach such documents to the application. However, such transfer documentation may be recorded separately, or at a later date, with the Copyright Office. The procedure for recording such documents is presented later in this chapter.

Space 5: Previous Registration

Space 5 requires that the applicant provide information about any previous copyright registrations for this work or earlier versions of the work. If the work has never been previously registered, simply check the NO box. For purposes of Space 5, the Copyright Office is only seeking information about earlier registrations of the particular work being registered. For example, the author Stephen King may register the novel *The Shining* as a literary work. If a revised version of the novel is published that includes new material, then the box marked YES would be checked.

However, if a movie was prepared based upon the novel, the registration for the motion picture would *not* list the novel as a previous registration. This is because the motion picture is considered to be an original work, distinct and separate from the novel. Assuming there were no other registrations for the motion picture or underlying screenplay, the box marked NO would be checked. If, however, the motion picture were revised and additional scenes were later added and released on video, the registration for that subsequent motion picture would indicate that an earlier registration had been issued.

Basis for Seeking New Registration

If the applicant has checked the YES box in Space 5, a new registration will be issued, provided that the applicant meets any one of the following conditions.

1. *Previously unpublished.* The work was registered in unpublished form and a second registration is now being sought to cover this first published edition; or

2. *Author seeking registration as claimant.* Someone other than the author is identified as a copyright claimant in the earlier registration, and the author is now seeking registration in his or her own name; or

3. *Changed version.* If the work was changed and the applicant now seeks registration to cover the additions or revisions.

Previous Registration Number and Year of Registration

If the applicant is unsure whether the work has been previously registered, a search of the Copyright Office records may be initiated, as explained in Chapter 6. In addition, several private companies perform copyright searches. Generally, the applicant will have access to information regarding the previous registration. The registration number is listed on the upper righthand corner of the registration and usually begins with the letters of the form (e.g., TX-334-821 or PA 334-821). Space 5 also should include the year that the previous registration was issued.

Space 6: Derivative Work or Compilation

The applicant completes Space 6 if the work being registered contains a *substantial* amount of material that:

- was previously published
- was previously registered in the U.S. Copyright Office
- is in the public domain
- is not included in the claim for registration.

In other words, Space 6 requires the applicant to determine if the work being registered is a derivative work or a compilation. Space 6 has two parts. If the work is derivative, then the applicant completes 6(a) and 6(b). If the work is a compilation, the applicant only provides information in 6b. The author of a **derivative work** has transformed, recast, or adapted the preexisting material, whereas the author of a **compilation** has assembled, selected, or organized the preexisting materials without transforming them. For example, the motion picture *The Addams Family* is a derivative work because it is derived from the cartoons of Charles Addams. The author of the motion picture would complete the form as follows:

LEGAL TERMS

derivative work
A work based upon one or more preexisting works, such as a translation, musical arrangement, dramatization, fictionalization, motion picture version, sound recording, art reproduction, abridgment, condensation, or any other form in which a work may be recast, transformed, or adapted. A work consisting of editorial revisions, annotations, elaborations, or other modifications that, as a whole, represent an original work of authorship is also a derivative work.

compilation
A work formed by the collection and assembling of preexisting materials or of data that are selected, coordinated, or arranged in such a way that the resulting work as a whole constitutes an original work of authorship. The term *compilation* includes collective works.

6a (preexisting material): original cartoons by Charles Addams
6b (material added): dramatization for motion picture

However, the use of selected cartoons by Charles Addams in a book, *Great Cartoons from the New Yorker,* would be a **collective work** constituting a compilation. Space 6 would be completed as follows:

6a (preexisting material): (blank)
6b (material added): compilation of cartoons, additional text, and introduction

Derivative Works

For some applicants, Space 6 creates confusion because it may be difficult to determine if the work is a derivative. A derivative is not created by minor variations or revisions to a work. To be protected, the derivative must contain an adequate amount of new material, and this new material should be capable of being separately protectible. If the derivative work is based upon a public domain work, copyright does not revive protection for the underlying work. For example, if an artist were to add color to black-and-white drawings by William Blake, copyright would extend only to the additional color, not to the Blake drawings that are in the public domain. Similarly, registration of a derivative work does not extend the life of the underlying work. For example, if the motion picture *Lawrence of Arabia* is reissued in 1990 with additional scenes and a new soundtrack, it does not extend protection for the underlying film, originally published in 1962.

Permission must still be obtained from the underlying copyright owner when creating a derivative based upon a protectible work. It is also a prudent practice to include language such as "Used with permission of . . . " when using such material.

Under some circumstances, a person may be preparing a second edition of a computer program or book. The registration in the derivative work (the second edition) will only cover the new material. Therefore, if the first edition has not been registered, it may be prudent to register that first work as well to guarantee protection for the material contained in that book. For example, Bill writes a computer program, *Cold Shower 1.0.* Later he makes major improvements in the basic program and publishes *Cold Shower 2.0.* He registers this second edition as a derivative work. However, because protection extends only to the major improvements, he also separately registers *Cold Shower 1.0* at the same time.

Table 5.3 compares derivative and nonderivative works.

Examples of Derivative Filings. Table 5.4 shows some examples of how Space 6 should be completed for a derivative work application.

Derivative Work	Not a Derivative Work
Addition of new routines or functions to a computer program	Correction of errors in a computer program
Translation of book into a different language	Publication of book with larger type to aid vision-impaired persons
Addition of scenes and sequences to a previously released motion picture	Reproduction of motion picture in videocassette format
A drawing created from a photograph	Duplication of photograph on a lunch box

TABLE 5.3
What Is and Is Not a
Derivative Work?

Compilations and Collective Works

When completing Space 6, an applicant also may be confused as to whether the work is a compilation. When an author creates a work by selecting various components and grouping them together in a unique manner, the result is a compilation. Copyright will protect a compilation only if the manner in which the work has been assembled is original and constitutes separately protectible authorship. Table 5.5 compares compilations and noncompilations.

Derivative Work	Space 6a (Preexisting Material)	Space 6b (Material Added to this Work)
Motion Picture *First Blood*	original novel *First Blood*	dramatization for motion picture
Musical arrangement "Mary Had a Little Lamb"	words and music	arrangement for saxophone trio
Book *An Analysis of Macbeth*	Shakespeare's *Macbeth*	introduction, foreword, and additional text
Catalog *1990 Urban Gardener*	*1989 Urban Gardener* catalog	editorial revisions and additional material (*note:* this revised catalog also may constitute a compilation)
Silkscreen print of *Elvis Presley* photograph	photograph	stencil and silkscreen reproduction
Sound recording reissue of Beatles' *Abbey Road*	1969 recording by the Beatles	remixed sounds from original multitrack sound sources
Map *Mountain Bike Routes in Northern California*	U.S. Geological Survey map of northern California	additional cartographic authorship and text

TABLE 5.4
Examples of Derivative
Works for Space 6

Compilation Work	Not a Compilation
Selection and arrangement of names and phone numbers by profession or political preference	Alphabetical listing of names and corresponding phone numbers
Selected *Doonesbury* comic strips	Chronological ordering of *Doonesbury* comic strips
Abridged version of *Moby Dick*	Publication of *Moby Dick* in two volumes
Specially paginated and arranged judicial opinions of the U.S. Supreme Court	Montly reproduction of official U.S. Supreme Court opinions

TABLE 5.5
What Is and Is Not a Compilation?

Examples of Compilation Filings.   Table 5.6 contains some examples of how Space 6 should be completed for a compilation work application.

Space 7: Deposit Account

Space 7 on all application forms (except Form TX, where it is Space 8), requires information as to whether the registration fee is to be charged to a deposit account. The Copyright Office maintains deposit accounts for persons who register works on a regular basis. If the applicant maintains a deposit account, the registration fee can be charged against the balance. This way the registrant does not have to send in a check each time an application is mailed. However, deposit accounts are not like commercial charge accounts.

Compilation Work	Space 6a (Preexisting Material)	Space 6b (Material Added to this Work)
Motion picture *Great Baseball Bloopers*		Compilation of various baseball motion picture sequences; introduction and accompanying soundtrack
Directory *Republican Dentists*		Compilation of names, addresses, and telephone numbers of Republican dentists and foreword
Encyclopedia *Home Brewing Tips*		Compilation of articles, index, and foreword
Sound recording *Marvin Gaye's Greatest Hits*		compilation of Marvin Gaye sound recordings

TABLE 5.6
Examples of Compilations for Space 6

Compilation and Derivative Works (Combined)		
Compilation & Derivative Work	Space 6a (Preexisting Material)	Space 6b (Material Added to this Work)
Book French translation— *Selected Stories of O. Henry*	Original stories by O. Henry	Translation in French and compilation
Automated database *Rules of Grammar II*	Previously published rules of English grammar	Revised and updated text; revised compilation
Sound recording *Donna Summer's Disco Hits (Remixed)*	Sound recordings by Donna Summer from 1977 through 1979	Remixed sounds from original multitrack sound sources and compilation

TABLE 5.6
(Continued)

They cannot be overdrawn. The funds must be in the account before an application can be accepted. The requirements for deposit accounts are as follows:

- The initial deposit must be at least $250
- All subsequent deposits must be $250 or more
- There must be at least 12 transactions a year
- The exact name and number of the deposit account must be on all applications or requests for services
- The deposit account holder must maintain a sufficient balance to cover all charges.

The Copyright Office will send holders monthly statements showing deposits, charges, and balances. However, the account holder is responsible for maintaining a sufficient balance to cover applications, so deposit account holders should establish an accounting system within their organization. For more information regarding Deposit Accounts, request Circular R5 from the Copyright Office. The form in figure 5-3 can be used to establish a deposit account.

Correspondence

The space for "correspondence" should contain the name, address, area code, and telephone number of the person to be consulted if correspondence about the application becomes necessary. For example, if the copyright examiner has a question regarding the application, the person named in this space will be contacted. If this space is not completed, the copyright examiner may attempt to contact the person named as copyright claimant regarding questions.

ESTABLISHING A DEPOSIT ACCOUNT

TO: Department DS
    Library of Congress
    Washington, DC 20540
    Attention: Deposit Accounts

Enclosed is my remittance of $_____ to establish a Deposit Account under
the name of _____ whose address is _____
                                              (street)

_____
(city)   (state)   (zip)

_____ _____
(area code) (telephone no.)
attention of _____
             (please give name of the person to whom you wish monthly
             statements and "no funds" notifications to be sent)

_____
(Signature)

FIGURE 5-3
Sample form for
establishing deposit
account

Certification

According to the Copyright Office, the "Certification" space on the copyright application "speaks directly" to the person filling out the application. The person must check one of the four boxes as either the author, other copyright claimant, owner of exclusive rights, or authorized agent.

Author. This box is checked if the person filling out the form is the person (or one of the persons) named in Space 2 of the application. This box would not be checked if the applicant is *not* the person named in Space 2.

Other Copyright Claimant. This box is checked if the person filling out the application has obtained ownership of all rights under the copyright initially belonging to the author. Generally this box is checked if the person filling out the copyright application is not the author, but is listed as the copyright claimant in Space 4 (along with an explanation of how the copyright was transferred).

Owner of Exclusive Right(s). This box is checked if the person filling out the application is not the author and is not the copyright claimant, but does own a limited right (for example, the exclusive right to reproduce the work for a period of years).

Authorized Agent. This box is checked if the person filling out the application is the authorized representative of the author, claimant, or owner of exclusive rights. For example, if the work is made for hire and the claimant is the Softco Company, this box would be checked and the space would be completed by writing "Softco Company."

Signature.   After checking the appropriate box, the person completing the application should type or print the name and date and sign it where marked. Note that the person who signs the application is certifying to the Copyright Office that the information contained in the application is correct to the best of his or her knowledge. Section 506(e) of the Copyright Act of 1976 provides that a "false representation of a material fact" in a copyright application may result in a fine of up to $2,500. It is in the best interest of the person signing the application to review the material and be sure of its accuracy. An application for registration of a published work will not be accepted if the date of certification is earlier than the date of publication given in the application.

Mailing Information

The address box in the final space of the application should be completed legibly. After the Copyright Office registers the work, a certificate that is a duplicate of the completed application, with a registration number and date of registration, will be issued. The registration will be mailed back in a window envelope; and this final space on the application will be viewed through the window envelope and will serve as a mailing address.

The Fee

Along with the copyright application, a filing fee and deposit material are also required. The fee is currently $20 per application. A check or money order, made payable to *Register of Copyrights,* should be enclosed with the application unless the applicant intends to authorize payment from a deposit account. If the application is rejected or if the applicant withdraws it, the fee will not be refunded. If the check is drawn against insufficient funds, the Copyright Office will not proceed with registration or will revoke the registration.

Application Cover Letter

A cover letter should be sent with the application, fee, and deposit materials. The cover letter should detail the contents of the package and provide any explanations, if required. In addition, a return postcard should be enclosed. The Copyright Office does not send the applicant a notice of receipt. Therefore, to guarantee that the materials have been received, a self-addressed return postcard detailing the name of the work should be enclosed.

Responding to the Copyright Office

If for some reason the Copyright Office has questions or requires changes in the application, the applicant will generally be granted a period of 120 days to respond to the Copyright Office request. The final date for response to such requests must be promptly docketed, as the failure to timely reply will result in the closing of the file at the Copyright Office. The applicant will be required to submit a new application, fee, and deposit materials. If the application is initially refused, the applicant can request a reexamination. If, after reexamination, the application is again refused, the applicant will be sent a notice of refusal by the head of the Examining Division. However, refusal is not final until the Chief of the Examining Division furnishes a final decision. This final refusal is necessary to proceed with infringement actions by the claimant or to appeal the Copyright Office decision in federal district court.

Effective Date of Registration

The effective date of registration is the date when the complete application is received (including the fee and deposit materials). If the application is not complete, the effective date of registration will be the date when the Copyright Office receives all the necessary materials. For example, suppose that an application is missing the name of the claimant. The examiner may telephone the applicant and obtain the name of the claimant. The date of the telephone call will become the effective date of registration. As explained in previous chapters, copyright protection is not triggered by registration. However, the effective date of registration may have an impact on whether certain remedies are available to a copyright claimant.

Certificate of Registration

Copies should be made of the certificate of registration. If the certificate is mailed to a law office representing the applicant, the client should be furnished the original with instructions as to its safekeeping. Copies should be retained. It is good practice to record the registration number and date in a separate table, as in Table 5.7, for example.

TABLE 5.7
Sample Listing of
Copyright Registrations

Softco COPYRIGHT CERTIFICATES Computer Programs		
Work	Registration	Date of Issue
Wild West	TX-38-0448	11/03/92
Harry the Hero	TX-56-7566	01/22/93
Mr. Camera	TX-33-6783	06/30/93

Duplicate Certificates

The Copyright Office will provide duplicate certificates. If requested, and upon payment of an additional fee, the duplicate will be certified. If known, the registration number and date of registration should be furnished. If the registration number is not known, a search of the Copyright Office should be performed to determine the correct registration number. The Copyright Office charges an hourly rate to search its records. Requests for specific information should be made to the following address: Reference and Bibliography Section, LM-450, Copyright Office, Library of Congress, Washington, DC 20559.

5.5 SPECIAL SITUATIONS

Many applications require special attention because of the nature of the work. For example, a mixed work or multimedia work may contain various types of works. An instructional program may include a text, filmstrip, and sound recording. In addition, certain works such as computer video games may involve textual program code and copyrightable audiovisual works. A serial publication may comprise many issues of a journal or periodical containing text and visual arts works. These works pose special problems for the applicant. This section lists some of the special situations encountered in copyright registration. Further information can be found in various Copyright Office circulars detailing registration of specific types of works.

Multimedia Works

One of the most common sources of confusion in the registration process is what to do if the work consists of two or more forms of authorship. For example, a book is published with illustrations or a filmstrip is published in conjunction with an audio cassette. Such works are considered "mixed" works, "mixed class" works, or multimedia works. A **multimedia work** is a work that combines authorship in two or more media.

A single registration may be used for a such work, provided that:

- the copyright claimant is the same for each element of the work; and
- the elements of the work are unpublished, or, if published, are published together as a single unit.

The applicant must identify all the copyrightable elements of the mixed work. For example, consider an instructional exercise program released on videotape. There are several copyrightable elements: the audiovisual work and the accompanying sounds, and the visual arts work embodied in the packaging of the tape (including photographs and graphic design). If the copyright claimant is the same for all of these elements and the work is either published as a unit (or is unpublished), then one registration can be used. If the copyright claimant for the packaging is different than the claimant for the

LEGAL TERMS

multimedia work
 Work that combines authorship in two or more media.

audiovisual work, two applications would be made: a Form PA for the audiovisual work and a Form VA for the visual arts work.

Choosing the Correct Application Form

The Copyright Office has established a procedure for selecting the appropriate registration to use in the case of a mixed work. The list here indicates the preferred application forms. Regardless of the form chosen, the application may include a claim in all of the accompanying authorship. An applicant should choose the form that first pertains to the work.

Use Form PA if the work contains an audiovisual element (e.g., a filmstrip, slides, film, or videotape) regardless of whether there are any sounds

Use Form SR if the work does *not* contain an audiovisual element, but contains an audiotape or disk in which sound recording authorship is claimed

Use Form VA if the work does *not* contain an audiovisual element or a sound recording, but does contain a visual works element, such as a pictorial, graphic, or sculptural work

Use Form SE if the work is a nondramatic literary work intended to be published in serial form (e.g., a journal, newspaper, or newsletter)

Use Form TX if the work contains only text, such as a manual and computer program that produces a textual screen display.

Table 5.8 gives some examples of multimedia works, the proper forms therefor, and a suggested description for the nature-of-authorship statement.

Deposit Materials

The application for a multimedia work varies according to the type of work being registered and whether the work has been published. Generally, for unpublished works, one complete multimedia work (or kit) containing all elements should be provided. All elements should bear the title of the work. For published works, one complete copy of the best published edition should be provided. The complete copy must include all of the elements in the kit or work. If the multimedia kit is first published outside the United States, the applicant should deposit one complete copy as first published. For more information on copyright registration for multimedia works, consult Copyright Office Circular R55.

Computer Programs

Preparing a registration for a computer program requires some knowledge of the programming process. A *computer program* is defined as a set of statements or instructions to be used directly or indirectly in a computer to bring about a certain result. Copyright protection for computer programs

Multimedia Work	Form	Nature of Authorship
Slides and booklet *First Aid Procedures for Sailboarders*	PA	"Entire Work" or "Text and Photography"
Filmstrip, booklet, and audio cassette *Repairing Hot Tub Leaks*	PA	"Entire Work" or "Text as printed and recorded; photography and sounds"
Videocassette, manual with text, and pictorial illustrations *How to Lose Weight in Your Hands and Feet*	PA	"Entire Work" or "Cinematography, text and illustrations"
Audio cassettes and manual *Building a House Out of Aluminum Cans*	SR	*DO NOT USE* the term "ENTIRE WORK" for FORM SR Instead, state "Text as printed and recorded, and sound recording"
Compact discs, sheet music, and manual *Play Accordion with Zydeco Masters*	SR	*DO NOT USE* the term "ENTIRE WORK" for FORM SR Instead, state "Text, music and sound recording"
Posters and manual *Paint by Example*	VA	"Entire Work" or "Artwork and text"
Manual and identifying materials for computer program on machine-readable diskette (or cassette) that produces textual screen display *Do the Write Thing*	TX	"Text of manual and computer program"

TABLE 5.8
Nature of Authorship for Various Multimedia Works

extends to all of the copyrightable expression embodied in the computer program. Copyright protection may extend to the screen display, or, in the case of certain works, such as a video game, protection may extend to the audiovisual aspects of the game. Computer programs are usually published and fixed in a form that cannot be perceived without the aid of a machine. For example, when you purchase a copy of *Microsoft® Word™,* the program cannot be perceived until it has been loaded into the computer's memory. Therefore, computer programs, because they are embodied on disks, magnetic tape, or computer chips, are referred to as *machine-readable works.* A program is usually written in one of various computer languages. These programming languages are generally known as *source code.* Source code can be expressed in letters and numbers and printed out on paper. The source code is eventually assembled into a very simple computer language called *object code* or *machine language,* which consists of a series of "0" and "1" symbols that set in motion "on" and "off" electrical impulses in the central processing unit of the computer. (See figure 5-4.) The software can be

FIGURE 5-4
Examples of machine
codes. *ASCII* stands for
American Standard
Code for Information
Interchange. *EBCDIC*
stands for Extended
Binary Coded Decimal
Interchange Code.

Character	Machine Codes		
	ASCII	ASCII-8	EBCDIC
1	0110001	01010001	11110001
2	0110010	01010010	11110010
A	1000001	10100001	11000001

FIGURE 5-4
Examples of machine codes. *ASCII* stands for American Standard Code for Information Interchange. *EBCDIC* stands for Extended Binary Coded Decimal Interchange Code.

embodied or stored in many ways, usually on diskettes. Many video game programs are stored on chips inside cartridges. These cartridges are inserted into the game machine. Most programs permit the user to save certain information, such as the score or the way a game was played. When information is saved, it is recorded on a disk, chip, or other device and may be retrieved by the user.

The Application

Form TX is generally used when registering a computer program. The principles for completing the TX application, as explained earlier in this chapter, apply for computer programs, with some exceptions. A single basic registration is made for all the elements of the work. The Copyright Office believes that the single basic registration is sufficient to protect the copyright in a computer program, including related screen displays, without a separate registration for screen displays or reference to the displays in the application. Therefore, in Space 2, the applicant for a computer program copyright may simply state: "entire work" or "entire computer program." If the registrant is primarily concerned with the program and not the audiovisual aspect, statements such as "entire program text," "program text," or a similar statement will suffice. However, if the statement given by the applicant is "Entire computer program including screen displays" or "Entire computer program including audiovisual material," then the registrant *must* deposit identifying material for the screens or audiovisual aspects, as explained in this section. For more information regarding the registration of computer programs, also see Copyright Office Circular 61.

The Program Manual

Generally, a computer program includes a manual or booklet that helps the user understand and use the computer program. The manual may be registered separately as textual work, but the Copyright Office will also permit the applicant to include the manual as part of the program registration, provided that the copyright claimant is the same for the manual and the program and the program and manual are published together as a single unit. For example, in the Commentary to this chapter, the manual for the software program *Crazy Clock* could be registered as part of the software program registration. The statement about nature of authorship should include the manual, (e.g., "entire text of computer program and user's manual").

Deposit Requirements

Because the copyrightable aspects of a computer program are its code, the Copyright Office will not accept diskettes or machine-readable copies of the computer program as suitable identifying materials. Instead, the Copyright Office prefers identifying materials that consist of source code of the program. The applicant should consult with the computer programmer as to the form of the deposit materials. For unpublished or published works, the applicant should deposit the first and last 25 pages of the program in source code form (along with the page containing the copyright notice, if any). If the entire program is less than 50 pages of source code, the entire source code should be deposited. The printouts for these deposit materials should be consecutively numbered. If the registration is for a revised version of a computer program, the same rules regarding identifying material apply unless the revisions are not located within the first and last 25 pages of source code, in which case any 50 pages representative of the revised material may be used (along with the page containing the copyright notice, if any). If the applicant is registering the user's manual with the program, a copy of the published user's manual or other printed documentation should accompany the other identifying material. The applicant also may deposit identifying materials for the screens. These identifying materials consist of printouts, photographs, or drawings clearly revealing the screens. If the work is predominantly audiovisual, such as a video game, a half-inch VHS videotape of the video game screen display is acceptable. If the applicant listed "screen display" or "audiovisual material" in the nature-of-authorship section of Space 2, this deposit requirement regarding screen displays is mandatory.

Computer Programs Containing Trade Secrets

Some computer programs contain valuable trade secrets (i.e., information that is not generally known and that gives the owner an advantage over competitors). In such cases, the copyright owner may not wish to disclose source code to the Copyright Office, as that information will be available to the public. When a computer program contains trade secrets, the applicant may deposit any of the following:

- First and last 25 pages of source code with some portions blocked out, provided that the blocked-out portions are proportionately less than the material still remaining; or
- First and last 10 pages of source code alone (with no blocked-out portions); or

- First and last 25 pages of object code plus any 10 or more consecutive pages of source code with no blocked-out portions.
- For programs 50 pages or less in length, the entire source code with trade secret portions blocked out.

If the work is revised and contains trade secrets, the previously stated deposit requirements apply unless the revisions are not present in the first and last 25 pages. If that is so, the applicant must deposit:

- 20 pages of source code containing the revisions, with no portions blocked out; or
- any 50 pages of source code containing the revisions, with some portions blocked out.

The Rule of Doubt

If the registrant of a computer program desires to protect trade secrets, the identifying materials may not be sufficient for the copyright examiner to verify originality. This same predicament may occur in registrations for other works. When the Copyright Office has a reasonable doubt as to the registration, it will be processed under the **rule of doubt.** This means that the Office has a reasonable doubt as to whether the requirements of the copyright act have been met or whether the deposit materials constitute protectible subject matter. If a dispute arises as to these issues, the final determination will be made by a federal court.

Automated Databases

An **automated database** is a body of facts, data, or other information assembled into an organized format suitable for use in a computer and comprising one or more files. As noted in the examples of compilations, an automated database is a compilation. For example, the collection of judicial opinions on a legal database such as WESTLAW or LEXIS is an example of an automated database. Often an automated database is a collection of facts, such as a directory of pharmaceutical compounds. Copyright protection only extends to the original expression of the compilation, not the underlying facts; that is, the original method by which the facts are compiled is the subject of copyright protection. Therefore, when the collection and arrangement of the material is solely a mechanical task, such as alphabetical or chronological order, there will be no protection of the compilation, because there is no original authorship.

The Registration Form

The registration for an automated database should include a completed Form TX, the appropriate deposit materials (as described later in this chapter), and the $20 filing fee. If the material in the database has been previously published, previously registered, or is in the public domain, the nature-of-authorship claim in Space 2 would be completed by writing "compilation." If the material in the database contained previously published information, Space 6a would be completed with "previously published data" or "public domain data," and Space 6b would be completed "compilation." If the database is revised or periodically updated, Space 6 would be completed as follows: Space 6a, "previously registered database"; Space 6b, "revised and updated text; revised compilation." If all, or a substantial portion, of the material represents copyrightable expression and is being published or registered for the first time, the nature-of-authorship claim also could extend to "text," "revised text," or "additional text." If the material contained in the database is entirely new and has never before been registered or published, Space 6 would be left blank.

Deposit Requirements

If the automated database is fixed or published only in machine-readable copies, the deposit requirements are the same for published and unpublished databases, *except* that, if the database was first published prior to March 1, 1989, the deposit also must include a representation of the page containing the copyright notice. The deposit material consists of two types of identifying material depending on whether the work is a single file database or a multiple file database. A **single file database** is a database that consists of data records pertaining to a single common subject matter, for example, a database of *Academy Award® Winners*. A **multiple file database** consists of separate and distinct groups of data records, for example, a database consisting of *Grammy® Awards, Academy Awards®, and Emmy® Awards*.

The identifying material for automated databases consists of one copy of the identifying portions reproduced in a form visually perceptible without the aid of a machine, either in paper or in microfilm. In the case of a single file database, that is the first and last 25 pages. In the case of a multiple file database, the requirement is to deposit a representative portion of each file (either 50 data records or the entire file, whichever is less). If the database has been revised, representative portions of the added or modified material are needed (50 pages or the entire revised portions, whichever is less). If the deposit is *encoded* (not written in a natural language), the deposit should include a key or explanation of the code. If the examiner is unable to determine the presence of copyrightable material, a rule-of-doubt registration may issue. Special relief also may be granted for trade secrets, as explained in the preceding section regarding computer program registrations.

Group Registration for Automated Database Revisions

Many automated databases are updated regularly. In this way, an automated database may be a combined derivative and compilation. For example, an automated database of *Baseball Pitching Statistics* would be a compilation,

LEGAL TERMS

rule of doubt
  Legal doctrine declaring that a work is registered even though a reasonable doubt exists at the Copyright Office as to whether the requirements of the Copyright Act have been met or whether the deposit materials constitute protectible subject matter under copyright law; the final determination will be made by a federal court.

automated database
  A body of facts, data, or other information assembled into an organized format suitable for use in a computer and comprising one or more files.

single file database
  Database that consists of data records pertaining to a single common subject matter.

multiple file database
  Collection of separate and distinct groups of data records.

but if the database were updated with new statistics, the subsequent version would be both a derivative and a compilation. Because automated databases are updated regularly, special provisions exist for registration of an automated database and its updates or other revisions. As of March 31, 1989, an automated database and its updates or revisions may be registered using a single application, deposit, and filing fee if the following conditions are met:

- All of the updates or revisions must be fixed (if unpublished) or (if published) published only in machine-readable copies. If the work is fixed or published in visually perceptible copies, group registration is *not* possible
- All of the updates or revisions (if unpublished) were created or (if published) were first published within a three-month period, all within the same calendar year
- All of the updates or revisions are owned by the same copyright claimant
- All of the updates or revisions have the same general title
- All of the updates or revisions are similar in their general content, including their subject
- All of the updates or revisions are similar in their organization
- The updates or revisions, if published before March 1, 1989, bear a copyright notice naming the owner of the copyright, and that name is the same in each notice.

Deposit Requirements. For group registrations of automated databases, the identifying material required for deposit includes 50 representative pages from a single file database or 50 records from each updated data file. In addition, the deposit material must include a brief, typed or printed descriptive statement indicating the title of the database, the name and address of the claimants, and certain information regarding the content, subject, origins, approximate number of data records, and nature, location, and frequency of changes. For specific information about registration of automated databases, see Copyright Office Circular 65.

Serials

A **serial** is a work issued or intended to be issued in successive parts bearing numerical or chronological designations and intended to be continued indefinitely. Examples of serials include periodicals, newspapers, magazines, bulletins, newsletters, annuals, journals, proceedings of societies, and similar works. Form SE is used to register serials.

A claim for a serial does not include individual contributions to the serial publication. Any individual contribution should be registered separately. For example, Josephine writes an article on copyright for a law school journal. If Josephine seeks to register her work, she should use Form TX. However, if the law school seeks to register the issue containing Josephine's article, the review would use Form SE. The Copyright Office provides specific information about copyright registration in Circular 62.

The Registration Form.   There are three possible forms that can be used for registering serials: Short Form SE, Form SE, and Form SE/Group. Form SE is the standard form and is appropriate for any serial. However, Short Form SE is one-page and can be used if all the following criteria can be met:

- The claim is in the entire collective work
- The collective work is essentially all new
- The author is a U.S. citizen or domiciliary
- The work is a work made for hire
- The author(s) and claimant(s) are the same; and
- The work is first published in the United States.

For example, Softco publishes *End User,* a monthly newsletter for purchasers of its computer programs. The material is all created by Softco employees and is first published in the United States, and the newsletter is essentially all new each month. Therefore, Short Form SE may be used. If any of the preceding criteria do not apply, or if the applicant is in doubt about using Short Form SE, then the standard Form SE should be used.

There are some differences between Form SE and other copyright applications. For example, Space 1 of Form SE requires information about the volume and number of the serial, as well as the frequency of publication. Space 2 also requires knowledge as to the ownership of the various contributions. In the case of *End User,* the newsletter just described, the author would be Softco Company. Under "Nature of Authorship," the box marked "Collective Work" would be checked and the statement "entire text," or "entire text and illustrations." If John Jones contributed an article to *End User* and assigned his rights, then he may listed as an author in Space 2b. Under "Nature of Authorship" for John Jones in Space 2b, the application may state "text of one article." In Space 4, a statement would be made indicating how Softco acquired the rights to John Jones's article, such as "Assignment of copyright in one article."

Rather than registering each issue separately, the Copyright Office permits the registration of a group of issues of a serial, if the following criteria apply:

- A complimentary subscription for two copies of the serial have been given to the Library of Congress, confirmed by letter to the General Counsel, Copyright Office. Subscription copies must be mailed separately to: Library of Congress, Group Periodicals Registration, Washington, D.C. 20540
- The claim must be in the collective works
- The collective works must be essentially all new
- The author is a U.S. citizen or domiciliary
- Each issue must be a work made for hire
- The author(s) and claimant(s) are the same
- Each issue must have been created no more than one year prior to publication
- All issues must have been published within the same calendar year.

LEGAL TERMS

serial
    Work, such as a newspaper, magazine, newsletter, or journal, issued or intended to be issued in successive parts bearing numerical or chronological designations and intended to be continued indefinitely.

Group Contributions to Periodicals

John is a cartoonist. Each month he creates a comic strip for a monthly magazine. He has retained copyright in the comic strips. Does he have to file 12 separate registrations for his monthly comic strips? No. Under a new Copyright Office procedure, a single copyright registration can be used for a group of works if *all* of the following conditions are met:

- All of the works must be published on or after March 1, 1989
- All of the works are by the same author who is an individual (not an employer for hire)
- All of the works are first published as contributions to periodicals (including newspapers) within a 12-month period
- All of the works have the same copyright claimant
- one copy of the entire periodical issue or newspaper section in which each contribution is first published is deposited with the application
- The application must identify each contribution separately, including the periodical containing it and the date of its first publication.

Two Application Forms Must Be Filed. To apply for a single registration to cover a group of contributions to periodicals, two application forms must be submitted. A basic application on either Form TX, Form PA, or Form VA must be completed, *except* that the title information and dates of publication should be left blank. For example, a cartoonist such as John would use Form VA, leave the title and date of publication blank, and complete the remainder of the Form VA. A columnist, such as Ann Landers or Jesse Jackson, would use Form TX. When completing the basic application form, the year of creation is the year that the last of the contributions was completed.

In addition to this basic application, the applicant also must submit Form GR/CP, which consists of two parts: Part A (Identification of Application) and Part B (Registration for Group of Contributions). Part A requires that the applicant identify the type of form (TX, VA, or PA) that is being submitted, as well as identifying the author and copyright claimant. Part B requires specific information about the title of each contribution, title of the periodical, date of first publication, volume, number, issue date, and nation of first publication. The two forms are submitted together with deposit materials and the appropriate fee.

Sound Recording

Applicants are sometimes confused when registering a sound recording because of the relationship between sound recordings and the underlying musical or textual works. For example, a musician writes a song, records it, and then releases an audio cassette containing the recording. Is it necessary to register the song and the sound recording as two separate works? Should Form PA or Form SR be used? If the author of the sound recording and the musical work are the same, it is possible to register both with one form. The chart in Table 5.9, prepared by the Copyright Office, demonstrates the appropriate copyright form to use in various sound recording situations. For more information about registration of sound recordings, the Copyright Office provides Circular 56.

Deposit Requirements for Sound Recordings. Generally, the deposit requirements for a claim in a sound recording are one or two phonorecords, depending on whether the work is published or unpublished. If the work is

How the work was created; what is being registered	Form	Description of authorship in Space 2, "Nature of Authorship"
Composer/author creates a song and wishes to claim copyright in the song	PA	"Music and words" *or* "Music"
Composer/author creates musical composition and wishes to claim copyright in the musical composition	PA	"Music"
Performer(s) (for example, vocalist and band) perform and record musical work; wish to claim copyright in the recorded performance only	SR	"Performance and sound recording"
Composer/author/performer creates music and performs it and then records the performance; wishes to claim copyright in both the music and the recording	SR	"Music and performance" *or* "Music, words, performance"
Author writes poem and records it, wishes to claim copyright only in the poem itself, not in recorded performance	TX	"Text"
Author writes a play and records it, wishes to claim copyright only in the play itself, not in recorded performance	PA	"Script"
Author writes a poem or narrative and records it, wishes to claim copyright in both text and recorded performance	SR	"Text and sound recording"
Author creates musical composition in machine-readable copy (computer disk) and wishes to claim copyright in only musical composition	PA	"Music" *or* "Music and words"
Author creates musical composition in machine-readable copy (computer disk) and wishes to claim copyright in both composition and performance	SR	"Music and performance" *or* "Music, words, and performance"

TABLE 5.9
Nature of Authorship
for a Musical Creation

published on or after January 1, 1978, deposit two complete copies of the best edition, along with any printed or other visually perceptible material such as record sleeves and jackets. If the work was first published prior to 1978, deposit two complete phonorecords of the work as first published. (Note that copyright protection did not extend to sound recordings until 1972.) If the sound recording was first published outside the United States, deposit one complete phonorecord of the work as first published. If the sound recording work is created in machine-readable form (e.g., computer disk), the Copyright Office will not accept the computer disk as deposit material; the author must deposit an audio cassette of the work.

Motion Pictures and Video Recordings

A **motion picture** is an audiovisual work consisting of a series of related images that, when shown in succession, impart an impression of motion, together with accompanying sounds, if any. Creating a motion picture or video recording is a collaborative effort involving the merger of many discrete elements. A screenplay or script is created, performers recite the material, photographers capture the activity, and editors and directors cut and splice the final result. Numerous technical contributions are made, including lighting, sound recording, set designs, and costume creation. The expression that is fixed in the motion picture or videotape (e.g., the dialogue, camera work, sounds, etc.) is protectible under copyright.

The *screenplay* is the script or scenario of the motion picture. Once the motion picture is made or fixed, the screenplay, to the extent that it is embodied in the motion picture, is considered to be an integral and protectible part of the motion picture. However, if the motion picture has not been made, the screenplay would be protectible as a performing arts work and would be registered using Form PA, which is intended for works to be performed before an audience or with the aid of a machine or device. Form TX would *not* be used to register the screenplay, because that form is only intended for use for *nondramatic* textual material.

The Registration Form

Form PA should be used to register the motion picture. In Space 1, the applicant should provide a statement of the nature of the work, such as "motion picture," or, in the event the work is part of a multimedia kit, "multimedia kit including motion picture and textual material." Generally, a motion picture is a work-for-hire, either because the individual contributions are made by employees within the scope of their employment or because the contribution is for a specially commissioned motion picture work. In either case, the applicant should confirm the work-for-hire status of all contributions. If the entire work was made for hire, the author would be the hiring party and Space 2, "Nature of Authorship," would be completed "entire motion picture." If the contributions were not works made for hire, then each author would be listed separately, along with his or her contribution, for example,

2a *Name of Author:* Mary Smith
   Nature of Authorship: Script
2b *Name of Author:* John Jones
   Nature of Authorship: Director, Producer
2c *Name of Author:* William Johnson
   Nature of Authorship: Camera work

Space 6 of Form PA would reflect any previously registered, previously published, or public domain material. Some examples of statements for Space 6 might include:

Feature film based on a screenplay that was previously registered:
Space 6a *Preexisting Material:* Previously registered screenplay
Space 6b *Material Added to this Work:* Motion picture dramatization
New version of training video that was previously registered:
Space 6a *Preexisting Material:* Previously registered video production
Space 6b *Material Added to this Work*: Revisions and some new cinematographic material
Television documentary;
Space 6a *Preexisting Material:* Previously published footage and photographs
Space 6b *Material Added to this Work:* Editing, narration, and some new footage.

Deposit Materials

The deposit materials for motion pictures are different than for other works. For unpublished or published motion pictures, the Copyright Office requires a separate description of the work. This description should be as complete as possible. If the work is a theatrical film or major television production, a shooting script or a press book is sufficient. In addition to the separate description, deposit materials for a published motion picture must include a complete copy, clear, undamaged, and free of splices and defects that would interfere with viewing the work. If the work is first published in the United States, the copy must be a complete copy of the best edition. If the work is first published outside the United States, the applicant should furnish one complete copy as first published. If the work is unpublished, a complete copy of the work containing all the visual and aural elements should be deposited.

An alternative deposit system is also available for unpublished motion pictures. The applicant may send either a recording of the complete sound track or reproductions of images from each 10-minute segment of the work. The written description for such alternative deposit must include the title,

LEGAL TERMS

motion picture
Audiovisual works consisting of a series of related images that, when shown in succession, impart an impression of motion, together with accompanying sounds, if any.

summary of the work, date the work was fixed, first telecast (if applicable), whether telecast was fixed simultaneous with transmission, running time, and the credits. It is important to remember that the performance or broadcast of a motion picture does not, by itself, constitute publication. Publication of a motion picture requires either that copies of the film have been made, be ready for distribution and offered for distribution, *or* that copies of the film be distributed to the public by sale, rental, lease, or lending. For more information about copyright registration for motion pictures, including video recordings, the Copyright Office provides Circular 45.

Architectural Works

The Copyright Act of 1976 was amended in 1990 to extend protection to architectural works. An **architectural work** is an original design of a building embodied in any tangible medium of expression, including a building, architectural plans, or drawings. An architectural work includes the overall form as well as the arrangement and composition of spaces and elements in the design, but does not include individual standard features such as windows, doors, and other staple features.

Only architectural works created on or after December 1, 1990 (or any architectural work that is unconstructed and embodied in unpublished plans or drawings on that date) are eligible for protection. Protection for any work that is unconstructed and embodied in unpublished plans or drawings on December 1, 1990, will terminate on December 31, 2002, unless the work is constructed by that date.

The Registration Form

Application Form VA may be used to file a claim in an architectural work. When completing Space 1 ("Title"), the applicant should indicate the title of the building *and* its date of construction. If the building has not yet been constructed, the applicant should note, after the title, "not yet constructed." The space for "Nature of this Work" should state "architectural work." The author of the architectural work is the creator of the architectural design. The "Nature of Authorship" section of Space 2 should state the basis for the claim, for example, "architectural work" or "building design."

In Space 3, the year of creation of the work is the year in which architectural plans or drawings for the building were completed. The date of publication is the first date of sale, or the first date of an offering for sale or public distribution of copies of the design embodied in blueprints, design plans, drawings, photographs, or models. The first date of sale may also be the first date of an offer to distribute copies to a group of persons for further distribution or public display. By way of example, the sale of copies of architectural plans or distribution of blueprint copies to contractors may be regarded as publication.

Deposit Requirements

The required deposit for an architectural work, whether or not the building has been constructed, is one complete copy of an architectural blueprint or drawings, in visually perceptible form, showing the overall form of the building and any interior arrangement of spaces or design elements in which copyright is claimed. If the claim covers a building for which construction has been completed, the deposit materials also should include identifying material in the form of photographs of the completed structure, clearly revealing the design elements on which the claim is based. In each case, the Copyright Office requires that the deposit be marked to show the date of publication, if any, and the date of completion of construction of the architectural work. For more information about copyright claims in architectural works, the Copyright Office provides Circular 41.

Secure Tests

What happens when a national testing service wants to register an examination such as the Scholastic Achievement Test (SAT)? The Copyright Office cannot guarantee the security or confidentiality of text materials mailed to the office. However, if the examination is a secure test, the Copyright Office provides for a special procedure to register the work. A **secure test** is a nonmarketed test administered under supervision at specified centers on specific dates, all copies of which are accounted for and either destroyed or returned to restricted locked storage following each administration. A test is *nonmarketed* if copies are not sold and the test is distributed and used in such a manner that ownership and control of copies remain with the test sponsor or publisher. The Copyright Office offers a special procedure to hand-carry the secure test material through the registration procedure. For more information about registration of secure tests, the Copyright Office provides Circular 64, or contact the Copyright Office, Information Section, LM-401, Library of Congress, Washington DC 20559.

5.6 DEPOSIT REQUIREMENTS

Imagine a library that receives all of the nation's books, movies, artwork, computer programs, and recordings. This is the Library of Congress. Since the copyright laws have required deposit of the best editions of copyrightable works, the Library of Congress has had access to an unequaled collection of artistic expression. The Copyright Act of 1976 requires that two complete copies of the best edition of each copyrightable work be deposited with the Library of Congress within three months of publication. Although this requirement may be fulfilled by the copyright registration process, it is still mandatory regardless of whether an application is filed.[15] In other words, even if the copyright owner does not register the work, copies must still be deposited. Certain works are exempt, for example, greeting cards; postcards;

stationery; three-dimensional sculptural works; works published on jewelry, textiles, or any useful article; scientific and technical drawings; advertising material; works first published as an individual contribution to a collective work; and automated databases available online.

This mandatory requirement is often disregarded by copyright owners. Why? Because the deposit requirement is not a condition of copyright protection. The owner will be penalized or fined only if the Copyright Office requests the deposit and the copyright owner *fails* to supply the requested materials within three months of the request. The fines shall not be more than $350 per work, but may rise to $2,500 if the copyright owner willfully or repeatedly fails to comply with the demand. In any event, validity of the copyright is not affected by such action.

Complete Copies

Generally, deposit requirements are satisfied by providing two complete copies of the best edition of the work. A **complete copy** includes all elements comprising the unit of publication of the best edition of the work, including elements that, if considered separately, would not be copyrightable subject matter or would otherwise be exempt from mandatory deposit requirements. In the case of a sound recording, for example, the deposit materials would include textual or pictorial matter embodied on the record sleeve or cover of the compact disc. In the case of a motion picture, a copy is complete if the reproduction of all of the visual and aural elements comprising the copyrightable subject matter in the work is clean, undeteriorated, and free of any splices or defects.

Best Edition

The **best edition** of a work is the edition, published in the United States at any time before the date of deposit, that the Library of Congress determines to be most suitable for its purposes. For works first published in a country other than the United States, the deposit should be the best edition of the work as *first* published.

When there is more than one published edition of a work, there are rules, set forth in 37 Code of Federal Regulations § 202.19(b) (see appendix C) and in Circular 7b to assist in determining the best edition. These rules are based upon common-sense principles: for example, a hardcover version of a book is preferred to the softcover; an illustrated book is better than an unillustrated work; a larger photograph is preferred to a smaller. The rules regarding best editions are set forth 37 C.F.R § 202.19 (see appendix C). These rules are the same for mandatory deposit or copyright registration except for computer programs. For purposes of mandatory deposit, the Copyright Office requires machine-readable copies of the program (i.e., computer disks). For purposes of registration, the Copyright Office requires printouts of the underlying computer code.

Determining the Number of Copies to Deposit

As a general rule, in the case of published works, two complete copies of the best edition of the work must be deposited. For unpublished works, only one copy should be deposited. When filing a registration, there are numerous exceptions in which only one copy of a work must be deposited with the application. These works are set forth in 37 C.F.R. § 202.20(c)(12) (see appendix C).

Special Relief

The Copyright Office has the discretion to relieve the copyright owner of deposit requirements. For example, under certain circumstances, the Copyright Office may permit the deposit of one copy of a work instead of two. In other situations, it may not be necessary for any copy of the work to be deposited. If an applicant for copyright registration seeks special relief from the deposit requirements, such request should be sent by separate letter to Chief, Examining Division, Copyright Office, Library of Congress, Washington, DC 20559.

Motion Pictures

Special rules regarding the deposit of motion pictures have been implemented by the Library of Congress. These rules permit the owner of copyright in a motion picture to sign a *motion picture agreement,* whereby the depositor of a motion picture may have the motion picture returned under certain conditions. For more information about the motion picture agreement, contact the Motion Picture Section, Motion Picture Broadcasting and Recorded Sound Division, Library of Congress, Washington DC 20540.

5.7 CORRECTING OR SUPPLEMENTING THE COPYRIGHT REGISTRATION

Occasionally, a copyright owner may wish to correct information in a basic registration (e.g., the author's name is misspelled) or may wish to add information, facts, or explanations that are necessary to protect the work. The Copyright Act of 1976 provides for the filing of an application for supplementary registration "to correct an error in copyright registration or to amplify the information given in registration." The supplementary application is made by using Form CA.

For example, Joe prepares Form PA for the song "Birdbrain" incorrectly and names Paul and Bob as the authors of that song. The real authors are Paul and Jane. The work is registered. The applicant would file Form CA. However, a supplementary registration should *not* be used if there is a change in ownership rights. For example, the song "Birdbrain" is sold to Sue. That transfer should be recorded separately in the Copyright Office pursuant

LEGAL TERMS

complete copy
All elements comprising the unit of publication of the best edition of the work, including elements that, if considered separately, would not be copyrightable subject matter or would otherwise be exempt from mandatory deposit requirements.

best edition
The edition, published in the United States at any time before the date of deposit, that the Library of Congress determines to be most suitable for its purposes.

to § 205 of the Copyright Act of 1976. A supplementary registration also should *not* be used to register changes in the work itself. For example, the song "Birdbrain" has no words when it is registered. Later, words are added.

Form CA.   Form CA is not a registration form. It is intended solely to correct or amplify information in a basic registration. The filing of a supplementary registration does not void the underlying basic registration; it merely expands the information in the basic registration. For example, Softco files a supplementary registration to correct its address as copyright claimant. This filing does not supersede or replace the earlier registration— it merely augments the information in the underlying registration.

Section A: The Basic Instructions.   The first section of the Form CA ("The Basic Instructions") requests information regarding the title of the work, the name(s) of the author(s), the registration number of the basic registration, the year of basic registration, and the names of copyright claimants. All the information in this section should correspond with the information in the basic registration. *Corrected* information should not be provided in this section; that should be provided in the "Correction" section.

Section B: Correction.   If the applicant intends to correct an error in the basic registration, then Space B is completed. If there is no correction, this section should be left blank. The line number referred to in Space B is the large numeral on the left side of the basic registration. The line heading or description refers to the phrase or heading indicating the location of the incorrect information. For example, if the publication date was incorrect in the basic registration, Space B would state: line number: "4"; and line heading or description: "Date of First Publication." The rest of Space B would indicate the "Incorrect Information As It Appears in Basic Registration" and "Corrected Information." The Copyright Office also provides an area for an "Explanation of Correction." As this portion is optional, the applicant has no obligation or responsibility to complete it. A lack of explanation will not prevent the processing of Form CA. If there is any confusion as to the correction, a copyright examiner will contact the applicant by letter or telephone.

Section C: Amplification.   If the applicant intends to amplify, expand, or augment information in a basic registration, then Space C is completed. If there is no amplification, this section should be left blank. As with Space B, the line number referred to in Space B is the large numeral on the left side of the basic registration. The line heading or description refers to the phrase or heading indicating the location of the incorrect information. If more than one section is to be augmented, then the line number and heading for a second or third section would be marked in Space C (or in Space D, a space provided for continuation of material). For example, if a song was first registered under the title "Theme from The Vampire Strikes Back," but later has been popularized and become known by the title "I Kiss Your Neck," the registrant may augment the basic registration by completing Space C as follows: line number: "1"; and line heading or description: "Previous or Alternative Title." Under "Amplified Information," the applicant would write "I Kiss Your Neck." The Copyright Office also provides an area for an "Explanation of Amplified Information." As with Space B, this portion is optional and the applicant has no obligation or responsibility to complete it. A lack of explanation will not prevent the processing of Form CA.

The remaining sections of the Form CA (E—Deposit Account, F—Certification, and G—Address for Return of Certificate) are similar to the final sections of the copyright application and should be completed as discussed previously in this chapter. For further information on supplementary registrations, review Circular R8, provided by the Copyright Office.

5.8 CANCELLATION OF COMPLETED REGISTRATIONS

If, after registration, the Copyright Office learns that a work is not copyrightable, the Copyright Office will commence a procedure that will result in cancellation of the registration. What could cause such action? One reason may be that the Copyright Office determines that registration should not have been issued because the work does not constitute copyrightable subject matter. For example, a dress designer registers her creations as "three-dimensional soft sculptures." The Copyright Office later determines that the works are useful articles (i.e., clothing) and not registrable. The registration will be canceled. Another reason for cancellation may be that the work does not meet legal or formal requirements. For example, if a work was first published before 1978 and copyright notice was omitted from the deposit materials, the Copyright Office will cancel the registration. Another reason for cancellation may be that the registration does not meet the requirements of the regulations. For example, the check used to pay the fee was written against insufficient funds, or the application and the deposit materials do not match, or the registration fails to list a claimant. In the case of minor substantive errors (such as the type normally rectified during the registration procedure), the Copyright Office will attempt to correct the problem through correspondence with the applicant. If a work has been registered in the wrong class, the Copyright Office will cancel the basic registration in the incorrect class and issue a new registration in the proper class. Prior to canceling any registration, the Copyright Office will provide notice to the registrant and give the registrant an opportunity to respond to the Copyright Office action. Further information on cancellation of completed registrations can be found in 37 C.F.R. § 201.7.

5.9 RECORDATION OF TRANSFERS AND OTHER DOCUMENTS

After a work has been registered, the owner may transfer some or all of the rights to a third party. This change in ownership would not be reflected in the Copyright Office records unless a copy of the written agreement is recorded. It is not mandatory to record a transfer of ownership or other documents relating to copyright, but there are certain advantages to recordation.[16] Recordation may:

- Be required for an infringement suit to be filed by the transferee
- Establish a priority between conflicting transfers or nonexclusive licenses
- Establish a public record of the contents of the transfer or document
- Provide constructive notice to the public (a legal concept that indicates that the public could have actual notice of the facts in the recorded document. There are several requirements for recording documents).

Document must "pertain to a copyright."   To be recorded, the document must pertain to a copyright. Such documents include any exclusive or nonexclusive license, contract, assignment, or other transfer of any right or exercise of rights; any document pertaining to the scope, duration, or identification of a copyright; any contract, security interest, mortgage, will, probate decree, or power of attorney.

Document must bear actual signature of person who executed it. Any grant, transfer, license, or assignment must be signed by the party giving up the rights. If a copy is furnished (not the original signed document), a certification must be included stating that the photocopy is a true reproduction of the original document (i.e., "I swear under penalty of perjury under the laws of the United States that the attached document is a true and correct copy of the original"). It is not necessary to have the document notarized. However, if the document is notarized or accompanied by a certificate of acknowledgment, it is considered to create a legal presumption or prima facie evidence of execution of the transfer.

Document must be complete and legible.   All of the required information to be recorded must be in the document. If, for example, a reference is made to an exhibit, schedule, or attachment, the referenced item should be recorded as well. The document must be of such quality and readability that it can be reproduced in legible microfilmed copies.

Fee and Cover Letter

The current fee for recording documents pursuant to § 205 can be determined by calling Public Information (1-202-479-0700) or Certification and

Documents (1-202-707-6850). The documents and fee should be mailed to Documents Unit LM-462, Cataloging Office, Library of Congress, Washington, DC 20559. A cover letter should be prepared (e.g., "Enclosed please find an original and one copy of the *name of document* for recording pursuant to Section 205 of the Copyright Act. Please return a copy of the document as it is recorded to this office"). If the document does not enumerate the works, the Copyright Office will allow them to be enumerated in an attachment to the cover letter and will record the document, provided that such fees are paid or authorized to be deducted from a deposit account. If recording the document on behalf of a third party or client, a copy of the letter should be sent to the client or transferee and a review should be calendared for eight weeks from the mailing to check on the recording of the document. For more information about the recordation of transfers and other documents, the Copyright Office provides Circular 12. See also Circular 96 Section 201.4 that includes the referenced section from the Code of Federal Regulations.

Unacceptable Documents

A document will be returned unrecorded if:

- The document purports to be a transfer but does not bear a signature of the transferor
- The capacity of the person signing for the transferor is unclear
- The date of certification or notarization is earlier than the date of execution
- The date of receipt is earlier than the date of execution
- The document submitted is not capable of being reproduced legibly
- The transferor or transferee is not clearly identified in the document
- The titles are listed in a cover letter but not in the document itself
- The document is incomplete by its own terms
- The document is marked as an exhibit
- The document purports to be a notice of termination but does not meet the formal requirements
- The complete recordation fee is not submitted
- It is unclear whether the document is to be recorded
- The document is submitted to the Copyright Office in error.

SUMMARY

5.1 Copyright notice is only used on copies that can be visually observed, either directly or with the aid of a machine or device. The copyright notice has three elements: the © symbol or word *Copyright;* the year of first publication; and the name or abbreviation of the owner of copyright. Sound recordings embodied on phonorecords are required to include a special notice—the letter "P" in a circle ℗ followed by the year of first publication of the sound recording and the name of the copyright holder. The notice should be affixed to the copies in such a manner and location as to give reasonable notice of the claim of copyright.

5.2 Under certain circumstances, the omission of copyright can result in the loss of copyright ownership. The effect of an omission depends upon the date of first publication of the work. For works published under the Copyright Act of 1909, protection could only be secured if the owner published the work with copyright notice. If an authorized copy of a work was published without notice, the work would be placed permanently in the public domain. For works published between January 1, 1978, and March 1, 1989, § 405 of the Copyright Act of 1976 provides a means of "saving" the copyright in the event of certain omissions. If copyright is omitted from works first published on or after March 1, 1989, the owner will not suffer a loss of copyright protection.

5.3 Registration is not necessary to obtain copyright protection. Although registration is permissive and not mandatory under the current copyright act, it is strongly recommended. The certificate of registration does not prove ownership of copyright, but registration within five years of first publication creates a legal presumption of ownership and validity. The Copyright Office permits one basic registration to be made for each version of a particular work. Registration is required prior to the filing of an infringement lawsuit if the plaintiff is to qualify for statutory damages or attorney fees.

5.4 To choose the correct application form, the registrant should consult Copyright Office regulations. Specific information as to completing each form is available in the "Line-by-Line Instructions" furnished with each copyright application. Information is required regarding the title, authorship, claimant, creation, and publication dates and information regarding correspondence. The applicant must know whether the work is a derivative or compilation to complete Space 6, which requests information about any preexisting material or material added to the registered work.

5.5 Certain applications require special attention. For example, a creation that combines authorship of multiple works, i.e., a multimedia work, can be registered so as to include all elements in one form, provided that the applicant meets certain criteria. Registration of a computer program or automated database may require some knowledge of the programming process to complete the form and prepare the deposit materials. Serial publications may be registered in various forms, and knowledge as to the authorship contributions is essential for assuring proper registration of the work. Copyright Office procedures also enable the author of a sound recording to register the work and the underlying text or musical work with one application.

5.6 The Copyright Act of 1976 requires that two complete copies of the best edition of each copyrightable work be deposited with the Library of Congress within three months of publication, a requirement that may be satisfied by the copyright registration process. A complete copy includes all elements comprising the unit of publication of the best edition of the work, including elements that, if considered separately, would not be copyrightable subject matter or would otherwise be exempt from mandatory deposit requirements. The best edition of a work is the edition, published in the United States at any time before the date of deposit, that the Library of Congress determines to be most suitable for its purposes. Regulations have been prepared by the Copyright Office to guide the person making the deposit.

5.7 The Copyright Act of 1976 provides for the filing of an application for supplementary registration to correct an error in copyright registration or to amplify the information given in registration. The supplementary application is made using Form CA.

5.8 If, after registration, the Copyright Office learns that a work is not copyrightable, or that the work or the application does not meet legal or formal requirements, the Copyright Office will commence a procedure to cancel the registration. Prior to canceling any registration, the Copyright Office will provide notice to the registrant and give the registrant an opportunity to respond to the Copyright Office action.

5.9 A change in ownership will not be reflected in the Copyright Office records unless a copy of the written agreement is recorded. It is not mandatory to record a transfer of ownership or other documents relating to copyright, but there are certain advantages to recordation and the recordation may establish legal presumptions. To qualify for recordation, the document must pertain to a copyright, must bear the actual signature of the person who executed it, and must be complete and legible.

NOTES

1. 17 U.S.C. § 401 (notice of copyright).
2. 17 U.S.C. § 404 (notice of copyright on contributions to collective works).
3. 17 U.S.C. § 402 (notice of copyright on phonorecords of sound recordings).
4. 17 U.S.C. § 403 (notice of copyright on publications incorporating U.S. government works).
5. 17 U.S.C. § 405 (omission of notice).
6. Peter Pan Fabrics, Inc. v. Martin Weiner Corp., 274 F.2d 487 (2d Cir. 1960).
7. 17 U.S.C. § 408 (copyright registration in general).
8. 17 U.S.C. § 410(c) (registration as presumption of validity.
9. 17 U.S.C. § 412 (registration as prerequisite to remedies in infringement action).
10. 17 U.S.C. § 411 (registration and infringement actions).
11. 17 U.S.C. § 411(a) (right to bring infringement action after refusal of registration).
12. 17 U.S.C. §§ 101, 411(a) (exemption from registration for Berne adherents).
13. 17 U.S.C. § 411(b) (simultaneous transmission exemption for infringement action).
14. 17 U.S.C. § 412 (registration as prerequisite to certain remedies).

15. 17 U.S.C. § 407 (deposit of copies).
16. 17 U.S.C. § 205 (recordation of transfer and other documents).

QUESTIONS FOR REVIEW AND DISCUSSION

1. Does a computer program constitute a visually perceptible copy?
2. What are the elements of copyright notice?
3. What effect does the year of first publication have upon notice requirements?
4. Where should copyright notice be placed on a motion picture?
5. Why is it important to notify the copyright owner when an omission of notice is discovered?
6. What legal presumption is created by copyright registration?
7. To what extent is registration necessary or beneficial in an infringement lawsuit?
8. What is the process for expediting registration?
9. What types of statement can be provided on the application to indicate a transfer of ownership?
10. Who may sign the copyright application?
11. What is the difference between the mandatory deposit requirements and the deposit requirements for copyright registration?
12. What is a multimedia or mixed class-work?
13. What is the rule of doubt?
14. What are the three possible forms that can be used for registering serial publications?
15. Can a composer register a sound recording and the underlying song with one application?
16. What form is used to correct a basic registration?
17. What are some advantages of recording a transfer of copyright ownership?

ACTIVITIES

1. Examine various types of works and review the copyright notices (or lack of notice). Review collective works, such as newspapers or magazines, to determine which notices are applicable to which works.
2. Review the Code of Federal Regulations Appendix D and determine the correct form of deposit materials or identifying material for motion picture works. Are these requirements different for registration and mandatory deposit?

3. Determine what advice to give a television producer who wishes to register a video program that will be broadcast over national television.

4. Locate a multimedia work (e.g., an instructional kit with a videotape and a book) and determine where to place the copyright notice and the proper form to use for the registration.

PROJECT

Consider the following: Thomas Bing wrote the novel *Lost in a Fog*. He retained all copyright to the novel but sold the movie rights to Clam City Productions. Clam City made it into a movie. Sally Ford wrote a title song for the movie, "Still Loving You," with the alternate title "Theme from Lost in a Fog." She owns all copyright in the song. A television series, *Fog*, is now being created by Clam City, based upon the motion picture. Identify the various basic registrations and determine which forms would be used for each. Determine how Space 6 would be completed on each form.

FOR MORE INFORMATION

Copyright Office Circulars

Applicants for copyright registration can simplify the process by reviewing two- or four-page materials published by the Copyright Office, known as *Copyright Office Circulars*. Many of these circulars are grouped according to subject matter ("Books," "Sound Recordings," etc.) and, as explained in chapter 2, an attorney's kit that groups most of these circulars in one packet can be obtained. The table of contents for this packet is reproduced in appendix A. These materials are available for the Publications Section, LM-455, Copyright Office, Library of Congress, Washington, D.C. 20559. Forms can be requested by calling the Forms Hotline number, 202-707-9100. General copyright information is available by calling 202-707-3000.

Copyright Applications

Application Instructions. Each copyright application is available in a four-page foldout format. Two pages (one double-sided sheet) consist of the application. The other two pages, which are removed, contain "Basic Information" and "Instructions" explaining how to fill out the application. Copies of each of these explanation pages are provided in appendix D; they are invaluable for preparing applications.

Application forms can be obtained by writing to the Copyright Office at Publications Section, LM-455, Copyright Office. Library of Congress, Washington, D.C. 20559. Forms can be requested by calling the Forms Hotline number, 202-707-9100. General copyright information is available by calling 202-707-3000.

J. E. Hawes, *Copyright Registration Practice* (Clark Boardman Callaghan 1990). A one-volume looseleaf treatise detailing registration procedures.

The Compendium of Copyright Office Practices

The *Compendium* is the manual used by copyright examiners when reviewing applications. Therefore, it is very helpful in avoiding problems when preparing applications. It is available from the Government Printing Office, Superintendent of Documents, P.O. Box 371954, Pittsburgh, PA 15250-7954.

Registering Computer Software

M. J. Salone, *How to Copyright Software* (Nolo Press 1991). A one-volume paperback explaining the process of protecting and registering software.

CHAPTER 6
Copyright Disputes: Avoidance and Resolution

Those who create are rare; those who cannot are numerous.
Therefore, the latter are stronger.

Gabrielle "Coco" Chanel (1961)

OUTLINE

COMMENTARY

A nature photographer spent a year in the Alaskan wilderness photographing the mating habits of freshwater trout. She has created a set of photographs and under her authorization several of the photos, including one entitled Trout Ecstasy, *were printed in a nature magazine. Two months after publication of the magazine, a friend sent the photographer a postcard purchased in the gift shop of a San Francisco museum. The postcard is an illustration that appears to be based on the photographer's* Trout Ecstasy *photograph. The postcard is not exactly the same as the photograph, but several people tell the photographer that it is very similar.*

OBJECTIVES

Chapters 2 through 5 introduced concepts of copyright protection and administration. Chapter 6 provides information about copyright disputes: how to avoid them and how to resolve them. After reading this chapter you will be able to:

- Describe the elements of copyright infringement.
- Outline the standards for substantial similarity.
- Identify potential copyright infringement defendants.
- Explain and contrast various defenses in a copyright infringement lawsuit.
- Distinguish the remedies available to a plaintiff in a copyright infringement lawsuit.
- Assist in the drafting of a cease and desist letter.
- Assist in the preparation of a copyright infringement complaint.
- Determine the appropriate means of discovering evidence during litigation.
- Interview a client involved in a copyright infringement lawsuit.
- Facilitate preparation for a copyright infringement trial.

6.1 ELEMENTS OF INFRINGEMENT

Infringement is the violation of one or more of the exclusive rights granted under copyright law. Infringement occurs when a party with access to a work copies it or interferes with a right granted under copyright law.[1] For example, infringement may occur when someone copies several chapters of a book or performs a copyrighted song without authorization of the owner.

There are two steps in proving infringement. First, the party claiming infringement must prove ownership and existence of the copyright. Second, the copyright owner must demonstrate that the alleged infringer violated one of the exclusive rights. For example, in the preceding case of the nature photographer, it must be shown that: (1) the photographer owns a copyright in the trout photo and has acquired a registration in the work (unless excused

LEGAL TERMS

infringement
Unauthorized use of a work protected by copyright; occurs when a party with access to a copyrighted work creates a substantially similar work without permission of the copyright owner and in violation of copyright laws.

under the Berne Amendment provisions or registration has been refused); and (2) the photo was copied to make the postcards. (Note that in February 1993, legislation (S. 373 and H.R. 897) was proposed that would eliminate the copyright registration requirement for filing suit (17 U.S.C. § 411(a)) and the registration requirement for statutory damages and attorney fees (17 U.S.C. § 412). Although this legislation has not been enacted as of the publication of this book, the legal assistant should review the current copyright law when researching this issue.) Copying does not have to be an exact duplication to qualify as an infringement. To prove that the photograph has been copied, evidence must be introduced that the postcard owner had access to the copyrighted photo and that the postcard is substantially similar to the copyrighted photo.

Ownership of Copyright

Proving ownership and validity of a copyright is generally accomplished by introducing the copyright registration as evidence. The copyright registration establishes prima facie proof of ownership (unless the work is registered more than five years after the first publication) and creates a presumption of copyright validity. In other words, the court will presume that the work is protected under copyright law and that the owner has properly acquired rights to the work.[2]

If the owner of copyright has transferred a right to a third party, that person may bring suit if that right is infringed. For example, if the nature photographer transferred the right to make painted derivatives of her trout photos to Joan Smith, then Joan could bring the lawsuit against the museum gift shop. However, Joan would have to prove ownership of *her* right. That is, she would have to introduce a recorded document that evidences the transfer from the photographer to Joan.

Access to the Copyrighted Work

It is difficult to prove direct evidence of copying. For example, in the case of the postcard and trout photo, it may be difficult to find a witness to testify that the painter of the postcard used the photo as the basis for the postcard. Instead, the courts will conclude that copying has occurred if it can be proven that the defendant had access to the copyrighted work and that the defendant's work is substantially similar to the copyrighted work. **Access** means that the defendant had the reasonable opportunity to view or hear the copyrighted work.

Often, if the infringement involves identical copies, access will be presumed. For example, it is not necessary to prove access in a case involving identical copies of architectural plans, word-for-word similarity of two 1,000-page novels, or photographic reproduction of a picture. In these cases of verbatim copying, it is virtually impossible that the two works could have been independently created. The defendant *had* to have had access to the plaintiff's work to create an exact duplicate.

Most infringements are not exact duplications. Therefore, the plaintiff must prove that the defendant had access to the work. There are many ways to prove access. For example, in a case involving infringement of copyrighted characters, the plaintiffs proved that the defendants had visited the plaintiff's headquarters and discussed use of the characters. The presence of the defendant at the plaintiff's office demonstrated that the defendant had had the reasonable opportunity to view the copyrighted work.

In another case, the copyright owner of the song "He's So Fine" sued songwriter George Harrison, alleging that Harrison's song "My Sweet Lord" infringed copyright. The plaintiff proved that Harrison had access to "He's So Fine" because the song was on the British pop charts in 1963, while a song by Harrison's group, the Beatles, was also on the British charts. Therefore, the court concluded, Harrison had a reasonable opportunity to hear the plaintiff's song.

Substantial Similarity

In addition to proving access, the plaintiff must prove that the infringing work is substantially similar to the copyrighted work. **Substantial similarity** means that the works have similarities that can result only from copying, rather than from coincidence, common source derivation, or independent creation.

There are numerous ways in which a work can be infringed. Works can be illegally performed, duplicated, altered, combined with other works, and reproduced on all manner of media. Measuring and proving substantial similarity requires an assessment of all the similarities between the plaintiff's and the defendant's work.

Literal Similarities

Some similarities may be *literal.* For example, if several chapters of a textbook were photocopied for sale to students, that would be a literal or *verbatim* form of copying. If a pop song was used as the background for an advertisement without permission of the songwriter, that also would be a literal similarity (i.e., the song had been duplicated without any change). Proving literal similarities is a straightforward matter. The court compares the duplications and assesses the infringement.

Nonliteral Similarities

Other infringements are not exact duplications. For example, in the case of the nature photographer cited in the Commentary at the beginning of this chapter, the painting on the postcard is not precisely similar to the photograph. The most common method of assessing substantial similarity is to consider the two works and create a list of the similarities. For example, the photographer may compare the shape and position of the animals, the

LEGAL TERMS

access
   The reasonable opportunity of the defendant to view or hear the copyrighted work.

substantial similarity
   Two works have similarities that can result only from copying, rather than from coincidence, common source derivation, or independent creation.

background, the proportions, the coloring, and the lighting. The list might be as follows:

1. Both works consist of a brown trout (*salmo trutta*) with a lightly speckled body. The speckles are turquoise and olive in both trout.
2. The trout in both works is three quarters above water in a jumping position with its head facing to the northwest portion of the frame.
3. A rapidly moving river with an indigo tint is shown in both works flowing from left to right and occupying approximately one-fourth of the bottom portion of the frames.
4. Two trees are depicted in both works: a weeping willow in the northwest corner of each frame and a maple tree in full bloom in the northwest corner of each frame.
5. A lush kelly-green riverbank is seen approximately two-thirds from the top of each frame and running along the length of the entire frame. Two large silvery-grey rocks are in the forefront of the bank on the far left side.
6. The tail of each trout is partially visible through the water.
7. A milky cirrus cloud is visible behind the weeping willow tree in both frames.

These similarities are considered *comprehensive* or *nonliteral* similarities. The greater the quality and the quantity of such similarities, the greater the likelihood of substantial similarity. For example, the owners of copyright in the movie *Star Wars* sued the owners of the television show *Battlestar Galactica* for copyright infringement. There was no duplication of actual dialogue, but there were several *nonliteral* similarities. The owners of *Star Wars* listed 34 such similarities, including the following:

1. The central conflict of each story is a war between the galaxy's democratic and totalitarian forces.
2. In *Star Wars* the young hero's father had been a leader of the democratic forces, and the present leader of the democratic forces is a father figure to the young hero. In *Battlestar* the young hero's father is a leader of the democratic forces.
3. The leader of the democratic forces is an older man, displaying great wisdom, and symbolizing goodness and leadership, with a mysterious mystical ability to dominate a leader of the totalitarian forces.
4. An entire planet central to the existence of the democratic forces is destroyed.
5. The heroine is imprisoned by the totalitarian forces.
6. A leading character returns to the family home to find it destroyed.
7. The search by the totalitarians and the liberation attempt by the democratic forces are depicted in alternating sequences between the totalitarian and democratic camps.

8. There is a romance between the hero's friend (the cynical fighter pilot) and the daughter of one of the leaders of the democratic forces.

9. A friendly robot who aids the democratic forces is severely injured (*Star Wars*) or destroyed (*Battlestar*) by the totalitarian forces.

10. There is a scene in a cantina (*Star Wars*) or casino (*Battlestar*), in which musical entertainment is offered by bizarre, nonhuman creatures.

11. Space vehicles, although futuristic, are made to look used and old, contrary to the stereotypical sleek, new appearance of space-age equipment.

12. The climax consists of an attack by the democratic fighter pilots on the totalitarian headquarters.

13. Each work ends with an awards ceremony in honor of the democratic heroes.

Copying Portions of a Work

Often, only part of a work is copied. For example, several pages from a book are taken, or two photographs from a book of photos are used, or one section of a song is borrowed. How much must be taken to amount to an infringement? No measurement can quantify exactly how much taking equals substantial similarity. In each case, the court examines the portion taken and determines whether the portion constitutes a substantial portion of

JUDGE LEARNED HAND ON COPYRIGHT: LETTY LYNTON AND THE DISHONORED LADY

In 1936, the author of a play, *Dishonored Lady,* sued the producer of a movie, *Letty Lynton,* for copyright infringement. Confusing the issue was the fact that the plaintiff's work was based on the true story of a 19th-century Scottish woman, a fact pattern over which no author could claim a monopoly. The defendant had borrowed the plot of the plaintiff's play but not any of the specific dialogue. The lower court held that there was no infringement. Judge Hand disagreed on appeal. According to Judge Hand, the issue was not whether the plaintiff got his idea from the public domain, but whether the defendant had copied the plaintiff's expression. After a careful review, Judge Hand determined that the play's expression had been copied by the film, even though no literal copying of the dialogue occurred. "Speech is only a small part of a dramatist's means of expression . . . the play may often be most effectively pirated by leaving out the speech."

the plaintiff's work. For example, the taking of one sentence from a work will generally not be considered an infringement. However, when that one sentence is "E.T., phone home," the court will consider that line to be a substantial portion of the movie, and the unauthorized reprinting of the sentence on cups and merchandise will amount to an infringement.

The Lay Observer Test

Different federal circuits may apply different standards in judging infringement. One of the most common standards is the *lay observer* test. First the court analyzes the specific list of literal and nonliteral similarities. After that, the court asks, "Would the ordinary observer, when examining both works, consider that the defendant has misappropriated the plaintiff's work?" By using this lay observer test, the court applies a personal "gut-level" inquiry (rather than an expert or technical opinion) as to whether an infringement has occurred.

Applying the Lay Observer Test.   The lay observer test can be applied informally prior to initiating an infringement suit. It is often a good idea to show the copyrighted work and the infringing works to friends or office workers to get their initial opinions as to whether they feel that the defendant has misappropriated something from the plaintiff. This casual review may alert the parties to issues or opinions that might not occur under normal scrutiny.

Special Issues in Infringement Cases

Special infringement issues may arise because of the nature of certain works. Courts may use different standards when reviewing copying or performance of musical works, computer programs, factual works, or compilations.

Factual Works and Compilations

Because of the nature of factual works, maps, charts, and factual compilations, the courts often use a higher standard for establishing infringement. The courts have indicated that proving infringement of these works requires very close paraphrasing or verbatim copying. Courts believe that there are only a limited number of ways to express facts and factual compilations and therefore similarities should be literal. For example, two authors write books about the ingredients and side effects of prescription drugs. There are only a limited number of ways in which to express this information. Therefore, for one author to prove infringement, there must be some indication of direct copying.

The Deliberate Mistake.   The author of a factual work or map may sometimes deliberately place unnecessary or incorrect information in the work in order to prove direct copying. For example, in the index of a map, the cartographer may insert the name of a fictitious city. If the same fictitious city appears in the index of the defendant's map, then there is proof of direct copying. However, proof of such copying does not always indicate that the copyright owner will prevail. Such copying may be excused if it qualifies as a fair use or if the court determines that the plaintiff's work is not protectible under copyright.

Musical Works and Sound Recordings

Certain infringement issues arise that are unique to musical works and sound recordings. As noted previously, for example, if the copied portion of a song is quantitatively small, the court will attempt to determine the importance of that portion to the plaintiff's work. For example, the copying of two bars of music in one song was held to be an infringement, while the copying of six bars of music in another song was not an infringement. If the song is reduced to sheet music, copying the sheet music is an infringement. If the words are altered without the authorization of the songwriter, that would infringe the derivative right of the songwriter.

Musical works can be infringed in many ways. If the song is performed without the authorization of the songwriter (either in a live performance or by the playing of a recording), that is an infringement of the performance right. Performance rights organizations such as BMI and ASCAP employ persons to visit clubs and stores and determine if illegal performances are being made of copyrighted works. These "spies" report back to the performance rights societies, who may sue the clubs or stores to require that licenses be obtained. The unauthorized use of a song as a background for a commercial will amount to an unauthorized performance. It also may give rise to other claims related to use of the performer's name or style as a commercial endorsement.

If the sounds embodied on a sound recording are duplicated, that is an infringement of the sound recording copyright. For example, if a record is illegally duplicated and sold, that is an infringement of the sound recording and underlying musical works. The digital recording process has also made it possible for persons to sample or digitize a portion of a sound recording. In this process, digital data are manipulated so that the user can modify or alter the recording. For example, a certain guitar part from a record by the group Van Halen could be reproduced in a rap song by Tone Lōc. This sample is not a computer program. It is a digital representation of a sound wave and, because it involves the literal duplication of a sound recording, it may be considered an infringement, provided that a court determines that the portion sampled is of qualitative or quantitative importance to the copyrighted work. Since copyright of sound recordings began in 1972, sampling a sound recording published prior to 1972 would not be a violation of copyright law, although it may be a violation of applicable state laws or a violation of the copyright on the underlying musical work.

An issue that often arises in musical infringements is the derivation of the copyrighted work. For example, a defendant may argue that both songs at issue are based upon common musical notation and language. Blues, rock, and country songs, for example, are usually based on traditional chord patterns and changes. The use of these common musical forms is considered public domain. Similarly, the use of a common phrase in a musical work, such as "got my mojo working," is considered to be a public domain or unprotectible phrase for which no author can claim a proprietary right.

Computer Programs

The nature of computer programs has created unique infringement issues. As noted in previous chapters, there is a difference between the ownership of most copyrighted works and the ownership of a computer program. It is the position of the software industry that when a consumer purchases a program, that consumer is acquiring a license to use the program, not ownership of the program. Under that license, and pursuant to the copyright law, the user may make an archival copy of the program. Any other duplication may be considered an infringement.

Computer programs may be infringed in various ways. For example, a video game has several copyrightable elements, including the programming code, the movement on the screen, the game's characters, and the general "plot" of the game. It is possible to infringe the program code controlling the video game action without infringing the visual aspect. For example, in one case, an infringing video game *played* exactly like *Pac-Man,* although using distinctly different characters and sounds. Conversely, in another case involving the game *Scramble* (in which players control a spaceship, release bombs, and fire lasers), a copy infringed the characters and appearance of the video game without infringing the computer program (the code) that controlled the action.

There are various methods of connecting computers and these systems may give rise to infringement claims. For example, the use of a computer bulletin board (BBS) may lead to infringement claims. With a BBS, users who connect via telephone lines to remote computers can retrieve or download information or programs. If the user is not authorized to download a certain program, an infringement may have occurred.

A *network* is another method by which computer users connect and exchange information. These systems are also known as *LANS* (local area networks) and *WANS* (wide area networks). Most networks are installed in offices or businesses because they provide an efficient means of exchanging information among workers. However, networks may create infringements if various workers are using unauthorized copies of *one* program. This would be an infringement, because the owner of a single computer program is only licensed to use one copy. Most software companies now offer network versions that license multiple users.

Recently issues were raised regarding the "look and feel" of computer programs. Even though the underlying code is different, can one copyright owner claim a proprietary right to the *interface,* the manner in which the user interacts with the computer? For example, the makers of the Macintosh computer fought a long and largely unsuccessful battle to prevent other software makers from using the graphic images of wastebaskets, pens, and other icons. Although caselaw is still evolving, the courts appear to be applying the same standards as to other infringement issues, analyzing the similarities between the works and weighing those similarities quantitatively and qualitatively.

Myths Regarding Infringement

There are several myths surrounding copyright infringement. Listed below are some of the more common falsehoods.

Four Bars of Music.   There is a common myth among musicians that four bars of music may be copied without an infringement occurring. As noted, when a judge examines the portion taken from the copyrighted work, the criterion is not the amount of taken, but the importance of the portion taken, as well as the four fair use factors.

Attribution.   Some persons presume that infringement cannot occur if attribution is made to the original source. They think that if a credit is given to the original author, then that author cannot complain of infringement. *This is not true.* Attribution will not prevent an infringement claim. In the case of advertisements, for example, attribution may even lead to additional claims of invasion of the right of publicity or false endorsement. For example, if a scientist's copyrighted article was quoted at length (with attribution) in an advertisement for cigarettes, that unauthorized use would be an infringement. If quoting portions of a copyrighted work for scholarly purposes or other purposes that may qualify as a fair use, it is sometimes suggested to include an attribution as to the source. Some commentators even suggest including information about how to purchase the source material, thereby turning the reference into a promotion and (it is hoped) avoiding a claim of infringement. Remember, however, that attribution will not *prevent* infringement claims.

Paraphrasing.   Paraphrasing a work will not defeat a claim of substantial similarity. For example, in the case of *Salinger v. Random House,*[3] the author paraphrased several copyrighted letters by novelist J. D. Salinger. In one example, Salinger had written, "She's a beautiful girl, except for her face." The paraphrase was written, "How would a girl feel if you told her she was stunning to look at but that facially there was something not quite right about her?" The court, in finding infringement, also took offense as to how inadequately the paraphrasing had been performed. The court further determined that an appreciable number of readers would have the impression they had read Salinger's words.

It's In the Mail. Many persons believe that mailing a work to oneself is proof of ownership or priority of creation of a work. They believe that the postmark will demonstrate that the material sealed inside was prepared on a certain date and therefore that the work was independently created prior to any alleged infringement. Such evidence is inconclusive in an infringement case because of the possibility that the envelope may have been opened and resealed after being postmarked.

Not for Profit. Some people incorrectly believe that if the purpose of the infringement is not for profit, there is no infringement. For example, if a non-profit charity uses a copyrighted character in its donation drive and mailings, the charity may be liable for infringement. Similarly, a not-for-profit political campaign cannot freely reproduce television footage of news events or other candidates without risking a claim of infringement. The not-for-profit status of a defendant may have a bearing on two issues, however: a defense of fair use or proof of lost profits.

6.2 LIABILITY FOR INFRINGEMENT

Everyone has probably infringed a copyright at one time. The copying of portions of a book or article, the duplication of several copies of a phonorecord, or the reproduction of a computer program or manual all may amount to infringing acts. An *infringer* is any person who is liable for an unauthorized use of the copyrighted material. When reviewing an infringement situation, the plaintiff must identify the parties who are legally culpable for the infringing acts. These parties will become the defendants in the action. General legal principles determine liability. For example, the acts of an employee within the scope of his or her duties are attributable to the employer. Therefore, if an employee infringes a book while working for a publishing company, the publishing company may be named as a defendant. A *corporation* is a legal entity that can sue or defend an action. However, a corporation's capacity to sue or defend is determined by the law of the state in which it was incorporated. In the case of an independent contractor who infringes in the course of doing work for a client, both client and contractor may be defendants. For example, suppose that an advertising agency infringes a photographic copyright when preparing an advertisement for a car company. The ad is published in a magazine. The car company, the magazine, and the ad agency could all be named in the copyright infringement lawsuit.

Prior to instituting an action for an alleged act of infringement, a prudent attorney and legal assistant will research the economics of litigation. Does the copyright owner simply want the acts of infringement to stop, or is one goal of the lawsuit to obtain monetary damages? Does the defendant have sufficient funds to pay a judgment? Can the copyright owner afford to maintain an infringement action? All these issues must be examined before instituting any litigation.

Infringer's Intent

The intent of the person performing the infringing acts is irrelevant for determining whether an infringement occurred. For example, in the situation of the museum that prints postcards of a photographer's photos, it does not matter if the gift shop innocently believed that it had the right to print post-cards. The intention of the museum or the printer may only be relevant for determining the remedy for the infringement, that is, the amount of damages or whether attorney fees will be awarded.

Contributory Infringement

Consider the example involving the gift shop and the infringing post-cards. The gift shop operates independently of the museum in which it is located. However, the museum is presented with samples of all merchandise prior to introduction of the merchandise at the gift shop, and the museum charges the gift shop rent and receives a percentage of its sales. Under these facts, the museum also may be named as a **contributory infringer** (also known as a **vicarious infringer**). A *contributory infringer* is one who, with knowledge or reason to know of infringing activity of another, induces, causes, or materially contributes to the infringement; or one who has the right and ability to supervise the infringing activities and also has a direct financial interest in such activities. The Supreme Court has also described a contributory infringer as one who was in a position to control the use of copyrighted works by others and has authorized the use without permission from the copyright owner.

The key elements in determining who is a contributory infringer are the knowledge or reason to know of the infringing activity and the extent to which the third party is involved in the infringement. The following are some examples of situations in which a person might be held to be a contributory infringer.

EXAMPLE

The Dance Club. A dance club hires bands and disk jockeys (deejays). Music is performed without a performance rights license. The deejays and bands are infringing the performance rights of the copyright owners of certain songs. The proprietor of the dance club will be liable as a contributory infringer for the infringing activities of hired bands or deejays. The proprietor has a reason to know of the infringing activity. In addition, the proprietor has a direct financial interest, that is, the dance club proprietor profits directly from the infringing activity. The landlord of the building in which the dance club is located is probably not a contributory infringer. The landlord does not supervise and does not have a reason to know of the infringing activity, and the landlord does not have a direct financial interest in the infringing activity.

LEGAL TERMS

contributory infringer (also called vicarious infringer)
  One who, with knowledge or reason to know of infringing activity of another, induces, causes or materially contributes to the infringement; or one who has the right and ability to supervise the infringing activities and also has a direct financial interest in such activities.

EXAMPLE

The Television Broadcast. A television station broadcasts a television movie that infringes the copyright of a motion picture owner. The producer of the television movie is an infringer. The television station supervises and reviews the television movie before it is broadcast. The station has the ability to supervise the infringing activity and has a direct financial interest. However, under a special exemption, a cable television broadcaster who has no control over the content or selection of a television signal is *not* a contributory infringer if it carries or transmits the infringing television movie.

EXAMPLE

The Videotape Duplicator. A person makes multiple copies of a motion picture using a videotape recording machine. The person is an infringer, but the suppliers of the videotape recording devices are *not* contributory infringers. The Supreme Court has ruled that when a device has multiple uses besides infringement, the suppliers of such devices are not contributory infringers. For example, manufacturers of photocopying machines are not considered contributory infringers simply because some persons illegally use the devices to infringe copyright.

EXAMPLE

The "Helpful" Copy Shop. A copy shop near a university rents required textbooks to customers. Students can illegally copy the necessary chapters without buying the books. The copy shop is a contributory infringer because it induces or materially contributes to the infringing activity. However, a special exemption provides that a library or archives is *not* a contributory infringer with respect to the unsupervised use of copy machines located on its premises.

6.3 DEFENSES TO INFRINGEMENT

When evaluating an infringement dispute, it is important to review the possible defenses. Most of these defenses have been introduced in previous chapters. For example, chapter 2 explained what items were not copyrightable. Therefore, similarities based upon uncopyrightable elements would not give rise to an infringement claim. Chapter 3 listed various statutory exceptions to the rights granted under copyright. Fair use, the first sale doctrine, and numerous statutory exemptions permit persons to make use of works that would otherwise appear to be infringing. Chapter 4 presented several formalities regarding copyright, including use of copyright notice and registration. If the plaintiff failed to follow the required formalities, the defendant may assert that failure as a defense. Certain defenses common to all litigation are also available in copyright infringement lawsuits. These defenses include estoppel, unclean hands, and expiration of the statute of limitations.

Attacking Ownership and Validity of Copyright

The defendant (infringer) can challenge the claim of ownership or validity of the copyright. The most common reasons to attack ownership are:

- The work is not original to the author
- The work is not copyrightable
- The owner has failed to comply with statutory formalities
- The plaintiff is not the author and has failed to prove the relationship demonstrating a transfer of rights.

There are other methods of defending based upon the plaintiff's lack of ownership. For example, if the work was first published before March 1, 1989, the defendant may attempt to discover any copies of the work published without notice. Depending upon the applicable copyright act and the facts of the case, publication without notice may invalidate copyright, thereby ending the infringement suit. In addition, there is some caselaw (although the courts are not in agreement as to this issue) indicating that the defendant may claim that the certificate of registration is invalid because the registrant made misrepresentations of fact when preparing it.

Attacking Access

If the defendant never had access to the plaintiff's work and can prove that fact to the court, the infringement suit will fail. As previously indicated, this can be very difficult when the two works are identical or when the similarities are striking, such as the inclusion of common errors. But absent such striking similarities, the plaintiff still must prove that the defendant had the reasonable opportunity to view or hear the copyrighted work.

Unsolicited Submissions.   A claim of access may be countered, for example, if the defendant can argue that the decision making and creative personnel of the company were insulated from unsolicited submissions. Even more common, many companies in the entertainment and publishing industries log all unsolicited materials and routinely return such works without opening them. This helps to defeat any claim of access. For example, if a demo tape of a song was mailed to Michael Jackson but returned unopened, then the owner of that demo tape would have difficulty asserting that Mr. Jackson had an opportunity to hear it.

Attacking Substantial Similarity

It is important to remember that not all similarities give rise to an infringement claim. For example, similarities based upon short phrases, facts, public domain material, or ideas would not prove substantial similarity. As discussed in chapter 2, these components of a work are not protectible. The following is a list of unprotectible elements.

- *Short phrases and standard designs.* Works and short phrases such as names, titles, and slogans; familiar symbols or designs; mere variations of typographic ornamentation, lettering or coloring; mere listing of ingredients or contents
- *Ideas and methods.* Ideas, plans, methods, systems, or devices, as distinguished from the particular manner in which they are expressed or described in a writing
- *Standard forms and measurements.* Blank forms, such as timecards, graph paper, account books, diaries, bank checks, scorecards, address books, report forms, order forms, and the like, that are designed for recording information and do not in themselves convey information
- *Facts and public domain elements.* Works consisting entirely of information that is common property containing no original authorship. For example: standard calendars, height and weight charts, tape measures and rulers, schedules of sporting events, and lists of tables taken from public documents or other common sources.

The following are some examples of similar but noninfringing works.

EXAMPLE

Novel Not Substantially Similar to Factual Work. An author writes a novel about a wealthy Jewish family in San Francisco. She borrows factual material and several short phrases from a social history of Jewish migration to San Francisco. Even though there are similarities between the two books, the novelist has not infringed the historical work because the only things borrowed were short phrases and facts, both unprotectible under copyright law.

EXAMPLE

Textiles with Public Domain Images Not Substantially Similar. One textile designer creates a fabric using public domain pictures of bees, flowers, and birds. Another designer uses the same public domain elements and creates a different design. Even though there are similarities, there is no infringement because neither author can claim a proprietary right to the public domain material—only to the manner in which the elements are combined.

EXAMPLE

Songs with Similar Phrases Not Substantially Similar. A songwriter writes a country song in which he uses the phrases, "I like to gamble, I like to smoke. I like to drink and tell a dirty joke." The defendant had written a song with dissimilar music. However, it contained the phrases, "She don't drink. She don't smoke. She can't stand a dirty joke." The court determined that the resemblance of such public domain phrases did not amount to substantial similarity.

EXAMPLE

Dramatic Works with Similar Elements Not Substantially Similar. The plaintiff wrote a play about aliens stranded on earth. The defendant created the motion picture *E.T.* The only similarity between the works was that in both scripts, aliens with powers of levitation and telepathy are stranded on earth, pursued by authoritarian characters, and finally bid their earthly friends farewell. The court determined that these similarities were only ideas and too general to be protected. The plaintiff could not claim infringement on the basis of such similarities.

Fair Use

As explained in chapter 3, *fair use* is the right to use copyrighted material for limited purposes and without authorization of the author. Whether the fair use defense is applicable is determined by a federal court after weighing several factors, including the purpose and character of the use, the amount and substantiality of the portion borrowed, and the effect of the use on the market for the copyrighted material. This latter factor, effect of the use on the market, is considered the most important factor. Under a fair use defense, it does not matter if the works are substantially similar, because the defendant has a right to use the copied materials under fair use principles. For example, videotaping an off-the-air television show for home use is an unauthorized use. However, the Supreme Court has determined that it is permitted because it is a fair use. The same rules apply for certain satires and parodies that are also excused under fair use principles. Examples of the criteria and standards applied in fair use defenses are provided in detail in chapter 3.

Estoppel

Suppose that a songwriter hears a parody of her song in a club. Although it is an infringement, she decides not to object. The infringer is led to believe that the copyright owner will not oppose the parody and continues using it in her nightclub act. Later, the songwriter decides to sue the parodist. The parodist may assert a defense called **estoppel**, which asserts that the plaintiff cannot contradict behavior upon which the defendant has justifiably relied. To assert successfully an estoppel defense, the plaintiff must know the facts of the defendant's conduct and the defendant must have a justifiable belief that the infringing conduct is permitted.

LEGAL TERMS

estoppel
A defense to infringement in which the defendant prevents the plaintiff from contradicting behavior upon which the defendant has justifiably relied. To assert successfully an estoppel defense, the plaintiff must know the facts of the defendant's conduct and the defendant must have a justifiable belief that the infringing conduct is permitted.

Unclean Hands

The **unclean hands** defense is asserted when the plaintiff has committed a serious act of wrongdoing in regard to the infringement—so serious that it would be inequitable for the court to allow the plaintiff to proceed. Because the plaintiff has unclean hands, the defendant argues that the infringement lawsuit must be dismissed. For example, if the plaintiff has falsified material facts, or made material misrepresentations when registering the work, a defense of unclean hands may be successful.

Laches

Laches is a defense asserted when the plaintiff has waited an unreasonable amount of time to bring the lawsuit. Even though the statute of limitations has not expired, the defendant contends that the delay is so unreasonable that it would be unfair to permit the plaintiff to proceed with the lawsuit. The laches defense, like that of unclean hands, is rarely successful in an infringement lawsuit.

Statute of Limitations

Section 507 of the Copyright Act of 1976 provides a three-year period for bringing a claim of copyright infringement. This is known as the **statute of limitations**, and it means that the owner of the copyrighted work has a time limit of three years from the time the infringing activity occurred to file a copyright infringement lawsuit. If the infringement is continuing (e.g., the infringer continues to publish the work over many years), then the three-year interval would begin at any time during the infringing activity. Some courts have held that the time limit for bringing a lawsuit begins when the copyright owner *should have reasonably known* that the infringement has occurred. In other words, if the copyright owner is unaware of the infringement because it has been concealed, the owner could not have reasonably known, and therefore the three-year period to bring the lawsuit would begin when the owner learns of the infringing activity. If more than three years have passed since the infringing activity was discovered or should have been discovered by the plaintiff, the defendant may be able to assert successfully that the litigation is barred because the statute of limitations has run out.

6.4   REMEDIES FOR COPYRIGHT INFRINGEMENT

One of the major factors in determining whether to pursue an infringement claim is the extent of the relief available if the copyright owner prevails. What will the court order the defendant to do? How much money will the copyright owner be awarded? How hard will it be to collect the judgment from the defendant? There are a variety of forms of judicial relief in an infringement lawsuit. Some remedies attempt to compensate the plaintiff for the damages resulting from the infringement. Payment for damages may be based upon actual losses suffered as a result of the infringement, as well as any profits by the defendant that are not included in the plaintiff's losses. In certain cases, the court may determine damages based upon a minimum and maximum established by the Copyright Act. Factors such as the innocence or willfulness of the defendant may result in higher or lower awards of damages.

In addition to these financial awards, the plaintiff may seek nonfinancial relief. For example, the plaintiff may want to impound all infringing copies and to destroy such copies. The plaintiff may seek an order of the court known as an *injunction* to prevent the defendant from continuing any infringing activity. In rare cases, the court also may award attorney fees to the prevailing party in the lawsuit.

Writ of Seizure

Prior to instituting a lawsuit, the copyright owner may be concerned that the infringer will relocate, destroy evidence, or attempt to sell the infringing merchandise. Under such circumstances, the copyright owner may seek to have the infringing merchandise and manufacturing materials impounded by the court. To impound the materials, as described later, a writ of seizure must be issued by the court. A **writ of seizure** is an order of the court directing the federal marshal to seize and hold infringing merchandise. It is usually granted only upon payment of a bond of not less than twice the value of the infringing articles. Under a judicial process known as *ex parte,* the writ may be obtained without consulting with the infringer. That is, upon sufficient showing of evidence, the copyright owner may obtain the writ without providing the defendant an opportunity to appear and contest the writ. The federal rules for the writ follow the annotations at the end of 17 U.S.C. § 501 of the Copyright Act of 1976. The writ can only be obtained upon or after the filing of the copyright infringement lawsuit. Alternatively, as explained later, during the course of the trial, the court may order the impounding of all infringing copies or phonorecords, as well as the items used in the manufacture of the infringing copies.

Injunctions

Generally, the plaintiff in a copyright infringement lawsuit seeks an order from the court enjoining the defendant from any further infringing activity. This court order, instructing the infringer to stop the infringing activity, is known as an **injunction.**[4] A court weighs several factors when determining whether to grant an injunction, including: (1) is the plaintiff likely to succeed in the lawsuit?; and (2) will the plaintiff suffer irreparable harm if the injunction is not granted? Normally, if the plaintiff can demonstrate copyright infringement, irreparable harm will be presumed.

There are three types of injunctions. Initially, the plaintiff may seek preliminary relief known as a **temporary restraining order** or **TRO**. The

LEGAL TERMS

unclean hands
A defense asserted when the plaintiff has committed a serious act of wrongdoing in regard to the lawsuit or the activity precipitating the lawsuit.

laches
A defense to infringement in which the defendant argues that the plaintiff's delay in bringing the lawsuit is so unreasonable that the plaintiff should be barred from proceeding.

statute of limitations
Time limit during which the plaintiff must file a lawsuit. In copyright, it is three years from the date when the infringing activity occurred (or when the copyright owner could have reasonably known that the infringing activity occurred).

writ of seizure
An order of the court directing the federal marshal to seize and hold infringing merchandise; granted only upon payment of a bond of not less than twice the value of the infringing articles.

injunction
A court order directing the defendant to stop certain activities.

temporary restraining order (TRO)
Injunction, often granted ex parte, that is of short duration and remains in effect only until the court has an opportunity to schedule a hearing for a preliminary injunction.

TRO may be granted ex parte, that is, without hearing an opposition from the defendant. The TRO is short in duration and remains in effect only until the court has an opportunity to schedule a hearing for the preliminary injunction. The **preliminary injunction** is granted after a noticed hearing where both parties have an opportunity to present evidence. Often such hearings are "mini-trials" and require considerable preparation. The court may request, for either the TRO or preliminary injunction, that a bond be posted by the plaintiff. The purpose of the bond is to cover any damages suffered by the defendant if the court determines that no infringement has occurred.

The preliminary injunction lasts until the end of the trial and a final judgment has been rendered. If the plaintiff prevails, a permanent injunction is granted. A **permanent injunction** is a durable injunction issued after a final judgment on the merits of the case. It permanently restrains the defendant from engaging in the infringing activity. If it is not probable that the defendant will continue the infringing activity, the court will not issue a permanent injunction.

To see how the injunction procedure works, consider the dispute about the trout postcards. The photographer may initially obtain a TRO preventing the gift shop from selling or transferring the cards. The photographer also may obtain a TRO preventing the printer from manufacturing the postcards for the gift shop. The TRO will restrain the defendants until a preliminary injunction hearing can be held, usually a period of a few weeks. At the preliminary injunction hearing, the photographer will emphasize several issues: her likelihood of success, whether the injunction would promote the public interest, the irreparable harm that could result from the infringement, and whether the balance of hardships favors the photographer. As to the likelihood of success, she will argue that she is likely to prevail at trial because she is the copyright owner, the defendants had access to the photographer's work, and the postcards are substantially similar to the photographs.

She will also argue that the harm she is suffering is irreparable, in that the sale and manufacture of the cards are a violation of her exclusive right to create derivative postcards and are disrupting her ability to market similar articles. After weighing the evidence, the court will either grant or deny the request for the preliminary injunction. If it is granted, the printer cannot manufacture the cards and the gift shop cannot sell them until the final judgment has been rendered. At that time, a permanent injunction may be issued, permanently preventing the sale of the postcards.

Any injunction issued in an copyright infringement action may be served anywhere in the United States on the person enjoined. The injunction is operative throughout the United States. If the defendant fails to abide by the orders, the injunction is enforceable by contempt proceedings.

Damages

If the copyright owner prevails, the court may award monetary damages. If the copyright owner has registered the work *prior* to the infringement, then the owner may elect, any time prior to final judgment, either actual damages or statutory damages. If registration has not occurred prior to infringement, the copyright owner may only recover actual damages.[5] (Note that in February 1993, legislation (S. 373 and H.R. 897) was proposed that would eliminate the copyright registration requirement for filing suit (17 U.S.C. § 411(a)) and the registration requirement for statutory damages and attorney fees (17 U.S.C. § 412). Although this legislation has not been enacted as of the publication of this book, the legal assistant should review the current copyright law when researching this issue.)

Actual damages are damages that are provable, for example, the profits from the sale of a pirated computer program or the loss resulting from the reduction in value of the copyrighted work. The determination of actual damages may be made by comparing costs, market values, anticipated revenues, and sales. Sometimes the court may use the defendant's profits as a benchmark for determining the plaintiff's damages. In establishing the infringer's profits, the copyright owner is required to present proof only of the infringer's gross revenue, and the infringer is required to prove its deductible expenses and the elements of profit attributable to factors other than the copyrighted work.

How does a copyright owner determine whether to seek actual or statutory damages? **Statutory damages** are monetary damages awarded for infringement of any one work in a sum of not less than $500 nor more than $20,000, as the court considers just. That is, the court may use its discretion to determine damages. This discretion is also affected by whether the court determines that the infringement was willful or innocent.

Although intent is irrelevant for proving infringement, it can be a factor in the award of statutory damages. In a case where the copyright owner sustains the burden of proving that the infringement was committed willfully, the court in its discretion may increase the award of statutory damages to a sum of not more than $100,000. A *willful infringement* is generally infringing activity committed with a reckless disregard for the plaintiff's rights. For example, in the case of the trout postcards, if the photographer can prove that the gift shop has a regular practice of infringing other works and was aware of the plaintiff's copyright, then the court may infer willfulness.

If a court finds that an infringement was innocent—that is, the infringer was not aware and had no reason to believe that his or her acts constituted an infringement of copyright—the court in its discretion may reduce the award of statutory damages to a sum of not less than $200. Regardless of whether an infringer is categorized as innocent, the plaintiff in a copyright infringement action can always elect to obtain the defendant's profits as actual damages. However, lack of knowledge of the law does not by itself prove innocent infringement. The defendant must demonstrate a good faith belief, based upon reasonable grounds, that the activities were not infringing; for example, if the plaintiff failed to include notice and the defendant reasonably believed that the work was in the public domain.

17 U.S.C. § 504 also provides an excuse for a certain class of innocent infringers, namely, nonprofit public broadcasting entities or employees of

LEGAL TERMS

preliminary injunction
Injunction granted after a noticed hearing where the parties have an opportunity to present evidence as to the likelihood of the plaintiff's success on the merits, the balancing of hardships, the public interest, and the irreparability of the harm to be suffered if the injunction is not granted; lasts until a final judgment has been rendered.

permanent injunction
Durable injunction issued after a final judgment on the merits of the case; permanently restrains the defendant from engaging in the infringing activity.

actual damages
The plaintiff's provable monetary damages resulting from the infringing acts.

statutory damages
Monetary damages awarded for infringement of any one work in a sum of not less than $500 nor more than $20,000, as the court considers just.

nonprofit educational facilities who had reasonable grounds for believing that the use of the copyrighted work was a fair use under § 107.

The copyright owner may elect statutory damages at any time before final judgment is rendered. Statutory damages are awarded per work infringed, not per infringement. If several works have been infringed, the statutory damages will be multiplied by the number of works. For example, if three separately copyrighted computer programs are infringed, the statutory damages may range from $1,500 to $60,000. But if the defendant only copied one program, or copied portions of one program into several other works, only one work has been infringed, and statutory damages would range between $500 and $20,000. In such a case the plaintiff may elect to prove and recover the actual damages. For the purposes of statutory damages, all the parts of a compilation or derivative work constitute one work.

Impoundment and Destruction of Infringing Articles

As part of a final judgment or decree, the court may order the destruction or disposal of all copies or phonorecords found to have been in violation of the copyright owner's exclusive rights.[6] In addition, the court may order the destruction of all plates, molds, matrices, masters, tapes, film negatives, or other means by which the infringing copies were reproduced. For example, in the case of the trout postcards, the court may order the destruction of all infringing cards. Instead of ordering destruction, some courts have ordered that the infringing copies be delivered to the plaintiff.

The court acquires control over the infringing copies by issuing a writ of seizure, described earlier. 17 U.S.C. § 503(a) provides for impoundment at any time after a copyright infringement action has been filed. The court may order the impounding of all infringing copies or phonorecords as well as the articles used to manufacture these copies.

Attorney Fees

Provided that the copyright owner has registered the work prior to the infringing activity, the prevailing party in a copyright infringement lawsuit may be awarded attorney fees.[7] (As of the publication of this book, legislation had been introduced (but not yet passed) eliminating the requirement that a work be registered prior to infringement in order for the plaintiff to obtain attorney fees.) By awarding fees, the losing party ends up paying *all* the attorney fees in the action. The award penalizes the loser and compensates the winner. However, the award of attorney fees is at the discretion of the court and such awards are rarely made.

Criminal Prosecution

Most people are familiar with the warning that appears at the beginning of a prerecorded videotape. The viewer is warned that violation of the copyright law could result in "severe criminal penalties." These criminal regulations are referenced in 17 U.S.C. § 506 and 18 U.S.C. § 2319, and provide penalties for the person or persons who, for commercial advantage, infringe a copyright. As amended in 1992, the revised sanctions for copyright infringement are: (1) up to five years imprisonment for at least 10 copies made during a 180-day period, if the copies have a retail value in excess of $2,500; (2) up to 10 years imprisonment for a second or subsequent offense; and (3) up to one year imprisonment in any other case.[8]

Fraudulent Use or Removal of Copyright Notice

A fine of up to $2,500 may be imposed when a copyright notice is fraudulently used or removed. For example, if a person illegally duplicates merchandise from the *Batman* movie and takes the copyright notice off it, the infringer may be liable for a criminal fine as well as other civil damages. In addition, a person who, with fraudulent intent, imports for public distribution any article bearing a fraudulent notice, may be fined up to $2,500.

Fraudulent Representation in a Copyright Application

Any person who knowingly makes a false representation of a material fact in the application for copyright registration or in any written statement filed in connection with the application may be liable for a criminal fine of not more than $2,500.

6.5 RESOLVING THE INFRINGEMENT DISPUTE PRIOR TO LITIGATION

Only a small fraction of infringing activity results in a copyright infringement trial and judgment. Most copyright infringement litigation is resolved before trial, and many copyright infringement actions are resolved without filing a lawsuit.

The goal of a copyright owner is to resolve disputes as fairly and efficiently as possible. Hiring an attorney and engaging in litigation are both very expensive. Therefore, it is in the best interest of all parties to conclude any infringement disputes equitably and quickly. To do this, both sides must make an accurate and realistic assessment of the facts and law. The copyright owner must determine the likelihood of prevailing in a federal court and the amount of any resulting award of damages. The defendant must review all possible defenses and understand its potential liability if the plaintiff prevails. These initial inquiries are time-consuming but well worth the effort if they can make the parties aware of the possible outcomes.

Registration

Many rights and remedies are conditioned upon timely registration of the work at issue. Registration is a prerequisite for filing the infringement action, and if registration has occurred prior to the infringing activity it will offer additional remedies, including statutory damages and attorney fees. The certificate of registration also has a powerful psychological effect when used in conjunction with the cease and desist letter; for lay persons, it implies a government certification of the plaintiff's argument. If registration has not occurred prior to the infringement, the copyright owner should consider expediting the registration, as explained in chapter 5. If the copyright owner has not acquired a registration, the cease and desist letter should still be mailed and should include a statement to the effect that the copyright application is currently being processed.

The Cease and Desist Letter

One of the most important steps in resolving an infringement dispute is the **cease and desist letter.** This letter informs the infringing party of the validity and ownership of the copyrighted work, the nature of the infringement, and the remedies available to the copyright owner. Most importantly, it requests the immediate cessation of all infringing activity and demands an accounting for all acts of infringement. It should provide an accurate assessment of the facts and anticipate any defenses. In short, it should convince the infringing party that illegal activity has occurred and that the copyright owner is very serious about enforcing statutory rights. In certain instances, when the copyright owner believes that the infringer may destroy evidence or transfer assets, the copyright owner may wish to consider obtaining an ex parte temporary restraining order or writ of seizure (discussed earlier in this chapter), in lieu of sending a cease and desist letter. In addition, the receipt of a cease and desist letter may trigger litigation called a **declaratory relief action**, as discussed later in this chapter. This is a process whereby the parties, in anticipation of a copyright infringement lawsuit, request that a court declare the legal rights and duties of the plaintiff and defendant.

Figure 6-1 shows a sample cease and desist letter as might be used in the situation involving the museum gift shop and the trout photographer. The letter should be faxed, if possible, and also sent by certified mail. Note that the middle paragraphs explaining substantial similarity would not be required in cases of exact duplication, such as copying of computer programs or photographs. The concluding paragraphs should state the remedies available under copyright law and demand an accounting (i.e., a statement of how many infringing copies have been manufactured or sold). If other claims have arisen as a result of the defendant's activities (e.g., trademark, right of publicity), those claims should be noted in the letter as well.

The cease and desist letter should have a dispassionate tone. It is important to remember that this letter, like all correspondence preceding infringement

LEGAL TERMS

cease and desist letter
Correspondence from the owner of a proprietary work that informs the infringing party of the validity and ownership of the proprietary work, the nature of the infringement, and the remedies available to the owner, and requests the cessation of all infringing activity.

declaratory relief action
Request that the court sort out the rights and legal obligations of the parties in the midst of an actual controversy.

VIA FACSIMILE & CERTIFIED MAIL

Josephine Shavez, President
Golden Egg Museum Gift Shop, Inc.
99 Golden Blvd.
San Francisco, CA 94913

Re: Copyright Infringement
"Trout" Postcard

Dear Ms. Shavez:

I represent K.R. Bickwhite, a photographer and California resident who is the owner of copyright of a photographic visual arts work entitled "Trout Ecstasy." The "Trout Ecstasy" work consists of a photographic image of a brown speckled trout in a three quarter pose jumping out of the water. The Trout Ecstasy photograph was created in December 1990 by Ms. Bickwhite and Ms. Bickwhite has licensed the use of the photograph to a national magazine. K.R. Bickwhite, Inc. has applied for a copyright registration for "Trout Ecstasy."

Ms. Bickwhite recently purchased a postcard from Golden Egg Gift Shop Museum, Inc. (the "Golden Egg Postcard"). The Golden Egg Postcard features a silkscreen painting of a brown speckled trout in a three quarter pose jumping out of the water.

It is clear that the Golden Egg Postcard illustration is substantially similar to the "Trout Ecstasy" illustration. Both works consist of a brown trout (*salmo trutta*) with a lightly speckled body. The speckles are turquoise and olive in both works. The trout in both works is three quarters above the water in a jumping position with its head facing to the northwest portion of the frame. A rapidly moving river with an indigo tint is shown in both works flowing from left to right and occupying approximately one-fourth of the bottom portion of the frames. Two trees are depicted in both works, a weeping willow in the northwest corner of each frame and a maple tree in full bloom in the northwest corner of each frame. A lush kelly-green riverbank is seen approximately two-thirds from the top of each frame and running along the length of the entire frame. Two large silvery-grey rocks are in the forefront of the bank on the far left side. The tail of each trout is partially visible through the water. A milky cirrus cloud is visible behind the weeping willow tree in both frames. All of this leads to the obvious conclusion that the "Trout Ecstasy" illustration was used as the source of the Golden Egg Postcard silkscreen.

Under such circumstances and under the standards expressed by the federal courts in this area, I am convinced that the Golden Egg Postcard illustration is an infringement of the "Trout Ecstasy" illustration copyright. It would be advisable and I do hereby demand that you cease any further copying, sale, distribution, or use of the Golden Egg Postcard illustration, whether on postcards or other merchandise. Any further infringing activity occurring after the receipt of this letter shall be considered a willful infringement.

K.R. Bickwhite vigorously protects her copyrights. As your attorney can advise you, infringement of copyright exposes you to extensive liability. Be advised that Title 17 of the United States Code § 504(c) provides that in the case of willful infringement, a court may award up to the sum of $100,000 in

FIGURE 6-1
Sample cease and desist letter

damages for each infringement, as well as full court costs and reasonable attorney's fees. If necessary, K.R. Bickwhite, Inc., is prepared to seek temporary restraining orders, injunctions, and other appropriate relief in addition to compensation for damages. Your attorney can undoubtedly advise you as to the relevant details.

I expect a prompt response from you or your attorney addressing the issues raised in this letter and providing (1) an accounting of all unauthorized copies produced or distributed by you; and (2) payment for all unauthorized copies distributed. If I do not hear from you within seven (7) days of the date of this letter, I will be compelled to advise Ms. Bickwhite to take appropriate legal action to protect her copyrights and to receive just compensation for any damage she has suffered. I look forward to hearing from you or your attorney.

Sincerely yours,

Susan R. James
Attorney for K.R. Bickwhite

FIGURE 6-1
(Continued)

litigation, may become an exhibit or an addendum to papers filed with the court. Therefore, a shrill or overbearing tone is unnecessary (and may be counterproductive), as the primary goal of the cease and desist letter is to convince the recipient that the plaintiff would prevail in a lawsuit. In addition, the copyright owner should assert that if the infringing activity continues after receipt of the letter, such continuing activity will amount to a willful infringement. The letter should be signed by the supervising attorney.

Alternative Dispute Resolution

Instead of resolving a dispute in a courtroom, some people agree to have their problem settled privately through informal procedures known as arbitration or mediation. **Arbitration** is the referral of a dispute to one or more impartial persons for an advisory or a binding determination. **Mediation** is an alternative to arbitration in which the parties submit their dispute to an impartial mediator, who assists the parties in reaching a settlement. However, unlike an arbitrator, a mediator does not have the authority to make a binding decision. Organizations such as the American Arbitration Association or the Volunteer Lawyers for the Arts provide arbitration and mediation services. If the parties have submitted to binding arbitration, the arbitrator's decision may be entered as a judgment in a court of competent jurisdiction. In mediation, a neutral party attempts to help the parties themselves resolve their dispute. Sometimes, parties may be compelled to arbitrate or mediate if they have previously entered into an agreement which requires arbitration or mediation for matters arising under or related to the contract.

Settlement

The parties may settle the case at any point prior to the final determination of the judge or jury. A **settlement** is an agreement between the parties in which the dispute is formally resolved. A settlement is a contract signed by both parties, usually executed at the time one party makes a payment to the other. For example, in the case of the trout photographer, the gift shop may pay an agreed-upon sum to the photographer at the time the settlement agreement is signed. State laws may contain code provisions regarding settlement agreements. For example, in some states, civil code provisions require inclusion of specific language regarding general releases. The federal district courts attempt to compel the parties into settlement during mandatory settlement conferences, usually held within the judge's chambers. An example of a settlement agreement is shown in figure 6-2. The terms of the settlement are sometimes presented in a document that is filed with the court in a form known as a *stipulated judgment.*

LEGAL TERMS

arbitration
Referral of a dispute to one or more impartial persons for final or advisory determination.

mediation
An alternative to arbitration in which the parties submit their dispute to an impartial mediator, who assists the parties in reaching a settlement.

settlement
Agreement between the parties in which the dispute is formally resolved.

MUTUAL RELEASE AND SETTLEMENT AGREEMENT

This Mutual Release Agreement (the "Agreement") is made and effective _____, 19___, by and between GOLDEN EGG MUSEUM GIFT SHOP, Inc., a California corporation with its principal place of business at 96 Golden Blvd., San Francisco, CA 94913 ("GOLDEN EGG") and K.R. BICKWHITE, a California resident with her principal place of business at 22 Lackburn Avenue, San Mateo, California 94991 ("BICKWHITE"), both referred to collectively as the "Parties." BICKWHITE is the author and copyright owner of a photographic visual arts work (attached hereto as Exhibit A and incorporated by reference), that features a brown speckled trout in a three quarter pose jumping out of the water. For purposes of this Agreement, the illustration and any substantially similar illustrations shall be referred to as the "BICKWHITE Copyright."

The parties now desire to settle all issues raised and arising from a dispute regarding the BICKWHITE Copyright. This Agreement is a compromise settlement and not an admission of any wrongdoing on the part of GOLDEN EGG. In consideration of the mutual promises and conditions enumerated herein, and for other consideration, the receipt and sufficiency of which are hereby acknowledged, the Parties agree and covenant as follows:

1. GOLDEN EGG acknowledges that: (a) the BICKWHITE Copyright is proprietary to BICKWHITE; (b) GOLDEN EGG is not authorized to reproduce, distribute, adapt, license, or display the BICKWHITE Copyright; and (c) GOLDEN EGG shall cease any further copying, manufacture, and distribution of the BICKWHITE Copyright in any form. Upon execution of this Release, GOLDEN EGG shall immediately deliver to BICKWHITE all silkscreens, negatives, and film positives containing the BICKWHITE Copyright.

FIGURE 6-2
Sample settlement agreement

2. GOLDEN EGG acknowledges that its failure to cease copying, manufacturing, or distribution of the BICKWHITE Copyright after execution of this Agreement: (a) will result in immediate and irremediable damage to BICKWHITE; (b) that there is no adequate remedy at law for such failure to cease copying, manufacture, or distribution; and (c) that in the event of such failure BICKWHITE shall be entitled to equitable relief by way of temporary and permanent injunctions and such other further relief as any court with jurisdiction may deem just and proper. Resort to any such remedies shall not be construed as a waiver of any other rights and remedies to which BICKWHITE is entitled under this Agreement or otherwise.

3. Upon execution of this Agreement GOLDEN EGG will pay to BICKWHITE the sum of five thousand dollars ($5,000) as a settlement fee.

4. Except for the covenants, terms, and obligations of this Agreement, BICKWHITE does hereby forever discharge GOLDEN EGG from any and all claims, demands, and causes of action, whether known or unknown, that BICKWHITE has against GOLDEN EGG arising out of or relating to the dispute over the BICKWHITE Copyright and occurring up until the execution of this Agreement.

5. This Agreement and Exhibits constitute the full, complete, and exclusive understanding of the Parties and may not be altered except by written consent of the Parties. This Agreement shall be deemed to be made and entered into pursuant to the laws of the State of California. In the event of any dispute hereunder, this Agreement shall be governed by and shall be construed and interpreted in accordance with the laws of the State of California and the Copyright laws of the United States. The prevailing party shall have the right to collect from the other party its reasonable costs and necessary disbursements and attorney fees incurred in enforcing this Agreement.

FIGURE 6-2
(Continued)

6.6 COPYRIGHT LITIGATION

Like all litigation, a copyright lawsuit requires a great deal of preparation and attention to procedural details. Missing a filing deadline, failing to respond to a document request, or making a misrepresentation to the court can have disastrous effects for a litigant. There is also a considerable business risk for the participants. For example, a plaintiff who owns a computer game sues a rival for infringement. The rival finds examples of the plaintiff's game published before 1989 without copyright notice. Suddenly, the plaintiff is on the defensive and may face the loss of copyright ownership. For this reason, considerable care must go into the investigation and preparation of the lawsuit.

Initially, a determination must be made as to which parties shall be named as defendants. Then determinations must be made as to *subject matter jurisdiction,* which is the right of a court to hear a certain case, and *venue,* which is the geographic location of the court. Then a complaint is drafted, stating the basis for the lawsuit. The complaint is filed with the court and served on each defendant. The defendant has a certain time period to respond to the complaint. After the defendant answers the complaint, a process of discovery begins, during which time, the parties, following legal rules, investigate the merits and defenses of the case. Each party may request orders from the court. These requests are known as *motions*. Finally, a trial will be held and a determination will be made as to liability. A judgment will then be issued by the court. If either party is dissatisfied with the result of the trial, an appeal may be made. Alternatively, the parties may, at any point, agree to settle the matter, regardless of the status of the litigation. In that event, the case is dismissed.

Federal Rules of Civil Procedure and Local Rules

The Federal Rules of Civil Procedure (Fed R. Civ. P.) are the procedural rules that govern the parties in federal litigation. These rules set forth the requirements for the parties when filing papers, appearing in court, or communicating with counsel. In addition, each federal district court has its own local rules. For example, the district court may have rules regarding the assignment of the case to a magistrate instead of a district court judge. Before commencing an action, it is important to acquire a copy of the local rules. These rules can usually be obtained in person or by sending a return envelope to the clerk of the court. *Always* review the local rules before preparing or filing any documents with a court.

Exclusive Federal Jurisdiction

The federal district courts have exclusive jurisdiction over any lawsuit arising under the copyright statute. **Exclusive jurisdiction** means that a court has the sole authority to hear a certain type of case. Every lawsuit for infringement of copyright must be brought in a federal district court.[9] Certain cases may relate to copyright law, but may not "arise under" the copyright law. For example, a computer company signs a contract to license the copyright of a computer program. The company is supposed to make payments for the license but fails to make one payment. A lawsuit is initiated. The issue is not copyright infringement, it is a breach of a contract. Therefore, the federal courts would not have exclusive jurisdiction over this matter, and it may be brought in a state court.

Venue

Venue is the proper geographic location of the federal court. The United States has 12 circuits. Each of the circuits has several districts. A copyright lawsuit may be brought in the district in which the defendant or the defendant's agent resides or may be found.[10] For example, in the case of the trout photographer, the infringing gift shop is located in San Francisco, which is in the Northern District of the Ninth Circuit. Therefore, the proper venue

LEGAL TERMS

exclusive jurisdiction
A court's sole authority to hear a certain type of case.

214 Intellectual Property

for the photographer to file the lawsuit would be in the Northern District. If the defendant is a corporation, the lawsuit may be brought in any district where the company is incorporated, licensed to do business, or doing business. In the interest of justice and for the convenience of parties and witnesses, the lawsuit may be transferred to another district court.

The Copyright Complaint

The **complaint** is the initial document filed in a lawsuit. It sets forth the basis of the plaintiff's claims and requests certain remedies. Like all complaints, the complaint for copyright infringement consists of a caption (which identifies the court, the parties, and the filing numbers), a statement of the facts, a prayer for relief (e.g., the remedies of compensation or injunctions), and a signature by the attorney who prepared the document.

Civil Cover Sheet and Summons

In addition to the complaint, the defendant is served with a summons and civil cover sheet, both of which are available from the clerk's office of the local federal court. The **summons** (figure 6-3) explains that the defendant has been sued and has a certain time limit in which to respond. The **civil cover sheet** (figure 6-4) is a form required for use by the court in maintaining statistical records.

Demand for Jury Trial

If the plaintiff desires a jury trial, that demand should be made in the complaint and reflected in the civil cover sheet. If the plaintiff has not sought a jury trial but the defendant wants one, the request for a jury trial should be made in the defendant's answer.

Report of a Copyright Action

The Copyright Act of 1976 requires that the clerk of the federal court report all copyright actions to the Register of Copyrights. The clerk's office may require the plaintiff to complete such a report form.

Drafting the Complaint

The sample clauses in this section illustrate the basic elements of a copyright complaint.

Jurisdiction. In federal court (unlike state court), all complaints must establish the basis for the court's jurisdiction. The first or second paragraph of a copyright complaint states the reason for filing in federal court.

AO 440 (Rev 1/90) Summons in a Civil Action

United States District Court

———————————— DISTRICT OF ————————————

SUMMONS IN A CIVIL ACTION

V.

CASE NUMBER:

TO: (Name and Address of Defendant)

YOU ARE HEREBY SUMMONED and required to file with the Clerk of this Court and serve upon

PLAINTIFF'S ATTORNEY (name and address)

an answer to the complaint which is herewith served upon you, within _____ days after service of this summons upon you, exclusive of the day of service. If you fail to do so, judgment by default will be taken against you for the relief demanded in the complaint.

CLERK _____   DATE _____

BY DEPUTY CLERK _____

FIGURE 6-3
Sample summons

JS 44
(Rev. 07/89)

CIVIL COVER SHEET

The JS-44 civil cover sheet and the information contained herein neither replace nor supplement the filing and service of pleadings or other papers as required by law, except as provided by local rules of court. This form, approved by the Judicial Conference of the United States in September 1974, is required for the use of the Clerk of Court for the purpose of initiating the civil docket sheet. **(SEE INSTRUCTIONS ON THE REVERSE OF THE FORM.)**

I (a) PLAINTIFFS

DEFENDANTS

(b) COUNTY OF RESIDENCE OF FIRST LISTED PLAINTIFF _____
(EXCEPT IN U.S. PLAINTIFF CASES)

COUNTY OF RESIDENCE OF FIRST LISTED DEFENDANT _____
(IN U.S. PLAINTIFF CASES ONLY)
NOTE: IN LAND CONDEMNATION CASES, USE THE LOCATION OF THE
TRACT OF LAND INVOLVED

(c) ATTORNEYS (FIRM NAME, ADDRESS, AND TELEPHONE NUMBER)

ATTORNEYS (IF KNOWN)

II. BASIS OF JURISDICTION *(PLACE AN × IN ONE BOX ONLY)*

☐ 1 U.S. Government
Plaintiff

☐ 2 U.S. Government
Defendant

☐ 3 Federal Question
(U.S. Government Not a Party)

☐ 4 Diversity
(Indicate Citizenship of
Parties in Item III)

III. CITIZENSHIP OF PRINCIPAL PARTIES *(PLACE AN × IN ONE BOX FOR PLAINTIFF AND ONE BOX FOR DEFENDANT)*
(For Diversity Cases Only)

	PTF	DEF		PTF	DEF
Citizen of This State	☐ 1	☐ 1	Incorporated or Principal Place of Business in This State	☐ 4	☐ 4
Citizen of Another State	☐ 2	☐ 2	Incorporated and Principal Place of Business in Another State	☐ 5	☐ 5
Citizen or Subject of a Foreign Country	☐ 3	☐ 3	Foreign Nation	☐ 6	☐ 6

IV. CAUSE OF ACTION *(CITE THE U.S. CIVIL STATUTE UNDER WHICH YOU ARE FILING AND WRITE A BRIEF STATEMENT OF CAUSE.*

DO NOT CITE JURISDICTIONAL STATUTES UNLESS DIVERSITY.)

V. NATURE OF SUIT *(PLACE AN × IN ONE BOX ONLY)*

CONTRACT	TORTS		FORFEITURE/PENALTY	BANKRUPTCY	OTHER STATUTES
☐ 110 Insurance ☐ 120 Marine ☐ 130 Miller Act ☐ 140 Negotiable Instrument ☐ 150 Recovery of Overpayment & Enforcement of Judgment ☐ 151 Medicare Act ☐ 152 Recovery of Defaulted Student Loans (Excl. Veterans) ☐ 153 Recovery of Overpayment of Veteran's Benefits ☐ 160 Stockholders' Suits ☐ 190 Other Contract ☐ 195 Contract Product Liability	**PERSONAL INJURY** ☐ 310 Airplane ☐ 315 Airplane Product Liability ☐ 320 Assault, Libel & Slander ☐ 330 Federal Employers' Liability ☐ 340 Marine ☐ 345 Marine Product Liability ☐ 350 Motor Vehicle ☐ 355 Motor Vehicle Product Liability ☐ 360 Other Personal Injury	**PERSONAL INJURY** ☐ 362 Personal Injury— Med Malpractice ☐ 365 Personal Injury— Product Liability ☐ 368 Asbestos Personal Injury Product Liability **PERSONAL PROPERTY** ☐ 370 Other Fraud ☐ 371 Truth in Lending ☐ 380 Other Personal Property Damage ☐ 385 Property Damage Product Liability	☐ 610 Agriculture ☐ 620 Other Food & Drug ☐ 625 Drug Related Seizure of Property 21 USC 881 ☐ 630 Liquor Laws ☐ 640 R.R & Truck ☐ 650 Airline Regs ☐ 660 Occupational Safety/Health ☐ 690 Other **LABOR** ☐ 710 Fair Labor Standards Act ☐ 720 Labor/Mgmt. Relations ☐ 730 Labor/Mgmt. Reporting & Disclosure Act ☐ 740 Railway Labor Act ☐ 790 Other Labor Litigation ☐ 791 Empl. Ret. Inc. Security Act	☐ 422 Appeal 28 USC 158 ☐ 423 Withdrawal 28 USC 157 **PROPERTY RIGHTS** ☐ 820 Copyrights ☐ 830 Patent ☐ 840 Trademark **SOCIAL SECURITY** ☐ 861 HIA (1395ff) ☐ 862 Black Lung (923) ☐ 863 DIWC/DIWW (405(g)) ☐ 864 SSID Title XVI ☐ 865 RSI (405(g)) **FEDERAL TAX SUITS** ☐ 870 Taxes (U.S. Plaintiff or Defendant) ☐ 871 IRS—Third Party 26 USC 7609	☐ 400 State Reapportionment ☐ 410 Antitrust ☐ 430 Banks and Banking ☐ 450 Commerce/ICC Rates/etc. ☐ 460 Deportation ☐ 470 Racketeer Influenced and Corrupt Organizations ☐ 810 Selective Service ☐ 850 Securities/Commodities/ Exchange ☐ 875 Customer Challenge 12 USC 3410 ☐ 891 Agricultural Acts ☐ 892 Economic Stabilization Act ☐ 893 Environmental Matters ☐ 894 Energy Allocation Act ☐ 895 Freedom of Information Act ☐ 900 Appeal of Fee Determination Under Equal Access to Justice ☐ 950 Constitutionality of State Statutes ☐ 890 Other Statutory Actions
REAL PROPERTY ☐ 210 Land Condemnation ☐ 220 Foreclosure ☐ 230 Rent Lease & Ejectment ☐ 240 Torts to Land ☐ 245 Tort Product Liability ☐ 290 All Other Real Property	**CIVIL RIGHTS** ☐ 441 Voting ☐ 442 Employment ☐ 443 Housing/ Accommodations ☐ 444 Welfare ☐ 440 Other Civil Rights	**PRISONER PETITIONS** ☐ 510 Motions to Vacate Sentence Habeas Corpus: ☐ 530 General ☐ 535 Death Penalty ☐ 540 Mandamus & Other ☐ 550 Other			

VI. ORIGIN *(PLACE AN × IN ONE BOX ONLY)*

☐ 1 Original
Proceeding

☐ 2 Removed from
State Court

☐ 3 Remanded from
Appellate Court

☐ 4 Reinstated or
Reopened

Transferred from
☐ 5 another district
(specify)

☐ 6 Multidistrict
Litigation

Appeal to District
☐ 7 Judge from
Magistrate
Judgment

VII. REQUESTED IN COMPLAINT:

CHECK IF THIS IS A **CLASS ACTION**
☐ UNDER F.R.C.P. 23

DEMAND $

Check YES only if demanded in complaint:
JURY DEMAND: ☐ YES ☐ NO

VIII. RELATED CASE(S) IF ANY *(See instructions):*

JUDGE _____ DOCKET NUMBER_____

DATE

SIGNATURE OF ATTORNEY OF RECORD

UNITED STATES DISTRICT COURT

FIGURE 6-4
Sample civil cover sheet

INSTRUCTIONS FOR ATTORNEYS COMPLETING CIVIL COVER SHEET FORM JS-44

Authority For Civil Cover Sheet

The JS-44 civil cover sheet and the information contained herein neither replaces nor supplements the filings and service of pleading or other papers as required by law, except as provided by local rules of court. This form, approved by the Judicial Conference of the United States in September 1974, is required for the use of the Clerk of Court for the purpose of initiating the civil docket sheet. Consequently a civil cover sheet is submitted to the Clerk of Court for each civil complaint filed. The attorney filing a case should complete the form as follows:

I. (a) Plaintiffs - Defendants. Enter names (last, first, middle initial) of plaintiff and defendant. If the plaintiff or defendant is a government agency, use only the full name or standard abbreviations. If the plaintiff or defendant is an official within a government agency, identify first the agency and then the official, giving both name and title.

(b) County of Residence. For each civil case filed, except U.S. plaintiff cases, enter the name of the county where the first listed plaintiff resides at the time of filing. In U.S. plaintiff cases, enter the name of the county in which the first listed defendant resides at the time of filing. (NOTE: In land condemnation cases, the county of residence of the "defendant" is the location of the tract of land involved).

(c) Attorneys. Enter firm name, address, telephone number, and attorney or record. If there are several attorneys, list them on an attachment, noting in this section "(see attachment)".

II. Jurisdiction. The basis of jurisdiction is set forth under Rule 8 (a), F.R.C.P., which requires that jurisdictions be shown in pleadings. Place an "X" in one of the boxes. If there is more than one basis of jurisdiction, precedence is given in the order shown below.

United States plaintiff. (1) Jurisdiction is based on 28 U.S.C. 1345 and 1348. Suits by agencies and officers of the United States are included here.

United States defendant. (2) When the plaintiff is suing the United States, its officers or agencies, place an X in this box.

Federal question. (3) This refers to suits under 28 U.S.C. 1331, where jurisdiction arises under the Constitution of the United States, an amendment to the Constitution, an act of Congress or a treaty of the United States. In cases where the U.S. is a party, the U.S. plaintiff or defendant code takes precedence, and box 1 or 2 should be marked.

Diversity of citizenship. (4) This refers to suits under 28 U.S.C. 1332, where parties are citizens of different states. When Box 4 is checked, the citizenship of the different parties must be checked. (See Section III below; federal question actions take precedence over diversity cases.)

III. Residence (citizenship) of Principal Parties. This section of the JS-44 is to be completed if diversity of citizenship was indicated above. Mark this section for each principal party.

IV. Cause of Action. Report the civil statute directly related to the cause of action and give a brief description of the cause.

V. Nature of Suit. Place an "X" in the appropriate box. If the nature of suit cannot be determined, be sure the cause of action, in Section IV above, is sufficient to enable the deputy clerk or the statistical clerks in the Administrative Office to determine the nature of suit. If the cause fits more than one nature of suit, select the most definitive.

VI. Origin. Place an "X" in one of the seven boxes.

Original Proceedings. (1) Cases which originate in the United States district courts.

Removed from State Court. (2) Proceedings initiated in state courts may be removed to the district courts under Title 28 U.S.C., Section 1441. When the petition for removal is granted, check this box.

Remanded from Appellate Court. (3) Check this box for cases remanded to the district court for further action. Use the date of remand as the filing date.

Reinstated or Reopened. (4) Check this box for cases reinstated or reopened in the district court. Use the reopening date as the filing date.

Transferred from Another District. (5) For cases transferred under Title 28 U.S.C. Section 1404(a). Do not use this for within district transfers or multidistrict litigation transfers.

Multidistrict Litigation. (6) Check this box when a multidistrict case is transferred into the district under authority of Title 28 U.S.C. Section 1407. When this box is checked, do not check (5) above.

Appeal to District Judge from Magistrate Judgment. (7) Check this box for an appeal from a magistrate's decision.

VII. Requested in Complaint. Class Action. Place an "X" in this box if you are filing a class action under Rule 23, F.R.Cv.P.

Demand. In this space enter the dollar amount (in thousands of dollars) being demanded or indicate other demand such as a preliminary injunction.

Jury Demand. Check the appropriate box to indicate whether or not a jury is being demanded.

VIII. Related Cases. This section of the JS-44 is used to reference relating pending cases if any. If there are related pending cases, insert the docket numbers and the corresponding judge names for such cases.

Date and Attorney Signature. Date and sign the civil cover sheet.

(rev. 07/89)   ★ U.S.GPO:1991-0-685-359/79002

FIGURE 6-4
(Continued)

1. This court has original jurisdiction under 28 U.S.C. § 1338(a) in that this action arises under the copyright laws of the United States, 17 U.S.C. § 101 *et seq.*

Venue.   Because the case may be filed where the defendant resides, venue is commonly established by stating the location of the defendant. Although not required, the complaint usually states the citizenship or location of the plaintiff.

2. Plaintiff is informed and believes that defendant Golden Egg Museum Gift Shop, Inc., is a corporation organized under the laws of the State of California, having its principal place of business in San Francisco, California.

3. Plaintiff K.R. Bickwhite is a resident of the City and County of San Francisco, California, and a citizen of the United States.

Establishing Plaintiff's Ownership of the Work.   The plaintiff must establish that he or she owns the work, either as a result of creation or transfer. The plaintiff also must demonstrate that the work has been registered.

4. Plaintiff is the creator and owner of an original photographic visual arts work entitled "Trout Ecstasy," that contains copyrightable subject matter under the laws of the United States.

5. Plaintiff complied in all respects with the copyright act, 17 U.S.C. *et seq.,* and all other laws governing copyright and secured the exclusive rights and privileges in copyright to the "Trout Ecstasy" visual arts image and received from the Register of Copyrights a certificate of registration, dated and identified as follows: January 12, 1991, Class:VA No. 657-980. A copy of the certificate of registration is attached to this Complaint as Exhibit A and is incorporated in this Complaint by reference.

6. "Trout Ecstasy" was first published with notice under plaintiff's authorization in February 1991, in *Back to Nature* Magazine. A copy of the publication is attached as Exhibit B and incorporated by reference in this Complaint.

7. Plaintiff has been and still is the sole proprietor of all rights, title, and interest in and to the copyright in "Trout Ecstasy."

Establishing the Infringement.   As succinctly as possible, the plaintiff should attempt to establish the basis of the infringement.

8. In February 1991, defendant infringed the copyright in "Trout Ecstasy" by publishing and selling a postcard containing a substantially similar visual arts image entitled, "Fish Delirium," which plaintiff is informed and believes was copied from "Trout Ecstasy." A copy of defendant's work is attached to this complaint as Exhibit C and incorporated by reference in this Complaint.

9. Plaintiff has notified defendant that defendant has infringed the "Trout Ecstasy" copyright of plaintiff and defendant has continued to infringe the copyright.

The Prayer.   The *prayer* is at the end of the complaint. It is the formal request for remedies provided under law (i.e., damages, injunctive relief, etc.).

Wherefore plaintiff demands that:

(1)   Defendant, its agents and servants be enjoined during the pendency of this action and permanently from infringing the "Trout Ecstasy" photograph in any manner and from publishing, selling, marketing, or otherwise disposing of copies of the work entitled "Fish Delirium."

(2)   Defendent be required to pay to plaintiff such damages as plaintiff has sustained in consequence of defendant's infringement of copyright and to account for all gains, profits, and advantages derived by defendant by its infringement or such damages as to the court shall appear proper within the provisions of the copyright statutes, but not less than $500.

(3)   Defendant be required to deliver up to be impounded during the pendency of this action all copies of the work entitled "Fish Delirium" in its possession or control and to deliver up for destruction all infringing copies, and all plates, molds, and other matter for making such infringing copies.

(4)   Defendant pay to plaintiff the costs of this action and reasonable attorney fees to be allowed to the plaintiff by the court.

(5)   Plaintiff have such other and further relief as is just.

Additional Claims

Not all copyright infringement suits are as simple as the situation involving the trout photographer. Often other claims are made besides copyright infringement. As explained in chapter 2, other claims, including nonfederal claims, may be brought along with the copyright claim, at the time of filing the complaint. For example, state claims may be brought under the principle of pendent jurisdiction, as explained in chapter 2. The complaint in figure 6-5 is an example of a lawsuit in which a programmer infringed copyright *and* also misappropriated trade secrets (confidential information that has a commercial value to its owner).

Declaratory Relief

Sometimes, after receiving a cease and desist letter, or after the breakdown of negotiations to settle a dispute, the alleged infringer may ask the federal courts for declaratory relief. This is not a claim for monetary damages, but instead a request that the court sort out the rights and obligations of the parties. For example, the computer company Softco claims that a competitor, Diskco, is infringing its new program. Diskco does not believe that its program is an infringement. However, Diskco is concerned that if it goes ahead with the sale of its program, Softco will later sue. Diskco also believes that Softco's copyright is invalid. Therefore, so that it can decide whether to release the program, Diskco may file a claim for declaratory relief. The party seeking declaratory relief need only establish that an actual controversy exists regarding a matter within federal court subject matter jurisdiction.

LAW OFFICES OF JOSEPH SMITH
One Embarcadero, Suite 1234
San Francisco, California 94111
(415) 555-1212

Attorneys for Plaintiff

IN THE UNITED STATES DISTRICT COURT
NORTHERN DISTRICT OF CALIFORNIA

SOFTCO, Inc,.,a California Corporation,	)))	No.
Plaintiff,	)))	COMPLAINT
v.	)))	
ROBERT PIRATE,	)))	
Defendant.	)))	

JURISDICTION

Jurisdiction is based upon the Copyright Act, 28 U.S. Code annotated Section 1338(a). Plaintiff is a valid California Corporation with its principal place of business in San Mateo County, California, within the Northern District of California. Defendant is an individual residing in San Francisco County within the Northern District of California.

FIRST CAUSE OF ACTION
(Copyright Infringement)

1. Plaintiff SOFTCO, INC. ("SOFTCO") is the creator and owner of an original software program, "$WORD," consisting of computer program source code. This source code was comprised of wholly original material.

2. On or about 27 June 1990, plaintiff secured exclusive rights and privileges on the copyright of the above entitled work and received from the Register of Copyrights a certificate of registration dated and identified as follows: $WORD, Registration No. TX 3 779 665, a true copy of which is attached to this Complaint and incorporated by reference.

3. Prior to and after the date the copyright was secured the above entitled work was published and distributed in compliance with the Copyright Act. At all times mentioned herein plaintiff has been and is the sole proprietor of all rights, title, and interest in and to the copyright in the above entitled work.

4. Defendant was hired by plaintiff in February of 1988 as a full-time computer software programmer. In June 1989, defendant left plaintiff's employ. Following defendant's departure, plaintiff determined that certain proprietary and valuable source code materials had been removed from plaintiff's computer storage system.

FIGURE 6-5
Sample complaint

5. Plaintiff is informed and believes that defendant has subsequently manufactured and sold $WORD to several parties, including sale through an electronic bulletin board service.

6. Plaintiff is informed and believes that it would require two programmers working six to twelve months to recreate the missing source code files. Plaintiff is informed and believes that the cost of recreating the missing source code files would be $150,000.

7. On or about December 1989 or January 1990 defendant infringed on plaintiff's copyright by copying on a disk, tape, or other medium the aforementioned source code and retained physical custody of such copy.

8. Plaintiff notified defendant that he had infringed upon said copyright and defendant has continued to infringe on said copyright.

9. Said acts were willful and malicious and were intended by defendant to cause harm to plaintiff in that said source code lacked commercial value to defendant and was of critical commercial significance to plaintiff, and was intended to impair the ability of plaintiff to maintain and support the source code.

10. As a proximate result of the acts alleged above, plaintiff has and will in the future incur replacement costs including, but not limited to, the cost of reconstructing the source code, in the approximate amount of $150,000.

11. As a further proximate result of the acts alleged above, and loss of the source code, plaintiff has and will in the future be unable to improve, upgrade, and create and sell enhancements of said software, which inability has and will in the future diminish, impair, and eventually destroy the marketability and commercial viability of said product, directly resulting in lost profits in the amount of $2,000,000.

WHEREFORE, plaintiff prays damages against defendant, as set forth.

SECOND CAUSE OF ACTION
(Uniform Trade Secrets Act)

Plaintiff alleges and incorporates herein each preceding paragraph of the complaint preceding as if set forth herein in full.

12. On or about December 1989, plaintiff was in possession of a trade secret, to wit, the source code for the $WORD software program. This code had an economic value in that it was an essential structural component of the software program that was for sale to the public. Plaintiff made reasonable efforts to ensure that the source code remain a secret, including but not limited to, strictly limiting access to employees of plaintiff who signed a confidentiality agreement or demonstrated a need to know such information.

13. On or about December 1989 and continuing until the present day, defendant misappropriated said trade secret by copying it from computer disk, tape, or other medium and removing it from the premises prior to the time he left plaintiff's employ.

14. As a proximate result of defendant's conduct plaintiff is no longer in possession of such code nor has access to it and has incurred and will in the future incur losses for the cost of replacement of the source code in the amount of $150,000.

15. As a further proximate result thereof plaintiff will suffer loss of use of the source code in the amount of $2,000,000.

FIGURE 6-5
(Continued)

16. Defendant's taking of said trade secret was willful and malicious and motivated by his pecuniary interest.

WHEREFORE, plaintiff prays damages against defendant, as follows:

ON THE FIRST AND SECOND CAUSES OF ACTION

1. Defendant be enjoined during the pendency of this action and thereafter from infringement on the copyright of plaintiff, and from selling, distributing, marketing, altering, destroying, using, copying, or disclosing the source code or any copies thereof;
2. Damages for replacement costs and lost profits in the amount of $2,150,000;
3. All gains or profits derived by defendant from his infringement;
4. Delivery of any copies of source code to plaintiff;
5. Punitive damages in the amount of $50,000;
6. Attorney fees and costs of suit; and
7. Any other relief the Court may deem proper.

DATED: _____

FIGURE 6-5
(Continued)

The Answer

A response to the copyright complaint must be received within 20 days of service. Unless the defendant attacks the complaint on procedural grounds (e.g., argues that service is improper or that the court has no jurisdiction), the proper response is an answer. The **answer** is a response to the complaint in which the defendant admits or denies the allegations and provides a list of defenses. The answer, like the complaint, includes a caption and is filed with the court.

In the answer, the defendent goes through each paragraph of the complaint and generally responds one of four ways:

1. *Defendant denies all allegations of the paragraph.* Example: In answer to Paragraph 16 of the Complaint, Defendant denies each and every allegation contained in that paragraph.
2. *Defendant admits all allegations of the paragraph.* Example: In answer to Paragraph 3 of the Complaint, Defendant admits each and every allegation contained in that paragraph.
3. *Defendant lacks information to form a response to a paragraph.* Example: In answer to Paragraph 5 of the Complaint, Defendant is without sufficient information or belief upon which to base an answer to the allegations of this paragraph and, based upon such lack of information and belief, denies each and every allegation in that paragraph.
4. *Defendant denies or admits part of a paragraph.* Example: In answer to Paragraph 7, Defendant admits it is the owner of a software product

named JETBOY. Except as expressly admitted, Defendant denies each and every remaining allegation of Paragraph 7.

In addition to responding to each allegation, the answer should provide a list of defenses. These defenses should each be listed separately. All that is necessary is that the basis for the defense be stated; no further elaboration is required. For example, if the defendant wished to offer the defense of unclean hands because the plaintiff had falsified a registration, the defense would be stated as follows:

First Affirmative Defense

Unclean Hands

Plaintiff is barred from obtaining relief on any of the claims alleged in the Complaint by its unclean hands in taking actions calculated to unfairly deceive the public by falsifying documents filed with the United States Copyright Office.

Counterclaims

If the defendant wishes to bring an action against the plaintiff, a counterclaim must be filed at the time the answer is filed. A **counterclaim** is a claim for relief usually asserted by the defendant against an opposing party, usually the plaintiff. For example, Diskco files a complaint against Softco claiming infringement of a program. Softco answers the complaint and files a counterclaim against Diskco for breach of contract. A counterclaim is compulsory (i.e., it *must* be brought) if the claim arises out of the transaction or occurrence that is the subject of the complaint. For example, consider the case of the trout photographer. After discovering the infringing postcards, the trout photographer physically attacked the owner of the gift shop. Then the photographer filed a complaint for copyright infringement. Because the physical attack arose out of the transaction or occurrence, the claim for personal injury against the photographer must be brought as a counterclaim.

Discovery

In every lawsuit, there is a procedure known as *discovery* during which the parties acquire facts and evidence relating to the case. There are specific rules regarding this process, and, if a dispute arises during the exchange of information, the federal district court will rule on the issues. The four common forms of discovery are interrogatories, production of documents, depositions, and requests for admissions. The Federal Rules of Civil Procedure provide rules regarding discovery, such as the number and format of interrogatories. In addition, local court rules also may set rules regarding discovery procedures and formats.

Interrogatories

Interrogatories are written questions that must be answered under oath. They are usually presented in special formats and include definitions of certain terms. There is a time limit for responding to interrogatories, and the recipient should carefully calendar the response. Interrogatories are only exchanged among parties to the lawsuit (i.e., persons named in the caption of the complaint or counterclaim).

Requests for Admissions

A **request for admission** is a request for a party to the lawsuit to admit the truthfulness of a fact or statement. For example, the plaintiff may request that the defendant admit or deny that the defendant is a corporation. This request is submitted in writing, and, like an interrogatory, the response should be calendared. Requests for admissions are only exchanged among parties to the lawsuit.

Depositions

A **deposition** is oral or written testimony of a party or witness, given under oath. An attorney may depose any person who may have information relevant to the lawsuit. The deposition is noticed by the transmission of a *notice of deposition*. Questions are asked and answered in the presence of a court reporter. Afterward, a transcript of the deposition is provided to the parties. Documents may also be requested at the deposition. It is through this means that documents are obtained from nonparties to the lawsuit.

Production of Documents

A **request for production of documents** is a method by which a party to the lawsuit may obtain documents or other physical evidence. The request is written and delivered to the other party. The time for response should be calendared.

Motions

A **motion** is a request for an order of the court. For example, if the venue is inconvenient, one party may request an order for a change of venue. This would be done as a motion for change of venue. If a party objects to a discovery request, a motion to compel may be made, requesting an order requiring the party to respond. One of the most common motions made in copyright infringement lawsuits is the **motion for summary judgment.** This is a request that the court order a judgment without having a trial because there is no genuine issue as to any material facts. For example, if the defendant in the trout photo litigation admitted copying the plaintiff's work, there may not be an issue of triable fact. There is nothing for a jury to deliberate over because there is no dispute as to liability. Therefore, a judge may determine that a trial is not necessary. The party responding to the motion would attempt to prove that there is an issue of material fact in dispute. For example, in the trout case, the defendant may argue that even though the photo was copied, it is not substantially similar to the defendant's postcard. A motion for summary judgment is a means of ending the litigation. It requires extensive proof and documentation, including declarations under oath from witnesses and parties.

Expert Witnesses

Sometimes the nature of the work at issue in a copyright infringement lawsuit requires the opinions or testimony of persons who are experts. For example, in a case involving infringement of a computer program, it may be necessary to have testimony from a programmer who is an expert on a particular type of software code. Information about expert witnesses and the subject matter and substance of their expected testimony is discoverable prior to trial. Normally, interrogatories are propounded which inquire into each party's choice of expert witnesses. Sometimes, expert witnesses are deposed prior to the litigation.

Trial

Trial is the court hearing in which the parties present their facts and evidence to a judge or jury. It requires extensive preparation. Evidence must be indexed, witnesses must be identified and prepared, and case law must be researched. The Federal Rules of Civil Procedure and local rules must be carefully examined to determine rules regarding marking and admission of evidence. In addition, certain matters may require pretrial motions. For example, a party may wish to limit the admission of certain evidence prior to trial. In that case, a motion in limine would be filed. A **motion in limine** is a request made to the court, usually prior to trial, that certain information not be presented to the jury. In addition, any list of expert witnesses should be prepared and exchanged among the parties. Finally, assistance may be required in the preparation of **jury instructions**, explanations of the legal rules that the jury shall use in reaching a verdict. For example, a jury instruction may state that access to the plaintiff's work is a required element of copyright infringement. As a result of the final deliberation of the judge or jury, a judgment will be issued. A **judgment** is the relief awarded by the court as the result of the judge or jury's verdict.

The Trial Notebook.   The paralegal assisting in a copyright infringement trial should utilize a *trial notebook,* a binder created to index and reference the important documentation necessary to litigate a case. Generally, the sections of a trial notebook include:

LEGAL TERMS

interrogatories
Written questions that must be answered under oath.

request for admission
Request for a party to the lawsuit to admit the truthfulness of a fact or statement.

deposition
Oral or written testimony of a party or witness, given under oath.

request for production of documents
Method by which a party to the lawsuit may obtain documents or other physical evidence.

motion
Request for an order of the court.

motion for summary judgment
Request that the court order a judgment without having a trial because there is no genuine issue as to any material facts.

motion in limine
Request made to the court, usually prior to trial, that certain information not be presented to the jury.

jury instructions
Explanations of the legal rules that the jury shall use in reaching a verdict.

judgment
Relief awarded by the court as the result of the judge or jury's verdict.

1. A directory of the parties and witnesses, including names, addresses, and telephone numbers with important notations. This should be maintained on a computer database and periodically reprinted as it is updated.

2. A listing of the litigation files and their contents. Each file should have a cover sheet listing its contents. These cover sheets should be reproduced and kept in the binder so that the paralegal can easily locate the document.

3. Either a copy of pleadings and motions, or at least a listing of such filings and their location in the litigation files.

4. A chronology of events and filings, including all events from creation of the work to the present.

5. Listings of all witnesses for each party. A separate portion should be devoted to expert witnesses.

6. Summaries of relevant discovery. If there is room, all deposition summaries should be included; if not, indexes of where the summaries are located should be provided.

7. Relevant legal research, either included or indexed.

8. Trial notes or plans, task lists, and attorney notes (in separate sections).

Appeal

Both parties may appeal the final determination of the trial court to the U.S. Court of Appeal in the appropriate circuit. Both sides submit appellate briefs. A three-member panel of judges will review the trial court record to determine if a legal error occurred. An example of a legal error is a judge's not permitting the introduction of evidence relevant to the case. An appellate court ruling requires a majority determination of the three judges. If the parties are not satisfied with the court of appeal's determination, an appeal may be sought by the U.S. Supreme Court. However, unlike the court of appeal, the U.S. Supreme Court determines which cases it will hear. If the U.S. Supreme Court refuses to hear the case, the determination of the court of appeal is the final determination in the case.

Litigation Checklists

The following checklists are for plaintiffs and defendants involved in a copyright infringement lawsuit.

Copyright Infringement Dispute: Plaintiff's Checklist

■ **Interview the client.**
  The following information should be obtained:
  ☐ The copyright owner's name, address, and business form (i.e., corporation, partnership, etc.).
  ☐ Information about all registrations or transfers regarding the work (i.e., the chain of title).

☐ Registration number. If registration has not been filed (or if registration has been filed but has not yet issued), or a transfer has not been filed, proceed with filing and consider expedited registration process. (Note that separate special handling fees apply for transfer documents and recordation.)

☐ Information about the copyright owner's publication and use of notice.

☐ Extent of distribution of the work (i.e., how widely has it been disseminated?).

☐ The owner's knowledge and discovery of the infringement.

■ **Acquire evidence of the infringement.** It is extremely difficult to make a case for copyright infringement without direct proof of the infringing activity.

☐ Purchase the infringing merchandise or witness the infringing activity and pay for infringing merchandise with check or credit card (the returned canceled check or credit card statement may provide more information about the name of the infringing business or the location of its bank account).

☐ Trace the chain of distribution of infringing merchandise (locate manufacturer, distributor, and retailers of infringing merchandise, as this may lead to other defendants).

☐ Review dates of infringement and compare with statute of limitations.

■ **Obtain information about all infringing parties.** The copyright owner should have researched the infringement to determine the names of the infringing parties.

☐ Determine name, address, and business form of all infringing parties (databases such as LEXIS®, Compuserve®, Dialog®, or Westlaw® may provide information regarding business form (i.e., corporation or partnership), and agent for service).

☐ Set up computer index (directory of all persons involved in litigation, facts, relationships and caselaw).

☐ Investigate whether the infringing party has been sued for copyright infringement previously.

☐ If the client can afford copyright search, order search regarding work.

■ **Review legal claims and possible defenses regarding infringement.** An infringer should not be confronted without first reviewing all possible claims and defenses. Untimely contact may tip off the infringer and result in the destruction of evidence. In the case of mobile infringers, such as t-shirt vendors, it may result in relocation. In addition, a confrontation may become heated and emotional, possibly leading to hostility resulting in additional causes of action. For example, a copyright owner might improperly take infringing materials, assault a vendor, or slander the infringer.

☐ Determine if additional claims, such as trade secrecy, trademark, or other contract, tort, or related claims can be made as a result of the infringing activity.

☐ List *all* possible copyright and equitable defenses and review the list with the client.

- ☐ Perform legal research and review caselaw and statutes regarding infringement issues. Consider special rules applying to specific works (e.g., no performance rights in sound recordings).

- ■ **Confront the infringer: Prepare cease and desist letter.** As explained earlier in this chapter, the cease and desist letter is a summary of the copyright owner's claims and a request that the recipient of the letter halt all infringing activity.

  - ☐ Consider whether a cease and desist letter will trigger destruction of evidence or the liquidation or transfer of assets. If so, proceed with an ex parte temporary restraining order or consider filing suit and securing a writ of seizure.

  - ☐ Consider whether the cease and desist letter will trigger a declaratory action. Discuss with the client.

- ■ **Attempt settlement of the dispute.** A settlement is a written agreement in which the parties formally resolve the infringement dispute.

  - ☐ Determine sums that will compensate the plaintiff for all damages (including attorney fees and related costs).

  - ☐ Review state law regarding required language for settlement agreements.

  - ☐ Consider what nonmonetary remedies are sought (i.e., does the plaintiff want the infringing merchandise?).

- ■ **Consider alternative dispute resolution.** If the parties cannot resolve their dispute among themselves, it is still possible to avoid litigation if the parties agree to alternative dispute resolution (also known as ADR), such as mediation or arbitration.

  - ☐ Is there an agreement between the parties compelling arbitration or mediation?

  - ☐ Will both parties submit to mediation or arbitration? If so, where?

  - ☐ Locate arbitration or mediation rules and procedures from arbitrating entity (e.g., American Arbitration Association).

- ■ **Filing the lawsuit.**

  - ☐ Review the Federal Rules of Civil Procedure and obtain local court rules.

  - ☐ Obtain a civil cover sheet and summons from the federal clerk.

  - ☐ Determine venue.

  - ☐ Assist in preparation of complaint.

  - ☐ Arrange for filing of complaint and issuance of summons.

  - ☐ Coordinate service of process.

- ■ **Discovery.** Coordination of discovery requires preparation of a discovery plan. Many attorneys begin the procedure with interrogatories to determine the names and addresses of relevant parties. This is often followed by depositions and requests for production of documents. Finally, requests for admissions are used to confirm or deny relevant information.

  - ☐ Calendar all discovery received and propounded for appropriate deadlines.

  - ☐ Summarize and index depositions, interrogatory responses, and documents for use at trial.

■ **Trial.**
- ☐ Prepare lists of witnesses (and expert witnesses).
- ☐ Review evidence regarding pretrial motions (e.g., motions in limine).
- ☐ Prepare trial notebook.
- ☐ Assist in preparation of jury instructions.

Copyright Infringement Dispute: Defendant's Checklist

■ **Interview the client.**
The following information should be obtained:
- ☐ The defendant's name, address, and business form (i.e., corporation, partnership, etc.).
- ☐ Information about all registrations or transfers regarding the work (i.e., the chain of title) for the defendant's work.
- ☐ Consider if registration should be made for the defendant's work.
- ☐ Information about the defendant's distribution of the work (i.e., how widely has it been disseminated?).
- ☐ The defendant's knowledge of the infringement and intent.
- ☐ The defendant's access to the plaintiff's work.
- ☐ Does the defendant have insurance that covers this type of dispute?

■ **Review the plaintiff's work and title to the work.**
- ☐ Review dates of infringement and compare with statute of limitations.
- ☐ Perform copyright search for the plaintiff's work regarding any questions of ownership.
- ☐ Acquire copies of the work and examine for notice and other issues of formality.

■ **Obtain information about all parties.**
- ☐ Determine name, address, and business form of all possible parties to lawsuit, including other potential defendants (databases such as LEXIS® CompuServe®, Dialog®, or Westlaw® may provide information regarding business form (i.e., corporation or partnership), and agent for service).
- ☐ Set up computer index (directory of all persons involved in litigation, facts, relationships, and caselaw).

■ **Review legal claims and possible defenses regarding infringement.**
- ☐ List *all* possible copyright and equitable defenses and review the list with the client.
- ☐ Perform legal research and review caselaw and statutes regarding infringement issues. Consider special rules applying to specific works (e.g., no performance rights in sound recordings).
- ☐ Are there any counterclaims that the defendant may wish to file?

■ **Responding to cease and desist letter.**
- ☐ Review and respond to accuracy of the allegations in the letter.
- ☐ Consider whether the defendant should cease activity pending resolution of the dispute.

□ Consider whether the defendant should file an action for declaratory relief.

■ **Attempt settlement of the dispute.** A settlement is a written agreement in which the parties formally resolve the infringement dispute. An example of a settlement is provided in figure 6-2.

■ **Consider alternative dispute resolution.**

□ Is there an agreement between the parties compelling arbitration or mediation?

□ Will both parties submit to mediation or arbitration?

■ **Responding to the Complaint.**

□ Calendar response—20 days from service.

□ Review the Federal Rules of Civil Procedure and obtain local court rules.

□ Determine whether venue or jurisdiction is improper.

□ Assist in preparation of the answer.

□ If appropriate, prepare a counterclaim.

■ **Discovery.** Coordination of discovery requires preparation of a discovery plan. Many attorneys begin the procedure with interrogatories to determine the names and addresses of relevant parties. This is often followed by depositions and requests for production of documents. Finally, requests for admissions are used to confirm or deny relevant information.

□ Calendar all discovery received and propounded for appropriate deadlines.

□ Summarize and index depositions, interrogatory responses, and documents for use at trial.

■ **Trial.**

□ Prepare lists of witnesses (and expert witnesses).

□ Review evidence regarding pretrial motions (e.g., motions in limine).

□ Prepare trial notebook.

□ Assist in preparation of jury instructions.

SUMMARY

6.1 Infringement is the unauthorized use of a work protected by copyright law. Infringement occurs when a party with access to a work copies it or interferes with a right granted under copyright law. Copying is proven by introducing evidence that the defendant had access to the copyrighted work and that the defendant's work is substantially similar to the plaintiff's work. Access means that the defendant had the reasonable opportunity to view or hear the copyrighted work. Substantial similarity means that the works have similarities that can result only from copying, rather than from coincidence, common source derivation, or independent creation. The copyright registration establishes prima facie proof of ownership and creates a presumption of copyright validity. One of the most common standards is the *lay observer* test. First, the court analyzes the specific list of literal and nonliteral similarities. After that, the court asks, "Would the ordinary observer, when examining both works, consider that the defendant has misappropriated the plaintiff's work?"

6.2 When reviewing an infringement situation, the plaintiff must identify the parties who are legally culpable for the infringing acts. These parties will become the defendants in the action. The intent of the person performing the infringing acts is irrelevant for determining whether an infringement occurred. A contributory infringer, also known as a *vicarious infringer,* is one who, with knowledge or reason to know of infringing activity of another, induces, causes, or materially contributes to the infringement; or one who has the right and ability to supervise the infringing activities and also has a direct financial interest in such activities.

6.3 Determining the defenses to a copyright infringement claim requires a review of the two works. Is the plaintiff's work copyrightable? Is the infringement excused by a statutory exception such as fair use? Has the plaintiff properly followed all formalities? Are any common law or equitable defenses, such as estoppel, laches, unclean hands, or the statute of limitations, available?

6.4 The plaintiff may seek damages as a remedy to compensate for any losses attributable to the infringement. If registration has been made in a timely fashion, the plaintiff may seek statutory damages rather than actual damages. The plaintiff may also seek to enjoin the defendant from any further infringing acts by requesting a preliminary or permanent injunction. At any time during the litigation, the court may order the impounding of all infringing copies or phonorecords, as well as the articles used to manufacture these copies. These copies may be destroyed upon court order following the verdict. In certain cases of copyright infringement, the infringer may be prosecuted for criminal violations of copyright law.

6.5 It is in the best interest of all parties to conclude any infringement disputes equitably and quickly. The cease and desist letter informs the infringing party of the validity and ownership of the copyrighted work, the nature of the infringement, and the remedies available to the copyright owner. Most importantly, it requests the immediate cessation of all infringing activity and demands an accounting for all acts of infringement. Instead of resolving a dispute in a courtroom, some people agree to have their problem settled privately through informal procedures known as arbitration or mediation. The parties may settle the case at any point prior to the final determination of the judge or jury. A settlement is an agreement between the parties in which the dispute is formally resolved.

6.6 After a decision is made as to which parties shall be named as defendants, determinations must be made as to jurisdiction, which is the right of a court to hear a certain case, and venue, which is the geographic location of the court. Then a complaint is drafted, stating the basis for the lawsuit, and served on each defendant. The defendant has a certain time period to respond to the complaint. After the defendant answers the complaint, a process of discovery begins, during which time the parties, following legal rules, investigate the merits and defenses of the case. Each party may request orders from the court. These requests are known as motions. Finally, a trial will be held and a determination will be made as to liability. A judgment will be issued by the court. If either party is dissatisfied with the result of the trial, an appeal may be made. Alternatively, the parties may, at any point, agree to settle the matter. In that event, the case is dismissed.

NOTES

1. 17 U.S.C. § 501 (infringement of copyright).
2. 17 U.S.C. § 410 (c) (registration as basis for presumption of validity).
3. Salinger v. Random House, 811 F.2d 90 (2d Cir. 1987).
4. 17 U.S.C. § 502 (injunctions).
5. 17 U.S.C. § 504 (damages and profits).
6. 17 U.S.C. § 503 (impoundment of infringing articles).
7. 17 U.S.C. § 505 (attorney fees).
8. 17 U.S.C. § 506 (criminal offenses).
9. 28 U.S.C. § 1338(a) (district court jurisdiction).
10. 17 U.S.C. § 1400 (district court venue).

QUESTIONS FOR REVIEW AND DISCUSSION

1. How does a copyright owner prove ownership of a copyrighted work?
2. What are ways of proving that an infringer had access to a copyrighted work?
3. What is the difference between a literal similarity and a nonliteral similarity?
4. Does paraphrasing a work shield the user of the work from an infringement claim?
5. What are the key elements in determining whether a person is a contributory infringer?
6. What are some examples of similarities between works that do not amount to substantial similarity?
7. How many years does the copyright owner have to bring an infringement lawsuit?
8. What are the elements necessary to obtain a preliminary injunction against a defendant?
9. On what basis can a plaintiff claim statutory damages for copyright infringement?

10. Under what circumstances can a copyright infringer be criminally prosecuted?
11. What are the elements of a cease and desist letter?
12. How is venue determined for a copyright infringement lawsuit?
13. What forms of discovery may be used on nonparties to the lawsuit?

ACTIVITIES

1. Review the Commentary regarding the trout photographer and draft questions to be asked by the plaintiff's and defendant's attorneys at the initial client interviews.
2. The defendant in the trout photograph lawsuit does not understand why she is being sued. She thought that anyone was free to paint a picture of a trout and sell it. Your supervising attorney asks you to prepare a brief explanation in response to the client's query.
3. Your office represents the plaintiff in the trout photography case. Your supervising attorney would like to establish that there are many ways that a trout can be depicted in nature photographs and paintings. She asks you to find expert witnesses who are knowledgeable in this field. Describe how you might obtain such information.

PROJECT

For this project, the class should split into two law offices, one representing Softco and the other representing Diskco. Softco, a California corporation, has recently released a computer game, *Snake City.* The object of the game is for the player to prevent giant animated snakes from controlling a nuclear plant in an imaginary East Coast city. One week after announcing the release of *Snake City,* Softco receives a cease and desist letter from Diskco. Diskco is the owner of a program, *Reptile Rumble,* in which the user attempts to prevent giant reptiles from taking over the water supply in a small mining town. Diskco has been manufacturing and selling *Reptile Rumble* for more than three years. First consider issues regarding jurisdiction and venue, that is, where to file the lawsuit. Then the students representing Diskco should draft a cease and desist letter. The students representing Softco should prepare an appropriate response.

CHAPTER 7
Trade Secrets

*He'd suck my brains, memorize my Rolodex, and use my telephone
to find some other guy who'd pay him twice the money.*

Ned Dewey (1986)

COMMENTARY

A toy manufacturer, Kidco, is preparing to release a children's toy called Webosaurus. *The toy is a fanciful creature like a dinosaur with two webbed legs that appear only when it is placed in water. Although Kidco has not yet offered the toy for sale, Dave, Kidco's top engineer, gives a speech to a convention of engineers about the water-triggered device used in the new toy. Kidco is in the midst of moving its facilities and a lot of the information about the new toy has been left in an open storage room in cardboard boxes. The president of Kidco is concerned that competitors will learn of the appearance, design, or marketing plans for the toy before its release. He seeks advice regarding the legal measures necessary to protect the secrecy of the toy.*

OBJECTIVES

The preceding chapters introduced you to principles of copyright protection. Trade secret law deals with the management and protection of confidential information. After reading this chapter, you will be able to:

- Distinguish between trade secret protection and copyright and patent protection.
- Identify examples of trade secrets.
- Locate the sources of trade secret law.
- Explain reverse engineering.
- Assist in the drafting of a confidentiality agreement.
- Discuss the principles of clean room research.
- Identify a covenant not to compete.
- Discuss the limitations on protecting customer lists.

- Know the principles of protecting trade secrets during litigation.
- Review a company's trade secret precautions.

7.1 WHAT IS PROTECTIBLE AS A TRADE SECRET?

According to legend, the *Coca-Cola* formula is locked inside a safe in Atlanta, Georgia, and only a handful of company employees, sworn to secrecy, have access. The Coca-Cola company believes that the formula is a trade secret and that if it were made available to the public, an advantage would be lost over competitors. A **trade secret** is defined as any formula, pattern, device, or compilation of information which is used in one's business that is treated with confidentiality and which gives the owner of the secret an opportunity to obtain an advantage over competitors who do not know or use it. To maintain ownership rights over a trade secret, the owner must treat the information with secrecy. It can only be disclosed to a person who agrees to maintain confidentiality. Any public disclosure will end trade secret status. The material will no longer be considered a trade secret and anyone is free to use it.

Genentech, Inc.
Genentech, Inc.
Genentech, Inc.
Genentech, Inc.
Genentech, Inc.

Genentech is a biotechnology firm whose products are very competitive. Trade secret laws protect the manufacturing of these products.

The owner of a copyright or a patent makes money from the publication and distribution of the copyrighted or patented material. In contrast, the owner of a trade secret makes money because the trade secret is *not* published or publicly distributed. Unlike other forms of proprietary rights, the secretive nature of trade secrets makes them unsuitable for public registration. With the exception of certain computer software and secure tests, a registered trade secret is no longer a "secret." Therefore, many companies use trade secret law to protect copyrightable or patentable material prior to registration or patent issuance. In addition, trade secrets are an important proprietary right, because they may be used to protect unpublished materials that may not qualify for copyright or patent protection.

The underlying principle of trade secret law is to encourage development and competition. The legal protection of confidential material creates an incentive for a business to invest in development and research. Because of trade secret law, a business can have some security in the knowledge that the unlawful misappropriation of confidential research will be punished and damages recovered. The protection of trade secrets helps to maintain an ethical standard for business competition. In addition to civil damages, some states have enacted penal code provisions establishing criminal sanctions for misappropriation. These statutes usually involve theft or fraud in the procurement of trade secrets.

State Statutes and Contract Law

Under certain circumstances, the theft of trade secrets may violate federal statutes. Generally, however, civil litigation regarding trade secrets is primarily determined under state law. Unlike copyright, patents and trademarks, there are no federal trade secret statutes. State law protects trade secrets in two ways. First, there are state laws prohibiting the misappropriation of trade secrets. **Misappropriation** is the improper acquisition of a trade secret by a person who has reason to know that the trade secret was obtained by improper means or the disclosure, or use of a trade secret without consent by a person who either had a duty to maintain secrecy or who used improper means to acquire the secret.

For example, in the Commentary to this chapter, the president of Kidco is concerned about competitors learning of his new toy, *Webosaurus,* before it is released. If someone were to bribe an employee or to break into Kidco for the secrets, this would constitute misappropriation. Under state trade secret law, the company could recover damages from the party using the improper means to get the secret.

Trade secrets are also protected under principles of state contract law. To prevent disclosure of a trade secret, a company may require a party to enter into a contract that is called (or includes) a **confidentiality** or **nondisclosure agreement.** For example, in the Commentary to this chapter, Kidco should enter into nondisclosure agreements with all employees, consultants, and independent contractors (e.g., advertising agencies, manufacturing plants). If any party then disclosed the secret material, Kidco would be able to sue for breach of the agreement. If Kidco prevailed, the company could recover all damages proximately caused by the employee's disclosure.

Sources of State Trade Secret Law

Trade secret law is derived from the common law, state statutes, and the *Restatement of Torts.* The **common law** is a system of legal rules derived from the precedents and principles established by court decisions.

Most states have specific statutes that express the rights and remedies of the owner of a trade secret. Some of these state statutes are based upon the Uniform Trade Secrets Act, a model act created by lawyers, judges, and scholars to conform the rules of different states. Almost half of the states have adopted some variation on the Uniform Trade Secrets Act. In addition to the Uniform Trade Secrets Act, the *Restatement of Torts* is an advisory document that elaborates on common law principles of trade secret protection. Many states that have not adopted the Uniform Trade Secrets Act have adopted the *Restatement* as the basis for state trade secret law.

Uniform Trade Secrets Act

The Uniform Trade Secrets Act, created in 1979 and amended in 1985, is part of a program to conform various state laws. A copy of the Uniform Trade Secrets Act and a listing of the states that have adopted it appear in appendix E. The Uniform Trade Secrets Act is considered to be a modern reflection of trade secret law, and, in states where it has been adopted, the principles of the Uniform Trade Secrets Act control over previous common

LEGAL TERMS

trade secret
  Any formula, pattern, device, or compilation of information that is used in a business, that is the subject of reasonable efforts to preserve confidentiality, and that gives the owner of the secret an opportunity to obtain an advantage over competitors who do not know or use it.

misappropriation
  Improper acquisition of a trade secret by a person who has reason to know that the trade secret was obtained by improper means, or the disclosure or use of a trade secret without consent by a person who either had a duty to maintain secrecy or who used improper means to acquire the secret.

confidentiality agreement (also known as nondisclosure agreement)
  Contract that restricts the disclosure of trade secrets.

common law
  A system of legal rules derived from the precedents and principles established by court decisions.

law. The following is a definition of *trade secret* as provided in the Uniform Trade Secrets Act:

> A trade secret is information, including a formula, pattern, compilation, program, device, method, technique or process that:
>
> (i) derives independent economic value, actual or potential, from not being generally known to, and not being readily ascertainable by proper means by, other persons who can obtain economic value from its disclosure or use, and
>
> (ii) is the subject of efforts that are reasonable under the circumstances to maintain its secrecy.

The Restatement (Second) of Torts

The American Law Institute (ALI) is an organization comprised of judges, attorneys, and law professors. Its goal is to clarify and simplify legal principles. The ALI publishes "Restatements" of the law on different topics and, although these Restatements do not have the force of law, they are commonly cited by judges and attorneys. In 1939, the ALI published the *Restatement (Second) of Torts*. Sections 757 through 759 of the *Restatement* summarize the law regarding trade secrets. The ALI is in the process of completing an update of this study and revised chapters are expected to be out sometime in 1993. The *Restatements* are available in law libraries.

Examples of Trade Secrets

Consider the trade secrets at a software company such as Diskco. The sales department has trade secrets such as customer characteristics, marketing plans, and forecasts. The management department has business strategies and unpublished financial information. The engineering and development departments have computer programs, documentation, programming procedures, and test results.

A *trade secret* is any confidential information developed in the course of a business which gives the business an advantage over competitors who do not know or use it. A trade secret comes into existence when the party developing the secret determines to treat it with secrecy and takes all steps necessary to prevent disclosure of the secret. Although trade secret protection differs from state to state, the same fundamental principles establish and define a trade secret. All three of the following elements must be present:

1. The information is not generally known or ascertainable by proper means
2. The information has economic value
3. The owner of the secret must use reasonable efforts to maintain secrecy.

One test for determining if material may qualify as a trade secret is to ask whether the business would be damaged if a competitor acquired the information. For example, Susie, a magician, would be damaged if Bob, a competing magician, learned the secrets behind Susie's magic tricks. Provided that the material and the manner in which it is protected meet the criteria of state law, almost anything may qualify as a trade secret. Customer lists may qualify as trade secrets under certain circumstances. By way of example, the following are some items that courts have determined to be protectible under trade secret law:

- Marketing strategies for propane gas
- Manufacturing techniques for veterinary vaccines
- Process for manufacturing marble picture frames
- Procedures for mixing concrete
- Process for manufacturing chocolate powder
- Design for a photo processing machine
- Expiration dates and gross revenues from insurance policies.

Information Not Generally Known or Ascertainable

One requirement of a trade secret is that it not be generally known or ascertainable. This does not mean that the secret has to be unique or novel. A trade secret may be the compilation or organization of information. For example, a salesperson's detailed notes about the demographics and buying habits of customers may not involve creativity or invention, but it can be protected as a trade secret if it is not generally known or ascertainable (except by a person who industriously and independently gathers such information). Similarly, a company's development of an invention, a restaurant chef's creation of a recipe, or a manufacturer's business forecast for the next year could all qualify as information not generally known or ascertainable.

Commentary to the Uniform Trade Secrets Act indicates that information is *readily ascertainable* if it is available in trade journals, reference books, or published materials. For example, a chef develops a recipe for nectarine ice cream. However, the chef created the recipe by using a published recipe for peach ice cream and substituting a nectarine. Anyone is free to use the same peach recipe and make the same substitution. Similarly, if the magician David Copperfield, through research in books and documents, learns how to do a magic trick, he cannot claim trade secret infringement if a second person uncovers the same information through similar legitimate research.

Information Has Economic Value

Only material that provides a business with a competitive edge can properly be claimed as a trade secret. However, this standard of *economic value* is easy to prove. A business can usually demonstrate that information has economic value by proving the cost of developing or acquiring the information. The fact that a competitor has made attempts to acquire the information may also demonstrate the value. For example, a restaurant has developed a popular barbecue sauce which it uses on its foods and also sells in bottles. A competitor offers the restaurant $10,000 for the recipe. If the recipe were stolen, its value could be proven by the sales of the sauce, the success of the restaurant, and the $10,000 offer. The owner of the secret may prove economic value by demonstrating the profits attributable to the secret, the effectiveness of the marketing resulting from the secret, or the savings made by use of the confidential material.

It is rare for material to lose trade secret status because the information has no economic value. However, this can occur if the value of the trade secret has dissipated over time. For example, a method of writing software code for CP/M-style computers may have lost its value since the CP/M operating system has largely been superseded by DOS-based computers.

Trade Secrets and Copyright

Copyright law does not exist separate from trade secret law. The two forms of protection exist concurrently, as explained here. Trade secret law exists as an important *first step* for a copyrightable work. For example, a software company, Softco, is preparing to distribute a new program, *Filer Compiler*. Although the *Filer Compiler* is protected under copyright law, certain elements of the work may not be protectible under copyright law. Therefore, prior to publication, Softco will treat *Filer Compiler* with confidentiality, requiring all employees to sign nondisclosure agreements and restricting access to the program.

Generally, the publication or distribution of a trade secret destroys the proprietary rights associated with trade secrets, because competitors may legitimately disassemble or evaluate the work and determine the elements of the trade secrets. However, this is not always true—it is determined by the nature of the trade secret, the nature of the publication or display, and the terms of any license with the person licensing the published material. For example, the publication of Softco's program, *Filer Compiler*, does not necessarily alert competing programmers to the underlying algorithms, source code, or formulas that form the published program. As explained in chapter 5, copyright law provides a means for Softco to deposit *Filer Compiler* with the Copyright Office without revealing trade secrecy elements of the computer code.

Trade Secrets and Patents

Owners of patentable inventions and devices who wish to preserve their trade secrecy rights must limit any disclosure prior to the issuance of a patent. Under U.S. patent law, there is a requirement that the inventor or owner of an invention must file a patent application within one year of commercial exploitation of the patent. For example, if Diskco begins selling a patentable armrest for computers, the company must file its patent application within one year of the debut of the product if they want to secure a U.S. patent. A patent attorney must carefully guide the inventor regarding these factors and must counsel the inventor so that trade secret security is maintained throughout the patent application process.

Unless authorized by the owner, federal law prohibits (with a few exceptions) the disclosure of information in pending patents and abandoned patent applications. This means that there is no loss of trade secrecy arising from the application process. It is only when the patent is issued that the information is made public and trade secret rights in previously unpublished information (now published) terminate. It is possible that some trade secret information associated with an invention need not be disclosed (e.g., the research method by which the inventor arrived at the conclusions or the inventor's test results). The trade secret information not required for the patent application can still be left unpublished and remain protected under state trade secret law.

In 1974, the U.S. Supreme Court ruled that trade secrets are protectible under state law regardless of their patentability. This was an important ruling because it established that state trade secret law and federal patent law did not necessarily clash (i.e., federal patent law did not preempt state trade secret law).

What Is Not Protected under Trade Secret Law?

It is not a misappropriation of a trade secret to independently create confidential information, even if the resulting creation is identical to a trade secret. For example, if a magician independently creates a trick identical to that of a competitor, without resorting to any improper means to acquire the information, there is no misappropriation of the trade secret. Similarly, if the secret is obtained through a legitimate means and without violating any limitation on making or receiving the disclosure, then the party who learns the secret in that way is free to use it. For example, in the facts in the Commentary to this chapter, Dave, an engineer employed by Kidco, disclosed trade secrets to a convention of engineers regarding an invention or process. The information publicly disclosed in that way was no longer a trade secret.

The Clean Room

To demonstrate that a company independently developed trade secrets, or to avoid a potential claim of infringement of proprietary rights, a company may want to demonstrate that its works were developed independently. The most reliable means of doing this is to employ **clean room** techniques in evaluation and development. There are various forms of clean rooms, but all of them involve isolating certain engineers or designers and filtering information to them. These engineers or designers are usually given an objective (e.g., create a software program that connects a telephone to a computer) and are then presented with publicly available materials, tools, and documents (which can include information obtained by reverse engineering, as explained

LEGAL TERMS

clean room
  A method of developing proprietary material in which an isolated development team is monitored; the purpose is to provide evidence that similarities in works or products are due to legitimate considerations and not copying.

later). The development team's progress is carefully monitored and documented, and any requests for further information by the team are reviewed by a technical expert or legal monitor. Records of the clean room development are saved to demonstrate that trade secrets were independently developed and to refute any claims that a work was copied. The clean room technique provides evidence that any similarities between two works or products are due to legitimate constraints and not copying or improper means. The clean room technique can come in many forms.

Reverse Engineering

The computer technologies created by HP can be discovered by reverse engineering. If there is nothing unique about the HP products, the reverse engineering and subsequent use of the discoveries would not violate trade secret laws.

Material that is ascertainable by legitimate means will not be protected under trade secret law. Therefore, the disassembly and examination of products that are available to the public is not a violation of trade secret protection. For example, a cabinetmaker has a secret formula for making glue. A person buys a cabinet, takes out the glue, chemically analyzes it, duplicates the formula, creates the exact same glue and opens a business selling the glue. The cabinetmaker's secret formula has been obtained by a legitimate means. This process is sometimes known as **reverse engineering.**

The same principle applies to computer programs. To perform reverse engineering on a video game program, a company made one unauthorized copy of the code. The purpose of the reverse engineering of the code was to determine what elements were in the public domain. A court ruled that the making of one copy for such a purpose was not a violation of copyright law and did not violate trade secret law. Despite this appellate court ruling, the making of copies for reverse engineering purposes may still, under some circumstances, violate U.S. copyright or patent law.

Trade secret protection is not lost simply because a trade secret could be discovered by reverse engineering. For example, the Food and Drug Administration (FDA) made a determination that a secret ingredient in a product was not a trade secret because it could easily be discovered by reverse engineering. However, a federal court later overruled the FDA determination because, despite the fact that the secret *could* have been discovered, no competitor *had* ever discovered the ingredient.

Reverse engineering may not be used to obtain trade secret information in some circumstances. If the parties have entered into a nondisclosure agreement or are in a fiduciary relationship, reverse engineering cannot be used to circumvent the agreement or relationship. If reverse engineering involves improper means (e.g., stealing products from a company), then the improper use of the trade secret will not be excused under the principle of reverse engineering.

7.2 MAINTAINING TRADE SECRETS

For 80 years, the Kellogg Company permitted tours of its cereal-making factory. But in 1986 the company discontinued the practice because corporate spies had been discovered on two occasions. The company feared that the tours provided the opportunity for competitors to learn about its trade secret technology, so the company terminated the popular promotional tours.

The failure of a trade secret owner to maintain reasonable security will result in the loss of trade secret status. A crucial issue in trade secret protection is the maintenance of a confidentiality program to assure the continued protection of the information. This requires vigilance. For example, in the Commentary to this chapter, the toy company, Kidco, apparently left much of the "secret" material in cardboard boxes in an open storeroom. A defendant in a trade secret lawsuit could argue that this demonstrated that Kidco had failed to take reasonable security precautions and, therefore, the material could not be categorized as a trade secret.

Many companies adopt a trade secret management and security plan. Trade secret material is kept in a restricted location and access to documents is controlled. Unauthorized personnel must be kept out of the restricted location. For example, confidential financial records should be stamped "confidential" and kept in locked file cabinets. Confidential computer programs should be used only on computers on which access is restricted. If the computer is hooked to a network, there must be a means of preventing access to the programs. In one case, a company failed to erase trade secrets from a hard disk before the company sold the computer. A court ruled that the material had lost its trade secret status. This section discusses some guidelines for establishing suitable trade secret standards.

Physical Security

The first defense for trade secrets is the workplace. The legal administrators responsible for maintaining proprietary rights should have a checklist for evaluating trade secret precautions. However, not all businesses require the same security. A business is only required to observe "reasonable" precautions. This does not include extreme or heroic measures to preserve secrecy. It generally means that anyone, except a person using improper means, would have difficulty in acquiring the information.

Trade Secret Workplace Security Checklist

- *Access to the building.* Is the entrance to the building secure? Are visitors or after-hours employees required to sign in? Does the building have a fence, an alarm, or a guard system?

- *Access to portions of the building.* Do employees wear name badges? Is employee access restricted in areas where confidential material is located? Are any closed-circuit cameras in place?

- *Precautions observed by employees.* Is there security education for employees? Are there reminders to employees about dealing with trade secrets? Are file cabinets and desks locked? Are persons leaving restricted areas subject to search? Is there a document control policy?

LEGAL TERMS

reverse engineering
Disassembly and examination of products that are available to the public.

- *Locations of computers, copying devices, and other devices.* Are machines in secure areas? Is access to machines restricted? Do users of machines log their usage? Is a machine (such as a paper shredder) used to destroy confidential material?

- *Systems used to access computer and telephone networks.* Are passwords required for access? Are the passwords changed frequently?

- *Stamps and signs.* Does the company use stamps such as "Confidential Material" or "Restricted"? Are signs posted throughout the workplace restricting access? Are security rules posted?

- *Documentation.* Are all notebooks or other materials used in the development or maintenance of trade secrets properly documented (e.g., labeled and filed in the restricted access area) and treated with confidentiality and secrecy? Is an official internal list of trade secret materials maintained? Is it is updated frequently? Is it sufficiently broad to cover any materials regarded as proprietary? (Note: Some companies prefer not to list trade secrets because they are concerned that such lists could limit the possible trade secrets.)

Employee Limitations

One of the most commonly litigated trade secret issues is the use or disclosure of confidential material by an employee. An employee may inadvertently disclose the information, for example, if it is accidentally faxed or mailed to the wrong party. An employee may deliberately disclose the secret for an illegal purpose (i.e., theft or bribery). Sometimes an employee acquires the confidential information legitimately during the course of employment and then uses it at a new job. For example, in the Commentary to this chapter, Dave, an engineer at Kidco, has used confidential information acquired while working at Kidco to make a competing product. Is this improper? The answer will depend on several factors, including the conditions of Dave's employment (e.g., employee or independent contractor), the nature of Dave's employment agreement, whether the material is confidential or publicly known, the safeguards used by the company to protect the material (e.g., did Kidco authorize Dave's speech to the programming convention?), and whether Dave has executed a confidentiality agreement with the company.

Employee Confidentiality Agreements

Companies often require that all employees enter into a confidentiality agreement before beginning employment. A *confidentiality agreement,* also known as a *nondisclosure agreement,* is a contract that restricts the disclosure of trade secrets. The terms of the confidentiality agreement are sometimes incorporated within an employment agreement. Although it is advisable to include information about the confidentiality policies of the company within the company's employee manual, the most effective means of preserving confidentiality is for each employee to execute an employment or confidentiality agreement acknowledging and accepting the company's terms for preserving trade secrecy. The duration and scope of employee confidentiality agreements may be limited by state law.

Figure 7-1 is an example of a confidentiality agreement for an employee.

The Departing Employee

If the company failed to execute a nondisclosure agreement or similar precautionary measures with a departing employee, the company should conduct an exit interview and, if possible, get the employee to execute an *exit agreement* indicating that the former employee will maintain confidentiality. An exit agreement is similar to a confidentiality agreement, except that it is signed by the employee when the employee is departing. If the company is particularly concerned about trade secrecy loss, the departing employee

---

DISKCO EMPLOYEE CONFIDENTIALITY AGREEMENT

In consideration of your employment and payment at Diskco ("Diskco" or "Employer"), you agree as follows:

You acknowledge that in the course of your employment by Diskco, you will be exposed to valuable confidential Diskco trade secret information. This information may include any material owned or possessed by Diskco that has economic or commercial value or information which, if disclosed without authorization, could be detrimental to Diskco.

You agree to treat all such information as confidential, regardless of whether it is marked as confidential, and to take all reasonable and necessary precautions against disclosure of such information to third parties during and after your employment with Diskco. You shall not use Diskco's trade secret information, except to the extent necessary in the course of your employment.

You agree that all materials furnished to you by Diskco, and all materials prepared by you in connection with your employment by Diskco, including but not limited to computer software and documentation, shall be returned promptly to Diskco upon termination of your employment.

You also agree that all works created by you or under your direction in connection with your work at Diskco shall be the sole property of Diskco and that any and all copyrights and other proprietary interests in those works shall belong to Diskco, and that the confidentiality provisions of this Agreement shall fully apply to all such works.

I ACKNOWLEDGE I HAVE READ AND RECEIVED A COPY OF THIS AGREEMENT AND THAT I UNDERSTAND ITS CONTENTS.

Dated: _____

_____   _____
Employee   Employer

[handwritten margin note: CONFIDENTIALITY / SIGNED IN ADDITION TO EMPLOYMENT AGREEMENT]

FIGURE 7-1
Sample employee confidentiality agreement

should be interviewed in the presence of a witness to obtain assurances that no confidential data remains in the employee's control. However, it is a violation of most state labor laws to refuse payment of salary until such an agreement has been executed. That is, an employer should not withhold payment of salary until the employee signs a confidentiality agreement. If the employee has not signed a confidentiality agreement at the time of employment and refuses to sign an exit agreement, the company may wish to send a confirming letter to the departing employee (see figure 7-2). The confirming letter does not have the force of a confidentiality agreement, because the employee has not agreed to the terms. However, in the absence of a confidentiality or exit agreement, the confirming letter serves to place the employee on notice as to confidentiality requirements. Whether conducting an exit interview, executing an exit agreement, or sending an exit confirmation letter, it is always prudent to advise the employee to seek independent legal advice. This is particularly important if the employee is dealing with a company attorney.

Contacting Competing Employers.   A business may contact a competing employer to request that the competing business avoid use of any confidential material to which a departing employee had access. For example, assume the facts presented in the letter in figure 7-2. If Jane was subsequently employed by

---

EXIT LETTER TO DEPARTING EMPLOYEE

Dear Jane:

Your recent departure from Softco makes it necessary to note that while employed by Softco you have had occasion to acquire and generate knowledge and information concerning our business and the businesses of our clients which we keep confidential or proprietary to protect its competitive value. We consider this information to be proprietary.

Let me mention certain areas by way of example which will require particular attention: [e.g., customer lists, source codes pertaining to products, marketing strategies for new products].

Let me also remind you that, except when permission to do so was expressly given in writing, you were not authorized to take any such documents or records with you when you left and no such permission was given. You may not use any of Softco's confidential information for any purpose, including its use in connection with any of your business activities, or the business activities of others, or in any other way use it to the disadvantage of Softco.

Please feel free to contact me if you have any questions with regard to your obligations under the Softco employment agreement.

Sincerely,

_____

FIGURE 7-2
Sample exit letter to departing employee

Diskco, Softco may write to Diskco and inform the company that Jane is bound to honor her confidentiality agreement with Softco. However, employers should be extremely careful when contacting the departing employee's new employer. Statements regarding the departing employee may lead to claims of libel, invasion of privacy, misrepresentation, or interference with a contractual relationship. Any such letter should be reviewed by an attorney.

Third-Party or Independent Contractor Confidentiality

Consultants, agents, vendors, and other persons who have access to trade secrets also should sign nondisclosure agreements. Such agreements may be mutual. For example, two software companies, Softco and Diskco, wish to exchange software programs. They could execute a mutual nondisclosure agreement, as shown in figure 7-3.

MUTUAL NONDISCLOSURE AGREEMENT

This Mutual Nondisclosure Agreement (the "Agreement") is entered into this _____ day of _____, 19____, by and between SOFTCO and DISKCO (collectively referred to as the "parties"), for the purpose of preventing the unauthorized disclosure of Confidential Information (as defined below).

1. The parties may disclose confidential and proprietary trade secret information to each other for the purpose of exploring a possible business relationship. The parties mutually agree to enter into a confidential relationship with respect to the disclosure by one or each (the "Disclosing Party") to the other (the "Receiving Party") of certain proprietary and confidential information (the "Confidential Information").

2. For purposes of this Agreement, "Confidential Information" shall include all information or material that has or could have commercial value or other utility in the business in which Disclosing Party is engaged. Confidential Information also includes any information described above which the Receiving Party obtains from another party which the Disclosing Party treats as proprietary or designates as confidential, whether or not owned or developed by the Disclosing Party. Confidential Information shall not include any information and data as the parties agree in writing is not proprietary or confidential. Information made available to the general public shall not be considered to be Confidential Information. The Receiving Party shall hold and maintain the Confidential Information of the other party in strictest confidence for the sole and exclusive benefit of the Disclosing Party. The Receiving Party shall carefully restrict access to any such Confidential Information to persons bound by this Agreement, only on a need-to-know basis. The Receiving Party shall not, without prior written approval of the Disclosing Party, use for the Receiving Party's own

---

FIGURE 7-3
Sample mutual nondisclosure agreement

benefit, publish, or otherwise disclose to others, or permit the use by others for their benefit or to the detriment of the Disclosing Party, any of the Confidential Information. The Receiving Party shall take all necessary action to protect the confidentiality of the Confidential Information and hereby agrees to indemnify the Disclosing Party against any and all losses, damages, claims, or expenses incurred or suffered by the Disclosing Party as a result of the Receiving Party's breach of this Agreement.

3. The nondisclosure and confidentiality provisions of this Agreement shall continue in full force and effect and shall survive the termination of any relationship between the Disclosing Party and the Receiving Party except that the Receiving Party's obligations under this Agreement shall not extend to information that is: (a) publicly known at the time of disclosure under this Agreement or subsequently becomes publicly known through no fault of the Receiving Party; (b) discovered or created by the Receiving Party independent of any involvement with the Disclosing Party or the Confidential Information; or (c) otherwise learned by the Receiving Party through legitimate means other than from the Disclosing Party or anyone connected with the Disclosing Party.

4. The Receiving Party understands and acknowledges that any disclosure or misappropriation of any of the Confidential Information in violation of this Agreement may cause the Disclosing Party irreparable harm, the amount of which may be difficult to ascertain, and therefore agrees that the Disclosing Party shall have the right to apply to a court of competent jurisdiction for an order restraining and enjoining any such further disclosure or misappropriation and for such other relief as the Disclosing Party shall deem appropriate. Such right of the Disclosing Party is to be in addition to the remedies otherwise available to Disclosing Party at law or in equity. The Receiving Party shall return to Disclosing Party any and all records, notes, and other written, printed, or tangible materials in its possession pertaining to the Confidential Information immediately on the written request of Disclosing Party.

5. This Agreement and each Party's obligations shall be binding on the representatives, assigns, and successors of such party and shall inure to the benefit of the assigns and successors of such Party. This Agreement shall be governed by and construed in accordance with the laws of the State of California. The parties hereby consent to the exclusive jurisdiction of the state and federal courts located in San Francisco County, California, in any action arising out of or relating to this Agreement, and waive any other venue to which either party might be entitled by domicile or otherwise. If any action is brought to enforce this Agreement, the prevailing party in such action shall be entitled to reimbursement for reasonable attorney's fees and costs. This Agreement expresses the full and complete understanding of the parties with respect to the subject matter and supersedes all prior proposals, agreements, representations, and understandings, whether written or oral. This Agreement may not be amended or modified except in writing signed by each of the parties to the Agreement.

I acknowledge that I have read, understood, and received a copy of, and agree to the terms of this Agreement.

FIGURE 7-3
(Continued)

Disclosure by U.S. Government

Information held by the U.S. government may be disclosed upon request of citizens under the Freedom of Information Act (5 U.S.C. § 552). In the event that a business has disclosed trade secret information, further disclosure may be prevented under the Freedom of Information Act if the trade secret documents are marked with the following notice:

Subject to exemption of 5 U.S.C. § 552(b)(4).

In addition, if a company contracts with the federal government, any proprietary materials licensed or transferred should be marked with a legend that restricts rights. This is particularly important in the case of software. The following legend is suggested, for example, in the case of software licensed to the federal government:

> The software is furnished with RESTRICTED RIGHTS. Use, duplication, or disclosure is subject to restrictions as set forth in paragraph (b)(3)(B) of the Rights in Technical Data and Computer Software Clause in DAR 7-104.9(a) and in subparagraph (c)(1)(ii) of 252.227-7013; 52.227-19(a) through (d) and applicable ADP Schedule Contract. Unpublished rights are reserved under the copyright laws of the United States. The U.S. Government agrees that any such products licensed which have appropriate RESTRICTED RIGHTS legends applied on them shall be provided only with RESTRICTED RIGHTS.

Noncompetition Provisions (Covenants Not to Compete)

A **covenant not to compete** is a contract that restrains a person from engaging in a business, trade, or profession. (See figure 7-4.) For example, if a software company, Softco, wished to prevent one of its founders from selling her shares in the company and starting a competing business, Softco might require a covenant not to compete. The regulation of such covenants is

LEGAL TERMS

covenant not to compete
Contract provision that restrains a person from engaging in a business, trade, or profession for a period of time; may not be enforceable in some states.

COVENANT NOT TO COMPETE
(Often Included in Employee Agreements)

Without the prior written consent of Diskco, Employee agrees not to solicit or to enter into any offers of employment, in any capacity, either directly or indirectly, with any competitor of Diskco, either directly or indirectly, for a period of one (1) year from the termination of this employment agreement. The term "competitor" as used in this agreement shall refer to any manufacturer or developer of game or entertainment software for microcomputers.

FIGURE 7-4
Sample covenant not to compete

a matter of state law. Some states, such as California, prohibit restraints on trade and "every contract by which anyone is restrained from engaging in a lawful profession, trade or business of any kind is to that extent void."[1] Even in states that prohibit restraint of trade, there are exceptions. One exception indicates that such an agreement will be valid when it involves either (1) the sale of goodwill of a business; (2) the sale or disposition of all the seller's shares in a corporation; or (3) the sale of all or substantially all the operating assets together with the goodwill of a corporation or the dissolution of a partnership.

Although a covenant not to compete may be invalid, it is always permissible to prohibit an employee from competing by using confidential information. Consider MicroCo, a software company in California. A former employee has misappropriated trade secrets and is using them in a rival business. Even though a covenant not to compete may be invalid in California, the courts will still prohibit the misappropriation of trade secrets used in the competing business.

In addition to covenants not to compete, ownership of employee inventions may also vary from state to state. In some states, a principle known as the *shop right rule* is enforced, which guarantees the employee's ownership of inventions created under certain circumstances (e.g., when an employee creates an invention at home using her own equipment).

Customer Lists

Perhaps the most litigated issue regarding trade secrets is the protection of customer lists. The issue of customer list protection often arises when an employee leaves a business and then uses a customer list to contact former clients. Although the law differs from state to state, the modern trend among courts is not to afford trade secret protection to customer lists if the information is ascertainable by other means. For example, a salesman works at a luxury car dealership. When the salesman leaves, he takes his card file of customers and contacts the customers from his new job at a rival luxury car dealership. The first dealership sues for misappropriation of a trade secret (the customer list). The court rules for the salesman, holding that the customer list is not a trade secret because the salesman has contributed to its creation and because the names of customers who could afford luxury cars in the vicinity are easily ascertainable by other means. When analyzing customer lists, courts often consider the following elements:

1. The information contained in the list (e.g., a list of names and addresses will be given less protection than a detailed analysis of customer characteristics)

2. The amount of effort required to assemble the list

3. The departing employee's contribution to the list

4. Whether the customer list is personal, longstanding, or exclusive.

EXAMPLES

Customer Lists.   In a federal case, a court permitted an employee to use the former employer's mailing list, indicating that the customer information was easily ascertainable and the compilation process was "neither sophisticated, nor difficult, nor particularly time consuming."

In another federal case, trade secret protection was denied for customer lists that could be readily derived from a telephone directory, even though the lists contained more detailed information than was available in the phone book.

In a California case, a court determined that employees who left a business could send out an announcement of their change of employment to former clients. The use of the former employer's mailing list did not infringe a trade secret because: (1) the clients became known to the ex-employees through personal contacts; *and* (2) because the use of the customer list (i.e., address cards) simply saved the ex-employees the minor inconvenience of looking up the information.

In a federal case, a defendant was enjoined from using customer information. In this case, the customer information was not readily ascertainable and would have required considerable expense to compile. In addition, the defendant had obtained the customer information through a confidential relationship with the plaintiff.

7.3 PROTECTING A SUBMISSION (PROTECTING AN IDEA)

Dan is a fisherman. One day he dreams up an idea for a television game show in which celebrities compete with contestants in televised fishing expeditions. Dan wants to present his TV show idea, tentatively titled *Superstar Fishin' Expedition,* to a television network. The information may not be protectible as a trade secret, for various reasons. As ideas are not protected under copyright law, how can Dan protect against the unauthorized use of his concept?

To protect against the unauthorized use of an idea or a concept, the parties should enter into a contract such as an **evaluation agreement** or a *submission agreement*. The evaluation agreement is similar to a nondisclosure agreement: One party promises to submit an idea; the other party promises to evaluate the idea; after evaluating the idea, the evaluator will either enter into an agreement to exploit the idea, or will not use or disclose the idea. For example, if Dan entered into an evaluation agreement with a television producer, the producer would either use Dan's idea and compensate him, or not use or disclose Dan's idea.

To protect his idea under contract law, Dan must show two things: (1) that the idea was solicited (i.e., the television producer asked to see the idea); and (2) that there was an expectation of compensation if the idea was used. Under limited circumstances the originator and proprietor of an idea may stop others from misappropriating the idea if there was a **fiduciary relationship** between the parties and if the idea was not one of general

Evaluation or submission agreement

LEGAL TERMS

evaluation agreement
Contract by which one party promises to submit an idea and the other party promises to evaluate the idea. After the evaluation, the evaluator will either enter into an agreement to exploit the idea or promise not to use or disclose the idea.

fiduciary relationship
A special relationship of trust, confidence, or responsibility between persons.

knowledge. In a fiduciary relationship, one person stands in a special relationship of trust, confidence, or responsibility. Fiduciary relationships are often defined by statute or caselaw. For example, the relationship of an attorney to a client is a fiduciary relationship, and the theft by an attorney of a client's idea would be a breach of the fiduciary relationship.

One problem with evaluation agreements is that there may be difficulty obtaining the evaluator's consent. Companies may be wary of signing an evaluation agreement because of fear of the repercussions of considering unsolicited ideas. For example, what if the company likes the idea but was already preparing a similar product? Does the evaluation agreement prohibit it from proceeding with the product it had developed internally? Because of this concern, some companies do not like to sign evaluation agreements, or they have their own submission agreements. Figure 7-5 is an example of an evaluation agreement.

The Option Agreement. In the *Art Buchwald* case, dicussed in this section, Mr. Buchwald and his partner signed an agreement regarding the submission of their idea for a movie. In return for an exclusive option to make a

---

EVALUATION AGREEMENT

This agreement is made between Roy Programmer ("Programmer") and Softco ("Softco"). Programmer wishes to have Softco examine and evaluate the video game product known as "$BATTLE" (the "Product"). Softco desires to examine and evaluate the Product in order to determine if it wishes to assist in the marketing, production, or distribution of the Product to the parties' mutual benefit. The materials furnished by Programmer shall be used by Softco solely to review or evaluate the Product.

After evaluating the submission, Softco will either offer to enter into an agreement with Programmer or return the submission to Programmer and agree not to market or participate in the marketing of the Product or any product derived from the Product. Softco agrees that the materials submitted under this agreement describing the Product contain valuable proprietary information of Programmer, constitute a trade secret of Programmer, and the loss or outside disclosure of these materials or the information contained within these materials will harm Programmer economically.

Softco agrees to hold the submission confidential and will not disclose it to any person other than its evaluators and other members of its staff who have reason to view the submission in connection with the evaluation that is contemplated by this agreement. Softco agrees to exercise a high degree of care to safeguard these materials and the information they contain from access or disclosure to all unauthorized persons. Softco acknowledges that all applicable rights to the submission remain vested in Programmer. Programmer retains the right to submit the submission to others while it is being evaluated by Softco.

FIGURE 7-5
Sample evaluation
agreement

The foregoing provisions apply with equal force to any additional
or supplemental submissions and other materials submitted or to be
submitted by Programmer to Softco with respect to the same subject
matter of the submission. This Evaluation Agreement shall be
governed by, and construed in accordance with, the laws of the State
of _____ .

FIGURE 7-5
(Continued)

movie based on this idea, Paramount paid $10,000 to Buchwald and his part-
ner. If a movie was made based upon the idea, Buchwald and his partner
would receive a percentage of the profits. This is known as an **option agreement.** If Paramount exercised its option to use the idea, the company would
pay Buchwald and his partner more money. In an option agreement, the company is not positive it will use the idea or submission, but it wants to have an
exclusive option to do so for a period of time. In return for this right, an initial payment is made to the creator of the idea.

The Art Buchwald Case. In 1983, humorist Art Buchwald and producer Alan Bernheim submitted an idea for a movie and signed an agreement
with Paramount Pictures. They received $10,000 and the agreement provided
that if Paramount ever made a movie *based upon* the submission, Buchwald
and Bernheim would be paid more money from the profits. The submission
was an idea for a movie about the king of an African country who comes to
America, loses his memory, works in a restaurant, marries an American woman,
and returns with her to his kingdom. A Paramount executive provided actor
and producer Eddie Murphy with the idea, based upon the Buchwald submission. After Paramount released the film *Coming to America,* Buchwald
and Bernheim successfully sued the studio for breaching the submission
agreement. An interesting aspect of the suit is that despite the fact that the

LEGAL TERMS

option agreement
    Agreement whereby
    one party pays
    the other for the
    opportunity to later
    exploit an idea or work.

Art Buchwald

film grossed $300 million, Paramount maintained that there were no profits. In 1992, Buchwald was awarded $150,000 and Bernheim was awarded $750,000.

7.4 TRADE SECRET LITIGATION

Trade secret litigation is usually based upon two theories. If the secret was acquired by misappropriation, then there has been a violation of the state trade secret law. Alternatively, if the trade secret is disclosed in violation of an agreement to maintain secrecy, the disclosing party has breached an agreement. Unlike copyright and patent litigation, trade secret litigation may be brought in state court or may be brought in federal court, provided the claim qualifies under federal jurisdiction rules. When a federal court rules on trade secrets, it applies the relevant state law. One of the most important and unique aspects of trade secret litigation is that the parties must limit the disclosure of the trade secret throughout the litigation. This requires attention to confidentiality agreements and use of federal and state rules of civil procedure.

A party defending against a claim of trade secret misappropriation will usually argue that the plaintiff failed to utilize reasonable efforts to maintain secrecy and therefore the material does not qualify as confidential. Alternatively, the defendant may argue that the information is publicly available and therefore does not qualify as a trade secret.

Misappropriation and Improper Means

Consider the Commentary to this chapter. What if a competitor bribes an employee of Kidco to disclose the secret information about the *Webosaurus* toy? In a state that has adopted the Uniform Trade Secrets Act, the competitor and the employee would have misappropriated the information and therefore violated state law. The following is the definition of *misappropriation* from the Uniform Trade Secrets Act:

"Misappropriation" means:

Acquisition of a trade secret of another by a person who knows or has reason to know that the trade secret was acquired by improper means; or

Disclosure or use of a trade secret of another without express or implied consent by a person who:

(A)   Used improper means to acquire knowledge of the trade secret; or

(B)   At the time of disclosure or use, knew or had reason to know that his or her knowledge of the trade secret was:

Derived from or through a person who had utilized improper means to acquire it;

Acquired under circumstances giving rise to a duty to maintain its secrecy or limit its use; or

Derived from or through a person who owed a duty to the person seeking relief to maintain its secrecy or limit its use; or

(C) Before a material change of his or her position, knew or had reason to know that it was a trade secret and that knowledge of it had been acquired by accident or mistake.

Improper means is defined by the Uniform Trade Secrets Act as "theft, bribery, misrepresentation, breach or inducement of a breach of a duty to maintain secrecy, or espionage through electronic or other means." If a trade secret is acquired by **improper means**, the remedy is to sue for damages and an injunction preventing any further use or dissemination of the secret. Depending upon the extent of disclosure by the thief or third party, the trade secret may have lost its confidential quality because the public became aware of the secret and its value was destroyed. For example, if the barbecue sauce recipe in a famous restaurant is stolen and printed, it may damage the restaurant. Competitors could imitate it and consumers could attempt to duplicate it at home. In such case, the restaurant would sue for the amount by which the business is damaged.

In other cases, the taking of the secret by improper means may not end trade secret protection. The owner may still assert trade secret ownership and sue for damages and to prevent any further disclosure of the material. For instance, an employee of Softco takes confidential software program code from the company and sells it to Diskco. Diskco uses a portion of the stolen code in its new program. A lawsuit is filed and Diskco agrees not to use the secret code, to destroy all copies, and to maintain the confidentiality of the secret. In this case, the theft of the secrets does not end their trade secret status.

Breach of Contract

If a party has breached an agreement not to disclose the secret, there has been a breach of contract. The breach-of-contract claim is a separate theory that may be brought in addition to bringing an action under the state trade secret statute. Section 7 of the Uniform Trade Secrets Act specifically provides that the Act "does not affect contractual remedies, whether or not based upon misappropriation of a trade secret." The measure of damages for breach of contract is the amount that will compensate the aggrieved party for all the detriment proximately caused by the breach. Similarly, if the disclosure results from a breach of fiduciary duty, the claim would be for a breach of fiduciary duty rather than a breach of contract.

Jurisdiction

A trade secret claim may be brought in a state court or, if the claim qualifies, in the federal district courts. There are several ways that a trade secret claim can be brought in federal court. Under rules known as **diversity,** a plaintiff may bring a claim in federal court if the parties are from different states and the matter in controversy is over $50,000. This can be done even if no federal question or issue is involved in the litigation. Alternatively, the claim may be brought in a federal court under rules known as

LEGAL TERMS

improper means
The illegal acquisition of trade secrets through theft, bribery, misrepresentation, breach, or inducement of a breach of a duty to maintain secrecy, or espionage through electronic or other means.

diversity
The right to file a lawsuit based upon nonfederal claims in federal court; parties must be from different states and the matter in controversy over $50,000.

pendent **jurisdiction**. If a claim is based upon federal law (e.g., a patent or copyright claim), the plaintiff may make any additional state claims, such as trade secret violation, as part of the complaint. Finally, the misappropriation of the trade secret may involve the violation of federal laws, for example, the transportation of stolen materials across state lines or the use of telephone communication to conspire to steal trade secrets. The final determination of whether to file in state or federal court is made by the supervising attorney based upon tactical and geographic factors.

Applying State Law

Even if a trade secret case is brought in federal court, state trade secret law is used to decide the case. That is, the federal court will apply the state law when dealing with the state trade secret claim. But which state's law shall be applied? If both parties are from the same state and the misappropriation occurred in that state, the choice of state law would be simple. However, if the parties are from different states, there are several variables. If there is a written agreement, such as a nondisclosure agreement, that contract may establish which state's law will apply. For example, in the nondisclosure agreement in figure 7-3, there is a provision stating that "This Agreement shall be governed by and construed in accordance with the laws of the State of California." Therefore, in the event of a dispute, the state law of California will govern the trade secret litigation, regardless of where the parties are from or where the misappropriation occurred.

If there is no written agreement regarding disclosure of trade secrets, then the court will determine which state's law should apply. This may be based upon factors such as the relationship of the parties, the domicile of the disclosing party, or the location(s) of the misappropriation. Under state *long-arm statutes*, a state may exercise jurisdiction over nonresident defendants in certain circumstances.

Rules of Civil Procedure

The parties in litigation are governed by rules of civil procedure. In federal court, these are the Federal Rules of Civil Procedure. If the matter is brought in state court, the parties will be governed by the rules of civil procedure for that state. These rules set forth the requirements for parties when filing papers, appearing in court, or communicating with counsel. In addition, each court, whether federal or state, usually has its own local rules. Before commencing an action, it is important to acquire a copy of the local rules. This can be accomplished by calling the local court clerk.

The Trade Secret Complaint

The *complaint* is the initial document filed in a lawsuit. It sets forth the basis of the plaintiff's claims and requests certain remedies. An example of a trade secret claim is joined with the complaint for copyright infringement in chapter 6. Trade secret claims are commonly joined with other claims, such as copyright infringement, patent infringement, unfair competition, trade dress or trademark infringement, or the tort of fraud. In addition to the complaint, the defendant is served with a summons and, in federal court and some state courts, a civil cover sheet. The *summons* explains that the defendant has been sued and has a certain time limit within which to respond. The *civil cover sheet* is a form required for use by the court in maintaining statistical records. If the plaintiff desires a jury trial, that demand should be made in the complaint and reflected in the civil cover sheet. If the plaintiff has not sought a jury trial, but the defendant wants one, the request for a jury trial should be made in the defendant's *answer.*

Statute of Limitations

The Uniform Trade Secrets Act has a three-year statute of limitations. This means that the trade secret misappropriation claim must be filed within three years of when the misappropriation is (or should reasonably have been) discovered. The failure to timely file the claim will prevent the plaintiff from proceeding with the case. A state that has not adopted the Uniform Trade Secrets Act may have a different statute of limitations.

Injunctive Relief

An *injunction* is a court order compelling the defendant to take some affirmative action or prohibiting the defendant from engaging in some activity. If a trade secret is misappropriated, the plaintiff will seek to enjoin the defendant's use of the confidential information. This injunction may even continue for a period of time *after* the trade secret has become publicly known. This prevents any commercial advantage resulting from the misappropriation. The Uniform Trade Secrets Act also permits a court to order the return of all trade secrets and related materials. If a court determines that an injunction would be unreasonable, the court can deny the request and instead condition the defendant's further use of the trade secret material upon the payment of a reasonable royalty. For example, Diskco has misappropriated Softco's trade secrets and is using them in a special program for the military. If a court determined that military personnel could be endangered by an injunction, the court may order Diskco to pay Softco royalties for the use of the trade secrets. Section 2 of the Uniform Trade Secrets Act covers injunctive relief.

Uniform Trade Secrets Act § 2:   Injunctive Relief

(a)   Actual or threatened misappropriation may be enjoined. Upon application to the court, an injunction shall be terminated when the trade secret has ceased to exist, but the injunction may be continued for an

LEGAL TERMS

jurisdiction
The authority of a court to hear a certain type of case.

additional period of time in order to eliminate commercial advantage that otherwise would be derived from the misappropriation.

(b) In exceptional circumstances, an injunction may condition future use upon payment of a reasonable royalty for no longer than the period of time the use could have been prohibited. Exceptional circumstances include, but are not limited to, a material and prejudicial change of position prior to acquiring knowledge or reason to know of misappropriation that renders a prohibive injunction inequitable.

(c) In appropriate circumstances, affirmative acts to protect a trade secret may be compelled by court order.

Damages and Attorney Fees

The complaining party may recover damages for actual loss, as well as for unjust enrichment caused by the misappropriation that is not taken into account in computing actual damages. Alternatively, the court may order payment of a reasonable royalty. Under some state laws, if the misappropriation is willful and malicious, the court may award punitive or exemplary damages (not to exceed twice the amount of actual damages) as well as attorney fees.

Disclosure of Trade Secrets During Litigation

During civil litigation (whether it is over trade secret misappropriation or other issues), one party may seek to force disclosure of a trade secret. Each state, and the federal government, has rules regarding the use of trade secret evidence. Generally, the owner of a trade secret may refuse to disclose a trade secret (and may prevent others from disclosing it) unless the failure to disclose would cause injustice or conceal a fraud. A court will balance the interests of the parties when determining whether to require the disclosure of a trade secret. Section 5 of the Uniform Trade Secrets Act establishes the right of the court to preserve the security of trade secrets.

Uniform Trade Secrets Act § 5: Preservation of Secrecy

In an action under this Act, a court shall preserve the secrecy of an alleged trade secret by reasonable means, which may include granting protective orders in connection with discovery proceedings, holding in-camera hearings, sealing the records of the action, and ordering any person involved in the litigation not to disclose an alleged trade secret without prior court approval.

The court may issue a protective order for confidential information. Alternatively, the parties may agree (or stipulate) to the protection of confidential information. A plaintiff in federal court would follow Federal Rule of Civil Procedure 26(c)(7), which authorizes a protective order concerning the disclosure of trade secret information. Figure 7-6 is an example of a stipulation for protection of confidential information. This form is intended for use in a

**UNITED STATES DISTRICT COURT
NORTHERN DISTRICT OF CALIFORNIA**

DISKCO, Plaintiff,   )
) STIPULATION
-against-   ) AND ORDER
) OF PROTECTION
SOFTCO, Defendant.   )

IT IS HEREBY STIPULATED AND AGREED by and between the undersigned attorneys of record for the parties that:

1. Confidential information of the type recognized by Rule 26(c)(7) of the Federal Rules of Civil Procedure, described more specifically in this Stipulation, and disclosed by Defendant, its officers, employees, or agents (collectively "Defendant"), and by third parties, shall be governed by this Order and may not be used by Plaintiff, its officers, employees, or agents (collectively "Plaintiff"), for any purpose other than in connection with this litigation, including but not limited to any use by Plaintiff for any competitive purpose.

2. The confidential Information includes:
   a. The *Filer Compiler* computer program, including both source code and object code versions;
   b. Any written, printed, recorded, or graphic matter, however produced or reproduced, pertaining to the *Filer Compiler* program. Such information shall be designated as confidential as follows: In the case of documents, by stamping or writing "CONFIDENTIAL," and in all other cases by any manner reasonably calculated to impart notice that confidential information is being disclosed.

3. Disclosure of the confidential information shall only be made to: (1) any person requested by counsel of record to assist in conducting this litigation, provided that such person executes a declaration in the form attached to this stipulation; (2) any members or paralegals of Plaintiff's law firm who are employed in the preparation of trial of this action or independent experts chosen by Plaintiff. All confidential information shall be kept in a secure, segregated location at Plaintiff's law firm. Access shall be permitted only to those persons described in this paragraph.

4. Prior to access to the confidential information, any person permitted access to Confidential Information shall execute an affidavit stating that he or she abides by the terms of this Order. An example of such affidavit shall be attached to this Order. Defendant's attorneys will retain these affidavits and provide them for inspection to Plaintiff's attorneys upon application to the Court.

5. Within ninety (90) days of final adjudication of this action, Plaintiff's attorneys shall return to Defendant all confidential information, including copies or extracts, and shall destroy any and all working notes made with respect to the confidential information.

6. This protective order shall not apply to information which is: (a) publicly known or subsequently becomes publicly known through no fault of the receiving party; (b) discovered or created by the receiving party independent of any involvement with the confidential information; or (c) otherwise

FIGURE 7-6
Sample stipulation for protection of confidential information

learned by the receiving party through legitimate means other than from the disclosing party or anyone connected with the disclosing party.

Dated: _____

_____
Attorney

_____
Attorney

SO ORDERED:

_____
U.S. District Court Judge

CONFIDENTIALITY DECLARATION
(Attached to Stipulated Protective Order)

I declare that:

1. I am employed as [a paralegal] by [law firm].
2. I have reviewed and understand the terms of the protective Order that has been entered in this action entitled [name of action].
3. I agree not to disclose the Confidential Information to persons not authorized by the protective Order to receive such Information.
4. I agree to abide by the terms of the protective Order and I hereby submit to the jurisdiction of [name of court] for the limited purpose of any proceeding to enforce the terms of the protective Order. I understand that I may be subject to contempt for violation of the protective Order if I violate the terms of this Declaration or the protective Order.
5. I declare under penalty of perjury under the laws of the State of [state] that the foregoing is true and correct and that this declaration is executed on _____, 19____.

_____
Signature

FIGURE 7-6
(Continued)

federal court case, but may be adapted for use in a state court action. To adapt it for use in a state court case, locate the state civil procedure provision which permits the protection of trade secret material in court and cite it instead of Federal Rule of Civil Procedure 26(c)(7) in paragraph 1.

Declaratory Relief

Sometimes, in anticipation of trade secret lawsuit, the alleged defendant asks the state or federal courts for **declaratory relief.** This is not a claim for monetary damages. Instead, it is a request that the court sort out the rights and obligations of the parties. The party seeking declaratory relief need only establish that an actual controversy exists regarding a matter within federal court subject matter jurisdiction. For example, an employee leaves the software company Diskco and begins a new business. Diskco claims that the employee is using its trade secrets and threatens to sue the employee. The employee may seek a declaratory action to prove that the trade secret information has not been misappropriated.

LEGAL TERMS

declaratory relief
Request that the court sort out the rights and legal obligations of the parties in the midst of an actual controversy.

Discovery

Discovery is the process during which the parties acquire facts and evidence relating to the case. The rules regarding this process are set forth in the state or federal code of civil procedure, depending on which court has jurisdiction. In addition, local court rules also may set rules regarding discovery procedures and formats. Much of the information regarding discovery and the various discovery tools (i.e., interrogatories, requests for admission and depositions) is presented in chapter 6 (copyright), chapter 10 (trademarks), and chapter 12 (patent infringement). The only major difference is that state discovery rules may apply and that certain information may have to be maintained as confidential during the pretrial and trial process.

State law may also require that a party filing a claim for misappropriation of a trade secret identify the trade secret with reasonable particularity before beginning the discovery process. For example, in California, Civil Procedure Code § 2019(d) requires that the trade secrets be identified in a court filing, as demonstrated in figure 7-7.

**SUPERIOR COURT OF CALIFORNIA
IN AND FOR THE CITY AND COUNTY OF SAN FRANCISCO**

DISKCO, Plaintiff,   )
)   Preliminary
-against-   )   Designation of
)   Trade Secrets
SOFTCO, Defendant.   )

    Pursuant to Code of Civil Procedure § 2019 and Civil Code § 3426.1, plaintiffs hereby designate the following information as their trade secrets. This designation is without prejudice to plaintiffs' rights to amend this designation of trade secrets, including their right to add or delete materials identified as trade secrets misappropriated by defendants. Plaintiffs claim that some or all of the following are trade secrets misappropriated by the defendants:

1. _____
2. _____

Dated: _____   _____
                                  Signature of Attorney

FIGURE 7-7
Sample trade secret designation

Pretrial Preparation

Trial is the court hearing in which the parties present their facts and evidence to a judge or jury. During trial, the plaintiff will attempt to limit by protective order the extent of disclosure of trade secrets. In addition, as in all trials, the trade secrets and related information must be indexed, witnesses must be identified and prepared, and caselaw must be researched. State or federal rules of civil procedure and local rules must be carefully examined to determine rules regarding marking and admission of evidence. Finally, assistance may be required in the preparation of jury instructions. **Jury instructions** are explanations of the legal rules that the jury shall use in reaching a verdict.

The following are examples of jury instructions that could be used in a trade secret case.

JURY INSTRUCTION NO. ___: Reverse Engineering

Matters which are fully disclosed by a product which is marketed to the public and which are readily ascertainable through reverse engineering of such a product cannot be protected as trade secrets.

Reverse engineering of a product is an accepted and lawful practice in industry. Reverse engineering involves starting with a product obtained by proper means and working backwards by examining the product and disassembling it to discover information about the manner in which the product was developed, designed, and manufactured.

JURY INSTRUCTION NO. ___: Proper Means of Acquiring a Trade Secret

It is not improper to acquire knowledge of a trade secret by any one of the following:

1. Discovery through published literature or other available sources; or
2. Discovery through independent development, research, or experimentation; or
3. Discovery through reverse engineering; or
4. Observation of the trade secret as used in public or on public display.

JURY INSTRUCTION NO. ___: Proper Means of Acquiring a Trade Secret by Former Employee

If plaintiff's former employees who left to work for defendant knew or learned about the alleged trade secrets before their employment at plaintiff, or if they learned of the alleged secrets by a means other than directly or indirectly through plaintiff after they left plaintiff's employ, these individuals did not acquire this knowledge improperly.

The Trial Notebook. As discussed in chapters 6, 10, and 12, the paralegal assisting in a trial should utilize a *trial notebook,* a binder created to index and reference the important documentation necessary to litigate a case. Generally, the sections of a trial notebook include:

1. A directory of the parties and witnesses, including names, addresses, and telephone numbers, with important notations. This should be maintained on a computer database and periodically reprinted as it is updated.

2. A listing of the litigation files and their contents. Each file should have a cover sheet listing its contents. These cover sheets should be reproduced and kept in the binder so that the paralegal can easily locate the document.

3. Either a copy of all pleadings and motions, or at least a listing of such filings and their location in the litigation files.

4. Chronology of events and filings, including all events from creation of the work to the present.

5. Listings of all witnesses for each party. A separate portion should be devoted to expert witnesses.

6. Summaries of relevant discovery. If there is room, all deposition summaries should be included; if not, indexes of where the summaries are located should be provided.

7. Relevant legal research, either included or indexed.

8. Trial notes or plans, task lists, and attorney notes, included in separate sections.

Litigation Checklists

The following checklists are for plaintiffs and defendants involved in a trade secret infringement lawsuit.

Trade Secret Misappropriation: Plaintiff's Checklist

■ **Interview the client.** The following information should be obtained:

☐ Trade secret owner's name, address, and business form (i.e., corporation, partnership, etc.).

☐ Information about the development and creation of the trade secret information.

— Security precautions taken regarding the trade secrets (review the security precautions provided earlier in this chapter).

— Method of labeling the trade secret.

— Origin of the secret (i.e., created by employees, consultants, or independent contractors?). Agreements that exist between the company and these parties?

☐ Future purpose of trade secret material under patent or copyright law. Is copyright or patent registration planned? Extent of overlap between trade secret misappropriation and patent or copyright claims?

LEGAL TERMS

jury instructions
Explanations of the legal rules that the jury shall use in reaching a verdict.

□ Extent of public exposure to the trade secret. Is the product on the market and capable of being reverse engineered?

□ Owner's knowledge and discovery of the trade secret misappropriation.

■ **Acquire evidence of the misappropriation.** It is usually difficult to make a case for trade secret misappropriation without direct proof of the improper means or evidence of the misappropriation.

□ Purchase the merchandise or product and reverse engineer it to confirm the use of trade secret material.

□ Trace the chain of development of the product containing the misappropriated trade secret. Did plaintiff's former employees or contractors work for defendant?

■ **Obtain information about all infringing parties.** The trade secret owner should have researched the misappropriation to determine the names of the infringing parties.

□ Determine name, address, and business form of all infringing parties (databases such as LEXIS®, Dialog®, or Westlaw® may provide information regarding business form (i.e., corporation or partnership) and agent for service).

□ Set up computer index (directory of all persons involved in litigation, facts, relationships, and caselaw).

□ Investigate whether infringing defendant has previously been sued for trade secret misappropriation.

■ **Review legal claims and possible defenses regarding misappropriation.**

□ Determine if additional claims, such as patent infringement, copyright infringement, unfair competition, contract, trade dress misappropriation, or other tort or related claims, can be made as a result of the trade secret misappropriation.

□ List *all* possible trade secret defenses (i.e., the information was acquired by proper means or that the information is not confidential) and equitable defenses and review the list with the client.

□ Perform legal research and review caselaw and statutes regarding misappropriation issues. Consider special state rules applying to trade secrets.

■ **Confront the infringer; Prepare cease and desist letter.** As explained in chapters 6 and 10, the cease and desist letter is a summary of the owner's claims and a request that the recipient of the letter halt all misappropriation or infringing activity.

□ Consider whether a cease and desist letter will trigger a declaratory action. Discuss with the client.

■ **Attempt settlement of the dispute.**

□ Determine sums that will compensate the plaintiff for all damages (including attorney fees and related costs).

□ Review state law regarding required language for settlement agreements.

□ Consider what nonmonetary remedies are sought (i.e., does the plaintiff want an injunction or destruction of trade secret materials?). Will the plaintiff consider a royalty as settlement?

■ **Consider alternative dispute resolution.**

☐ Are there agreements between the parties compelling arbitration or mediation?

☐ Consider whether both parties will submit to mediation or arbitration. If so, where?

☐ Locate arbitration or mediation rules and procedures from arbitrating entity (e.g., American Arbitration Association).

■ **Filing the lawsuit.**

☐ Determine if the case will be brought in state or federal court and determine which state's law will apply.

☐ Review appropriate rules of civil procedure and obtain local court rules.

☐ Obtain civil cover sheet and summons from local clerk.

☐ Determine venue.

☐ Assist in preparation of complaint and initial discovery.

☐ Arrange for filing of complaint and issuance of summons.

☐ Coordinate service of process.

☐ Be prepared to establish protective orders to preserve secrecy.

■ **Discovery.** Coordination of discovery and related protective orders requires preparation of a discovery plan.

☐ Calendar all discovery received and propounded for appropriate deadlines.

☐ Summarize and index depositions, interrogatory responses, and documents for use at trial.

■ **Trial.**

☐ Have protective order in place.

☐ Prepare lists of witnesses (and, if necessary, expert witnesses).

☐ Review evidence regarding pretrial motions (e.g., motions in limine).

☐ Prepare trial notebook.

☐ Assist in preparation of jury instructions.

Trade Secret Misappropriation: Defendant's Checklist

■ **Interview the client.** The following information should be obtained:

☐ Defendant's name, address, and business form (i.e., corporation, partnership, etc.).

☐ Information about the defendant's proprietary rights (i.e., all copyright and patent registrations, licenses, and assignments).

☐ Information regarding the defendant's access to the plaintiff's trade secrets. If the defendant is a former employee or contractor of the plaintiff, or if the defendant acquired information from a former employee or contractor, obtain any agreements between the parties.

☐ Extent of sales of the defendant's product containing the alleged trade secrets or extent of display to the public. Extent of advertising.

☐ Defendant's knowledge of the alleged misappropriation and intent.

☐ Review the defendant's insurance, if any, covering this type of dispute. Acquire a copy of the defendant's policy.

- **Review the plaintiff's trade secret ownership.**
  - ☐ Review issues of trade secret ownership. Does the plaintiff *own* the trade secret (e.g., can it be argued that a former employee or consultant who developed the information is actually the owner of the confidential material)?
  - ☐ Acquire information regarding the trade secret protection plan used by the plaintiff to preserve secrecy. (Has ownership been lost by a failure to maintain reasonable efforts for preserving secrecy?)
- **Obtain information about all parties.**
  - ☐ Determine name, address, and business form of all possible parties to the lawsuit, including other potential defendants (databases such as LEXIS®, Dialog®, or Westlaw® may provide information regarding business form (i.e., corporation or partnership), and agent for service).
  - ☐ Set up computer index (directory of all persons involved in litigation, facts, relationships, and caselaw).
- **Review legal claims and possible defenses regarding misappropriation.**
  - ☐ List *all* possible trade secret and equitable defenses and review the list with the client.
  - ☐ Determine if the material is a trade secret (i.e., derives independent economic value, actual or potential, from not being generally known and is the subject of efforts that are reasonable under the circumstances to maintain its secrecy).
  - ☐ Examine the method by which the alleged secret was acquired (i.e., through proper means?):
    - — Discovery through published literature or other available sources; or
    - — Discovery through independent development, research, or experimentation; or
    - — Discovery through reverse engineering; or
    - — Observation of the trade secret as used in public or on public display.
    - — Did a former employee learn about the alleged trade secrets before employment at the plaintiff's business, or by a means other than directly or indirectly through the plaintiff after the employee left the plaintiff's employ?
  - ☐ Perform legal research and review caselaw and statutes regarding misappropriation issues.
  - ☐ Consider whether any counterclaims will be filed.
- **Respond to cease and desist letter.**
  - ☐ Review and respond to accuracy of the allegations in the letter.
  - ☐ Consider whether the defendant should cease activity pending resolution of the dispute.
  - ☐ Consider whether the defendant should file an action for declaratory relief.
- **Attempt settlement of the dispute.** A settlement is a written agreement in which the parties formally resolve the misappropriation dispute.
- **Consider alternative dispute resolution.**

☐ Is there an agreement between the parties compelling arbitration or mediation?

☐ Will both parties submit to mediation or arbitration?

■ **Responding to the complaint.**

☐ Calendar response—20 days from service in federal court (see appropriate state statute for date of response).

☐ Review rules of civil procedure and obtain local court rules.

☐ Determine whether venue or jurisdiction is improper.

☐ Assist in preparation of answer.

☐ If appropriate, prepare counterclaim.

■ **Discovery.** Coordination of discovery requires preparation of a discovery plan. Determine if a protective order should be opposed.

☐ Calendar all discovery received and propounded for appropriate deadlines.

☐ Summarize and index depositions, interrogatory responses, and documents for use at trial.

■ **Trial.**

☐ Prepare lists of witnesses (and expert witnesses).

☐ Prepare trial notebook.

☐ Assist in preparation of jury instructions.

SUMMARY

7.1 A trade secret is any formula, pattern, device, or compilation of information which is used in one's business and which gives the owner of the secret an opportunity to obtain an advantage over competitors who do not know or use it. To maintain ownership rights over a trade secret, the owner must treat the information with secrecy. Trade secrets are protected under state laws, many of which are modeled on the Uniform Trade Secrets Act. Trade secrets can also be protected under state contract law. It is not a misappropriation of a trade secret to independently create confidential information, even if the resulting creation is identical to a trade secret. If the secret is obtained through a legitimate means and without any limitation on disclosure, then the party who learns the secret is free to use it.

7.2 The failure of the trade secret owner to maintain reasonable security will result in the loss of trade secret status. A business is only required to observe reasonable precautions. A confidentiality agreement, also known as a nondisclosure agreement, is a contract that restricts the disclosure of trade secrets. Employees, contractors, and consultants are often required to execute nondisclosure agreements. A covenant not to compete is a contract that restrains a person from engaging in a business, trade, or profession. Courts will prohibit an employee from misappropriating a trade secret and using it to compete.

7.3 To protect against the unauthorized use of an idea or a concept, the parties should enter into a contract such as an evaluation agreement or a submission agreement. Under limited circumstances, the originator and proprietor of an idea may stop others from misappropriating the idea if there was a fiduciary relationship between the parties and if the idea was not one of general knowledge.

7.4 Unlike copyright and patent litigation, trade secret litigation may be brought in state court, or may be brought in federal court if the claim qualifies under federal jurisdiction rules. When a federal court rules on trade secrets, it applies the relevant state law. A party has acquired a trade secret by improper means if it did so by theft, bribery, misrepresentation, breach or inducement of a breach of a duty to maintain secrecy, or espionage through electronic or other methods. An injunction will prevent the defendant's continued use of the trade secret. Sometimes a court will require payment of a royalty rather than enjoin the trade secret. Limiting disclosure of the trade secret during litigation is accomplished by protective orders or other methods of securing the evidence.

NOTES

1. Cal. Bus. & Prof. Code § 16600 *et seq.*

QUESTIONS FOR REVIEW AND DISCUSSION

1. What are the two bases for protecting trade secrets under state law?
2. What are some ways of losing trade secret protection?
3. How does a nondisclosure agreement protect a trade secret?
4. What are some differences between copyright protection and trade secret protection? Between patent and trade secret protection?
5. What is a clean room? What is reverse engineering?
6. What is the relationship between trade secrets and a covenant not to compete?
7. What dangers are there in contacting the new employer of a former employee?
8. On what basis was Art Buchwald compensated?
9. What is "misappropriation" under the Uniform Trade Secrets Act?
10. How can disclosure of trade secrets be limited during litigation?

ACTIVITIES

1. Review the factual situation in the Commentary. What problems would Kidco have protecting the design of the water-trigger device if the company had authorized Dave's speech to the convention of engineers?

2. Locate the state trade secret statute in your state. Is your state statute modeled after the Uniform Trade Secrets Act?

3. The software company Diskco is located in your state. Could the president prohibit employees from competing with the company after they left Diskco? Could the president protect the company's mailing list of customers as a trade secret?

4. Consider that the building where you attend class has been transformed into a software business. What steps would you take to preserve trade secrets at the location?

PROJECT

Review the facts in the Commentary. The president of Kidco has asked the law firm where you work to prepare a series of posters regarding trade secrets. The posters will be displayed throughout the building. Each poster should include the slogan "PROTECT KIDCO TRADE SECRETS" and two or three sentences advising employees on some aspect of trade secret protection. For example, one poster might say, "PROTECT KIDCO TRADE SECRETS—KEEP FILE CABINETS LOCKED—CONFIDENTIAL INFORMATION CAN DISAPPEAR FROM OPEN DRAWERS." What other posters might be suitable?

FOR MORE INFORMATION

The Restatement of the Law

The Restatements are published by the American Law Institute, 4025 Chestnut Street, Philadelphia, PA 19104-3099.

Locating State Secret Law

There are various ways to learn about the trade secret laws in your jurisdiction. Any compendium or legal encyclopedia or collection of state law, such as *CALJUR* in California or *NYJUR* in New York, will list state law under the trade secrets index. The index to the appropriate state codes will also lead to state trade secret law. There are several texts on trade secret law:

R. Milgrim, *Milgrim on Trade Secrets* (Matthew Bender 1967). A two-volume treatise.

M. F. JAGER, *Trade Secrets Law* (Clark Boardman Callaghan 1987).

CHAPTER 8
Principles of Trademarks

*[A logo] should look just as good in 15-foot letters on top company headquarters
as it does one sixteenth of an inch tall on company stationery.*

Steven Gilliatt (1987)

OUTLINE

COMMENTARY

Jane and Julie are two graphic artists who have an idea to create a calendar highlighting famous achievements of women. They plan to name their product The Galendar *and they want to promote it with the slogan, "Woman's Day—Every Day." Before producing any calendars, Jane and Julie form a corporation named The Galendar Corporation. Then, after spending several months perfecting the calendar product, they begin distributing it. The calendar is very popular and the company sells several thousand within the first month. Jane and Julie take out advertisements in* Ms. Magazine *and are interviewed on two cable television shows. The following month, two things happen. Another company publishes a feminist calendar called* The Galendar. *Second, Jane and Julie receive a letter from* Woman's Day *magazine requesting that the Galendar Corporation cease any further use of the slogan. The Galendar Corporation is a client of the law office where you work. Your supervising attorney asks you to perform preliminary research regarding the rival calendar and the letter from the magazine.*

OBJECTIVES

This chapter provides a basic understanding of the principles of trademark law, including the origin and types of protectible trademarks. After reading this chapter you will be able to:

- Explain the relationship between good will and a trademark.
- Describe what can function as a trademark.
- Distinguish between a trademark, a service mark, a collective mark, and a certification mark.
- Determine what is and what is not protectible under trademark law.
- Explain the difference between strong and weak marks.
- Contrast a trademark with generic goods.
- Differentiate a geographically descriptive mark and a geographic certification mark.

- Know the rights associated with a trade name and trade dress.
- Describe the extent of protection for a senior user of a strong trademark.
- Discuss the relationship between the federal Lanham Act, state trademark laws, and the common law.

8.1 TRADEMARKS AND UNFAIR COMPETITION

The **common law** is a system of legal rules derived from the precedents and principles established by court decisions. Certain statutes and common law principles are grouped together under the title of **unfair competition**, a very broad body of law aimed at maintaining ethical ideals in business transactions. As explained in this chapter, trademark laws are derived from these **common law** principles that prohibit companies from competing unfairly. For example, imagine that Smith is a popular clothmaker in 18th-century England. Smith's fabrics are known for their excellent quality and unique designs. Jones, another clothmaker, fraudulently claims that his cloth is made by Smith. Consumers are mistakenly led to believe that Jones's cloth comes from Smith. Under common law principles of unfair competition, the English courts would have prohibited Jones from competing unfairly—that is, attempting to pass off his goods as those of Smith.

Unfair Competition

The general purpose of **unfair competition** law is to prevent business practices that "hinder rather than promote the efficient operation of the market." By way of example, consider Ratco, a manufacturer of rodent poison. Ratco's competitor sells *Kill-o-Ratt,* the top-selling poison. To increase sales, Ratco copies the appearance and unique product shape of *Kill-o-Ratt* and calls its product *Kill-A-Rat.* In its ads, Ratco tells consumers that it will refund one dollar under a special rebate program. However, the company has no plan actually to repay customers. Ratco fraudulently claims that its poison is a patented formula and threatens to sue other rat poison manufacturers. Ratco advertises that its poison has been approved by numerous environmental organizations and that it is the safest rodent poison on the market. None of these statements is true. Finally, Ratco hires hooligans to slash the tires of its competitor's delivery trucks.

Under principles of common law unfair competition, Ratco could be enjoined and liable for damages from each of these deceptive or unfair activities. Every state has common law rules of unfair competition. In addition, many state legislatures have drafted statutes based on the Unfair Trade Practices and Protection Act, a model act prepared by attorneys, scholars, and judges. (A listing of state unfair competition statutes is provided in appendix F.) A federal unfair competition statute, commonly known as § 43(a) of the Lanham Act,[1] also prohibits unfair business practices. As explained in chapter 10, activities such as those engaged in by Ratco give rise to violations of *both* common law unfair competition and statutory unfair competition.

Trademarks and Service Marks

The law of trademarks is part of the family of unfair competition law. Trademark law is derived from a simple principle of commerce: When two businesses are competing for the same consumers, each business will attempt to attract the consumer's attention and gain the purchaser's loyalty. For example, if Kelloggs and Nabisco, two food companies, each sell corn flakes, they will attempt to distinguish their cereals with distinctive names, packages, and logos. They will attempt to create a brand loyalty based upon these trademarks. For this reason, manufacturers create special names, logos, and other devices to distinguish one product from another and to avoid consumer confusion. Any word, symbol, design, device, logo, or slogan that identifies and distinguishes one product from another is a **trademark.** A mark that is used in the sale or advertising of services to identify and distinguish services performed for the benefit of others is known as a **service mark.** The same principles of law govern trademarks and service marks. Throughout this text, all references to trademark law also apply to service marks unless a specific exception is noted.

Good Will

A trademark separated from goods and services has little value. There is no property right, for example, in the hyphenated words *Coca-Cola.* The value or property rights associated with a trademark are in connection with the good will created by the trademark. **Good will** is the tendency or likelihood of a consumer to repurchase goods based upon the name or source. It is an expectation of continued public patronage. If a company uses a distinctive mark or logo and the consumer establishes a loyalty or association to that product, the company earns good will. For example, a waitress at a restaurant may inform Andre, a customer, that the only available cola is *Pepsi Cola.* Andre is a loyal drinker of *Coca-Cola* and will not purchase *Pepsi.* In other words, *Coca-Cola* has established good will with Andre. A transfer of rights of a trademark has little value unless the good will is also transferred.

Trade Names

A **trade name** is the name of a business or company. For example, Diskco is the trade name of the company that owns the rights to the trademark *Brontosaurus* for a computer game. When the term *Diskco* is used to identify the business (e.g., on company stationery, business cards, and in business directories), the name functions as a trade name and not as a trademark. It identifies the business but it is not used to create a consumer association with specific goods or services. Although *Diskco* may be protected under state statutes or principles of unfair competition as a trade name, it will be protected as a trademark only if the company uses *Diskco* to identify and distinguish its goods.

This is an example of a trademark.

LEGAL TERMS

common law
A system of legal rules derived from the precedents and principles established by court decisions.

unfair competition
A collection of common law principles and precedents, many of which have been adopted as state laws, that protect against unfair business practices.

trademark
Any word, symbol, design, slogan, or combination that identifies and distinguishes goods.

service mark
Mark used in the sale or advertising of services to identify and distinguish services performed for the benefit of others.

good will
Tendency or likelihood of a consumer to repurchase goods or services based upon the name or source of the goods or services.

trade name
Name of a business or company; generally not protectible as a trademark unless used to identify and distinguish goods or services.

Many trade names *do* function as a trademark. For example, *Sony* is both a trade name and a trademark for consumer electronics goods and services. When "Sony" is used on company letterhead (for example, the Sony Corporation of America), it is a trade name. But when *Sony* is used on consumer electronics goods, it is a trademark.

Trademark Myth: Corporate or DBA Name Clearance Equals Trademark Clearance. During its formation, a business may register a fictitious business name (also known as a "dba," short for "doing business as") in the state or county, or may register the business name for purposes of incorporation within the state. These processes often involve a "name clearance" through which the state or local government approves the use of a name for the business. Sometimes a business mistakenly assumes that because a name has been approved for purposes of corporation registration, the term is now "owned" by the company and can be used on goods. For example, in the case in the Commentary to this chapter, Jane and Julie incorporated under the name "The Galendar Corporation." However, incorporation does not necessarily indicate that the company can use the name to identify its products or services. Corporate registration only assures the company of the right to use the name for the corporation, not to identify the corporation's products or services. As explained in this chapter, the Galendar Corporation acquires trademark rights once the company begins using the mark in commerce (e.g., selling copies of the calendar).

Trade Dress

This is an example of Trade dress.

Often a business uses other identifying features for a product or service besides a trademark. For example, *Advil* is a registered trademark for pharmaceutical pain relievers. However, in addition to the trademark, *Advil* is packaged in a distinctive dark blue box with yellow lettering. The total image and overall appearance of a product or service is its **trade dress**. Trade dress may include the shape, size, color or color combinations, texture, graphics, or even particular sales techniques. With some exceptions (e.g., distinctively shaped bottles or containers), trade dress cannot be registered like a trademark. However, federal and state unfair competition laws protect trade dress under principles similar to trademark law. In 1992, for example, the U.S. Supreme Court protected the distinctive trade dress of a chain of Mexican restaurants. One chain of Mexican restaurants had adopted similar decor and design elements as a competitor. To avoid consumer confusion, the chain that had imitated the decor and design was barred from further use of such similar elements.[2]

Trademark Infringement

If another company were to copy the distinctive lettering and use a similar name such as *Coco Cola,* consumers would likely be confused when purchasing soft drinks. By using a similar name and style of lettering, *Coco*

Cola is trading off *Coca-Cola*'s good will with consumers and is infringing the trademark of *Coca-Cola.* This is an unfair method of competing. When a second user of a substantially similar trademark creates a likelihood of causing consumer confusion, **trademark infringement** occurs.

Federal law provides a means of protecting and registering marks for goods or services that are in commerce regulated by the federal government (i.e., generally any product or service sold in interstate commerce) or that are intended to be used in interstate commerce. However, unlike copyright law and patent law, trademarks are not exclusively within the control of the federal government. Each state also has its own trademark registration process.

Dilution

Sometimes a trademark owner may be able to preclude the use of a similar mark on unrelated or noncompetitive goods, under a principle known as **dilution**. Dilution occurs when a similar mark adversely affects the reputation of a distinctive mark, even though it may not confuse consumers. Dilution does not result in customer confusion, but it tarnishes or damages the selling power of a distinctive mark. For example, the *Garbage Pail Kids* trading cards, with their rude and violent characters, tarnished and diluted the strength of the wholesome *Cabbage Patch Kids* mark. Many states have special statutes addressing dilution. (A listing of state dilution statutes is provided in appendix F.)

Federal Trademark Law and the Lanham Act

Unlike protection granted to copyrights and patents under Article 1, § 8, clause 8 of the U.S. Constitution, there is no specific authorization in the Constitution regarding trademarks. However, Article 1, § 8, clause 3 of the Constitution authorizes Congress to regulate interstate commerce. Therefore, under this authority, Congress passed the Lanham Act, codified at 15 U.S.C. § 1051 *et seq.* One of the primary purposes of the Lanham Act is to protect the public from confusion or deception by enabling purchasers to identify and obtain desired goods or services. The Lanham Act provides for a federal registration system and establishes remedies for infringement of federally registered trademarks. A trademark or service mark that is federally registered is identified by the symbol ® or language noting federal registration. In addition to federal trademark protection, the Lanham Act is also used to protect against other forms of unfair competition. The Lanham Act has been the basis for lawsuits regarding trade dress infringement, false advertising, and other forms of consumer deception.

Trademarks and service marks may be federally registered on the Principal Register or the Supplemental Register of the U.S. Patent and Trademark Office. The Principal Register is preferred because it offers a stronger range of rights and remedies. However, as explained in chapter 9, certain marks

LEGAL TERMS

trade dress
The total image and overall appearance of a product or service; protected under common law principles similar to trademark law.

trademark infringement
Use of a substantially similar mark by a junior user that creates a likelihood of consumer confusion.

dilution
The adverse effect of use of a similar mark on the reputation of a distinctive mark, even though the use may not confuse consumers as to the source of the goods or services.

will not qualify for the Principal Register, but may qualify for the limited rights and remedies of the Supplemental Register.

Regulations regarding federal trademark practice are located in Title 37 of the Code of Federal Regulations (C.F.R.). If there is a clash between federal and state trademark laws, federal law will preempt state trademark law. **Preemption** is the authority of the federal government to preclude the states from exercising powers granted to the federal government. Even if a trademark is not registered with the federal government (or under state law), it may still be protected under common law principles prohibiting unfair competition. This is because the Lanham Act does not *create* trademark rights—it merely provides a registration scheme and certain remedies for the owners of valid trademarks.

Trademark Law Revision Act of 1988

Under the Lanham Act, as it was originally enacted in 1946, a trademark owner could only apply for registration *after* the mark had been used in interstate commerce. In 1988, the Lanham Act was overhauled. The effective date of this trademark revision was November 16, 1989. Among the changes was a provision for a new system under which a trademark owner can apply for registration prior to using the mark, based upon the owner's bona fide **intent to use** the mark.[3] If the application is *allowed* (i.e., approved and published without opposition), the trademark owner is given a period of up to three years to submit evidence that the mark is in use. Only upon meeting these conditions will a trademark registration issue. The intent-to-use (or ITU) provision was very important for companies seeking protection. For example, prior to ITU, a company might invest a large amount of money preparing labels and advertising, even though an application for registration could not be made until after the product was released in commerce. If, for some reason, the trademark could not be federally registered, the owner would have wasted a great deal of money. The ITU provision enhances predictability for the business introducing a new product, because it can acquire an assurance as to whether registration will occur prior to the preparation of advertising and labels.

As originally passed, the Lanham Act protected federally registered marks for an initial period of 20 years. Because many trademarks were abandoned before the 20 years, this created a great deal of "deadwood" in the Patent and Trademark Office files. The 1988 revision of the Lanham Act also revised the period of protection for federally registered marks. Marks registered after November 16, 1989, are protected for an initial 10-year period, after which the registrant may renew the registration for subsequent 10-year periods.[4]

State Trademark Law and the Model Trademark Act

Some trademarks will not qualify for federal registration because the mark is not used on goods in interstate commerce, commerce between the

United States and a foreign country, or in any other commerce regulated by the federal government. For example, the owner of a floor-polishing business in New York City uses the trademark *Big Apple Polisher.* There is no interstate commerce involved in advertising or providing the floor-waxing services. The business is only concerned about protecting its rights within the state of New York. Therefore, the owner may register the mark in New York under state law.

If the floor-waxing business advertises in New Jersey, begins performing services in New Jersey, or intends to do either of these things, the owner may apply for federal registration. There is an advantage in federal registration. For example, the owner of the New York state registration for *Big Apple Polishers* will not be able to stop a similarly named floor-polishing business from registering in the state of Connecticut. However, with a federal registration, the owner would be able to stop the subsequent Connecticut user.

Each state has its own trademark law. Most of these laws are patterned on the Model State Trademark Bill, which in turn is based upon principles in the Lanham Act. A chart of the various state trademark laws is provided in appendix F. Generally, state registrations occur through the offices of the respective Secretary of State. If a dispute arises as to state trademark rights, the litigation is usually brought in the state where the mark is registered.

The Patent and Trademark Office

The U.S. Patent and Trademark Office (PTO) is responsible for the federal registration of trademarks. The PTO is a division of the Department of Commerce, and although located in Virginia, all correspondence is mailed to the Patent and Trademark Office, Washington DC 20231. Rules and regulations for PTO activities are established in the Lanham Act, in the Code of Federal Regulations, and in special Patent and Trademark Office publications, such as the *Trademark Manual of Examining Procedure* (TMEP). If there is a conflict between trademark owners regarding the registration of a federally registered mark, the parties may resolve the conflict through an **inter partes proceeding** at the Trademark Trial and Appeal Board (TTAB), a division of the Patent and Trademark Office. An inter partes proceeding is a formal administrative hearing governed by the Federal Rules of Civil Procedure and Evidence. An appeal from a TTAB proceeding may be taken to the United States Court of Appeal for the Federal Circuit (located in Washington, D.C.), or it may be brought in any federal district court.

The Restatement of Law: Unfair Competition and Trademarks

The American Law Institute (ALI) is an organization comprised of judges, attorneys, and law professors. The goal of the organization is to clarify and simplify legal principles. The ALI publishes "Restatements" of the law on different topics and, although these Restatements do not have the

LEGAL TERMS

preemption
The authority of the federal government to preclude the states from exercising powers granted to the federal government.

intent-to-use application
Application for federal trademark registration based upon the trademark owner's bona fide intention to use the mark in commerce.

inter partes proceeding
Formal administrative hearing governed by the Federal Rules of Civil Procedure and Evidence.

force of law, they are commonly cited by judges and attorneys. In 1946, the ALI published a *Restatement of the Law of Trademarks and Unfair Competition.* The ALI is in the process of completing an update of this study, *Restatement (Third) of the Law of Unfair Competition.* Chapters 1 and 2 are entitled, "The Freedom to Compete and Deceptive Marketing," chapter 3 of the four volumes deals exclusively with trademarks, and chapter 4 deals with appropriation of trade values. These revised chapters are expected to be out in 1993. This Restatement of Law is available in law libraries and is a valuable source of guidance for trademark practitioners and judges.

8.2 ACQUIRING TRADEMARK RIGHTS

Unlike copyright and patent laws, trademark laws do not reward creativity. That is, trademark rights do not arise from invention, discovery, or creativity. Trademark laws grant protection to the person who first uses the mark in commerce. Consider the trademark *Cracker Jack.* In the 1890s, two German immigrants, the Ruekheim brothers, sold a snack food consisting of popcorn and peanuts covered with molasses. A customer eating the snack supposedly remarked, "This is crackerjack," which was an expression meaning that the product was excellent. The brothers decided to use the term *Cracker Jack* as the trademark for their snack food. A few years later, another customer supposedly told the brothers, "The more you eat, the more you want." This became the slogan (and another trademark), for the *Cracker Jack* snack food. It does not matter who first created the term *Cracker Jack* or the slogan *"The more you eat, the more you want."* What matters is who *first* used it on goods in commerce. That person acquires trademark rights. Why? Because trademark law is based upon the principle of protecting the consumer and allowing companies to compete fairly. The first user of the mark on goods in commerce creates an association with consumers. Subsequent users are likely to confuse consumers as to the source. To avoid confusion and to encourage fair competition, trademark laws grant rights to the first user of the mark in commerce. The extent of trademark rights is affected by five factors: the distinctiveness of the mark, the goods or services, the date of first use in commerce, the geographic area in which the mark is used, and the registration of the mark, if any.

Goods and Services

One of the cornerstones of trademark law is that protection for a mark extends only to the particular goods or services with which the mark is used, intended to be used, or likely to be used. For example, one company may own a trademark for the term *Camel* for cigarettes. This company will have difficulty stopping another company from using *Camel* as a trademark for water storage containers. The rationale is that the purpose of trademark is to avoid consumer confusion among competitive or related goods. Water storage containers and cigarettes are not competitive or related goods. They are not sold through the same channels of distribution or in the same retail outlets. However, if a company made cigarette holders or ashtrays and used the *Camel* trademark, these are arguably goods related to cigarettes, and therefore may confuse consumers as to their source. In the case of the fact pattern presented in the Commentary to this chapter, *Woman's Day* magazine has used the mark on printed goods for women. Therefore the use of the *Woman's Day* mark within the *Galendar* logo may cause confusion as to the source of the related calendar goods. Determining whether goods or services are related is a decision made by the Patent and Trademark Office and the courts. In some cases, as described in chapter 10, the owner of an extremely well-known mark may be able to stop use of a similar mark on seemingly unrelated goods.

Date of First Use in Commerce

When two trademark owners use a substantially similar mark on goods in commerce, the first party to adopt and use a particular mark in connection

JUDGE LEARNED HAND ON TRADEMARKS: The "Yale" Lock Case

In 1928, a company that manufactured flashlights and batteries was prevented from using the trademark *Yale* on its goods or any other article manufactured out of metal. The reason for this injunction was that another company was using the same trademark on locks. Judge Hand invoked an important standard for determining trademark protection—the opinion of the relevant trade. On this basis, Judge Hand affirmed the injunction preventing the use of the term on flashlights and batteries; however, he limited the injunction and refused to prohibit the use of *Yale* on all metal goods.

In the *Yale Electric* case (*Yale Electric Corp. v. Robertson*, 26 F.2d 974 (2d Cir. 1928)), Judge Hand stated one of the important tenets of trademark law:

> "A merchant may have significant economic interest in the use of his mark outside the field of his own exploitation. . . . His mark is his authentic seal; by it he vouches for the goods that bear it; it carries his name for good or ill. If another use it, he borrows the owner's reputation, whose quality no longer lies within his control. This is an injury, even though the borrower does not tarnish it, or divert any sales by its use; for a reputation, like a face, is the symbol of its possessor and creator and another can use it only as a mask."

with its goods or services is known as the **senior user**. A party who adopts and uses a trademark similar to the mark previously adopted and used by the senior user is known as a **junior user**. A senior user will have priority over junior users. For example, the Diskco company releases a new accounting program called *Bean Counter.* A few weeks later, Softco introduces an accounting program called *Mr. Bean Counter.* The marks are substantially similar and are used on similar goods in commerce. Diskco, as the senior user, can stop Softco from its use of the *Mr. Bean Counter* mark. Even if Softco federally registers its mark prior to Diskco's registration, Diskco will still be able to stop Softco from using its mark, because Diskco first used the mark in commerce.

However, this rule regarding first use in commerce may not always control the disposition of the case. As explained later in this chapter, certain marks, because of their descriptive nature, do not qualify for protection until the marks have acquired secondary meaning. **Secondary meaning** is a demonstration that the consuming public associates the mark with a single source. This does not mean that the public knows the name or location of the company that manufactures the goods; it only means that the consuming public thinks that there is one particular source for certain trademarked goods. For example, in the case described in the Commentary to this chapter, the term *Galendar* describes a calendar for "gals" or women. To stop subsequent users of the same mark, the company must demonstrate through its sales, advertising, or promotion that the public associates *Galendar* with its products. In the case of descriptive marks, the first company to establish secondary meaning would be able to stop the other user. In other words, the company with the most extensive advertising, promotion, and sales is more likely to preclude the other from its use of a descriptive trademark.

In addition, it is not enough for a company to establish that it was the first user of a mark in commerce. In addition to its prior use, the company must be able to establish that the use has been continuous. As explained in the next chapter, a long period of nonuse may result in the loss of trademark rights.

One exception of the senior user–junior user issue of priority occurs when a party has filed an intent-to-use application with the Patent and Trademark Office. In that case, the party that has filed its bona fide intent-to-use application will have priority over a subsequent party who first uses the mark, *provided* the ITU application is eventually issued as a registration on the Principal Register.

Abandonment

Trademark rights derive from the continued use of the mark in commerce. If the mark is no longer used in commerce and there is sufficient evidence that the owner intends to discontinue use of the mark, then **abandonment** occurs. For example, if the owner of a mark for hotel services closes its hotels and fails to use the mark on similar services for a period of 30 years, there is sufficient proof that the mark is no longer in use and that, by nonuse of the mark, the owner intended to abandon the mark. Abandonment may also result from the loss of distinctiveness of a mark or from the trademark owner's misuse of trademark rights. Abandonment is discussed in more detail in chapter 10.

8.3 TYPES OF MARKS

The Lanham Act defines a *trademark* as any word, name, symbol, or device, or any combination thereof, used, or intended to be used, by a person to identify and distinguish goods from those manufactured or sold by others.[5] There is no limit to what can function as a trademark. Consider, for example, the ice cream company with trucks that make street sales. The ice cream company may use a distinctive name for its products, such as *Polar Bars,* and may use a distinctive design for the product, shaping each bar like a polar bear. The trucks for the company may have a distinctive "igloo" shape. Each truck also may use a distinctive series of four bell-like tones. When consumers hear the tones, see the trucks, view the ice cream bars, or identify the name *Polar Bar,* they will associate these names, symbols, or devices with a certain company's ice cream products. Because these indicia distinguish the company's goods, each of them functions as a trademark. When a mark functions to identify and distinguish services, it is a service mark. The vast majority of marks are either trademarks or service marks. In addition to trademarks and service marks, the Lanham Act provides protection for two other types of marks: *collective marks,* which signify membership in an organization; and *certification marks,* which attest to regional origin, quality, or method of manufacture. As noted earlier, the term *trademark* or *mark* is used in this book interchangeably to describe trademarks, service marks, collective marks, or certification marks, unless the specific type of mark is distinguished by the context.

Names, Words, and Numbers

Most trademarks are in alphanumeric form—that is, they consist of letters, words, numbers, or a combination thereof. The most popular marks are words. For example, *Lotus, Applause, Quicken,* or *WordPerfect* are all words that distinguish various computer software goods. Letters by themselves also may function as trademarks. *CNN, MTV,* and *ESPN* are all marks that distinguish various cable television broadcast services. Numbers can function as marks. For example, *20/20* and *60 Minutes* are marks that distinguish television news services. A combination of letters and numbers also may function as a mark. For example, *UB40, MX-80,* and *U2* are all marks that distinguish the entertainment services of various musical groups. A combination of words that functions as a slogan also may qualify as a trademark. For example, *"You're in good hands with Allstate,"* and *"Like a good neighbor, State Farm is there,"* distinguish insurance services. Names, under

LEGAL TERMS

senior user
  The first party to adopt and use a particular mark in connection with its goods or services.

junior user
  A party that adopts and uses a trademark similar to a mark previously adopted and used by a senior user.

secondary meaning
  Demonstration that the consuming public associates a descriptive mark with a single source; usually proved by advertising, promotion, and sales.

abandonment
  Loss of trademark rights resulting from nonuse of the mark; demonstrated by sufficient evidence that the owner intends to discontinue use of the mark. May also occur when a mark has lost its distinctiveness or through the owner's misuse of trademark rights.

certain circumstances, also can function as trademarks. *Gallo, Mondavi,* and *Manischevitz* are all names that distinguish various wines. Even the abbreviation of a trademark can become a trademark. For example, *Coke* and *RC Cola* are both abbreviations (for *Coca-Cola,* and *Royal Crown Cola,* respectively) that distinguish cola soft drinks.

Logos, Symbols, and Devices

In addition to alphanumeric trademarks, logos, symbols, and devices have functioned for centuries as marks. **Logos** (short for logotypes) are graphic symbols that may use stylized lettering or concise imagery. For example, the image of a dog listening to the open cone of an old-style phonograph functioned for many years as the logo trademark for the RCA Corporation. Furniture and crockery makers historically differentiated their goods by special symbols and shapes, usually placed on the bottom or underside of their wares. Geometric shapes also can function as marks. The unique star shape used by the Mercedes Benz company and the open-banded cross used by the Chevrolet company both serve to distinguish goods supplied by automobile manufacturers. A **device** can be anything that serves to differentiate the goods or services. Some example of devices that function as marks include:

- the distinctive chimes used to identify a radio station
- a statue used to identify a restaurant
- a fictional character, such as *Betty Crocker* or *Uncle Ben,* used to identify food products
- the uniquely shaped cypress tree used to identify Pebble Beach's sports and entertainment services
- the yellow arches of the McDonald's fast food franchise
- the color pink when applied to fiberglass insulation
- the distinctive fragrance applied to a fabric to distinguish it from competitive fabrics.

Trademarks: Using the Mark with Goods

A trademark is a mark used in conjunction with goods or products. One factor that sometimes helps in determining if something functions as a trademark is whether the mark is used as an adjective and "announces" a product's identity to the consumer. A walk down a supermarket aisle will illustrate this principle: *Windex* describes a type of glass cleaner; *Jell-O* describes a type of gelatin dessert; *Sanka* describes a brand of decaffeinated coffee; and *Sweet 'n Low* depicts a type of sugar substitute. All these trademarks are placed on labels or containers for the goods and are used in advertising for the goods are described. If a trademark is federally registered, the owner may use the symbol ®. If not federally registered, the owner may use the symbol ™ to signify a claim to the mark.

Service Marks: Using the Mark in Conjunction with a Service

Many parties perform services for the benefit of others. For example, the company that owns the *Hilton* resort chain performs hotel services for travelers. The rock group *R.E.M.* provides entertainment services. When any party performs services or labor for the benefit of others, then the mark that identifies those services is a *service mark.*[6] The federal courts have interpreted a *service* to be an activity that is (1) real; (2) for the benefit of someone other than the applicant; and (3) qualitatively different from what is necessarily done in connection with the sale of goods.

For example, the computer company CompCo sells computers. The routine repairs necessitated by CompCo warranties are not a service that would give rise to a service mark, because it is expected and legally required in connection with the sale of CompCo's goods. However, if Compco is a company that performs computer repairs and troubleshooting for many brands of computers (not merely its own), that service would qualify for protection under trademark law. Recently, the Patent and Trademark Office provided examples of activities that may or may not qualify as a service for purposes of trademark protection. Some of those examples are presented in Table 8.1.

A trademark is usually applied or affixed to containers or labels for the goods. A service mark, however, is used in advertisements or promotional material that identifies the services rendered in commerce. A mark can function as both a trademark and a service mark. For example, the mark *Abba* is used by a Swedish pop singing group. When the group provides entertainment services such as concerts, *Abba* functions as a service mark. When the

Activity	Service	Not a Service
Contest	The party conducts contests as its sole business.	The contest is incidental to the sale of goods or services.
Personnel	The party recruits and places workers for other companies.	The party operates a personnel department to employ workers for itself.
Guarantee/ Warranty	The guarantee for the goods is paid separately; the guarantee or warranty is above the industry norm; the goods are offered for sale with the guarantee; or the guarantee is not limited by time like a manufacturer's guarantee.	A manufacturer's warranty of its own goods and which is not charged, promoted, or offered separately.
Publishing	The publication of books or magazines for others.	The publication of one's own newspaper; or advertising or design services for the benefit of one's own publication.

TABLE 8.1
Services That May or May Not Have Trademark Protection

group releases record albums, *Abba* functions as a trademark. Although the Lanham Act provides protection for both trademarks and service marks, some state trademark statutes do not provide for registration of service marks.

The AMA logo is a collective mark.

Collective Marks

A **collective mark** is used by members of a cooperative, an association, or another collective group or organization to indicate membership.[7] This is the purpose of a collective mark—to indicate that the user is a member of an organization. For example, the distinctive eagle, placed within the arrow-head-shaped crest with the letters "GS," is a collective mark that indicates membership in the Girl Scouts of America.

Certification Marks

Certification marks have been described as a "special creature" of trademark law. The function of a certification mark is different from that of a trademark. A certification mark is used in connection with products and services to certify regional or other origin, material, mode of manufacture, quality, accuracy, or other characteristics.[8] A certification mark is always used in conjunction with another mark, because the owner of the certification mark does not produce or sell goods—it only certifies some quality of the goods or services. For example, various companies grow and sell potatoes under different trademarks. However, if a consumer purchased a brand of potatoes that had the *IDAHO* certification mark, then the consumer would have certification as to the geographic origin of the product. Similarly, the purchaser of *WASHINGTON* apples receives an assurance that the goods are in fact from the state of Washington. When a consumer purchases cheese with the certification *ROQUEFORT,* there is an authentication that the cheese was manufactured from sheep's milk in the caves of Roquefort, France, according to long-established methods.

A certification mark may also attest to materials used, the mode of manufacture or quality, accuracy, or other characteristics. The presence of the mark *UL* from the Underwriters Laboratory certifies that representative samplings of electrical equipment meet certain safety standards. The Good Housekeeping *Seal of Approval* is a well-known certification mark indicating that products have been tested and meet certain standards. A certification mark may also indicate that labor was performed by a certain organization. For example, *ILGWU-UNION MADE* certifies that the garment (bearing its own trademark) was manufactured by members of the International Ladies Garment Workers Union.

Multiple Marks

A manufacturer or provider of services can use any number of trademarks to distinguish its goods or services. For example, an advertisement for

Diet Coke may include numerous trademarks, including the distinctive name, the abbreviation *Coke,* the slogan *"Things Go Better With Coke,"* the distinctive red-and-white "wave" shapes, the distinctively shaped *Coca-Cola* bottle, and even the trademark for *NutraSweet,* a licensed product that is incorporated within the *Diet Coke* product. There is no prohibition on the use of more than one mark for a product, and numerous goods and services use multiple marks. The most common combination of multiple marks occurs when a house mark is combined with a mark for a product. A **house mark** is often a trade name (used as a trademark) that functions as the source for various products or services from one company. For example, *Sony* is the house mark for a variety of products from an electronics manufacturer. *Sony* also maintains various product marks, such as *Trinitron* for televisions, *Walkman* for personal stereos, and *My First Sony* for children's consumer electronics. Often a combination of house and product marks is used, for example, *Sony*® *Walkman.*

8.4   STRONG MARKS VERSUS WEAK MARKS

Why is it that some trademarks immediately attract the consumer's attention and others take a long time to become established? For example, the trademark *Apple* is a distinctive and memorable mark for computers. Unlike marks such as *Microsoft* and *Compudyne,* the *Apple* mark does not describe the qualities or characteristics of microcomputers or software. The creators of the Apple computer company wanted a term that could have many meanings and also that symbolized knowledge (alluding to the Biblical story in which Adam and Eve bite an apple from the tree of knowledge). When the Apple computer company offered a new computer line, the company used the name of another type of apple, the *Macintosh.* Unlike marks that merely describe the qualities of the goods or services, both the *Apple* and *Macintosh* marks were immediately distinctive and had inherently distinctive qualities. Because some marks are more distinctive than others, trademark laws provide for a two-step analysis of marks. If a mark is *inherently distinctive,* it is considered to be "strong," and trademark protection begins upon its use in commerce. The owner of an inherently distinctive mark will immediately be able to stop subsequent users of similar marks on similar goods and services. However, if a mark is not inherently distinctive, and merely describes a product or its nature, quality, characteristics, ingredients, or origin, it is considered "weak" because it is *descriptive.* A descriptive mark will not acquire trademark protection until the owner can demonstrate that consumers associate the mark in identifying the goods or services as originating from a particular source. This proof of consumer association is known as *secondary meaning.*

The company may want a descriptive mark rather than a memorable or clever mark because a descriptive mark such as *Clean & Smooth* (for antibacterial soap) or *Healthy Favorites* provides information about the product to the consumer. When choosing a mark, the attorney advising the

LEGAL TERMS

collective mark
  Mark used by members of a cooperative, an association, or other collective group or organization to signify or indicate membership.

certification mark
  Mark indicating that third-party goods or services meet certain standards, such as regional origin, material, mode of manufacture, quality, or accuracy, or that the work or labor was performed by a member of a certain organization.

house mark
  Mark that functions as the source for various products or services from one company.

company may encourage an inherently distinctive mark because it provides immediate legal protection.

Inherently Distinctive Marks: Strong Marks

Certain trademarks are memorable because they exhibit a creative twist. Consider popular breakfast cereals like *Cheerios* and *Trix,* or candy bars such as *Three Musketeers* or *Milky Way,* all terms that have either fanciful, playful, or suggestive qualities—yet do not actually describe the goods. Experts in trademark law consider these marks to be strong because they are inherently distinctive or memorable. These distinctive trademarks are generally classified into three groups: fanciful, arbitrary, or suggestive marks.

Fanciful Marks.   A **fanciful mark** is a term that is invented, coined, or made up. It is generally a word or a combination of letters that has no dictionary meaning. For example, the Standard Oil Company once used the trademark *Esso* (a phonetic soundalike for the letters "S" and "O") for gasoline and automotive products. To update the company's image, the company

coined a more modern term in the 1960s, *Exxon. Exxon* is fanciful. Exxon does not describe anything and has no meaning. Similarly, *Xerox* was invented as a term to identify a brand of photocopy machines. *Kodak* was coined for photographic products. Although fanciful marks are strong and acquire trademark rights immediately upon use in commerce, they are often disfavored by trademark owners. Why? Because the public must be educated as to the consumer association—that is, what the term is supposedly identifying. Not all made-up words are fanciful.

Not All Coined Terms Are Fanciful.   Some terms may have a recognized meaning to consumers or may have a meaning when considered phonetically. For example, *Breadspred* (for jams and jellies) is not a fanciful mark because it has a meaning to consumers and is descriptive of the qualities of the goods—i.e., that they can be spread on bread. Similarly, the mark *Galendar,* as used in the Commentary to this chapter, is not a fanciful mark because it has a meaning that is descriptive of the goods—i.e., a calendar for "gals" or women.

Arbitrary Marks.   An **arbitrary mark** is a word or image that has a common meaning that does not describe or suggest the goods or services; for example, *Apple* for computers, *Black and White* for scotch liquor, *Arm & Hammer* for baking soda, *Lucky Strike* for cigarettes, or *Arrow* for shirts. Most service marks used by pop and rock groups are arbitrary—the *Rolling Stones, Parliament,* the *Psychedelic Furs,* the *Ventures*—because such words do not describe or pertain to entertainment services. Arbitrary marks, like fanciful marks, require education of consumers as to the association between the mark and the goods or services.

Suggestive Marks.   A *suggestive mark* alludes to or hints at (without describing) the nature or quality of the goods. For example, *Roach Motel* suggests, without describing, the nature of a trap for catching insects. *Coppertone* suggests, without describing, the results of using a brand of suntan oil. *Rain Dance* does not describe a car wax, but suggests that rain will "dance" off the wax. Like fanciful and arbitrary marks, suggestive marks are also inherently distinctive and are registrable on the Principal Register without any proof of secondary meaning.

Descriptive Marks: Weak Marks

Many manufacturers or providers of services choose to use marks that are descriptive. For example, *Beef & Brew* describes what is available at a restaurant. *Vision Center* describes a place where eyeglasses can be purchased. *Bufferin* describes a product that consists of buffered aspirin. *Shake 'N Bake* describes the method of using a food product. *Chap Stick* describes a stick-shaped compound used to heal chapped lips. All of these marks are descriptive of goods or services. A descriptive mark describes a product or service, or its purpose, function, use, nature, quality, characteristics, ingredients, or geographic origin. Marks that are merely descriptive generally are registrable only on the Supplemental Register, and will obtain protection only if the trademark owner can prove secondary meaning. This does not mean that the public knows the company that manufactures the goods; it only means that the consuming public thinks that there is one particular source for certain trademarked goods. For example, when the consumer sees *Bufferin* or *Chap Stick,* an association is made. The consumer associates the mark with one particular brand, not all buffered aspirins or stick applications for chapped lips. Secondary meaning does not mean that the consumer knows the name of the business that supplies the goods. For example, a consumer may not know the name of the company that publishes the *World Book Encyclopedia,* but the consumer associates the mark with a single source of encyclopedias. For purposes of federal registration, secondary meaning may be assumed after five years of continuous and exclusive use of the mark. However, a trademark owner does not have to wait five years if it can be proven through advertising, promotion, or sales that secondary meaning has been established earlier.

For example, suppose that a company uses a descriptive mark, *Nut Case,* for a mixed-nut snack sold in a tin case. The company spends a large amount of money on a massive advertising campaign and within one month has sold over a million units of *Nut Case* snacks. This extensive advertising and sales demonstrate secondary meaning. Secondary meaning also can be demonstrated by consumer surveys or other proof that consumers associate a specific source for the goods.

If a descriptive mark cannot be registered until after a showing of secondary meaning, why would a company choose to use a weak mark instead of a strong, inherently distinctive mark? Because many businesses prefer

LEGAL TERMS

fanciful mark
Term that is invented, coined, or made up; generally a word or combination of letters that has no dictionary meaning.

arbitrary mark
Word or image that has a common meaning that does not describe or suggest the goods or services with which it is associated.

trademarks that describe the purpose or nature of their goods and services. With a descriptive mark, the consumer immediately knows, for example, that *Food Fair* is a supermarket and that *Raisin Bran* is a cereal made with raisins and bran. The informative nature of a descriptive mark is invaluable for a company that wants to familiarize consumers quickly with a new product or service. When the otherwise descriptive mark has become distinctive through secondary meaning, registration will be permitted on the Principal Register.

Geographically Descriptive Marks.   As noted earlier, if a mark is used to certify a geographic source, that mark can be registered as a certification mark. A certification mark is always used in conjunction with a trademark or service mark. For example, a company in Idaho uses the mark *Little Farmer* for frozen french-fried potatoes. Like other companies selling potatoes grown in Idaho, the company may use the certification mark *Idaho Potatoes* (in conjunction with its own trademark) to authenticate the geographic origin of the potatoes.

However, if the company were to use the term *Little Idaho Farmer* as a trademark for its frozen foods, then the term "Idaho" is not being used as a certification mark, but as part of a trademark. In this instance, "Idaho" describes the geographic location or origin of the goods. Unlike a certification mark, *Little Idaho Farmer* does not make a guarantee of authentication. When a geographic term is used to describe the location or origin of the goods, it is considered to be descriptive and is therefore not inherently distinctive. It is a weak mark that requires proof of secondary meaning to obtain trademark protection. The geographic designation may be to any location, including streets, rivers, cities, or even nicknames. For example, *Quaker State* is a geographically descriptive nickname for Pennsylvania, and therefore its use in a trademark for oil produced in Pennsylvania is descriptive. When a geographic term does not describe the location or the origin of the goods, then the mark is considered to be arbitrary. For example, *European* health spas or *Atlantic* magazine are uses that do not describe the source of the goods or services. Note that if the goods do not come from the place that is named, but the public is deceived into believing they are from the geographic area, the mark is considered to be geographically deceptively misdescriptive. For example, if a sausage product from Florida is called *Neapolitan* Italian sausage and features an Italian flag, that would be geographically deceptively misdescriptive and would be refused federal registration, as discussed in chapter 9.

Personal Names (Surnames).   Many goods and services use marks based upon personal names. For example, clothing manufacturers commonly use designers' names to indicate the source of the goods. *Chanel, Gucci,* and *Levis* all use personal names as trademarks. Personal names, like descriptive marks, acquire trademark protection only upon proof of secondary meaning. This rule may seem at odds with trademark principles. After all, a name like

Jones for pants and jeans seems to be arbitrary and not descriptive of the clothing. However, one rationale offered by a leading trademark expert is that personal names *do* describe an attribute of the goods—they characterize the goods as being from someone named Jones. But which Jones? Only after the *Jones* Jeans company has established secondary meaning can it be assumed that the public knows (and associates) Jones with jeans.

8.5 WHAT IS NOT PROTECTIBLE AS A TRADEMARK?

Not every term, designation, or title can function as a trademark, even when used with a product or service. For example, the Patent and Trademark Office may refuse registration if the matter furnished is merely an adornment or decoration and does not function to distinguish or identify the goods. For example, the use of a blue ring around the outside of a plate, or a white circle around the inside of a tire, is more likely to function as an embellishment, than as an identification of the source of the goods. Similarly, functional designs will not qualify as trademarks. A descriptive term also may not be protectible as a trademark until there is proof of secondary meaning. A **generic term**, a term that describes an entire group or class of goods or services, can never function as trademark. For example, the term *telephone* describes a class of goods, and no manufacturer of telephones would be able to acquire a trademark solely for the term *telephone*. The rest of this section elaborates on some of the things that cannot function as trademarks.

Generic Terms

During the mid-1980s, several supermarket chains began offering "generic" products. For example, beer was sold in plain white cans that simply said "beer," and paper towels were sold in packages that just said "paper towels." The logic was that the supermarket could offer lower prices because the cost to manufacture and sell these products did not include the expense of labeling and advertising. However, the negative aspect of the promotion was that consumers could not identify the source or quality of the goods. For the manufacturers, there was an added disincentive: Any company was free to use the generic packaging and labeling, and therefore there was no way to protect against competitive use or to encourage brand loyalty.

This is the major problem with a generic term. It can never function as trademark because it describes an entire group or class of goods. If the principal significance of a term is that it is the name of the article, then the term is generic. For example, the principal significance of the term *bicycle* is that it is the name of a chain-driven, human-powered device with wheels, pedals, a seat, and handlebars. No company can trademark the term *bicycle* although any company can create a trademark such as *Specialized*, *Fuji*, or *Schwinn* that indicates the source of a brand of bicycle. As a general rule, the generic term almost always follows the trademark, as shown in Table 8.2.

LEGAL TERMS

generic term
Term that describes an entire group or class of goods.

Trademark	Generic Term
Crest	toothpaste
PageMaker	desktop publishing program
Dustbuster	portable vacuum

TABLE 8.2
Trademarks of generic terms

Literary and Movie Titles

The title of a single book, play, or movie is usually not protected as a trademark, because the primary purpose of the title is to describe the book or movie. A title of a single book or movie may achieve protection, however, if the owner can demonstrate secondary meaning. Titles of literary or audiovisual works generally achieve protection only if the work is serialized. Some examples of titles that may achieve protection include: the title of a magazine (i.e., *Newsweek* or *New York* magazine); the title of a series of books (*Cult Movies,* volumes 1 and 2); the title of a film with sequels (*The Godfather* (I–III); or the title of a television series (*All in the Family, The Dating Game*).

Functional Features

Trademark law, like copyright law, will not protect an object whose design is dictated by its function. By way of example, consider a guitar. It would be very difficult to acquire trademark protection for the metal tuning nuts that hold the guitar strings. These mechanical devices serve a specific utilitarian function and their design is dictated almost exclusively by their function. However, the body of the guitar, if it is uniquely cast or molded, may become a trademark, because the shape of the body is not necessarily dictated by function (as evidenced by the rounded, wide-bottom shape of the *Ovation* brand of guitars).

Trademark law will not protect functional objects that are part of the packaging of a product. For example, if the design of a spray nozzle is based primarily upon its function (i.e., spraying a liquid), it will not be protected as a trademark. However, if the design of a wine bottle is based primarily on ornamental rather than functional considerations, as in the case of the *Mogen David* wine bottle, then the bottle may achieve protection as a trademark. In addition, nonfunctional design features may be protected under trade dress principles or under principles for design patents.

Descriptive Marks

As previously noted, descriptive terms, geographically descriptive terms, and personal names are not protectible until the owner can demonstrate secondary meaning. For example, the mark *Arthriticare*, as used for an analgesic gel to relieve arthritis pain, is descriptive because it describes the general use to which the product is put. Until the owner of the mark can show that a significant number of prospective purchasers associate the mark with the product as originating from a particular source, the mark lacks secondary meaning and cannot be protected.

SUMMARY

8.1 Trademark laws are derived from common law principles that prohibit companies from competing unfairly. Unfair competition is a body of law aimed at maintaining ethical ideals in business transactions. Trademark law is part of the law of unfair competition; its purpose is to prevent the unauthorized use of a word, logo, design, or device that distinguishes goods or services. A trade name is the name of a business and also may function as a trademark. Trade dress is the overall appearance of a product or service. Trademark infringement occurs when a substantially similar mark used on similar goods is likely to cause consumer confusion. Dilution occurs when a similar mark adversely affects the reputation of a distinctive mark.

8.2 The extent of trademark rights is affected by the distinctiveness of the mark, the goods or services, the date of first use in commerce, the geographic area in which the mark is used, and the registration of the mark, if any. Protection of a mark extends to the goods or services and to related goods or services. The first party to adopt and use a distinctive mark in commerce on goods or services establishes a priority over subsequent users on similar goods and services. Trademark rights derive from the continued use of the mark. The failure to continuously use a mark may result in its abandonment.

8.3 A trademark is a mark used to distinguish goods, whereas a service mark is used to distinguish services. A collective mark is a mark used to indicate membership in an organization. A certification mark is used to certify regional origin or quality of goods or services. A certification mark is always used in conjunction with a trademark or service mark.

8.4 If a trademark is inherently distinctive, protection begins upon its use in commerce. If a trademark is descriptive of the goods or services, then protection will begin only upon a showing that prospective purchasers associate the mark with the product as originating from a particular source. This showing is known as secondary meaning and is demonstrated by sales, advertising, and length of use of the mark.

8.5 Trademark law does not protect terms that describe an entire group or class of goods. These generic terms, such as *telephone* and *automobile* are for all to use in the description of their goods. Although a descriptive term may achieve protection upon a showing of secondary meaning, a generic term can never be protected under trademark law.

NOTES

1. 15 U.S.C. § 1125 (federal unfair competition law; § 43(a) of the Lanham Act).
2. Two Pesos, Inc. v. Taco Cabana International, Inc., 112 S. Ct. 2753 (1992).
3. 15 U.S.C. § 1051(b)-(d) (intent to use trademark).
4. 15 U.S.C. § 1058 (duration of federal trademark registration).
5. 15 U.S.C. § 1127 (Lanham Act definitions).
6. 15 U.S.C. § 1053 (service marks; § 3 of Lanham Act).
7. 15 U.S.C. § 1054 (collective marks; § 4 of the Lanham Act).
8. 15 U.S.C. § 1054 (certification marks; § 4 of the Lanham Act).

QUESTIONS FOR REVIEW AND DISCUSSION

1. What is the purpose of trademark law?
2. What is the importance of the date when a company first uses a trademark in commerce?
3. What is good will?
4. Does the right to use a corporate trade name guarantee trademark rights?
5. Will trademark law protect a personal name used as a trademark?
6. What federal office manages trademark registration?
7. What is the difference between the Lanham Act and the Model Trademark Act?
8. What are some important changes brought about by the Trademark Law Revision Act of 1988?
9. What is a house mark?
10. Why are marks separated according to strength and weakness?
11. What is secondary meaning?
12. Why can't a generic term achieve trademark protection?

ACTIVITIES

1. Review the factual situation in the Commentary. Determine if the Galendar Corporation can stop the subsequent user of the *Galendar* mark. What criteria are important in making this determination?
2. Examine various products and make a chart separating the trademark from the generic term that it describes.
3. Find the Lanham Act in the United States Code. Locate Title 37 of the Code of Federal Regulations.
4. Make a list of literary and movie titles that may have achieved trademark status.

PROJECT

Obtain a copy of a Sunday newspaper supplement for local supermarkets or grocery products. Identify the various trademarks and try to determine which are federally registered. List the terms and discuss the strength or weakness of each mark by categorizing the marks as arbitrary, fanciful, suggestive, or descriptive.

FOR MORE INFORMATION

Trademark Law

Many secondary sources of trademark information are presented throughout this and subsequent chapters. This list includes some treatises and guides that may be helpful in understanding trademark law.

J. Thomas McCarthy, *McCarthy on Trademarks and Unfair Competition*, 3d ed. (Clark Boardman Callaghan 1992). A three-volume looseleaf treatise commonly cited in legal opinions.

Kramer & Brufsky, *Trademark Law Practice Forms* (Clark Boardman Callghan 1991). A three-volume looseleaf treatise emphasizing practice forms.

S. D. Kane, *Trademark Law* (Practising Law Institute 1991). A one-volume practitioner's guide.

United States Trademark Association, *State Trademark and Unfair Competition* (Clark Boardman Callaghan 1987). A one-volume treatise offering state by state analysis of trademark, unfair competition and related business statutes.

McGrath, Elias, & Shena, *Trademark: How to Name Your Business and Product* (Nolo Press 1992). A one-volume paperback designed for small business.

The International Trademark Association

A helpful secondary source for information about trademark practice is the International Trademark Association (ITA). This association helped to draft the Model Trademark Act, as well as the 1988 revisions to the Lanham Act. The ITA offers numerous publications, handbooks, and documentation regarding trademarks. The ITA is located at 6 East 45th Street, New York, NY, 10017.

The Restatement of the Law

The *Restatements* are published by the American Law Institute, 4025 Chestnut Street, Philadelphia, PA 19104-3099.

CHAPTER 9
Trademarks: Selection, Evaluation, and Registration

*Dozens of meetings, hundreds of man-hours, millions of dollars and months of angst . . .
went into the name change . . . the most sweeping of changes brought
about by the most persnickity attention to detail.*

Lisa Belkin

COMMENTARY

The law office where you work represents Diskco. Diskco is developing a new computer software program that enables a user to double the information stored on a floppy disk. This method allows the user to save space on disks using a system called data compression. Diskco has developed five possible marks for their new product. These names include: Disk Compressor, Space Saver, Jam Session, The Big Squeeze, *and* Scrooge. *Diskco would like to apply for federal registration for its trademark before preparing its labels, advertisements, and promotion. Your supervising attorney requests that you search and review these marks and indicate your recommendation for Diskco's course of action.*

OBJECTIVES

Chapter 8 provided a basic understanding of what can be protected under trademark law. In this chapter, you will be exposed to the methods of selecting, evaluating, and registering a trademark. After reading this chapter you will be able to:

- Outline the method for evaluating a proposed trademark and prepare a trademark evaluation form.
- Identify the appropriate goods or services used in connection with a trademark.
- Use preliminary screening procedures, such as online computer searching and CD-ROM databases, to evaluate a proposed trademark.
- Perform a preliminary analysis of a trademark search.
- Contrast the benefits of state and federal trademark registration.

- Determine if a trademark applicant may be barred by statutory provisions of the Lanham Act.
- Prepare a federal trademark application and drawing.
- Contrast registration on the Principal and Supplemental Registers.
- Assist in preparation of a response to a trademark examiner's rejection of a proposed mark.
- Identify appropriate state trademark statutes and registration information.

9.1 SELECTING AND EVALUATING A TRADEMARK

How does a company decide on a mark? Sometimes inspiration just strikes! For example, the manager of the Continental baking plant in Chicago looked out the window and saw a billboard for "Twinkle Toe Shoes" and was thus inspired to come up with the name of the company's new cream-filled finger-shaped shortcakes, *Twinkies*. The Hormel company held a contest and paid $100 for the winning trademark for its ham and pork shoulder meat cooked in a can. The winner: *Spam,* for "spiced ham."

There are innumerable methods of selecting a mark. For a new business, the selection process may provoke the first argument. Everybody has an idea; everybody has a strong opinion. Some companies hire professional firms to perform "naming" services. An analysis of the goods or services often leads to specific qualities or attributes of the product that may assist in creating a trademark. For example, *ore* is a Scandinavian term for "coin" (derived from the Latin, *aurum,* for gold coin). Therefore, *Oreo* is a good choice for a black cookie shaped like a coin.

Very often, a company will survey its market to determine the consumer reaction—a recommended method because it helps determine consumer response. In addition to these methods, numerous books and articles, as well as computer programs, have been written to aid in the process of choosing a competitive trademark. Selecting the mark often involves identifying the market for the goods or services and examining the competition.

After selecting a mark, it is important that the mark be screened and evaluated for use as a trademark and for its registrability. If a company rushes to market, unaware that a similar trademark is already being used, the effect can be devastating. At worst, a court may issue a preliminary injunction and the company will have to cease and desist from any further use of the infringing mark, as well as pay damages and attorney fees to the competitor. At best, the two companies will reach an agreement that permits mutual use. In either case, there will be considerable expense and annoyance while they attempt to sort out the trademark dispute, generally at a time when a company wishes to put all its efforts into marketing instead of legal wrangling.

A law office versed in trademark law can guide a company through the selection process and assist in searching the marketplace to determine if competitors are using a similar mark. In addition, the law office can determine the extent of trademark protection required. For example, is federal registration anticipated, or will state registration suffice? All these considerations, along with expert guidance, can help to avoid unnecessary problems and confusion.

Eliminate the Generic

Before selecting a mark, the client must identify its goods and services. What is the client selling? For example, if a company acts as a broker for a person selling a home, then the company is offering "real estate brokerage services." If the company is selling jars of homemade salad dressing, then the goods are "salad dressing." The goods (salad dressing) or services (real estate brokerage services) are generic. That is, no one should be able to claim a proprietary right to these generic terms. As explained in chapter 8, a generic term cannot function as a mark.

Therefore, one simple rule for selecting a mark is that it should never be the generic term for the goods or services. For example, in the factual situation presented in the Commentary, what is Diskco selling? The answer is a "computer program that compresses disks" or a "disk compressor." Therefore the term *Disk Compressor* would make a very poor choice for a mark because it is unlikely to acquire trademark protection. It does not merely describe the product—it *is* the product.

Analyze the Competition

A second important step in selecting a mark is to analyze the competition. What marks are being used by competitors on similar goods or services? A review of competition helps to avoid any marks that might deceive or confuse the public. Second, an analysis of the competition might help to determine what types of marks have success. For example, the personal names of designers or celebrities are often successful marks in the garment industry. Romantic terms are obvious choices for fragrances. Geographic locations are common choices for banking services. Note, however (as discussed further in this chapter), that geographically descriptive (and misdescriptive) marks and marks using surnames may pose obstacles in the state or federal registration process.

Review Multi-Language Marks

Word marks that are in languages other than English should be evaluated carefully. If the average consumer in the United States is familiar with the English equivalent of the foreign term, the mark may be considered confusingly similar. For example, the mark *Toro Rojo* was considered to be confusingly similar to the mark *Red Bull*.

Similarly, it is a good idea to perform foreign translations of English words. This may be required as part of the registration process and it may help to avoid unnecessary embarrassment. For example, the term *Nova* has the same sound as the words meaning "no go" in Spanish. Therefore, it might not be a good choice as a trademark for an automobile sold to Spanish-speaking customers.

Avoid Marks Protected by Federal Statute

Congress has granted exclusive rights to certain marks. The most famous example is the *Olympic* mark and symbol (the five connected rings), which are protected by a federal statute.[1] Only the U.S. Olympic Committee can use or license these marks. Federal protection has also been extended to various military and veterans groups, as well as to certain historical societies. U.S. statutes also protect "Little League" Baseball, the Boy Scouts of America, and the Girl Scouts of America. Also, as explained later in this chapter, certain uses of the American flag may require either a license from the Secretary of Defense or disclaimers at the time of trademark registration.

Trademark Evaluation Form

Based upon the standards established in this chapter, it is a good idea to prepare and use a trademark evaluation form. This form will assist the paralegal in keeping track of the potential conflicts with the mark as well as the other issues raised, such as international considerations or generic terms.

A trademark evaluation form should include the sections shown in figure 9-1.

Identification of Elements of Mark

Once a mark or group of marks have been selected for further evaluation and screening, the paralegal and attorney must isolate the protectible elements. Generally, the client seeks to register a word, group of words, or words in connection with a design. For purposes of evaluating the mark, the initial screening focuses on the word or words used in the mark (rather than design or graphic elements). One reason for this is that it is difficult to perform preliminary searching of graphic or design marks using standard online databases and print media; these resources are geared toward alphanumeric searching. However, professional search companies and certain CD-ROM and online databases, described later, can analyze design and graphic trademarks.

Strength or Weakness of Proposed Mark

As discussed in chapter 8, marks are classified according to their distinctiveness. A strong mark is *inherently distinctive;* that is, it is immediately memorable because it is playful, fanciful, suggestive, or because it is an invented term such as *Rolex* or *Kodak.* A company's new mark must be evaluated according to its strength or weakness. If a mark is inherently distinctive (strong), it will have an advantage in terms of its ability to acquire trademark protection or to be federally registered. For example, the name *Space Saver,*

Proposed Mark		
CLIENT		
CLIENT INFORMATION	Name, address, phone, fax	
	Client business	
	Other marks currently used by client	
GOODS OR SERVICES	Generic term for goods or services	
	International classification	
	Identification of Goods or Services (Review resources such as the TMEP)	
	Identification of purchasers	
USE OF MARK	Is client using mark now?	
	Date (or anticipated date) of first use in commerce	
	Date (or anticipated date) of first use in interstate commerce	
	In which states is use anticipated?	
	In which countries is use anticipated?	
PROPOSED MARK	How was the mark selected or created?	
	Is mark a word, design, device, or combination?	
	Does the mark (or phonetic soundalike) have a meaning within the trade?	
	Does the mark have a meaning in a foreign language?	
	Is the mark weak (descriptive) or strong (inherently distinctive)?	
SEARCH RESULTS	Type of Search	Potential Conflict

FIGURE 9-1
Trademark evaluation form

as presented in the Commentary to this chapter, describes a quality or characteristic of the Diskco program, namely, the ability of the software program to save space on a computer disk. Because it is descriptive, it is *not* inherently distinctive and is likely to be classified as a weak mark. If the mark is descriptive, it cannot be protected under trademark law until Diskco can prove secondary meaning. However, the terms *The Big Squeeze* and *Scrooge* are likely to be considered suggestive and nondescriptive because they allude to or hint at the space-saving quality of the software program without describing it. Unlike *Space Saver,* these marks may be registrable on the Principal Register without proof of secondary meaning. In addition, a nondescriptive mark may be reserved for use under the intent-to-use provisions of the Lanham Act. A descriptive mark that lacks proof of secondary meaning cannot be registered under the intent-to-use provisions because there is no way of proving secondary meaning *before* a mark is introduced into commerce. Sometimes it is difficult to predict whether a mark is descriptive or distinctive (e.g., suggestive). In such cases, some attorneys consider it a good idea to alert the client that either a descriptive or distinctive interpretation is possible. This will prepare the client in the event the examining attorney at the Patent and Trademark Office maintains that the mark is descriptive.

Preliminary Screening Methods: Locating Conflicting Marks

After identifying the potential marks that a company wants to use, research must be done to determine if there is a potential conflict. The most complete analysis of possible trademark conflicts is offered by professional trademark searching firms. However, these firms often charge hundreds of dollars to report on one mark. If a company is considering multiple marks, the cost could quickly exceed a thousand dollars. Therefore, before hiring a professional trademark searching firm, it is a good idea to perform preliminary searches. To keep costs at a minimum, the client may wish to perform some of the preliminary investigations itself (e.g., investigating standard trade publications, major metropolitan telephone directories, or reviewing the marketplace).

Trade Publications and Directories

One simple method of evaluating marks is to have the client or the paralegal review trade publications. Almost every trade or business has a journal, publication, or directory published for the benefit of the companies competing within the trade. Directories are particularly helpful because they contain indexes that may allow fast cross-referencing of product or service titles. For example, many members of the toy and hobby industry subscribe to the trade publication *Playthings.* This publication also distributes an annual "Buyer's Directory" issue. By reviewing the Buyer's Directory, it may be possible to determine if a similar mark is being used on toy or hobby products. If you are unsure of which directory or publication is applicable, ask the client, or investigate publications such as *Directories in Print, Gale Directory of Publications, Information Industry Directory, National Directory of Catalogs, Oxbridge Directory of Newsletters,* or *The Standard Periodical Directory.*

Many publications and directories are available at local libraries and are also available on online databases. As explained later, it is faster and easier to find information that is stored on an online database, because a specific search can be designed to search through the computer's data.

Online Computer Databases

An *online database* is a collection of information that is accessed by a person using a computer connected to a telephone line. Online databases such as *CompuServe, Prodigy, America Online, Nexis,* and *The Knowledge Index* contain articles from news magazines, trade publications, and journals. Each online database has a system of searching, storing, and printing information. Various fees may be charged to users of an online database. Initially, most services charge an annual or subscription fee (which includes the introductory software). There may also be a monthly fee. Some systems charge a fee for each search as well for the total time on the system during each session. There may be additional charges for downloading or printing database information. (*Downloading* means that the user is saving certain information to disk for later use.)

The *Nexis* database is particularly helpful because this is one of the databases used by the Patent and Trademark Office when attempting to determine if a mark is used as a descriptive term within a trade or business.

Database Search Techniques

The first-time user of an online database may be shocked by the fees that quickly accumulate while searching. When used haphazardly, these online systems become very expensive. Poorly executed searches, unnecessary browsing, and large amounts of downloading and printing may turn one hour of online database searching into a bill running several hundred dollars. If you are concerned about online expenses, the following tips may assist online database users:

1. Take advantage of any free training offered by the search company, whether it is a seminar, software-driven training, or free time offered to new subscribers.
2. Never go online without first working out the details of your search. If you have questions about fashioning a search, call online database customer assistance *before* going online.
3. Search during off-hours when rates are lower.
4. Group searches of titles rather than running one search for each title. For example, instead of doing two separate searches for the terms *The Big Squeeze* and *Scrooge,* try to put both terms in one search. In the *Nexis* online database, such a search might look like:

   (BIG PRE/1 SQUEEZ!) OR SCROOGE W/10 ("SOFTWARE" OR "COMPUT!")

Note: In online database searches, certain characters such as "*" or "!" may have wildcard capabilities. For example, on *Nexis,* the term **c*t** would locate *cat, cut,* or *cot.* The term *comput!* would locate *computer, compute, computation,* etc. The user must become familiar with the idiosyncrasies of each system. Consult the appropriate software manual or the company's technical support system.

If the results of an online database search turn up numerous articles with matching terms, the attorney supervising the trademark evaluation should review the materials to determine if there are any conflicts or if the terms are used as descriptive designations within the trade. The supervising attorney may then wish to eliminate such terms from further evaluation.

CD-ROM and Trademark Database Searching

After using the preliminary search techniques just discussed, a second level of searching can be made of any federal or state registered trademarks. In the past decade, new technologies and searching techniques have emerged that enable users to search state and federal trademark registrations with a computer. The two most common methods are the trademark online databases, similar to the ones previously described, and CD-ROM trademark products.

Searching a trademark online database is similar to using any other online database. It requires some knowledge of computers, a computer modem and telephone line to connect with the database, and a subscription agreement with the database company. The difference between a trademark online database and databases such as *Nexis* and *America Online* is that the trademark databases contain information about state and federally registered trademarks. The online databases used in the preliminary search techniques contain articles from magazines and newspapers.

Dialog provides access to *Trademarkscan®—Federal* and *Trademarkscan®—State,* both of which are databases assembled by the Thomson & Thomson Company. *Trademarkscan®—Federal* provides information on all active registered trademarks and applications for registration. Any registered or pending marks that become inactive or are canceled or abandoned are also retained in the database, but their current status is reflected. Trademarks that were inactive prior to January 1984 are not in the database. *Trademarkscan®—State* provides records of trademarks and service marks registered with the Secretaries of State of all 50 U.S. states and Puerto Rico. (There are also country-specific *Trademarkscan* services.) Generally, both databases, like most trademark databases, will cross-reference to assist retrieval of corrupted spellings, soundalikes, and unconventional presentations of words. *Dialog* also provides the *Trade Names Database* from Gale Research, Inc., which is a database containing over 280,000 trade names. There is a charge for each individual search performed. The *CompuServe* service also provides access to a trademark database, the Trademark Research Center, that contains nongraphic federal and state trademarks. There is a charge for each individual

Compu-Mark

search. CompuServe users can access the database by typing GO TRADERC. *Compu-Mark,* also owned by the Thomson & Thomson Company, offers a unique method of database searching known as the "Hitlist," which is a work sheet referencing registered marks according to their similarities, including identical marks and phonetic equivalents as well as marks sharing the same phonetic prefixes and suffixes in selected classes. A portion of a "Hitlist" search for the mark *The Big Squeeze* (mentioned in the factual situation in the Commentary to this chapter) appears in figure 9-2.

Page 3
Your Mark   : BIG SQUEEZE / COMPUTER SOFTWARE
References   : \CR-CED

NUMBER	LINE	S	CLASS	TRADEMARKS FOUND
IA0851327	50	A	[35]	BIG SQUIRT
MN0703099	51	A	[37]	BIG SKY LOG HOMES, INC.
MT2000575	52	A	[37]	BIG SKY - HI - TECH, INC.
AZ2022233	53	A	[37]	BIG SKY CONSTRUCTION
R1576844	54	A	[37]	THE BIG SQUIRT
R0786351	55	I	[28]	BIG SKY
R1165669	56	I	[28]	BIG SKI
MT0850049	57	A	[28]	THE BIG SKY TRIVIA GAME
R0617778	58	A	[28]	BIG SCOOP
R0964634	59	I	[28]	BIG SCOOP
R0985863	60	A	[28]	"THE BIG SCOOP"
74133551	61	P	[28]	THE BIG SCORE
R1086076	62	A	[28]	BIG SCOOT
CA2005603	63	A	[28]	BIG SQUIRT
74238899	64	P	[28]	BIG SQUIRT
72113279	65	I	[28]	BIG SQUIRT
MT0850388	66	A	[41]	BIG SKY STATE GAME
R1693819	67	A	[41]	BIG SKY MUSIC FESTIVAL
MT0141993	68	A	[38]	BIG SKY BEEPER COMPANY
MT0850284	69	A	[38]	BIG SKY INSTITUTE BSI
IN2000090	70	A	[38]	THE BIG SCREEN
MT0131311	71	A	[0]	BIG SKY MONTANA
MT0850551	72	A	[0]	BIG SKY TOPPERS

KWESE 5 LETTER SUFFIX IN SELECTED
(and related) CLASS(ES) (PHONETIC)
71 HITS FOUND —   — 0 HIGH FREQUENCIES FOUND

NUMBER	LINE	S	CLASS	TRADEMARKS FOUND
SN793776	73	I	[9]	EZE THE QUEEZE
R0898710	74	A	[9]	SQUEEZE-METER
SN406848	75	I	[9]	SQUEEZE-N-POUR
R1460691	76	A	[9]	FLIP & SQUEEZE
R1438531	77	A	[9]	SQUEEZE-N-EASY
R1461739	78	A	[9]	* SQUEEZE

FIGURE 9-2
Sample Compu-Mark
Hitlist

```
NUMBER          LINE  S   CLASS          TRADEMARKS FOUND
SN771097        79    I   [9]          * DS SQUEEZE
MA0500929       80    A   [9-16-28]-     SQUEEZE ME'S
                          11-17-20-
                          22
TN0251621       81    A   [9-16]         SQUEEZEE
R1667995        82    A   [9]            SQUEEZE-BOX
R1207048        83    A   [9]            TIMESQUEEZE
R1662929        84    A   [9]          * COLORSQUEEZE
R1450748        85    A   [16]           SQUEEZE-IT
74073933        86    P   [16]-2         SQUEEZE A SHAPE
0150762         87    A   [16]           COMFORTABLE SQUEEZE


Your Mark          : BIG SQUEEZE / COMPUTER SOFTWARE
Reference          : \CR-CED

FULLTEXT for       : R1461739
Mark Retrieved     : SQUEEZE
Design Phase       : (no design)
Registration No    : R1461739        dated 1987/10/20
Serial No          : SN636894        dated 1986/12/22
Publication Date   : 1987/07/28
Status             : A REGISTRATION ON THE PRINCIPAL REGISTER
Goods/Services     : COMPUTER PROGRAMS AND INSTRUCTION
                     MANUALS SOLD AND SHIPPED THEREWITH USE:
                     01 JUN 1982 COMM: 01 JUN 1982

U.S. Class(es)     : 038
Intl. Class(es)    : 9

Owner Information  : QUANTUMN INFORMATION SYSTEM, INC.
                     (WASHINGTON CORPORATION) SUITE H 98037
                     18609 SEVENTY-SIXTH AVENUE
                     WEST LYNNWOOD WASHINGTON
```

FIGURE 9-2
(Continued)

Some companies offer CD-ROM technology for searching federal and state registrations. *CD-ROM* stands for "Compact Disc-Read Only Memory." CD-ROM technology uses compact discs similar to the discs sold for sound recordings, except that these discs contain data instead of sounds. Although the CD-ROM drive cannot presently save data as a traditional computer drive can, the compact discs used for CD-ROM can store an incredible amount of information, including complete encyclopedias. There is no need for a telephone line or modem because the CD-ROM system hooks to the computer. Many computer users already own CD-ROM drives (note however, that a standard audio compact disc player cannot function as a CD-ROM drive). A subscriber to CD-ROM services receives discs containing databases of federal or state registrations. These discs are periodically updated. For example, all of the *Trademarkscan*® databases listed earlier are available in CD-ROM format. Users of these services may lease CD-ROM drives and pay a monthly or annual subscription fee. However, there are no charges for each search performed. Therefore, for a business that performs numerous trademark searches, it may be less expensive to use a CD-ROM service rather than pay for the searching charges associated with a trademark online database.

It is important to remember that the trademark database search facilities, both online and CD-ROM, are suitable as preliminary screening tools. However, neither of these methods provides screening and searching of common law marks. Therefore, they are not completely conclusive. If a client is planning to adopt a new mark for goods or services, it is recommended that the client order a full trademark search, as described later.

EXAMPLE: Compu-Mark Online Database Hitlist Search for "Squeeze" Mark

Figure 9-2 shows a sample page from the Compu-Mark online trademark database Hitlist search for the mark *Squeeze*. The Compu-Mark Hitlist search scans all state and federal trademark records to find any pertinent marks and classes that "match" the searched term—in this case, *Squeeze* for Class 9 goods, namely computer software. The method of reading a Hitlist search and the appropriate symbols are shown here. As noted, the Hitlist can result in a search of all classes and can include various phonetic variations (e.g., SKWESE instead of SQUEEZE). The Hitlist in figure 9-2 was prepared on order from Compu-Mark as part of a trademark search report and includes symbols ("+" or "-") indicating which of the Hitlist terms have been included in the full search report.

For example, the HITLIST reference: **-R1461739 78 A [9] * SQUEEZE**

"-"   indicates that the mark has been prepared included in the full search report

"R"   indicates a federal registration followed by the registration number. For state registrations, the letters of the state are shown (e.g., MA or CA). If the application is pending for federal registration, the symbol "SN" is used, and intent-to-use applications are preceded by the number "74."

"78"   is the "line number" that is an internal reference. Every term that is uncovered on the Hitlist is placed in numerical order.

"A"   indicates that the registration is active (i.e., it has not been canceled or abandoned).

[9]   indicates the class in which the registration was made (i.e., International Class 9).

*   is a reference used by Compu-Mark analysts to indicate that a key element of the word pertinent to the goods has been searched.

SQUEEZE is the potentially conflicting mark.

International Considerations

Another concern in the process of evaluating a mark is the worldwide use of the mark. Does the client intend to use the mark in countries other than the United States? If so, it is now possible to search online for certain foreign countries. Companies such as Thomson & Thomson also offer worldwide, regional, and country-specific searches for similar trademarks. The trademark applicant also may need the assistance of an international trademark agent, located in each country. Such agents are often necessary if the U.S. applicant wishes to register the trademark in a foreign country. Listings of these agents can be found in trademark publications or may be obtained from the International Trademark Association (INTA). As an attorney may have to obtain an opinion of registrability from a competent agent in each country considered, the cost of such international evaluation can rise into the thousands of dollars.

Trademark Search Reports

A few companies perform extensive trademark research functions, including trademark searches. These companies may search federal and state registrations as well as international and common law marks. After performing the research, an extensive written report is provided to the client. The report breaks the information into sections, along with reproductions of the potentially conflicting marks. These professional searching companies use sophisticated searching techniques and computer software. Using these methods, the companies can find matching marks that are phonetically similar or that share similar root words, prefixes, suffixes, or variants. For example, the search for the mark *Jam Session* for computer software also located marks identical or similar to *jam,* such as *Jam Factory, Jam/Reportwriter, Jamis, James, ITC Jamille, Vam, Bam,* and *Jims.* Similarly, the search located matches and similar terms for *session,* such as *Business Session, Color Session, Conversessions, Supersession,* and *Sessionnet.*

The most expedient method of initiating a search is to call and discuss the search with a company representative. Many businesses and law firms maintain accounts with these companies. The search company representative is prepared to assist in identifying related classes of goods or services. After initiating the search, a confirmation letter should be sent or faxed to the trademark search company. Normally a trademark search can be performed within 7 to 10 days, but search companies can expedite the searches for higher fees. In addition, other types of research facilities are available from these companies, including "watching" services (discussed in chapter 10).

Analyzing Trademark Research Reports

The analysis of a trademark search report should always be performed under the supervision of an attorney. The paralegal may initially examine and review the results, but it is important that an attorney review the search for any potential conflicts. The purpose of the trademark search is to determine if there are any potential conflicts that could affect the registration process, *not* to determine whether a mark can be registered.

The trademark search report consists of three main portions. The first section contains information from the Patent and Trademark Office. This portion of the report consists of similar federally registered marks and pending marks, as well as marks that have been canceled or abandoned. The second portion of the report is a survey of state registrations. Included are similar marks that are registered under state trademark law. The third portion of the report consists of common law information. It is in this area that trademark search reports are especially helpful. The search companies examine numerous sources to locate unregistered users of similar marks, brand names, and even trade names. Still another portion of the search report lists citations to reported decisions of the courts or the Trademark Trial and Appeal Board of the Patent and Trademark Office concerning the same or closely similar marks.

EXAMPLE

The "Scrooge" Search. In the Commentary to this chapter, one of the potential marks considered by the client is *Scrooge*. The trademark search for this mark, in discussing each potentially conflicting mark, would indicate the search report number (usually the number in the upper righthand corner of each frame).

The federal registration portion of the search indicates the following:

- *SCROOGE MACDOC* (REF. 1) is federally registered in International Class 9 (the same class of goods as sought by Diskco). The federally registered mark *SCROOGE MACDOC* is used in connection with a software program designed for physicians' office management and billing. The mark has been used in commerce since May 1, 1990, and was federally registered on June 4, 1991. The party registering the mark is an individual, David A. Lowe.
- *$CROOGE* (REF. 2) is an abandoned application. Apparently the applicant failed to respond to a Patent and Trademark Office inquiry and as a result the application was abandoned.
- *SCROOGE* (REF. 4) is a canceled registration. Apparently the owner of the mark failed to file a Section 8 affidavit indicating continued use.
- *SCREWGE* (REF. 12) is a phonetic soundalike for the *Scrooge* mark, also in Class 9. However, it is also a canceled registration. Apparently the owner of the mark failed to file a Section 8 affidavit indicating continued use.

The state registration and common law sections do not provide any conflicting users with similar goods. There also were no reported decisions of the courts or the Trademark Trial and Appeal Board of the Patent and Trademark Office concerning the same or closely similar marks.

Conclusion. After reviewing the *Scrooge* trademark search, the only potential conflict is *SCROOGE MACDOC,* used in connection with a computer software program designed for physicians' office management and billing. From the information presented, it is not possible to determine if the two marks, as they are used in commerce and in their channels of trade, would be likely to be confused. More investigation is needed. For example, is the mark still in use? Does the "Macdoc" prefix indicate use of the program on Macintosh-style computers? (The Diskco program is not for Macintosh use.) In chapter 10, several factors for determining likelihood of confusion are presented. These factors would apply when making an assessment as to the adoption or use of a mark. Even if a law office determines that two marks are not likely to be confused, the client should be advised that, despite this opinion, the owner of a potentially conflicting mark may still oppose the registration or use of the mark.

EXAMPLE

The "Jam Session" Search. In the Commentary to this chapter, one of the potential marks considered by the client is *Jam Session.*

The federal registration portion of the search indicates that:

- *JAM SESSION* (F-1) is federally registered in International Class 9 (the same class of goods as sought by Diskco.) The federally registered mark *JAM SESSION* is used in connection with a program designed for composing music. The mark has been used in commerce since November 1987, and was federally registered on December 18, 1990. The party registering the mark is Broderbund Software of San Rafael, California.

- *JAM FACTORY* (F-2) is a federally registered in Class 9 and is also a mark used in connection with a program designed for composing music. The mark has been used in commerce since December 20, 1986, and was federally registered on January 8, 1991. The registrant is Intelligent Computer Music System, Inc., a New York corporation. This report also indicates that the trademark has been assigned. The registrant assigned it to Dr. T's Music Software, Inc., a Massachusetts corporation. Finally, there is information about an inter partes proceeding at the Trademark Trial and Appeals Board (TTAB). A party JYACC, who owns the trademark *JAM,* opposed the registration of *JAM FACTORY* in August 1989, but terminated the opposition on September 28, 1990. As explained later in this chapter, a party that opposes the registration of a trademark may oppose that application in a proceeding at the TTAB. In this case, the opposition was terminated before the TTAB ruled on the matter, possibly because the opposer withdrew its claims or the parties reached a settlement.

- *JAM* (F-3) is a federally registered mark for computer programs and manuals for use in developing user interfaces for application programs. The owner of the *JAM,* JYACC, Inc., also owns *JAM/DBI* (F-4),

JAM/REPORTWRITER (F-5) and *JAM/PRESENTATION INTER-FACE* (F-6).

- The owner of the *JAM* mark is the party that initiated the proceeding in opposition to the application of the mark *JAM FACTORY.*

- The stylized mark *JAM* (F-7), with its unique lettering, was *not* federally registered. An attempt was made to register the mark in 1987 by an Australian company. However, registration of the mark was opposed by JYACC, Inc., owners of the *JAM* marks shown in F-3, F-4, F-5, and F-6. The registration was abandoned after the TTAB proceeding.

- The state registration portion of the trademark search indicates that there are three marks using the term "Jam Session": *Jam Sessions Sack Lunch (S-3),* owned by Volunteer Ventures (and no goods or services indicated), *Jimmy's Jam Session How Sweet It Is* (and design) (S-4) for guitar instruction services, and *Polka Jam Session* (and design) (S-5) for polka music services. None of these marks appears to be used in conjunction with goods or service similar to computer programs.

- The common law portion of the trademark search indicates references of previously cited federally registered marks, along with *JAMPACK* (ICP-1) for software.

Conclusion.   After reviewing the *Jam Session* trademark search, it is clear that there are potential conflicts. As indicated in the Commentary to this chapter, Diskco wants to use the term for computer software that aids in disk compression. The obvious problem is that the term *Jam Session* is already registered for computer software. It is arguable that the purchasers of these items would not be confused because the software is for different purposes; however, it is likely that the Patent and Trademark Office would refuse registration. It is also possible that the Broderbund Company, the registrant of the reference mark, would oppose the mark after publication. It is also likely that the registration would be opposed by JYACC, Inc., the company that already owns federal registrations for four *JAM*-related marks. As the trademark search indicates, JYACC, Inc., has a history of aggressively opposing registrations of *JAM* marks. Therefore, Diskco's attempt to register and use *Jam Session* is likely to run into resistance.

Informing Client of Results

As a general practice, the paralegal should *never* contact the client regarding a search report until a supervising attorney has thoroughly reviewed any conflicting uses. The letter to the client must make several points, including the status of any potentially conflicting marks. Generally the client simply wants to know, "Can I use the mark?" Unfortunately the answer may not be a simple yes or no. The letter to the client should include the following:

- *Purpose of the search report.*   The client should be informed that the purpose of the search report is to assist in determining whether there are any confusingly similar marks on similar goods or services. The search does *not* prove registrability, but it may help determine the likelihood of refusal from the Patent and Trademark Office or opposition from other users.

- *Potentially conflicting marks.* The client should be informed of any potentially conflicting marks located by the search. This information should be clearly stated and should include the information about the owners of these marks and dates of use.
- *Attorney opinion.* The attorney should provide the client with an opinion as to use of the mark. The opinion may be positive (i.e., "We believe the mark is available for your exclusive use"); it may be negative (i.e., "It is our opinion that the mark is not available for use because of the presence of a confusingly similar mark"); or the opinion may be that the attorney is unsure (i.e., "Based upon the information furnished, we are unable to determine if the mark is available") and more investigation is necessary.
- *Accuracy of the search.* The client should be informed that a trademark search company report may not be completely faultless. Marks may exist that have not been located by the search company. In addition, the search is only accurate as of a certain date (usually indicated on the front page of the report).

The client should receive a copy of the search report and the law office should retain a copy for its records.

Resolving Potential Conflicts

Sometimes a client wants to find a way to use the mark despite the potential conflicts, or the client may have already begun using the mark and want to continue using it. The fact that a conflict exists does not preclude a company from moving ahead with its choice of marks.

Consider the facts mentioned in the Commentary to this chapter. Imagine if Diskco had adopted and used in commerce the mark *Jam Session* on its disk compression software product. As the trademark search indicates, there are two major obstacles to continued use. One is the current federal registrant for the mark and the other is the owner of the series of four *JAM* marks (i.e., *JAM, JAM/DBI, JAM/REPORTWRITER,* and *JAM/PRESENTATION INTERFACE).*

There are various ways of resolving or avoiding the conflict. The most obvious one is to reach an agreement with the owner of the conflicting mark. Sometimes the owner of a conflicting mark will simply agree not to oppose registration or use. Such agreements may be in the form of a letter agreement and may or may not involve any payment.

Research Conflicting Users

The first step in analyzing a trademark conflict issue is to research the conflicting users. This can be done by the client or the law office. The client may prefer to do the work to avoid legal expenses and because of a familiarity with the trade. Online business databases may help to determine the relative size, current business form (i.e., corporation, limited partnership, etc.), and current sales or use of the mark. Private research companies also can perform such functions. Most major cities have private research companies that will investigate businesses and provide reports. Another helpful research technique is to search the reported proceedings of the Trademark Trial and Appeals Board and the Federal Circuits to determine if a company has a record of actively opposing and policing trademarks. These reported proceedings are located on databases such as *Lexis* and *Westlaw.*

Abandonment

There are many ways to determine if a company is still using a trademark. The simplest method is to call the company and ask if the product can be purchased. If the response is something like, "No, we haven't sold that product in years," then there is a chance that the trademark has been abandoned, as discussed in chapter 10. Although there is no fixed period of time of nonuse that conclusively proves abandonment, a presumption arises under the Lanham Act if the mark has not been used for two years.[2] If more resources are available, professional investigators may be hired to determine the extent of the company's use. If the supervising attorney concludes that the mark may have been abandoned, a Petition for Cancellation of the registration based upon abandonment of the mark may be filed with the Patent and Trademark Office.

Failure to File Section 8 Affidavit

How many years have passed since registration? Between the fifth and sixth year following registration, a trademark owner must file an affidavit declaring the continued use of the mark.[3] This is known as a **Section 8 affidavit.** If the company fails to timely file the affidavit, the registration will be canceled and federal trademark rights may be lost, whereupon a subsequent user could claim rights to the mark.

Assignment

If the company with the rights to the mark is small or financially strapped, there is always the possibility of purchasing the mark and the associated good will. If the mark has not been abandoned, but the company has discontinued use for a period of time, it also may be possible to buy the rights to the trademark and any associated good will. Sometimes, as part of an agreement to purchase trademark rights, the buyer will also pay to search and register a new mark for the seller. The purchase of the trademark and its accompanying good will, together with the registration, can be accomplished by an assignment of trademark rights, which should be recorded with the Patent and Trademark Office.[4]

Concurrent Use

The Lanham Act permits two users of a similar mark to register concurrently (i.e., at the same time).[5] This **concurrent use** results from a determination by the Commissioner of the Patent and Trademark Office or by a determination by a court of competent jurisdiction. For example, Diskco files an application to register the mark *The Big Squeeze* in Class 9 for computer compression programs. After filing, Diskco learns of a small computer software developer that has been using the same mark for computer programs to teach accordion music. Diskco's use of the mark in interstate commerce began in 1992. The other software company has been using the mark in the New Orleans and Texas areas since 1988. If the Commissioner determines that confusion is not likely to result from the concurrent use of the mark in separate geographic regions, a concurrent use registration will be permitted. Concurrent use registrations are not common.

Revising the Mark

Sometimes it may be possible to change or revise the trademark in a manner that avoids the conflict. If the parties owning the conflicting marks agree upon the client's use of its house mark in combination with the desired mark, (e.g., *Diskco Jam Session),* then the dispute will terminate. Similarly, as there may be an issue registering *Squeeze,* the client and a conflicting user may modify the desired mark to *The Big Squeezy.* The modified mark should be searched and evaluated with the same level of care as the original form of the mark.

9.2 FEDERAL REGISTRATION

This section introduces the process of obtaining federal and state trademark registration. Although registration of trademarks is strongly recommended, it is important to remember that registration, whether state or federal, does not *create* a trademark and is not essential to proving that the trademark is valid. The ownership and right to the exclusive use of a trademark derive from the owner's adoption and use of the mark, not from the registration of the mark. These are principles of common law and, as indicated in chapter 8, the owner of a valid mark can *always* enforce these common law rights, regardless of whether a trademark registration has issued. For example, if a company is using the unregistered mark in commerce, it will have priority over a subsequent user of a similar mark on similar goods. However, despite the common law protection, registration of one's trademarks is strongly recommended. Generally, federal registration is preferred because of its wide range of benefits and national-scope consistency. There

---

LEGAL TERMS

Section 8 affidavit
Declaration of continued use of a federally registered trademark filed between the fifth and sixth year following registration. Failure to file in this time period will result in the registration being cancelled and may result in loss of trademark rights.

concurrent use
When more than one person is entitled to use a similar mark; results from a determination by either the Commissioner of the Patent and Trademark Office or by a court of competent jurisdiction.

are certain limitations on trademark registration, including bars against registration of descriptive marks on the Principal Register and marks that conflict with other registered marks. The process to achieve federal registration includes three major steps: (1) filing the application; (2) examination by the Patent and Trademark Office; and (3) publication for opposition in the *Official Gazette* of the Patent and Trademark Office. If all these steps are achieved and there is no opposition preventing registration, the Patent and Trademark Office issues a Certificate of Registration.

State or Federal Registration?

Which registration is suitable for the client—state or federal? Are both types of registration necessary? As a general rule, if the product or service will be used in any commerce lawfully regulated by the United States, then the mark should be federally registered. The most common forms of such commerce are interstate commerce or commerce between the United States and a foreign country. If the owner anticipates using the mark only in intrastate commerce (within one state), then state registration will suffice. Dual registration on federal and state trademark registers also should be considered. As discussed in chapter 10, many states offer a form of trademark remedy known as *dilution* that is unavailable under federal law. Claims for recovery of attorney fees also may be easier to maintain under some state laws. Prior to making a final determination, the appropriate state trademark laws should be reviewed and compared to the list of benefits offered by federal registration.

Benefits of Federal Registration

There are several benefits of federal registration.

- *Right to use the ® symbol.* Only the owner of a federally registered mark may use the symbol ® in conjunction with the mark. If a mark is not federally registered, it is a violation of the statute to use the ® symbol or to state that the mark is federally registered.
- *Constructive notice of date of first use.* The filing date of the application is the constructive date of first use of the mark in commerce and gives the registrant nationwide notice of priority as of that date. This applies to intent-to-use applications that issue into registrations on the Principal Register. The only exceptions to this are for certain prior users, prior trademark registration applicants, or persons who have filed a Section 44 application claiming priority of an earlier filed foreign application. A **Section 44 application** is an application for federal trademark registration by the foreign owner of a mark registered (or for which an application has been filed) in a foreign country (provided that the foreign country is a party to an international convention or treaty of which the United States is a member).

- *Right to sue in federal court.* The registration grants the right to sue in federal court for trademark infringement. In addition, the trademark owner can assert related nonfederal claims under the principle of pendent jurisdiction. Note, however, that owners of unregistered marks also can sue in federal court under the provisions of § 1125(a) of the Lanham Act, discussed in chapter 10.

- *Statutory damages and attorney fees.* The owner of a registered mark may recover lost profits, damages, and costs in a federal court trademark infringement action. In addition, in some cases, the owner may be awarded treble damages and attorney fees.

- *Prima facie evidence.* Federal registration of a trademark on the Principal Register provides prima facie evidence of the validity of the registration, the registrant's ownership of the mark, and of the registrant's exclusive right to use the mark in commerce for the specified goods.

- *Constructive notice of ownership claim.* Federal registration of a trademark on the Principal Register provides constructive notice of a claim of ownership. If a second party adopts the mark after the federal registration, this second party is prohibited from arguing that it was acting in good faith when it adopted the mark.

- *Criminal penalties and damages.* Certain criminal penalties and treble damages may be assessed in an action for counterfeiting a registered mark on the Principal Register. **Counterfeiting** is an extreme form of trademark infringement in which an identical or indistinguishable trademark is used on goods or services for which the original mark is still being used. For example, if a company deliberately imitated the *Reebok* trademark and used that on running shoes, this would constitute counterfeiting, and the counterfeiter would be subject to criminal penalties.

- *Right to stop importation of infringing marks.* The owner of a mark registered on the Principal Register can deposit a copy of the registration with U.S. Customs to stop the importation of goods bearing an infringing mark. For example, in the preceding example, if the manufacturer of the counterfeit *Reebok* running shoes was located in Mexico, the owners of the federally registered *Reebok* trademark, working with the Department of the Treasury and U.S. Customs, could prevent the importation of those counterfeit goods into the United States.

- *Incontestability.* Under certain conditions, a federally registered mark may become **incontestable.** A mark that is incontestable is immune from challenge except for certain grounds specified in § 33(b) of the Lanham Act. In addition, incontestability is conclusive evidence of the registrant's exclusive right to use the registered mark in commerce in connection with the specified goods or services. Incontestability occurs after the mark has been used for five consecutive years following registration, provided that the registrant files a declaration or affidavit in the Patent and Trademark Office evidencing that the mark is not: (1) the common descriptive name of the goods; (2) the subject of any final adverse decision as to ownership or registration; and (3) the subject of any pending proceeding

LEGAL TERMS

Section 44 application
Application for federal trademark registration by the foreign owner of a mark registered in a foreign country, provided that country is a party to an international convention or treaty of which the United States is a member.

counterfeiting
Extreme form of trademark infringement in which an identical or indistinguishable trademark is used on goods or services for which the original mark is still being used.

incontestable
Trademark that is immune to challenge except for certain grounds specified in Lanham Act § 33(b). Incontestability is conclusive evidence of the registrant's exclusive right to use the registered mark in commerce in connection with the specified goods or services.

involving such rights. The filing of such a declaration is provided for by § 15 of the Lanham Act and applies only to marks registered on the Principal Register.

- *Limited grounds for attacking trademark after five years.* After five years of registration, the grounds for attacking trademarks federally registered on the Principal Register are limited.
- *Basis for foreign applications.* A federal registration may serve as the basis for filing a trademark application in certain foreign countries.

Statutory Bars to Registration

A trademark will be refused for federal registration for several reasons.[6] The following grounds for refusal should be reviewed prior to making any final determination on federal registration.

Descriptive Marks

A mark that is merely descriptive or deceptively misdescriptive of the goods or services cannot be federally registered on the Principal Register. As discussed in chapter 8, a *descriptive mark* is a mark that is not inherently distinctive because it merely describes a product or its nature, quality, characteristics, ingredients, or origin. This bar to registration is commonly known as a "Section 2(e)" bar (referencing the section in the Lanham Act), and also applies to a mark that is primarily a surname or that is primarily geographically descriptive or deceptively misdescriptive. As discussed later in this chapter, a refusal to register based upon descriptiveness may be overcome if the applicant can demonstrate sufficient secondary meaning. For purposes of registration on the Principal Register, five years of continuous use is considered to be prima facie proof that the mark has acquired secondary meaning.

Mark Is Immoral, Scandalous, or Creates a False Representation

A mark will not be registered if it consists of immoral, deceptive, or scandalous material or if it falsely suggests a connection with persons, institutions, beliefs, or national symbols or brings those things into contempt or disrepute. This bar to registration is commonly known as a "Section 2(a)" bar.

Scandalous and Immoral. The refusal to register based upon scandalous or immoral content is rarely exercised by the Patent and Trademark Office, and many attempts at such bars have been reversed by the Trademark Trial and Appeals Board. For example, registration of *Week-End Sex* was permitted as a mark for a magazine and registration of *Acapulco Gold* was permitted as a mark for suntan oil. However, a picture of a nude man and woman kissing and embracing was refused, as was the word *Bullshit* for use on handbags and wallets. It should be noted that the definition of "scandalous" is considered to require a lower threshold of offensiveness than obscenity.

False Connections.   The remaining bar under Section 2(a)—falsely suggesting a connection with persons, institutions, beliefs, or national symbols—may be a matter of concern for persons choosing certain marks. If it can be demonstrated that there is a false suggestion or connection resulting from a mark that is similar or a close approximation of the name or identity of a person or institution, then registration of the mark will be refused. For example, the mark *Bama* was refused registration for footwear because it was established that "Bama" is a well-known nickname for the University of Alabama and its football team. This nickname and the university's identity were of sufficient fame that the use of *Bama* on socks created a false connection with the University of Alabama. In another case, however, the use of *Notre Dame* on cheese was not barred, despite opposition from the University of Notre Dame, because the Trademark Trial and Appeals Board determined that the term *Notre Dame* had significance apart from the university. Therefore, consumers were not likely to be misled into believing there was a connection between the cheese and the university.

Confusingly Similar to Registered Mark

The PTO cannot register a mark that is confusingly similar to a registered mark still in use on similar goods and services. This bar to registration is known as a "Section 2(d)" bar. For example, under the facts in the Commentary to this chapter, if Diskco attempted to register the mark *Jam Session,* the registration would be refused because that mark is confusingly similar to a federally registered mark for computer software goods. It is possible that Diskco could argue that the goods are not the same, as the registered mark is used for entertainment software and Diskco's mark is for compression software. However, Diskco will have the burden of overcoming the refusal.

Unauthorized Use of Living Person or Deceased President

A mark will not be registered if it consists of a name, portrait, or signature identifying a particular living individual, except by his or her written consent. This bar to registration is known as a "Section 2(c)" bar. In addition, Section 2(c) prohibits registration for marks consisting of the name, portrait, or signature of a deceased President of the United States during the lifetime of the president's surviving spouse, except by written permission.

Flags or Coat of Arms

A mark is barred from registration if it is consists of or comprises the flag or coat of arms or other insignia of the United States or any state, municipality, reign country. However, registration is permitted if the applicant is disclaim any trademark rights to the use of such flag in its mark.

ꜱ Not Used as Trademark

not listed as a bar to registration in Section 2, the definition the Lanham Act prohibits the registration of any matter that ꞇ as a trademark, that is, which does not identify the goods ꞇing from a particular source. For example, ornamentation ꞇcle on the side of a tire (i.e., "white- walled tires") could ꞇsidered a trademark.

Supplemental Register

The drafters of the Lanham Act created two registers for marks, the *Principal Register* and the *Supplemental Register.* Registration of a mark on the Principal Register conveys numerous substantive rights and, as a result, is the preferred method of federal trademark protection. Registration on the Supplemental Register does not convey the bundle of rights and protections granted to marks registered on the Principal Register. For example, registration on the Supplemental Register is *not* prima facie evidence of the registrant's exclusive right to use the mark in connection with the goods or services, and the owner of a mark on the Supplemental Register cannot utilize the power of the Customs Service to stop importation of infringing goods.

However, like the owner of a mark registered on the Principal Register, the owner of a mark registered on the Supplemental Register may sue in federal court and may use the ® symbol. In some circumstances, the Patent and Trademark Office will permit an application made on the Principal Register to be converted to one on the Supplemental Register.[7]

Actual Use and Bona Fide Intent to Use

One of the decisions that must be made prior to federal registration is the basis for the federal application. The most important question is whether the registration is based upon actual **use in commerce** or upon a bona fide intent to use the mark in commerce. For purposes of federal registration, **commerce** is any commerce lawfully regulated by the United States. For state registration, it is generally any commerce occurring within the state of registration.

What constitutes use in commerce? The Lanham Act defines *use in commerce* as the bona fide use of a mark in the ordinary course of trade and not made merely to reserve a right.[8] A mark is deemed to be in use in commerce on goods when it is placed on the goods or containers, tags or labels, or displays associated with the goods (or, if otherwise impracticable, on documents associated with the goods) and the goods are sold or transported in interstate commerce or in commerce between the United States and a foreign country. An applicant may qualify under the interstate commerce requirement if the goods are shipped or delivered across state lines (for example, a customer is fitted for a suit and pays for it in New York but has it shipped to California).

For a service mark, *use in commerce* is the use or display of the mark in the sale or advertising of services, when the services are rendered in commerce lawfully regulated by Congress or the services are rendered in more than one state or between the United States and a foreign country. If services are *only* performed in one state, but the services are rendered to out-of-state customers, that may qualify as use in interstate commerce. Generally, rendering services to approximately 15 percent (or more) out-of-state customers is the threshold standard. For example, imagine that the *No-Tell Motel* operates in Indiana but 20 percent of its customers are from Kentucky. That hotel may obtain federal registration of its service mark.

Use in commerce does not occur as a result of "sweetheart sales" or "sweetheart shipments," which are generally shipments or transactions within a company and performed solely to qualify for registration or make a claim as to priority of use. The commerce should be more than a token sale to a personal friend, and the initial transaction should be followed by a demonstration that the trademark owner intends to maintain and continuously use the mark in commerce.

9.3 APPLICATION FOR FEDERAL REGISTRATION

Since 1990, the Patent and Trademark Office has processed approximately 120,000 trademark applications a year. Because of this vast number of applications, it is important to prepare the application and attached documentation properly. An application for registration based upon use in commerce should include (in addition to the application form) a drawing, the proper fee, and three specimens of the mark as used in connection with the goods or services. The specimens are not required for intent-to-use applications. This package of materials is delivered to the Patent and Trademark Office, where the application is given a number and assigned to a PTO examining attorney (also known as the trademark examiner). If the examining attorney has no objections, the mark is published in the *Official Gazette*. However, if there is an error or inconsistency in the application, or if the examiner believes that registration is inappropriate because of a statutory bar, the trademark examiner corresponds with the applicant. The applicant may respond to the objections or errors or may abandon the application. Normally, a trademark examiner completes an analysis of the application within three months. After publication of the mark on the Principal Register, the public has 30 days to oppose registration of the mark. If there is no opposition, a trademark registration will be issued.

The Federal Trademark Application

A trademark application for registration on the Principal Register is shown in figure 9-3. The application must be completed in the English language.

LEGAL TERMS

use in commerce
Use of a trademark by placing it on goods or containers, tags or labels, displays associated with the goods (or, if otherwise impracticable, on documents associated with the goods) and selling or transporting the goods in interstate commerce or commerce between the United States and a foreign country.
Also, use of a service mark when the mark is used or displayed in the sale or advertising of services and the services are rendered in commerce or in more than one state or in the United States and a foreign country.

commerce
For federal trademark registration purposes, any commerce lawfully regulated by the United States. For state registration purposes, generally any commerce occurring within the state of registration.

[SER]VICE MARK [P]RINCIPAL [DE]CLARATION	MARK (Word(s) and/or Design)	CLASS NO. (If known)

[SECR]ETARY AND COMMISSIONER OF PATENTS AND TRADEMARKS:

[AD]DRESS: _____
_____
_____
_____

[ENTITY T]YPE: (Check one and supply requested information)

[ ] - Citizen of (Country): _____

[ ] Partnership - State where organized (Country, if appropriate): _____
Names and Citizenship (Country) of General Partners: _____
_____
_____

| [ ] | Corporation - State (Country, if appropriate) of Incorporation: |
| [ ] | Other (Specify Nature of Entity and Domicile): |

GOODS AND/OR SERVICES:

Applicant requests registration of the trademark/service mark shown in the accompanying drawing in the United States Patent and Trademark Office on the Principal Register established by the Act of July 5, 1946 (15 U.S.C. 1051 et. seq., as amended) for the following goods/services (SPECIFIC GOODS AND/OR SERVICES MUST BE INSERTED HERE):

_____
_____
_____
_____

BASIS FOR APPLICATION: (Check boxes which apply, but never both the first AND second boxes, and supply requested information related to each box checked.)

[ ]	Applicant is using the mark in commerce on or in connection with the above identified goods/services. (15 U.S.C. 1051(a), as amended.) Three specimens showing the mark as used in commerce are submitted with this application. •Date of first use of the mark in commerce which the U.S. Congress may regulate (for example, interstate or between the U.S. and a foreign country): _____ •Specify the type of commerce: _____ (for example, interstate or between the U.S. and a specified foreign country) •Date of first use anywhere (the same as or before use in commerce date): _____ •Specify manner or mode of use of mark on or in connection with the goods/services: _____ (for example, trademark is applied to labels, service mark is used in advertisements)
[ ]	Applicant has a bona fide intention to use the mark in commerce on or in connection with the above identified goods/services. (15 U.S.C. 1051(b), as amended.) •Specify intended manner or mode of use of mark on or in connection with the goods/services: _____ (for example, trademark will be applied to labels, service mark will be used in advertisements)
[ ]	Applicant has a bona fide intention to use the mark in commerce on or in connection with the above identified goods/services, and asserts a claim of priority based upon a foreign application in accordance with 15 U.S.C. 1126(d), as amended. • Country of foreign filing: _____ • Date of foreign filing: _____
[ ]	Applicant has a bona fide intention to use the mark in commerce on or in connection with the above identified goods/services and, accompanying this application, submits a certification or certified copy of a foreign registration in accordance with 15 U.S.C. 1126(e), as amended. • Country of registration: _____ • Registration number: _____
	NOTE: Declaration, on Reverse Side, MUST be Signed

PTO Form 1478 (REV. 8/92)
OMB No. 0651-0009 (Exp. 6/30/95)

U.S. DEPARTMENT OF COMMERCE/Patent and Trademark Office

FIGURE 9-3
Trademark registration application, Principal Register

DECLARATION

The undersigned being hereby warned that willful false statements and the like so made are punishable by fine or imprisonment, or both, under 18 U.S.C. 1001, and that such willful false statements may jeopardize the validity of the application or any resulting registration, declares that he/she is properly authorized to execute this application on behalf of the applicant; he/she believes the applicant to be the owner of the trademark/service mark sought to be registered, or, if the application is being filed under 15 U.S.C. 1051(b), he/she believes applicant to be entitled to use such mark in commerce; to the best of his/her knowledge and belief no other person, firm, corporation, or association has the right to use the above identified mark in commerce, either in the identical form thereof or in such near resemblance thereto as to be likely, when used on or in connection with the goods/services of such other person, to cause confusion, or to cause mistake, or to deceive; and that all statements made of his/her own knowledge are true and that all statements made on information and belief are believed to be true.

DATE   SIGNATURE

TELEPHONE NUMBER   PRINT OR TYPE NAME AND POSITION

INSTRUCTIONS AND INFORMATION FOR APPLICANT

TO RECEIVE A FILING DATE, THE APPLICATION <u>MUST</u> BE COMPLETED AND SIGNED BY THE APPLICANT AND SUBMITTED ALONG WITH:

1. The prescribed **FEE ($210.00)** for each class of goods/services listed in the application;
2. A **DRAWING PAGE** displaying the mark in conformance with 37 CFR 2.52;
3. If the application is based on use of the mark in commerce, **THREE (3) SPECIMENS** (evidence) of the mark as used in commerce for each class of goods/services listed in the application. All three specimens may be in the nature of: (a) labels showing the mark which are placed on the goods; (b) photographs of the mark as it appears on the goods, (c) brochures or advertisements showing the mark as used in connection with the services.
4. An **APPLICATION WITH DECLARATION** (this form) - The application must be signed in order for the application to receive a filing date. Only the following person may sign the declaration, depending on the applicant's legal entity: (a) the individual applicant; (b) an officer of the corporate applicant; (c) one general partner of a partnership applicant; (d) all joint applicants.

SEND APPLICATION FORM, DRAWING PAGE, FEE, AND SPECIMENS (IF APPROPRIATE) TO:

U.S. DEPARTMENT OF COMMERCE
Patent and Trademark Office, Box TRADEMARK
Washington, D.C. 20231

Additional information concerning the requirements for filing an application is available in a booklet entitled **Basic Facts About Trademarks**, which may be obtained by writing to the above address or by calling: (703) 308-HELP.

This form is estimated to take an average of 1 hour to complete, including time required for reading and understanding instructions, gathering necessary information, recordkeeping, and acutally providing the information. Any comments on this form, including the amount of time required to complete this form, should be sent to the Office of Management and Organization, U.S. Patent and Trademark Office, U.S. Department of Commerce, Washington, D.C. 20231, and to Paperwork Reduction Project 0651-0009, Office of Information and Regulatory Affairs, Office of Management and Budget, Washington, D.C. 20503. Do NOT send completed forms to either of these addresses.

FIGURE 9-3
(Continued)

There is no requirement that the "official" form be used. Instead of filling out a trademark application form, many applicants create their own applications by typing all the information. Many law offices that perform federal registrations prepare disk formats of the application forms. This way, the paralegal or administrator only has to type in the appropriate information and print out the result. (See figure 9-9.)

The application should be printed on one side of the paper. The Patent and Trademark Office prefers typewritten, doublespaced applications on 8.5 x 11-inch paper with a 1.5-inch margin on the left and top of the page. A federal trademark application consists of the following basic elements[9]:

- Identification of the mark
- Identification of the class of goods or services, if known
- Information about the applicant, including name, address, and business form
- A description of the goods or services
- Basis for application (i.e., whether the mark is presently being used or whether the applicant has a bona fide intent to use the mark) and appropriate dates of use
- A declaration by the applicant.

Identification of the Mark

The first space of the application form requires that the applicant identify the mark. The paralegal and attorney must determine if the mark is a word or group of words, a stylized presentation of the word, a graphic symbol, a logo, a design, or any of the devices permitted under trademark law. If the mark is already in use, the specimens should be examined. If the mark is a word or group of words, the identification is straightforward. If it is a word, the mark may be identified simply as "JELL-O" or "THE WORD JELL-O," for instance.

Stylized Word Marks

Some companies use a word mark with a specific style of lettering. The lettering for the *JELL-O* gelatin dessert mark is often used in a capital letter format with a narrow elongated font style that does not include serifs. (*Serifs* are the fine lines that finish off the main strokes of a letter.) If the applicant intends to register the mark in its stylized format, the identification of the mark must reflect this by stating, for example, "JELL-O AND DESIGN" or "THE WORD JELL-O AND DESIGN." If the client is using the mark in commerce, the description should conform to the specimens provided with the application.

The broadest protection for a word mark will occur if a word mark is registered free of any lettering style. This way, for example, if the company decides to change its lettering, a new registration may not be necessary. However, this may preclude the company from stopping a competitor from using a similar style of lettering with a different word or words. For example, the Coca-Cola company desires to protect the mark *Coca-Cola* in its stylized and unstylized format. Both versions may be registered (i.e., with and without a specific lettering style). However, if a client is concerned about costs, the focus should be on the unstylized term rather than the appearance of the lettering.

Design Marks

In some cases, the mark may be primarily a graphic or design configuration. A succinct description of the graphic should be provided. For example, the design in figure 9-4 is a trademark for the Make-A-Wish Foundation of America. It is identified as "THE MARK CONSISTS OF A STYLIZED WISHBONE DESIGN." The design in figure 9-5 for a trademark of Huls America, Inc., is used for printing inks and colorants. The registrant described it as "TWO VERTICAL BANDS INTERRUPTED BY WHAT MAY BE DESCRIBED AS A PARTIALLY COMPRESSED 'C' SHAPED PROJECTION."

Color

As explained later in this chapter, trademarks that include colors are presented in drawings using special lining and shading sometimes known as *stippling*. Different types of lining and stippling are used to identify colors. For example, the identification for the mark in figure 9-4 also includes the additional statement, "THE MARK IS LINED FOR THE COLORS PURPLE, BLUE, GREEN, YELLOW, ORANGE AND RED."

If the mark uses lining and shading, but the applicant does not intend for that to convey a color, the applicant must so state in the identification of the mark. For example, "THE LINING IS A FEATURE OF THE MARK AND DOES NOT INDICATE COLOR."

FIGURE 9-4
Trademark of Make-A-Wish Foundation of America

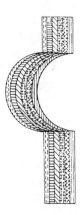

FIGURE 9-5
Trademark of Huls America, Inc.

Errors in Description

If the trademark examiner disagrees with the description of the mark, an alternative description may be suggested. In such a case, the application will be amended to conform to the trademark examiner's description.

Some examples of marks and their descriptions are provided in Table 9.1.

Identification of Class

The heading of the federal application includes a space for "Class Number (if known)." The Commissioner of Patents and Trademarks, under authority granted in the Lanham Act, has authorized a classification of goods and services.[10] The applicant does not need to list a class of goods or services. If the applicant leaves the space blank, or if the class chosen by the applicant is incorrect, the trademark examiner will select the appropriate class. If an applicant would like guidance on choosing a classification, the Patent and Trademark Office can offer assistance.

The purpose of the classification system is administrative: to group related goods in order to facilitate comparisons of the mark. The identification of class is different from the identification of goods (which is presented at another point in the application). The listing of a class of goods in the application does not mean that the applicant will be able to preclude all others in that class from using a similar mark.

Multiple Classes

The applicant may apply for registration in multiple classes. For example, the registration of the stylized letter "U" mark in Table 9.1 is a service

Mark	Identification
	THE MARK CONSISTS OF A STYLIZED LETTER "U" FEATURING STYLIZED REPRESENTATIONS OF HORNS AND A TAIL. THE MARK IS LINED FOR THE COLORS RED AND GREEN.
	THE MARK CONSISTS OF THE WORD "DIMARCO" AND A DESIGN OF AN OUTER WREATH IN GREEN AND INNER WREATH IN RED. THE DRAWING IS LINED FOR THE COLORS GREEN AND RED.
	THE MARK CONSISTS OF A STYLIZED LETTER "B" DESIGN. THE LINING SHOWN IN THE DRAWING IS A FEATURE OF THE MARK, AND IS NOT INTENDED TO INDICATE COLOR.
	THE MARK CONSISTS OF THE WORD "PARAMOUNT" IN STYLIZED LETTERS ABOUT FIVE SHADOW MOUNTAIN WITH AN ARC OF STARS SURROUNDING IT ALL.

TABLE 9.1
Identification
of Marks

mark for a professional hockey team *and* a trademark for various merchandise sold in connection with professional hockey exhibitions. The goods include key rings (Intl. Class 6), tote bags (Intl. Class 18), lapel badges and novelty items, namely foam fingers (Intl. Class 20), plastic drinking cups (Intl. Class 21), pennants (Intl. Class 24), shirts, caps, sweaters, jackets, sweatshirts, sweatpants, jerseys (Intl. Class 25), hockey pucks (Class 28), and programs for professional hockey exhibitions, team photographs, calendars, and hockey yearbooks (Intl. Class 16). The mark is a service mark for the entertainment services of professional hockey competitions and exhibitions (Class 41). All of these classes may be listed in the application. However, there is a separate registration fee for each class. For example, the application described here would cost $1890 ($210 multiplied by 9 classes).

International Schedule of Classes of Goods and Services

The current classification system is known as the **International Schedule of Classes of Goods and Services** and is applicable to applications filed on or after September 1, 1973. This schedule is shown in figure 9-6.

U.S. Classification System

For all trademark applications filed prior to September 1, 1973, the *U.S. Classification System* was used to categorize goods and services. Some state trademark offices still use this system and knowledge of the system may be necessary for analysis of trademark research reports. The U.S. Classification System appears in figure 9-7.

Class	Goods
1	Chemical products used in industry, science, photography, agriculture, horticulture, forestry; artificial and synthetic resins; plastics in the form of powders, liquids or pastes, for industrial use; manures (natural and artificial); fire extinguishing compositions; tempering substances and chemical preparations for soldering; chemical substances for preserving foodstuffs; tanning substances; adhesive substances used in industry.
2	Paints, varnishes, lacquers; preservatives against rust and against deterioration of wood; coloring matters, dyestuffs; mordants; natural resins; metals in foil and powder form for painters and decorators.
3	Bleaching preparations and other substances for laundry use; cleaning, polishing, scouring and abrasive preparations; soaps; perfumery, essential oils, cosmetics, hair lotions; dentifrices.
4	Industrial oils and greases (other than oils and fats and essential oils); lubricants; dust laying and absorbing compositions; fuels (including motor spirit) and illuminants; candles, tapers, night lights and wicks.
5	Pharmaceutical, veterinary, and sanitary substances; infants' and invalids' foods; plasters, material for bandaging; material for stopping teeth, dental wax, disinfectants; preparations for killing weeds and destroying vermin.
6	Unwrought and partly wrought common metals and their alloys; anchors, anvils, bells, rolled and cast building materials; rails and other metallic materials for railway tracks; chains (except driving chains for vehicles); cables and wires (nonelectric); locksmiths' work; metallic pipes and tubes; safes and cash boxes; steel balls; horseshoes; nails and screws; other goods in nonprecious metal not included in other classes; ores.
7	Machines and machine tools; motors (except for land vehicles); machine couplings and belting (except for land vehicles); large size agricultural implements; incubators.
8	Hand tools and instruments; cutlery, forks, and spoons; side arms.
9	Scientific, nautical, surveying and electrical apparatus and instruments (including wireless), photographic, cinematographic, optical, weighing, measuring, signalling, checking (supervision),

FIGURE 9-6
International Schedule
of Classes of Goods
and Services

	life-saving and teaching apparatus and instruments; coin or counterfreed apparatus; talking machines; cash registers; calculating machines; fire extinguishing apparatus.
10	Surgical, medical, dental, and veterinary instruments and apparatus (including artificial limbs, eyes, and teeth).
11	Installations for lighting, heating, steam generating, cooking, refrigerating, drying, ventilating, water supply, and sanitary purposes.
12	Vehicles; apparatus for locomotion by land, air, or water.
13	Firearms; ammunition and projectiles; explosive substances; fireworks.
14	Precious metals and their alloys and goods in precious metals or coated therewith (except cutlery, forks and spoons); jewelry, precious stones, horological and other chronometric instruments.
15	Musical instruments (other than talking machines and wireless apparatus).
16	Paper and paper articles, cardboard and cardboard articles; printed matter, newspaper and periodicals, books; bookbinding material; photographs; stationery, adhesive materials (stationery); artists' materials; paint brushes; typewriters and office requisites (other than furniture); instructional and teaching material (other than apparatus); playing cards; printers' type and cliches (stereotype).
17	Gutta percha, india rubber, balata and substitutes, articles made from these substances and not included in other classes; plastics in the form of sheets, blocks and rods, being for use in manufacture; materials for packing, stopping or insulating; asbestos, mica and their products; hose pipes (nonmetallic).
18	Leather and imitations of leather, and articles made from these materials and not included in other classes; skins, hides; trunks and travelling bags; umbrellas, parasols and walking sticks; whips, harness and saddlery.
19	Building materials, natural and artificial stone, cement, lime, mortar, plaster and gravel; pipes of earthenware or cement; roadmaking materials; asphalt, pitch and bitumen; portable buildings; stone monuments; chimney pots.
20	Furniture, mirrors, picture frames; articles (not included in other classes) of wood, cork, reeds, cane, wicker, horn, bone, ivory, whalebone, shell, amber, mother-of-pearl, meerschaum, celluloid, substitutes for all these materials, or of plastics.
21	Small domestic utensils and containers (not of precious metals, or coated therewith); combs and sponges; brushes (other than paint brushes); brushmaking materials; instruments and material for cleaning purposes, steel wool; unworked or semiworked glass (excluding glass used in building); glassware, procelain and earthenware, not included in other classes.
22	Ropes, string, nets, tents, awnings, tarpaulins, sails, sacks; padding and stuffing materials (hair, kapok, feathers, seaweed, etc.); raw fibrous textile materials
23	Yarns, threads
24	Tissues (piece goods); bed and table covers; textile articles not included in other classes.
25	Clothing, including boots, shoes and slippers.
26	Lace and embroidery, ribbons and braid; buttons, press buttons, hooks and eyes, pins and needles; artificial flowers.
27	Carpets, rugs, mats and matting; linoleums and other materials for covering existing floors; wall hangings (nontextile).

FIGURE 9-6
(Continued)

28	Games and playthings; gymnastic and sporting articles (except clothing); ornaments and decorations for Christmas trees.
29	Meats, fish, poultry and game; meat extracts; preserved, dried and cooked fruits and vegetables; jellies, jams; eggs, milk and other dairy products; edible oils and fats; preserves, pickles.
30	Coffee, tea, cocoa, sugar, rice, tapioca, sago, coffee substitutes; flour, and preparations made from cereals; bread, biscuits, cakes, pastry and confectionary, ices; honey, treacle; yeast, baking powder; salt, mustard, pepper, vinegar, sauces, spices; ice.
31	Agricultural, horticultural and forestry products and grains not included in other classes; living animals; fresh fruits and vegetables; seeds; live plants and flowers; foodstuffs for animals, malt.
32	Beer, ale and porter; mineral and aerated waters and other nonalcoholic drinks; syrups and other preparations for making beverages.
33	Wines, spirits and liqueurs.
34	Tobacco, raw or manufactured; smokers' articles; matches.
Class	**Services**
35	Advertising and business.
36	Insurance and financial.
37	Construction and repair.
38	Communication.
39	Transportation and storage.
40	Material treatment.
41	Education and entertainment.
42	Miscellaneous.

FIGURE 9-6
(Continued)

Class	**Goods**
1	Raw or partly prepared materials.
2	Receptacles.
3	Baggage, animal equipments, portfolios, and pocket books.
4	Abrasives and polishing materials.
5	Adhesives.
6	Chemicals and chemical compositions.
7	Cordage.
8	Smokers' articles, not including tobacco products.
9	Explosives, firearms, equipments, and projectiles.
10	Fertilizers.
11	Inks and inking materials.
12	Construction materials.
13	Hardware and plumbing and steamfitting supplies.
14	Metals and metal castings and forgings.
15	Oils and greases.
16	Protective and decorative coatings.
17	Tobacco products.
18	Medicines and pharmaceutical preparations.
19	Vehicles.

FIGURE 9-7
U.S. Classification System (prior system)

20	Linoleum and oiled cloth.
21	Electrical apparatus, machines, and supplies.
22	Games, toys, and sporting goods.
23	Cutlery, machinery, and tools, and parts thereof.
24	Laundry appliances and machines.
25	Locks and safes.
26	Measuring and scientific appliances.
27	Horological instruments.
28	Jewelry and precious-metal ware.
29	Brooms, brushes, and dusters.
30	Crockery, earthenware, and porcelain.
31	Filters and refrigerators.
32	Furniture and upholstery.
33	Glassware.
34	Heating, lighting, and ventilating apparatus.
35	Belting, hose, machinery packing, and nonmetallic tires.
36	Musical instruments and supplies.
37	Paper and stationery.
38	Prints and publications.
39	Clothing.
40	Fancy goods, furnishings, and notions.
41	Canes, parasols, and umbrellas.
42	Knitted, netted, and textile fabrics, and substitutes therefor.
43	Tread and yarn.
44	Dental, medical, and surgical appliances.
45	Soft drinks and carbonated waters.
46	Foods and ingredients of foods.
47	Wines.
48	Malt beverages and liquors.
49	Distilled alcoholic liquors.
50	Merchandise not otherwise classified.
51	Cosmetics and toilet preparations.
52	Detergents and soaps.
Class	**Services**
100	Miscellaneous.
101	Advertising and business.
102	Insurance and financial.
103	Construction and repair.
104	Communication.
105	Transportation and storage.
106	Material treatment.
107	Education and entertainment.

FIGURE 9-7
(Continued)

The Applicant

The applicant is the owner of the mark—the party that controls the nature and quality of the goods or services offered in connection with the mark. The applicant can be an individual, a partnership, a corporation, an association such as a union, social club, or cooperative, or a joint ownership by a combination of any these forms.

Partnership—Include the names and citizenship of the general partners and the domicile of the partnership.

Corporation—Include the name under which the business or group is incorporated and the state or foreign nation under which it is organized.

The applicant's citizenship also is required, as well as a post office address. If the applicant is doing business under a fictitious name, that information should also be included, especially if it is included on any specimens furnished with the application. If the mark is owned jointly by two entities (an individual and a corporation, two corporations, etc.), that should be stated as well.

EXAMPLE

Individual/Sole Proprietor. "Applicant is an individual and citizen of the United States of America doing business as *Palm Tree Furniture.*"

EXAMPLE

Partnership. "Applicant is a partnership organized under the laws of the State of Florida and comprised of Sally Hepburn and Bob Smith, both citizens of the United States of America."

EXAMPLE

Corporation (or Association.) "Applicant is a corporation [or non-profit corporation, etc.] organized under the laws of the state of Maryland."

EXAMPLE

Joint Applicants. "Applicants are Herbert Clawson, an individual, and FoodCo, a corporation organized under the laws of the state of California, joint owners."

Other Entities

Other business entities, such as banking institutions, government entities, conservatorships, trusts, estates, and universities, may own trademarks. Listings for these bodies generally follow the style used by these entities when they acquire other forms of property. For example, the executors of an estate should be listed as owners of a trademark in respect to their capacity administering the estate (i.e., "The executors of the Herbert Clawson estate, comprised of Sam Clawson and Mary Clawson, both citizens of the United States").

Consistency

It is important that the proper entity be listed as the owner/applicant. If the name of the owner is filed incorrectly, the subsequent registration will be void. (If the applicant is using the mark in commerce, examine the specimens of the mark as it is used.) The name of the applicant should be consistent with the name of the owner or company on the specimen (if listed). If the names are not the same, the applicant must explain the relationship between the applicant and the party listed in the specimen. The applicant also must explain how any use of the mark by that party inures to the applicant's benefit.

Identification of Goods and Services

The applicant must supply an identification of the goods and services for which the trademark will be used. This description should be specific; the descriptions of items listed in the International Classification of Goods and Services are not considered definite enough to serve as proper identification. For instance, if the trademark owner is selling key rings, the listing should state "key rings" and not "nonprecious metal goods" as listed in International Class 6.

The description should be precise. Often an applicant uses broad or incorrect language and the trademark examiner must question the accuracy of the identification. Alternatively, the examiner will negotiate an appropriate identification with the applicant. In fact, a survey of the Patent and Trademark Office in 1986 indicated that more than 50 percent of the trademark applications involved a questioned identification of goods or a negotiated identification adjustment. The choice of language for the identification also may be important in the context of a trademark infringement lawsuit.

Two sources for guidance in identifying goods are the *Trademark Examiners Manual of Procedure (TMEP),* available from the Government Printing Office, and the *U.S. Patent and Trademark Office Acceptable Identification of Goods and Services Manual,* published by the USTA. The latter guide lists appropriate choices of identification of goods and services in alphabetical order and by class. The Patent and Trademark Office also will provide information about classification over the telephone. In 1986, the former Chairman of the Trademark Trial and Appeal Board published several tips for applicants preparing identifications. Some of these tips are incorporated in the following suggestions:

1. *Keep it concise and use common terminology.* Technical language and lengthy descriptions are ordinarily not appropriate. Identifications should be clear, concise, and as brief as possible, using current and common marketplace terminology. Review the specimens that will be submitted and confirm that the identification is consistent. If it is helpful, consider identifying the use of the goods or services. If the mark is the title of a periodical publication, the identification should specify the

subject matter of the publication and the form of the publication, unless the mark itself includes this information.

EXAMPLES

[Salsa Sauce] FOR SALSA SAUCE, GARNISHES, AND MARINADES FOR USE AS CONDIMENTS, DRESSINGS, OR DIP.
[Guard Services] FOR PROVIDING UNIFORMED GUARD AND INVESTIGATING SERVICES.
[Record Label] FOR PHONOGRAPH RECORDS, COMPACT DISC RECORDINGS, AND PRERECORDED AUDIOTAPES FEATURING VARIOUS MUSICAL ENTERTAINMENT.
[Electronic Parts Catalog] FOR CATALOG OF ELECTRONIC COMPONENTS.
[Hospital ID Bracelets] FOR PLASTIC OR VINYL IDENTIFICATION BRACELETS FOR MEDICAL OR HOSPITAL USE.
[Running Shoes] FOR ATHLETIC FOOTWEAR.
[Direct Mail Promotion] FOR PROVIDING DIRECT MAIL ADVERTISING SERVICES FOR RETAIL BUSINESSES.
[Database Computer Program] FOR COMPUTER SOFTWARE PROGRAMS FOR DATABASE MANAGEMENT FOR USE IN BUSINESS AND PERSONAL APPLICATIONS.
[Music Magazine] FOR MAGAZINES DEALING WITH MUSIC AND POPULAR CULTURE.

2. *Avoid broad terminology.* Terms that are ambiguous (e.g., "metallic parts" or "beauty products") are not acceptable. Many applicants desire to list a broad category first and then follow it with specific items. For example, "alcoholic beverages—cognac brandy and champagne." In such cases the applicant should not use "linking" terminology like "including" or "such as." Instead, definite phrases like "namely" or "consisting of" should be used.

EXAMPLES

FOR ALCOHOLIC BEVERAGES, NAMELY COGNAC, BRANDY, AND CHAMPAGNE. FOR HAIR CARE PRODUCTS, NAMELY HAIR SHAMPOO, HAIR CONDITIONER, HAIR MOISTURIZER, CONTROL AND FINISHING SPRAY FOR HAIR.
FOR PROCESSED FOOD, NAMELY NATURAL FROZEN FRUIT BARS AND ICE CREAM BARS.
FOR CLOTHING, NAMELY T-SHIRTS, JACKETS, AND SHORTS.

On some occasions, broad terminology, without elaboration (e.g., "paper," "furniture," "ammunition"), is acceptable, provided that the mark is actually being used on a number of products of the same general type and the broad term identifies the group as a whole with reasonable certainty.

Also, "accessories therefor" is normally considered unacceptably indefinite, but "parts therefor" is acceptable when related to machinery or equipment that itself has been described with particularity (e.g., "motorcycles and parts therefor").

3. *Avoid or limit identifying terms that cross classes.* Avoid or qualify terms that identify goods in different classes. For example, terms such as "equipment," "parts," "hardware," or "instruments" could each refer to goods in various classes. In such cases a qualifier should be used. For example, "*computer* hardware" or "*electrical* instruments." Similarly, qualifiers such as "*hair* brush" or "*surgical* table" should be used.

4. *Avoid using the trademark in the identification.* Just as a dictionary definition should not include the word being defined, an identification of goods or services should not include the trademark or service mark in the identification. For example, the *Xerox* mark is *not* used for xerographic services, it is used for photocopy services.

5. *Describe the goods or services, not the advertising medium.* An identification should not include the medium in which the goods or services are communicated or advertised. For example, a woman who advertises for her entertainment services should not identify her services as "entertainment services and advertising." The Patent and Trademark Office considers advertising to be a service that is rendered by advertising agencies. Similarly, the Patent and Trademark Office has indicated that "signs and menus" should not be included in the identification of restaurant services. The menus and signs are the media through which the mark is communicated.

Basis for Application

The Patent and Trademark Office trademark form provides four bases for trademark application in the official form: (1) use in commerce; (2) bona fide intention to use the mark; (3) bona fide intention to use the mark and applicant asserts priority because of a foreign application for registration; and (4) bona fide intention to use the mark and applicant has acquired a certification or copy of a foreign registration. The most common applications are the first two choices. The latter two choices, based upon foreign registration or application, are sometimes known as *Section 44 applications* and are often grouped together for classification purposes (see Table 9.2). Section 44 applications are only available to foreign applicants.

When using the Patent and Trademark Office form, the applicant checks one of the four choices and completes the blank. An application cannot be based on *both* Section 1(a), actual use, and Section 1(b), intent to use. If *both* the first two boxes are checked, the Patent and Trademark Office will not accept the application and will return it to the applicant without processing. When preparing the application without the Patent and Trademark Office form, the applicant need only specify the particular basis and not list the other choices. The basis for registration is dependent upon use in commerce.

Section 1(a): Actual Use	The applicant is using the mark in commerce at the time of execution of the trademark application.
Section 1(b): Bona Fide Intent to Use	The applicant has a bona fide intention to use the mark in commerce but has not yet used the mark in commerce at the time of execution of the application.
Section 44: Intent to Use Based on Foreign Registration or Foreign Application for Registration	The applicant has a bona fide intention to use the mark and applicant asserts priority because of a foreign registration.
	The applicant has a bona fide intention to use the mark and applicant asserts priority because of a foreign application for registration.

TABLE 9.2
Basis for Trademark
Application

If the applicant is using the mark in commerce regulated by the United States on or before the day the application is executed, then the basis for the application is "use in commerce." If not, it is one of the three "intent-to-use" bases.

If the application is filed under Section 44 based on a foreign registration, a certified copy of the foriegn registration must accompany the U.S. application. If the Section 44 application is based on a foreign application, the U.S. application must be filed within six months of the foreign filing date. In the latter instance, the U.S. registration will not issue until a certified copy of the foreign registration, when it issues, is filed in the Patent and Trademark Office.

As explained earlier, a trademark is deemed to be in use in commerce on goods when it is placed on the goods or containers, tags or labels, or displays associated with the goods (or, if otherwise impracticable, on documents associated with the goods) and the goods are sold or transported in commerce in more than one state or between the United States and a foreign country. A service mark is deemed to be in use in commerce when it is used or displayed in the sale or advertising of services and the services are rendered in commerce, or the services are rendered in more than one state or between the United States and a foreign country. For federal registration, commerce is any commerce lawfully regulated by the United States. For state registration, it is generally any commerce occurring within the state of registration.

Use in Commerce: Dates of First Use and Type of Commerce

An applicant who is using the mark in commerce must state that the mark is presently being used in commerce and provide dates of use and type of commerce.

EXAMPLE

The trademark was first used on the goods on June 1, 1986; was first used on the goods in interstate commerce on June 1, 1986; and is now in use in such commerce.

Dates of Use

Applicants must supply the date of: (1) first use in commerce; and (2) first use in commerce that the United States may regulate. Often both dates are the same. However, in some cases the dates are different. For example, the service mark *Big Apple Floor Polishers* is first used for floor-polishing services in New York City on June 1, 1992. The following month, on July 1, 1992, the service mark is used in an advertisement distributed to New Jersey citizens. The first use in commerce is June 1, 1992; the first use in interstate commerce is July 1, 1992.

If the law office is preparing the application on behalf of the client, it is advisable to have the client provide some supporting documentation for these dates. For example, if the first use of a service mark is a newspaper advertisement, then the law office should retain a copy of the advertisement. If the trademark is used on goods, then a copy of the invoice should be kept in the file.

If the client is unwilling or unable to furnish documentation and it is difficult to discern the exact date, it is permissible to generalize the date. In such case, the Patent and Trademark Office will consider the date as the last possible date. For example, "January 1993" would be January 31, 1993 or "sometime before April 1, 1993" would be March 31, 1993.

Type of Commerce

The type of commerce should be described. For example, "interstate commerce" or "commerce between the United States and [*foreign country*]." Do not state "foreign commerce."

Specifying the Manner or Mode of Use

An applicant (excluding applicants based on foreign filings or registrations) must provide information about the "manner or mode of use." For a trademark, the mode and manner of use is generally on containers, labels, or tags. For a service mark, the mark is generally used in advertisements, business cards, or promotional literature. If the application is based upon an intent to use, the applicant would state the "intention" to use the mark. The manner or mode of use should be consistent with the specimens that will be furnished with the mark.

EXAMPLES

The mark is used on labels that are affixed to the goods.
The mark is used in advertisements for the services.
[For Intent to Use]
The intended manner of use of the mark is by applying it to containers for the goods.

First Use by a Predecessor

If the first use of the mark was by a predecessor of the applicant, that fact should be noted in the application. For example, if the first use of the *Doctor Clone* mark was by Softco and Softco later was acquired and merged into Diskco, then Diskco's application for the *Doctor Clone* mark should state:

> The trademark was first used on the goods in interstate commerce on June 1, 1986 by applicant's predecessor in title and is now in use in such commerce.

First Use by a Related Party

If the first use of the mark was by a related party, that fact should be noted in the application. For example, the mark may be used by another corporation, Subsidco, which may be either a wholly owned subsidiary or a licensee of the applicant. The applicant should state:

> The trademark was first on the goods in interstate commerce on June 1, 1986 by Subsidco, a related company which is a wholly owned subsidiary of applicant, and is now in use in such commerce. Applicant controls the nature and quality of the goods sold under the mark, and claims that all use of the mark by the related company inures to applicant's benefit.

If the related company is a licensee, that fact should be included in the preceding example in place of the words "wholly owned subsidiary." The Patent and Trademark Office will accept the statement that the applicant controls the nature and quality of the goods when the related company is a wholly owned subsidiary. In the case of use by a licensee, the application should include provisions from the license agreement to support the assertion that the applicant controls the nature and quality of the goods sold by its licensee under the mark.

Foreign Meanings

Additional material may be required in an application. If, for example, the trademark has a meaning in a foreign language, a statement including a translation should be provided.

FIGURE 9-8
Sample trademark with foreign meaning.

EXAMPLE

When attempting to register the mark in figure 9-8, which includes the words *Parfums* and *L'Arome,* the applicant includes a statement, "THE ENGLISH TRANSLATION OF THE WORDS 'PARFUMS' IS 'PERFUME' AND 'L'AROME' IS 'THE AROMA' OR 'PERFUME.'

Disclaimers

Many trademarks include words or phrases that, by themselves, cannot be protected under trademark law. For example, no person can claim an exclusive right to the common words *salsa* or *computer*. To allow one person a monopoly or exclusive right to use such terms would prevent others from also using these generic terms. Therefore, the trademark office requires a **disclaimer** as to certain portions of trademarks. A *disclaimer* is a statement that a trademark owner does not claim exclusive right in a specific portion of a mark, apart from its use within the mark.[11] For example, if a party wanted to register the mark, *Lucky Driving School,* the applicant would be required to disclaim "driving school." This means that, apart from the use as a part of the trademark, the applicant claims no exclusive right to use the words *driving school.*

In some cases, it is easy to discern what must be disclaimed. Any term that would be generic when applied to the goods is normally disclaimed (e.g., terms such as *oil, table, telephone, coffee, productions,* etc.). If the applicant is unsure and no disclaimer is made, the trademark examiner may request and negotiate a disclaimer with the applicant. The application will be amended accordingly. The disclaimer in a federal application does not prevent the trademark owner from asserting common law rights. That is, even though the applicant cannot claim an exclusive right to use a portion of a mark, that does not prevent the applicant from claiming an exclusive right under common law principles.

EXAMPLES

 NO CLAIM IS MADE TO THE EXCLUSIVE RIGHT TO USE "BABY", APART FROM THE MARK AS SHOWN.

For foreign terms with generic meanings:

 NO CLAIM IS MADE TO THE EXCLUSIVE RIGHT TO USE "PARFUMS" AND "L'AROME", APART FROM THE MARK AS SHOWN.

Surnames

A trademark which is primarily the surname of an individual (i.e., Jones) cannot be registered on the Principal Register without a showing of distinctiveness (i.e., secondary meaning). Because of this requirement, surnames are typically relegated to the Supplemental Register. In addition, as indicated earlier in this chapter, a trademark containing the name of a living person cannot be registered unless the consent of that person has been provided. If the mark contains the name of an individual (or wording that could be interpreted to be the name of an individual), the applicant should advise the Patent and Trademark Office accordingly.

EXAMPLE

frank Meisler THE NAME "Frank Meisler" IDENTIFIES A LIVING INDIVIDUAL WHOSE CONSENT IS OF RECORD.

Proof of Secondary Meaning; Distinctiveness

A descriptive mark can be registered on the Principal Register if the applicant can demonstrate distinctiveness. As indicated previously, a demonstration of continued use over a period of five years or a demonstration of sales and advertising may overcome a presumption of descriptiveness. Some applicants, in anticipation of an objection for descriptiveness, prepare a statement demonstrating secondary meaning. If the applicant has used the mark continuously for five years, the following type of statement will suffice:

THE MARK HAS BECOME DISTINCTIVE OF APPLICANT'S GOODS AS A RESULT OF SUBSTANTIALLY EXCLUSIVE AND CONTINUOUS USE IN INTERSTATE COMMERCE FOR THE FIVE YEARS NEXT PRECEDING THE DATE OF FILING OF THIS APPLICATION.

If the applicant has not used the mark for five years, a showing may be made in support of registrability. This would be included in a separate document furnished with the application. The applicant would submit affidavits, declarations, depositions, or other appropriate evidence showing the duration, extent, and nature of use in commerce and advertising expenditures in connection with advertising (identifying types of media and attaching typical advertisements). In addition, the applicant can furnish affidavits, declarations, letters or statements from the trade or public, or other appropriate evidence tending to show that the mark distinguishes the goods. In the event of such a showing, the following statement should be included in the application:

THE MARK HAS BECOME DISTINCTIVE OF APPLICANT'S GOODS AS EVIDENCED BY THE SHOWING SUBMITTED SEPARATELY.

Some trademark attorneys and paralegals prefer not to make a showing of distinctiveness. Instead, they wait to see if the examining attorney considers the mark to be descriptive. In that case, a response is then prepared demonstrating distinctiveness. Any declarations furnished in support of the application must meet the requirements of § 2.20 of the Title 37 of the Code of Federal Regulations, as discussed later.

Declaration

The owner of the mark is required to provide a sworn statement or other verification that the facts in the trademark application are true, or, if the statements are made on information and belief, that the owner believes the statements to be true.[12] In lieu of making a sworn statement, the applicant may provide a signed declaration, testifying to the truthfulness of the facts and indicating that the declarant has been warned that willful false statements may jeopardize the application and are punishable by fine or imprisonment or both. The declaration should be executed by the applicant or member of the firm or an officer of the corporation or association making the application. A sample declaration is included on the back of the Patent and Trademark Office application form. When you include declaration for use on a self-prepared form, you should edit it to accommodate the status of the person executing it. For example, if the applicant is a corporation, the declaration should indicate the position of the person signing (i.e., president, director, chief executive officer).

Use in Commerce Declarations. In addition to the general requirements for a declaratiom, an applicant for a mark used in commerce must attest to the following:

- That the applicant is believed to be the owner of the mark sought to be registered
- That the mark is in use in commerce and specifying the nature of such commerce
- That no other entity, to the best of the declarant's knowledge and belief, has the right to use such mark in commerce, either in the identical form or in such near resemblance as to be likely, when applied to the goods or services of such other entity, to cause confusion, or to cause mistake, or to deceive
- That the specimens or facsimiles show the mark as used on or in connection with the goods or services
- That the facts set forth in the application are true.

EXAMPLE: Declaration by President of Corporation— Mark Used in Commerce

HAROLD HAWTHORNE, being hereby warned that willful false statements and the like so made are punishable by fine or imprisonment, or both under Section 1001 of Title 18 of the United States Code and that such willful false statements may jeopardize the validity of the application or any registration resulting therefrom, states that he is *President* of applicant corporation and is authorized to execute this instrument on behalf of said corporation; he believes said corporation to be the owner of the mark sought to be registered; that said mark is in use in the type of commerce specified in this application; to the best of his knowledge and belief no other person, firm, corporation, or association has the right to use said mark in commerce either in the identical form thereof or in such near resemblance thereto as to be likely, when applied to the goods of such other person, to cause confusion, or to cause mistake, or to deceive; that the specimens or facsimiles accompanying this application show said mark as actually used in connection with the goods; that the facts set forth in this application are true; and that all statements made of his own knowledge are true and statements made on information and belief are believed to be true.

Intent-to-Use Declarations

In an intent-to-use application, the applicant must attest to the following:

- That the applicant is believed to be the owner of the mark sought to be registered
- That the applicant has a bona fide intention to use the mark in commerce on or in connection with the specified goods or services
- That no other entity, to the best of the declarant's knowledge and belief, has the right to use such mark in commerce, either in the identical form or in such near resemblance as to be likely, when applied to the goods or services of such other entity, to cause confusion, or to cause mistake, or to deceive
- That the facts set forth in the application are true.

EXAMPLE: Declaration of Partner—Bona Fide Intent-to-Use Application

DONNA LUTHER, being hereby warned that willful false statements and the like so made are punishable by fine or imprisonment, or both under Section 1001 of Title 18 of the United States Code and that such willful false statements may jeopardize the validity of the application or any registration resulting therefrom, states that she is a *Partner* of applicant partnership, organized under the laws of the State of Florida, and is authorized to execute this instrument on behalf of said partnership; she believes said partnership to be the owner of the mark sought to be registered; that she believes applicant is entitled to use the mark in the type of commerce specified in this application; to the best of her knowledge and belief no other person, firm, corporation, or association has the right to use said mark in commerce either in the identical form thereof or in such near resemblance thereto as to be likely, when applied to the goods of such other person, to cause confusion, or to cause mistake, or to deceive; that the facts set forth in this application are true; and that all statements made of her own knowledge are true and statements made on information and belief are believed to be true.

Power of Attorney

For an attorney to assist in the processing of a trademark application, the applicant must provide authorization.[13] Such authorization is usually added at the bottom of the application.

EXAMPLE: Power of Attorney

Applicant hereby appoints **Sam C. Follow, Esq.**, One South Street, Santa Wanda, California, 94411 (415-771-5222), a member of the bar of the State of California, to act as attorney for Aunt Pauline's Foods, applicant herein, with full power to prosecute this application, to transact all relevant business with the Patent and Trademark Office in connection therewith and to receive all official communications in connection with this application.

If the applicant intends to have an attorney assist in processing the application after it has been submitted, a separate power of attorney may be furnished. This document should be signed by the applicant and should include the serial number of the application, the name of the applicant, the mark, and the date of signature of the applicant.

Domestic Representative

If an applicant is not domiciled in the United States, the applicant must designate the name and address of some person who resides in the United States. That person will receive notices affecting the mark. This designation may be incorporated in the application. Official communications of the Patent and Trademark Office will be addressed to the domestic representative unless the application is being prosecuted by an attorney at law or other qualified person. The designation of a domestic representative does not authorize the person designated to prosecute the application. The domestic representative can be a person, a corporation, or some other recognized business entity.

EXAMPLE: Designation of Domestic Representative

Barbi Josephs, whose postal address is 2727 South Lock Road, Baltimore, Maryland, 03241, is hereby designated applicant's representative upon whom notice or process in proceedings affecting the mark may be served.

Figure 9-9 shows a self-generated application.

Application for Registration Based Upon Use
Principal Register—Partnership—Power of Attorney

TRADEMARK APPLICATION, PRINCIPAL
REGISTER, WITH DECLARATION
(Partnership)

Mark: **BROTHER BOB'S BIG BEANJAM**

Class No.: (*if known*)

TO THE COMMISSIONER OF PATENTS AND TRADEMARKS:
Name of partnership: **BROTHER BOB'S FOODS,** a California general partnership
Names and citizenship of partners: **Robert Bowman, California; Linda Lionel, California**
Business address of partnership: **321 25th Avenue, San Francisco, CA 94121**
Telephone: **415 722-5242**

The above identified applicant has adopted and is using the trademark shown in the accompanying drawing for the following goods: **food dressings and marinades for use with salads, vegetables, fish, poultry, pasta and meat,** and requests that said mark be registered in the United States Patent and Trademark Office on the Principal Register established by the Act of July 5, 1946.

The trademark was first used on the goods on **May 20, 1991**; was first used on the goods in **interstate** commerce on **July 1, 1991**; and is now in use in such commerce. The mark is used by applying it to **containers for the goods** and three specimens showing the mark as actually used are presented herewith.

Robert Bowman, being hereby warned that willful false statements and the like so made are punishable by fine or imprisonment, or both under Section 1001 of Title 18 of the United States Code and that such willful false statements may jeopardize the validity of the application or any registration resulting therefrom, states that he is a **General Partner** of applicant partnership and is authorized to execute this instrument on behalf of said partnership; he believes said partnership to be the owner of the mark sought to be registered; that said mark is in use in the type of commerce specified in this application; to the best of his knowledge and belief no other person, firm, corporation, or association has the right to use said mark in commerce either in the identical form thereof or in such near resemblance thereto as to be likely, when applied to the goods of such other person, to cause confusion, or to cause mistake, or to deceive; that the specimens or facsimiles accompanying this application show said mark as actually used in connection with the goods; that the facts set forth in this application are true; and that all statements made of his own knowledge are true and statements made on information and belief are believed to be true.

POWER OF ATTORNEY AT LAW

Applicant hereby appoints Wilma Richards, Esq., One Maritime Plaza, Suite 1110, San Francisco, California, 94111 (415-711-5121), a member of the bar of the State of California, to act as attorney for Brother Bob's Foods, applicant herein, with full power to prosecute this application, to transact all relevant business with the Patent and Trademark Office in connection therewith, and to receive all official

FIGURE 9-9
Sample trademark
application

communications in connection with this application.

BROTHER BOB'S FOODS

Dated _____   By:_____
                                  ROBERT BOWMAN, General Partner

FIGURE 9-9
(Continued)

Intent-to-Use Application

The application for federal trademark registration based upon a bona fide intent to use ("also known as *Section 1(b)* or *ITU application*) is similar to the registration based upon actual use, except that: (1) no dates of use are supplied; (2) the applicant does not state that the mark has been used in commerce; (3) no specimens are provided with the application; and (4) additional fees, documents, and specimens must be provided to the Patent and Trademark Office once the applicant uses the mark in commerce. The advantage is obvious: the applicant can "reserve" a mark prior to actual use on goods or services. An example of an ITU application is shown in figure 9-10.

Application for Registration Based upon Bona Fide Intent to Use

Principal Register—Corporation
TRADEMARK APPLICATION,   Mark: **the words "THE BIG SQUEEZY"**
  PRINCIPAL   Class No.: (*if known*) **CLASS 9**
REGISTER, WITH DECLARATION
  (Corporation)

TO THE COMMISSIONER OF PATENTS AND TRADEMARKS:

Name of corporation: **Diskco**
State of incorporation: **CALIFORNIA**
Business address: **3200 PRINCETON ROAD, LOS ANGELES, CALIFORNIA, 94022**
Telephone: **312-111-1434**

FIGURE 9-10
Sample intent-to-use application

Applicant requests registration of the above-identified trademark shown in the accompanying drawing in the United States Patent and Trademark Office on the Principal Register established by the Act of July 5, 1946 for the following goods: **computer software programs and accompanying instruction manuals sold as a unit for use in compressing data on magnetic storage devices and other computer disk storage devices in business and personal applications.**

Applicant has a bona fide intention to use the mark in commerce on or in connection with the above identified goods. (15 USC § 1051(b) as amended.) Applicant intends to use the mark by applying it to **containers for the goods.**

Terrence Stumpfel, being hereby warned that willful false statements and the like so made are punishable by fine or imprisonment, or both under Section 1001 of Title 18 of the United States Code and that such willful false statements may jeopardize the validity of the application or any registration resulting therefrom, states that he is **Chief Executive Officer** of applicant corporation and is authorized to execute this instrument on behalf of said corporation; he believes said corporation to be the owner of the mark sought to be registered; to the best of his knowledge and belief no other person, firm, corporation, or association has the right to use said mark in commerce either in the identical form thereof or in such near resemblance thereto as to be likely, when applied to the goods of such other person, to cause confusion, or to cause mistake, or to deceive; that the facts set forth in this application are true; and that all statements made of his own knowledge are true and statements made on information and belief are believed to be true.

POWER OF ATTORNEY AT LAW

Applicant hereby appoints Wilma Richards, Esq., One Maritime Plaza, Suite 1110, San Francisco, California, 94111 (415-711-5121), a member of the bar of the State of California, to act as attorney for Diskco, applicant herein, with full power to prosecute this application, to transact all relevant business with the Patent and Trademark Office in connection therewith, and to receive all official communications in connection with this application.

Dated:_____   **Diskco**

                         By: _____
                             Terrence Stumpfel,
                             Chief Executive Officer
                             August 8, 1992

FIGURE 9-10
(Continued)

Drawing

Every trademark application must contain a trademark drawing. A trademark **drawing** is a substantially exact representation of the mark as used or, in the case of an intent-to-use application, as intended to be used. The trademark drawing is not required if the mark is not capable of representation by a drawing (e.g., a smell or an audio trademark), but in such cases the application must contain an adequate description of the mark. The requirements for the drawing are set forth in the Code of Federal Regulations.

37 C.F.R. § 2.52 Requirements for drawings.

(a) **Character of drawing**. All drawings, except as otherwise provided, must be made with the pen or by a process that will provide high definition upon reproduction. A photolithographic reproduction or printer's proof copy may be used if otherwise suitable. Every line and letter, including color lining and lines used for shading, must be black. All lines must be clean, sharp, and solid, and must not be fine or crowded. Gray tones or tints may not be used for surface shading or any other purpose.

(b) **Paper and ink**. The drawing must be made upon paper that is flexible, strong, smooth, non shiny, white and durable. A good grade of bond paper is suitable; however, water marks should not be prominent. India ink or its equivalent in quality must be used for pen drawings to secure perfectly black solid lines. The use of white pigment to cover lines is not acceptable.

(c) **Size of paper and margins**. The size of the sheet on which a drawing is made must be 8 to 8 1/2 inches (20.3 to 21.6 cm.) wide and 11 inches (27.9 cm.) long. One of the shorter sides of the sheet should be regarded as its top. It is preferable that the drawing be 2.5 inches (6.1 cm.) high and/or wide, but in no case may it be larger than 4 inches (10.3 cm) wide. If the amount of detail in the mark precludes a reduction to this size, such detail may be verbally described in the body of the application. There must be a margin of at least 1 inch (2.5 cm.) on the sides and bottom of the paper and at least 1 inch (2.5 cm.) between the drawing and the heading.

(d) **Heading**. Across the top of the drawing, beginning one inch (2.5 cm.) from the top edge and not exceeding one third of the sheet, there must be placed a heading, listing in separate lines, applicant's complete name; applicant's post office address; the dates of first use of the mark and first use of the mark in commerce in an application under section 1(a) of the Act; the priority filing date of the relevant foreign application in an application claiming the benefit of a prior foreign application in accordance with section 44(d) of the Act; and the goods or services recited in the application or a typical item of the goods or services if a number of items are recited in the application. This heading should be typewritten. If the drawing is in special form, the heading should include a description of the essential elements of the mark.

(e) **Linings for color**. Where color is a feature of a mark, the color or colors employed may be designated by means of conventional linings as shown in the . . . color chart . . . .

Preparing the Drawing.   If color is claimed as a component of the mark, that should be demonstrated by special lining or stipling incorporated in the drawing. If the mark is a group of letters, words, or words and numbers and no special lettering design is claimed, then the drawing may be prepared by simply inserting the words in the drawing as shown for the drawing of *Brother Bob's Big Beanjam.* (figure 9-11). When preparing a drawing for an unstylized word

LEGAL TERMS

drawing
A substantially exact representation of the mark as used (or, in the case of intent-to-use applications, as intended to be used). A drawing is required for all federal trademark applications and for many state trademark applications.

Drawing for Mark "BROTHER BOB'S BIG BEANJAM"
Partnership Application based upon Use in Commerce

Applicant: **BROTHER BOB'S FOODS**, a California general partnership
Address: **321 25th Avenue, San Francisco, CA 94121**
Date of First Use: **May 20, 1991**
Date of First Use In Interstate Commerce: **July 1, 1991.**
Goods: **food dressings and marinades for use with salads, vegetables, fish, poultry, pasta and meat.**

BROTHER BOB'S BIG BEANJAM

FIGURE 9-11
Sample drawing to accompany application

or words, capitalized standard "Courier"-style lettering (found on most word processor programs and typewriters) should be used, as shown in figure 9-11.

If the drawing is a design or image, a professional graphics designer should be consulted. This drawing becomes the basis for the reproduction in the *Official Gazette* of the U.S. Patent and Trademark Office. Therefore, all lines should be sharp and clear to avoid any disintegration in the image. Photocopy reductions or similar quality facsimiles may not be suitable.

Using Computers to Prepare a Drawing. When drawings incorporate design elements or graphics, it may be possible to prepare the drawing using a computer and a laser printer. Many law offices own scanners that can produce a computer format of a design. If the office does not own a scanner, the design also may be scanned by a computer services company (easy to locate through the local Yellow Pages). Some clients may have prepared the logo in a scanned disk format. The scanned computer image can then be loaded into a word processing program such as *Word for Windows* or *WordPerfect for Windows*. If the laser printer quality in the office is not sufficient, computer service companies can reproduce the disk file with better reproduction quality.

Specimens

Three specimens of the mark as used in commerce must be furnished as part of the application process. A *specimen* is an actual example of the trademark in use. In the case of an application based upon actual use in commerce, the specimens are furnished with the application and the fee. In the case of an application based upon a bona fide intent to use the mark, the specimens are furnished with an amendment alleging use or a statement of use. The specimen should be smaller than 8½ x 11 inches and should be capable of being arranged flat, that is, one-dimensional. Three-dimensional or bulky material is not acceptable. The specimens do not have to be identical. Specimens should never be generated solely for the purpose of trademark registration. The specimen must be *as used* in commerce. If it is not possible to furnish the specimen in a flat format, then a photographic or other reproduction may be furnished.[14] For example, a company that embosses its bicycle tires with a trademark may furnish a photograph of the embossed portion of the tire, no larger than 8½ x 11 inches. The trademark drawing should not be used as a specimen. Special rules and regulations regarding the submission of reproductions (known as *facsimiles*) are located in the *Trademark Manual of Examining Procedure.*

Specimens for Trademarks. Trademark application specimens can include labels, containers (such as a box or package bearing the mark), tags that are tied or attached to the goods, and point-of-sale displays, such as windows, menus, banners, and window displays. A point-of-sale display is intended to catch a consumer's attention *at the time of purchase* and should prominently identify the goods. Advertising, such as a print ad in a magazine, is not considered an acceptable specimen for a trademark application because the ad promotes the goods separate and apart from the purchase and is not used "on or in connection with the goods in commerce." Similarly, a letterhead or business card is unacceptable as a trademark specimen because it is not used in connection with the goods in commerce.

Specimens for Service Marks. Specimens for service marks may include advertisements, brochures about the services, or business cards or stationery used in connection with the services. An advertisement, such as a billboard, magazine advertisement, or direct mailing is suitable provided that the applicant is capable of rendering the service at the time of the advertisement. For example, if a company advertises its hotel services but is not yet able to render such services, the advertisement would be unacceptable as a specimen. A press release, invoice, or use of the mark on goods (i.e., as a trademark) would not be an acceptable specimen. In the case of an audio service mark (e.g., chimes or tones) not used or printed in written form, three audio cassette tape recordings will be accepted. If the mark is used for motion picture or television services, the specimen should be a film stripnegative or positive print of the title card at the beginning of the program.[15]

Entertainers often register service marks. The specimens for such services must identify the services and not simply provide the entertainer's name. The specimen should provide the name *in connection* with specific services.

EXAMPLE

When registering the service mark *Johnny Carson,* an acceptable specimen would be an advertisement for Mr. Carson showing his name in close proximity to the words, "In Concert" and identifying information about performance time, place, and ticket availability.

Applications for Collective Marks

A *collective mark* is used by the members of a cooperative, an association, or other collective group to indicate membership. If the association wants to certify that their work *is performed* by the organization, then a certification mark should be registered as described in the following section. The application process for a collective mark is similar to registration for trademarks and service marks. However, the opening paragraph for the collective mark application must state the class of persons entitled to use the mark, indicate their relationship to the applicant, and the nature of the applicant's control over use of the mark. The same information must be stated for an intent-to-use application for a collective mark.

EXAMPLE: Opening Paragraph for Application— Collective Mark for Dentiopathy International

The above identified applicant has adopted and is exercising legitimate control over the use of the collective membership mark shown in the accompanying drawing to indicate membership in the applicant organization that is a trade association for dentists practicing homeopathic dental procedures.

Specimens for a collective mark could include any means by which the members identify their association, for example, membership cards or decals. As with trademarks and service marks, if the collective mark is not inherently distinctive (descriptive), the applicant will be required to submit proof of secondary meaning to register the mark on the Principal Register.[16]

Applications for Certification Marks

A *certification mark* is used in connection with products and services to certify regional or other origin, material, mode of manufacture, quality, accuracy, or other characteristics. A certification mark is always used in conjunction with another mark because the owner of the certification mark does not produce or sell goods; it only certifies some quality of the goods or services. The application for a certification mark includes the same information as an application for a trademark (see figure 9-12), but the applicant also must specify:

- The conditions under which the certification mark is used
- That the applicant exercises legitimate control over the use of the goods or services
- That the applicant is not engaged in the production or marketing of the goods or services.[17]

Application for Certification Mark
Registration Based Upon Use—Principal Register—Association

CERTIFICATION MARK APPLICATION, PRINCIPAL REGISTER, WITH DECLARATION
(Association)

Mark: **ROCK MUSICIANS LABORATORIES**

Class
  A. Goods
  B. Services

TO THE COMMISSIONER OF PATENTS AND TRADEMARKS:
Name of Applicant: **Association of Musical Manufacturers**
Business address: **One Music Way, Nashville, TN 37202**
Telephone: **615 432-5742**
Citizenship of Applicant: **United States**

The above identified applicant has adopted and is exercising legitimate control over the use of the certification mark shown in the accompanying drawing for the following goods, **electric and acoustic guitars, electric bass guitars, acoustic drums, electronic drums, portable public amplification systems, microphones, and electronic musical keyboards.** The mark as used by the applicant or by persons authorized by the applicant certifies that the goods meet the applicant's standards for durability for touring and performing musicians.

The certification mark was first used on the goods by a person authorized by applicant on **May 20, 1991**; and was first used by a person authorized by applicant on the goods in **interstate** commerce on **July 1, 1991**; and is now in use in such commerce. The mark is used by applying it to **containers for the goods** and three specimens showing the mark as actually used are presented herewith. Applicant is not engaged in the production or marketing of any goods or services to which the mark is applied.

Donald Duccone, being hereby warned that willful false statements and the like so made are punishable by fine or imprisonment, or both under Section 1001 of Title 18 of the United States Code and that such willful false statements may jeopardize the validity of the application or any registration resulting therefrom, states that he is

FIGURE 9-12
Sample application for certification mark

President of applicant association and is authorized to execute this instrument on behalf of said association; he believes said association to be the owner of the mark sought to be registered; that said mark is in use in the type of commerce specified in this application; that to the best of his knowledge and belief no other person, firm, corporation, or association has the right to use said mark in commerce either in the identical form thereof or in such near resemblance thereto as to be likely, when applied to the goods of such other person, to cause confusion, or to cause mistake, or to deceive; that the specimens or facsimiles accompanying this application show said mark as actually used in connection with the goods; that the facts set forth in this application are true; and that all statements made of his own knowledge are true and statements made on information and belief are believed to be true.

POWER OF ATTORNEY AT LAW

Applicant hereby appoints Wilma Richards, Esq., One Maritime Plaza, Suite 1110, San Francisco, California, 94111 (415-711-5121), a member of the bar of the State of California, to act as attorney for **Association of Musical Manufacturers**, applicant herein, with full power to prosecute this application, to transact all relevant business with the Patent and Trademark Office in connection therewith, and to receive all official communications in connection with this application.

Association of Musical Manufacturers

Dated:_____   **By:** _____
                                    DONALD DUCCONE, President

FIGURE 9-12
(Continued)

Section 44 Applications

A *Section 44 application* is an application by a foreign applicant for federal registration. However, this application is based upon the fact that the foreign owner of the mark either has applied for or has received registration for the mark in a foreign country. The foreign country must be a party to an international convention or treaty of which the United States is a member.

A Section 44 application also must include the language used in a Section 1(b) intent-to-use application. That is, application in the United States is based upon the bona fide intention to use the "foreign" mark in U. S. commerce. If the Section 44 application is based on a foreign application, the U.S. application must specify the filing date and the country of the first regularly filed foreign application, and must be filed within six months of the foreign filing date. The U.S. registration will not be issued until the foreign registration issues and a certified copy of the registration, together with an English translation, is filed in the U.S. case. If the Section 44 application is based on a foreign registration, the U.S. application must specify the registration number and the country in which the registration issued, and the certified copy of the foreign registration must accompany the filing papers of the U.S. application.[18] The application is the same as any other Section 1(b) intent-to-use application except that it also contains the following statement:

> The applicant has a bona fide intent to use the mark in commerce on or in connection with the above identified goods and asserts a claim of priority based upon the foreign application or registration identified below in accordance with 15 U.S.C. § 1126, as amended:

Country:
Date of Foreign Filing *(if applicable)*
Serial Number: *(if applicable, but not required)*
Registration Number: *(if applicable)*
Registration Issue Date: *(if applicable, but not required)*

Applications on the Supplemental Register

As indicated earlier in this chapter, registration on the Principal Register, with its wide range of benefits, is preferred to registration on the Supplemental Register. However, in the case of descriptive marks, geographically descriptive marks, or surnames, the applicant may choose to apply on the Supplemental Register. A sample application for the Supplemental Register is provided in figure 9-13. Registration on the Supplemental Register may also serve as the basis for foreign protection of the mark. A Section 1(b) intent-to-use application cannot be made on the Supplemental Register.

Application on the Supplemental Register
Corporation

TRADEMARK APPLICATION, SUPPLEMENTAL
REGISTER, WITH DECLARATION
(Corporation)

Mark: **NASAL NO-HAIR**
Class No.: *(if known)*

TO THE COMMISSIONER OF PATENTS AND TRADEMARKS:
Name of corporation: **EPINOSE,** a California corporation
Citizenship of Applicant: **California, U.S.A.**
Business address: **45 Bell Towers, San Francisco, CA 94121**
Telephone: **415 722-3332**

The above identified applicant has adopted and is using the trademark shown in the accompanying drawing for the following goods: **hand held devices used for the**

FIGURE 9-13

Sample application on Supplemental Register

cutting and trimming of human nose hairs, and requests that said mark be registered in the United States Patent and Trademark Office on the Supplemental Register established by the Act of July 5, 1946.

The trademark was first used on the goods on **May 20, 1991**; was first used on the goods in **interstate** commerce on **July 1, 1991**; and is now in use in such commerce. The mark is used by applying it to **containers for the goods** and three specimens showing the mark as actually used are presented herewith.
Class

Will Mathison, being hereby warned that willful false statements and the like so made are punishable by fine or imprisonment, or both under Section 1001 of Title 18 of the United States Code and that such willful false statements may jeopardize the validity of the application or any registration resulting therefrom, states that he is **President** of applicant corporation and is authorized to execute this instrument on behalf of said corporation; he believes said corporation to be the owner of the mark sought to be registered; that said mark is in use in the type of commerce specified in this application; that to the best of his knowledge and belief no other person, firm, corporation, or association has the right to use said mark in commerce either in the identical form thereof or in such near resemblance thereto as to be likely, when applied to the goods of such other person, to cause confusion, or to cause mistake, or to deceive; that the specimens or facsimiles accompanying this application show said mark as actually used in connection with the goods; that the facts set forth in this application are true; and that all statements made of his own knowledge are true and statements made on information and belief are believed to be true.

POWER OF ATTORNEY AT LAW

Applicant hereby appoints Wilma Richards, Esq., One Maritime Plaza, Suite 1110, San Francisco, California, 94111 (415-711-5121), a member of the bar of the State of California, to act as attorney for Epinose, applicant herein, with full power to prosecute this application, to transact all relevant business with the Patent and Trademark Office in connection therewith, and to receive all official communications in connection with this application.

EPINOSE
By:_____

Dated:_____   **WILL MATHISON, President**

FIGURE 9-13
(Continued)

Fee

Along with the application and drawing (and specimens, if applicable), the applicant must submit the required fee. The fees for filing trademark applications frequently change. Therefor, prior to filing, it is wise to review current fees by calling the Patent and Trademark Office or reviewing the current fees as published in the *Official Gazette.* As of October 1, 1993, the required fee is expected to be raised to $245 per class.[19] That is, if all the goods are in one class, a fee of $245 should be enclosed. If the goods are in four classes, a fee of $980 would be enclosed. For example, when an application is being made for a trademark used with key rings (Intl. Class 6), tote bags (Intl. Class 18), lapel badges (Intl. Class 20), plastic drinking cups (Intl. Class 21), and pennants (Intl. Class 24), the applicant should furnish a fee of $1,225. However, if the registration is for carpets, rugs, and mats (Intl. Class 27), the fee would be $245. All application fees are nonrefundable. Money orders, certified checks, or personal and business checks are all acceptable. Cash also may be sent, but the sender assumes the risk. Payments from foreign countries should be immediately payable and negotiable in the United States for the full amount of the fee.

Businesses or law offices that deal with the Patent and Trademark Office on a regular basis may want to establish a Patent and Trademark Office deposit account. A sum is placed in the deposit account and fees are charged against the balance. For general information about establishing a Patent and Trademark Office deposit account, call 703-308-0902.

Filing Receipt

When the Patent and Trademark Office receives the complete application, a serial number is assigned and the materials are forwarded to a trademark examining attorney. Within a month, a *Filing Receipt for Trademark Application* is mailed to the applicant. The Filing Receipt contains information about the application, including the serial number. The applicant should review the Filing Receipt for accuracy. Any corrections should be sent to the attention of the OATP Data Base Maintenance Staff, Commissioner of Patents and Trademarks, Washington, DC 20231.

Along with the application, the applicant should include a self-addressed, stamped postcard with the information shown in the example. In this way, the applicant can verify receipt and acquire information that may be necessary to track the mark's progress. The return postcard arrives earlier than the Filing Receipt. In addition to the filing of a trademark application, it is a good idea to send a return postcard with every form of document to be filed with the Patent and Trademark Office.

EXAMPLE: Return Postcard Enclosed with Trademark Application

To Comm. of Pats & Tmks.
Washington, DC 20231

Applicant: **Diskco**
Mark: **THE BIG SQUEEZY**

Please confirm receipt of the "THE BIG SQUEEZY" trademark application (including drawing, specimens, and check) by applying your date stamp and serial number, below.

Express Mailing. If the applicant is submitting the trademark application by the U.S. Postal Service's express mailing procedure, a Certificate of Express Mailing must be included, pursuant to 37 C.F.R. § 1.10. Use of the procedure establishes a filing date of the application as of the date the envelope is delivered to the Postal Service. If the application is sent to the Patent and Trademark Office using regular mail service, the filing date of the application will be the date the envelope is received in the Patent and Trademark Office.

EXAMPLE: Statement Required for Express Mailing

CERTIFICATE OF EXPRESS MAILING—37 C.F.R § 10
Express Mail Mailing Label Number: **OB071328928**
Date of Deposit: **August 9, 1992**

I hereby certify that the enclosed Intent-to-Use Application, drawing, and fee is being deposited with the United States Postal Service, "Express Mail Post Office to Addressee" service under 37 CFR § 1.10 on the date indicated above and is addressed to the Commissioner of Patents and Trademarks, Washington, D.C. 20231.

[Signature]

Table 9.3 lists things to check before mailing an application.

Application Process

At the time the trademark application is mailed, the paralegal and attorney should institute a system for tracking the progress of the application. Many things can happen on the road to registration. The *tracking log* is a diary of the application process, summarizing correspondence and telephone conversations between the Patent and Trademark Office and the applicant. A copy of the log should be placed in the client's application file and a copy should also be maintained and updated weekly in a "registration log" binder, containing all of the trademark registrations-in-progress in the office. This can be handy, for example, when calling the trademark status line and inquiring about several marks in one call.

Examination Process

If the application and accompanying materials have been prepared properly *and* if the trademark examiner determines that there is no basis for objection, the mark will be approved for publication and a Notice of Publication will be issued to the applicant. However, it is quite common for an obstacle to arise on the way to publication.

Checklist: Mailing Trademark Application	
Application	Declaration must be signed by the applicant.
	If an attorney will represent the applicant, a power of attorney is required.
	Only one basis for filing should be marked (i.e., Section 1(a), Section 1(b). However, a foreign applicant may base its filing on both Section 1(b) and Section 44.
	If the applicant is based upon actual use (i.e., a Section 1(a) application), the dates of first use should be confirmed by the client.
Drawing	The goods listed in the drawing should match the application. If registering a word or words in an unstylized form, the drawing should use a simple Courier lettering style.
Specimens	If the application is based on use (i.e., a Section 1(a) application), three specimens must be included. The specimens do not have to be identical.
Fee	The fee is $245 per *class*. Confirm with the client if the registration is for goods or services in one class or multiple classes.
Return Card	Enclose a stamped, self-addressed postcard to receive a prompt notification of the filing date and serial number.
After mailing: Tracking Chart	Create a log tracking all correspondence and telephone calls. Coordinate docket management and set 10 days from mailing to confirm receipt of return postcard. Send a copy of the application to the client.

TABLE 9.3
Checklist before
Mailing
Application

Sometimes the person preparing the application creates delay by erring in the preparation of the materials. The Patent and Trademark Office recently listed some examples of common errors.

Name of applicant. Through carelessness, the application lists the wrong owner. For example, the founder of a company may mistakenly believe that he, not the corporation, owns the mark.

Authority for applicant. The authority and position of the person signing the application is ambiguous. Officers of a corporation, for example, should be specifically identified by their titles.

Using the class heading as listing of goods. Instead of identifying the specific goods or services in the application, an applicant describes the goods by the International Class heading. For example, the owner of a mark for key rings identifies the goods as *nonprecious metal goods* instead of *key rings.*

Scattered listing of goods. A multiclass filing includes a scattered mix of goods. The Patent and Trademark Office prefers that the goods be grouped according to class, in ascending order, in the description of goods and in the drawing.

Use of indefinite terminology. An applicant uses ambiguous terms such as "parts," "accessories," and "attachments."

Incorrect listing of goods. The application does not accurately reflect the goods or services.

Section 44 applicant fails to state intent to use. The applicant under a Section 44 application (foreign registration or filing as basis for priority) fails to include a statement of a bona fide intent to use the mark in the United States. The applicant under a Section 44 application *must* affirmatively state a bona fide intent to use the mark in U.S. regulated commerce.

In addition to these "self-inflicted" errors in the trademark application, the trademark examining attorney also may require changes or conclude that there is a statutory bar to the registration. For example:

Likelihood of confusion. The trademark examining attorney determines that the mark when used on the identified goods is likely to be confused with a registered mark. For example, a running shoe manufacturer attempts to register *KNIKE* for running shoes.

Disclaimer. The trademark examining attorney determines that a portion of the mark is generic and must be disclaimed. For example, the owner of the service mark *Nebraska Opry* may have to disclaim the word *Opry,* as it is a generic term for country and western music entertainment.

Descriptive mark. The trademark examining attorney determines that the mark when used on the identified goods is merely descriptive of the goods. For example, the mark *Nasal No-Hair* for a nose-hair clipper.

The examining attorney may communicate by telephone or mail. Patent and Trademark Office correspondence includes an adhesive-label "caption," as shown in in figure 9-14. The label includes a mailing date. This date must be calendared, because a response is usually required within a specific time period (set forth in the letter). The correspondence also should be summarized and placed in the trademark registration log. The supervising attorney will direct that the client be informed of the current activity regarding the mark. The client should not be notified of the Patent and Trademark Office action until the supervising attorney has directed such contact. Naturally, if the Patent and Trademark Office has determined that the mark will be published, the attorney will direct that this good news be forwarded to the client.

Responding to a Patent and Trademark Office Objection

In the event of an objection by the Patent and Trademark Office, the supervising attorney will direct a reply. It may be necessary to amend the

Caption Heading: **Amendment to Application**
UNITED STATES DEPARTMENT OF COMMERCE
PATENT AND TRADEMARK OFFICE

APPLICANT: **Diskco**   Trademark Law Office **No. 10**
MARK: **THE BIG SQUEEZY**   Attention
SERIAL NO. **74/277201**   Trademark Attorney: **BARBARA JONES**
FILED: **December 1, 1992**

AMENDMENT

In response to an Office Action No. [*The Office Action Number is on the
correspondence from the Patent and Trademark Office*] from Trademark Attorney
_____ [*the name and law office of the trademark attorney is usually at the end
of the correspondence*] dated _____, please amend the above referenced
application as follows:

FIGURE 9-14
Sample caption
heading for Amendment

application or to provide a response to a rejection. An *Amendment* is a correction usually made in response to a request by the Patent and Trademark Office. A *Response* is a legal argument advanced by the applicant to overcome an objection. Both of these replies use a standard caption heading as shown in figure 9-14. In the case of a response to a rejection, the word *Amendment* would be replaced with *Response*. A response *must* be provided to the Patent and Trademark Office within six months of the date of mailing of the office action. If it is not, the application will be abandoned.

A dispute may develop between the applicant and the Patent and Trademark Office as to the registrability of the mark. Sometimes the law office must prepare extensive legal and factual arguments to overcome objections. Because these arguments are often similar to the arguments made in infringement lawsuits (e.g., likelihood of confusion or descriptiveness), the bases for such responses are included in chapter 10. The procedure for preparing such responses is also documented in treatises such as *McCarthy on Trademarks and Unfair Competition, Trademark Registration Practice,* and *Trademark Law Practice Forms,* all listed at the end of in this chapter. Many excellent articles on related subjects are included in the *Trademark Reporter,* published by the International Trademark Association (INTA).

If, after the applicant files a response, the Patent and Trademark Office still determines that the mark is not registrable, a Final Rejection will be mailed to the applicant. In the event of a Final Rejection, the applicant can:

- Appeal the determination to the Trademark Trial and Appeal Board (TTAB)
- File a Petition to the Commissioner

- Request further reconsideration
- Abandon or suspend the application
- Amend the application to seek registration on the Supplemental Register (37 C.F.R. § 2.75).[20]

An appeal to the TTAB is made when the basis for the final rejection is *substantive,* that is, based upon a statutory bar to registration such as descriptiveness or likelihood of confusion. A Petition to the Commissioner is used when the basis for the formal rejection is *procedural,* that is, when the applicant or the Patent and Trademark Office failed to adhere to established procedural rules. For example, a final rejection that is based upon an improper time limit for response would be a procedural basis for a Petition to the Commissioner. The format and rules regarding Petitions to the Commissioner are set forth in chapter 10. A request for further reconsideration generally will not be considered unless the applicant is responding to an outstanding requirement of the trademark examiner or the applicant is raising a new issue not previously considered. When the mark has been ruled descriptive and the applicant is unable to establish distinctiveness (secondary meaning), the applicant often amends the application to convert it to the Supplemental Register.

Publication

If on examination or reexamination of an application, the Patent and Trademark Office determines that the mark meets the requirements for registration, the mark will be published in the *Official Gazette.* The purpose of publication is to alert the public to the pending registration and to give an opportunity to object to the registration. If the mark is not opposed within 30 days of publication in the *Official Gazette,* or within any extended period approved by the Patent and Trademark Office, the Certificate of Registration will be issued. However, if the mark is filed under an intent-to-use application and an Amendment to Allege Use has not been filed, a Notice of Allowance will be issued instead of a Certificate of Registration.

When an opposition is filed, the Trademark Trial and Appeal Board begins an *inter partes proceeding.* As described in chapter 10, this proceeding is very similar to a federal lawsuit and includes initial pleadings, discovery, motions, and a trial.

The applicant will be notified of the pending publication date and how to order a copy of the *Official Gazette,* which is published weekly. Many law offices and businesses subscribe to the *Official Gazette.* It is for sale by the U.S. Government Printing Office, SSOP, Washington, DC 20402-9328.

Certificate of Registration

If there is no opposition (and, in the case of intent-to-use applications, all additional requirements have been met), a Certificate of Registration will be issued. A copy of the certificate should be retained by the law office and a letter should be sent to the client that contains the following points:

- The date of registration and the registration number
- The fact that the registration remains in place for 10 years, *provided* that a Section 8 affidavit is filed at the proper time evidencing continued use of the mark.
- A Section 8 affidavit must be filed between the fifth and sixth year following registration. For example, if a registration issued on April 1, 1992, the Section 8 affidavit must be filed between April 1, 1997 and April 1, 1998. The client and the law office should calendar this date for filing. The Section 8 affidavit states that the mark is still in use in commerce (or explains the basis for any nonuse).
- A Section 15 affidavit should be filed when the mark has been in continuous use for five years from the date of registration. This can be filed at any time during the term of the registration, provided the applicant satisfies the five-year continuous use requirement and there are no proceedings pending that would affect the validity of the registration or ownership of the mark. If the mark has been in continuous use for five years since the date of registration, the Section 15 affidavit may be filed at the same time as the Section 8 affidavit. A Section 15 affidavit is a request to have the mark declared incontestable except for certain limited exceptions.
- The registration will expire 10 years from the date of registration. It must be renewed six months before the date of expiration. For example, if a registration was issued on August 1, 1992, the renewal should be filed before February 1, 2002 (i.e., six months before August 1, 2002). A three-month grace period is permitted for filing the renewal application, subject to the payment of a late filing fee.
- The mark should be used in conjunction with the symbol ® or the words "Registered in the U.S. Patent and Trademark Office" or "Reg. U.S. Pat & Tm. Off." The notice must be sufficient to alert persons that the mark is federally registered. Failure to use the notice may limit the recovery in a trademark infringement action.

Additional Requirements for Intent-to-Use Applicants

The Patent and Trademark Office will not register a trademark until the applicant uses the mark in commerce. The intent-to-use applicant must begin using the mark on the goods during the registration process in order to acquire registration. For an intent-to-use applicant, the process for registration consists of:

1. Filing of the application
2. Examination of the application by the Patent and Trademark Office
3. Publication of the mark in the *Official Gazette*

4. Either registration or issuance of a Notice of Allowance, depending on whether the applicant has demonstrated use of the mark in commerce.

A *Notice of Allowance* is a statement by the Patent and Trademark Office that the mark has been published without opposition in the *Official Gazette* and that registration will occur once actual use of the mark on the goods or services commences and a **Statement of Use** is filed (along with three specimens of the mark and the appropriate fee). If the applicant uses the mark before the Notice of Allowance is issued, then the applicant may file an **Amendment to Allege Use** (along with the specimens and fee). In that case, registration will occur after the mark is published without opposition.[21]

The Amendment to Allege Use (figure 9-15) and the Statement of Use (figure 9-16) serve the same purpose: to notify the Patent and Trademark Office that the applicant has commenced use of the mark on the goods in commerce. The only difference between the Amendment to Allege Use and a Statement of Use is the timing of the filing. An Amendment to Allege Use can only be filed before approval of the mark for publication (or, if there is a rejection, within six months of the response period). A Statement of Use can only be filed after a Notice of Allowance has been issued. During the period between approval of the mark for publication and issuance of a Notice of Allowance, neither an Amendment to Allege Use nor a Statement of Use can be filed.

Before filing either of these documents, the applicant must have used the mark in connection with *all* of the goods or services for which the applicant is seeking registration. That is, if the applicant seeks registration based upon a bona fide intent to use the mark on shirts, shoes, and parkas, the mark must have been used on all of the goods. If the applicant has not used the mark on all of goods, the applicant will have to delete from the application those goods not yet in use. However, the applicant can make a **request to divide out** the goods not yet in use, which would form the basis of a continuing application for such goods. A request to divide out is included in an Amendment to Allege Use or a Statement of Use, asking to separate from the application certain goods for which the trademark has not been used.

Extension of Time to File Statement of Use. The intent-to-use applicant must file a Statement of Use within six months of the date of mailing of the Notice of Allowance. However, the Patent and Trademark Office will grant five separate and consecutive six-month extensions, provided they are filed at the proper time. The maximum extended term for filing the Statement of Use cannot extend beyond three years from the date of the Notice of Allowance.

EXAMPLE

Diskco files an application based upon a bona fide intent to use the mark *The Big Squeezy* for its disk compression program. The Patent and Trademark Office publishes the mark and issues a Notice of Allowance. However, Diskco has not used the mark on goods in commerce within six months of the date of mailing of the Notice of Allowance. Within six months of the Notice of Allowance, Diskco files a Request for an Extension of Time.

AMENDMENT TO ALLEGE USE UNDER 37 CFR 2.76 WITH DECLARATION

Mark: the words "THE BIG SQUEEZY"
Serial No. 74/024724

TO THE ASSISTANT SECRETARY AND COMMISSIONER OF PATENTS AND TRADEMARKS:

Applicant Name: **Diskco** State of incorporation: **CALIFORNIA**
Applicant requests registration of the above-identified trademark shown in the accompanying drawing in the United States Patent and Trademark Office on the Principal Register established by the Act of July 5, 1946 (15 U.S.C. § 1051 et seq. as amended). Three specimens showing the mark as used in commerce are submitted with this amendment.

    Check here if Request to Divide Under 37 CFR § 2.87 is being submitted with this amendment.

Applicant is using the mark in commerce on or in connection with the following goods: **computer software programs and accompanying instruction manuals sold as a unit for use in compressing data on magnetic storage devices and other computer disk storage devices in business and personal applications.**
Date of first use of mark anywhere: **September 1, 1992**
Date of first use of mark in commerce that the U.S. Congress may regulate:
September 1, 1992
Specify type of commerce: **interstate**
Specify manner or mode of use of mark on or in connection with the goods:
trademark is applied to containers for the goods.

Terrence Stumpfel, being hereby warned that willful false statements and the like so made are punishable by fine or imprisonment, or both under Section 1001 of Title 18 of the United States Code and that such willful false statements may jeopardize the validity of the application or any registration resulting therefrom, states that he is **Chief Executive Officer** of applicant corporation and is authorized to execute this instrument on behalf of said corporation; that he believes said corporation to be the owner of the mark sought to be registered; that said mark is in use in the type of commerce specified in this application; that and the facts set forth in this application are true; and that all statements made of his own knowledge are true and statements made on information and belief are believed to be true.

Diskco
By: _____

Dated:_____   **Terrence Stumpfel,**
                               Chief Executive Officer

FIGURE 9-15

Sample Amendment to Allege Use

STATEMENT OF USE UNDER   Mark: **the words "THE BIG SQUEEZY"**
37 CFR 2.88 WITH DECLARATION   Serial No. **74/024724**
TO THE ASSISTANT SECRETARY AND COMMISSIONER OF PATENTS AND TRADEMARKS:

Applicant Name: **Diskco**
State of Incorporation: **CALIFORNIA**
Notice of Allowance Issue Date: **December 15, 1992**
Applicant requests registration of above-identified trademark/service mark in the United States Patent and Trademark Office on the Principal Register established by the Act of July 5, 1946 (15 U.S.C. 1051 et seq., as amended). **Three (3)** specimens showing the mark as used in commerce are submitted with this statement.

     Check here only if a Request to Divide Under 37 CFR 2.87 is being submitted with this Statement.

Applicant is using the mark in commerce or in connection with the following goods/services:

     Those goods/services identified in the Notice of Allowance in this application.
     Those goods/services identified in the Notice of Allowance in this application except (Identify goods/services to be deleted from application).

Date of first use of mark anywhere: **December 1, 1992**
Date of first use of mark in commerce that the U.S. Congress may regulate:
December 1, 1992
Specify type of commerce: **interstate**
The mark is used by applying it to **containers for the goods.**

Terrence Stumpfel, being hereby warned that willful false statements and the like so made are punishable by fine or imprisonment, or both under Section 1001 of Title 18 of the United States Code and that such willful false statements may jeopardize the validity of the application or any registration resulting therefrom, states that he is **Chief Executive Officer** of applicant corporation and is authorized to execute this Statement of Use on behalf of said corporation; that he believes said corporation to be the owner of the mark sought to be registered; that said mark is in use in the type of commerce specified in this application; to the best of his knowledge and belief no other person, firm, corporation, or association has the right to use said mark in commerce either in the identical form thereof or in such near resemblance thereto as to be likely, when applied to the goods of such other person, to cause confusion, or to cause mistake, or to deceive; that the specimens or facsimiles accompanying this application show said mark as actually used in connection with the goods; that the facts set forth in this application are true; and that all statements made of his own knowledge are true and statements made on information and belief are believed to be true.

                                       Disko

Date: **December 20, 1992**   **By** _____
Telephone Number: **312-111-1434**   **Terrence Stumpfel,**
                                      Chief Executive Officer

FIGURE 9-16
Sample Statement of Use

State Registration

The state registration process varies. Most states have adopted the Model State Trademark Act, which is patterned after federal registration procedures. The advantage of a state trademark registration is that it grants rights within a certain state. In some states, the registrant may use antidilution statutes as a basis for a trademark lawsuit, as explained further in chapter 10. A listing of state trademark statutes and dilution statutes is provided in appendix F. All state trademark registrations are based upon actual use, and there presently is no provision for an intent-to-use application in any state trademark program.

SUMMARY

9.1 After selecting a mark, the mark should be screened and evaluated for use. The screening should include an analysis of the competition, strengths and weaknesses of the mark, and any statutory prohibitions on registration. A preliminary screening may be performed using online databases or CD-ROM technology. A trademark search report should be performed to confirm any conflicting marks.

9.2 Although registration of trademarks does not create trademark rights, it is strongly recommended to preserve rights. There are many benefits of federal registration on the Principal Register, including the right to use the ® symbol, constructive notice of date of first use, right to sue in federal court, statutory damages and attorney fees, constructive notice of ownership claim, criminal penalties and damages, and the right to stop importation of infringing marks. Federal registration also serves as the basis for foreign applications. The Supplemental Register grants limited rights, specifically the right to use the ® symbol and the right to sue in federal court. There are certain statutory bars to registration, for example, if the mark is descriptive or is confusingly similar to a registered mark.

9.3 The federal application process provides for three bases for registration on the Principal Register: actual use of the mark, intent to use the mark, or registration based upon foreign registration or filing (Section 44). The applicant must provide an accurate description of the class of goods, the identification of the goods, and the description of the mark. In addition, the application must include a declaration or verification of the facts. A power-of-attorney section also may be included in the application. All applications must attach a drawing of the mark, and specimens are required before a certificate of registration will issue. After the examination process is completed, the mark is published. If there is no opposition to the publication, a certificate of registration is issued. In addition to the requirements of application, an intent-to-use applicant must furnish proof of actual use in the form of either a Statement of Use or an Amendment to Allege Use.

NOTES

1. 36 U.S.C. § 380 (protection of Olympic symbol).
2. 15 U.S.C. § 1127 (definition of abandonment; Lenham Act § 45).
3. 15 U.S.C. § 1058 (Section 8 affidavit; Lanham Act § 8).
4. 15 U.S.C. § 1060 (assignment; Lanham Act § 10).
5. 15 U.S.C. § 1052(d) (concurrent use; Lanham Act § 2(d); 37 C.F.R. §§ 2.24, 2.49.
6. 15 U.S.C. § 1052 (bars to registration on the Principal Register; Lanham Act § 2).
7. 15 U.S.C. § 1091 *et seq.* (Supplemental Register; Lanham Act § 23 (*et seq.*).
8. 15 U.S.C. § 1127 (definition of *use in commerce;* Lanham Act § 45).
9. 15 U.S.C. § 1051 (requirements for application; Lanham Act § 1); 37 C.F.R. §§ 2.21, 2.23.
10. 15 U.S.C. § 1112 (trademark classification; Lanham Act § 30).
11. 15 U.S.C. § 1056 (disclaimers; Lanham Act § 6).
12. 27 C.F.R. § 2.20 (trademark declarations).
13. 37 C.F.R. § 2.17 (legal representation).
14. 37 C.F.R. § 2.56-2.59 (submission of reproductions).
15. 37 C.F.R. § 2.56 *et seq.* (specimens).
16. 15 U.S.C. § 1054 (collective marks; Lanham Act § 4).
17. 15 U.S.C. § 1054 (certification marks; Lanhan Act § 4).
18. 15 U.S.C. § 1126 (Section 44 applications; Lanham Act § 44); 37 C.F.R. § 2.39.
19. 15 U.S.C. § 1113 (trademark fees; Lanham Act § 31); 37 C.F.R. § 2.6.
20. 15 U.S.C. § 2.75 (conversion of application to Supplemental Register).
21. 37 C.F.R. §§ 2.76, 2.87-2.89 (Amendment to Allege Use; State of Use).

QUESTIONS FOR REVIEW AND DISCUSSION

1. Why is it necessary to evaluate the non-English meaning of trademarks?
2. Why should a prospective trademark user be concerned about use of terms such as "little league baseball" or "olympics"?
3. What is the difference between an online computer database and a CD-ROM database?
4. What system of classification of goods and services is presently used for trademarks?
5. What are some methods of resolving a potential trademark conflict?
6. What are two benefits of registration on the Principal and Supplemental Registers?
7. For what activity does the Lanham Act provide criminal penalties?
8. What is a Section 44 application?
9. What are the statutory bars to federal registration of a trademark?
10. What book establishes the procedure for federal trademark examiners?

11. What type of specimens can be furnished with a service mark application?

12. Prior to issuance of registration, what document(s) must be furnished by an intent-to-use applicant?

13. If an attorney wishes to receive all communications regarding a client's trademark application, what should be submitted with the application?

14. What is a Section 8 affidavit?

15. Under what circumstances should a petition be used in a trademark proceeding?

ACTIVITIES

1. Review the trademark research report for the *Scrooge* mark. On the basis of this report, is there any anticipated conflict for registration of the mark for a business that offered retail and mail order services in the field of records and tapes? What about for use of the mark for retail gift-shop services?

2. The factual situation in the Commentary to this chapter deals with software products that perform data compression. Using directories, catalogues, and other resources, locate the names of three commercial software products that perform this function.

PROJECT

A fictitious soft drink company, DrinkCo, is preparing to unveil a new software drink—a coconut-flavored cola. The company has proposed three potential trademarks for registration. *Coca-nut Cola, Koka Cola,* and *Kokola.* What problems may exist in the attempted registration of any of these marks? Review the current soft drink marks (i.e., soft drink names such as *Dr. Pepper, 7-Up,* and *Snapple)* and create potential trademarks for the new soft drink. Review the evaluation form in the process of creating the mark for foreign meanings, strength and weakness, ans so forth. Remember, a trademark does not have to be a word; it can also be a slogan or a combination of a word and design.

FOR MORE INFORMATION

Trademark Online Search Companies

Three companies that provide trademark online database searching are:

Dialog Information Services, Inc., 3460 Hillview Avenue, Palo Alto, CA 94304.

Compu-Mark, 500 Victory Road, North Quincy Ma 02171-1545.

Trademark Research Center (accesible through CompuServe by typing GO TRADERC), P.O. Box 20212, 5000 Arlington Centre Boulevard, Columbus, OH 43220.

CD-To, Trademark Searching

Companies that provide trademark CD-Rom databases are:

Thomson & Thomson, 500 Victory Road, North Quincy, MA 021 1-1545.

Trademark Research Corporation, 300 Park Avenue South, New York, NY 10010.

Ordering the Trademark Search

The two leading companies that perform trademark searches are:

Thomson & Thomson, 500 Victory Road, North Quincy, MA 02171-1545.

Trademark Research Corporation, 300 Park Avenue South, New York, NY 10010.

Federal Trademark Application Resources

Trademark Application Forms. Copies of federal trademarks application forms are located in the publication *Basic Fact About Trademarks,* U.S. Department of Commerce, Patent & Trademark Office, Washington, D.C. 20231. This publication is also available through the Goverment Printing Offices and its local outlets. Copies of all federal trademark forms are also located in the *Trademark Manual of Examining Procedure (TMEP),* Superintendent of Documents, U.S. Government Printing Office, Washington, DC 20402.

If the preparer owns a computer, a software program called *Mark Your Words* has been created to assist in the drafting of trademark applications and supporting documentation. It is available from Patent Vidoes, Inc., Suite 606A, 19 Chenango Street, Binghamton, NY 13901.

Trademark filing forms in CD-ROM format are available from Prentice Hall Legal & Financial Services, 300 Franklin Center, 29100 Northwestern Highway, Southfield, MI 48034-1095. Prenticce Hall offers a product, *Master Trademark Forms,* which, like *Mark Your Words,* is interactive—that is, the program requests information, the user furnishes the answers, and the program prepares the final trademark application or form. A CD-ROM drive, hooked to the preparer's computer, is necessary to use the *Master Trademark Forms* software

A collection of trademark application forms is reprinted in most trademark treatises, such as *McCarthy on Trademark and Unfair Competition,* as well as in:

Patent and Trademark Office Forms in Trademark Cases, available from the USTA, 6 East 45th Street, New York, NY 10017.

Kramer & Brufsky, *Trademark Law Practice Forms* (Clark Boardman Callaghan 1991). A three-volume looseleaf treatise emphasizing practice forms.

McGrath, Elias, & Shena, *Trademark: How to Name Your Business and Product* Nolo Press 1991). A one-volume paperback designed for small business.

J. Hawes, *Trademark Registration Practice* (Clark Boardman Callaghan 1992). A one-volume treatise devoted primarily to federal trademark registration.

A law office or business that regularly prepares trademark applications or forms should subscribe to the *Trademark Manual of Examining Procedure* (also known as the *TMEP*), an annual publication available from the Govermant Printing Office. The *TMEP* is the guide used by examinig attorneys when evaluating trademark applications. Information about current prices and availability can be obtained by calling 202-783-3238 or writing to Superintendent of Documents, Government Printing Office, Washington DC 20402-9325. (Fax: 202-512-2250.) Note: some of the treatises mentioned here may include portions of the *TMEP*.

State Trademark Registration

Specific information about state registrations can be obtained from the Secretary of State, located in each state capital. A listing of state trademark offices is provided in appendix F. The International Trademark Association (INTA) has created a reference text for state registration law, *State Trademark and Unfair Competition Law* (Clark Boardman Callaghan 1987).

CHAPTER 10
Trademark: Administration and Protection

Good design keeps the user happy, the manufacturer in the black and the aesthete unoffended.

Raymond Loewy, "The Father of Streamlining," recalled on his death (1986)

OUTLINE

COMMENTARY

Softco, a computer software company, hires Nancy, a graphic artist, to create a logo for the company's new software program, The Big Squeezy. *Nancy creates a design but Softco rejects it. Nancy is not an employee of Softco and she did not execute a work-for-hire agreement. She sells the logo to Diskco, a rival software company. Diskco plans to use the logo with its new program* Easy Squeezee. *Like* The Big Squeezy, Easy Squeezee *is a computer program that compresses data, allowing more information to be stored on a disk. After Softco commences nationwide sales, the company files a federal registration for the words* The Big Squeezy. *A month later, Softco learns that Diskco has begun selling the* Easy Squeezee *program with the logo. Softco wants to stop Diskco from using the words and logo.*

OBJECTIVES

The previous chapter introduced principles of selecting, evaluating, and federally registering a trademark. This chapter provides information on administering and protecting trademark rights. After reading this chapter, you will be able to:

- Prepare and organize trademark maintenance and administration files.
- Assist in the preparation of a company trademark guide.
- Calendar appropriate federal trademark deadlines, including renewal.
- Distinguish and prepare Section 8, 9, and 15 affidavits.
- Identify the forms of abandonment and assist the client in avoiding trademark abandonment.
- Know the basic principles of trademark use, including use of competitor's marks.
- Contrast a trademark license and a trademark assignment.
- Outline the basic types of inter partes trademark proceedings, including opposition and cancellation proceedings.
- Differentiate the basic claims and defenses in a trademark infringement lawsuit.

- Know the remedies for trademark infringement.
- Explain the methods of resolving an infringement lawsuit without litigation.

10.1 TRADEMARK PROTECTION AND MAINTENANCE

In 1988, a study was made of 30 product categories. In 27 of the product categories, the same brand had led the category for 60 years. This consumer loyalty is a tribute to the power of trademarks. It is also a tribute to the lawyers and paralegals who maintain and protect these trademarks and prevent the loss of trademark rights.

Legal administrators use a variety of tools to maintain a constant vigil over their marks. These tools include computer databases, calendaring, trademark "watches," and international trademark reviews. Federal trademark rights are also maintained by timely filing of Section 8, 9, or 15 affidavits, and by initiating, if necessary, opposition actions within the Patent and Trademark Office. All these efforts are made to preserve the good will associated with the mark and to prevent the damage that results from abandonment, infringement, and dilution.

Maintaining Trademark Files

The legal administrator is historian and caretaker for the trademark. Maintaining accurate records can prevent problems and can assist in defending against infringement claims. For a small company with a single trademark, all the trademark documentation may fit into one multileaf file. For a large company with a popular mark, several floors of file cabinet space may be required to document all trademark activities. Generally, all trademark documentation can be categorized in one of five types of trademark files: use, registration, postregistration documents, licensing, and infringement.

The following list shows the five categories of trademark files and what they should include.

1. *Use files.* Materials regarding use, including samples of the mark as used, dates of first use, evidence of continued use, and efforts to maintain proper trademark usage. Samples of the labels or other uses of the mark should be preserved. If the labels or containers for the mark are too cumbersome to maintain within the trademark files, graphic reproductions or photographs should be used.
2. *Registration files.* All documentation during the registration process, including applications, publication, and the certificate of registration.
3. *PTO actions postregistration.* Petitions, oppositions, amendments to registration, and Section 8, 9, and 15 affidavits.
4. *Licensing files.* Often a trademark owner licenses rights. For example, if a person aquires a *McDonald's* franchise, the buyer acquires a limited license from the McDonald Corporation to use the *McDonald*

trademarks. A mark also may be licensed for uses not related to the original product. For example, the *Harley Davidson* company sells motorcycles, but licenses the use of its mark on clothing and other merchandise. All such licenses must be recorded, tracked, and periodically monitored to guarantee conformance with quality standards.

5. *Infringement files.* Similar to traditional litigation files, but also includes evidence of infringement, "watching" service reports, and cease and desist letters.

Proper Trademark Usage: The Company Handbook

Administering trademarks is like managing a garden. Inattentiveness results in damage and loss. Therefore, to preserve trademark rights, legal administrators must actively encourage trademark owners to follow basic rules of usage. Often this education takes the form of a trademark handbook. For example, the Coca-Cola Company, Dow Chemical, and Chevron Corporation Law Departments are among many law departments that have prepared guides to trademark law. These handbooks offer a brief explanation of trademark law, answer basic questions, and establish principles of use. All trademark guides should include the "rules of usage" information provided in Table 10.1.

In addition to printed handbooks, some companies have prepared video presentations to explain the interaction of the corporate legal department with the business team. For example, Dow Chemical has prepared a video that explains the need for involving the corporate legal department in the trademark selection and evaluation process. After internal and external searches are completed, an opinion is rendered. If the trademark is determined to be suitable for use, the registration program is initiated. Following registration, the trademark is included in the corporate maintenance program.

Notice Provisions

The ® symbol should be used only in connection with a mark that is federally registered, and should be applied only when the mark is used in connection with the goods.[1] For example, Diskco has federally registered *Write-On* for word processing software. If the company began publishing *Write-On* Magazine, the ®symbol should not be used with the magazine until the mark has been federally registered for such goods.

Similarly, it is not necessary to use the ® symbol when using the mark for trade name purposes. For example, if Diskco federally registered *Diskco* for computer software goods, the company would not need to use the ® symbol in connection with the mark on its stationery or business cards. However, for service mark purposes, the ® symbol should be used on stationery and cards.

There is no requirement that the ® symbol *must* be used for federally registered marks. However, if the ® symbol or the phrases "Registered in U.S. Patent & Trademark Office" or "Reg.U.S. Pat. & Tm. Off." are not

Rule of Usage	DO	DON'T
1. Use the mark as an adjective, not as a noun or verb.	"Buy a *Walkman* personal stereo."	"Buy a *Walkman*."
	"I'm going to make a *Xerox* photocopy."	"I'm going to *Xerox* that."
2. Avoid using the mark in the plural or possessive	"Many people use *Nordic Track* exercise systems."	"We sell a lot of *Nordic Tracks*."
	"The advantage of the *Nautilus* exercise system is that you can control your workout."	"*Nautilus*'s advantage is that the user can control the workout."
3. Always distinguish the mark; never merge the mark with other words.	*WORDSTAR* word processing program	wordstar word processor
	Xywrite word processing program	xywrite-word-processor
4. Always use proper notice	(If registered, use ®) *Frito's*® corn chips	*Frito's*(R) corn chips
	(If not federally registered, use ™ or ˢᴹ) Hippy Farmer™ popped corn	Hippy Farmerˢᴹ popped corn (ˢᴹ is used only for service marks that are not federally registered).
5. Use the mark consistently	Use the mark in the same manner. For example, *Coca-Cola* always has a hyphen and both letter "C"'s are capitalized. If the mark is a graphic image, establish standards for the appearance and use of the graphic image.	Avoid inconsistences such as *Coca Cola* or *Coca-Cola* or *coca-cola*.
6. Treat other trademarks with respect	"In constructing our home, we used *Styrofoam** insulation." * *Styrofoam* is a trademark of the Dow Chemical company.	"We purchased styrofoam."

TABLE 10.1
Proper Trademark
Usage

used, a federal court is not empowered to award monetary damages to the plaintiff in a federal trademark infringement case, unless the defendant had actual notice of the registration. In addition, these forms of notice serve as constructive notice of the registration, so a subsequent infringer cannot argue that it adopted a similar mark in good faith. This may be relevant as a factor in a determination of likelihood of confusion and damages for infringement.

It is not necessary to place the ® symbol on every use of the mark on the product. For example, if the trademark is used repeatedly on the box of a software program (i.e., on the cover, within the advertising text, or as part of the program explanation), it is only necessary to apply the ® symbol once on the most prominent version of the mark on each product.

Improper use of the ® symbol may have a negative impact on the mark. If, for example, the use of the ® symbol is fraudulent (i.e., intended to deceive), then the Patent and Trademark Office or competitors may object to or prevent subsequent federal registration of the mark. A ® symbol cannot be used for an intent-to-use mark until the certificate of registration has been issued.

The symbols ™ and SM are often used when a mark is not federally registered, to signify common law ownership rights. No special symbol or form of notice is associated with any kind of state registration. That is, no particular symbol such as ® is used in connection with the issuance of a state registration. Although there is no particular statutory significance to the ™ and SM symbols, a trademark owner may argue that the use of these symbols provides notice of a proprietary claim under common law. Sometimes the ® and ™ symbols are used in conjunction, for example, *Microsoft® Word™ for Windows™*.

Calendaring

Every trademark administration program uses a calendaring system, sometimes known as a *docket management* or *tickler* system. These programs provide warnings of due dates or trademark administration requirements. A simple calendaring system can be maintained with a 3 x 5 card file. However, most offices now maintain calendar programs on computer software. For federal or state registered marks, the calendar system must be programmed to include renewal and affidavit dates. For inter partes proceedings and infringement actions, relative due dates should be calendared.

Often a licensing agreement may be terminated only if notice is provided during a certain time period. Therefore, the dates of execution and termination of licensing agreements also should be included in the calendar program. Large law offices or companies often have a docket clerk whose only job is to enter such information. In smaller companies or law offices, a legal administrator may document the appropriate dates. Because offices often change computer systems and software, it is important to maintain consistency of the timing events over many years. Three dates that should be calendared automatically are the dates for the filing of the Section 8, Section 15, and Section 9 affidavits, as discussed later.

Section 8 Affidavit: Continued Use

Sometime during the sixth year after registration, the trademark owner must file a **Section 8 affidavit** (see figure 10-1) declaring its continued

UNITED STATES DEPARTMENT OF COMMERCE
Patent and Trademark Office

Registrant: **Diskco**
Mark: *THE BIG SQUEEZY*
Registration No. **7867574**
Class No. **9**

The Commissioner of Patents and Trademarks
Washington, D.C. 20231

Declaration of Use

Terrence Stumpfel, being hereby warned that willful false statements and the like so made are punishable by fine or imprisonment, or both, under Section 1001 of Title 18 of the United States Code and that such willful false statements may jeopardize the validity of this document, declares that **Diskco,** a California corporation, owns the above identified registration, issued March 1, 1991, as shown by records in the Patent and Trademark Office. The mark shown in said registration is still in use in **interstate** commerce, in connection with the goods. The mark is still in use, as evidenced by the specimen of the mark attached to this declaration. All statements made of his own knowledge are true and all statements made on information and belief are believed to be true.

Dated:_____

By: _____
Terrence Stumpfel
Chief Executive Officer

FIGURE 10-1
Section 8 affidavit
(declaration)

use of the mark or an explanation as to the special circumstances for any period of nonuse.[2] If the mark was assigned to a new owner after registration, the change in ownership should be reflected in the Patent and Trademark Office and the Section 8 affidavit must be executed by the current owner of the mark. The fee must be enclosed, along with a specimen of the mark as it is currently used for each class of goods or services. In lieu of the specimen, the applicant may recite facts as to sales or advertising that demonstrate that the mark is in use. If the owner fails to timely file the affidavit, federal trademark rights will be canceled and a subsequent user could claim rights to the mark.

It is not sufficient to simply state that the mark is "in use." The declarant must state that the mark is "in use in commerce" and specify the type of commerce. In 1991, a company called *Mother Tucker's Food Experience* filed three Section 8 affidavits. The affidavits stated that the marks were "still in use," but the words "in commerce" were not used. The Patent and Trademark Office examiner refused to accept the affidavits and, because the

LEGAL TERMS

Section 8 affidavit
Declaration of continued use of a federally registered trademark filed between the fifth and sixth year following registration. Failure to file in this time period may result in loss of trademark rights.

time period for filing had expired, all three marks were canceled. The company claimed that the omission was inadvertent, but the examiner's decision to cancel the marks was upheld on appeal. If, however, the mark is not currently in use, facts explaining the circumstances for the nonuse must be included. The Section 8 affidavit *must* be filed during the sixth year after registration.

> *Calendar Requirement:* During the sixth year after registration (i.e., between fifth and sixth anniversary of federal registration).
>
> *Example*: Diskco registers the mark *The Big Squeezy* on March 1, 1991. Sometime between March 1, 1996, and March 1, 1997, Diskco must file its Section 8 affidavit.
>
> *Filing Requirements:* Enclose the appropriate fee (consult 37 C.F.R. § 2.6 for current fee) and a specimen of the mark. As of August 1993, the fee was $100 per class. Enclose specimen for each class or facts evidencing sales and advertising.

Note: The PTO provides a form for filing a Section 8 declaration (PTO Form 1583; see appendix F).

Section 15 Affidavit: Incontestability

As explained in Chapter 9, one advantage of federal trademark registration is that after five years of consecutive use from the date of registration (or amendment of the registration), the mark may be declared **incontestable.**[3] A mark that is incontestable is immune from challenge except if it has become the generic term for the goods, has been abandoned for nonuse, or was obtained under fraudulent conditions. To acquire incontestability, the owner must file an affidavit stating: (1) that the mark has not become the common descriptive term for the goods (i.e., the generic term); (2) that the mark has not been the subject of a final decision adverse to the registrant's claim of ownership; and (3) that there is no proceeding involving such trademark rights pending in the Patent and Trademark Office or in a court that has not been finally disposed. A **Section 15 affidavit** (see figure 10-2) is not necessary for maintaining ownership or rights under trademark law. The failure to file the affidavit does not result in the loss of any rights. The filing of the Section 15 affidavit expands the rights of the owner of a federally registered mark on the Principal Register.

Combined Section 8 and 15 Affidavits.   The Section 8 affidavit and the Section 15 affidavit may be combined into one affidavit (see figure 10-3). However the filing fees for both affidavits must be included.

> *Calendar Requirement:* During the sixth year after registration (i.e., between fifth and sixth anniversary of federal registration).
>
> *Example*: Diskco registers the mark *The Big Squeezy* on March 1, 1986. Diskco uses the mark for five consecutive years. Sometime

---

LEGAL TERMS

incontestable
A trademark that is immune from challenge except for certain grounds specified in § 33(b) of the Lanham Act; provides conclusive evidence of the registrant's exclusive right to use the registered mark in commerce in connection with the specified goods or services.

UNITED STATES DEPARTMENT OF COMMERCE
Patent and Trademark Office

Registrant: **Diskco**
Mark: *THE BIG SQUEEZY*
Registration No. **7867574**
Class No. **9**

The Commissioner of Patents and Trademarks
Washington, D.C. 20231

Affidavit of Incontestability

   Terrence Stumpfel, being hereby warned that willful false statements and the like so made are punishable by fine or imprisonment, or both, under Section 1001 of Title 18 of the United States Code and that such willful false statements may jeopardize the validity of this document, declares that **Diskco,** a California corporation, owns the above identified registration, issued March 1, 1986, as shown by records in the Patent and Trademark Office; that the mark shown in said registration has been in continuous use in **interstate** commerce for five consecutive years from February 1, 1986 to the present, in connection with all of the goods that are stated in the registration; that such mark is still in use in interstate commerce; that there has been no final decision adverse to registrant's claim of ownership of such mark for such goods or to registrant's right to register the mark or to keep the same on the register; and that there is no proceeding involving said rights pending and not disposed of either in the Patent and Trademark Office or in the courts.

Dated: February 1, 1992

By: _____
       Terrence Stumpfel
       Chief Executive Officer

FIGURE 10-2
Section 15 affidavit

between March 1, 1991, and March 1, 1992, Diskco must file its
Section 8 Affidavit, and may include the Section 15 Affidavit.
Filing Requirements: Enclose appropriate fee (consult 37 C.F.R. § 2.6
for current fee) and a specimen of the mark. As of October 1992,
the fee was $100 per class.

Note: The PTO provides a form for filing a joint Sections 8 and 15 affidavit (PTO FB-TM) and for filing a Section 15 affidavit (PTO Form 4.16). See appendix F.

Section 9 Affidavit: Renewal

   A trademark registration issued after November 16, 1989, is valid for 10 years. A trademark registration issued prior to November 16, 1989,

LEGAL TERMS

Section 15 affidavit
Declaration of five years of continuous use of a federally registered trademark on the Principal Register; if filed and accepted by the Patent and Trademark Office, the mark becomes incontestable.

UNITED STATES DEPARTMENT OF COMMERCE
Patent and Trademark Office

Registrant: **Diskco**
Mark: *THE BIG SQUEEZY*
Registration No. **7867574**
Class No. **9**

The Commissioner of Patents and Trademarks
Washington, D.C. 20231

Combined Declaration of Use and Incontestability
(Sections 8 & 15)

    Terrence Stumpfel, being hereby warned that willful false statements and the like so made are punishable by fine or imprisonment, or both, under Section 1001 of Title 18 of the United States Code and that such willful false statements may jeopardize the validity of this document, declares that: **Diskco,** a California corporation, owns the above identified registration, issued March 1, 1986, as shown by records in the Patent and Trademark Office; the mark shown in said registration is still in use in **interstate** commerce, in connection with the goods; the mark is still in use as evidenced by the specimen of the mark attached to this declaration; the mark shown in said registration has been in continuous use in **interstate** commerce for five consecutive years from February 1, 1986 to the present in connection with all of the goods that are stated in the registration; such mark is still in use in interstate commerce; there has been no final decision adverse to registrant's claim of ownership of such mark for such goods or to registrant's right to register the mark or to keep the same on the register; and there is no proceeding involving said rights pending and not disposed of either in the Patent and Trademark Office or in the courts.

Dated: February 1, 1992

By: _____

Terrence Stumpfel
Chief Executive Officer

FIGURE 10-3
Combined Section 8
and Section 15
affidavit

LEGAL TERMS

Section 9 affidavit
Declaration seeking renewal of a federal trademark registration; must be filed within six months of the expiration of the term of trademark registration, or within three months thereafter, in which event the applicant must also pay a late filing fee.

is valid for 20 years. If the registrant wishes to renew either of these registrations for an additional 10-year period, a **Section 9 affidavit** (see figure 10-4) must be filed.[4] A Section 9 affidavit is a renewal of the registration, and the requirements for it are set forth in § 9 of the Lanham Act (15 U.S.C. § 1059). The affidavit sets forth facts regarding the use of the mark in connection with the goods or services in each class for which renewal is sought.

Calendar Requirement:
For marks registered after November 16, 1989, file within six months prior to the end of the 10th year of registration.

UNITED STATES DEPARTMENT OF COMMERCE
Patent and Trademark Office

Registrant: **Diskco**
Mark: *THE BIG SQUEEZY*
Registration No. **7867574**
Class No. **9**

The Commissioner of Patents and Trademarks
Washington, D.C. 20231

Application for Renewal of a Federal Registration

The applicant for renewal is Diskco, a corporation organized under the laws of the State of California with its principal place of business at 1234 Main Street, Los Angeles, California, 90069.

The above identified applicant for renewal requests that the above identified registration, granted to **Diskco** on **March 1, 1991**, which applicant for renewal now owns, as shown by records in the Patent and Trademark Office, be renewed in accordance with the provisions of Section 9 of the Act of July 5, 1946.

The mark shown in said registration is still in use in **interstate** commerce in connection with all of the goods that are recited in the registration, the attached specimen showing the mark as currently used.

Terrence Stumpfel, being hereby warned that willful false statements and the like so made are punishable by fine or imprisonment, or both, under Section 1001 of Title 18 of the United States Code and that such willful false statements may jeopardize the validity of this document, declares that all statements made in this application of his knowledge are true and all statements made on information and belief are believed to be true.

Dated:_____   By:_____

Terrence Stumpfel
Chief Executive Officer

FIGURE 10-4
Section 9 affidavit
(declaration)

For marks registered before November 16, 1989, file within six months prior to the end of the 20th year of registration.

If the owner of the mark misses these deadlines and the mark expires before renewal, the applicant may pay an additional fee and file the Section 9 affidavit, provided the renewal is filed within three months after the 10- or 20-year term, as applicable.

Example: Diskco registers the mark *The Big Squeezy* on March 1, 1991. Diskco should file its Section 9 affidavit between September 1, 2000, and March 1, 2001. If it misses this "window" of filing time, Diskco may pay an additional fee and file the Section 9 affidavit by June 1, 2001.

Filing Requirements: Enclose appropriate fee (consult 37 C.F.R. § 2.6 for current fee). As of August 1993, the fee was $300 per class. The late filing fee is an additional $100 per class. Enclose a specimen for each class of goods.

Note: The PTO provides a form for filing a Section 9 affidavit (PTO Form 4.13a; see appendix F).

Abandonment

A major concern for any trademark owner is the loss of rights through abandonment. The Lanham Act provides that a mark is deemed to be abandoned if: (1) the mark has become the generic term for the goods or services; or (2) use of the mark has been discontinued with intent not to resume such use.[5]

A mark becomes the generic term for goods when consumers begin to think of the trademark as the descriptive name for the goods. For example, the term *thermos* was once a trademark for vacuum-sealed drinking containers. Over time, however, consumers used the word *thermos* to describe the goods and as a result, a court determined that *thermos* no longer functioned as a trademark. This process, described more fully below, is nicknamed **genericide.**

The second and more common means of abandonment is the loss of trademark rights because of nonuse. Two elements must be proven to show this type of abandonment. First, it must be proven that the mark is no longer in use in commerce. Second, it must be demonstrated that the owner did not intend to resume use of the mark. A failure to use the mark for two consecutive years is considered prima facie evidence of abandonment. In other words, the failure to use the mark on the goods for a period of two years creates a presumption of abandonment. This presumption shifts the burden of proof to the trademark owner, who must rebut that presumption with evidence that the mark has not been abandoned. Because abandonment is such a drastic act of forfeiture, the Patent and Trademark Office and the courts require clear and convincing proof.

Intent Not to Resume Use. The Lanham Act does not require proof that the owner intended to *stop the use* of the mark. Instead, the drafters of the Lanham Act required proof that the owner did not intend to *resume use*. The courts have interpreted this to mean that the owner did not intend to resume use in the reasonably foreseeable future. This intention may be inferred from the circumstances.

For example, CBS television owned the trademark *Amos & Andy* for entertainment services. The network took the television show *Amos & Andy* off the air after complaints from civil rights groups. For 20 years the network did not use the mark. However, when a new musical was created using the *Amos & Andy* trademark, CBS sued for trademark infringement. The owner of the musical claimed that CBS had abandoned the mark. The court acknowledged that CBS intended at some time to resume use, but the intent to resume use was not in the reasonably foreseeable future. Therefore, the court determined that CBS had abandoned the mark.

The actions of the trademark owner create the most determinative evidence regarding intent. Foreign use of the mark cannot be used to infer an intent to resume. For example, the Lever Brothers Company federally registered the mark, *Sunsilk* for hair shampoo in 1974. The Shaklee company began using the mark *Rainsilk* for hair shampoo and conditioner in 1978. Lever Brothers opposed Shaklee's registration of the *Rainsilk* mark, claiming it was likely to cause confusion among consumers.

Shaklee defended its position by arguing that Lever Brothers had abandoned the *Sunsilk* mark. It was determined that Lever Brothers had not used the mark at all between 1965 (when the mark was first created) and 1975. Between 1975 and 1978, the total sales of *Sunsilk* products in the United States were under $100. Lever Brothers stated that it did not intend to abandon the mark and demonstrated that there had been substantial use of the *Sunsilk* mark in the United Kingdom. The court disregarded foreign sales as being irrelevant to U.S. usage and determined that the scattered American sales did not demonstrate an intent to resume use. The court determined that Lever Brothers had abandoned the *Sunsilk* mark and the registration for *Sunsilk* was canceled.

Sometimes a trademark owner may alter or abandon elements of a trademark over time. For example, the owner of the mark *UNBURN* changed its mark to *UN-BURN*. Such minor changes do not result in an abandonment of the previous version of the mark. Similarly, a modernization or slight customization of a mark will not result in abandonment or loss of trademark rights. Nevertheless, it is a prudent practice to register each new version of a trademark.

An owner of a mark also may abandon the mark by an intentional act of abandonment. For example, it was determined by one company that, for tax purposes, abandonment of trademark rights to the mark *Duraflame* would result in a tax benefit that outweighed any possible sale of the mark. The company published a statement of its intent to abandon the mark. When a mark is abandoned for nonuse, whether voluntarily or involuntarily, anyone may claim the mark.

The forms of abandonment described here are different from abandonment of a trademark application. Abandonment of a trademark application occurs when a trademark owner files a federal application for registration and later withdraws the application or fails to respond in a timely manner to a rejection by the Patent and Trademark Office. In such event, the application is considered abandoned. *See* 37 C.F.R. §§ 2.65–2.68. This form of abandonment does not affect any common law rights.

LEGAL TERMS

genericide
Process by which trademark rights are abandoned because consumers have begun to think of the trademark as the descriptive name for the goods; results from a judicial determination or inter partes proceeding at the Patent and Trademark Office.

Genericide

As indicated earlier, trademark rights are abandoned when consumers begin to think of the trademark as the descriptive name for the goods.[6] This process, nicknamed *genericide,* appears to be a contradiction in trademark theory. After all, the purpose of a mark is to create consumer recognition as to the source of the goods. But if the mark becomes *too* popular, consumers may think of it as the descriptive term for the goods.

For example, the term "cellophane" was originally a registered trademark of E. I. du Pont de Nemours and Company. However, the product became so popular that consumers began to think of *cellophane* as the generic term for the plastic sheets. Other marks that have turned into generic terms are *kerosene, escalator, shredded wheat,* and *yo-yo.* One of the most famous terms to move from trademark to generic term was *aspirin.*

Genericide, like abandonment from nonuse, is triggered by a trademark infringement lawsuit or an inter partes proceeding in the Patent and Trademark Office. For example, a linguist created a new "logical language" and coined the term *Loglan* to identify the language. The term was federally registered as a trademark for dictionaries. Later, the owner of the mark attempted to prevent use of the term *Loglan* for a competitor's dictionary. The competitor defended itself by arguing that *Loglan* was generic and the trademark registration should be canceled. The federal court agreed that *Loglan* was a generic designation of a language and was unprotectable. The trademark registration was canceled and the mark was considered to be abandoned. The term *Loglan* is considered free for all to use.

To prevent genericide, the owner of the mark must maintain proper rules of usage and should make an effort to educate the public that the mark

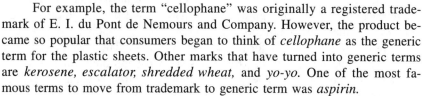

JUDGE LEARNED HAND ON TRADEMARK LAW: The Aspirin Case

In 1921, the Bayer Company filed a trademark infringement lawsuit against the United Drug Company, alleging infringement of its trademark, *aspirin.* United Drug Company argued that Bayer could not claim *aspirin* as a trademark because it was a generic term. Judge Learned Hand asked, "The single question in all these cases is merely one of fact. What do buyers understand by the word . . . ? If they understand by it only the kind of goods sold, then, I take it, it makes no difference whatever what efforts the plaintiff has made to get them to understand more. He has failed . . . ." Judge Hand was concerned with the perception of the "general consuming public"; on that basis, he held that *aspirin* had become a generic term.

is not a generic term. For example, the Kimberly-Clark corporation regularly provides promotional materials to writers and advertisers indicating that *Kleenex* is a registered trademark for a line of disposable paper products and should always be used with a capital "K" and followed by a generic term such as *tissue*. The Dow Chemical Company regularly writes to persons who misuse the *Styrofoam* mark to inform them that *Styrofoam* is a registered trademark for certain foam products, including insulation, nautical billets, and billets sold in the floral and craft industries. Dow Chemical informs those who misuse the mark that *Styrofoam* plastic foam is not, as often mistakenly believed, used in the manufacture of cups, plates, food containers, or packaging materials such as loose-fill plastic foams.

The Xerox corporation regularly runs advertisements stating that "Not Even Xerox Can Xerox," which indicate that the *Xerox* trademark is not a verb. The company urges people to make a copy of the advertisement and "place it near your *Xerox* copier." Efforts such as these may aid in preventing genericide of popular and valuable trademarks.

Using Other Trademarks

It is not necessary, when writing about other marks, to include the ® or ™ symbols. However, it is prudent to indicate that the term is a trademark and to identify the owner. For example, if writing about the WordPerfect Corporation's word processing program in a commercial publication such as a software manual or an advertisement, particularly in a commercial publication, the reader should be informed that "*WordPerfect* is a trademark of the WordPerfect Corporation." Usually this is done by means of a footnote. Permission is not required to use a trademark for editorial purposes. However, when a trademark includes copyrightable expression, it may be necessary to acquire permission of the copyright owner. For example, if a trademark included a photograph, permission of the copyright owner of the photograph might be required.

When a trademark is used for comparative advertising purposes, the trademark usage should be reviewed by an attorney. For example, if Softco wants to use the trademarks of its rival, Diskco, in an advertisement comparing products, it is a good idea to have the comparative advertising reviewed, as such marketing efforts are carefully scrutinized by competitors and may give rise to claims such as dilution, trademark infringement, or false advertising.

Using a Hallmark or a House Mark.   A **house mark** is a mark that functions to identify the source for various products or services from one company. The term **hallmark** is often used interchangeably with house mark, but generally refers to a graphic icon rather than a word or group of words. For example, *Sony* is a house mark, whereas the red-and-white "wave" mark used on *Coca-Cola* beverages is a hallmark.

Sometimes a house mark or hallmark is used in conjunction with a new product mark. For example, the term *Publisher* is descriptive of a desktop publishing computer program. However, the descriptive quality of the term did not stop the Microsoft company from introducing the *Publisher* program by using it in conjunction with its house mark as *Microsoft*® *Publisher*™. There is no guarantee that the use of a house mark in conjunction with a descriptive mark will extend protection to the descriptive term or protect against a claim of confusion. However, many companies prefer to use the combination initially because the house mark (e.g., *Sony*) already has high consumer recognition and will aid in creating brand loyalty to the new mark (e.g., *Walkman*). Some companies prefer *not* to use a house mark with a trademark because they believe that such a use is confusing. For example, the trademark guide prepared by Dow Chemical urges its employees not to use "Dow" with its company marks because such usage implies that someone other than Dow may also make that product.

Policing the Mark

Legal administrators perform two types of surveillance. First, they screen marks likely to cause confusion. Sometimes the client encounters potential or actual infringers in the marketplace; sometimes similar marks are reported by the public. The legal administrator also uncovers potentially infringing marks by reviewing the marks published for state, federal, or international registration.

Many law offices and companies subscribe to the weekly *Official Gazette* of the Patent and Trademark Office, which includes all marks allowed for publication on the Principal and Supplemental Register. Many companies hire "watching" services, such as those offered by the Thomson & Thomson company. Domestic watching (i.e., within the United States) by such services may include review of the *Official Gazette,* Patent and Trademark Office records, state registration records, common law marks, or trade and industry publications. Reports are furnished either on order or on a weekly basis. The *Wiss/Riss/Kiss* services offered by Thomson & Thomson/Compu-Mark are worldwide screening tools.

The second type of surveillance involves use within the company and among licensees. The legal administrator should provide standards of review for advertising, packaging, and promotion involving the trademark. Note, for example, that the Chevron trademark guide advises employees on how to create and use trademarks and what to do if an employee notices an improper imitation of any Chevron marks.

Licensees of the trademark also must be monitored to guarantee that the goods or services offered meet the standard of quality associated with the trademark. Some trademark owners require samples of licensed merchandise to be furnished periodically for examination. Other companies send investigators to review products in the field. For example, the Coca-Cola company has investigators that visit eating establishments. The investigators order

Coca-Cola or *Coke* and then send the drink to Atlanta for analysis. This is done to guarantee that the establishment is using *Coca-Cola* syrup when producing fountain drinks. It is part of the company's ongoing effort to document the quality associated with the mark. If the quality of the goods does not match company standards, then the mark loses some of its good will.

10.2 OWNERSHIP OF TRADEMARKS

Trademark rights are created by the first use of the mark in commerce. Trademark ownership rights are not acquired by designing the trademark or creating the term or words used in a mark. If there is copyrightable authorship in the creation of a trademark (e.g., an original illustration or photo reproduction), then the author may claim copyright ownership, but this copyright claim is separate and apart from trademark ownership.

For example, in the facts in the Commentary to this chapter, it appears that Nancy owns the copyright to the logo (dependent on the terms of her agreement with Diskco). She can sue for any unauthorized reproduction of her copyrightable expression. But Nancy does not own any trademark rights to the logo. She has not used the logo to sell goods or services. Because Diskco has used the logo throughout the United States in connection with the sale of its computer programs, the company has acquired rights as the first or senior user of the trademark. It has acquired these trademark rights even though the marks have not been federally registered.

Any form of business can own a trademark. A sole proprietor, a profit or nonprofit corporation, an association, or even a cooperative can acquire and register trademark rights. Often these trademarks and the associated good will are sold or licensed.

Sometimes a dispute as to ownership of a trademark may arise among members of a partnership. For example, it is not uncommon in the music business for a dispute to arise among members of musical groups as to ownership of the name. Group names such as *The Kingsmen, Herman's Hermits, Buffalo Springfield, Lynyrd Skynyrd,* and *Yes* were all the subject of trademark infringement actions, as members of the groups fought over the right to use the band's name. Such battles can be avoided if the group members agree as to ownership of the trademark or service mark. For example, the members might agree that if the group disbands, no member may acquire rights to continued use of the name or, alternatively, only certain members of the group may acquire rights to the name. In all cases, and regardless of the business form that owns the mark, trademark rights may be transferred in the form of a *license* or an *assignment.*

Trademark Licensing

The ownership of trademark rights can be transferred. A limited transfer of rights is generally known as a **trademark license.** For example, if Softco enters into an agreement with a mail order distributor to sell its products or

LEGAL TERMS

trademark license
  Agreement granting limited trademark rights.

to bundle its products for sale with other products, that distributor would acquire a limited license to use the trademark in connection with sales of the goods. Within the sales agreement, there would be a provision regarding trademark usage, as shown in the example.

Because the license transfers some of the goodwill associated with the mark, the trademark owner must maintain quality control over the mark. Without such control, the agreement is called a "naked license" and it may be argued that the owner has abandoned trademark rights. Therefore all provisions for the licensing of trademarks should provide some means of regulating the nature and quality of the licensee's goods or services associated with the mark.

EXAMPLE: Contract Provision Limiting Trademark Usage in License Agreement

TRADEMARK RIGHTS. All copies of any advertising, promotional, or display material bearing the title of the Software shall have the notices specified below conspicuously placed on such materials.

SOFTCO and *THE BIG SQUEEZY* are trademarks of SOFTCO.

Distributor shall only use the terms *SOFTCO* or *THE BIG SQUEEZY* or any other proprietary trademark of SOFTCO in conjunction with the sale or promotion of the Software. Distributor acknowledges and agrees that Distributor's right to use any such trademark or trade name of SOFTCO is only by virtue of this Agreement, and that Distributor shall acquire no rights in any such trademark or trade name through Distributor's use. If any such trademark or trade name is used in signs, advertising, or in any other manner by Distributor, Distributor will, upon termination of this Agreement, immediately discontinue all such use and display. Distributor shall not remove, deface, cover, or otherwise alter any SOFTCO proprietary notices.

From time to time after Distributor has commenced marketing of the Software, and upon SOFTCO's written request, Distributor shall furnish without cost to SOFTCO not more than two random samples of the Software as sold by Distributor together with any cartons, containers, and packing and wrapping material used in connection with it.

Another example of a trademark license is in a franchise agreement. A franchise agreement occurs when a company authorizes someone to sell its products within a certain territory. For example, the *Polar Bar* ice cream company may sell franchises to different store owners. These owners would have a license to use the trademark in connection with the sale of the *Polar Bar* goods. Depending upon the provisions of the agreement, the license may limit what goods can be sold.

Similarly, a trademark owner may license rights to use the mark on certain merchandise. The agreement may provide for certain sales quotas or payments. If these payments or quotas are not met, the rights of trademark use would be terminated. Such agreements also provide for standards of quality control. A simple version of a trademark license is reproduced in figure 10-5.

LICENSE AGREEMENT

This trademark license agreement (the "Agreement") is effective as of the date of execution shown below. TEAMCO ("TEAMCO") is a New York corporation with its principal place of business at 2727 Whisper Lane, Wantagh, New York 11793. SELLCO ("SELLCO) is a California corporation with its principal place of business at 1822 74th Avenue, San Francisco, California, 94122.

TEAMCO is the owner of the trademark *New York Yakkers* (the "Trademark"). SELLCO desires to license from TEAMCO the exclusive rights to use the trademark on t-shirts, hats, and jackets (the "Goods") within the United States. Therefore, the parties agree as follows:

1. License. TEAMCO grants to SELLCO and SELLCO accepts an exclusive nontransferable right to use the Trademark on the Goods within the United States. Except for the rights granted under this license, all other rights are reserved to TEAMCO. TEAMCO retains all ownership of the trademark and any applications or registrations resulting from such ownership.

2. Payment. SELLCO agrees to pay TEAMCO a royalty of ten percent (10%) for all Net Revenues of the Goods. Net Revenues are defined as all gross receipts minus returns.

3. Minimum Sales. As a material requirement for maintaining the exclusive license, SELLCO agrees to meet the minimum sales requirements as set forth in this provision: $100,000 in royalties in the first year of this Agreement; and $200,000 during the second year of this Agreement.

4. Use of Trademark. SELLCO shall only use the Trademark in conjunction with the sale or promotion of the Goods. SELLCO acknowledges and agrees that SELLCO's right to use any such trademark or trade name of TEAMCO is only by virtue of this Agreement, and that SELLCO shall acquire no rights in any such trademark or trade name through SELLCO's use. If any such trademark or trade name is used in signs, advertising, or in any other manner by SELLCO, SELLCO will, upon termination of this Agreement, immediately discontinue all such use and display. SELLCO shall not remove, deface, cover, or otherwise alter any TEAMCO proprietary notices. Periodically, after SELLCO has commenced marketing of the Goods, and upon TEAMCO's written request, SELLCO shall furnish without cost to TEAMCO at least two random samples of each of the Goods as sold by SELLCO, together with any cartons, containers, and packing and wrapping material used in connection with it. SELLCO shall not attack TEAMCO's title or any rights of TEAMCO to the Trademark and SELLCO shall assist TEAMCO to the extent necessary in the procurement of any protection of TEAMCO's rights to the Trademark arising under this Agreement.

FIGURE 10-5
Sample trademark license agreement

5. Quality of Goods. SELLCO warrants that the sale of the Goods covered by this Agreement and SELLCO's policy of sale, distribution, and exploitation shall be of such style, appearance, and quality as to be adequate and suited to the best advantage and to the protection and enhancement of the Goods. The Goods will be sold or distributed in accordance with all applicable laws, rules, and regulations. SELLCO will not engage in any deceptive, misleading, or unethical practices that are or might be detrimental to TEAMCO, the Trademark, or the Goods.

6. Indemnification. SELLCO shall indemnify TEAMCO and hold TEAMCO harmless from any claims arising out of any defects in the Goods or arising from SELLCO's marketing of the Goods or any of SELLCO's business activities under this Agreement.

7. Term. The license granted in this Agreement shall be effective as of the Date of Execution and shall continue for a period of two (2) years, unless terminated sooner according to the provisions in Section 9.

8. Payment; Books. SELLCO shall pay TEAMCO, within thirty (30) days of the end of each calendar quarter, all sums due to TEAMCO for sales and transfers of the Goods during the preceding calendar quarter. SELLCO shall keep accurate books of account and records covering all transactions relating to the license granted in this Agreement, and TEAMCO's authorized representatives shall have the right upon two (2) days prior written notice, and during normal business hours, to inspect, audit, and analyze all of SELLCO's records relating to the trademark licensed under this Agreement, and all of SELLCO's shipping and manufacturing records relating to the Goods. All books of account and records shall be kept available for at least two (2) years after the termination of this Agreement.

9. Right to Terminate. TEAMCO or SELLCO shall have the right to terminate this Agreement and the appointment granted in this Agreement as follows: TEAMCO shall have the right to terminate this Agreement at any time if SELLCO fails to meet its minimum sales requirement as set forth in Section 3; and either party shall have the right to terminate this Agreement at any time if the other party breaches any of its obligations under this Agreement and such breach is not cured within thirty (30) days after written notice from the nonbreaching party

10. General Provisions. This Agreement may not be modified or altered except by written instrument duly executed by both parties. Dates or times by which either party is required to make performance under this Agreement shall be postponed automatically to the extent that either party is prevented from meeting them by strikes, Acts of God, war, or other causes beyond their reasonable control. If any provision of this Agreement is invalid under any applicable statute or rule of law, it is to that extent to be deemed omitted and the remaining provisions of this Agreement shall in no way be affected or impaired as a result of such invalidity. This Agreement may not be assigned or transferred by SELLCO without the prior written approval of TEAMCO. Neither party shall represent itself to be the agent, employee, franchise, joint venturer, officer, or partner of the other party. Nothing contained in this Agreement shall be construed to place the parties in the relationship of partners or joint venturers, and neither party shall have the power to obligate or bind the other in any manner whatsoever, other than as specified in this Agreement. The prevailing party shall have the right to collect from the other party its reasonable costs and necessary disbursements and attorney fees incurred in enforcing this Agreement. The waiver or failure of either party to exercise in any respect any right provided for in this Agreement shall not be deemed a waiver of any further

FIGURE 10-5
(Continued)

right under this Agreement. This Agreement shall be governed by and construed in accordance with the laws of the State of New York. SELLCO consents to the exclusive jurisdiction of the state and federal courts located in Nassau County, New York, in any action arising out of or relating to this Agreement and waives any other venue to which SELLCO might be entitled by domicile or otherwise. This Agreement expresses the full, complete, and exclusive understanding of the parties with respect to the subject matter and supersedes all prior proposals, representations, agreements, and understandings, whether written or oral.

Date of Execution: _____

FIGURE 10-5
(Continued)

Trademark Assignment

An *assignment of trademark rights* is a transfer of all ownership rights and good will associated with the mark.[7] Sometimes this transfer may occur as a result of the acquisition of a business. By way of example, if a company were to purchase the *Big Apple Polisher* floor-waxing business, the purchase agreement would provide for the transfer of all assets, including the assignment of the *Big Apple Polisher* mark and its attendant good will. The same is true for the acquisition of billion-dollar companies. In 1992, the RJR Nabisco company sold its cereal division to General Mills, thereby assigning its rights to *Nabisco Shredded Wheat* and other trademarks.

Like a trademark license, an assignment of trademark rights should be drafted and reviewed by an attorney. A trademark is considered to be inseparable from its good will; therefore, any assignment of trademark rights *must* include a transfer of the good will associated with the mark. An assignment of a trademark that is made without mention of the associated good will is considered to be an *assignment in gross* and is invalid.

Figure 10-6 shows a very simple trademark assignment for a federally registered trademark. In the event that the mark is not federally registered, reference would be made to either state registration or common law rights, as the case may be.

Recording Assignments

Assignments of federally registered trademarks should be recorded with the Patent and Trademark Office. This enables the new owner of the mark to commence and defend actions at the PTO. Recording the assignment also provides constructive notice of the claim to ownership.

In July 1992, the Patent and Trademark Office amended its rules regarding the recording of assignments. Under these new rules, a cover letter

---

ASSIGNMENT OF "VULCAN WARRIOR" TRADEMARK

Softco ("Softco"), a New York corporation with its principal offices at Ten Industrial Avenue, New York, New York, 10151, is the owner of the trademark *Vulcan Warrior,* which is presently registered in the United States Patent and Trademark Office as follows:

> Registration Number 4456879
> For computer software games
> Date of Registration: May 27, 1977

Diskco ("Diskco"), a California corporation, with its principal offices at 1234 Main Street, Los Angeles, California, 90061, desires to acquire all right, title, and interest in the trademark *Vulcan Warrior,* the good will symbolized by the mark, and the registration of the trademark.

Now, therefore, for good and valuable consideration, the receipt and sufficiency of which are hereby acknowledged, Softco does hereby sell, assign, transfer, and set over to Diskco, its successors, and assigns, all right, title, and interest in said mark, along with the registrations thereof, together with the good will symbolized by the mark.

Softco warrants that it is the legal owner of all right, title, and interest in the aforementioned trademark, that the trademark has not been otherwise previously licensed, pledged, assigned, or encumbered, and that this assignment does not infringe on the rights of any person.

Softco agrees to cooperate with Diskco and to execute and deliver all papers, instruments, and assignments as may be necessary to vest all right, title, and interest in and to the aforesaid trademark, including, without limitation, recordation of the assignment in the United States Patent and Trademark Office.

SOFTCO
By: _____
    [signature]

On this _____ day of _____, 19___, before me, _____, the undersigned Notary Public, personally appeared _____ and proved to me on the basis of satisfactory evidence to be the person who executed the within instrument. WITNESS my hand and official seal.

_____
Notary Public

FIGURE 10-6
Sample trademark
assignment agreement

containing specific information about the assignment must be included. A sample of the appropriate form is included in the appendix to that section of the Code of Federal Regulations.[8] In addition, the new rules permit an assignment of an intent-to-use trademark application and also permit the recording of a non-English assignment, provided that the document is accompanied by a verified English translation signed by the translator. If the assignee is not domiciled in the United States, a separate paper must be included designating a domestic representative upon whom notice or process in proceedings affecting the mark may be served. All such requests for recording documents should be accompanied by the appropriate fee.

> *Calendar Requirement:* As soon as possible after execution of the assignment of trademark rights.
> *Filing Requirements:* Enclose appropriate fee (consult 37 C.F.R. § 2.6 for current fee). As of August 1993, the fee was $40 for the first mark per document and $25 for the second and subsequent marks in the same document.

Note: The PTO provides a form for recording assignments and transfers (PTO Form 1594).

10.3 INTER PARTES PROCEEDINGS

An application for registration of a federal trademark on the Principal Register may be opposed prior to registration in an **opposition proceeding**. This opposition action is an inter-partes proceeding. That is, the arguments opposing the registration and the responses are all presented to the Trademark Trial and Appeal Board. A registration issued by the Patent and Trademark Office also may be canceled upon sufficient proof. This proceeding is known as a **cancellation proceeding** and it is brought before the Trademark Trial and Appeal Board. An opposition proceeding is initiated by filing a **Notice of Opposition.** A cancellation proceeding is instituted by filing a **Petition to Cancel.**[9]

The rules in these proceedings are very similar to the rules in civil litigation. The documents that start the actions are similar to complaints and the procedural regulations are found in Rule 8 of the Federal Rules of Civil Procedure.

The bases for opposition and cancellation are very similar. An application may be opposed or a registration may be canceled if the party (i.e., the "Opposer" in the case of an opposition, or the "Petitioner" in the case of cancellation) can demonstrate that it will be damaged by the registration and show sufficient grounds for opposition or cancellation. The most common grounds for opposition and cancellation are:

1. *Likelihood of confusion.* The opposer or party seeking to cancel can demonstrate that the mark, when used on similar goods or services, is likely to cause confusion among consumers (i.e., the basis for refusing registration under § 2(d) of the Lanham Act).

2. *Descriptiveness.* The opposer or party seeking to cancel can demonstrate that the mark is merely descriptive (i.e., has not acquired secondary meaning) or is deceptively misdescriptive. This basis for refusing registration is based upon § 2(e) of the Lanham Act.

LEGAL TERMS

opposition proceeding
Action brought before the Trademark Trial and Appeal Board to prevent the federal registration of a mark; must be based upon one of the statutory grounds provided in the Lanham Act and the party bringing the action must prove that it would be damaged.

cancellation proceeding
Action brought before the Trademark Trial and Appeal Board to cancel a federal registration of a mark; must be based upon one of the statutory grounds provided in the Lanham Act and the party bringing the action must prove that it would be damaged.

Notice of Opposition
Initial pleading filed by the petitioner in an opposition proceeding.

Petition to Cancel
Initial pleading filed by the petitioner in a cancellation proceeding.

3. *Abandonment.* The trademark owner has lost rights because of misuse, loss of distinctiveness, or as a result of nonuse of the mark (as demonstrated by sufficient evidence that the owner intends not to resume use of the mark).

In addition, a mark may be opposed or canceled if it can be demonstrated that the trademark was acquired fraudulently, the mark includes immoral or scandalous matter, the mark identifies a living individual without written consent, or the registration violates or is precluded by an agreement between the parties or by a prior judicial determination. All of these bases are provided in the Lanham Act and are discussed further in this chapter. State claims, such as dilution, may not be used for opposition or cancellation purposes. An application for registration of a federal trademark on the Supplemental Register is not subject to opposition. A Supplemental Registration may be challenged in the Patent and Trademark Office by filing a Petition to Cancel.

In addition to these requirements, the party bringing the proceeding must have a personal interest in the matter. To bring a proceeding, the party must be able to demonstrate that it will be damaged. For example, a women's action group dislikes the trademark for a men's magazine and claims that the magazine is demeaning to women. The women's group would not have a personal interest in the matter and would not have standing to oppose registration. However, a competing men's magazine with a similar name would have standing to oppose the registration.

Opposition

An *opposition proceeding* is an action to prevent the federal registration of a mark. It must be based upon one of the statutory grounds provided in the Lanham Act and the party bringing the action must prove that it would be damaged if the registration were to issue. The *Notice of Opposition* is similar to a complaint in a civil lawsuit and sets forth the basis of the opposer's claims (see figure 10-7).

Calendar Requirement: The opposition proceeding can be filed any time prior to the expiration of the 30-day period following publication of the mark in the *Official Gazette.* However, an extension of time will be granted if filed prior to expiration of the time period.

Example: If the mark described in figure 10-8 were published on March 31, 1992, the opposer would have until April 30, 1992 to file a Notice of Opposition.

Filing Requirements: Enclose appropriate fee (consult 37 C.F.R. § 2.6 for current fee). As of August 1993, the fee was $200. File the Notice in duplicate and provide a statement of proof of mailing.

If the opposer is unable to prepare and file the opposition within 30 days of the publication in the *Official Gazette,* the opposer may file a Request to Extend Time for Filing Notice of Opposition (Figure 10-8).[10]

IN THE UNITED STATES PATENT AND TRADEMARK OFFICE
BEFORE THE TRADEMARK TRIAL AND APPEAL BOARD

In the Matter of Trademark Application, Serial No. 74/123,456
Published in the Official Gazette of March 31, 1992, Page TM 191

ANGEL'S FOODS, INC.	)	
	)	
Opposer,	)	
	)	
v.	)	Opposition No. _____
	)	
BROTHER BOB'S FOODS,	)	
	)	
Applicant.	)	
	)	

Commissioner of Patents and Trademarks
U.S. Patent and Trademark Office
Box TTAB
Washington, DC 20231

NOTICE OF OPPOSITION

Angel's Foods, Inc., a corporation duly organized, incorporated, and existing under the laws of the state of Michigan, and having its principal place of business at 14 47th Avenue, Flint, Michigan, 48509, believes that it will be damaged by the registration of the mark shown in Trademark Application Serial No. 74/123,456 filed April 7, 1991, and published in the Official Gazette of March 31, 1992, Page TM 191, and opposes registration of said mark in Class 29.

As grounds of opposition, it is alleged that:

1. Continuously, since well prior to the filing of the application opposed or any use by Applicant, Opposer has engaged in business relating to the making and selling of relishes and bean sauces using the mark *Angel and Rob's Beanjam.*

2. Opposer has, since well prior to Applicant's filing date, advertised and promoted its relishes and bean sauces under its mark, including on the label a design representing an angel and a halo, as shown in Exhibit A, attached hereto.

3. As a result of such continuous use, advertising, promotion, and sales of goods under the mark *Angel and Rob's Beanjam* together with the design, the mark has become identified in the minds of Opposer's customers, and in the minds of other users of Opposer's goods, throughout the United States, as distinguishing Opposer's goods from the goods of others. The image of the angel has created an impression associated with spiritual symbolism.

4. Applicant's proposed goods as listed in the application opposed, upon information and belief, include goods which are closely related to or the same as the goods of the Opposer and are sold to the same class of purchasers and through the same channels of trade.

FIGURE 10-7
Sample Notice of
Opposition

5. Opposer is the owner of United States Trademark Registration No. 1,234,567 registered October 1, 1986 for relishes and bean sauces in class 30, a copy of which is attached as Exhibit B.

6. Applicant's mark sought to be registered comprises *Brother Bob's Heavenly Beanjam,* which appears similar to and when pronounced sounds similar to opposer's mark, and, therefore, is a mere colorable imitation of Opposer's previously used and registered mark *Angel and Rob's Beanjam,*

7. Applicant's mark sought to be registered, namely *Brother Bob's Heavenly Beanjam,* is likely to cause a belief there is an association of Applicant with Opposer.

8. Opposer believes that it will be damaged by registration of the mark *Brother Bob's Heavenly Beanjam,* as shown in Trademark Application, Serial No. 74/123,456, because prospective and actual purchasers and users of goods from Applicant will be likely to believe that such goods emanate from, or are in some way produced by or associated or affiliated with, Opposer.

9. Applicant should be denied registration of the mark shown in Trademark Application, Serial No. 74/123,456, because the mark consists of or comprises matter that may falsely suggest a connection or association with Opposer.

10. Applicant's mark sought to be registered incorporates the word "Heavenly", which is commonly associated with spiritual or religious symbolism. Opposer's label, as shown in Exhibit A, includes an angel. Opposer believes that Applicant's use of the word "Heavenly", which has a spiritual connotation, also is likely to cause confusion or mistake by creating a connection or association with Opposer in the minds of purchasers of Applicant's goods.

11. Applicant's mark sought to be registered, namely *Brother Bob's Heavenly Beanjam,* sounds strikingly similar to opposer's mark, *Angel and Rob's Beanjam.* Opposer believes this will falsely suggest a connection or association with Opposer.

12. The mark sought to be registered by Applicant so resembles Opposer's mark so as to falsely suggest a connection with the Opposer, and also so as to be likely to cause confusion, or to cause mistake, or to deceive, all to the damage of Opposer, and therefore, the registration of Applicant's mark should be refused under the provisions of 15 U.S.C. § 1052(d).

13. For the foregoing reasons, Opposer believes that registration of the mark sought to be registered by Applicant will seriously damage Opposer.

WHEREFORE, Opposer believes it will be damaged by registration of the mark sought to be registered by Applicant and prays that such registration be denied.

The filing fee for this opposition in the amount of $200.00 is enclosed.

Dated: _____   Respectfully submitted,

_____
Opposer

Proof of Mailing

I hereby certify that this paper is being sent by U.S. Mail, First Class, to the Commissioner of Patents and Trademarks, Washington, DC 20231, this _____ day of _____, 19____.

_____
Attorney

FIGURE 10-7
(Continued)

**IN THE UNITED STATES PATENT AND TRADEMARK OFFICE
BEFORE THE TRADEMARK TRIAL AND APPEAL BOARD**

Serial No. 74/123,456
Filed April 7, 1991
Published: March 31, 1992, Page TM 191
Trademark: *Brother Bob's Heavenly Beanjam*

**Request under Rule 2.102 to Extend Time for
Filing Notice of Opposition**

Commissioner of Patents and Trademarks
U.S. Patent and Trademark Office
Box 5: Attn: TTAB
Washington, DC 20231

Angel's Foods, Inc., a corporation duly organized, incorporated, and existing under the laws of the state of Michigan, and having its principal place of business at 14 47th Avenue, Flint, Michigan, 48509, by and through its attorney requests that the Board grant a thirty (30) day Extension of Time to and including May 30, 1992, to file a Notice of Opposition in the above-identified matter.

The Extension of Time is necessary in order for Angel's Foods, Inc. to further investigate and evaluate the necessity of filing a Notice of Opposition. This request is being submitted in triplicate as required by 37 C.F.R. § 2.102(d).

Respectfully submitted,

_____
Attorney

I hereby certify that this paper is being sent by U.S. Mail, First Class, to the Commissioner of Patents and Trademarks, Washington, DC 20231, this _____ day of _____, 19_____.

_____
Attorney

FIGURE 10-8
Sample request for extension of time to file opposition

Petition to Cancel

A *Petition to Cancel* is basically the same as a Notice of Opposition except that the Petition is filed *after* registration of the mark at issue. Instead of opposing registration, the petitioner is seeking to cancel the registration (e.g., if the petitioner believes that a registered mark has been abandoned by nonuse or genericide; or if the petitioner is a prior user of the mark and, when the respondent's mark is registered on the Principal Register, the Petition is filed within five years from the date of registration). The statement of facts would be similar to the Notice of Opposition and should also include a request for relief (i.e., "WHEREFORE, Petitioner believes it will be damaged by the above identified registration and petitions to cancel the same"). Figure 10-9 is an example of the format for a Petition to Cancel.

Answering the Notice or Petition

The Patent and Trademark Office will notify the applicant or registrant of the opposition or cancellation proceeding, furnish a copy of the Notice of Opposition or Petition for Cancellation, and grant the applicant a 40-day period to answer. The answer is similar to an answer filed in a civil lawsuit. It should have a caption (heading) similar to the Petition or Notice and should state in short and plain terms the applicant's defenses to each claim asserted. The applicant should admit or deny the allegations. Denials may take any of

---

IN THE UNITED STATES PATENT AND TRADEMARK OFFICE
BEFORE THE TRADEMARK TRIAL AND APPEAL BOARD

In the Matter of Trademark Registration No. 123,456
Registered on March 1, 1991

ANGEL'S FOODS, INC.   )
)
            Petitioner,   )
)
v.   )   Cancellation No. _____
)
BROTHER BOB'S FOODS,   )
)
            Respondent.   )
)

Commissioner of Patents and Trademarks
U.S. Patent and Trademark Office
Box TTAB
Washington, DC 20231

PETITION FOR CANCELLATION

Angel's Foods, Inc., a corporation duly organized, incorporated, and existing under the laws of the state of Michigan, and having its principal place of business at 14 47th Avenue, Flint, Michigan, 48509, believes that it will be damaged by the above identified registration and hereby petitions to cancel the same.

The grounds for cancellation are as follows: [state grounds].

FIGURE 10-9
Sample Petition
to Cancel

the forms specified in Rule 8(b) of the Federal Rules of Civil Procedure. An answer may contain any defense, including the affirmative defenses of unclean hands, laches, estoppel, acquiescence, fraud, mistake, prior judgment, or any other matter constituting an avoidance or affirmative defense. Counterclaims may also be filed with the answer. If the answering party wishes to challenge the validity of the opposer or petitioner's trademark registration, that counterclaim is compulsory and must be brought.[11]

Inter Partes Proceeding: Discovery, Motions, and Trial

An *inter partes proceeding* is as complex as civil litigation in federal court. Discovery is conducted pursuant to the Federal Rules of Civil Procedure (*see* 37 C.F.R. § 2.120.) Rules regarding motions are set forth in 37 C.F.R. § 2.127. Inter partes proceedings may involve the same variety of motions typically filed in civil litigation, such as a motions for judgment on the pleadings, motions for protective order, motions to strike, motions to dismiss, motions for a more definite statement, motions to compel discovery, motions for summary judgment, motions to amend, or motions for a new trial.

After all the discovery and testimony has been completed, closing briefs are submitted by each party and, if requested by either party, oral arguments are set before three members of the Trademark Trial and Appeal Board in Washington, D.C. Usually within four to six weeks, a decision is rendered. That decision may be appealed to the United States Court of Appeal for the Federal Circuit or to any United States District Court.

Interference Proceedings

The Lanham Act provides that when two trademark applications are pending that conflict, or when a pending application conflicts with a registered mark that is not incontestable, an **interference proceeding** may be declared.[12] The interference proceeding is a form of a trial before the Trademark Trial and Appeal Board. However, the Patent and Trademark Office will declare an interference only under "extraordinary circumstances," and generally prefers that such actions be brought as opposition or cancellation proceedings.

Concurrent Use Proceedings

If the user of a trademark desires to register a trademark concurrently with another person already using the mark in a geographic area, a **concurrent use proceeding** may be instituted.[13] The underlying principle of a concurrent use proceeding is that the junior user did not know (or had no reason to know) of the senior user's use of the trademark. This is known as a "good faith" standard. For the Patent and Trademark Office to have jurisdiction, the junior user must have begun using the mark before the earliest filing date of any application seeking registration of a confusingly similar mark.

LEGAL TERMS

interference proceeding
    Mini-trial before the Trademark Trial and Appeal Board, brought when two trademark applications are pending that conflict, or when a pending application conflicts with a registered mark that is not incontestable; permitted only under extraordinary circumstances.

concurrent use proceeding
    When the user of a trademark desires to federally register a trademark concurrently with another person already using the mark in a geographic area; provided that the junior user did not know (or had no reason to know) of the senior user's use of the trademark.

10.4 LIKELIHOOD OF CONFUSION

In the Commentary to this chapter, Softco sells a computer program under the registered trademark *The Big Squeezy.* Softco learns that Diskco has begun selling a program that performs similar functions, called *Easy Squeezee.* Softco wants to stop Diskco from using the words *Easy Squeezee.* For Softco to prevail in an infringement lawsuit, the company will have to demonstrate that consumers are likely to be confused. Issues of *likelihood of confusion* arise in three ways: registration; inter partes proceedings; and infringement litigation. In each case, the standard is the same—is it probable, under all of the circumstances, that consumers of the relevant goods will be confused? When it is probable that purchasers of goods will be confused by a junior user's trademark, there is a likelihood of confusion. Every circuit court in the United States uses a multifactor analysis in determining if there is a likelihood of confusion. Although the number of factors may vary from each circuit, the principles are similar and all relate in some way to consumer perception.

Strength of the Mark

A mark is *weak* if it is descriptive and has not acquired sufficient secondary meaning. A mark is *strong* when it has acquired secondary meaning, or if it is arbitrary, fanciful, or suggestive. The owner of a weak mark will have more difficulty proving likelihood of confusion. For example, the mark, *Maid in America* for cleaning services was determined to be descriptive. The owner was unable to demonstrate a sufficient showing of advertising or sales to prove secondary meaning. Therefore, the trademark owner did not prevail in a claim of infringement against a similar mark. If descriptiveness is an issue in an infringement action, a survey may be conducted to prove secondary meaning.

Similarity of the Marks

As a general rule, marks must be compared in their entirety, including appearance, sound, connotation, and commercial impression. However, determining whether two marks are similar may require dissecting and comparing the elements of each mark. For example, in the facts to the Commentary of this chapter, Softco owns the mark *The Big Squeezy,* and wants to stop Diskco's use of *Easy Squeezee* on similar goods. "Squeezy" (which is phonetically identical to "Squeezee") is an arbitrary term and the dominant element of both marks. Therefore, a court may not place much emphasis on the words "The Big" or "Easy" when comparing these two marks, because the dominant element in both marks is a virtually identical arbitrary term.

In one case, the owner of the mark *OAG Travel Planner* sued the owner of the mark *The Travel Planner.* The court determined that the mark *Travel Planner* was descriptive and weak, but that the use of *OAG* in conjunction with "Travel Planner" created an arbitrary mark. Because there were similarities in sight and sound, the court determined that the marks were likely to confuse customers. Similarly, a court found similarity between *Dutch Masters* and *Little Dutchman* for cigars, because of the common use of the dominant term "Dutch."

Generally, adding a prefix or suffix, changing letters, or adding clarifying information may not avoid a claim of similarity of marks. For example, the following marks were found to be similar: *Magnavox* and *Multivox*; *Simoniz* and *Permanize*; *Platinum Puff* and *Platinum Plus*; *Zirco* and *Cozirc*; and *Maternally Yours* and *Your Maternity Shop*.

In addition, the similarity of the meaning of the marks may also be taken into consideration. For example, the following marks were held to be similar: *Mr. Clean* and *Mr. Rust* and *Mr. Stain; Thirty Forty Fifty* and *60 40 20;* and *Pledge* and *Promise.*

Similarity of the Goods

The standard of infringement is whether an ordinary prudent purchaser would be likely to purchase one item, believing he was purchasing the other. For example, *Chlorit* when used on bleach is likely to be confused with *Clorox*. As a general rule, a trademark owner is permitted to use a similar mark as long as it is on completely dissimilar goods. For example, the use of the mark *Lexus* on automobiles was determined not to confuse consumers of the *LEXIS* database services.

The protection afforded to a trademark owner may extend to related goods. For example, a trademark for canned salmon may also extend to other canned fish. Use of a mark on kerosene lamps may extend to electric lamps. In such cases, the courts consider whether the buying public would reasonably expect that the goods came from the same source. The more extensively used and the more popular the mark, the more likely it is that consumers will expect an expansion of the product base. For example, would consumers confuse the *McDonald's* trademark for food establishments with Quality Inn's *McSleep* for motel services? Yes, according to a federal court. The reason is because the "Mc" prefix has been used so extensively by the McDonald's Corporation that its expansion into nonfood categories is expected. In fact, the company already has expanded into children's clothing with its *McKids* clothing line. The same is true for the *Coca-Cola* mark, which has been licensed for clothing, glassware, puzzles, watches, bags, and other nonfood items. The *Coca-Cola* mark also has been infringed when used on unlikely goods. (For example, the trademark has been used on "can wraps," which are labels intended to be wrapped around an alcoholic beverage to disguise its contents.)

The courts also consider the similarity of the advertising and distribution channels. Many courts weigh this evidence separately to determine if consumers or distributors may be exposed to potential confusion. For example, if the plaintiff sells salami directly to consumers, but the defendant only sells salami in bulk to delicatessens, that may be an important factor in avoiding a claim of infringement.

What if: (1) the marks are similar; (2) the goods or services are related but not identical; and (3) many large companies purchase both types of goods? In one case, no confusion was found between the mark *EDS* for computing programming services and *EDS* for power supplies for battery chargers, even though both companies conducted business with many of the same corporate customers. The Federal Circuit Court determined that the departments that purchased computer services and battery chargers in large purchasing institutions were separate and thus not likely to be confused by the identical marks. In other words, likelihood of confusion must be shown to exist for the actual purchaser, not the purchasing institution as a whole.

Degree of Care Exercised by the Consumer

The degree of care exercised by the consumer varies according to the purchase. Generally, a buyer making a very expensive purchase is more likely to be discriminating and is less likely to be easily confused by similar marks. The reason for this higher degree of care is because the consumer buys expensive items less frequently. Therefore, the courts assume that such purchasers are likely to be more discriminating and source-conscious when purchasing real estate services, insurance, or other "high ticket" items. Under these circumstances, the courts require a more substantial showing of similarity to justify a claim of likelihood of confusion. The same is true for items purchased by professional buyers. A *professional buyer* is a person who arrives at the purchasing point already knowledgeable about the goods (e.g., pharmacists, physicians, architects, builders, etc.). Professional buyers are less likely to be confused because of their superior knowledge as to purchasing decisions.

An ordinary purchaser, particularly one who buys inexpensive items on impulse, is the most likely to be confused by similar marks. This consumer, for example, may quickly scan the aisle of a supermarket and impulsively purchase a box of garbage bags without realizing that she or he has been confused as to the choice of brands. In this instance, a lesser degree of care has been exercised. Therefore, less similarity may be necessary to prove likelihood of confusion.

Defendant's Intent

Although the intent of the defendant is not essential in proving infringement, it is a relevant factor. According to the *Restatement of Trademarks*, it is appropriate to consider the defendant's intent because a party intending to cause confusion will generally be successful in doing so. Direct evidence of the defendant's intention to deceive is usually unavailable, and the plaintiff must depend on circumstantial evidence, such as the defendant's knowledge of the plaintiff's mark, the method by which the defendant's mark was chosen, and whether the defendant continued use of the mark after the plaintiff's warning. Factors that may mitigate a claim of bad faith are the defendant's request for a trademark search and the defendant's good faith reliance on the advice of legal counsel.

Actual Confusion

Proof of actual confusion is not essential in determining trademark infringement. However, such evidence might be compelling in an infringement case. For example, in the Commentary to this chapter, Softco was concerned about the use of a similar mark by Diskco. If software retailers or distributors reported complaints because of such confusion, or if Softco received notification from disgruntled consumers, those facts might be sufficient to prove the potential damage to Softco's mark. Sometimes companies conduct surveys to determine actual confusion. These surveys are expensive, however, and if improperly performed may subvert the plaintiff's case.

10.5 RELATED TRADEMARK CLAIMS

Trademark infringement actions are often related to other injuries or claims. For example, if the defendant copied artwork from the plaintiff's packaging, that might give rise to a claim of copyright infringement. If a patented design were copied, that might give rise to a claim of patent infringement. When the trade dress of the package is copied, this may be characterized as a claim of unfair competition under federal or state law. False or deceptive sales statements may give rise to a claim of false advertising. The owner of a federal trademark registration may also bring claims for common law unfair competition and for violation of state trademark laws, as well as dilution. Some of these additional claims are discussed in this section.

Dilution

What if a defendant is using a similar trademark on noncompetitive goods and there is no likelihood of confusion? For example, if the trademark *Playboy* is used by an auto body shop, does the owner of the *Playboy* mark for publishing have a claim? Under certain state statutes, the trademark owner may claim that the defendant's use dilutes the distinctive quality of the mark. In the *Playboy* case, the court determined that the magazine company had a valid claim for dilution.

The **dilution** remedy is available only under state law. There is no federal dilution statute. Because dilution does not require proof of likelihood of confusion, judges and trademark scholars have expressed concern about its application. For example, a New York state trial court determined that the *Lexus* mark for automobiles diluted the *Lexis* mark for computer databases. On appeal, however, that decision was reversed. In another case, a federal court determined that the defendant's use of the mark *Bagzilla* (for storage

LEGAL TERMS

dilution
When the defendant's use weakens or reduces the distinctive quality of the mark. A claim of dilution is available only under state laws sometimes known as *antidilution* statutes.

bags) *did not* dilute the plaintiff's trademark for entertainment services, *Godzilla.* In a Georgia case involving a dilution statute, use of the *Pillsbury* doughboy in a pornographic magazine, engaging in sexual acts with a female counterpart, was considered to dilute the *Pillsbury* trademark. The use of *The Greatest Used Car Show on Earth* was held to dilute *The Greatest Show on Earth,* a mark for circus productions.

The authors of the *Restatement of the Law of Trademarks* take the position that claims of dilution should be allowed only when authorized by state statute and when the defendant's use of the mark is in a commercial trademark sense (as opposed to use in literature, comparative advertising, or parody). In addition, the trademark that has allegedly been diluted must have a degree of distinctiveness beyond the minimum level needed to function as a trademark. A party would be liable for dilution under such conditions if the use causes a "reduction in the distinctiveness of the other's mark" or the use is likely to cause a consumer association that results in a disparagement or tarnishing of the other's goods or services. For a listing of state dilution statutes, see the chart in appendix F.

Section 43(a) False Advertising (Unfair Competition)

Section 43(a) of the Lanham Act creates a federal remedy against any false description of origin or false representation in competition.[14] It has been labeled a federal unfair competition statute and has been used broadly against claims of false advertising and trade dress infringement, and for claims of infringement of unregistered marks. Under this statute, a defendant is prohibited from knowingly making false claims or false designations in connection with goods or services (e.g., the use of pictures of a competitor's products, claimed to be defendant's products in a mail order catalogue). The ultimate test under § 43(a) is whether the public is likely to be deceived by the defendant's acts. For example, the use of *Dallas Cowboys* cheerleader outfits in the adult film *Debbie Does Dallas* was considered to deceive the public as to the origin of the film or representation of the Dallas Cowboy Cheerleaders in the film. By suing under § 43(a), the owner of an unregistered trademark may obtain federal court jurisdiction, provided that the infringement occurred within the context of interstate or other commerce regulated by the federal government. The following are some examples of the variety of claims that may be brought under § 43(a):

EXAMPLE: Trade Dress

A manufacturer of a metal polish obtained an injunction preventing a competitor from selling a metal polish in a similarly shaped and sized container in either silver or red colors.

EXAMPLE: Product Configuration

A manufacturer of a wall-mounted jewelry organizer obtained an injunction preventing a competitor from selling an almost identical product.

EXAMPLE: Unregistered Marks

A retail store using the unregistered mark *Bath & Beyond* obtained an injunction against another retail store using the mark *Bed, Bath & Beyond.*

EXAMPLE: Image and Appearance

A Mexican restaurant chain with a distinctive appearance and image obtained a judgment against a competing restaurant chain using a similar image and appearance.

EXAMPLE: Color

A company that had manufactured and sold green-gold dry cleaning press pads for 30 years obtained a judgment against a competitor that used the same color on its dry cleaning press pads.

EXAMPLE: False Advertising

A company was ordered to pay $100,000 in damages for falsely advertising that its product was "100% Florida juice" when it actually contained sugar and pulpwash.

EXAMPLE: Misappropriation of Voice

Tom Waits, a singer with a distinctive "gravelly" voice, was awarded a judgment (including $2 million in punitive damages) when a food company used an imitation of Mr. Waits's voice to sell corn chip products.

Common Law Unfair Competition Claims

Common law claims are usually added to a claim of federal trademark infringement. If the mark is not registered, the case may be brought solely on the basis of common law claims. As explained in chapter 8, the common law is a system of legal rules derived from the precedents and principles established by court decisions. Certain common law principles are grouped together as unfair competition laws. Under these principles, a senior user is entitled to relief and remedies regardless of whether the mark is registered.

10.6 DEFENSES TO INFRINGEMENT

Most of the defenses to infringement have been previously introduced, for example, genericide, abandonment through nonuse, lack of secondary meaning, or a failure to follow statutory formalities. Certain defenses common to all litigation are also available in trademark infringement lawsuits. These defenses include estoppel, unclean hands, and laches.

Use of Generic Terms

Sometimes a court determines that a mark is generic, and therefore the owner of the registered mark cannot preclude others from using that generic term. This defense was successfully used in the case of "toll house" cookies, "lite" beer, and "chocolate fudge" beverages. Similarly, the owners of the registered mark *Grand Ole Opry* could not prevent the use of the mark *The Carolina Opry*. The term "Opry" is generic for country-and-western music presentations, and a federal court ruled that the two marks, when considered as a whole, were not confusingly similar.

Abandonment

A defendant will avoid an infringement claim if it can be proven that the plaintiff abandoned the mark prior to the defendant's use. As indicated earlier in this chapter, the elements are a period of nonuse (two years is prima facie proof) and an intent by the trademark owner not to resume use in the foreseeable future. Abandonment may also occur as a result of improper licensing, as, for instance, when the trademark owner executes numerous licenses for the mark but fails to exercise the requisite control over the quality of the goods.

Lack of Secondary Meaning

If the defendant can demonstrate that the plaintiff's mark is descriptive and has not acquired secondary meaning, then the plaintiff will not have a protectible mark. Therefore, there can be no infringement. For example, the owner of the descriptive mark *Lip Renewal Cream* failed to prove secondary meaning and therefore did not prevail against a defendant using a similar mark.

Fraud in Obtaining Trademark Registration

If the defendant can prove that the plaintiff's registration was fraudulently procured, then the registration would be invalid and the plaintiff's claims of *federal* trademark infringement would be defeated. Examples of such fraud are false statements of material fact in a trademark registration or declaration (e.g., that the plaintiff had begun use in commerce when in fact it had not). The defendant must also demonstrate that the plaintiff's fraud has damaged the defendant. The defendant must prove such facts by a clear and convincing showing.

Estoppel

The **estoppel** defense asserts that the plaintiff cannot contradict the plaintiff's behavior upon which the defendant has justifiably relied. To successfully assert an estoppel defense, the plaintiff must know the facts of the defendant's allegedly infringing conduct and the defendant must have a justifiable belief that such infringing conduct is permitted. **Collateral estoppel** is a form of estoppel that occurs when a plaintiff is prevented from bringing an action because of facts that were determined in a previous action. For example, Softco sued Diskco for trademark infringement and a court determined that Diskco's mark was not likely to cause confusion. Softco sues again in a different court on the same issues. Diskco would defend by claiming collateral estoppel.

Unclean Hands

Unclean hands is a defense asserted when the plaintiff has committed a serious act of wrongdoing in regard to the infringement—so serious that it would be inequitable for the court to allow the plaintiff to proceed. For example, in one case the court sustained an unclean hands defense when the plaintiff had used the ® symbol even though the mark was not federally registered.

Laches

The **Laches** defense is asserted when the plaintiff has waited an unreasonable amount of time to bring the lawsuit and the defendant is prejudiced as a result. As expressed by Judge Learned Hand, "The defense is in substance that the defendant has built up its business upon the faith of the plaintiff's implicit assurance that it had no grievance." In a case before Judge Hand, one company had permitted another to use the mark "White House" without objection for over 15 years. Judge Hand asked, "How can [the plaintiff] expect us to stifle a competition which with complete complaisance, and even with active encouragement, it has allowed for years to grow like the mustard tree?"

10.7 REMEDIES FOR TRADEMARK INFRINGEMENT

There are a variety of forms of judicial relief in a trademark infringement lawsuit. Perhaps the most important is to prevent the defendant from any further use of the infringing mark. This can be accomplished by a court-ordered **injunction**. In addition, the plaintiff will seek payment for damages

---

LEGAL TERMS

estoppel
Defense to infringment in which the defendant prevents the plaintiff from contradicting behavior upon which the defendant has justifiably relied. To assert successfully an estoppel defense, the plaintiff must know the facts of the defendant's conduct and the defendant must have a justifiable belief that such infringing conduct is permitted.

collateral estoppel
When a plaintiff is restricted because of facts that were determined in a previous action.

unclean hands
Defense asserted when the plaintiff has committed a serious act of wrongdoing in regard to the lawsuit or the activity precipitating the lawsuit.

laches
Defense to infringement in which the defendant argues that the plaintiff's delay in bringing the lawsuit is so unreasonable that the plaintiff should be barred from proceeding.

injunction
Court order directing the defendant to stop certain activities.

based upon actual losses suffered as a result of the infringement, as well as any profits by the defendant that are not included in the plaintiff's losses. Pursuant to § 35 of the Lanham Act, the court may increase the amount of the judgment (up to three times the actual damages) and, in exceptional circumstances, may award attorney fees. However, such awards are rare and in such cases the plaintiff must prove compelling circumstances (e.g., willful misconduct on the defendant's part).

Injunctions

Generally, the plaintiff in a trademark infringement lawsuit seeks an order from the court enjoining the defendant from any further infringing activity. This court order, instructing the infringer to stop the infringing activity, is known as an *injunction*.[15]

There are three types of injunctions. Initially, the plaintiff may seek preliminary relief known as a **temporary restraining order** or **TRO**. The TRO may be granted *ex parte,* that is, without hearing an opposition from the defendant. The TRO is short in duration and remains in effect only until the court has an opportunity to schedule a hearing for the preliminary injunction. The **preliminary injunction** is granted after a noticed hearing where both parties have an opportunity to present evidence. Often such hearings are "mini-trials" and require considerable preparation. The court may request, for either the TRO or a preliminary injunction, that a bond be posted by the plaintiff, to cover any damages suffered by the defendant in case the court determines that no infringement has occurred.

According to the leading trademark treatise, *McCarthy on Trademarks and Unfair Competition,* each federal circuit generally applies a formulation that includes five factors when determiningwhether to grant a preliminary injunction: (1) whether the plaintiff can show a probability of success on the merits of the claim; (2) whether the plaintiff can show that it will suffer irreparable injury pending a full trial on the merits; (3) whether a preliminary injunction will preserve the status quo preceding the dispute; (4) whether the hardships tip in the plaintiff's favor; and (5) whether a preliminary injunction would favor the public interest (i.e., is it necessary to protect third parties?). Irreparable harm is considered to be an injury for which a monetary award will not provide adequate compensation. For example, if customers are likely to be confused by a similar mark, that is harm which may be irreparable.

The preliminary injunction lasts until the trial ends and a final judgment has been rendered. If the plaintiff prevails, a **permanent injunction** is granted. A permanent injunction is a durable injunction issued after a final judgment on the merits of the case. It permanently restrains the defendant from engaging in the infringing activity. If it is not probable that the defendant will continue the infringing activity, the court will not issue the a permanent injunction. A suggested checklist for filing a motion for a preliminary injunction is provided in § 10.9.

Damages

Monetary compensation is not always the major concern for a plaintiff seeking to stop an infringing trademark. In some cases, for example, a court may order an injunction without ordering the payment of any damages. This may occur if the defendant's use of the mark was not in bad faith and there was no deliberate attempt to cause confusion.

The Lanham Act provides standards for the award of damages for infringement of a federally registered trademark.[16] Damages are to be awarded under principles of equity (or fairness), and the plaintiff may recover: (1) the defendant's profits; (2) any damages sustained by the plaintiff; and (3) the costs of the action. *Costs* are defined as the incidental expenses involved in the handling of the lawsuit, such as filing fees. In assessing profits, the plaintiff is required to prove the defendant's sales income and the defendant must prove any deductions (e.g., business overhead) from such sales. For example, consider the facts in the Commentary to this chapter. Diskco is found liable for federal trademark infringement. Softco proves that the total sales revenues from Diskco's product was $100,000. Diskco must now prove the expenses, such as manufacturing or promotion, that should be deducted from the $100,000 sales figure to arrive at the actual profit.

If the court finds that the amount of recovery for profits is inadequate or excessive, the court may, in its discretion, enter judgment for a sum it finds to be just. In exceptional cases, the court may award attorney fees.

Under the Lanham Act, a court is not empowered to award damages if the defendant did not have actual notice of the plaintiff's registration. Therefore, if the plaintiff failed to use the proper form of notice (i.e., the ® symbol or "Registered in U.S. Patent & Trademark Office" or "Reg.U.S. Pat. & Tm. Off."), it cannot rely on the constructive notice provision of the statute and no profits or damages will be awarded until such time as the defendant received actual notice of the plaintiff's registration.

In the event of a counterfeit trademark, as defined in § 32 of the Lanham Act (15 U.S.C. § 1114), the court is required to award three times the profits or damages (whichever is greater) together with reasonable attorney fees. Only in extenuating circumstances are these damages waived by the courts.

Impoundment and Destruction of Infringing Articles

As part of a final judgment or decree of a violation of the Lanham Act, a federal court may order the delivery and destruction or disposal of all labels, signs, prints, packages, wrappers, receptacles, and advertisements in the possession of the defendant which bear the infringing mark.[17] For example, in the case of Diskco's mark, *Easy Squeezee,* mentioned in the Commentary to this chapter, the plaintiff, Softco, may ask the court for an order that Diskco deliver all packages, disk labels, and promotional materials bearing the *Easy Squeezee* mark.

LEGAL TERMS

temporary restraining order (TRO)
An injunction, often granted ex parte, that is short in duration and remains in effect only until the court has an opportunity to schedule a hearing for the preliminary injunction.

preliminary injunction
Injunction granted after a noticed hearing at which the parties have an opportunity to present evidence as to the likelihood of the plaintiff's success on the merits and irreparability of the harm to be suffered if the injunction is not granted; lasts until a final judgment has been rendered.

permanent injunction
Durable injunction issued after a final judgment on the merits of the case; permanently restrains the defendant from engaging in the infringing activity.

Fraudulent Representation in a Trademark Registration

Under the Lanham Act, any person who knowingly makes a false representation of a material fact, whether oral or written, in the process of procuring a federal trademark registration may be liable in a civil action by any person who is injured as a result of that false statement.[18] This is of particular importance for legal administrators who assist in the preparation and administration of federal applications.

10.8 RESOLVING THE INFRINGEMENT DISPUTE PRIOR TO LITIGATION

The goal of a trademark owner is to stop infringing activities as quickly and efficiently as possible. In addition, a trademark owner may fear that the failure to assert trademark rights will later be used as a defense (i.e., laches or estoppel) by the alleged infringer. For owners of popular trademarks such as *Coca-Cola,* the assertion of rights is a mandatory element of the maintenance program. In the case of the *McDonald's* trademark, the aggressive assertion of trademark rights has virtually precluded any service or food business from using the "Mc" prefix or the trade dress of golden arches.

For a smaller business, the trademark owner must carefully weigh the chances of prevailing in court and any resulting award of damages. The defendant must review all possible defenses and understand the potential liability if the plaintiff prevails. In addition, the plaintiff must be concerned about the possible use of defenses, such as abandonment, which could result in loss of the plaintiff's trademark rights. These initial inquiries are time-consuming but well worth the effort if they can make the parties aware of the possible outcome.

The Cease and Desist Letter

As explained earlier in this book, one of the most important steps in resolving a dispute over proprietary rights is the **cease and desist letter**. This letter informs the infringing party of the ownership of the trademark, the nature of the infringement, and the remedies available to the trademark owner. Most importantly, it requests the immediate cessation of all infringing activity and demands an accounting for all acts of infringement. It should provide an accurate assessment of the facts and anticipate any defenses. In short, it should convince the infringing party that illegal activity has occurred and that the trademark owner is very serious about enforcing its statutory rights.

In certain instances, such as in the case of counterfeit trademarks, the infringer may destroy evidence or transfer assets (e.g., an infringer that is selling counterfeit *Rolex* watches). The trademark owner may wish to consider obtaining a temporary restraining order in lieu of sending a cease and desist letter. This order could be obtained ex parte, that is, without informing the infringer about the request for the injunction.

The receipt of a cease and desist letter may trigger litigation called a *declaratory relief action*, as discussed in § 10.9. This is a process whereby the accused party, in anticipation of a trademark infringement lawsuit, request that a court declare the legal rights or duties of the plaintiff and the defendant.

It is important to remember that the cease and desist letter, like all correspondence preceding infringement, may become an exhibit or addendum to papers filed with the court. The trademark owner should assert that if the infringing activity continues after receipt of the letter, such continuing activity will amount to bad faith and shall be a factor in assessing likelihood of confusion.

Figure 10-10 is an example of a cease and desist letter that might be used in a situation involving an unregistered mark. If the mark is registered, evidence of the registration should be included. The letter should be faxed, if possible, and also sent by certified mail. The concluding paragraphs should state the remedies available under trademark law and demand an accounting (i.e., a statement of profits from sales of goods or services with the infringing mark).

Alternative Dispute Resolution

Instead of resolving a dispute in a courtroom, some parties agree to have their problem settled privately through informal procedures known as arbitration or mediation. *Arbitration* is the referral of a dispute to one or more impartial persons for a determination. The determination may be binding or advisory. *Mediation* is an alternative to arbitration in which the parties submit their dispute to an impartial mediator who assists the parties in reaching a settlement. However, unlike an arbitrator, a mediator does not have the authority to make a binding decision.

Settlement

The parties may settle the case at any point prior to the final determination of the judge or jury. A **settlement** is an agreement between the parties in which the dispute is formally resolved. When properly drafted, a settlement is a contract signed by both parties and usually executed at the time one party makes a payment to the other. It is possible that a trademark infringement settlement may not involve payment of money; instead, may provide simply for the cessation of any alleged infringing activity. For example, in the case of Softco and Diskco, it may simply be an agreement that Diskco will cease any further use of the *Easy Squeezee* mark. The terms of the settlement are sometimes presented in a document that is filed with the court in a form known as a *stipulated judgment.*

To achieve a settlement, several variables are considered. For example, if a large fast food franchise wanted to stop a small restaurant from using a

LEGAL TERMS

cease and desist letter
Correspondence from the owner of a proprietary work that informs the infringing party of the validity and ownership of the proprietary work, the nature of the infringement, and remedies available to the owner; requests the cessation of all infringing activity.

settlement
Agreement between the parties in which the dispute is formally resolved.

Re: Use of *Vulcan Warrior* trademark

Please be advised that this office represents Softco International (Softco), a software developer and manufacturer located in Los Angeles, California.

Softco has been using the trademark *Vulcan Warrior* on certain computer video game programs and accompanying instruction manuals in interstate commerce since January 1991. Softco currently has a federal trademark application on file with the U.S. Patent and Trademark Office for the trademark *Vulcan Warrior.* The serial number of that application is 74/134567.

It has come to our attention that your company, Valkuyrie Technology, Inc. of Boulder, Colorado ("**Valkuyrie**") has been using the term "Vulcan Warrior" on a new product which, according to a recent article from *Infoworld,* is marketed to players of personal computer game systems.

The use of the term "Vulcan Warrior" by Valkuyrie has become a source of consumer confusion. Softco already has received several telephone inquiries from distributors interested in Valkuyrie's products. Since both companies are engaged in the software game business, and since Softco can demonstrate substantial sales and extensive national advertising throughout the United States, Softco has a claim of priority of use. On this basis, Softco hereby demands that Valkuyrie Technology, Inc., cease and desist from any further use of the term "Vulcan Warrior" in connection with its goods and services.

As your attorney can advise you, Valkuyrie's failure to cease its infringing acts may subject you to a court-ordered injunction; substantial damages; attorney fees; and the costs of the action. Further, your failure to cease such use may be considered bad faith and reflect on any assessment of damages. We expect a prompt response to this letter addressing the issues raised in this letter and a settlement of these claims. If we do not hear from you within seven (7) days of the date of this letter, I will be compelled to recommend that my client take appropriate legal action to protect its proprietary rights and to receive just compensation for any damage it has suffered.

Sincerely,

_____

Josephine Jones
Attorney for Softco International

FIGURE 10-10
Sample cease and
desist letter

similar name, the large company might offer to pay the defendant to change its name. This may sound strange—paying an alleged infringer to stop use of a mark—but from a business perspective, it may cost far less than litigation and be the most economical means of ending the infringement. It also may make the defendant more likely to settle if the defendant company knows that the expenses for new letterhead, business cards, and signs will be paid by the plaintiff.

Similarly, a plaintiff may offer the defendant a period to sell off goods bearing the infringing mark. This also gives the defendant an incentive to end the dispute. However, this is usually done only when the defendant's outstanding inventory is reasonable and not likely to substantially affect the plaintiff's marketing efforts.

In situations where infringement is very clear and the defendant is aware that it is not likely to prevail, it may be possible to agree on a *structured settlement*. In this situation, the defendant agrees to make a series of payments over a period of time. These payments are often secured by a promissory note. If the defendant fails to make payments, the plaintiff can sue for relief based upon the promissory note.

10.9 TRADEMARK LITIGATION

Unlike many forms of civil litigation, trademark infringement is often intended to halt the infringing activity, not collect damages. For some larger companies, such as McDonald's, the goal of trademark litigation may be to aggressively expand its proprietary rights by forcing others to stop using its marks. In the case of McDonald's, this is not limited to marks with a "Mc" prefix. For example, the McDonald's corporation acquired a court order preventing the Arche computer company from using the color yellow with its "arch" logo.

In other types of trademark infringement lawsuits, the issues may revolve around the transfer of rights or the validity of trademarks. Consider the many issues raised in the *Gallo* case.

The Gallo Case

Ernest and Julio Gallo founded a winery business in 1933. A third brother, Joseph Gallo, decided not to join the brothers in the winery. Under Ernest and Julio's guidance, the winery became the world's largest producer of wine, with an estimated $1 billion dollars in revenues. The winery federally registered 11 Gallo trademarks. In 1959, a company began selling salami to consumers under the *Gallo Salame* mark. In 1970, the salami company also began selling cheese. The salami company federally registered two trademarks for *Gallo Salame*. In 1979, the winery sued the salami company for trademark infringement and dilution. Five years later, the parties entered into a settlement, under which the salami company assigned all rights in its marks to the winery. That way the winery would own all the meat and cheese trademark rights. The winery then licensed the marks back to the salami company.

The third Gallo brother, Joseph, raised grapes and sold cattle. In 1984, he began selling cheese to consumers under the *Joseph Gallo* trade name. The salami company complained that the winery, as it now owned the *Gallo* trademark for cheese, should stop Joseph from using "Gallo" in conjunction with his goods. The Gallo brothers entered into lengthy litigation. The winery

sued for trademark infringement, trademark dilution, and unfair competition, and sought an injunction preventing Joseph from marketing, advertising, selling, or distributing cheese bearing any trademark containing the word "Gallo."

The winery was able to successfully enjoin Joseph from using "Gallo" and "Joseph Gallo" as trademarks on retail cheese sold to consumers. The court determined that wine, cheese, and salami were sold and advertised in the same channels. The court also determined that the marks were similar because of the shared use of "Gallo" as the dominant element. As for Joseph's intent, the court reviewed evidence that Joseph had made an oral agreement not to use the "Gallo" name and had later changed his mind when he was convinced that he could sell more cheese by using the name. These findings supported a determination that Joseph intended to take advantage of the good will of the *Gallo* mark. Joseph was, however, permitted to use the trade names, "Gallo Cattle Company," "Joseph Gallo Farms," or "Joseph Gallo" in connection with nonretail sales of cheese.

As indicated by the *Gallo* case, the issues in trademark litigation may be complex and involve extensive and complicated transfers of rights. Each of the elements in the *Gallo* lawsuit, including the trademark registrations and the assignments, licenses, and other agreements, were subject to judicial scrutiny during the litigation. It is with this perspective that the trademark paralegal should perform similar tasks—realizing that all of the work may someday be reviewed during an infringement lawsuit or a challenge to trademark rights.

Rules of Civil Procedure

The parties in litigation are governed by rules of civil procedure. In federal court and actions before the Trademark Trial and Appeal Board, these are the Federal Rules of Civil Procedure (Fed. R. Civ. P.). If the matter is brought in state court, the parties are governed by the rules of civil procedure for that state. These rules set forth the requirements for the parties when filing papers, appearing in court, or communicating with counsel. In addition, each court, whether federal or state, usually has its own local rules. Before commencing an action, it is important to acquire a copy of the local rules.

Jurisdiction

The federal district courts have **jurisdiction** over any lawsuit arising under the Lanham Act, that is, any claim of infringement of a federally registered trademark or violation of the false advertising section, § 43(a).[19] This also includes the right to maintain any additional state claims as part of the complaint (i.e., claims of common law trademark infringement, unfair competition, and dilution). A plaintiff with an unregistered mark also may bring a claim in federal court under § 43(a) based on the defendant's use of a confusingly similar mark so as to convey a false designation of origin of the defendant's goods or services. In addition, under rules known as **diversity,** a plaintiff may bring a claim in federal court if the parties are from different states and the matter in controversy is more than $50,000. This can be done even if no federal question or issue is involved in the litigation.

Venue

Venue is the proper geographic location of the court. For federal actions, the United States federal court system has 12 circuits, each of which has districts. When the lawsuit is based upon a federal question (i.e., the Lanham Act) or instituted pursuant to the rules of diversity, the case may be brought either in the judicial district where any defendant resides (however, if there are several defendants, all of the defendants must reside in the same state) or in the district where a substantial part of the events giving rise to the claim occurred.[20]

If the lawsuit is based on a federal question *and* there is no district in which the action may otherwise be brought, the suit may be brought in the district where any defendant may be found. If the lawsuit is based on diversity, the suit may also be brought in the district in which the defendants are subject to personal jurisdiction at the time the action is commenced.

The word *reside* has a special meaning with regard to venue. If the defendant is a corporation, the defendant is deemed to "reside" in any judicial district in which it is subject to personal jurisdiction at the time the action is commenced. If a case is filed in a state court, the state venue statute determines the appropriate geographic location of the court.

The Trademark Infringement Complaint

The **complaint** is the initial document filed in a lawsuit. It sets forth the basis of the plaintiff's claims and requests certain remedies. Like all complaints, the complaint for trademark infringement consists of a caption (which identifies the court, the parties, and filing numbers), a statement of the facts, a prayer for relief (e.g., the remedies of compensation or injunctions), and the signature of the attorney preparing the document.

Civil Cover Sheet and Summons

In addition to the complaint, the defendant is served with a **summons**. Also, in federal court and in some state courts, a form referred to as a **civil cover sheet** is required at the time of filing of the complaint, for use by the court in maintaining statistical records. The summons explains that the defendant has been sued and has a certain time limit within which to respond.

LEGAL TERMS

jurisdiction
A court's authority to hear a certain type of case.

diversity
The right to file a lawsuit based upon nonfederal claims in federal court; parties must be from different states and the matter in controversy must be more than $50,000.

complaint
Initial document filed in a lawsuit; sets forth the basis of the plaintiff's claims and requests certain remedies.

summons
Document served with the complaint that explains that the defendant has been sued and has a certain time limit in which to respond.

civil cover sheet
Form required at the time of filing of the complaint for court use in maintaining certain statistical records.

Demand for Jury Trial

If the plaintiff desires a jury trial, that demand should be made in the complaint and reflected in the civil cover sheet. If the plaintiff has not sought a jury trial but the defendant wants one, the request for a jury trial should be made in the defendant's answer.

Report of a Trademark Action

The Lanham Act requires that the clerk of the federal court report all actions brought under the Act to the Commissioner of Patents and Trademarks.[21] A notice of the action will appear in the *Official Gazette* for trademarks.

Drafting the Complaint

The example figure 10-11 provides the basic elements of a trademark complaint based upon a claim of infringement of a federally registered trademark, common law infringement, violation of section 43(a) and dilution.

TRADEMARK COMPLAINT

LAW OFFICES OF JOSEPH SMITH
One Embarcadero, Suite 2727
San Francisco, California 94111
(415) 777-2727

Attorneys for Plaintiff

**IN THE UNITED STATES DISTRICT COURT
NORTHERN DISTRICT OF CALIFORNIA**

Softco, Inc., a California corporation,	)	No.
	)	
	)	
Plaintiff,	)	COMPLAINT
	)	
v.	)	
	)	
Diskco, Inc., a New York corporation	)	
	)	
	)	
Defendant.	)	
	)	

FIGURE 10-11
Sample trademark complaint

JURISDICTION

1. Jurisdiction is based upon the Federal Trademark Act, 15 U.S.C. § 1052 *et seq.*, and 28 U.S.C. § 1338(a) for claims relating to infringement of federal trademark rights, and 15 U.S.C. § 1125(a) for claims relating to false designation under the Lanham Act. Jurisdiction over all related common law and state claims is based upon the provisions of 15 U.S.C. § 1338(b).

THE PARTIES

2. Softco, Inc. (referred to in this Complaint as "plaintiff") is a valid California corporation with its principal place of business in San Mateo County, California, within the Northern District of California.

3. On information and belief, Diskco, Inc. (referred to in this Complaint as "defendant") is a valid New York corporation with its principal place of business in Albany, New York.

COUNT ONE
(Federal Trademark Infringement—15 U.S.C. § 1051 *et seq.*)

4. On or about January 1, 1991, plaintiff adopted and first used the trademark THE BIG SQUEEZY on computer software for use in compressing data on magnetic storage devices. Plaintiff is the owner of a federal registration of the mark for such products which issued on March 1, 1991. Plaintiff's registration is currently in full force and effect.

5. A copy of plaintiff's referenced federal registration is attached to this Complaint as Exhibit A.

6. Continuously since January 1, 1991, plaintiff has used the trademark THE BIG SQUEEZY to identify its software products and to distinguish them from those made by others.

7. Plaintiff extensively advertises its software products bearing its federally registered trademark, THE BIG SQUEEZY, to the consuming public and to the software distributing trade. Plaintiff's trademark THE BIG SQUEEZY has become and is widely and generally known to the consuming public and software trade and has acquired significant meaning as a symbol of plaintiff's good will in the industry.

8. Sales of plaintiff's software products bearing the trademark THE BIG SQUEEZY in the United States alone have been in excess of one million dollars ($1,000,000) for the year ending in 1991 and plaintiff has spent in excess of two hundred thousand dollars ($200,000) advertising and promoting its software products bearing THE BIG SQUEEZY trademark over that same time period.

9. Plaintiff is informed and believes that defendant has infringed plaintiff's trademark by defendant's adoption and use of the name EASY SQUEEZEE.

10. Plaintiff is informed and believes that defendant has offered and continues to offer for sale to the public, in interstate commerce, software products which are used for purposes of data compression bearing the name, EASY SQUEEZEE.

11. Plaintiff is informed and believes that plaintiff's software products bearing the trademark THE BIG SQUEEZY are distributed through the same trade channels, are offered for sale to the public through the same retail outlets, and are purchased

FIGURE 10-11
(Continued)

by the same class of customers as defendant's software products which bear the designation EASY SQUEEZEE.

12.   Since acquiring federal registration on March 1, 1991, plaintiff has given notice that its mark is registered in the U.S. Patent and Trademark Office. Prior to the commencement of this action, plaintiff duly advised defendant by a letter dated February 1, 1992, of plaintiff's claims with respect to defendant's use of the name EASY SQUEEZEE. A copy of that letter is attached to this Complaint as Exhibit B.

13.   Plaintiff's trademark THE BIG SQUEEZY and defendant's designation EASY SQUEEZEE are similar in sound and appearance, convey the same commercial impression, and increase the likelihood of public confusion.

14.   Defendant's alleged acts of infringement are without permission or authority of plaintiff and plaintiff is informed and believes that defendant's use of its name, EASY SQUEEZEE, is likely, when applied to defendant's software products, to cause confusion, or to cause mistake, or to deceive.

15.   Unless the relief prayed for is granted, plaintiff will be hindered and obstructed by defendant's use of the designation EASY SQUEEZEE upon its software products, and will suffer irreparable loss by the diversion of its customers and trade. It would be difficult to ascertain the amount of compensation which could afford plaintiff adequate relief for such continuing acts. Plaintiff's remedy at law is not adequate to compensate it for the injuries threatened.

COUNT TWO
(Unfair Competition by Infringement of
Common Law Trademark Rights)

16.   Plaintiff repeats and realleges Paragraphs 1 through 12 inclusive.

17.   Plaintiff's claim for common law trademark infringement is joined with a substantial and related claim under the trademark laws of the United States, 15 U.S.C. § 1051 *et seq.*

18.   By virtue of defendant's actions pleaded above, defendant has infringed upon the common law trademark rights of plaintiff.

19.   The conduct of defendant as herein alleged has damaged plaintiff and will, unless restrained, further impair, if not destroy, plaintiff's trademark and good will and plaintiff has no adequate remedy at law.

COUNT THREE
(False Designation—Lanham Act § 43(a))

20.   Plaintiff repeats and realleges Paragraphs 1 through 12, inclusive, and Paragraphs 15 through 16, inclusive.

21.   This is a claim for federal unfair competition arising under section 43(a) of the Federal Trademark Act of 1946, as amended (15 U.S.C. § 1125(a)).

22.   Plaintiff is informed and believes that defendant has, through its use of the designation EASY SQUEEZEE, knowingly caused goods to enter into commerce, which goods bear a false description and a false designation of origin. The false description and false designation of origin cause irreparable damage to the plaintiff and deceive the public, as purchasers will be confused as to the true source, sponsorship, or affiliation of said goods of defendant.

FIGURE 10-11
(Continued)

23. Defendant has engaged in acts of unfair competition with plaintiff which are in violation of 15 U.S.C. § 1125(a).

24. The conduct of defendant as herein alleged has damaged plaintiff and will, unless restrained, further impair, if not destroy, plaintiff's trademark and good will and plaintiff has no adequate remedy at law.

COUNT IV
(Dilution—Cal. Bus & Prof. Code § 14330)

25. Plaintiff repeats and realleges Paragraphs 1 through 12, 15 through 16, and 19 through 21, inclusive.

26. This is a claim for dilution of plaintiff's trademark pursuant to Cal. Bus & Prof. Code § 14330, which is joined with a substantial and related claim under the trademark laws of the United States.

27. The defendant has, by its use of the designation EASY SQUEEZEE on the same or similar products of the same class as plaintiff's software, diluted the distinctive quality of plaintiff's mark and thereby injured plaintiff's business reputation.

28. The conduct of defendant as herein alleged has damaged plaintiff and will, unless restrained, further impair, if not destroy, plaintiff's trademark and good will and plaintiff has no adequate remedy at law and is therefore entitled to invoke the injunctive provisions of Cal. Bus. & Prof. Code §§ 14330 and 14340.

WHEREFORE, plaintiff prays for:

1. This Court to grant an injunction enjoining defendant from directly or indirectly using EASY SQUEEZEE or any other mark, word, name, or device which by colorable imitation or otherwise is likely to cause confusion, mistake, or to deceive and from otherwise unfairly competing with plaintiff.

2. Damages against defendant in the amount of $500,000 and that defendant be required to account to plaintiff for any and all profits derived by defendant by reason of its trademark infringement and unfair competition and for all damages sustained by plaintiff by reason of the acts complained of.

3. An order requiring defendant to deliver to plaintiff for destruction all labels, containers, literature, advertising, and other materials bearing the EASY SQUEEZEE trademark.

4. The Court to grant such other and further relief as it shall deem just.

FIGURE 10-11
(Continued)

Declaratory Relief

Sometimes, after receiving a cease and desist letter, or after the breakdown of negotiations to settle a dispute, the alleged infringer may ask the federal courts for **declaratory relief.** This is not a claim for monetary damages, but instead is a request that the court sort out the rights and obligations of the parties. The party seeking declaratory relief need only establish that an actual controversy exists regarding a matter within federal court subject matter jurisdiction.

The Answer

In federal court, a response to the trademark complaint must be served within 20 days of service. In state court, the period for responding may vary depending upon the state statute. Unless the defendant attacks the complaint or service (e.g., argues that service is improper or that the court has no jurisdiction), the proper response is an **answer**. The answer is a response to the complaint in which the defendant admits or denies the complaint's allegations and provides a list of defenses. The answer, like the complaint, includes a caption and is filed with the court.

In the answer to a federal court complaint, the plaintiff goes through each paragraph of the complaint and generally responds one of four ways:

1. **Defendant denies all allegations of the paragraph.**
   Example— In answer to Paragraph 16 of the Complaint, Defendant denies each and every allegation contained in that paragraph.

2. **Defendant admits all allegations of the paragraph.**
   Example— In answer to Paragraph 3 of the Complaint, Defendant admits each and every allegation contained in that paragraph.

3. **Defendant lacks information to form a response to a paragraph.**
   Example— In answer to Paragraph 5 of the Complaint, defendant is without sufficient information or belief upon which to base an answer to the allegations of this paragraph and, based upon such lack of information and belief, denies each and every allegation in that paragraph.

4. **Defendant denies or admits part of a paragraph.**
   Example— In answer to Paragraph 7 of the Complaint, defendant admits it is the owner of a trademark *Easy Squeezee*. Except as expressly admitted, defendant denies each and every remaining allegation of this paragraph.

In addition to responding to each allegation, the answer should provide a list of defenses. These defenses should each be listed separately. All that is necessary is that the basis for the defense be stated; no further elaboration is required. For example, if the defendant wished to offer the defense of unclean hands because the plaintiff had falsified a registration, the defense would be stated as follows:

EXAMPLE: First Affirmative Defense—Unclean Hands

Plaintiff is barred from obtaining relief on any of the claims alleged in the Complaint by its unclean hands in taking actions calculated to unfairly deceive the public by falsifying documents filed with the United States Patent and Trademark Office.

Counterclaims

If the defendant wishes to bring an action against the plaintiff, a **counterclaim** must be filed at the time the answer is filed. A counterclaim is a claim for relief usually asserted by the defendant against an opposing party, usually the plaintiff. A counterclaim is compulsory (i.e., it *must* be brought) if the claim arises out of the same transaction or occurrence that is the subject of the complaint.

Discovery

The issues regarding trademark infringement are primarily factual. Are the marks similar? Are the goods similar? Did the defendant know of the plaintiff's mark? Is there actual confusion? Although legal research is an important element in the preparation of a trademark lawsuit, factual research is crucial. Therefore, the discovery process is invaluable in resolving trademark litigation.

There are specific rules regarding the discovery process, and if a dispute arises during the exchange of information, the federal district court will rule on the issues. The four common forms of discovery are interrogatories, production of documents, depositions, and requests for admissions. The Federal Rules of Civil Procedure provide rules regarding discovery, such as the format of interrogatories and the time in which to respond.[22] In addition, local court rules also may set rules regarding discovery procedures and formats.

Interrogatories

Interrogatories are written questions that must be answered under oath. They are usually presented in special formats and include definitions of certain terms. There is a time limit for responding to interrogatories and the recipient should carefully calendar the response. Interrogatories are only exchanged among parties to the lawsuit (i.e., persons named in the caption of the complaint or counterclaim). Often, local rules may affect the content of interrogatories (e.g., limiting them to identification of claims, damages, documents, or witnesses).

Requests for Admissions

A **request for admission** is a request for a party to the lawsuit to admit the truthfulness of a fact or statement. For example, the plaintiff may request that the defendant admit or deny the authenticity of annual sales figures. This request is submitted in writing and, like an interrogatory, the response should be calendared. Requests for admissions are only exchanged among parties to the lawsuit and are commonly used to verify the authenticity

LEGAL TERMS

answer
Written response to the complaint, in which the defendant admits or denies the complaint's allegations and provides a list of defenses.

counterclaim
Claim for relief usually asserted by the defendant against an opposing party, usually the plaintiff.

interrogatories
Written questions that must be answered under oath.

request for admissions
Request for a party to the lawsuit to admit the truthfulness of a fact or statement.

of documents. Some attorneys combine the use of interrogatories and requests for admissions. For example, if the defendant does not admit a request for admission, the plaintiff may include an interrogatory requesting information or facts regarding the failure to admit.

Depositions

Perhaps the most effective tool for obtaining information is the **deposition.** A deposition is oral or written testimony of a party or witness, given under oath. An attorney may depose any person who may have information relevant to the lawsuit. The deposition is noticed by the transmission of a Notice of Deposition. If the witness is not a party to the lawsuit, the deposing party may have to subpoena the witness to assure that the deposition may be taken. Questions are asked and answered in the presence of a court reporter. Afterward, a transcript of the deposition is provided to the parties. Documents may also be requested at the deposition. It is through this means that documents are obtained from nonparties to the lawsuit. Many attorneys prefer to combine the use of depositions and document requests.

Production of Documents

A **request for production of documents** is a method by which a party to the lawsuit may obtain documents or other physical evidence. The request is written and served on the other party. The time for response should be calendared.

Motion for Preliminary Injunction

As explained in chapter 6, a **motion** is a request for an order of the court. If a party seeks an order to preliminarily enjoin the use of an allegedly infringing mark, the moving party would make a **motion for preliminary injunction.**

Previously in this chapter, we discussed the standards for a temporary restraining order and a preliminary injunction. The documentation required for these motions is extensive. Intensive factual and legal research must be performed in a short time period. Occasionally, a party may make a request for expedited discovery. The moving party requests an order shortening the normal discovery periods so that information can be gathered prior to the hearing on the motion for a preliminary injunction. In addition, the moving party must anticipate payment of a bond, to insure payment for any damages suffered by a party who is found to have been wrongfully enjoined. Other documentation that must be furnished includes affidavits from persons supporting or verifying the moving party's position. For example, if a person is seeking to enjoin use of a similar mark for real estate mortgage brokerage services, affidavits should be prepared from persons who consume or transact such services (e.g., real estate brokers, lenders, sellers of real property). A checklist for a motion for a preliminary injunction is provided later in this chapter.

Motion for Summary Judgment

Either party in a trademark infringement lawsuit also may bring a **motion for summary judgment.** This a request that the court order a judgment without having a trial because there is no genuine issue as to any material facts. This may prove challenging in a trademark case because secondary meaning and likelihood of confusion are both considered factual issues. As one judge stated, it is rare that the facts in a trademark case are so black and white that it can be stated unequivocally there is no genuine issue as to any material fact.

However, certain cases may lend themselves to summary judgment. For example, in the *Gallo* case, the trial court's final determination was based upon the plaintiff's motion for summary judgment. A motion for summary judgment is a means of ending the litigation. It requires extensive proof and documentation, including declarations under oath from witnesses and parties.

Expert Witnesses

A trademark infringement lawsuit may require the opinion or testimony of a person who is an expert. For example, in a case involving use of survey evidence, it may be necessary to have testimony from a survey expert who can explain the survey procedures and the accuracy of the survey. Information about expert witnesses and the subject matter and substance of their expected testimony is discoverable prior to trial. Normally, interrogatories are propounded which inquire into each party's choice of expert witnesses. Prior to trial, each party identifies its expert witnesses by means of an "Identification of Expert Witness," an example of which is provided in chapter 12.

Pretrial Activities

The procedures and documentation required for trial are fully explained in other publications for paralegals, such as *Civil Litigation for the Paralegal* by Peggy Kerley *et al.* Preparation for trial includes researching law, indexing evidence, and identifying witnesses. The Federal Rules of Civil Procedure and local rules must be carefully examined to determine rules regarding marking and admission of evidence. Trademark trials almost always require admission of evidence as to the ownership and validity of the mark at issue. These are matters of factual proof and require documentation and testimony from the owners of the mark, consumers, distributors, and other relevant persons in the field of goods or services. The legal assistant may be required to organize this evidence for assistance in trial presentation. During trial, the paralegal may also be involved in the management and organization

LEGAL TERMS

deposition
　Oral or written testimony of a party or witness, given under oath.

request for production of documents
　Means by which a party to a lawsuit may obtain documents or other physical evidence.

motion
　Request for an order of the court.

motion for preliminary injunction
　Request that the court issue an order directing the defendant to stop certain activities.

motion for summary judgment
　Request that the court order a judgment without having a trial, because there is no genuine issue as to any material fact(s).

of physical evidence, such as product containers or advertisements documenting use.

In addition, trademark litigation requires the use of survey evidence. For example, a survey may be used to prove that the public now considers a mark to have become the generic term for the goods. Surveys are not conducted by the attorney or the staff, but the attorney may be involved in the creation or direction of the survey. A survey expert is generally used to introduce the results of any survey.

The paralegal assisting in a trademark infringement trial should use a *trial notebook,* a binder created to index and reference the important documentation necessary to litigate a case. Generally, the sections of a trial notebook include:

1. A directory of the parties and witnesses, including names, addresses, and telephone numbers, with important notations. This should be maintained on a computer database and periodically reprinted as it is updated.

2. A listing of the litigation files and their contents. Each file should have a cover sheet listing its contents. These cover sheets should be reproduced and kept in the binder so that the paralegal can easily locate documents.

3. Either a copy of pleadings and motions, or at least a listing of such filings and their location in the litigation files.

4. A chronology of events and filings, including all events from creation of the mark to the present.

5. Listings of all witnesses for each party. A separate portion should be devoted to expert witnesses.

6. Summaries of relevant discovery. If there is room, all deposition summaries should be included; if not, indexes of where the summaries are located should be provided.

7. Relevant legal research, whether included in full or indexed.

8. Trial notes or plans, task lists, and attorney notes, each included in a separate section.

In any event, evidence must be indexed, witnesses must be identified and prepared, and case law must be researched

In addition, certain matters may require pretrial motions. For example, a party may wish to limit the admission of certain evidence prior to trial. In that case, a **motion in limine** would be filed. A motion in limine is a request made to the court, usually prior to trial, that certain information not be presented to the jury. In addition, lists of expert witnesses should be prepared and exchanged amoung the parties.

One factor that will determine the extent and direction of the preparation is wether the trial will be by jury. If the trial is to a jury, the attorney may direct preparation of exhibits, jury instructions, and other jury-oriented materials. **Jury instructions** are explanations of the legal rules that the jury shall use in reaching a verdict. For example, a jury instruction may state that registration creates a presumption of validity of the registered mark, of the registrant's ownership of the mark, and of the exclusive rights to use the registered mark in commerce on or in connection with the goods or services specified in the registration.

The Trial

The procedures and documentation required for trial are fully explained in other publications for paralegals, such as *Civil Litigation for the Paralegal* by Peggy Kerley *et al.* However, certain aspects of trademark litigation require activity by legal assistance. As mentioned, trademark trials almost always require admission of evidence as to the ownership and validity of the mark at issue.

In addition, a trademark infringement trial very often requires the admission of survey evidence. The purpose of the survey evidence is to convince the judge or jury as to how a targeted group of consumers perceives the issues in the case (e.g., does the target audience believe that the plaintiff's mark is really the generic term for the goods?). The Federal Judicial Center's *Manual for Coplex Litigation* offers some recommendation as to the presentation of survey evidence, as does *McCarthy on Trademarks and Unfair Competition.*

Appeal

Either party may appeal the final determination of the trial court. An appeal in federal court would be made to the U.S. Court of Appeals in the appropriate circuit. A state court appeal would be made to the appropriate state appellate court. Both sides submit appellate briefs. A three-member panel of judges will review the trial court record to determine if a legal error occurred. An example of a legal is a judge not permitting the introduction of evidence relevant to the case. An appellate court ruling requires a majority determination of the three judges. A ruling from the U.S. Supreme Court or a state supreme court also requires a majority of the panel hearing the case.

Litigation Checklists

The following checklists are for plaintiffs and defendants involved in a trademark infringement lawsuit.

Trademark Infringement Dispute: Plaintiff's Checklist

■ **Interview the Client**. The following information should be obtained:
  ☐ Trademark owner's name, address, and business form (i.e., corporation, partnership, etc.).
  ☐ Information about all registrations, licenses, and assignments regarding the trademark.

LEGAL TERMS

motion in limine
Request made to the court, usually prior to the trial, that certain information not be presented to the jury.

jury instructions
Explanations of the legal rules that the jury shall use in reaching a verdict.

    ☐ If registration has not been made or an assignment has not been filed, proceed with filing at Patent and Trademark Office.

    ☐ Information about trademark owner's use of notice (i.e., the ® or ™ symbol).

    ☐ Extent of sales and advertising of the trademark.

    ☐ Owner's knowledge and discovery of the trademark infringement.

■ **Acquire Evidence of the Infringement.** It is extremely difficult to make a case for trademark infringement without direct proof of the infringing activity.

    ☐ Purchase the infringing merchandise or acquire evidence of advertising.

    ☐ Trace the chain of distribution of goods with the infringing trademark (locate distributors and retailers of infringing merchandise, as this may lead to other defendants).

■ **Obtain Information about All Infringing Parties.** The trademark owner should have researched the infringement to determine the names of the infringing parties.

    ☐ Determine name, address and business form of all infringing parties (databases such as LEXIS®, Dialog® or Westlaw® may provide information regarding business form (i.e., corporation or partnership) and agent for service).

    ☐ Set up a computer index (a directory of all persons involved in litigation, the facts, relationships, and caselaw).

    ☐ Investigate whether the infringing party has been sued for trademark infringement previously.

    ☐ Order a trademark search regarding the infringing trademark.

■ **Review Legal Claims and Possible Defenses Regarding Infringement.**

    ☐ Determine if additional claims, such as trade secrecy, contract, trade dress infringement, or other contract, tort, or related claims, can be made as a result of the infringing activity.

    ☐ List *all* possible trademark and equitable defenses and review the list with the client.

    ☐ Perform legal research and review caselaw and statutes regarding infringement issues.

    ☐ Consider special rules applying to specific trademarks (e.g., rights regarding surnames, geographic marks, etc).

■ **Confront the Infringer: Prepare Cease and Desist Letter.** As explained earlier in this chapter, the cease and desist letter is a summary of the trademark owner's claims and a request that the recipient of the letter halt all infringing activity.

    ☐ Consider whether a cease and desist letter will trigger destruction of evidence or a declaratory action. Discuss with the client.

■ **Attempt Settlement of the Dispute.**

    ☐ Determine sums that will compensate the plaintiff for all damages (including attorney fees and related costs).

    ☐ Review state law regarding required language for settlement agreements.

☐ Consider what nonmonetary remedies are sought (i.e., does the plaintiff want destruction of infringing merchandise?).

■ **Consider Alternative Dispute Resolution.**

☐ Is there an agreement between the parties compelling arbitration or mediation?

☐ Will both parties submit to mediation or arbitration? If so, where?

☐ Locate arbitration or mediation rules and procedures for the arbitrating entity (e.g., American Arbitration Association).

■ **File the Lawsuit.**

☐ Review appropriate rules of civil procedure and obtain local court rules.

☐ Obtain the civil cover sheet and summons from the federal court clerk.

☐ Determine venue.

☐ Assist in preparation of the complaint.

☐ Arrange for filing of the complaint and issuance of a summons.

☐ Coordinate service of process.

■ **Discovery.** Coordination of discovery requires preparation of a discovery plan. Many attorneys begin the procedure with interrogatories to determine names and addresses of relevant parties. This is often followed by depositions and requests for production of documents. Finally, requests for admissions are used to confirm or deny relevant information.

☐ Calendar all discovery received and propounded for appropriate deadlines.

☐ Summarize and index depositions, interrogatory responses, and documents for use at trial.

■ **Trial.**

☐ Prepare lists of witnesses (and expert witnesses).

☐ Review evidence regarding pretrial motions (e.g., motions in limine).

☐ Prepare trial notebook.

☐ Assist in preparation of jury instructions.

Checklist for Motion for Preliminary Injunction or Temporary Restraining Order

(The following documents may required.)

■ **Motion** (or Order to Show Cause, for a TRO).

■ **Complaint**—Pleading upon which the claim of infringement is based.

■ **Affidavits or Declarations in Support**—Statements by experts, industry authorities, trade persons, advertising companies, or the parties, to provide a foundation for demonstrating likelihood of success and irreparable harm.

■ **Points and Authorities (Memorandum of Law)**—Statement incorporating evidence and law and demonstrating the basis for the grant of injunctive relief.

■ **Proposed Order**—A proposed order that the court may use to grant the injunctive relief.

■ **Bond**—If required by the court.

- **Order for Impoundment**—If required.
- **Request for Expedited Discovery**—If necessary, a "fast-track" plan for discovery of evidence (deposition notices, schedule, and document requests should be prepared).

Note: Preliminary injunctions brought under the Trademark Counterfeiting Act of 1984 require affidavits relevant to that statute (15 U.S.C. §§ 1051, 1116, and 1117(b)).

Trademark Infringement Dispute: Defendant's Checklist

- **Interview the Client.** The following information should be obtained:
  - ☐ Defendant's name, address, and business form (i.e., corporation, partnership, etc.).
  - ☐ Information about all registrations, licenses, and assignments regarding the defendant's trademark.
  - ☐ If registration of the defendant's mark has not been made, consider registration.
  - ☐ Information about the defendant's use of notice (i.e., the ® or ™ symbol).
  - ☐ Extent of sales and advertising of the trademark.
  - ☐ Defendant's knowledge of the infringement and intent.
  - ☐ Information regarding the defendant's access to the plaintiff's trademark.
  - ☐ Does the defendant have insurance that covers this type of dispute?
- **Review the Plaintiff's Trademark and Title to the Trademark.**
  - ☐ Perform a trademark search for the plaintiff's trademark regarding any questions of ownership.
  - ☐ Acquire copies of the trademark and examine for notice and other issues of formality.
- **Obtain Information about All Parties.**
  - ☐ Determine name, address, and business form of all possible parties to the lawsuit, including other potential defendants (databases such as LEXIS®, Dialog®, or Westlaw® may provide information regarding business form (i.e., corporation or partnership) and agent for service).
  - ☐ Set up a computer index (a directory of all persons involved in the litigation, the facts, relationships, and caselaw).
- **Review Legal Claims and Possible Defenses Regarding Infringement.**
  - ☐ List *all* possible trademark and equitable defenses and review the list with the client.
  - ☐ Perform legal research and review caselaw and statutes regarding infringement issues. Consider special rules applying to specific trademarks (e.g., geographic marks, surnames, etc).
  - ☐ Are there any counterclaims that the defendant may wish to file?
- **Respond to Cease and Desist Letter.**
  - ☐ Review and respond to the accuracy of any allegations in the letter.

- □ Consider whether the defendant should cease activity pending resolution of the dispute.
- □ Consider whether the defendant should file an action for declaratory relief.
- ■ **Attempt Settlement of the Dispute.** A settlement is a written agreement in which the parties formally resolve the infringement dispute.
- ■ **Consider Alternative Dispute Resolution.**
  - □ Is there an agreement between the parties compelling arbitration or mediation?
  - □ Will both parties submit to mediation or arbitration?
- ■ **Respond to the Complaint.**
  - □ Calendar response—20 days from service.
  - □ Review rules of civil procedure and obtain local court rules.
  - □ Determine whether venue or jurisdiction is improper.
  - □ Assist in preparation of the answer.
  - □ If appropriate, prepare a counterclaim.
- ■ **Discovery.** Coordination of discovery requires preparation of a discovery plan. Many attorneys begin the procedure with interrogatories to determine names and addresses of relevant parties. This is often followed by depositions and requests for production of documents. Finally, requests for admissions are used to confirm or deny relevant information.
  - □ Calendar all discovery received and propounded for appropriate deadlines.
  - □ Summarize and index depositions, interrogatory responses, and documents for use at trial.
- ■ **Trial.**
  - □ Prepare lists of witnesses (and expert witnesses).
  - □ Review evidence regarding pretrial motions (e.g., motions in limine).
  - □ Prepare trial notebook.
  - □ Assist in preparation of jury instructions.

SUMMARY

10.1 Trademark documentation generally can be categorized in one of five types of trademark files: use, registration, postregistration documents, licensing, and infringement. Rules of proper trademark usage can be summarized in a company's trademark handbook. Proper notice of a federal trademark registration (i.e., the ® symbol or "Registered in U.S. Patent & Trademark Office") should be included with use of the mark. The continued use, renewability, and incontestability of a federal trademark are determined by filing specific affidavits with the Patent and Trademark Office. Genericide is the process by which trademark rights are abandoned because consumers have begun to think of the trademark as the descriptive name for the goods.

10.2   Ownership of trademark rights is created by their use in commerce, not by creation of the trademark. A trademark license is an agreement granting limited rights to a trademark. An assignment is a transfer of ownership and also requires a transfer of the good will associated with the mark.

10.3   An application for a federal trademark may be opposed at any time prior to registration in an opposition proceeding. A registration issued by the Patent and Trademark Office also may be canceled upon sufficient proof in a proceeding known as a cancellation proceeding. These inter partes proceedings are before the Trademark Trial and Appeal Board and involve many of the same procedures used in other federal civil litigation.

10.4   Likelihood of confusion occurs when it is probable that purchasers of goods will be confused by a junior user's trademark. The various factors in weighing likelihood of confusion include strength of the mark, similarity of the goods, similarity of the marks, degree of care exercised by the consumer, the defendant's intent, and actual confusion, if any.

10.5   A trademark infringement lawsuit may involve additional claims, such as dilution (in which the distinctive quality of a mark is reduced), common law unfair competition, and false advertising or false designation of origin (also known as a Section 43(a) claim).

10.6   Defenses to infringement include genericide, abandonment through nonuse, lack of secondary meaning, or a failure to follow statutory formalities. In addition, trademark defenses include defenses common to all litigation, such as estoppel, unclean hands, and laches.

10.7   The most important remedy sought in trademark infringement litigation is a cessation of use of the infringing mark, usually accomplished by an injunction. In addition, the plaintiff may obtain damages based upon actual losses suffered as a result of the infringement, as well as any profits by the defendant that are not included in the plaintiff's losses. On rare occasions, attorney fees are awarded.

10.8   It is in the best interest of all parties to conclude any infringement disputes equitably and quickly. The cease and desist letter informs the infringing party of the nature of the infringement and the remedies available to the trademark owner, and requests the immediate cessation of all infringing activity. Instead of resolving a dispute in a courtroom, some parties agree to have their problem settled privately through informal procedures known as arbitration or mediation. The parties may settle the case at any point prior to the final determination by the judge or jury. A settlement is an agreement between the parties in which the dispute is resolved.

10.9   After a decision is made as to which parties shall be named as defendants, determinations must be made as to jurisdiction, which is the right of a court to hear a certain case, and venue, which is the geographic location of the court. Then a complaint is drafted, stating the basis for the lawsuit, and served on each defendant. The defendant has a certain time period to respond to the complaint. After the defendant answers the complaint, a process of discovery begins, during which time the parties, following legal rules, investigate the merits and defenses of the case. Each party may request orders from the court. These requests are known as motions. Finally, a trial is held and a determination made as to liability. A judgment is then issued by the court. If either party is dissatisfied with the result of the trial, an appeal may be taken. Alternatively, the parties may, at any point, agree to settle the matter. In that event, the case is dismissed.

NOTES

1. 15 U.S.C. § 1111 (notice of registration; Lanham Act § 29).
2. 15 U.S.C. § 1058 (Section 8 affidavit; Lanham Act § 8).
3. 15 U.S.C. § 1065 (incontestability; Lanham Act § 15).
4. 15 U.S.C. § 1059 (renewal; Lanham Act § 9).
5. 15 U.S.C. § 1127 (definition of trademark abandonment; Lanham Act § 45). *See also* 15 U.S.C. §§ 1051, 1062, 1064, 1115.
6. 15 U.S.C. §§ 1064, 1065 (generic terms; Lanham Act §§ 14, 15).
7. 15 U.S.C. § 1060 (assignment; Lanham Act § 10).
8. 37 C.F.R. § 3.1 *et seq.* (recording assignment).
9. 15 U.S.C. § 1064 (cancellation; Lanham Act § 14); 15 U.S.C. § 1063 (opposition; Lanham Act § 13).
10. 37 C.F.R. § 2.102 (extension of time for filing opposition).
11. 37 C.F.R. § 2.106 (answer to notice of opposition); 37 C.F.R. § 2.114 (answer to petition for cancellation).
12. 15 U.S.C. § 1066 (interference proceedings; Lanham Act § 16); 37 C.F.R. §§ 2.91-2.98.
13. 15 U.S.C. § 1067 (concurrent use; Lanham Act § 17); 37 C.F.R. §§ 2.42, 2.49.
14. 15 U.S.C. § 1125(a) (Lanham Act § 43(a)).
15. 15 U.S.C. § 1116 (injunctions; Lanham Act § 34).
16. 15 U.S.C. § 1117 (damages; Lanham Act § 35).
17. 15 U.S.C. § 1118 (destruction of material bearing infringing mark; Lanham Act § 36).
18. 15 U.S.C. § 1120 (fraudulent statement; Lanham Act § 38).
19. 28 U.S.C. §§ 1331, 1338 (federal jurisdiction); 15 U.S.C. § 1221 (Lanham Act § 39).
20. 28 U.S.C. § 1391(a)-(c) (trademark infringment venue).
21. 15 U.S.C. § 1116(a) (report of trademark action; Lanham Act § 34(c)).
22. Fed. R. Civ. P. 26 (federal discovery).

QUESTIONS FOR REVIEW AND DISCUSSION

1. Why do companies discourage the use of a trademark as a noun or verb?

2. Under what circumstances should the ® symbol be used? What alternative notice may be used instead of the ® symbol?

3. What is the danger of not using the ® symbol on a federally registered mark?

4. Why do some companies choose to use house marks in conjuction with product marks (i.e., Microsoft® Windows™) while other companies choose not to use house marks?

5. What is the calendaring requirement for a section 8 affidavit? What affidavit is often filed at the same time?

6. When should a renewal application (Section 9 affidavit) be filed?

7. What are the different forms of abandonment under the Lanham Act?

8. How does genericide occur?

9. What must always be transferred when assigning a trademark?

10. What is the advantage of recording an assignment with the Patent and Trademark Office?

11. What is the difference between an opposition proceeding and a cancellation proceeding?

12. What are the factors used to make a likelihood of confusion determination?

ACTIVITIES

1. Review the factual situation in the Commentary. Could Nancy be prohibited from creating a similar logo design for a third software company?

2. What is the difference between the materials that might be kept in office files for a service mark rather than a trademark? What differences might there be in litigating a dispute over service mark infringement instead of trademark infringement?

3. Locate the state trademark act and antidilution statute, if any, for your state in your state codes.

4. Pick a famous trademark and prepare an assignment of trademark rights. What factors would be important to consider when preparing such a document?

PROJECT

Review the facts in the *Gallo* case (§ 10.9). Imagine that a new company began selling *Gallows* wine, which is intended as a parody of the *Gallo* trademark. Divide the class into parties representing the E&J Gallo company and the parodist wine company. What arguments could each party make? What settlement, if any, might be proposed? Is there any reason why the E&J Gallo company might not want to settle?

FOR MORE INFORMATION

Trademark Jury Instructions

Examples of jury instructions for use in trademark litigation can be found in:

American Bar Association, *Model Jury Instructions For Business Tort Litigation* (1980). Available from the American Bar Association, 750 North Lakeshore Drive, Chicago, IL 60611.

Kramer & Brufsky, *Trademark Law Practice Forms* (Clark Boardman Callaghan 1986).

CHAPTER 11
Patents: Rights and Limitations

An idea can turn to dust or magic, depending on the talent that rubs against it.

William Bernbach (1982)

OUTLINE

COMMENTARY

On March 1, 1992, a California company, Effectsco, begins selling Fogarama, *a fog-producing device used for theatrical purposes and at amusement parks. Unlike other fog-making devices,* Fogarama *does not use potentially hazardous combustion products and does not leave an oily residue. Instead, the device atomizes water and ejects the atomized liquid in small clusters by means of a series of stainless steel jets. The* Fogarama *produces a fog without odor or contamination problems and is capable of producing substantial volumes of fog at a very modest cost. On January 15, 1992, Dave, an engineer at Effectsco (and the inventor of the fog machine) gives a speech about how the device works to a convention of special effects engineers in New York. At the convention, Dave describes how he invented the fog machine at home. He distributes a printed handout detailing the methodology of the invention. On April 1, 1993, the president of Effectsco asks the law office where you work to file a patent application for the* Fogarama *machine.*

OBJECTIVES

In the previous chapter you learned about trade secrets and the methods of protecting confidential business information. In this chapter you will be introduced to the concepts of patent law. After reading Chapter 11, you will be able to:

- Locate sources of patent law.
- Explain the underlying rationale for granting patent protection.
- Outline the requirements for granting a utility patent.
- Distinguish between a utility patent and a plant or design patent.
- Explain patent rights and the limitations on patent rights.
- Describe the statutory classes for a utility patent.
- Differentiate between a design patent and a copyright.
- Discuss the principle of nonobviousness.
- Identify an article of manufacture, a machine, or a process.
- Define file wrapper estoppel and the doctrine of equivalents.
- Prepare an assignment of patent rights.

11.1 SOURCES OF PATENT LAW

In 1849, Walter Hunt registered a patent for a small metal device—a pin that fastened pieces of cloth together. What was remarkable about Hunt's device was that it could be used without leaving a protruding point (e.g., enabling parents to diaper babies without fear that the infant would be injured). Hunt's safety pin is now taken for granted, but at the time of its debut, it was innovative.

To encourage new inventions, a limited monopoly is granted to the patent owner, officially known as the grant of *Letters Patent*. In the United States, this grant of patent rights occurs only upon registration of the invention with the U.S. Patent and Trademark Office (acting under the authority of the U.S. patent statutes). Unlike copyright and trademark law, no rights are granted under patent law until the invention or discovery has been registered. Assuming the patent owner pays certain maintenance fees, the patent expires after 17 years from the date of registration. After that time, the public is free to make, use, or sell the invention. The grant of patent rights has been compared to an agreement between the United States and an inventor. The inventor discloses the invention and for a limited time (17 years) the inventor can monopolize the rights to it. However, when the patent expires, the invention enters the public domain where any person may freely make, sell, or use it. The laws protecting U.S. patent rights are derived from the Constitution, and the patent owner may resort to litigation in the federal courts to enforce these rights.

Federal Law and Preemption

Article 1, § 8, clause 8 of the U.S. Constitution grants Congress the power "to promote the progress of science and useful arts, by securing for a limited time to authors and inventors the exclusive right to their respective writings and discoveries." As explained in chapter 2, this constitutional grant became the basis for America's copyright and patent laws. Based upon this constitutional grant, Congress passed several patent acts, the most recent of which was the Patent Act of 1952, codified at Title 35 of the United States Code.[1] There have been various amendments to the Patent Act of 1952, and various proposals have also been made to modify the patent laws to conform to the laws of other countries. Regulations regarding patent law and operation of the Patent and Trademark Office are established in Title 37 of the Code of Federal Regulations (C.F.R.).

Although the states may create laws regarding ownership and transfer of ownership of patents, only the federal government can create laws regarding the standards of validity of patents and the grant of patent rights. The federal courts interpret patent laws and are the proper forum for filing patent infringement actions. The resulting judicial precedents are set forth in case reporters such as the *Federal Supplement, Federal Reporter, U.S. Supreme Court Reports,* and *United States Patent Quarterly.* The federal government preempts state law regarding patent validity and infringement. **Preemption** is the authority of the federal government to preclude the states from exercising powers granted to the federal government.

Litigants can appeal federal district court patent decisions to the United States Court of Appeals for the Federal Circuit, also known as the Federal Circuit. The Federal Circuit replaced the Court of Customs and Patent Appeals and Court of Claims in 1982. One of the goals of the Federal Circuit is to create predictability in the interpretation of U.S. patent law. Litigants may appeal decisions rendered by the Federal Circuit to the U.S. Supreme Court. However, the Supreme Court has discretion as to which cases it will hear.

The Patent and Trademark Office

The Patent and Trademark Office (PTO) is responsible for initially determining patentability and issuing federal registration of patents. The Patent and Trademark Office is part of the Department of Commerce and is under the direction of the Commissioner of Patents and Trademarks. The Patent and Trademark Office is located in Virginia, but its mailing address is: Commissioner of Patents and Trademarks, Patent and Trademark Office, Washington DC 20231. Rules and regulations for Patent and Trademark Office activities are established in Title 37 of the Code of Federal Regulations. Other rules are provided in special Patent and Trademark Office publications such as the *Manual of Patent Examining Procedure* (MPEP). When an application is made for a patent that, in the opinion of the Commissioner of Patent and Trademark Office, would interfere with any pending application (or an unexpired patent), a proceeding known as a **patent interference** is instituted in the Patent and Trademark Office and held before the Board of Patent Appeals and Interferences.

LEGAL TERMS

preemption
Authority of the federal government to preclude the states from exercising powers granted to the federal government.

patent interference (also called interference proceeding)
Proceeding instituted in the Patent and Trademark Office to determine any question of priority of invention between two or more parties claiming the same patentable invention.

If a patent examiner finally rejects a patent application (or the claims of patent rights in an application), the applicant may appeal to the Board of Patent Appeals and Interferences. A dissatisfied applicant may seek judicial review of a decision of the Board of Patent Appeals and Interferences in either the United States Court of Appeals for the Federal Circuit or in the U.S. District Court for the District of Columbia.

Registered Attorneys and Agents

An inventor is free to prepare his or her own patent application. However, most inventors prefer to use the services of a certified patent specialist with a scientific or technical background. To represent an inventor, an attorney or agent must be able to converse with the inventor in the technical language of the invention. For this reason, the Patent and Trademark Office established a certification process. Attorneys and nonattorneys alike may take an examination (the Patent Agent's Exam), provided they have a college degree or the equivalent in one of the physical sciences. A **patent agent** is a nonattorney certified and licensed by the Patent and Trademark Office to prepare and prosecute patent applications. Patent agents cannot represent parties in litigation or perform any activity amounting to the practice of law. For example, Susan is a patent agent who represents Dave. She can prepare and file his patent application. She can respond to letters (also known as "office actions") from the examiners at the Patent and Trademark Office and participate in the amendment of the application, but she cannot advise Dave as to the legal consequences of his ownership of the invention (e.g., in a divorce or for purposes of making a will).

A **patent attorney** is an attorney licensed by the Patent and Trademark Office to prepare and prosecute patent applications and to perform other legal tasks. When employing a patent attorney, the inventor executes a **power of attorney**. When employing a patent agent, the inventor executes an **authorization of agent**. These documents must be filed on an application-by-application basis with the Patent and Trademark Office. (Examples of both documents are provided in chapter 12.) The patent attorney or patent agent will prepare the application and respond to objections from the examiner. Often, the inventor's assistance is required. The process of shepherding a patent application through the Patent and Trademark Office is known as **prosecution** of the patent application. The term *patent practitioner* is used to include both patent attorneys and patent agents.

LEGAL TERMS

patent agent
  A nonattorney licensed by the Patent and Trademark Office to prepare and prosecute patent applications.

11.2 SUBJECT MATTER OF PATENTS

Congress has established the subject matter that can be protected under U.S. patent law. This subject matter includes processes, machines, articles of manufacture, and compositions of matter, all of which are considered utility patents. In addition to utility patents, the statutory subject matter also includes ornamental design patents and plant patents. Utility patents are the most common; throughout this chapter, all references will be to utility patents, unless otherwise indicated. Throughout this chapter and chapter 12, the term *invention* will be used to connote both inventions and discoveries.

Utility Patents

Utility patents are granted for inventions or discoveries that are categorized as machines, processes, compositions, articles of manufacture, or new uses of any of these. A utility patent protects any invention of any new and useful process, machine, article of manufacture, composition of matter, or any new and useful improvements to such inventions. (See figure 11-1 for an example.)

A **process** is a method of accomplishing a result through a series of steps involving physical or chemical interactions. For example, in 1927, George Washington Carver patented a process for producing paints and stains. In 1973, Patsy Sherman and Samuel Smith patented a process for treating carpets, commonly known as the *Scotchgard®* process. In 1909, Leo Baekeland patented a method for creating condensation products that led to the modern age of synthetic plastics. The method by which caffeine is extracted from green coffee is a process. A mathematical formula that is applied through a computer process may be patented, and certain computer software programs may also qualify for patent protection. A discussion of the relationship of computer software and patent protection is provided at the end of this section.

The Patent and Trademark Office can also issue a patent for a process considered to be a new or useful improvement of a patented substance or invention. For example, suppose that, during an emergency, a man uses a household plunger to induce respiration. If this *new* use of an old device had never been considered by the medical community, then (in the event the man applies to patent this use), the scope of the resulting patent grant would cover *only* the specific new process—a method for performing emergency resuscitation.

A **machine** is a device, such as engine or an apparatus, that accomplishes a result by the interaction of its parts. For example, in 1844, Linus Yale patented a machine that enabled doors and buildings to be secured (the cylinder lock). In 1855, Isaac Singer patented a device that enabled fabric to be sewn together (the sewing machine). Devices that transmit or transform energy, such as an electrical circuit, can also be machines.

An **article of manufacture** (also known as a *manufacture*) is usually a single object without movable parts, such as a chair, a pencil, or a garden rake. There may be some overlap between machines and an article of manufacture. For example, an article of manufacture may have movable parts that are incidental to the device (e.g., a folding chair). In 1892, Sarah Boone patented an article of manufacture with folding legs that enabled the user to press clothing (the ironing board). In 1841, John Rand patented the collapsible tube, an article of manufacture that became the container for numerous items such as toothpaste and glue.

patent attorney
An attorney licensed by the Patent and Trademark Office to prepare and prosecute applications and perform other legal tasks.

power of attorney
Inventor's or patent owner's authorization of representation by a patent attorney.

authorization of agent
Inventor's or patent owner's authorization of representation by a patent agent.

prosecution
Process by which an inventor or patent practitioner guides the application through the Patent and Trademark Office.

utility patents
Patents granted for inventions or discoveries that are categorized as machines, processes, compositions, articles of manufacture, or new uses of any of these.

process
Method of accomplishing a result through a series of steps involving physical or chemical interactions.

machine
Device such as an engine or apparatus that accomplishes a result by the interaction of its parts.

article of manufacture
A single object without movable parts or an object whose movable parts are incidental to its function.

United States Patent [19]

Nauta

[11] **4,142,270**

[45] **Mar. 6, 1979**

[54] **WET-DRY VACUUM CLEANER BAFFLE STRAINER SYSTEM**

[76] Inventor: Jelle G. Nauta, R.R. #4, Stouffville, Ontario, Canada

[21] Appl. No.: **774,316**

[22] Filed: **Mar. 4, 1977**

[51] Int. Cl.² A47L 7/00
[52] U.S. Cl. 15/353; 15/321; 55/216; 55/413; 55/462
[58] Field of Search 15/320, 321, 353; 55/216, 413, 462, 465

[56] **References Cited**

U.S. PATENT DOCUMENTS

2,639,005	5/1953	Gerstmann	15/353 X
2,671,527	3/1954	Moon	55/216
3,082,465	3/1963	Wood	15/353 X
3,165,774	1/1965	Barba	15/353 X
3,618,297	11/1971	Hamrick	15/353 X
3,911,524	10/1975	Parise	15/321 X

FOREIGN PATENT DOCUMENTS

1801921 5/1969 Fed. Rep. of Germany 15/353

Primary Examiner—Christopher K. Moore
Attorney, Agent, or Firm—E. H. Oldham

[57] **ABSTRACT**

This invention relates to a vacuum cleaning machine which is capable of operating in a wet or dry environment. It may also be used as a "steam" cleaning machine by applying a hot solution of cleaning solution to a surface to be cleaned and subsequently vacuuming up the deposited cleaning solution. The machine may also be used as a "dry" vacuum cleaner without substantial modification. The particular aspects of the machine to which this application is directed is a baffle system which when combined with a strainer-float system and a right angled elbow member, combine to permit operation in a "wet" mode, but prevent the ingress of the detergent and foreign matter into the air motivating system of the machine.

3 Claims, 5 Drawing Figures

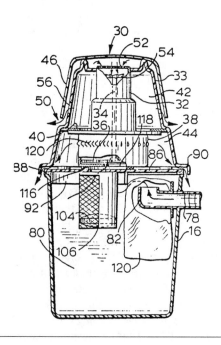

FIGURE 11-1
The wet-dry vacuum patent is an example of a utility patent.

A *composition of matter* is any combination of chemical or other materials. For example, Roy Plunkett received a patent in 1941 for poly tetrafluoroethylene—a chemical composition of matter commonly sold under the trademark *Teflon*. Although naturally occurring substances (in their natural state) cannot be patented, combinations of such elements or extracts of such materials may qualify for patent protection. For example, in 1900 Felix Hoffman patented acetyl salicylic acid (aspirin). In 1980, the Supreme Court permitted a grant of patent protection to living organisms as being within the statutory definition of patentable subject matter. Such inventions or discoveries are generally classified as compositions of matter. In 1988, amid great controversy, Harvard University acquired the first patent for a new animal life form, a genetically altered mouse. After a hiatus created by popular and political reaction to the patent, granting of such patents has recently resumed.

Plant Patents

Can a plant be *invented*? In 1930, the United States began granting patents for plants, and in 1931, the first **plant patent** was issued to Henry Bosenberg for his climbing, ever-blooming rose. Under U.S. patent law, the inventor of a plant is the person who first appreciates the distinctive qualities of a plant and reproduces it asexually.[2] In other words, a plant can be *created* (i.e., by breeding or grafting), or it can be *discovered*. Plants discovered in the wild or uncultivated state cannot be patented, because they occur freely in nature. A plant discovered in a cultivated area and thereafter asexually reproduced can be patented, even if it was discovered in a cultivated area owned by someone else. However, a tuber-propagated plant such as a potato cannot be patented.

To acquire a plant patent, the inventor must have actually asexually reproduced the plant. Asexual reproduction means that the plant is reproduced by means other than seeds, usually by cutting or grafting of the plant tissue culture. Asexual reproduction is the cornerstone of plant patents because it is what proves that the inventor (or discoverer) can duplicate the plant. The patented plant also must be novel and distinctive. For example, consider the *Smooth Angel* rose plant (see figure 11-2) patented by Henry Davidson of Orinda, California. It is described as follows in its patent:

> A new rose variety of the hybrid tea class distinctive in its character by being near thornless and by having blooms which open with the outer petals being a cream color and the center petals yellow-orange as hereafter shown and described.

This rose is novel and distinctive from previous rose plants in the following ways: (1) near thornlessness (i.e., only a few thorns appear on some bushes); (2) an attractive full-foliaged spreading plant; and (3) a medium to large, tight-centered, full, symmetrical, two-toned cream and yellow-orange bloom. Asexual reproduction of the *Smooth Angel* was performed in California and was continued through succeeding propagations.

LEGAL TERMS

plant patent
  Patent granted to the person who first appreciates the distinctive qualities of a plant and reproduces it by means other than seeds.

FIGURE 11-2
The *Smooth Angel* rose patent is an example of a plant patent.

If a plant has existed in nature and has reproduced, it is not novel. In other words, if the patent examiner can find a previously reproducing version of the plant in nature, a patent will not be granted. However, a patent may be granted for a spontaneous, one-time aberration (sometimes known as a *sport*) that is incapable of reproducing (provided that the person claiming the patent has asexually reproduced the plant). To be distinctive, a plant must have characteristics that make it distinguishable from other varieties.

Plant varieties produced sexually (i.e., by seed) cannot be protected under patent law, but can be protected under a federal law enacted in 1970 known as the Plant Variety Protection Act.[3] This law is administered by the Department of Agriculture.

Design Patents

A **design patent** is available for a new, original, and ornamental design for an article of manufacture. Unlike a U.S. utility patent (which can remain in force for 17 years), a U.S. design patent lasts for 14 years.[4] Generally, design patents are used to protect the shape, visually perceptible ornamental features, or other aesthetic appearance of functional articles (e.g., the unique shape of a wine bottle, a desk, computer case, an amusement car ride, or a shower head). (See figure 11-3 for an example.)

The design patent protects only the aesthetic appearance of an article, not its structure or utilitarian features. For example, Carco, an automobile company, creates a new van with a high-tech design. The exterior appearance of the van is protectible as a design patent. However, any new functional features of the van (such as double-locking doors, retractable windows, or double cutaway sun roof) are protectible by utility patents. Both types of patents can be obtained to protect the respective aspects of the same device. In this way, design and utility patents coexist. One way to separate design and utility concepts is to inquire whether the absence of the novel design feature affects the function of the device. For example, consider the patented design of various electric guitars. The method by which the electric guitar functions is unaffected by the various designs. Therefore, the designs are protectible.

The requirements for a design patent are that the design be new, original, and ornamental. The requirement of ornamentality means that the design is not primarily utilitarian. Also, to be patentable, the design must be visible during normal intended use or at some other commercially important time. This requirement can be satisfied if the design is visible at the time of sale or in an advertisement. For example, the design of a hip prosthesis may not be visible when in use, but it is visible at the time of purchase and in advertisements.

Design Patents and Copyright

The rights protected by a design patent and copyright can overlap. Both forms of law protect artistic design and visual imagery. For example, a three-dimensional cartoon character on a belt buckle could qualify for

---

United States Patent [19]

Davidow

[11] **3,739,975**

[45] **June 19, 1973**

[54] **NOVELTY PARTY CUP**

[76] Inventor: **Jodell Davidow,** 7116 Hillside Avenue, Los Angeles, Calif. 90046

[22] Filed: **Jan. 13, 1972**

[21] Appl. No.: **217,465**

[52] U.S. Cl. .... 229/8, 206/DIG. 35, 222/78, 229/1.5 B, D9/220, D9/217, D44/9 B, 46/11
[51] Int. Cl. B65d 3/00
[58] Field of Search .... 229/8, 1.5 B; 206/DIG. 35; D9/198, 199, 195, 217, 220; 46/11; D34/156; 2/199, 185 R, 173, 206 S, 200; 222/78; 161/12, 7; 215/100 R

[56] **References Cited**
UNITED STATES PATENTS

997,063	7/1911	Hordich	229/8 UX
2,000,242	5/1935	Manning	2/173
2,294,538	9/1942	Chaffin	46/11
2,454,906	11/1948	Amberg	229/1.5 B UX
2,659,527	11/1953	Liebenow	229/1.5 B UX
3,099,017	7/1963	Sullivan	229/8 X

3,109,252	11/1963	Schellenberg	229/8 X
3,357,623	12/1967	Wommelsdorf	229/1.5 B

Primary Examiner—Davis T. Moorhead
Attorney—Flam and Flam

[57] **ABSTRACT**

The invention is typically embodied in a disposable paper cup. The paper cup is provided with flaps that fold outwardly from the sides of the cup. The insides of the flaps (that is, the sides hidden from view before folded outwardly) are provided with suitable designs of fanciful facial features. The flaps cooperate with fanciful facial features printed on the bottom of the cup to constitute a suitable mask or caricature that can be held to the user's face. Since the caricature components of the mask are normally concealed, the secondary mask use of the cup has a surprise element. Since the flaps are normally in place along the sides of the cup, the cups are nestable notwithstanding the secondary function.

20 Claims, 9 Drawing Figures

FIGURE 11-3
The novelty party cup patent is an example of a design patent.

copyright protection as a work of visual art. The same belt buckle also could qualify for a design patent because it is a new, original, and ornamental design for an article of manufacture (the a belt buckle). Not all designs are protectible under both copyright *and* design patent law. The Patent and Trademark Office will not issue design patents for mere pictures or surface ornamentation per se (i.e., abstract designs). Purely aesthetic works, such as a photographs, drawings, or sculptures, are protected only under copyright law. Copyright and design patents differ substantially as to the extent of rights and the registration or patenting process. In choosing the appropriate form of protection, an attorney and client usually weigh several factors. The total cost (including attorney fees) of acquiring copyright protection is inexpensive (usually under $300) and a registration is usually issued within six months. The cost of acquiring a patent is several thousand dollars and the patenting process usually takes approximately 18 months.

[handwritten margin note: Copyright, much less expensive.]

The protection provided by design patents is broader (e.g., it is not necessary to prove copying to demonstrate infringement) but a design patent only lasts 14 years. Copyright protection lasts for either the life of the author plus 50 years or 75 or 100 years for a work made for hire. Design patents are best suited for protecting shapes and appearances of useful objects, particularly when that shape may not qualify for copyright protection (i.e., shapes of office equipment, kitchenware, appliances, certain jewelry, furniture, musical instruments, and motor vehicles). Copyright protection is best suited for flat art on functional objects (e.g., a map imprinted on fabric) or three-dimensional art that is separable from the function (e.g., licensed character on belt buckle, ornate sculpture on lamp base).

Design Patents and Trademarks

As explained in chapter 8, the image and overall appearance of a product can be protected under principles of trademark law. Similarly, the unique shape or appearance of a product can qualify for design patent protection. Design patent protection does not preclude trademark protection for the same design or appearance. For example, in a case involving the unique shape of the *Mogen David* wine bottle, a federal judge stated that both design patent and trademark protection could be claimed for the same container appearance. This is because the purposes of trademark and design patent law differ. The purpose of design patent law is to encourage creation of ornamental designs; the purpose of trademark law is to protect the trademark owner and the public from confusion and deception. Therefore, the expiration of a design patent does not terminate trademark rights.

Computer Software and Patent Protection

As explained earlier in this book, computer software programs are protectible under various laws. Prior to its publication, a program may be protected under trade secret law. The Copyright Act of 1976 extends copyright protection to both published and unpublished computer programs. In addition, a program that is expressed as a mask work on a semiconductor chip is protectible under the Semiconductor Chip Act of 1988.

In 1981, in the case of *Diamond v. Diehr,*[5] the U.S. Supreme Court held that a mathematical formula contained in a computer program was protectible by means of a utility patent. As a result of this decision, there has been increasing interest and debate about the use of patents to protect software. Not all programs are protectible under patent law. For example, patent law will not protect mathematical expressions or certain algorithms. In the competitive world of software programming, an applicant may have difficulty meeting patent requirements, and the one year bar, as explained later in this chapter, will pose problems if the program has been for sale for more than one year before a patent application is filed. In addition, the patent application process is much slower than the copyright registration process. In addition, no protection exists under patent law until the patent is granted. Copyright protection begins once the work is fixed.

Despite these drawbacks of patents, there is a trend among some attorneys to seek patent protection for computer programs, because the protection is so broad and because competitors cannot reproduce a patented program by reverse engineering. Under patent law the patent owner can stop the manufacture, use, and sale of a similar program, even if the other party's program was independently created. It is further possible that the ornamental design, such as screen interface or screen icons (e.g., the opening screen of an accounting program) may, under some circumstances, be protectible as a design patent. However, recent decisions by the Board of Patent Appeals and Interferences have rejected the granting of design patents for screen icons. Table 11.1 charts the different forms of protection afforded to computer software programs.

11.3 RIGHTS UNDER PATENT LAW

The rights granted under patent law are exclusionary. That is, the owner of a patent may exclude others from making, using, or selling the patented subject matter (i.e., the invention, design, or plant) throughout the United States. Patent rights are divisible. The owner of a patent may split these exclusionary rights and assign or license various rights to different parties. If a party, without authorization from the patent holder, makes, sells, or uses the patented subject matter, that is an infringement of the patent. It also is an infringement if a party makes an immaterial variation of the patented invention. Unlike other forms of intellectual property law, patent law can prevent the use of the infringing device by a consumer. For example, if a consumer buys and uses an infringing device, the patent owner has the right to sue the purchaser for infringement. This right is not usually asserted

	Extent of Protection	Advantage	Disadvantage
Copyright	Federal protection for life of author plus 50 years or 75 years from publication (if a work for hire).	Inexpensive and relatively easy to obtain	Protection may be limited to the literal expression of software code; cannot stop others who, without access to copyrighted code, independently develop similar code.
Trade Secret	State law protection for as long as software remains confidential.	Easy to protect confidential information prior to release.	Difficult to maintain protection after publication, due to ability of competitors to decompile or reverse engineer the code; cannot stop others who, without access, independently develop similar code.
Semiconductor Chip	Federal protection for 10 years.	Inexpensive and relatively easy to obtain.	Limited to the integrated circuit patterns provided on semiconductor chips.
Design Patent	Federal protection for 14 years.	May be used to protect look and feel of computer program.	Only protects the ornamental aspects (not the functional aspects) of the program. Recent design patent applications for screen icons have been rejected by the Patent and Trademark Office.
Utility Patent	Federal protection for 17 years.	Can be used to prevent similar programs even if independently created; software code cannot be reverse engineered.	Not all software programs qualify for patent protection; relatively expensive to obtain.

TABLE 11.1
Comparison of Legal Protection Offered for Computer Software

against consumers of mass-produced devices, but it may be exercised in the case of expensive or limited-production inventions.

Curiously, a patent does not guarantee the owner the right to use, sell, or make the invention. One reason for this is that not all patented matter may be made, used, or sold. For example, the government may prohibit the manufacture or use of a certain weapon. In addition, certain patents require the use of other patented devices or processes. The use or sale of such derivative inventions without permission from the owners of the basic patents would result in patent infringement. For example, consider the fog-making apparatus invention in the Commentary to this chapter. Perhaps a special effects company patented a method of combining the fog-making apparatus with a pump so as to spread the fog through several rooms. This may qualify for a new patent, but Effectsco could exclude the special effects company from manufacturing the new invention if it infringes upon Effectsco's underlying basic patent.

First to Invent (Priority of Invention)

Thomas Edison once stated, "Invention is 1 percent inspiration and 99 percent perspiration." The "inspiration" of which Edison spoke is the conception or mental idea for the invention. The "perspiration" results from physical acts—the developing, testing, or revising of the mental concept so that a useful, working invention is created. In patent law, this latter process is known as **reduction to practice**. In addition to the building and testing of an invention, the act of preparing and filing a patent application also is considered a reduction to practice (known as *constructive reduction to practice*). The **date of invention** is either the date the invention was conceived (providing that the applicant diligently reduced the invention to practice) or the actual date of reduction to practice. For example, on January 1, 1990, an inventor conceived of an idea for a motorized eight-wheeled folding chair. She diligently developed and tested her idea until June 1, 1991. At that she point, she gave up on the idea, believing it could not be perfected or commercialized. A year later, she decided to resume work on the chair again. She finally tested and perfected her invention on January 1, 1993. The date of invention would be January 1, 1993. If, however, she had not abandoned her development for the one-year period, the date of invention would have been January 1, 1990. As discussed later in this chapter, the date of invention is important when reviewing the issue of novelty and prior art. Because the dates associated with inventorship are often crucial in patent disputes or in preparing patent applications, inventors often maintain detailed notebooks documenting their progress on an invention and have these notebooks signed by witnesses (who must not be co-inventors.)

In the United States, patents are granted to the first person to invent (the "first to invent" system). The first person to invent has **priority of invention** and, assuming all other statutory requirements have been met, is granted a patent. Under United States law, the party who first files a patent application is *presumed* to be the first inventor. However, disputes may arise as to which party was actually the first to invent. When an application is made for a patent that, in the opinion of the Commissioner of the Patent and Trademark Office, would interfere with any pending application (or an unexpired patent), a proceeding known as a *patent interference* is instituted in the Patent and Trademark Office and held before the Board of Patent Appeals. Similar issues regarding priority of invention may also arise in a patent infringement lawsuit. Rules for determining priority of invention are discussed in chapter 12.

Note: In most countries, patents are granted to the person who first files for a patent application. This is known as a "first to file" system. At the

LEGAL TERMS

reduction to practice
Contemplation of the actual and complete use of the invention for its intended purpose, (e.g., the physical prototyping and successful testing of the invention); the act of preparing and filing a patent application is considered a constructive reduction to practice.

date of invention
Either the date the invention was conceived (providing that the applicant diligently reduced the invention to practice) or the actual date of reduction to practice.

priority of invention
U.S. patent policy awarding a patent to the first person to invent over persons who subsequently invent the same patentable concept.

time of writing of this book, the United States is considering proposals to change the American patent system to a "first to file" system. This change is proposed as part of efforts to harmonize U.S. patent law with the patent laws of other countries.

Patent Claims

The rights granted under patent law extend only to the invention as defined in the **claims** published in the patent. 35 U.S.C. § 112 states that the patent application specification must "conclude with one or more claims particularly pointing out and distinctly claiming the subject matter which the applicant regards as his invention." Patent claims, therefore, are the legal description or definition of the invention. It has been said that the claims paint a picture of what the inventor seeks to protect. The inventor (or patent attorney or agent) writes the proposed claims for defining the invention and the patent examiner reviews them in comparison to previous patents, inventions, and discoveries in the field to determine if the invention is patentable. Some commentators have compared patent claims to the description of real property because both define the boundaries of the property. In 1992, an inventor obtained a patent for a scented postcard (e.g., if the postcard had an illustration of Florida orange groves, the card might emit an orange scent). The following is an example of the claims for a utility patent for the scented postcard.

EXAMPLE: Claims for Scented Postcard

Patent No. 5,148,983 Sept. 22, 1992 Muniz

1.   A souvenir device comprising:

a pair of members joined together to define an internal storage cavity between their opposing surfaces;

graphic indicia carried on at least one exterior face of said joined pair of members;

a pad carried in said internal storage cavity holding a quantity of a scented substance;

means internally communicating said scented substance exteriorly of said joined pair of members;

said communicating means comprises a plurality of open-ended passageways extending between said internal storage cavity and edge marginal regions of said joined pair of members; and

said plurality of passageways are defined between opposing surfaces of said members and opposing surfaces of a plurality of raised portions carried on a selected one of said members.

As is apparent from this example, above, the drafting of claims is an acquired skill. Because it defines the extent of rights for the invention, the drafting should be performed only by the inventor or a patent agent or attorney. The rights granted under the patent are limited to the claims, so these claims are drafted as broadly and completely as possible. The goal of the inventor is to maximize the extent of protection under the patent. More sample claims are presented in chapter 12.

Doctrine of Equivalents

The patent owner has the right to exclude anyone from literally infringing the claims of the patent. Even if the competing method or thing is not a literal copy, the patent owner has the right to prevent the sale, use, or manufacture of a competing method or thing if it employs substantially the same means to achieve substantially the same results in substantially the same way as that claimed. Consider a company, Lightco, that owns a patent on a device that detects lightning and displays its location and distance. Another company, Brightco, manufactures a similar device, without authorization from Lightco. Brightco's device achieves the same result in the same manner. Lightco sues for patent infringement. Brightco argues that its device receives data from a wider frequency range, processes the data in a special way, and employs a more sophisticated display than the Lightco device. The court, however, finds that these elements are *equivalent* to the elements disclosed in Lightco's patent specification and recited in the patent claims. The owner of a utility patent may prohibit the use, sale, or manufacture of an invention or discovery that it is substantially similar even though it does not correspond literally to what is called for by the claims of the patent. This principle, known as the **doctrine of equivalents,** is a parallel to the principles of substantial similarity and derivative rights in copyright law. Generally, under the doctrine of equivalents, a patent owner can prevent sale, use, or manufacture of a discovery or invention if it performs substantially the same function in substantially the same way to obtain the same result.

Patent Suppression

The ability to patent an invention in the United States reserves to the owner the right *not to* manufacture or license rights to the item.[6] For example, Dan invents a new device that connects a shortwave radio to a computer. Several companies offer to license it, but Dan does not like the terms of the offers. He wants more money so he refuses to license it. In some countries, the failure to commercialize or license the invention within a specific time period may result in loss of patent rights. However, if Dan deliberately conceals his invention or fails to apply for a patent within a reasonable time after invention, these activities may cause Dan to lose out on his claim of *priority* over a rival inventor in the United States. These principles of concealing or suppressing the invention are generally referred to as **suppression** and are codified at 35 U.S.C. § 102(g).

LEGAL TERMS

claims
  Statements that define the novel and nonobvious elements of the invention or discovery; protection under patent law extends only to matter within the scope of the claims.

doctrine of equivalents
  Right of patent owner to prevent sale, use, or manufacture of a discovery or invention if it employs substantially the same means to achieve substantially the same results in substantially the same way as that claimed.

suppression
  Concealment or acts of delay in introducing an invention, which can result in loss of the inventor's claim of priority of invention.

11.4 Patent Requirements

The four requirements for a utility patent are:

1. The invention falls within one of the classes described in the statute;
2. The invention is useful;
3. The invention, when made, is novel; and
4. The invention, when made, is nonobvious.[7]

Statutory Classes

To qualify for utility patent rights, an invention or discovery must fall within one of the statutory classes provided in 35 U.S.C. § 101 (i.e., a useful process, machine, manufacture, or composition of matter, or any new and useful improvement of such items). These broad categories may include, as established by the Supreme Court, "anything under the sun that is made by man" provided that it meets the statutory requirements. It is possible that an invention or discovery may overlap two categories. For example, in the facts to the Commentary of this chapter, the inventor of the *Fogarama* has devised both a process for creating fog and a machine that accomplishes the process. When filing for patent protection, an applicant is not required to indicate the statutory class. As long as a patent examiner determines that the invention falls within one of the categories (and a court does not later disagree), the invention will meet the requirement of statutory subject matter. However, if an examiner at the Patent and Trademark Office determines that the *Fogarama* does not fall into one of the statutory categories, a patent will not be granted unless the examiner's evaluation is reversed on appeal.

Usefulness

Books and movies about the Old West often portray a clever con man who sells an elixir known as a "patent medicine," which he claims can cure common ills. Had anyone attempted to patent such substances, the Patent and Trademark Office would have rejected the application unless the applicant could demonstrate that the substance was actually effective. The Patent and Trademark Office is only empowered to grant utility patents on useful inventions or discoveries. To be *useful*, an invention must have a use or purpose and must work (i.e., be capable of performing its intended purpose). Therefore, unless the inventor of the patent medicine could demonstrate that the medicine *worked*, a patent would not be issued. Patent medicine aside, **usefulness** is generally the easiest requirement to establish because most inventions are created or discovered for some useful purpose. For example, in the Commentary to this chapter, the *Fogarama*, an artificial fog-producing apparatus, has an obvious use for persons in the fields of film, theater, special effects, and amusements parks.

The Patent and Trademark Office may reject an application if utility has not been established (e.g., a drug whose usefulness has not yet been demonstrated) or if the only use would be illegal or deceptive. For example, a man invented a method of putting spots on tobacco plants to make the plants resemble, but not otherwise have the characteristics of, tobacco plants of higher quality. The process did not improve the plants or change the quality of the tobacco. The sole purpose was to deceive purchasers. A federal court invalidated this patent. Similarly, an invention of a way to counterfeit American currency would not be able to acquire patent protection unless the inventor could demonstrate some alternative noncounterfeiting use of the device. The Atomic Energy Act of 1954 prohibits the patenting of any atomic weapon.

Novelty and Prior Art

In 1951, Edwin Land was granted a patent for a revolutionary process—instant photography. The resulting *Polaroid* camera was a novel concept for persons who had previously been accustomed to waiting days or weeks for developed pictures. Using Mr. Land's invention, a photograph would appear fully developed within minutes. Mr. Land's invention was new to the world. **Novelty** is a statutory requirement of U.S. patent law. Subsequent instant camera and instant film patents obtained by the Polaroid company in the early 1970s were used to prevent the Kodak company from manufacturing and selling Kodak's version of an instant camera. An invention such as the process for instant photography must be novel. It must differ in some way from the **prior art,** that is, the publicly known or existing knowledge in the field of photography. When assessing the prior art, the patent examiner or courts will consider the following:

Polaroid

1. Prior patents that issued more than one year before the filing date of the patent or before the date of invention
2. Prior publications having a publication date more than one year before the filing date of the patent or before the date of invention
3. U.S. patents that have an effective application filing date prior to the date of invention of the application at issue
4. Anything in public use or on sale in United States more than one year before the effective filing date of the patent application at issue
5. Anything that was publicly known or used by others in this country before the date of invention of the invention defined in the claims in question
6. Anything that was made or built in this country by another person before the date of invention of the invention defined in the claims in question, when the thing made or built by the other party was not abandoned, suppressed, or concealed.

The requirement for novelty (set forth in 35 U.S.C. § 102) provides that a patent will *not* be issued (or if issued, will not be held valid) if the invention

LEGAL TERMS

usefulness
An invention must have a use or purpose and must work (i.e., be capable of performing its intended purpose).

novelty
Statutory requirement that an invention must differ in some way from the publicly known or existing knowledge in the field.

prior art
Publicly known or existing knowledge in the field of the invention or discovery which is available prior to, or at the time of, the invention.

was known or used by others in this country or patented or described in a printed publication in this or a foreign country before the date of invention. In addition, the Patent and Trademark Office will not consider an invention to be novel if the application for the patent is made more than one year after sale, public disclosure, use, offer of sale in the United States, or patenting anywhere in the world. This is known as the *one year grace period* or *on sale bar* and is explained in more detail in § 11.5.

Nonobviousness

Approximately 100 years ago, Earl Dickson combined pieces of surgical tape with gauze. The result was the first adhesive strip bandage. His creation was intended for his wife, who suffered burns and cuts while working in the kitchen. Mr. Dickson's employer, the Johnson & Johnson Company acquired the patent to this invention and soon became the leading manufacturer of these *Band-Aid*® products. Today, we consider adhesive strip bandages to be an obvious invention, but at the turn of the century, nobody had ever created prepackaged gauze adhesive bandages. So many of the inventions discussed in this chapter (the safety pin, the ironing board, the sewing machine, the collapsible tube, and the cylinder lock) all seem obvious—now. This is one of the paradoxes of great inventions: once created, they seem obvious.

All inventions must meet a requirement of **nonobviousness**. This requirement demands an inquiry into whether persons working in the field would consider the invention obvious.[8] For example, in the case of the *Fogarama* device discussed in the Commentary to this chapter, the examiner at the Patent and Trademark Office would inquire as to whether the subject matter of the patent application (i.e., a method of suspending atomized water in the air) was sufficiently different from what had been used or previously described. In other words, would the *Fogarama* device be obvious to a person having ordinary skill in the science or technological field of special effects devices? Does the *Fogarama* have any novel features that produce an unexpected or surprising result? If previous fog-making machines did not use water and did not operate as efficiently, then the *Fogarama's* method of suspending water would be nonobvious to someone skilled in the field.

It is possible to create an invention that is novel but is not nonobvious. For example, an inventor created a system for clearing manure from a barn without using human labor. The system combined a water tank, flushing system, and a sloping barn floor. No prior system had performed this function, so the invention was novel. However, the Supreme Court held that the combination of a water tank and a sloping barn floor was not patentable because it was obvious at the time the invention was made. If the Patent and Trademark Office rejects the application for nonobviousness, the applicant can attempt to prove that the invention produces a result that would not have been expected by persons of ordinary skill in the art.

In 1966, the U.S. Supreme Court grappled with the definition of *nonobviousness* in the case of *Graham v. John Deere Co.*[9] The court established a four-part analysis, inquiring into the following:

1. What is the scope and content of the prior art to which the invention pertains?
2. What are the differences between the prior art and the claims at issue?
3. What is the level of ordinary skill in the pertinent art?
4. What objective evidence is there of secondary considerations? For example, has the invention enjoyed commercial success? Has there been a need in industry for the invention? Have others tried but failed to achieve the same result? Did the inventor do what others said could not be done? Have other copied the invention? Has the invention been praised by others in the field?

11.5 LIMITATIONS ON PATENT RIGHTS

An inventor's right to patent protection is limited by statutes and by caselaw (i.e., the federal court interpretation of U.S. patent law). For example,

JUDGE LEARNED HAND ON PATENT LAW: Nonobviousness

In 1910, Judge Hand adjudicated *Hartford v. Moore*, 181 F. 132 (S.D.N.Y. 1910), in which the inventor of an automobile shock absorber apparatus sued a competitor for making an infringing device. The defendant argued that the plaintiff's patent was invalid because the invention would have been obvious to a skilled mechanic trained in automotive skills. Judge Hand asked, "if the solution was obvious, why did not one of these skilled mechanics who have studied the machine inch by inch and screw by screw discover so simple a device?" The nonobviousness of the invention was corroborated by the fact that until 1905 "no device of any similar character appeared for use upon motor cars." Judge Hand provided a succinct statement as to the nature of the inventor's mind when he wrote, "It certainly cannot be necessary to repeat the well-known principle that it is no indication of noninvention that the device should seem obvious after it has been discovered. Many great inventions are of this character, and the reason why the ordinary man does not discover them although they are so plain when some one else has done so is that habit has limited his power to see what he has not been accustomed to see, and his selective attention is fast bound by his past experience."

LEGAL TERMS

nonobviousness
Requirement that, to acquire a U.S. patent, the subject matter of the patent application be sufficiently different from what has been used or described before so that it would not have been obvious to a person having ordinary skill in the area of technology related to the invention.

statutory law limits utility patent terms to 17 years and prevents the grant of a patent if the invention is offered for sale more than one year prior to the filing of the application. Certain caselaw limitations are based upon fairness. For example, it is unfair to permit an inventor to assert patent rights if the inventor has concealed important facts from the Patent and Trademark Office. The reason for such a caselaw limitation is to balance the interests of the public and to provide rules of fairness for persons attempting to create similar but not noninfringing inventions. The limitations set forth in this section are often used as defenses to claims of patent infringement.

One Year Grace Period/On Sale Bar

An inventor is barred from acquiring patent protection if the application is filed more than one year after the earliest date of sale, offer of sale, or public use of the invention in the United States (the **on sale bar**, sometimes known as the *one year grace period*) or more than one year after the date of a printed publication (in which the invention is described) in any country.[10] For example, in the facts in the Commentary to this Chapter, Effectsco has invented a fog-making apparatus. However, in January 1992, the invention was disclosed in a printed publication to a convention of engineers. In March 1992, the company began selling the *Fogarama* device. In April 1993, Effectsco applies to patent the device. It is over a year since the printed publication describing the device and it is over a year since the first sale. Therefore, an application for a patent would be rejected.

Printed Publication

Because the one year rule can have such a disastrous impact on an inventor, there has been a great deal of litigation, which generated substantial caselaw regarding what constitutes a sale or printed publication describing the invention. A *printed publication* includes the result of use of any method of recording information (i.e., paper, microfilm, or computer disk). If a person reasonably skilled in the field can make the invention based upon the publication, then the inventor will be barred from patent protection if the application is filed more than one year after publication. Publication occurs when there is public accessibility to the printed publication. For example, Dave, the inventor of the *Fogarama* device in the Commentary to this chapter, writes a master's thesis on his invention and delivers it to a university. The date of publication for purposes of the one year bar would be the date the university catalogs the thesis in and makes the thesis available in its library. Because of the impact of the printed publication rule, engineers and scientists eager to publish their findings are advised to determine the editorial policy of the publication and the publication date. In addition, submissions should be treated as confidential and should include a prominent notice such as the one in the following example.

EXAMPLE: Notice on Submissions to Scientific or Technical Journals

This paper is submitted solely for purposes of consideration for future publication. The contents of this paper shall not be disclosed or disseminated prior to publication and all persons with access to this paper shall agree not to use the knowledge included in this paper for any improper purposes.

Public Use or Sale

A sale need not be consummated to trigger the one-year period because the "offer to sell" the invention also starts the time period. The offer or sale is generally measured by several variables, including whether: (1) the invention was embodied in the thing for sale; (2) the invention was sufficiently operable to be commercially marketed; and (3) the sale was primarily for profit and not purposes of testing or experimentation. However, this standard is flexible, and any determination as to public use or sale depends on the facts and circumstances of each case.

Experimental Use Doctrine

The **experimental use doctrine** is a factor that can be considered by a court evaluating the on sale bar or public use bar to patent protection. If the inventor can prove that an alleged sale or public use was primarily for the purpose of perfecting or testing the invention, then this sale or use will not bar the grant of a patent. The Supreme Court established this principle in 1877. An inventor with a patent for a wooden pavement system sued an infringer. The infringer claimed that the patent was invalid because the invention had been in public use for six years prior to filing of the patent application. The inventor had installed the wooden pavement on a road and tested and evaluated the road's performance on a daily basis during the six-year period. The Supreme Court held that the use of an invention by an inventor or a person under the inventor's direction, by way of experiment and in order to bring the invention to perfection, is not regarded as a public use. In a 1984 case, however, the Federal Circuit determined that the use of a planting device to cultivate 40,000 acres of corn was a commercial and not an experimental use.

The On Sale Bar and International Patents

Despite the severe consequences of the one year rule, it is a much more liberal rule than the comparable rules applied in most foreign countries, where *any* sale, public disclosure, use, or offer of sale prior to filing a patent application will bar the grant of patent protection. For example, Jack, an American inventor, sells his toenail clipper invention in the United States on January 1, 1991. He has one year to file his patent application. After January

LEGAL TERMS

on sale bar (also called one year grace period or one year bar)
Doctrine that prevents an inventor from acquiring patent protection if the application is filed more than one year after the earliest date of sale or offer of sale or public use of the invention in the United States.

experimental use doctrine
Rule excusing an inventor from the one year bar, provided that the alleged sale or public use was primarily for the purpose of perfecting or testing the invention.

1, 1992, the invention is no longer novel and the patent would be barred. However, if Jacques, a French inventor, were to sell *his* toenail clipper prior to applying to patent it in France, he would be barred from obtaining patent protection in France. Therefore, if an American inventor desires to file a foreign patent application, it is advisable for that inventor to avoid any use, publication, sale, or offer to sell the invention anywhere until a foreign application has been filed, either in the foreign country or the United States.

Patent Misuse

Patent misuse is a caselaw limitation that prevents a patent owner who has abused patent law from enforcing patent rights. What does it mean to *misuse a patent* or to *abuse patent law?* The most common examples of misuse are violation of the antitrust laws or unethical business practices. The antitrust laws seek to prevent certain unfair monopolistic behavior. A conspiracy to fix prices may be a violation of antitrust laws. For example, if all of the patent owners of bicycle parts joined together and conspired to fix prices, this would be unfair to consumers and would violate antitrust laws. Under the doctrine of patent misuse, such behavior would not be permitted.

It also may be a violation of antitrust laws to require, as a condition of a transaction, that a buyer of a patented device purchase an additional, unpatented product. This is known as **tying** (or a *tie-in*), a coercive and prohibited business practice. In a famous case, *Morton Salt Co. v. G.S. Suppiger Co.,*[11] the U.S. Supreme Court held that it was a tying arrangement and a violation of the antitrust law for the seller of a patented machine to require purchasers also to buy unpatented salt tablets. The Supreme Court agreed with the defendant that the seller of the machine had misused its patent rights and should be prevented from suing for infringement.

Patent misuse is an affirmative defense to patent infringement, but it cannot be used to claim damages or seek an injunction. In other words, a defendant in a patent infringement lawsuit could avoid liability, but could not be awarded any money because of the plaintiff's patent misuse. That is why patent misuse has been characterized as a "shield, not a sword." In 1988, Congress enacted the Patent Misuse Amendments. These amendments apply to cases filed on or after the date of enactment and require that courts apply a "rule of reason" standard.[12] Under the rule of reason, the court must view all the relevant factors to determine if the tying arrangement is in any way justified. For example, imagine that Softco, a computer software company, had patented a disk-duplicating device that copies materials on computer disks at high speed. Persons who license the patented machine pay Softco based upon use, that is, upon the number of disks copied. To determine the number of copies made, Softco could require that the licensee also buy a metering device that counts the number of copies. Alternatively, Softco could require that the licensee purchase blank disks from Softco, because the sale of these disks may be a less expensive way of determining the number of copies made. In the case of the meter or the disk purchase, the tying arrangement does not restrain competition and may be justified under the 1988 Patent Misuse Amendments. In addition, a patent owner cannot be refused relief under these amendments simply because the patent owner refused to license or use any rights to the patent; (it is not patent misuse to suppress the invention in the United States).

Exhaustion Doctrine

Imagine that in the facts to the Commentary to this chapter, Effectsco were to acquire a patent on the *Fogarama* fog-making invention. Effectsco sells a *Fogarama* machine to Bill, and the company then has no further rights to the resale of Bill's fog-making machine. For example, Bill could resell the *Fogarama* at a different price or in a different area of the country. This principle is known as the **exhaustion doctrine**: once the authorized item is sold, patent rights to that article are exhausted. The rules are similar for products resulting from use of a process covered by a claim of a patent. For example, consider the inventor of a method for breeding fleas (see figure 11-4). The method requires construction of a special cage having a membrane screen. If the inventor licensed rights to a manufacturer, the first sale doctrine would apply to cages that used the process (i.e., a method for breeding fleas with a feeding membrane). The exhaustion doctrine will not apply to unauthorized purchasers of an invention. If a consumer purchases and uses an

United States Patent [19]

Georgi

[11] Patent Number: 5,133,289

[45] Date of Patent: Jul. 28, 1992

US005133289A

[54] ARTIFICIAL SYSTEM AND METHOD FOR BREEDING FLEAS

[75] Inventor: Jay R. Georgi, Freeville, N.Y.

[73] Assignee: Cornell Research Foundation, Inc., Ithaca, N.Y.

[21] Appl. No.: 755,141

[22] Filed: Sep. 5, 1991

[51] Int. Cl.5 .... A01K 67/00
[52] U.S. Cl. 119/6.6
[58] Field of Search 119/6.6, 6.5, 15, 174

[56] References Cited

U.S. PATENT DOCUMENTS

3,893,420 7/1975 Andreeu et al. 119/6.6
4,850,305 7/1989 Georgi et al. 119/1

OTHER PUBLICATIONS

Rutledge, L. C. et al., Mosquito News, pp. 407–419, Dec./64.
Sgovina, K., Parasitenk, 7:539–571 (1935).
Totze, R., Zentralbl, Bakt Parasitenk Infekt. 132:382–384 (1934).
Wade, S. E., et al., J. Med. Ent., 25, No. 3, 186–190 (May/88).
Bar-Zeev, M., et al., Entomol. Exp. & Appl. 5:60–68, 1962.

Bernardo, M. J., et al., J. Med. Ent. 23, No. 6, 666–679, Dec./86.
Cerwonka, R. H., et al., J. Parasitology, 44, ·No. 5, 565–566, 1958.
Galun, R., Life Sciences, 5:1335–1342, 1966.
Kartman, L., Experimental Parasitology, 525–537 (1954).
Lauer, D. M., et al., J. Med. Ent. 14, No. 5, 595–596 (Feb./78).

Primary Examiner—John G. Weiss

[57] **ABSTRACT**

A system for breeding fleas comprises a blood reservoir with a feeding membrane and a cage adjacent to the feeding membrane and containing a screen which supports the fleas during feeding, divides the cage into a feeding chamber and an egg collection chamber and provides access by the fleas between these chambers. The fleas are confined in the cage and stand on the screen to feed by penetrating the membrane with their mouth parts to obtain blood from the reservoir. The access between the feeding and egg collection chambers allows the cage to contain more fleas than if such access were not provided and open interiors of the feeding and egg collection chambers allow easy cleaning and egg collection.

10 Claims, 2 Drawing Sheets

FIGURE 11-4
The flea breeding patent

infringing invention, the patent owner can sue the purchaser for infringement and prevent any further use of the device.

A limitation similar to the exhaustion doctrine is the **repair doctrine**. The owner of a patent cannot prevent the licensor of the invention from repairing the device and replacing worn-out components that are not separately covered by patent claims. For example, a company owned a patent for a convertible top apparatus used in automobiles. The fabric part of the top was not separately patented. Under the repair doctrine, the "unauthorized" sale by a second company of the fabric part to legitimate purchasers and licensees of the complete patented convertible top was not an infringement or contributory infringement. However, a third company was making an infringing version of the convertible top apparatus. The sale of these devices was unauthorized and any repair made on these devices was also unauthorized. The sale of fabric parts for these infringing devices of the third company was not permitted under the repair doctrine, because the infringing convertible tops were not authorized by the patent owner.

File Wrapper/Prosecution History Estoppel

The official file in which a patent is contained at the Patent and Trademark Office is known as a *file wrapper.* All statements, admissions, correspondence, or documentation relating to the invention are placed in the file wrapper. If, during the patent application process, the inventor admits limitations to the invention or disclaims certain rights, those admissions or disclaimers will also become part of the file wrapper. If the patent owner later sues for infringement and claims rights that were previously disclaimed, the defendant can assert the affirmative defense of **file wrapper estoppel** (also known as **prosecution history estoppel**). For example, Effectsco furnishes an application for the *Fogarama* device. The patent examiner requests that one of the claims be amended so as to exclude an element of the transducer that causes the water to atomize. The patent is issued. If Effectsco later sues an infringer, Effectsco is precluded on the basis of file wrapper estoppel from claiming the disclaimed element of the transducer as a protectible element of its claims. The nature of file wrapper estoppel therefore requires that all correspondence or communication to the Patent and Trademark Office be reviewed by the supervising attorney, because any statement that diminishes the extent of the patent claims may give rise to a file wrapper estoppel defense.

Regulatory Testing

Consider the pharmaceutical company, Medco, that patents an artificial rib in 1977. In 1994, the patent will expire and competitors can copy the device freely. Healthco, a competitor, is waiting for the patent to expire so that it may begin making copies freely. However, Healthco will need government approval (which may take several years) before it can release its version. If Healthco had to wait until the patent expired to make its prototypes and then had to wait for government approval, it would not be able to release its rib until several years after the Medco patent expires. This effectively extends the period of time during which Medco can monopolize the manufacture of the rib device. To encourage competition and speed up the release of human health care and certain animal products, Congress passed an amendment to the Patent Act that applies to inventions for which premarketing regulatory approval is required.[13] Under the amendment, a competitor may engage in activities that would otherwise be considered infringement, if such activities are necessary for regulatory approval. Under this statute, Healthco could, during the term of Medco's patent, manufacture versions of its competing artificial rib, if those versions were used exclusively for purposes of government testing and approval. However, even if Healthco obtained approval in 1992, it could not legally sell its version until Medco's patent expired in 1994.

Reverse Doctrine of Equivalents

As indicated previously, the doctrine of equivalents protects the patent owner from infringers who create or sell substantially similar inventions. However, in some situations a competitor may create an invention that performs the same function in a substantially different way. In 1950, the U.S. Supreme Court held that "where a device is so far changed in principle from a patented article that it performs the same or a similar function in a substantially different way, but nevertheless falls within the literal words of the claim, the doctrine of equivalents may be used [in reverse] to restrict the claim and defeat the patentee's action for infringement." This principle is known as the **reverse doctrine of equivalents**. For example, in the facts to the Commentary of this chapter, if an inventor creates an apparatus that atomizes water in a substantially different way than the *Fogarama* device, the resulting invention would not be an infringement.

Inequitable Conduct/Fraud on Patent Office

An applicant for a patent has a special responsibility to be candid during the application process, that is, not to conceal or mislead the examiner.[14] If the applicant intentionally misleads the patent examiner, or if the applicant should have known that any withheld information was material to the examination process, then the issued patentable is unenforceable. This affirmative defense is known as *inequitable conduct* (and was previously titled *fraud on the patent office*). For example, in one case an applicant misled the patent examiner as to the use of plastic fibers in a fiber optic device. All rights to the invention were effectively lost.

Duration of Patent Rights

Although best known as a glamorous film actress, Hedy Lamarr also possessed scientific and engineering skills. In the early 1940s she co-invented

LEGAL TERMS

repair doctrine
   Right of an authorized licensor of a patented device to repair and replace unpatented components.

file wrapper estoppel (also called prosecution history estoppel)
   Affirmative defense used in patent infringement litigation that precludes patent owner from asserting rights that were disclaimed during the patent application process.

reverse doctrine of equivalents
   Affirmative defense used in patent infringement when the allegedly infringing device performs the same function in a substantially different way.

a sophisticated radar-jamming device. She offered to license the device to several parties, including the U.S. government (to help in World War II). However, no interest was taken in her device, and eventually the patent expired. After the patent expired, several companies adopted the device and it is now used to speed satellite communications. Because these uses were made after the expiration of the patent, Ms. Lamarr received no money from the exploitation of her invention.

Absent the rules regarding patent term extension, the right to exclude others from using, selling, or manufacturing the subject matter of a utility or plant patent is limited to a maximum of 17 years. A design patent lasts for 14 years. This monopoly begins when the Patent and Trademark Office issues the patent and, in the case of utility patents, continues as long as the patent owner pays the appropriate maintenance fees. At present, there are no maintenance fees for keeping design or plant patents in force for the full term.[15] After the monopoly on the patent ends, competitors are free to copy the patented material without infringing. If the patent owner is unable to exploit the invention during the term, then it is unlikely, as in the case of Ms. Lamarr, that any money will be earned by the inventor.

Under certain circumstances, the patent period may be extended if the commercial marketing of the product is delayed by government regulations or review. For example, the patent term for certain human and animal drugs may be extended for up to five years to compensate for government review.[16]

Patent rights do not begin until the patent is issued. However, upon issuance, the owner of the patent can prevent any continuing infringing activity that began earlier, during the **pendency period**. The pendency period is the time between filing of the application and issuance of a patent (usually 18 months or more). For example, Swimco applied for a patent for a new type of swimming goggles. During the pendency period, H2O-Co, a rival swimming products company, manufactured an infringing pair of goggles. Once the patent is issued, Swimco can prevent any infringing activity by H2O-Co.

11.6 PATENT OWNERSHIP

Like other intellectual property, a patent is a form of personal property that can be assigned, sold, licensed, transferred, or left in a will. The application for the patent must be made in the name of the inventor. However, the inventor does not always become the owner of the patent. Employees of companies, as a consequence of employment agreements or company policies, routinely assign their inventions to their employers. For example, in the facts to this Commentary, Dave, an engineer employed by Effectsco, has developed a fog-making apparatus during the course of his employment. Dave has agreed to give Effectsco rights to all inventions he creates through his employment. The patent application must be signed by Dave as inventor. But, simultaneous with filing the application, Dave will file an assignment of all rights to the invention to Effectsco. When the patent issues, Effectsco will own all rights to the patent. Sometimes independent inventors contract to create devices and, as part of the agreement, also assign all patent rights.[17]

Joint Ownership

If, according to the facts in the Commentary to this chapter, Dave invented the fog-making device with other Effectsco engineers, those other engineers would be named as joint inventors. The U.S. Code provides that inventors may apply for a patent jointly even though (1) they did not physically work together or at the same time, (2) each did not make the same type or amount of contribution, or (3) each did not make a contribution to the subject matter of every claim of the patent.[18] A named joint inventor should be an actual inventor, a true originator of the invention. That is, he or she should have personally contributed to the inventive idea. If, for some reason, a joint inventor cannot be located or refuses to join in the application, the omitted inventor may subsequently join in the application. If a person is incorrectly named as an inventor and the error arose without any deceptive intent, the Commissioner of Patents and Trademarks may permit the inventorship, as stated in the application, to be amended.

When joint inventors produce an invention and it is not part of an employment arrangement, they can detail their respective obligations and ownership of the invention with a **joint ownership agreement**. There are four essential elements of such an agreement:

1. A method of making decisions regarding the invention (e.g., each decision requires two-thirds approval);
2. The percentage interest and proportionate sharing of revenues from the interests (e.g., each partner receives one-third of the revenue)
3. Rights to manufacture or sell (e.g., the right to sublicense the invention in a geographic area); and
4. A method of resolving disputes between the parties.

Sometimes a dispute develops as to who is the inventor. For example, two different people may claim to be the first inventor. The first to conceive and diligently reduce the invention to practice is the first inventor. In the event of a dispute, an *interference proceeding* is instituted in the Patent and Trademark Office. An interference is a proceeding directed by the Patent and Trademark Office to determine who has priority of an invention. This process is discussed in chapter 12.

Government Ownership

What happens when a contractor creates a patentable invention while working under a government contract? According to a federal policy implemented in 1983, government agencies may waive or omit reservation of patent rights when awarding government contracts.[19] This permits the private

LEGAL TERMS

pendency period
    Time between filing of the patent application and issuance of a patent (usually 18 months or more).
joint ownership agreement
    Contract detailing the conditions, obligations, and ownership interest of the joint creators of an invention.

developer to retain patent rights to a co-sponsored invention (i.e., resulting from the government's contracting with a private company). Certain government contracts for space research, nuclear energy, or defense may be subject to separate statutory requirements.

Employee Inventions

Ownership of an employee's invention may depend on the contents of the employment agreement, and also may be affected by a principle governed by state law and known as the **shop right** rule. A shop right is the power of an employer to claim the nonexclusive right to use in its business an invention made by an employee. This right is determined from the nature of the employer's business, the character of the invention involved, the circumstances under which it was created, and the relation, conduct, and intention of the parties. The shop right is often triggered when an employee, not hired to invent, conceives of an invention during working hours. In some states, the shop right rule may grant ownership of an invention to the employee but allow the employer to have a nonexclusive, royalty-free right to use it. Rather than simply rely on shop right, most employers also require employees to sign an employment agreement whereby any rights in inventions will be assigned to the company. For example, in the facts to this Commentary, it is not clear what type of employment agreement Effectsco has with Dave, the inventor. However, if Dave signed an employment agreement that contained a provision requiring assignment of all innovations relating to Effectsco's business, then the company owns the patent rights from Dave's invention, provided the agreement does not violate state law.

If an employer is concerned about ownership of employee-created inventions, the employment agreement should require that the employer acquires ownership of an invention if it is created within the course of employment or relates to the employer's business. The employment agreement also should provide that the employee must disclose all inventions created during the term of the employment. Some states statutes limit the employee from giving up rights unless the underlying invention was (1) created within the scope of the employee's duties; (2) made during the period of the employment; (3) relates to the employer's existing or contemplated business; or (4) uses the employer's time, facilities, or materials. Any employment agreement with provisions broader than the state law may be subject to invalidation. For example, if an employment agreement provided that the employer owned any invention made by the employee, and that provision was broader than the state law, the provision might be unenforceable. The employment agreement provisions in figure 11-5 are written in anticipation of a California labor statute that limits employer ownership of inventions. Note that the provisions also grant the company a power of attorney to "apply for, prosecute, obtain, or enforce any patent." This is established so that in the event the employee is not available or refuses to cooperate, the company may represent the inventor for patent purposes. If a state statute limits employer ownership, it is prudent for the employer to include a copy of that statute within or as an exhibit to the employment agreement.

Commissioned Inventions

Some companies may be unable to afford the in-house research and development costs expended by larger companies. For this reason, companies

---

**EMPLOYMENT AGREEMENT: PATENT
OWNERSHIP BY EMPLOYER**
(reflecting California limitations on employer ownership)

Assignment of Intellectual Property Rights. Employee understands and agrees that the rights to any works of authorship, trade secrets, innovations, inventions, processes, systems, or patentable creations, whether or not registrable or patentable ("Intellectual Property"), written, conceived, originated, discovered, or developed in whole or in part by Employee (1) as a result of any work performed by Employee with Company's equipment, supplies, facilities, trade secret information, or other Company resources; or (2) on Company's time shall be the sole and exclusive property of Company, provided that any such Intellectual Property created by Employee either relates to Company's business or anticipated research. However, rights to the Intellectual Property that qualify fully under the provisions of California Labor Code § 2870 *et seq.* shall not be subject to this provision. Employee hereby assigns to Company all right, title, and interest Employee may have or acquire in and to all such Intellectual Property. To the extent that any such Intellectual Property created for Company by Employee or with Employee's assistance is not a work made for hire as defined under the U.S. Copyright Act, Employee hereby assigns and transfers to Company all rights, title, and interest Employee has or may acquire to all such works. Employee agrees to sign and deliver to Company, either during or subsequent to the term of this Agreement, such other documents as Company considers desirable to evidence (a) the assignment of all rights of Employee to Company, if any, in any such Intellectual Property, or (b) Company's ownership of any such Intellectual Property. Employee recognizes that U.S. patent laws require that patent applications be filed in the name of the true and actual inventor of the subject matter to be patented. Employee agrees to be named in any such U.S. patent applications although actual ownership shall vest in Company.

Power of Attorney. In the event Company is unable to secure Employee's signature on any document necessary to apply for, prosecute, obtain, or enforce any patent, copyright, or other right or protection relating to any innovation or copyrightable work referred to above, Employee irrevocably designates and appoints Company and each of its duly authorized officers and agents as his agent and attorney-in-fact, to act for and in his behalf and to execute and file any such document and to do all other lawfully permitted acts to further the prosecution, issuance, and enforcement of patents, copyrights, or other rights.

FIGURE 11-5
Sample patent ownership provisions for employment agreement

Disclosure. Employee agrees to promptly disclose in writing to Company all discoveries, developments, designs, programs, code, ideas, innovations, improvements, inventions, formulas, processes, techniques, know-how, and data (whether or not patentable or registerable under copyright or similar statutes) made, written, conceived, reduced to practice, or learned by Employee (either alone or jointly with others) during the period of his employment, that are related to or useful in Company's business, or that result from tasks assigned to Employee by Company, or from the use of facilities owned, leased, or otherwise acquired by Company.

FIGURE 11-5
(Continued)

often commission consultants or outside contractors to create necessary discoveries or devices. The major concern in such arrangements is to ensure that the company will own the resulting discovery, invention, or work. To guarantee company ownership, a consulting or professional services agreement is executed. Figure 11-6 is an example of a consulting agreement that might be used by Effectsco with a partnership that will create a computer program to be used inside the *Fogarama* device. The assignment of rights in this agreement includes not only patent rights, but also trade secret, copyright, and other proprietary rights.

PROFESSIONAL SERVICES AGREEMENT
(with Assignment of Patent Rights)

This PROFESSIONAL SERVICES AGREEMENT (the "Agreement") is made between Laurie Jolar and Bill Stoker *dba* Vertigo Programming, a partnership (jointly and severally referred to as "Contractor") with its principal place of business at 1234 Main Street, New York, New York, 10016, and Effectsco, a California corporation ("**Effectsco**" or the "**Company**"), with its principal place of business at 5678 Smallway, San Francisco, California, 94129. The parties agree as follows:
    Services. Contractor shall perform certain computer software consulting services as follows:

_____

_____

_____

Contractor shall be responsible for all specifications, development, and testing of the programs from inception to conclusion of the development. Contractor agrees and

FIGURE 11-6
Sample professional services agreement with rights assignment

acknowledges that the services described in this Agreement shall be completed no later than December 15, 1993. Contractor acknowledges that time is of the essence in the completion of the services.

Equipment Loan. Effectsco agrees to lend Contractor, without charge, sufficient hardware and documentation necessary to perform the services. A listing and inventory of such equipment shall be provided to and signed by Contractor upon receipt of such equipment. Upon termination of this Agreement, Contractor shall immediately return all such equipment to Effectsco.

Payment. Unless terminated prior to completion of the services, Company shall pay Contractor as follows: _____.
Contractor acknowledges the adequacy of the consideration. Company shall reimburse Contractor for all reasonable preapproved expenses incurred, including but not limited to travel, telephone, and facsimile transmissions, which are incidental to the services performed under this Agreement.

Contractor Responsibilities. Contractor has full responsibility and liability for the acts of its partners or employees. Contractor transacts business under the name *Vertigo Programming* and represents that this business has filed a Fictitious Business Name Statement, possesses any necessary business licenses, and timely pays all applicable taxes in installments or as otherwise required by the Internal Revenue Service or other taxing agency. Company shall not pay for, or in any way provide Contractor with, insurance, for example, liability, health, unemployment, workers' compensation, disability, or social security insurance. Contractor represents that it possesses any and all insurance required by law.

Confidential Information. Contractor acknowledges that Contractor may be furnished or may otherwise receive or have access to information that relates to Company's business and the affairs of its clients (the "Information"). Contractor agrees to preserve and protect the confidentiality of the Information disclosed to Contractor before this Agreement is signed and afterward. In addition, Contractor agrees not to disclose the Information to any third party without the consent of Company, and shall not use the Information for its own benefit or for the benefit of any third party without the consent of Company. These obligations shall not apply to any information that is: (a) already publicly known; (b) discovered or created independent of any involvement with Company or the Information; or (c) otherwise learned through legitimate means other than from Company or anyone connected with Company.

Representations. Contractor represents and warrants that (a) Contractor is able to perform the Professional Services and that Contractor does not have any understanding or agreement with anyone else which restricts Contractor's ability to perform such services or creates a potential or actual conflict of interest; (b) that any services Contractor provides and information or materials Contractor develops for or discloses to Company shall not in any way be based upon any confidential or proprietary information derived from any source other than Company, unless Contractor is specifically authorized in writing by such source to use such proprietary information; and (c) that Contractor shall not sublicense any work assigned under this Agreement to parties others than those named in this Agreement without the prior written consent of Company.

Indemnification. Contractor hereby agrees to indemnify and hold Company and other successors in interest harmless from and against any and all claims, including reasonable attorney fees, which may be incurred by reason of the breach of

FIGURE 11-6
(Continued)

any representations or warranties made by Contractor under this Agreement.

Assignment of Intellectual Property Rights. Contractor understands and agrees that any works of authorship, trade secrets, innovations, inventions, processes, systems, or patentable creations ("Intellectual Property Rights") written, conceived, originated, discovered, or developed in whole or in part by Contractor pursuant to this Agreement, whether or not registrable or patentable, shall be the sole and exclusive property of Company, including, without limitation, all exclusive rights granted to an author or inventor under the laws of the United States. To the extent that any such Intellectual Property created for Company by Contractor or with Contractor's assistance is not a work made for hire belonging to Company, Contractor hereby assigns and transfers to Company all rights, title, and interest Contractor has or may acquire to all such works. Contractor agrees to sign and deliver to the company, either during or subsequent to the term of this Agreement, such other documents as Company considers desirable to evidence (a) the assignment of all rights of Contractor to Company, if any, in any such Intellectual Property, or (b) Company's ownership of any such Intellectual Property. Contractor recognizes that U.S. patent laws require that patent application must be filed in the name of the true and actual inventor of the subject matter to be patented. Contractor agrees to be named in any such U.S. patent applications although actual ownership shall vest in Company.

Termination. Contractor's obligations, performance, and compensation pursuant to this Agreement may be terminated at any time, with or without cause, at the sole discretion and option of Effectsco. Contractor may terminate this Agreement at any time, with or without cause, at its sole discretion. Contractor hereby acknowledges that no representations to the contrary, oral or written, have been made. If this Agreement is terminated, Company can require Contractor to give it all work in progress in exchange for reasonable compensation based on the percentage of the work completed.

Independent Contractor. Contractor is performing services for Company as an independent contractor. Nothing contained in this Agreement shall be deemed to constitute either Contractor or Company an agent, representative, partner, joint venturer, or employee of the other party for any purpose.

Miscellaneous. This agreement may not be amended except by an instrument in writing signed by both parties. Each and all of the several rights and remedies provided for in this Agreement shall be cumulative. No one right or remedy shall be exclusive of the others or of any right or remedy allowed in law or in equity. No waiver or indulgence by Company of any failure by Contractor to keep or perform any promise or condition of this Agreement shall be a waiver of any preceding or succeeding breach of the same or any other promise or condition. No waiver by Company of any right shall be construed as a waiver of any other right. If a court finds any provision of this Agreement invalid or unenforceable as applied to any circumstance, the remainder of this Agreement and the application of such provision to other persons or circumstances shall be interpreted so as best to effect the intent of the parties. This Agreement shall be governed by the laws of the State of California. Contractor irrevocably consents to the exclusive jurisdiction of the state and federal courts in San Francisco County in any action arising out of or relating to this Agreement, and waives any other venue to which Contractor might be entitled by domicile or otherwise. This Agreement and any attachments or exhibits express the complete understanding of the parties with respect to the subject matter and

FIGURE 11-6
(Continued)

supersedes all prior proposals, representations, agreements, and understandings, whether written or oral.

By my signature below, I acknowledge that I have read and received a copy of this Agreement and I understand its contents.

Laurie Jolar and Bill Stoker   **EFFECTSCO**
dba **VERTIGO PROGRAMMING**

_____   **By:** _____
Laurie Jolar   **Wendy Wilding, President**

_____
Bill Stoker

Dated: _____   **Dated:** _____

FIGURE 11-6
(Continued)

Assignments and Licenses

Although this chapter has highlighted many successful inventions, the majority of discoveries and inventions that are patented are not commercially successful. There are two reasons for this: (1) the inventor is unaware that the invention has little commercial potential; or (2) no effort has been made to successfully commercialize the invention. For example, Dave invents a new high-speed nose-hair clipper. Presently, the most popular nose-hair clipper operates on batteries and costs $15. However, Dave is shocked to learn that his clipper will cost $60 per unit to produce the first million units. The retail price would be $90. It is unlikely that consumers will purchase Dave's invention at that price when the popular battery-operated version sells for $15. Therefore, it is unlikely that Dave's patent will be exploited.

A patent attorney or agent will sometimes advise the inventor as to the commercial potential of an invention. If there is no commercial potential, there is little sense spending the money to acquire a patent. If there is commercial potential, an inventor must exploit this potential or locate a company that will evaluate, manufacture, and distribute the subject matter of the patent. If a company desires to participate in commercialization of the product, the parties may enter into an agreement whereby the rights are either assigned or licensed. An *assignment* is a transfer of the ownership of the patent, for which the inventor may receive a lump-sum payment, continuing royalties during the life of the patent, or both. A *license* is a grant of rights as to the patent. It may be for all of the rights, or the rights may be limited as to time, territory, or subject matter.

Assignments

A *patent assignment* is a transfer of ownership interest in the patent. An assignment may transfer all rights encompassed by the patent grant, or it may transfer a percentage interest in the rights (e.g., 20 percent). In addition, an assignment may involve a transfer of all rights as to a specific geographic portion of the United States (e.g., all rights within the state of Wyoming). An assignment of patent rights can be made before the patent application is filed, during the application process, or after a patent has issued. Although federal law governs patent assignments, a lawsuit regarding the enforcement or validity of a *contract* assigning patent rights will be subject to state law. An assignment should be recorded in the Patent and Trademark Office.

Figure 11-7 shows an assignment for all proprietary rights in a children's toy. The party that grants rights is the *assignor* and the party acquiring rights (Toyco) is the *assignee.* If the assignor has already obtained a patent, a different assignment is used, as described in the following section, which specifically cites the patent number and other information.

FIGURE 11-7
Sample assignment
before issuance of
patent.

ASSIGNMENT OF INTELLECTUAL PROPERTY RIGHTS
(Prior to Issuance of Patent)

WHEREAS, _____ ("Assignor") is the owner of all proprietary
and intellectual property rights, including copyrights and patents, in the concepts and
technologies more specifically described in Attachment A to this Assignment
(and referred to collectively as the "Product") and the right to registrations to the
Product; and

WHEREAS, Toyco, a New Jersey corporation, ("Assignee" or "Toyco") desires
to acquire the ownership of all proprietary rights, including but not limited to the
copyrights and patent rights in the Product;

NOW THEREFORE, for good and valuable consideration, the receipt and
sufficiency of which are hereby acknowledged, Assignor hereby sells, assigns,
transfers, and sets over to Assignee, its successors, and assigns:

(1) all right, title, and interest in the Product, including all copyrights
and all United States Letters Patent and U.S. copyright registrations which
have been or may hereafter be granted on the Product;

(2) all reissues and extensions of such patents and registrations;

(3) all priority rights under the International Convention for the
Protection of Industrial Property for every member country;

(4) all applications for patents, copyright registrations, or patents or
copyright registrations (including related rights and all extensions,

renewals, and reissues) applied for or granted on the Product and improvements in any foreign countries;

(5)   all derivative rights to the Product;

(6)   the original material object(s) in which any copyright in the Product was first fixed; and

(7)   the right to sue and recover for past infringements.

Assignor warrants that: (1) she is the legal owner of all right, title, and interest in the Product; (2) she has no knowledge of any conduct regarding the Product in violation of U.S. antitrust laws; (3) she has no knowledge of any third-party claims regarding the Product; (4) that such rights have not been previously licensed, pledged, assigned, or encumbered; and (5) that this assignment does not infringe on the rights of any third party. Assignor agrees to cooperate with Assignee and to execute and deliver all papers, instruments, and assignments as may be necessary to vest all right, title, and interest in and to the intellectual property rights to the Product in Assignor. Assignor further covenants and agrees to communicate to Assignee any facts known to her respecting improvements or modifications to the Product and testify in any legal proceeding, sign all lawful papers, execute all applications, whether divisional, continuation, continuations in part, substitute and reissue applications, and make all rightful oaths and generally do everything possible to aid Assignee to obtain and enforce proper protection for the Product and any improvements in all countries.

DATED: _____, 1992   _____
                                                                  (Assignor)

On this _____ day of _____, 19____ , before me, _____ ,
the undersigned Notary Public, personally appeared _____ (Assignor) and proved
to me on the basis of satisfactory evidence to be the person who executed the within
instrument.
WITNESS my hand and official seal.

_____
Notary Public

FIGURE 11-7
(Continued)

If a patent has already been issued, or if the patent owner intends to assign a pending patent application, a different form of assignment can be used, as provided in figures 11-8 and 11-9.

Licenses

Patent rights are divisible. Different companies can acquire different rights from the patent owner. These grants are usually in the form of a license.

ASSIGNMENT OF RIGHTS

Toper M. Bradley of Woodsprings, Colorado ("Bradley") is the sole inventor and owner of (1) U. S. Patent Number: 1,234,567, dated August 1, 1989, for SYSTEM FOR CREATING CUSTOM-MADE INFLATABLE HEADPHONES (the "Patent"); and (2) the corresponding patent application PCT 89/12345, having an international filing date of **June 30, 1989** and a priority date of **April 12, 1988** (the "Application") and the invention(s) disclosed and claimed therein.

Jerry Swine of San Diego, California ("Swine") desires to acquire all rights in and to said inventions and under the Patent and the Application.

Therefore, for valuable consideration, the receipt of which is acknowledged, Bradley assigns all his right, title, and interest in said invention(s) and the Patent and Application to Swine for the entire term of the Patent and for the entire terms of any and all Letters Patent and Registrations which may issue from foreign applications filed or to be filed claiming the benefit of the Application or disclosing and claiming the invention(s). The right, title, and interest is to be held and enjoyed by Swine and Swine's successors and assigns as fully and exclusively as it would have been held and enjoyed by Bradley had this assignment not been made, for the full term of the Patent and of any and all Letters Patent and patents or registrations which may be granted thereon, or of any division, renewal, continuation in whole or in part, substitution, conversion, reissue, prolongation or extension thereof.

Bradley further agrees to: (a) cooperate with Swine in the prosecution of the Application and foreign counterparts; (b) execute, verify, acknowledge, and deliver all such further papers, including patent applications and instruments of transfer; and (c) perform such other acts as Swine lawfully may request to obtain or maintain the Patent and any and all Letters Patent and Registrations for the invention and improvements in any and all countries, and to vest title thereto in Swine or Swine's successors and assigns.

Date: _____

_____
Toper M. Bradley

STATE OF COLORADO)
) ss.
COUNTY OF WOODSPRINGS)

On this _____ day of _____, 19 ___, before me, _____, the undersigned Notary Public, personally appeared **TOPER M. BRADLEY**, personally known to me (or proved to me on the basis of satisfactory evidence) to be the person whose name is subscribed to the within instrument, and acknowledged to me that he executed the same.

WITNESS my hand and official seal in _____ County of _____ on the date set forth in this certificate.

_____
Notary Public   My Commission Expires: _____

FIGURE 11-8
Sample assignment after issuance of patent.

ASSIGNMENT OF PATENT

     Whereas I, _____, of _____, County of _____, State of _____, did obtain letters patent of the United States for an improvement in _____, numbered _____, and dated _____; and

     Whereas I am now the sole owner of said patent; and

     Whereas _____ of _____ County, of _____, and State of _____, is desirous of acquiring the entire interest in the same:

    Now, therfore, in consideration of the sum of _____ ($____) Dollars, the receipt whereof is hereby acknowledged, I, _____, by these presents, do sell, assign, and transfer unto _____, the whole right, title, and interest in and to the said letters patent therefor aforesaid; the same to be held and enjoyed by _____, for his own use, and for his legal representatives, to the full end of the term for which said letters patent are granted, as fully and entirely as the same would have been held by me had this assignment and sale not been made.

[Date—Investor's Signature and Seal—Acknowledgment by Inventor]

FIGURE 11-9
Sample assignment after issuance of patent (alternate).

For example, Susan, an inventor, may own rights to a new type of amusement ride. She can license the right to manufacture the amusement ride to one company and the right to sell the ride to another company. Rights as to use of the invention may be limited according to territory or according to time (e.g., the right to use the invention is limited to 10 years). Each of these rights is provided for in a *license agreement,* a document that permits certain uses in return for compensation. Some legal experts view the license as an agreement by the patent owner *not to sue* for the licensee's use. The payment for this right may be in the form of an up-front payment (i.e., paid at the time of execution of the agreement), or by way of royalties (i.e., continuing payments based upon sales or use), or a combination of these forms. There may be minimum and maximum royalties for a year, and there may also be engineering fees for continued improvements or maintenance of the patented invention. In addition, the patent owner may license ancillary rights, such as the trademark name or copyrighted artwork associated with the amusement ride. Rights may be licensed on an exclusive or nonexclusive basis. A patent license and agreements providing for patent licenses are interpreted under state law.

    It is common to license rights to an invention prior to issuance of a patent. Because the patent application process is so lengthy, a company will want a head start on advertising and manufacturing plans. A license agreement generally includes the following elements.

Description of the Invention. A full description of the invention or, if patented or registered, reference to the patent or registration, title, date, and number.

Rights Granted. Grant of exclusive or nonexclusive rights as to time period, territory, and right to use, manufacture, or sell. Contingency or termination rights if the patent is not issued. Term (i.e., length of time) for grant of rights.

Obligations of the Parties. Duties of licensee to manufacture or sell (and provision for termination or conversion from exclusivity to nonexclusivity if licensee discontinues sales or manufacture for a period of time or does not achieve or maintain certain sales targets). Duty of licensor to license subsequent inventions and to provide continuing support of patented subject matter.

Payments and Records. System for payment of fees and royalties. System for recordkeeping to guarantee accurate payments and provision to analyze licensee's accounting and books.

Right to Sublicense. Provision as to whether rights under the agreement can be granted by the licensee to another party (e.g., can the originally licensed company sell its rights to manufacture the invention to another company?).

Patent Prosecution and Infringement. Method by which the parties apportion rights and responsibilities in the event of: patent prosecution problems at the Patent and Trademark Office; claim of infringement by a third party; or claim of infringement by inventor against a third party.

Warranties and Indemnity. A *warranty* is a guarantee. Usually the inventor guarantees that the device does not infringe any another invention. *Indemnity* is an agreement to pay for any damages or claims if a lawsuit develops. For example, an inventor might warrant that the licensed invention will not infringe anyone else's patent. A third party sues for infringement. If there is an indemnity provision, the inventor may have to pay for all costs (including the licensee's costs) of defending the lawsuit.

SUMMARY

11.1 Patent law is derived from a constitutional grant. Federal laws establish patent rights and the federal courts interpret patent laws. The Patent and Trademark Office is responsible for the federal registration of patents and only certified patent attorneys or patent agents may prepare patent applications on behalf of inventors.

11.2 There are three types of patents: utility patents, design patents, and plant patents. Utility patents are granted for inventions or discoveries that are categorized as machines, processes, compositions, articles of manufactures, or new uses.

11.3   A patent owner can exclude others from making, using, or selling the invention throughout the United States. Patent rights are divisible and the owner of a patent may assign or license various rights to different parties. It is an infringement if a party, without authorization from the patent holder, makes, sells, or uses the patented invention. The rights granted under patent law extend only to the claims published in the patent application.

11.4   To qualify for a utility patent, the invention must be useful, novel, nonobvious, and fall within one of the classes described in the statute. In addition, an inventor must file a patent application within one year from the date of sale, use, or offer of sale of the invention in the United States or one year from the date of a printed publication (in which the invention is described) in any country.

11.5   Patent rights in the case of a utility or plant patent expire after 17 years, providing maintenance fees are paid. A design patent lasts for 14 years. The patent owner who abuses patent law may lose patent rights, under the doctrine of patent misuse. Under the principle of prosecution history estoppel (also called file wrapper estoppel), a patent owner cannot assert rights that were disclaimed during the patent application process. Once a patented product (or product resulting from a patented process) is sold or licensed, the patent owner has no further rights as to the resale of that particular item.

11.6   The initial owner of the patent is the inventor. However, employment laws and employment contracts may require transfer of ownership of inventions from employees to their employers. In addition, state shop right rules may affect employee ownership. Joint inventors can establish their rights and obligations with a joint ownership agreement. Patent rights may be transferred by assignments or licenses.

NOTES

1. 35 U.S.C. § 100 *et seq.* (U.S. patent law).
2. 35 U.S.C. §§ 161-164 (plant patents).
3. 7 U.S.C. §§ 2421, 2422, 2541 (Plant Variety Protection Act).
4. 35 U.S.C. § 171 (design patents).
5. Diamond v. Diehr, 450 U.S. 175 (1981).
6. 35 U.S.C. § 271(d)(4) (patent suppression).
7. 35 U.S.C. §§ 101-103 (requirements for patentability).
8. 35 U.S.C. § 103 (nonobviousness).
9. Graham v. John Deere Co., 383 U.S. 1 (1966).
10. 35 U.S.C. § 102 (one-year bar).
11. Morton Salt Co. v. G.S. Suppiger Co., 314 U.S. 488 (1942).
12. 35 U.S.C. § 271(d)(5) (patent misuse).

13. 35 U.S.C. § 271(e)(1) (patent regulatory testing).
14. 37 C.F.R. § 1.56 (patent applicant's duty of candor).
15. 35 U.S.C. § 154 (patent term).
16. 35 U.S.C. § 156 (regulatory extension).
17. 35 U.S.C. § 261 (ownership and assignment of patents).
18. 35 U.S.C. § 116 (joint inventors).
19. 35 U.S.C. § 200-11 *et seq.* (inventions made with government assistance).

QUESTIONS FOR REVIEW AND DISCUSSION

1. Who is permitted to prepare a patent application, besides the inventor?
2. What are the four requirements for a utility patent?
3. What is the meaning of asexual reproduction?
4. Name the statutory classes for utility patents.
5. What is the meaning of prior art?
6. How does the U.S. patent system differ from first-to-file systems?
7. What is the one year rule?
8. Can a device be novel without being nonobvious?
9. What are some differences between a design patent and a copyright?
10. What aspect of the patent application determines the extent of patent protection?
11. Under what doctrine can a patent owner stop another invention that performs substantially the same function in substantially the same way?
12. Why are some tying agreements unjustified?
13. What is the meaning of file wrapper estoppel?
14. How long are the rights for a utility patent? Design patent? Plant patent?

ACTIVITIES

1. Examine the classroom for examples of discoveries or inventions that may have qualified for utility patents. How many potential processes, machines, articles of manufacture, compositions of matter, or any new and useful improvements can you locate?
2. List and examine designs used on functional objects in the classroom. Discuss whether such designs would qualify for copyright, trade dress, or design protection.
3. Find the patent law in the United States Code and locate the sections on plant patents. Locate Title 37 of the Code of Federal Regulations.
4. Review the factual summary in the Commentary to this chapter. What if, instead of atomizing water, the patented device was designed as a means of atomizing and spreading poison gas? What complications

might there be in the process of acquiring patent protection? What if the device atomized medicine for purposes of curing respiratory infections?

PROJECT

Think of a common problem (i.e., losing car keys, lack of security at bank machines, using a telephone with one hand) and then imagine a device that would solve that problem. Designate the device with a trademark and then prepare a rough drawing of it. Organize a fictitious company that will own intellectual property rights to the device. Review your state's shop right laws and prepare a checklist to make sure that the company properly acquires ownership rights to the invention (i.e., prepare an assignment or employment agreement transferring rights.) Prepare a license agreement for the manufacture and sale of the device.

FOR MORE INFORMATION

Patent Law

P. Rosenberg, *Patent Law Fundamentals* (Clark Boardman Callaghan 1989). A thorough, multivolume patent treatise.

P. Rosenberg, *Patent Law Basics* (Clark Boardman Callaghan 1992). A single-volume, "lite" version of the *Fundamentals* treatise.

D. Chisum, *Patents* (Matthew Bender 1990). A classic multivolume patent treatise.

General Information about Patents. An introductory pamphlet about patents and the operations of the Patent and Trademark Office. Available from the Superintendent of Documents, Government Printing Office, Washington, DC 20402.

The Patentable Idea. A 22-minute videotape explaining the basics of patent law. Designed to help companies identify ideas warranting patent protection. Available from Salzman & Levy, The Press Building, Suite 606, 19 Chenango Street, Binghamton, NY 13901.

The Patent Office

The Story of the United States Patent Office. Short guide detailing the history and workings of the U.S. Patent Office. Available from the Superintendent of Documents, Government Printing Office, Washington, DC 20402.

Registered Patent Attorneys and Agents

Directory of Registered Patent Attorneys and Agents Arranged by States and Countries. An alphabetical and geographical listing of patent attorneys and agents registered to practice before the Patent and Trademark Office. Available from the Superintendent of Documents, Government Printing Office, Washington, DC 20402.

Patents Agent's Exam. An application to take the patent agent's examination can be obtained from: Clerk of the Committee on Enrollment, Patent and Trademark Office, Washington, DC 20231. The exam is given throughout the United States in April and October of each year.

Documenting an Inventor's Records

Grissom & Pressman, *The Inventor's Notebook* (Nolo Press, 1985). A user-friendly manual with a step-by-step procedure for the documentation of records and notes of an invention. Includes forms, patent law references, bibliography, and nonlegal aids.

Women Inventors

A. L. MacDonald, *Feminine Ingenuity.* Hedy Lamarr was one of many American women inventors. Because married women had no property rights until the 20th century, and because mechanical aptitude was previously considered "unladylike," many women inventors relinquished credit for their talents to husbands, brothers, and fathers. For example, it was Catherine Greene who reportedly helped her farm mechanic, Eli Whitney, create the first cotton gin; Ann Harned Manning reportedly created the mower that formed the basis of Cyrus McCormack's reaper. Neither woman was credited as inventor in the patent application. Fortunately, the situation for women has changed, and many female inventors and scientists have been credited for valuable patents, including the flat-bottomed paper bag, the bulletproof vest, the dishwasher, the fire escape, and curative drugs for herpes and cancer. Ms. MacDonald's book is an excellent 200-year history of women inventors and scientists.

Patent License Agreements

Mayers & Brunsvold, *Drafting Patent License Agreements* (BNA Books, 1991). One-volume source for patent licensing information.

Epstein & Politano, *Drafting License Agreements* (Prentice-Hall Law & Business, 1991). One-volume book with numberous form agreements.

R. M. Milgrim, *Milgrim on Licensing* (Matthew Bender, 1990). One volume, with license provisions and annotations.

J. Dratler, Jr., *Licensing of Intellectual Property Law* (New York Law Publishing, 1992). One-volume treatise with steps and procedures for all forms of intellectual property licenses.

Bell & Simon, eds., *The Law & Business of Licensing* (Clark Boardman Callaghan 1990). One-volume collection of articles on licensing issues.

CHAPTER 12
Patent Research, Application, and Dispute Resolution

We have become a people unable to comprehend the technology we invent.

Association of American Colleges (1985)

OUTLINE

COMMENTARY

Effectsco, a California company, has been selling its Fogarama *fog-making machine since March 1, 1990. Its customers are amusement parks, theaters, and special-effects companies. On September 1, 1990, the company files a patent application for the invention and on June 30, 1992, the patent is issued. SpecialFX, a competitor, has patents on two fog-making machines. One is sold under the trademark,* Fog-A-Wonder *and the other is called* In-a-Fog. *SpecialFX writes to Effectsco and charges that* Fogarama *infringes on the* In-a-Fog *patent and the* Fog-A-Wonder *trademark. The president of Effectsco asks the law office where you work to review these claims.*

OBJECTIVES

The previous chapter introduced patent concepts and discussed patent rights. This chapter provides information on researching prior art and other relevant patent information, filing patent applications, and resolving patent disputes. After reading this chapter you will be able to:

- Define terms such as *reexamination, best mode,* and *reissuance.*
- Differentiate between literal infringement and the doctrine of equivalents.
- Assemble the elements required for a patent application.
- Prepare a power of attorney for an inventor.
- Analyze the types of evidence used for patent litigation.
- Describe the ramifications of willful infringement.
- Discuss inducing infringement and contributory infringement.
- Draft a patent arbitration provision for a license agreement.
- Outline the types of injunctive relief available in patent litigation.
- Determine if an inventor qualifies for small entity status.
- Identify the elements of the patent specifications.
- Prepare a civil cover sheet for patent litigation.

12.1 THE PATENT SEARCH PROCESS

The patent application process usually begins with research of the prior art. The attorney (or someone on his or her behalf) examines previous patent records and other publications about prior inventions and forms an opinion as to patentability. If the search results indicate that a patent is likely to be granted (if promptly applied for), the application, text, and drawings are drafted. In addition, the attorney, if requested, may perform research as to the potential for commercial exploitation of the invention.

The Novelty Search

Prior to drafting the application, a patent attorney usually orders a **patent search** (sometimes known as a **novelty search**). The purpose of the search is to try to determine whether the invention may be novel and nonobvious, and therefore whether to file a patent application. If the determination is made to file the application, the search also offers background and provides technical and commercial information regarding similar inventions. Some patent practitioners distinguish the novelty search from a more comprehensive search used by patent attorneys to assess the facts in patent litigation or patent licensing contexts.

The average cost for a novelty search is usually $1,000, depending on the complexity of the invention, and it is usually performed by a professional searcher familiar with the area of technology of the invention. The searcher reviews the published patents (and often other publications) at the Patent and Trademark Office or elsewhere, identifies the documents that seem to be relevant, obtains copies of these documents, and furnishes them to the patent attorney or inventor. Most patent attorneys retain a listing of searchers in different technologies; others refer to the *Directory of Registered Patent Attorneys and Agents Arranged by States and Countries*. Because the searching often is performed at the Patent and Trademark Office in Arlington, Virginia, an attorney or paralegal may be able to locate a suitable person located in that area to perform a search. A suitable searcher is generally one who has knowledge in a specific field (for example, computer, electrical, or chemical sciences) as well as having familiarity with the search room, library, or database to be searched.

The Search Request

A good search request should include a drawing of the invention; a copy of a related patent, if available, to help the searcher to identify the appropriate class of prior patents to be searched; identification of the believed novel features of the invention; and any required deadlines. Because it expresses the believed novel features of the invention and because it sets forth the guidelines for investigating patentability, the search letter should generally be drafted by the patent attorney or patent agent. Figure 12-1 is an example of a search request letter.

After the results of the novelty search are received, the patent attorney will review them and advise the inventor of the potential for patentability. If the opinion of the attorney is that the invention would not have been obvious, and if there appears to be a potential for commercialization of the product, the attorney likely will advise proceeding with the preparation and filing of a patent application. For example, if, according to the facts in the Commentary, a novelty search had been ordered for the *Fogarama* device, it would have located the following patent for a fog-producing apparatus. A reading of the patent indicates that it was invented by Marshall M. Monroe of Glendale,

---

LETTER TO PATENT SEARCHER

Dear Searcher:

Re: *Fogarama* artificial fog-producing apparatus

Please conduct a novelty search of the files at the United States Patent Office in regard to the above-referenced invention. The search should, at this time, be limited to prior U.S. patents. The *Fogarama* artificial fog-producing apparatus utilizes ultrasonic transducers in a water-filled container. A dispersed fog effect is produced with the aid of compressed air. Unlike the prior art, the *Fogarama* device does not use a high-pressure nozzle system, combustion, smoke-producing materials, or chemical fog effects. Enclosed find drawings of the *Fogarama* device.

We need the search results within four weeks. If this deadline is not possible, please let me know. If you believe there is a need to expand the search beyond the scope of this request, please contact me for further authorization. You estimated the cost for this search as $750. Enclosed is a check for that amount.

FIGURE 12-1
Sample search request letter

California, and was assigned to the Walt Disney Company of Burbank, California. The patent also provides the application number, the date of filing, international and U.S. classifications, and other information. As should be clear from the sample abstract, there is a question as to the *Fogarama* invention's patentability, based upon the Monroe patent.

Abstract for Monroe's Fog-Producing Apparatus: No. 4,911,866

A fog-producing apparatus for suspending fine particles of water in air in an economical and reliable manner. Ultrasonic transducers potted in an electrically insulative and liquidproof material are placed in a container in which a predetermined water level is maintained by a float and valve device. Alternatively, the potted transducers are suspended below floats floating on the surface of the water whereby the critical water depth over the transducers is automatically maintained. In addition compressed air is conducted through the emanating fog plumes to provide a more homogeneous and dispersed fog effect. A copious amount of fog can thereby be efficiently and reliably produced to create theatrical or visual effects.

If the attorney believes that the Patent and Trademark Office will consider the *Fogarama* invention to be only an obvious modification of prior art, then the attorney likely will advise against the application process. All such letters to the client should also describe the limitations of the scope of the novelty search, such as informing the client that the search only covers U.S. patents (if that was the case), that the searching is only in the seemingly most relevant class, and that a relevant patent may be missing because it

LEGAL TERMS

patent search (also called novelty search)
Noncomprehensive prior art search intended to help the inventor determine whether to file a patent application.

was absent from the file at the time of the search. A paralegal should *never* forward the search results to a client without review by the supervising patent attorney. Prior to proceeding with the application, the attorney also will advise the client to review the market for the invention. Because the costs for a patent application may easily exceed $3,000, it is advisable to consider potential future revenue.

Independent Patent Searching

Although generally not recommended, it is possible for anyone to perform a novelty search without the aid of a searcher. There may be occasions when an attorney or inventor needs patent information other than for a novelty search. There are various procedures for performing patent research. One method is to travel to the Patent and Trademark Office in Arlington, Virginia, and perform the research there. The advantage is that the Patent and Trademark Office patent records are organized by subject matter. Searches can be made in the public search room or in the examiners' search files upstairs. There are search assistants who can help. A second method of searching is to use a collection of search files in a specific area. You may work at a business or law firm, or be affiliated with a business or law firm, that has a collection of patent files in a particular area of technology. A third method of searching is to use one of the Patent Depository Libraries (PDL). Each state has one or more PDL and a listing of the Patent Depository Libraries is included in appendix G. However, searching these libraries is more difficult than searching at the Patent and Trademark Office because not all PDLs have all patents and because the patents are not organized by subject matter. For example, some libraries have patents going back to 1790, whereas others have only the most recent patents. Each PDL has an online computer database called *CASIS* (Classification and Search Support Information System) which provides numbers of patents assigned to classifications, an index, and abstracts. An **abstract** is a summary of the invention, which enables the reader, regardless of his or her familiarity with patents, to quickly determine the character of the patentable subject matter.

Although abstract searching is easy, it is not as reliable as reviewing the whole patent. The following example is an abstract for a mechanical conveyor for live chickens and turkeys.

Live Fowl Conveyor: No. 2,345,678

A conveyor for supporting live fowl to be inoculated, inseminated, debeaked, or to have another operation performed on them. The conveyor includes a base, a pair of spindles mounted to the base, one at each of opposite ends, and a generally horizontally-disposed moving conveyor surface supported by the base. The conveyor surface is defined by an endless web encircling the spindles and is intended to receive thereon fowl which are to have an operation performed on them. The conveyor also includes apparatus for holding each bird in a defined position on the conveyor surface, including a pair of elongated, generally-parallel members spaced upward from the conveyor surface to define a slot therebetween. The elongated members are disposed such that the vertical distance between them can be varied.

If an abstract seems relevant, the full patent should be ordered from the Patent and Trademark Office.

Computer Searching

Patent searching can also be accomplished by computer via an online database. An *online database* is a collection of information accessed by a person using a computer connected to a telephone line. Each online database has a system of searching, storing, and printing information. The content of each online database is different.

Mead Data's *Lexis*® Patent Library is the most complete patent database available, because it includes the full text and abstracts of patents (though not drawings), the Patent and Trademark Office *Manual of Classification,* records of Patent and Trademark Office interference proceedings, and federal statutes and regulations. In addition, the *LEXPAT* library offers extensive prior art searching capability. That is, it is possible to review technical journals and magazines to determine if inventions have been disclosed in publications. Such technical publications are extremely relevant in determining whether an invention is patentable.

The Dialog® Claims™ service is a group of databases including, among other libraries, *Claims™ Uniterm* (chemical and chemically related patents); *Claims™ U.S. Patent Abstracts* (a collection of general, chemical, electrical, and mechanical patent abstracts); *Claims™ Reference Library* (a dictionary index to subject classifications used in the Dialog family of patent libraries); and *Claims™ Reassignment & Reexamination* (information on the current status of U.S. patents, including reassignment, reexamination, extensions, and expirations). Prentice Hall's *REFERENCEMASTER*™ system combines several databases, such as Dialog, Orbit Search, and NewsNet, to allow a user to search multiple database companies. *CLAIMS* is a patent database, available from IFI/Plenum, which contains approximately 2 million U.S. patents. Various fees may be involved when using an online database.

12.2 THE PATENT APPLICATION PROCESS

The drafter of a patent application must possess a relevant scientific or technical background as well as skillful application-drafting style. A patent application should *not* be prepared by an unsupervised paralegal unless that paralegal is also a patent agent. Only the inventor, a patent attorney, or patent agent should draft an application. However, there are activities that a legal assistant may perform, including assembly of the elements of the application

LEGAL TERMS

abstract
  Summary of the invention that enables the reader to determine the character of the patentable subject matter.

package and assistance in patent searching. Even though the paralegal may not be directly involved in preparation of the application, it is helpful to have some knowledge of the terminology. The application includes a summary of the background of the invention, the objectives and advantages of the invention, a description of the drawings, an explanation of how the invention works, a conclusion, a discussion of ramifications, and the aspects claimed for patent protection. The application and drawing are submitted with appropriate fees and supporting statements, petitions, and declarations. Fees depend on the size of the entity registering the patent (smaller companies can pay lower fees, providing they also file a necessary declaration regarding their small size).

Specification

The **specification** consists of several elements: a title, an abstract of the disclosure, cross-references to any related applications, a background and summary of the invention, a brief description of the views of the drawings, a detailed description of the invention and how it works, the claim or claims, and a signature.[1] The purpose of the specification is to sufficiently disclose the invention so that an individual skilled in the art to which the invention pertains could, after reading the patent, make and use the invention without the necessity of further experiment. The specification must set forth the **best mode** contemplated by the inventor of carrying out the invention. An inventor may envision several ways of embodying the invention or may hold back one method of carrying out the invention, in order to keep it a secret. However, if the inventor knew of a better mode and failed to disclose it, that failure may result in the loss of patent rights. For example, an infringer may defend against a patent lawsuit by arguing that the patent owner failed to disclose the best mode at the time of filing the application. If this is true, the infringer will prevail in the lawsuit because the patent will be invalidated.

Cross-References

If an applicant files a patent application claiming an invention disclosed in a prior-filed, co-pending application by the same inventor, the second application must contain (or be amended to contain) a reference to the prior application.[2] This cross-reference must identify the prior application by serial number and filing date and must indicate the relationship of the applications. Cross-references are necessary if the applicant is seeking the benefit of the filing date of the prior invention.

Background

The background section of the specification is really a method of promoting the discovery by criticizing the prior art and explaining the necessity of the invention. For instance, the following background example disparages previous conventional air poppers and explains the need for a low-headroom popcorn popper.

Background
3,456,789: Low-headroom popcorn popper

The present invention relates to kitchen appliances and, more particularly, to popcorn poppers.

One type of popcorn popper, with which the present invention is particularly concerned, employs a flow of heated air through unpopped kernels of corn to raise their temperature to a value high enough to generate steam within the kernels, thereby forcing explosive expansion of the hard kernels into the familiar soft popped corn. An air popper preferably includes means for separating the popped corn from the unpopped kernels. One way for performing such separation includes permitting the heated air to escape in an upward direction. The larger cross section of the popped corn permits it to be carried upward and to exit the corn popper while the smaller cross section of the unpopped kernels tends to permit them to remain in the bottom of the popper for additional heating until substantially all of the corn is popped and delivered from the popper by the exiting flow of air.

Balancing the requirements for attaining satisfactory popping while separating the popped corn from the unpopped kernels presents a critical problem in an air popper. The air flow through a popping chamber must be high enough to keep the unpopped kernels stirred for even heating. Excessive air flow velocity, however, tends to drive an unacceptable proportion of unpopped kernels out of the popping chamber along with the popped corn. Conventional air poppers position a fan below the popping chamber and provide for feeding kernels through a top opening and for permitting exit of the popped corn through the same top opening. The assignee of the present invention has developed a popular line of kitchen appliances to be mounted on the underside of suspended cabinets. The line is characterized by small vertical dimensions in order to provide minimum interference with counter space frequently disposed below the cabinets. The present invention is a member of this low-headroom family. Under-cabinet mounting denies access to the top of the popper for adding kernels or for receiving the popped corn. In addition, the vertical alignment of blower, popping chamber and fill/delivery chamber increases the vertical dimension of prior art devices beyond acceptable limits for a device mounted under suspended cabinets and over a counter. All air poppers tend to leave debris in the popping chamber. Debris from the popping chamber of a conventional air popper can be dumped out by inverting the air popper and can be cleaned through its top opening. Undercabinet mounting prevents both of these actions.

Summary of Invention

The *summary* is a short and general statement of the invention that explains how the invention resolves the criticisms of the prior art (posed in the

---

LEGAL TERMS

specification
Patent application disclosure by the inventor; drafted so that an individual skilled in the art to which the invention pertains could, by reading the patent, make and use the invention without the necessity of further experiment.

best mode
The inventor's principal and preferred method of embodying the invention.

background section).[3] The summary should be understandable by a judge or jury and should summarize the claims. The next example is a summary for a food-turning mechanism.

Summary
Turning Mechanism: No. 4,567,890

The present invention provides a particularly simple method and compact mechanism for automatically turning, or otherwise moving or manipulating a food item during cooking. A mechanism according to the present invention is able to turn the food item from one side to another following the same type of turning action conventionally provided manually by the chef. The method is applicable for automatically flipping over such generally planar-shaped foods as steaks, hamburgers, and fish filets as well as for automatically turning bulkier items such as roasts or fowl.

The invention is driven by a horizontally rotating drive shaft such as the drive shaft disclosed in my copending U.S. patent application Ser. No. 07/140,176 filed Dec. 31, 1987. Briefly, according to the invention a food item may be automatically turned about the horizontal rotation axis by a mechanism which provides a moment arm extending generally perpendicular to said horizontal axis. The moment arm is flexibly linked to the food item at an end of the food item, the link being made at one or more positions spaced apart from the horizontal rotation axis. The moment arm is then automatically rotated about the horizontal axis so as to drag the food item about the horizontal axis.

The turning mechanism of the invention is particularly suited for use with the automatic cooking apparatus disclosed in U.S. Pat. No. 4,649,810, described above. However, it may also be used with other automatic cooking arrangements or, as described above, as a stand-alone device associated with an appropriate drive mechanism.

Claims

The patent claims define the boundaries of the invention in the same way that a deed establishes the boundaries of real property. Two different types of claims may be filed in a patent application. The first and more important type, called an *independent claim*, broadly determines the scope of the invention. The second type is a *dependent claim*, which is narrower but incorporates the independent claim. For example, the independent claim may describe the invention, but the dependent claim may describe the type of material of which the invention is comprised. In the claim in the following example, dependent claim 3 states that the invention is formed of cellular plastic to provide insulation. The arcane rules of patent drafting require that the claims use only one sentence, that is, with an initial capital letter, one period, and no quotation marks or parentheses (except in mathematical or chemical formulas). The example contains the claims for a portable security box suitable for use by beachgoers. This thermally insulated cooler device emits an alarm when an unauthorized person attempts to take it. Note that the claims consist of one independent claim and eight dependent claims.

Claims
Secured valuable box for beachgoers: No. 5,678,901

What is claimed is:

1.   A portable container for valuables which comprises:

a.   a closed receptacle having a interior chamber with an access opening in its top surface;

b.   a cover hinged to said receptacle and moveable between an open position and a closed position totally closing said opening;

c.   a lock including a latch carried on said top cover and cooperative with a clasp carried on said receptacle;

d.   resilient means in said lock biasing said latch into a locked engagement with said clasp, and a solenoid carried on said container and cooperative with said lock to release said lock against the bias of said resilient means;

e.   a keypad carried on said top cover at a location exposed to view and free access;

f.   an electrical power supply carried by said container; and

g.   an alarm and control circuit carried on said top cover and in circuit with said power supply, keypad and solenoid including storage means whereby a code can be stored in said alarm and control circuit and accessed through said keypad to activate said solenoid;

h.   alarm means carried by said container;

i.   motion detection means also carried by said top cover and in circuit between said power supply, alarm and control circuit and said alarm means, whereby said keypad can arm said alarm to respond to a signal from said motion detection means, or disarm said alarm.

2.   The container of claim 1 whereby said keypad is the only operator-input device for said alarm and control circuit.

3.   The container of claim 1 wherein said receptacle is a box formed entirely of cellular plastic foam to provide thermally insulating walls to provide a portable cooler.

4.   The container of claim 1 wherein said keypad is carried on the top surface of said top cover.

5.   The container of claim 1 wherein said power supply includes a panel of solar cells carried on the top surface of said top cover.

6.   The container of claim 1 including a carrying handle on said top cover of said container.

7.   The container of claim 6 wherein said handle is centrally located on said cover.

8.   The container of claim 1 wherein said receptacle is a box with opposite end side walls and including a carrying strap attached to said opposite end walls of said container.

9.   The container of claim 8 wherein opposite ends of said strap are attached to said opposite end walls of said container.

Drawings

Drawings of the invention are required if such drawings are necessary to understand the subject matter of the patent. If a drawing is necessary, it must be included as part of the application, or else a filing date will not be granted. If a filing date is given by mistake (when a necessary drawing was not included as part of the application), the examiner may later find the application to be fatally defective. Patent drawings have strict standards as to materials, size, form, symbols, and shading.[4] Patent drawings are usually accomplished by experienced graphic artists using pen and ink. However, with the advent of computer-assisted design and drawing programs (CADDs), some patent practitioners have begun preparing their own drawings. There are many patent drawing services located in the Arlington, Virginia and Washington, D.C. area. If time is short or resources are stretched, it is possible to file a patent application with "informal drawings," e.g., photocopies of pencil-drawn drawings that show all of the details but are not as well drawn as will eventually be required.

Declaration

The oath or declaration serves several purposes: (1) identification of the inventor or joint inventors; (2) attestation of truthfulness and that the inventor understands the contents of the claim and specifications and has fully disclosed all material information[5]; and (3) identification of any prior U.S. or foreign patent applications that disclose the invention and upon which priority is claimed or not claimed.[6] The identification of foreign patents may enable the inventor to claim the benefit of the foreign filing date. This earlier date may help the inventor establish priority over other U.S. applicants who may have applied earlier in the United States, but do not have a prior foreign application date to rely upon. The Patent and Trademark Office provides a form for such a declaration, but the applicant may create a similar form provided that it includes all the required information.

An application for a plant patent must also contain a statement that the applicant has asexually reproduced the plant, or, if the subject is a recently discovered plant, it must state that the plant was found in a cultivated area. If the applicant is seeking to acquire a reissue patent, the declaration must contain additional statements as provided in 37 C.F.R. § 1.75(a).

Power of Attorney

As explained previously, only an inventor, a registered patent agent, or a registered patent attorney may prosecute a patent application. A *power of attorney* must be executed to authorize the patent attorney or agent to act on behalf of the inventor.[7] The power of attorney form may be combined with the declaration or oath (see figure 12-2). If the rights to the patent have been assigned, the assignee usually executes the power of attorney.

POWER OF ATTORNEY

Kimberly Simpson, inventor and owner of the application United States Letters Patent for a Portable Popcorn Popper, does hereby appoint as attorney of record with full power of substitution and revocation to prosecute this application and transact all business in the Patent and Trademark Office: Mark E. Marson, Reg. No. 12,345, 27 Windfall Rd., Wantagh, NY 11793 (516-555-1212).

I declare that I am the owner of the above-identified application and that I am authorized to make this appointment and I further declare that all statements made herein of my own knowledge are true and that all statements made on information and belief are believed to be true; and further that these statements were made with the knowledge that willful false statements and the like so made are punishable by fine or imprisonment, or both, under section 1001 of Title 18 of the United States Code, and that such willful false statements may jeopardize the validity of the application of any patent issuing thereon.

_____

Kimberly Simpson
1234 Homey Avenue, Levittown, NY 11793

FIGURE 12-2
Sample power of attorney

Information Disclosure Statement

Applicants for U.S. patents have a duty to inform the Patent and Trademark Office of any material prior art, related patents, or other pertinent information, such as related foreign applications and related litigation. New rules regarding such disclosures took effect on March 16, 1992. Under these new rules, information is considered "material" if it is not cumulative to information already of record in the application and: (1) if it establishes (by itself or with other information) the unpatentability of a claim; or (2) it refutes or is inconsistent with a position that the applicant takes in asserting an argument of patentability or in opposing an argument of unpatentability. This obligation of disclosure may be fulfilled by the filing of an **information disclosure statement** (sometimes known as an IDS) at the time of filing of the application or within three months of the filing of the application. The failure to disclose material information can have a disastrous effect on the application and may render the subsequent patent invalid. The information disclosure statement must include a listing of patents, publications, or other information and an explanation of the relevance of each listed item. A copy of each listed patent or publication or other item of information (or relevant portion) should be included. If the documentation is not in the English language, a translation should be provided. To assist in the filing, the Patent and Trademark Office encourages applicants to use Form PTO-1449, "Information Disclosure Citation."

LEGAL TERMS

information disclosure statement (IDS)
Pertinent information regarding an application provided to the Patent and Trademark Office; includes prior art, any related patents, and printed publications by the inventor.

Small Entity Declaration Form

To encourage small business, independent inventors, and nonprofit companies to obtain patents, fees are reduced for these entities. At the time of filing the application (or within 60 days of payment of the higher fee), the applicant desiring to pay the fee at the reduced rate (or obtain a refund of the overpayment) must file a small entity declaration for qualifying for this exception. There are three types of small entity exceptions: (1) independent inventors; (2) nonprofit organizations; and (3) small business concerns.[8] An *independent inventor* is a person who has either maintained rights or has transferred rights to a small entity or nonprofit company. *Nonprofit organizations* are defined and listed in the Code of Federal Regulations. A *small business concern* is a business with 500 or fewer employees (computed by averaging the number of full- and part-time employees during a fiscal year). Small entity status is lost if patent rights are transferred to an entity that does not qualify as small entity.

Assignment

The rights to a patent and patent application may be transferred by assignment (examples of such assignments are provided in chapter 11). It is wise to file the assignment at the same time the application is filed (or no later than when the issue fee is paid for issuing a patent), because that filing permits the patent to be issued in the name of the assignee (the party to whom rights are transferred) and also provides notice of the ownership of the application and patent in Patent and Trademark Office records. By providing the assignment with the application, the applicant also acquires the earliest possible date of recordation, a factor that may be important in a subsequent dispute as to ownership rights. It is not required that the assignment be notarized, but notarization can create a presumption of validity and may be required in some foreign countries. A cover sheet containing specific information must accompany an assignment that is being filed for recordation.[9]

Transmittal Letter and Mailing

The *transmittal letter* is more than a cover letter listing the enclosed documents. It is a formal requirement of the application and must include the name of the inventor, the title of the invention, the total number of pages of specifications and claims, and the number of sheets of drawings. If a small entity declaration is enclosed, that should also be noted. If the applicant is claiming priority on the basis of a foreign application, the following statement should be included:

> Pursuant to 35 U.S.C. 119, Applicant claims priority on the basis of Patent Application No. _____, in _____ filed on _____.
> A certified copy of the priority document is enclosed.

The Patent and Trademark Office has provided a form for the transmittal letter; however, the information may be retyped or keyed into a word processor, as shown in figure 12-3.

TRANSMITTAL LETTER

Date:
Commissioner of Patents & Trademarks
Washington, DC 20231

Enclosed for filing is the patent application of [Inventor]
For: [Title of Invention]
Enclosed are
( ) Specifications, Claims and Abstract (No. of sheets) _____
( ) Drawing (No. of Sheets) _____
( ) Declaration & Power of Attorney
( ) Information Disclosure
( ) Small Entity Declaration
( ) Assignment of the Invention to _____
( ) Return postcard
( ) Other _____
( ) Filing fee of $ _____ as calculated below:

FOR	No. Filed	No. Extra	Claims Filed / Small Entity		Other than small entity	
			Rate	Fee	Rate	Fee
Basic Fee				$345		$690
Total Claims			×10	$	×20	$
Independent Claims			×36	$	×72	$
			+110	$	+220	$
Multiple Dependent Claims Presented			Total	$	Total	$

Signed: _____

Certificate of Express Mailing

Express Mail Mailing Label Number: **OB071328928** Date of Deposit: **August 9, 1992**
I hereby certify that the enclosed documents are being deposited with the United States Postal Service, "Express Mail Post Office to Addressee" service under 37 CFR § 1.10 on the date indicated above and is addressed to the Commissioner of Patents and Trademarks, Washington, DC 20231.
[*Signature*]

FIGURE 12-3
Sample transmittal letter

Certificate of Mailing

Documents or fees filed with the Patent and Trademark Office should include a certificate of mailing. This statement may be appended to any document and should be signed and dated.

Certificate of Mailing

I hereby certify that this document is being deposited with the United States Postal Service, as first-class mail on the date indicated above in an envelope addressed to the Commissioner of Patents and Trademarks, Washington, DC 20231.

If the applicant is submitting the patent application or any other document by an overnight express mailing procedure, a certificate of express mailing must be included. An example is provided in the transmittal letter in figure 12-3.

Return Postcard

Along with the patent application, the applicant should include a self-addressed stamped postcard in order to verify receipt and track the application. The postcard should list each document enclosed in the envelope and provide a check box so that the person opening the application at the Patent and Trademark Office can confirm receipt.

Petition to Make Special

Under certain circumstances, processing of a patent application may be accelerated. Reasons for this may include: the applicant is in ill health or over age 65; the device will result in energy savings, enhancement of environment quality, or advancement of superconductivity; the invention involves recombinant DNA; infringement exists; the application is based on the results of a professional search; or the inventor has located a manufacturer for the device. If the inventor desires to speed up the process, a **Petition to Make Special** is filed along with supporting declarations and documentation. This petition may be filed with the application or at any time after filing.[10]

Filing Fees

The filing fees for patent applications change periodically and therefore the schedule shown in the sample transmittal letter (figure 12-3) may not be accurate when you read this. Always consult the Patent and Trademark Office for the current fees. Companies, firms, and individuals that deal regularly with the Patent and Trademark Office may establish a *deposit account*. A sum is placed in the deposit account and fees are charged against the balance. Rules regarding deposit accounts are at 37 C.F.R. § 1.25.

Checklist for Patent Application

The patent application should include the following:

- **Patent Application Transmittal Letter**—Should include a certificate of mailing or certificate of express mailing.
- **Specification**—Confirm that pages and claims are correctly and consecutively numbered and that figure numbers correspond to the application.
- **Power of Attorney**—Confirm that it is signed and dated.
- **Declaration**—Confirm that it is signed, dated, and that the addresses and telephone numbers are accurate.
- **Information Disclosure Statement**—Confirm listing of documents, comments regarding pertinent documents, copies of documents, and translations (if necessary).
- **Fee Payment**—Confirm that fees are accurate and the check is signed.
- **Return Postcard**
- **Express Mail**—Enclose certificate of express mailing.
- **Envelope**—Addressed to Commissioner of Patents and Trademarks, Washington, DC 20231; marked on the outside "PATENT APPLICATION."
- **Calendar**—Notify docket or calendar clerk of date of mailing.

If Required

- **Assignment**—Verify that it is properly executed and dated.
- **Small Entity Form**—Determine if applicant qualifies as independent inventor, small entity, or nonprofit business.
- **Petition to Make Special**—Confirm that Petition and declaration in support are properly executed and dated.
- **Copies**—Copies should be made of all documentation; copies should be furnished to client.

Processing of the Patent Application

It takes approximately 18 months for the Patent and Trademark Office to process a patent application. On the average, the Patent and Trademark Office issues two *office actions* during the processing period. In a large number of cases, the patent examiner initially finds some fault in the application (e.g., the examiner determines that the claims are too broad and requests that the applicant amend the claims to more narrowly define the invention). The office action from the patent examiner may require more research by the inventor or owner in order to provide information for contesting issues raised by the examiner regarding prior art references cited in the examiner's letter. The applicant is usually given three months to prepare and file an amendment in response to an office action. However, two three-month extensions (for a total period of six months) may be obtained upon payment of a fee. Although the claims can be amended, the drawings and text cannot be altered if the change involves **new matter**. What is new matter? Although one legal writer stated that "any effort to define new matter is hopeless," as a general

LEGAL TERMS

Petition to Make Special
Request to accelerate processing of a patent application.

new matter
New subject matter that does not conform to and is not supported by the original patent application; material that cannot be added to the patent application by amendment.

rule, *new matter* is considered to be any new subject matter that does not conform to or is not supported by the original patent application. New matter cannot be added to a pending application. As discussed later, however, new matter can only be added to a "continuation in part" application.

If possible, the applicant will prepare claim amendments that satisfy the patent examiner. If the amendment does not result in allowance of the patent, the examiner may issue a final rejection in the second office action. At this point, the applicant will either: (1) correct the claims according to the examiner's request or submit a narrower claim; (2) attempt to persuade the examiner to reconsider; (3) appeal the matter to the Board of Appeals and Patent Interferences (BAPI) or petition the Patent and Trademark Office Commissioner; (4) file a continuation application; or (5) abandon the application.

If the patent examiner allows (i.e., approves) the application, a Notice of Allowance is issued. After the Notice of Allowance, the applicant must pay an issue fee. Upon receipt of the issue fee, the patent will be issued within a matter of a few weeks.

Portions of the patent will be published in the weekly issue of the patent part of the *Official Gazette.* Most large libraries subscribe to the *Official Gazette,* and single copies can be obtained from the Superintendent of Documents, U.S. Government Printing Office, Washington, DC 20402. The purpose of the publication is to provide current information about patents, including patents available for license or sale and patents granted during the publication period, as well as changes in patent law or regulations.

Continuation and Divisional Applications

A **continuation application** is a second application for the same invention claimed in an earlier patent application. It must be filed before the original (or *parent*) application becomes abandoned. A *continuation* is a method of resubmitting the application with further evidence in support of patentability (e.g., revised or new claims). For example, if in the facts of the Commentary in this chapter, an examiner disallowed the claims for the original patent application for the *Fogarama* invention and the applicant later revised the claims based upon newly discovered evidence in support of patentability, the applicant could submit a continuation application. The refiled application acquires a new serial number and is reexamined. The continuation application must be filed by the same applicant and must cross-reference the first application. The filing date for the continuation application is the same as the filing date of the original application.

A **continuation in part application** is a second application for the same invention, filed while the first (or parent) application is still pending, and which includes new matter not covered in the original application. The difference between a continuation application and a continuation in part is that the latter adds new matter not disclosed in the earlier application (e.g., an improvement, correction of an error, or important information missing

LEGAL TERMS

continuation application
   Application filed after an earlier filed patent application has been disallowed (but not yet abandoned); a method of resubmitting the application with new claims or further evidence in support of patentability.

from the original application). For example, if in the facts of the Commentary, the inventor of the *Fogarama* device created an improved method of disbursing the fog *after* the original patent application was filed, a continuation in part application could be used. The filing date for the continuation in part application will be the same as the filing date for the original application, but only as to matter covered in the original submission. A second filing date will be issued to the applicant for the *in part* submission (i.e., the new matter).

A continuation application and a continuation in part application are distinguished from a **divisional application**, which is usually filed because an examiner has determined that the original application (the parent) contains two or more inventions. Only one patent may be issued per invention. For this reason, the applicant files a divisional application to carve out each separate invention. The filing date for the divisional application will be considered the same as the date for the parent or original application.

Reissue Patents

The purpose of a **reissue patent** is to correct errors made in a patent that is in effect (i.e., an *in-force patent*) and which, as the result of such error, is rendered wholly or partially inoperative or invalid. Such errors can relate to defective specifications or drawings. However, errors resulting from fraud or deceptive intent cannot be corrected by means of a reissue patent. Occasionally, the basis for correction is that the claims are too narrow or too broad. A reissue patent that seeks to broaden claims must be filed within two years of the issue date of the original patent.

For example, the inventor of *Fogarama* has received a patent that details use of stainless steel for the outer casing. Later, it is determined that other alloys work as well, if not better. The claims can be reissued with this broader statement provided that a reissue application explaining the error is filed within the time period. The expiration date for the reissued patent would be the same as for the original patent. The oath required in support of a reissue application must contain additional averments.[11]

Patent Interference

When an application is made for a patent that, in the opinion of the Commissioner of the Patent and Trademark Office, would interfere with any pending application (or an unexpired patent), a proceeding known as a **patent interference** is instituted in the Patent and Trademark Office and held before the Board of Patent Appeals. The purpose of this adversarial proceeding is to determine any question of **priority of invention**. A patent interference is an expensive and time-consuming process that involves most of the same procedures and rules as federal litigation. Approximately 1 percent of applications are subject to interference proceedings.

---

continuation in part application
A second subsequent application containing new material not previously disclosed in an earlier filed patent application; a method of supplementing an earlier patent application with new matter to cover improvements.

divisional application
Application made for an independent invention that has grown out of an earlier application; a method of dividing an original application that contains two or more inventions.

reissue patent
Patent granted to correct errors made in a patent that is in effect (i.e., an in-force patent) and that, as the result of such error, is rendered wholly or partially inoperative or invalid. Errors resulting from fraud or deceptive intent cannot be corrected by means of a reissue patent.

patent interference
Proceeding instituted in the Patent and Trademark Office to determine any question of priority of invention between two or more parties claiming the same patentable invention.

priority of invention
U.S. patent policy awarding a patent to the first person to invent over persons who subsequently invent the same patentable concept.

When a dispute arises as to priority of invention, the first party who files a patent application is known as the *senior party* and the second party is known as the *junior party*. To prevail, the junior party has the burden of proving either: (1) **reduction to practice** before the filing date of the senior party; or (2) conception of the invention before the senior party's filing date, coupled with a reasonably diligent effort to reduce to practice.

The final determination in a patent interference may be appealed to the United States Court of Appeals for the Federal Circuit or to the United States District Court for the District of Columbia. Many of the same issues that arise in a patent interference may also arise in patent litigation (e.g., questions of patentability, conception of the invention, reduction to practice, and priority of invention between the parties).

Maintenance Fees

To maintain the validity of a utility patent (i.e., to keep it "in force"), certain fees must be periodically paid to the Patent and Trademark Office.[12] Although a utility patent is granted for 17 years, the patent may be forfeited prior to expiration if maintenance fees are not timely paid. The initial issuance fee, paid at the time the patent is granted, guarantees patent rights for four years from the date of the grant. After that date, however, the patent may be forfeited unless a payment was made during the years preceding the four-year anniversary. The payment may be made during the first half of the preceding year (i.e., between year 3.0 and 3.5) or paid with a penalty during the second half of that year. Maintenance fees must also be paid during the years preceding the eighth anniversary and twelfth anniversary of the date of the patent grant. These payments may not be made prior to these time periods. That is, the maintenance fee due during the seventh year cannot be paid during the sixth year. (See table 12.1.) Businesses or inventors that qualify under the small entity exception and have filed small entity declarations may pay reduced maintenance fees. A patent that is forfeited due to failure to pay maintenance fees may be revived if a petition is made and the patent owner demonstrates that the delay was unavoidable. The payment of maintenance fees should be docketed and calendared when the patent issues.

Patent Notice

During the pendency period (between the filing and issuance of the patent), the inventor may use the notice "Patent Pending," "Pat. Pend.," "Patent Applied For," or similar variations. The notice informs the public that the inventor is seeking a patent. However, there is no enforcement power behind such notice. That is, the inventor cannot sue under the patent law, because a patent has not yet been issued. The "patent pending" notice simply informs the public that if a patent is issued, the inventor will enforce rights. Use of such notice when an application is not pending can subject the party to penalties. After the patent has issued, the owner should mark the invention with

Schedule of Patent Maintenance Fees	
Between 3 and 3.5 years	First maintenance fee
Between 3.5 and 4 years	First maintenance fee with penalty
Between 7 and 7.5 years	Second maintenance fee
Between 7.5 and 8 years	Second maintenance fee with penalty
Between 11 and 11.5 years	Third maintenance fee
Between 11.5 and 12 years	Third maintenance fee with penalty

TABLE 12.1
Patent Maintenance
Fees

"Pat." or "Patent" and the number of the patent. If this notice is used, the owner may recover damages from an infringer from the time that the infringement began. The notice must be applied to the patent owner's products that embody the patented invention, not merely to advertising or promotional materials. If the notice is not used, the owner can only recover damages as of the date the infringer is informed of the patent and charged with infringing it, usually in the form of a cease and desist letter.[13]

Design Patent Applications

Compared to a utility or plant patent application, the design patent application is relatively simple. Only one claim is permitted and the specification follows a short, set form. This means that the drawings are correspondingly more important; therefore, they must be complete and well drawn. If the examiner, when issuing an office action, requests any changes to a design patent application, they are usually straightforward and simple. There are no maintenance fees for a design patent.

Reexamination

If there is a "substantial new question of patentability," documented by printed publications or patents, the Patent and Trademark Office will reexamine an in-force patent to make a determination of the patentability of one or more of its claims. This **reexamination** procedure is a possible alternative to patent litigation. If a defendant claims that a plaintiff's patent is invalid, either the plaintiff or the defendant may request reexamination. The parties may stipulate or may request that the court suspend or stay the litigation until the reexamination is completed. The advantage of this procedure is that reexamination is often less expensive than litigation and may provide information that will help the parties settle the matter.

LEGAL TERMS

reduction to practice
The contemplation of the actual and complete use of the invention for its intended purpose (e.g., prototyping and successfully testing the invention). The act of preparing and filing a patent application is considered a *constructive reduction to practice.*

reexamination
Review by the Patent and Trademark Office of the patentability of one or more claims of an in-force patent, based upon substantial new evidence of prior art not previously considered.

12.3 PATENT INFRINGEMENT

In the early 1970s, the Polaroid Corporation received several patents for its innovative SX-70 instant camera and instant film process. Four years later, the Eastman Kodak Company debuted *its* instant camera. Lawyers at the Polaroid Corporation believed that the Kodak camera infringed on the SX-70 camera patents and, in 1976, filed a patent infringement suit. Kodak defended itself by claiming that the Polaroid patents were invalid, unenforceable, and, in any case were not infringed by the Kodak system. Over the next five years, the parties participated in pretrial conferences, filed numerous motions, and engaged in extensive discovery, accounting for more than 1,000 entries in the district court's docket. After 75 days of trial, the district court issued its judgment that 7 of 10 Polaroid patents were infringed. Damages were assessed at more than $900 million. (The infringement case had another unusual aspect. The trial judge was forced to disqualify herself when, in the midst of the litigation, she inherited 1,000 shares of Kodak stock.)

Kodak lost its appeal of the trial court decision and announced it was ending its instant camera business (which had provided annual revenues of about $200 million). Kodak offered a voluntary exchange plan to the estimated 16 million owners of its instant cameras. In 1990, after more discovery and motions, the $909.5 million award was confirmed by a written opinion of the district court. The massive award was an attempt to assess profits, royalties, and interest to Polaroid for Kodak's infringement. Polaroid's lawyers expressed disappointment because they had hoped to obtain triple damages ($2.7 billion). The patent law provides that a judge may award up to three times the actual damages—a decision occasionally made in cases of willful infringement.

For another year, the parties battled over the payment of damages. In 1991, 15 years after filing the lawsuit, Kodak and Polaroid reached a final settlement. Kodak agreed to pay Polaroid $925 million, including $873 million in damages and $53 million in interest. As part of the settlement, Kodak and Polaroid also agreed to end similar patent litigation in Canada and the United Kingdom. Curiously, the underlying patent on the Polaroid SX-70 instant camera expired prior to the settlement. Even more interesting, the instant photography market peaked in 1978, two years after the lawsuit was filed. Since then, both Kodak and Polaroid have sought new devices to exploit. Kodak has emphasized electronics and computerized information-retrieval systems and Polaroid has highlighted commercial and industrial uses of instant photography. For example, 30 states now use Polaroid instant photographs on driver's licenses.

As the Kodak-Polaroid case demonstrates, the pursuit and defense of patent infringement is expensive and often risky. Hundreds of thousands of dollars may be expended before the parties even reach the trial stage. The plaintiff risks a declaration of invalidity as to its patent and the defendant risks multimillion-dollar damage awards. The very subject of the patent dispute may lose its value during the lengthy litigation process.

There are two ways in which a patent can be infringed. In a *literal infringement*, the defendant makes, uses, or sells all of the components of a patent claim exactly as the claim is stated. The alleged infringement is a duplicate of the claim in the patent. The second type of infringement, *infringement under the doctrine of equivalents*, occurs if the defendant makes, sells, or uses a substantially similar device that varies from the exact wording of the patent claim. The infringing invention employs substantially the same means to achieve substantially the same results in substantially the same way as that claimed. As demonstrated in the Polaroid case, a suit for patent infringement usually triggers a defensive attack on the validity of the patent. The litigation becomes two separate battles, one in which the plaintiff claims damage from infringement and the other in which the defendant attempts to invalidate the plaintiff's patent rights. In the Polaroid case, for example, Polaroid proved infringement of seven patents, but Kodak proved invalidity of three of Polaroid's patents.

Literal Infringement

Both literal infringement and infringement under the doctrine of equivalents refer to infringement of the patent claims. Because the claims define the boundaries of the invention, they serve as the reference for infringement. A literal infringement occurs if a defendant makes, sells, or uses the invention exactly as defined in the plaintiff's patent claim. By way of example, in the facts to this chapter's Commentary, a rival company has duplicated Effectsco's fog-making apparatus. The infringing machine includes each and every component, part, or step in Effectsco's fog-making apparatus. It is a literal infringement because the defendant's device is indisputably the *same* invention as in Effectsco's patent claim.

Doctrine of Equivalents

A second way in which a claim can be infringed is if the defendant's invention employs substantially the same means to achieve substantially the same results in substantially the same way as that claimed. As explained in chapter 11, this is known as the **doctrine of equivalents**. There is no formula to determine equivalency. In the case of chemical compositions, for example, a defendant may change one or more ingredients so that there is no literal infringement. The jury or judge must determine if the changed ingredient has the same purpose, quality, and function as the ingredient in the patent claim. If so, unless negated by information in the patent application or prior art, there has been infringement under the doctrine of equivalents.

Improvement Infringement

A patent can be infringed by means of an improvement. For example, a company improves the *Fogarama* device discussed in the Commentary to

LEGAL TERMS

doctrine of equivalents
Right of patent owner to prevent sale, use, or manufacture of a discovery or invention if it employs substantially the same means to achieve substantially the same results in substantially the same way as that claimed.

this chapter by adding an exhaust and venting system. The company may even obtain a patent on this improvement. However, this does not give the rival company the right to manufacture or use the *Fogarama* device. Such unauthorized improvement may be an infringement of the claim or claims of the original patent.

Inducing Infringement and Contributory Infringement

Persons who induce[14] or contribute to[15] patent infringement will also be liable for the infringement. The elements of contributory infringement are (1) sale (2) of a material component of the invention defined by the claims (that is not a staple item of commerce capable of noninfringing use) (3) with knowledge that the component was especially made for use that would infringe the patent. For example, a large stainless steel atomizer is one aspect of the *Fogarama* device in the facts in the Commentary. If the atomizer were a component protected under the patent claim, it would be a contributory infringement for a manufacturer to knowingly make and sell the component to a company that intended to create an infringing fog-making apparatus. It is also contributory infringement to actively induce or persuade another to make, use, or sell the invention covered by the patent claims.

Willful Infringement

The infringer's intent is generally irrelevant to a finding of patent infringement (although intent may be a factor in contributory infringement and in assessing damages). Patent infringement does not require that the defendant have *intended* to infringe. However, if willful patent infringement occurred, the damages for that infringement may be increased up to triple the amount of damages actually proved. Infringement is *willful* if the defendant knew of the plaintiff's patent and knew that the making, using, or selling of the defendant's device infringed at least one claim of the plaintiff's patent. This determination may be based on the defendant's bad faith activities or on the fact that the defendant failed to exercise due care. For example, in the facts described in the Polaroid case, the Polaroid Corporation argued that Kodak willfully infringed seven of Polaroid's instant camera patents. The trial court disagreed and determined that the infringement was not willful. If the infringement had been determined to be willful, Polaroid could have been awarded up to $2.7 billion, rather than $900 million, and in addition might have been awarded attorney fees. A finding of willfulness can also result from the defendant's failing to reasonably investigate whether conflicting patent claims existed prior to making, using, or selling the new product and failing to obtain the opinion of a knowledgeable patent attorney about such conflicting claims. If a defendant has been accused of infringement, it may amount to willful infringement to continue the allegedly infringing activity without seeking the advice of counsel.

Design Patent Infringement

Infringement of a design patent occurs if the resemblance between the two devices is so similar that a consumer would be deceived. The resemblance must be due to the presence in both the patented design and the accused article of features that are primarily ornamental and that were novel in the patented invention. The judge or jury compares the design drawing in the plaintiff's patent (not the plaintiff's product) with the defendant's product. The comparison must be based upon the novel features of the design, because these are the design features that distinguish the design from the prior art. For example, Guitarco has a patent for a guitar body that resembles a telephone. Guitarco sues Musico for making a similar guitar. At trial, the jury will compare the drawing in Guitarco's patent with the Musico guitar. If, after comparing the distinguishing features, the jury determines that consumers would be confused as to the two designs, then an infringement has occurred.

Affirmative Defenses

A defendant in a patent infringement lawsuit generally argues that the defendant's device is noninfringing or that the plaintiff's patent is invalid and unenforceable. The basis for arguing invalidity and unenforceability was presented in chapter 11; these defenses include inequitable conduct (also known as fraud on the Patent Office), antitrust violations, patent misuse, obviousness, lack of novelty (also known as *anticipation*), or sale, use, or publication of the patented device more than one year prior to filing of application.

Statute of Limitations

Damages cannot be recovered for any infringement committed more than six years prior to the filing of the complaint (or counterclaim) for infringement.[16]

Burden of Proof

There are two standards or burdens of proof by which the jury or judge weighs the evidence in a patent infringement case. The plaintiff has the burden of establishing infringement by a **preponderance of the evidence**. The defendant has the burden of establishing patent invalidity and unenforceability by **clear and convincing proof**. A preponderance of evidence is proof that seems more true than not true. Clear and convincing proof means that the evidence is highly probable and free from serious doubt. A U.S. patent is presumed to be valid.[17] This means that a defendant attacking the validity of a patent has a significant burden of proof when attacking the validity of a patent.

LEGAL TERMS

preponderance of the evidence
Proof that produces the belief that the facts are more likely true than not.

clear and convincing proof
Evidence that is highly probable and free from serious doubt.

Damages and Attorney Fees

If the court finds that patent infringement has occurred, proof of damages will be offered by the patent owner and the court will award damages adequate to compensate for the infringement. In exceptional cases, such as willful infringement, this amount may be increased, at the discretion of the court, up to triple the amount of damages proved.[18] Often the measurement of patent infringement damages is what the plaintiff would have obtained as a reasonable royalty from the sale of the defendant's device. For example, if the plaintiff had entered into a license agreement with the defendant, what royalties would it have received from the defendant's sale of the device? This determination may require expert testimony. It took a great deal of time and testimony for the judge in the Kodak-Polaroid lawsuit to assess the amount of the damages for infringement of Polaroid's patents. In exceptional cases, a court may award attorney fees to the winning side, as, for example, in a case of willful infringement.[19] In addition to damages and attorney fees, injunctive relief may also be granted, as discussed in § 12.4.

JUDGE LEARNED HAND ON PATENT LAW: Patent Infringement

One reason Judge Hand was able to analyze and efficiently resolve patent infringement cases was because he understood the craft of drafting patent claims. In *Parke-Davis & Co. v. H.K. Mulford Co.,* 189 F. 95 (S.D.N.Y. 1911) Judge Hand commented on the modern standard of claim drafting. "There is nothing improper, so far as I can see, in first putting your claims as broadly as in good faith you can, and then, *ex abundante cautela* [from an abundance of caution], following them successively with narrower claims designed to protect you against possible anticipations of which you are not yet aware . . . . To pass between this Scylla and the Charybdis, I think a patentee may fairly be entitled to bend sails upon many yards." In the case of *Gibbs v. Triumph Trap Co.,* 26 F.2d 312 (2d Cir. 1928), Judge Hand enunciated the principles by which a court analyzes patent claims. "Courts do indeed treat the language of claims plastically, now stretching to save the whole scope of the invention, now squeezing to limit the claim so that it can survive. There are no absolutes; when justice requires, it is a question of filling the language as full as it will bear without bursting, or of pressing it so long as it will not quite break, though of course the words have their limits."

Judge Hand's patent decisions were not without humor. In 1910, the company founded by the Wright brothers sued a company that had infringed the rudder on its new flying machine. The defendant argued that the flying machine's rudder was not novel. Judge Hand disagreed, noting mankind's previous difficulty in becoming airborne: "The number of persons who can fly at all is so limited that it is not surprising that infringers have not arisen in great numbers . . . ."

12.4 PATENT LITIGATION

In patent litigation, the plaintiff's objective is usually to halt the defendant's infringing activity and recover damages for the infringement. The initial appearance of the parties in court may be in regard to a request by the patent holder for a preliminary injunction (an order that the defendant immediately halt the infringing activity). This pretrial battle alone can cost hundreds of thousands of dollars. Consider the litigation over the Black & Decker *Dustbuster*. In 1987, Black & Decker sued the Hoover Company for patent and trademark infringement and sought a preliminary injunction to prevent Hoover from making and selling its *DUBL-DUTY* wet-dry vacuum. Hoover counterclaimed that Black & Decker violated antitrust laws by the way Black & Decker marketed the *Dustbuster* wet-dry vacuum. In 1988, a trial court denied Black & Decker's request for a preliminary injunction. The ruling on the preliminary injunction was appealed to the Federal Circuit. On appeal, the Federal Circuit considered two issues: (1) trademark infringement and (2) patent infringement.

The claim of trademark infringement was based upon the shape of the "bowl" used in the Black & Decker wet-dry *Dustbuster*. Black & Decker maintained that the shape of the bowl in the *Dustbuster* was protectible under trademark law because the shape had acquired secondary meaning as a form of trade dress. Hoover argued that the bowl shape was functional and functional features cannot be trademarks. The Federal Circuit vacated and remanded this matter to the trial court for further consideration, because the appellate court was unable to make a determination based upon the record of the proceedings developed by the trial court.

The patent infringement issues focused on the patent claim wording describing the position of the intake nozzle and chamber in the wet-dry vacuum. The positioning of these components permitted the vacuum to separate liquids from the air that was also being sucked into the machine. The Federal Circuit agreed that it was not likely that Black & Decker would succeed on a claim of literal infringement. However, the Federal Circuit did determine that Hoover's air-liquid separation apparatus was "merely an insubstantially altered form of that set forth in the [Black & Decker] claim, and every claimed element or its equivalent is present in Hoover's cleaner." In other words, it was possible that the *DUBL-DUTY* vacuum infringed under the doctrine of equivalents. The Federal Circuit did not grant Black & Decker's preliminary injunction. Instead, the appellate court instructed the lower court to rehear the matter in light of its findings. For paralegals, one interesting aspect of the appeal is that the federal court castigated both sides for their failure to adhere to local court rules, including rules regarding the length of briefs and usage of appendices. As discussed later in this chapter, a review of each court's local rules is necessary when assisting in the preparation of litigation documents.

The Cease and Desist Letter

A **cease and desist letter** informs the party that makes, uses, or sells an unauthorized product or process of the nature of the believed infringement and the remedies that may be pursued. Most importantly, the letter requests the immediate cessation of all infringing activity and demands an accounting for all acts of infringement. The principles underlying the cease and desist letter are explained in chapters 6 and 9. In a patent infringement dispute, the cease and desist letter has certain risks and should never be used to bluff an alleged infringer. The reason for this is that the recipient of the letter can file a declaratory action to contest the validity of the patent that has been asserted against it. This may result in a loss of patent rights, particularly if the patent owner is not able to withstand the cost of the litigation. If the alleged infringer argues that the patent is invalid, one possible alternative (or accompaniment) to patent litigation is the process of reexamination, as discussed in § 12.2.

Jurisdiction

The federal courts have **exclusive jurisdiction** over disputes involving cancellation, infringement, and validity of patents. The reason that the federal courts have the sole authority to hear these types of cases is because patent law qualifies as a question of law arising under the U.S. Constitution or federal laws. Most of the litigation principles used in copyright litigation (as explained in chapter 6) apply to patent litigation. For example, the Federal Rules of Civil Procedure and local federal court rules govern the procedures to be followed in patent litigation. Despite the fact that federal courts have exclusive jurisdiction, not all claims *relating* to patent rights must go to federal court. For example, an inventor signs an exclusive agreement granting all rights in an invention to a company. Later, a dispute arises because the inventor previously signed a contract giving the same rights to another company. The federal courts would not have exclusive jurisdiction over this dispute, because the dispute is not over patent validity or infringement, but rather is about contractual rights to property (i.e., a patent). The case may still be brought in federal courts under diversity principles, as discussed in chapter 10.

Venue

Venue is the geographic location of the proper federal court where patent litigation is brought. Venue in federal patent litigation is determined by the basis of the lawsuit.[20] If the litigation is regarding patent infringement, venue is determined by 28 U.S.C. § 1400(b), which provides:

> Any civil action for patent infringement may be brought in the judicial district where the defendant resides, or where the defendant has committed acts of infringement and has a regular and established place of business.

The purpose of this patent venue statute is to limit the plaintiff's choice of forum to the district where the defendant is domiciled or districts that are related in particular ways to the defendant and the location of infringing activities.

If a controversy arises under the patent laws but does not include a charge of patent infringement (e.g., an action to declare that a patent is invalid), the action may be brought according to the provisions of 28 U.S.C. § 1391(b), which provides:

> (b) A civil action wherein jurisdiction is not founded solely on diversity of citizenship may, except as otherwise provided by law, be brought only in (1) a judicial district where any defendant resides, if all defendants reside in the same State, (2) a judicial district in which a substantial part of the events or omissions giving rise to the claim occurred, or a substantial part of property that is the subject of the action is situated, or (3) a judicial district in which any defendant may be found, if there is no district in which the action may otherwise be brought.

If the defendant is a corporation, the corporation "resides" in any district where the corporation is subject to personal jurisdiction at the time the action is commenced. For example, SpecialFX, Inc., believes that Effectsco's *Fogarama* patent is invalid. It seeks a declaration by the federal courts that the patent is invalid. Because this is not a claim for infringement, the venue would be determined by 28 U.S.C. § 1391(b) and the case could be brought where Effectsco resides (i.e., any district where it is subject to personal jurisdiction).

If the defendant believes that the venue is improper, a motion to dismiss the action may be made pursuant to Fed. R. Civ. P. 12(b)(3). In the interest of justice and for the convenience of parties and witnesses, the lawsuit may be transferred to another district court pursuant to a motion to change venue. As with all such motions, local rules should be checked for format and any special requirements.

Civil Cover Sheet and Summons. The plaintiff in a patent infringement lawsuit prepares three documents, a *complaint*, a *summons*, and a *civil cover sheet*. The plaintiff files the complaint and **summons** with the federal court clerk. The original summons is stamped and returned to the plaintiff and a copy is retained by the clerk. At the time of filing the complaint, a **civil cover sheet** must also be filed (copies are available from the clerk's office of the local federal court). These three documents must be served on the defendant pursuant to the rules of service of process of the state in which the district court is located, or by mailing a copy along with a notice and acknowledgement (according to Fed. R. Civ. P. 4(c)(2)(C)(ii)).

LEGAL TERMS

cease and desist letter
Correspondence from the owner of proprietary work that informs the infringing party of the validity and ownership of the proprietary work, the nature of the infringement, and the remedies available to the owner; requests the cessation of all infringing activity.

exclusive jurisdiction
The sole authority of a court to hear a certain type of case.

summons
Document served with the complaint which explains that the defendant has been sued and has a certain time limit within which to respond.

civil cover sheet
Form required at the time of filing of the complaint for use by the court in maintaining certain statistical records.

To fill out the civil cover sheet, information is needed as to the basis of jurisdiction and the citizenship of the parties. If jurisdiction is based upon the infringement or validity of a patent, it would be a "Federal Question" as provided in Box II. In Box V ("Nature of Suit"), the selection that most accurately defines the cause of action should be checked (e.g., No. 830, Patent). This information is provided for purposes of preparing statistical analyses of the types of cases filed in federal court. If a jury trial is requested, that information must also be provided in the civil cover sheet.

The Patent Infringement Complaint

The complaint for patent infringement sets forth the facts of the infringement and requests remedies such as compensation and injunctive relief for the infringement. If the plaintiff desires a jury trial, that demand should be made in the complaint. If the plaintiff has not sought a jury trial but the defendant wants one, the request for a jury trial should be made in the defendant's answer. Sometimes, two parties with similar patents may litigate against one another, and each side will file a claim of patent infringement against the other. For example, in the case of the *Fogarama* and *In-a-Fog* machines described in the Commentary to this chapter, both companies might bring claims of patent infringement against one another. SpecialFX, Inc., may file a patent infringement complaint against Effectsco. Effectsco may answer the complaint and file a counterclaim of patent infringement against SpecialFX.

A complaint for patent infringement is almost always combined with a request for *injunctive relief* (an order by the court that the accused party cease all infringing activity). For example, as in the Black & Decker *Dustbuster* litigation, the complaint was filed in conjunction with a motion for preliminary injunction. This section provides some basics on drafting the patent infringement complaint.

Drafting the Complaint

Below are the basic elements of a patent infringement complaint.

Jurisdiction and venue. The first and second paragraphs of a patent infringement complaint state the reasons for filing in federal court. As the case may be filed where the defendant resides, venue is often established by stating the location of the defendant. Although not required, the complaint usually states the citizenship or location of the plaintiff.

1. This is an action which arises under the Patent Laws of the United States, United States Code, Title 35. Jurisdiction and venue are pursuant to United States Code, Title 28, Sections 1338 and 1400.
2. Plaintiff SpecialFX, Inc., is a corporation organized and existing under the laws of the State of California and having its principal place of business at Orinda, California.

3. Defendant Effectsco is a corporation organized and existing under the laws of the State of California and having its principal place of business at San Francisco, California.

Establishing Plaintiff's Patent Ownership. The plaintiff must establish ownership rights to the patent.

4. For approximately 10 years, plaintiff has been engaged in the development, manufacture, and sale of special-effects devices for use in theatrical and motion picture presentations and amusement parks. Plaintiff is widely recognized as a source of innovative special-effects apparatus.
5. In 1989 and 1990, plaintiff expended considerable effort and expense to develop a fog-making apparatus which only used water to achieve a fog effect. In the early part of 1991, plaintiff introduced its fog-making apparatus and has sold it throughout the world under the trademark *In-a-Fog*.
6. The *In-a-Fog* apparatus achieved extensive acceptance in the special-effects field and generated substantial revenues for plaintiff.
7. Plaintiff filed an application for United States Letters Patent Serial No. 1,234,567 filed June 1, 1991. This application was filed in the name of Douglas Thornbey and was assigned to plaintiff by an assignment executed on April 23, 1991, and was recorded in the United States Patent and Trademark Office on _____ at Reel ____, Frame ____.
8. The aforementioned application was allowed by the United States Patent and Trademark Office and granted on June 7, 1992 as United States Letters Patent No. 2,345,678. Plaintiff is and has continuously been the owner of all right, title, and interest in and to the invention of United States Letters Patent No. 2,345,678.

Establishing the Infringement. The plaintiff must establish the elements of the infringement by detailing the defendant's infringing activities.

9. At or about the time of its introduction of the apparatus, now covered by the aforesaid patent, into the marketplace, plaintiff identified the *In-a-Fog* apparatus in its literature and labels as the subject matter of a pending patent application by placing in such literature the statement "patent pending."
10. Within a short period of time after the successful commercial introduction of the *In-a-Fog* apparatus, Defendant first offered for sale an apparatus closely simulating the subject matter of plaintiff's apparatus. Defendant's apparatus is titled and sold under the trademark *Fogarama*.
11. Upon information and belief, defendant's *Fogarama* apparatus closely simulates the properties and characteristics of plaintiff's *In-a-Fog* apparatus and infringes the following claims: _____.
12. Upon information and belief, such actions by defendant have been for the purposes of trading upon the substantial commercial acceptance of plaintiff's patented apparatus.

13. Defendant is making, using, and selling, within this District and elsewhere, the *Fogarama* apparatus which infringes United States Letters Patent No. 2,345,678.

14. As a result of defendant's competitive activities and infringement, plaintiff has suffered and will continue to suffer damage.

15. Defendant's infringement of said United States Letters Patent No. 2,345,678 will continue unless and until enjoined by this Court.

The Prayer.   The complaint concludes with the *prayer*, a formal request for remedies.

WHEREFORE plaintiff prays that this Court enter judgment:

1. Enjoining Effectsco and its subsidiaries, agents, officers, and employees, and all others acting in concert with it, from the manufacture, use, offer for sale, and sale of the apparatus encompassed by United States Letters Patent No. 2,345,678.

2. Ordering defendant to account for its profits and the damages to plaintiff from such infringement.

3. Assessing costs and interest against defendant.

4. Granting plaintiff such other and further relief as the court deems proper.

Additional Claims

Often, additional claims are present besides patent infringement. For example, the infringer also may be using the plaintiff's trademark, or may be breaching a contract. State claims may be brought along with the federal claims under the principle of pendent jurisdiction, as explained in chapter 2. The complaint in figure 12-4 is an example of a lawsuit in which the owner of a design patent is suing a company for patent infringement and unfair competition.

Declaratory Relief

Declaratory relief is a request that a court sort out the rights and obligations of the parties. For example, Effectsco believes that a patent owned by a rival company, SpecialFX, Inc., is invalid and that SpecialFX is preparing to sue Effectsco. Effectsco would file a claim for declaratory relief. Effectsco need only establish that it has a reasonable apprehension of a patent lawsuit or that an actual controversy exists regarding a matter within federal court subject matter jurisdiction. The request for declaratory relief is made in the form of a complaint (e.g., a "Complaint for Declaratory Relief" or a "Complaint for Declaratory Judgment").

Figure 12-5 shows is a complaint for a declaratory judgment based upon the situation described here, between Effectsco and SpecialFX, Inc.

LEGAL TERMS

declaratory relief
Request that the court sort out the rights and legal obligations of the parties in the midst of an actual controversy.

DESIGN PATENT COMPLAINT

LAW OFFICES OF SMITH & SMITH
One Embarcadero, Suite 2727
San Francisco, California 94111
(415) 555-1212

Attorneys for Plaintiff

IN THE UNITED STATES DISTRICT COURT
SOUTHERN DISTRICT OF NEW YORK

GUITARCO, a New York corporation,	) No._____))
Plaintiff,	) COMPLAINT FOR) DESIGN PATENT INFRINGEMENT
v.	) AND UNFAIR COMPETITION)
MUSICO, a Michigan corporation,	)))
Defendant.	))

JURISDICTION

Guitarco, Plaintiff, alleges as follows:

1. This action arises under the Patent Laws of the United States, 35 U.S.C. §§ 271 and 281, for patent infringement and under § 43(a) of the Lanham Act, 15 U.S.C. § 1125(a) for false designation of origin.

2. Plaintiff is a New York corporation having its principal offices at 1234 Main Street, New York City, New York.

3. Defendant, Musico, is a Michigan corporation having offices and a principal place of business at 2345 Major Street, Flint, Michigan.

4. Jurisdiction over the subject matter is conferred on the Court under 28 U.S.C. § 1338(a) and (b). Jurisdiction over the unfair competition count is also conferred on this Court by 28 U.S.C. § 1332 because of the existing diversity of citizenship between the parties and because the matter in controversy, exclusive of interest and costs, exceeds the sum of [amount]. Jurisdiction over the defendant is conferred upon this Court by Fed. R. Civ. P. 4(e).

COUNT I
Design Patent Infringement

5. On November 27, 1987, United States Design Patent No. 3,456,789 was issued in the name of Billy Ray Broustis as inventor of a design for an electric guitar as specified in Exhibit A to this complaint and incorporated by reference.

6. Plaintiff, Guitarco, is the owner by assignment of the entire right, title, and interest to Design Patent No. 3,456,789.

FIGURE 12-4

Sample design patent complaint

7. Defendant, Musico, has been and still is infringing the United States Design Patent No. 3,456,789 by making and selling, without authorization form Plaintiff, the molds, bodies, and attachment parts, all having the design covered by the claim in Plaintiff's design patent within this District and elsewhere.

8. Plaintiff, Guitarco, manufactures and sells goods, namely guitars and musical instruments embodying Design Patent No. 3,456,789 and all of the goods sold by Guitarco since the issuance of the patent have proper notice of the patent, pursuant to 35 U.S.C. § 287. Plaintiff caused notice to be given to defendant of the existence of defendant's infringement of Design Patent No. 3,456,789.

9. Defendant, Musico, deliberately, knowingly, and with willful disregard of the rights of the plaintiff, proceeded with the manufacture and sale of the infringing goods, and has been, and upon information and belief is still, manufacturing or causing to be sold such infringing goods. Defendant is deriving unlawful profits, and will continue to do so by continued infringement of the patent, to plaintiff's irreparable damage, unless restrained by this Court.

10. Plaintiff has been damaged by the infringing acts of the defendant in an amount unknown to plaintiff, but plaintiff asks leave to insert by amendment the amount of damages when the same is ascertained.

COUNT II
Unfair Competition: False Designation of Origin

11. Plaintiff, Guitarco, is in the business of developing, manufacturing, and selling musical instruments, including guitars of the type disclosed in the Design Patent 3,456,789.

12. Plaintiff has, over a period of years, expended time, money, and effort in promoting a series of guitars, based upon its patented design. Sales of guitars embodying the design patent have accounted for over three million dollars worth of sales in the United States.

13. As a result of this association by purchasers and potential purchasers, the distinctive designs embodied on these guitars represent property and goodwill owned by plaintiff.

14. Upon information and belief, defendant has now copied the distinctive design of plaintiff and has sold such guitar products within this jurisdiction and elsewhere for the sole purpose of passing off these guitars as those of plaintiff.

15. These acts of unfair competition of defendant fall within the meaning of 15 U.S.C. § 1125(a), were done to divert to defendant the profits arising from plaintiff's goodwill, and have damaged plaintiff in an amount in excess of [amount], exclusive of interest and costs.

WHEREFORE, plaintiff prays:

1. For an accounting and determination of the damages plaintiff has suffered in consequence of defendant's acts of patent infringement and of the profits gained by defendant, by copying plaintiff's product, unfair competition, and misappropriation.

2. For judgment treble the amount determined by said accounting to be attributable to acts of patent infringement by defendant.

3. For an injunction strictly commanding defendant, its agents, servants, and employees, and those in active concert or participation with it to refrain from further acts of patent infringement, unfair competition, and unjust enrichment as aforesaid.

FIGURE 12-4
(Continued)

4. For judgment against defendant in the amount necessary to compensate plaintiff for its reasonable costs, interest, and attorney fees incurred and expended in conjunction with this action.

5. For such other and further relief as this Court shall deem proper and necessary to adequately compensate plaintiff.

By:_____
Attorney for Plaintiff, Guitarco

Dated: _____

FIGURE 12-4
(*Continued*)

COMPLAINT FOR DECLARATORY RELIEF

LAW OFFICES OF SMITH & SMITH
One Embarcadero, Suite 2727
San Francisco, California 94111
(415) 555-1212

Attorneys for Plaintiff

IN THE UNITED STATES DISTRICT COURT
NORTHERN DISTRICT OF CALIFORNIA

EFFECTSCO, a New York corporation,	) No._____))
Plaintiff,	) COMPLAINT FOR) DECLARATORY
v.	) JUDGMENT)
SPECIALFX, INC., a California corporation,	))
Defendant.	)))

JURISDICTION

Plaintiff Effectsco alleges as follows:

1. This action arises under the Declaratory Judgment and Patent Laws of the United States including 28 U.S.C. §§ 2201 and 2202 and 35 U.S.C. § 1 *et seq.*

FIGURE 12-5
Sample complaint for declaratory judgment

Venue for this action is proper in this district pursuant to the Judiciary and Judicial Procedure Laws of the United States, 28 U.S.C. § 1391.

2. Plaintiff Effectsco is a corporation organized and existing under the laws of the State of California and having its principal place of business at New York, New York.

3. Plaintiff is informed and believes that SpecialFX, Inc., is a corporation organized and existing under the laws of the State of California and having its principal place of business at Orinda, California.

4. For approximately three years, plaintiff has been engaged in the development, manufacture, and sale of special-effects devices for use in theatrical and motion picture presentations and amusement parks.

5. Defendant, in a letter of June 3, 1992 (a true copy of which is attached hereto and incorporated by reference in this complaint), stated that it was the owner of a patent granted on June 7, 1992 as United States Letters Patent No. 1,234,567 and further stated that plaintiff's product, commonly known as the *Fogarama,* constituted an infringement of defendant's patent.

6. An actual controversy now exists between plaintiff and defendant with respect to the validity, infringement, and enforceability of defendant's patent.

7. Defendant's patent in this suit is limited in scope and is invalid and void for the following reasons:

(a) the applicant for the patent in this suit did not herself invent the subject matter sought to be patented;

(b) the alleged invention was known or used by others in this country, or patented or described in a printed publication in this or a foreign country before the alleged invention by the applicant for the patent in this suit; and

(c) any differences between the patent in this suit and the prior art are such that the subject matter as a whole would have been obvious at the time the alleged invention was made to a person having ordinary skill in the art of the subject matter.

8. Defendant's patent in this suit is not infringed by plaintiff.

WHEREFORE, plaintiff prays for judgment as follows:

1. Defendant's patent and the claims in this suit are invalid and unenforceable;
2. Plaintiff has not infringed defendant's patent;
3. Defendant is enjoined from asserting such patent against plaintiff, its representatives, and its agents;
4. Plaintiff recover its costs and reasonable attorney fees; and
5. Such other and further relief as this Court deems proper.

By:_____

Attorney for Plaintiff, Effectsco

Dated: _____

FIGURE 12-5
(Continued)

The Answer

A response to the complaint must be served within 20 days of service. The **answer** is a response to the complaint in which the defendant admits or denies the allegations and provides a set of defenses. The answer, like the complaint, includes a caption and is filed with the court.

In the answer, the defendant goes through each paragraph of the complaint and responds by admitting or denying the allegations, as appropriate. Examples of such admissions and denials are provided in chapters 2 and 6. In addition to responding to each allegation, the answer should provide a set of defenses. General affirmative defenses, such as failure to join necessary parties, laches, and unclean hands, are also discussed in chapters 2 and 6. Just as charges of infringement must not be irresponsibly made, without any adequate basis developed by investigation, affirmative defenses should not be made unless there is a good reason to believe that they can be proved. The following examples are affirmative defenses specifically applicable to patent litigation.

EXAMPLE: Affirmative Defense—Patent Invalidity

Plaintiff's patent in this suit is invalid for failure to comply with the criteria and regulations of the Patent Laws, specially §§ 10, 11, and 12 of Title 35 of the United States Code.

EXAMPLE: Affirmative Defense—Fraud on Patent Office

Plaintiff's patent in this suit is unenforceable because it was obtained by fraud, in that the applicant had knowledge that the alleged invention was not patentable.

EXAMPLE: Affirmative Defense—Patent Misuse

Plaintiff's patent in this suit is unenforceable because plaintiff has misused the patent.

EXAMPLE: Affirmative Defense—Noninfringement

Defendant's actions do not constitute infringement of Plaintiff's Patent No. _____.

EXAMPLE: Affirmative Defense—Prosecution History Estoppel

Plaintiff is estopped on the basis of representations made to the United States Patent and Trademark Office during prosecution of the application for Plaintiff's patent in this suit.

LEGAL TERMS

answer
  Written response to the complaint, in which the defendant admits or denies the allegations and provides a set of defenses.

Counterclaims

If the defendant wishes to bring an action against the plaintiff, a **counterclaim** must be filed at the time the answer is filed. A counterclaim is a claim for relief usually asserted by the defendant against an opposing party, usually the plaintiff. A counterclaim is compulsory (i.e., it *must* be brought) if the claim arises out of a transaction or occurrence that is the subject of a complaint.

Injunctions

As the Black & Decker litigation indicates, injunctive relief can be extremely important in patent litigation, and the motion for preliminary injunction, the response, and the hearing form an important battleground. If a patent is being infringed, the plaintiff desires to halt the infringing activity prior to trial. As explained in chapter 6, the **injunction** is a court order that prevents the defendant from engaging in infringing activity. The following factors are considered when determining whether a preliminary injunction will be granted:

1. Does the plaintiff have a reasonable likelihood of success on the merits of the lawsuit?
2. Does the plaintiff have an adequate remedy at law, and will the plaintiff suffer irreparable harm if the injunction is not granted?
3. Does the threatened injury to the patent owner outweigh the threatened harm that the injunction may cause the accused?
4. Will the granting of a preliminary injunction cause a disservice to the public interest?

A court may grant a **preliminary injunction** on the basis of the likelihood of success of proving literal infringement or infringement under the doctrine of equivalents. For example, the maker of a plastic cervical extrication collar was entitled to a preliminary injunction against the manufacturer of a competing plastic collar because the judge determined that the patent owner had a likelihood of success on the basis of both literal infringement and the doctrine of equivalents.

Initially, the plaintiff may seek preliminary relief known as a **temporary restraining order** or **TRO,** which is short in duration and remains in effect only until the court has an opportunity to schedule a hearing on a motion for a preliminary injunction. The preliminary injunction is granted after a hearing where both parties have had an opportunity to present evidence. Such an injunction may last until the final judgment has been rendered in the lawsuit. If the plaintiff prevails, a **permanent injunction** may be granted that replaces the preliminary injunction and permanently restrains the defendant from engaging in the infringing activity. Fed. R. Civ. P. 65 establishes the statutory requirement for a preliminary injunction and for a temporary restraining order. These provisions include:

Notice—A preliminary injunction will not be issued unless the adverse party has received sufficient notice of the proceeding and has had an opportunity to provide a response.

Consolidation of hearing with trial on merits—The court is empowered to order that the trial of the patent litigation be advanced on the court calendar and consolidated with the hearing on the motion for preliminary injunction. In other words, the trial date can be moved up so that the trial coincides with the preliminary injunction hearing. Even if the court does not consolidate the trial and the motion hearing, any evidence admitted at the preliminary injunction hearing usually becomes part of the record and is later admissible at the trial.

Temporary Restraining Order

A temporary restraining order may be granted without notice to the adverse party if it appears from specific facts shown by affidavit or by the verified complaint that immediate and irreparable injury, loss, or damage will result to the applicant unless one is granted. For example, if it is clear that evidence will be destroyed or that the defendant will sell all of the infringing inventory, the court may issue a TRO without any notice to the defendant. However, the attorney for the party seeking the TRO must certify to the court in writing any efforts that have been made to give the notice and the reasons supporting the claim that notice should not be required. If a TRO is granted without notice, the motion for a preliminary injunction must be set for hearing at the earliest possible time.

Security

In any case in which a TRO or preliminary injunction is issued, the court may require that the party seeking the injunction post a bond as the court deems proper. The purpose of the bond is to cover any costs and damages that may be incurred if the defendant prevails.

Form and Scope

Every order granting an injunction and every restraining order shall: (1) set forth the reasons for its issuance; (2) be specific in terms; (3) describe in reasonable detail, and not by reference to the complaint or other document, the act or acts sought to be restrained; and (4) bind only the parties to the action, and their agents and employees.

A motion for a preliminary injunction or temporary restraining order requires extensive research and preparation of a memorandum of law that effectively mixes the facts of the case and the appropriate law. The memorandum is supported by affidavits and declarations, made under penalty of

LEGAL TERMS

counterclaim
  Claim for relief usually asserted by the defendant against an opposing party, usually the plaintiff.

injunction
  Court order directing the defendant to stop certain activities.

preliminary injunction
  Injunction granted after a noticed hearing where the parties have an opportunity to present evidence as to the likelihood of the plaintiff's success on the merits and the irreparability of the harm to be suffered if the injunction is not granted; lasts until a final judgment has been rendered.

temporary restraining order (TRO)
  Injunction, often granted ex parte, that is short in duration and remains in effect only until the court has an opportunity to schedule a hearing for and rule on a motion for a preliminary injunction.

permanent injunction
  Durable injunction issued after a final judgment on the merits of the case; if issued against a defendant-infringer, it permanently restrains the defendant from engaging in the infringing activity.

perjury, which provide statements from witnesses or parties supporting the request. In addition, the motion is accompanied by a proposed order. The proposed order sets forth what activities are restrained and also indicates the date when the injunction will expire. In the case of a TRO, the order will state the date for hearing on the preliminary injunction. Figure 12-6 is a proposed temporary restraining order.

PROPOSED TEMPORARY RESTRAINING ORDER

IN THE UNITED STATES DISTRICT COURT
NORTHERN DISTRICT OF CALIFORNIA

EFFECTSCO, a New York corporation,	) No._____
	)
	)
Plaintiff,	) PROPOSED
	) TEMPORARY
v.	) RESTRAINING ORDER
	) & ORDER TO SHOW
SPECIALFX, INC., a California corporation,	) CAUSE
	)
Defendant.	)
	)

TO DEFENDANT SPECIALFX, INC.

YOU ARE HEREBY ORDERED to show cause at 9 a.m. on November 20, 1992, or, as soon thereafter as counsel may be heard in the courtroom of the Honorable Wilma Weston, located at 450 Golden Gate Avenue, San Francisco, California, why you, your officers, agents, servants, employees, and attorneys and those in active concert or participation with you or them should not be restrained and enjoined pending trial of this action from

(a) infringement of plaintiff's U.S. Patent No. 1,234,567; and are directed to:

(b) surrender for destruction, pending a full adjudication on the merits, all molds, articles, signs, brochures, catalogs, advertisements, and other material promoting and leading to infringement of plaintiff's patent.

PENDING HEARING on the above Order to Show Cause you, your officers, agents, servants, employees, and attorneys and those in active concert or participation with you ARE HEREBY RESTRAINED AND ENJOINED FROM

(a) infringement of plaintiff's U.S. Patent No. 1,234,567; and are directed to:

(b) surrender for destruction, pending a full adjudication on the merits, all molds, articles, signs, brochures, catalogs, advertisements, and other material promoting and leading to infringement of plaintiff's patent.

FURTHER ORDERED that this temporary restraining order shall expire at 5 p.m. on November 20, 1992 unless it is extended by order of this Court. It is:

FURTHER ORDERED that a copy of this Order shall be served forthwith upon the defendants, together with the summons, complaint, affidavits, motion for temporary restraining order, and motion for preliminary injunction, in the manner prescribed by Fed. R. Civ. P. 4. It is:

FIGURE 12-6
Sample proposed temporary restraining order

FURTHER ORDERED that pursuant to Fed. R. Civ. P. 65(c) the plaintiff shall give security in the amount of $3,000.00.

Dated: _____   _____
U.S. District Court Judge

FIGURE 12-6
(Continued)

Discovery

The procedure for discovery is outlined in this book in chapters 6 and 10. The four common forms of discovery are **interrogatories, requests for production of documents, depositions**, and **requests for admissions**. The Federal Rules of Civil Procedure provide rules regarding discovery, such as the format of interrogatories.[21] In addition, local court rules also may set rules regarding discovery procedures and formats.

Rule 26 of the Federal Rules of Civil Procedure provides the general provisions governing discovery. Unless otherwise directed by the court, the parties may implement the various discovery techniques by any means. However, the parties may not always agree on the timing or length of discovery. If the parties cannot agree upon a means of implementing discovery, then Rule 26(b)(4)(f) provides that the court may direct the attorneys to appear and provide a plan and schedule of discovery.

Protective Orders

As explained in chapter 7, Federal Rule of Civil Procedure 26(c)(7) authorizes a protective order to limit the disclosure of trade secret information. Patent litigation may require investigation and discovery of confidential information. For example, in the facts to this Commentary, SpecialFX, Inc., has acquired a patent for its fog-making device, *In-a-Fog*. However, the method of manufacturing the device or the specific requirements or modifications requested by customers may be confidential, trade secret information. The parties may stipulate to protect and limit the disclosure of such information, or, in the event the parties cannot reach an agreement, the court, upon request of one of the parties, may issue a protective order. A sample of a stipulation and order of protection is provided in chapter 7.

Expert Witnesses

Expert witnesses in patent litigation are selected not simply on the basis of their technical knowledge but also upon their ability to effectively present their views. Some patent practitioners believe that experts tend to cancel each

LEGAL TERMS

interrogatories
Written questions that must be answered under oath.

request for production of documents
Method by which a party to a lawsuit may obtain documents or other physical evidence from another party.

deposition
Oral or written testimony of a party or witness, given under oath.

request for admission
Request for a party to the lawsuit to admit the truthfulness of a fact or statement.

other out, and juries in patent trials sometimes find that experts do more harm than good. However, the technical and scientific nature of patent law demands that experts in the field testify on behalf of each party. Fed. R. Civ. P. 26(b)(4) provides that the experts may be identified by means of interrogatories. Possible topics for expert testimony may include technical expertise as to aspects of the claimed invention or an expert opinion regarding the proof or assessment of damages. Prior to trial, each party identifies its expert witnesses by means of an "Identification of Expert Witness," an example of which is provided in figure 12-7.

IDENTIFICATION OF EXPERT WITNESS

IN THE UNITED STATES DISTRICT COURT
NORTHERN DISTRICT OF CALIFORNIA

EFFECTSCO, a New York corporation,	) No._____
	)
	)
Plaintiff,	) PLAINTIFF'S
	) IDENTIFICATION OF
v.	) EXPERT WITNESSES
	)
SPECIALFX, INC., a California corporation,	)
	)
Defendant.	)
	)

PLAINTIFF'S IDENTIFICATION OF ITS EXPERT WITNESS

Pursuant to Federal Rule of Civil Procedure 26(B)(4) and this Court's Order dated January 8, 1993, Plaintiffs hereby notify the Court that they intend to call the following expert witnesses at trial:

Dan Nelson
555 Franklin Street
Newark, New Jersey

Ken Torkelson
2000 Gateway Ave.
Magenta, Ohio

Both witnesses will testify as experts concerning the validity and prior art in relation to Patent No. 1,234,567.

By:_____
Attorney for Plaintiff, Effectsco

Dated: _____

FIGURE 12-7
Sample identification
of expert witness

Pretrial Activities

Prior to commencement of trial, the judge issues a pretrial memorandum or pretrial order that is intended to establish certain issues. Each party must submit claims of fact that are undisputed. For example, the parties may stipulate as to the operation of an invention or as to contractual agreements executed by them. Each party must also submit proposed findings of fact (along with specification of related witnesses and evidence) as to each disputed claim for relief or affirmative defense. In addition, the parties must indicate exhibits, witnesses, and other evidence to be submitted at trial. Local court rules may require more extensive pretrial briefs or statements.

If the parties wish to consent to a trial before a **magistrate** (instead of a district court judge), that should also be indicated. A magistrate is an officer of the court, who may exercise some of the authority of a judge, including the authority to conduct a jury or nonjury trial. Fed. R. Civ. P. 73 sets forth the powers and requirements of magistrates.

If the trial is to be a jury trial, voir dire questions are also submitted. **Voir dire** is the process by which attorneys question potential jurors. Common voir dire questions include "Have you ever been sued?" "Have you ever served before on a jury?" "Do you know anything about the parties to this lawsuit or their attorneys?" In the factual situation in the Commentary to this chapter, examples of voir dire questions might include, "Does anyone in your family own a patent?" "Do you or does any member of your family work in a business related to or using special-effects devices?" "Do you have any technical or engineering background or training?"

To guarantee the appearance of certain witnesses at trial, the court may issue a subpoena commanding the witness to attend and give testimony or to produce and permit inspection of documents and other evidence. The procedures for obtaining a subpoena are set forth in Fed. R. Civ. P. 45.

As part of the pretrial preparation for a jury trial, the parties must prepare **jury instructions**, which are explanations of the legal rules that the jury shall use in reaching a verdict. Examples of model jury instructions are available in various form books, including Kramer & Brufsky's *Patent Law Practice Forms* (cited at the end of this chapter). Examples of patent jury instructions from *Patent Law Practice Forms* follow.

JURY INSTRUCTION NO. _____

Anticipation

In order to negate novelty and anticipate an invention under 35 U.S.C. § 102, it is necessary that all the elements of an invention, as expressed in a claim, be found identically in a single prior art device or reference, and that the elements so found must function in substantially the same way to do substantially the same work as the elements of the claimed invention.

LEGAL TERMS

magistrate
An officer of the court who may exercise some of the authority of a federal district court judge, including the authority to conduct a jury or nonjury trial.

voir dire
Process by which the judge and attorneys for the parties question potential jurors.

jury instructions
Explanations of the legal rules that the jury members are instructed by the judge to use in reaching a verdict.

JURY INSTRUCTION NO. _____

Claim Infringement

Before you can decide whether defendant has infringed plaintiff's patent, you will have to understand the patent "claims." The patent claims are the numbered paragraphs at the end of the patent. The patent claims involved here are claims [claim numbers], beginning at column [column numbers], line [line numbers] of the patent. The claims are "word pictures" and therefore define, in words, the exact boundaries of the invention described, illustrated, and covered by the patent. Only the claims of the patent can be infringed. Neither the specification, which is the written description, nor the drawings of a patent can be infringed. Further, each of the claims must be considered individually and not all claims of a patent have to be infringed before the patent is infringed. To have patent infringement, only one claim need be infringed.

As part of preparation for trial, the paralegal may be required to prepare a *trial notebook*, a binder created to index and reference the important documentation necessary to litigate a case. The procedure and requirements for arranging trial notebooks are explained in chapters 2, 6, and 7.

Trial

As in most trials, the paralegal will be required to assist in the management, organization, and presentation of evidence. After jury selection (if it is a jury trial), the trial begins with opening statements from the parties, followed by presentation of the plaintiff's case and then the defendant's case. The following list covers some forms of evidence used in patent litigation:

Glossary—Because of the large number of technical terms and scientific language, it is often advisable to prepare a glossary of terms. This glossary may help to simplify the complex terms for the judge or jury. It may form part of the pretrial statement or it may serve as a reference for attorneys so that they use language consistently.

Expert witness testimony—The organization of statements and background of the expert witnesses must be catalogued. Each party must be prepared to support its selection of experts and to attack the other party's choice.

Claim charts—Because it is important to educate the judge or jury as to the patent claims, many attorneys use enlarged copies of claims or charts comparing the claims to the invention or to the accused process or product. Sometimes such information is shown by way of overhead transparencies.

Time line charts—Some attorneys use charts to illustrate the sequence of events from conception of the invention to the issuance of patents.

Documents and illustrations—If certain documents, photographs, drawings, or portions of documents are fundamental to a case, an enlargement or overhead transparency is often prepared to illustrate the information.

Physical evidence—If possible, parties should attempt to provide or demonstrate the inventions at issue. If an actual demonstration is not practical, a videotape presentation or computer-graphics reproduction should be prepared.

Deposition testimony—Deposition testimony is used for several purposes. A witness may not be able to attend trial, so his or her deposition testimony will have to be introduced. This can be accomplished by selective readings, reproduction, or use of video depositions. In addition, indexing of all deposition testimony is necessary to contradict adverse witnesses or refresh friendly witnesses.

Following presentation of each side's case and cross-examination, each side provides a closing statement. If it is a jury trial, the judge instructs the jury; the jury deliberates and issues a verdict, which the judge will confirm as a judgment. On some occasions, the judge will set aside the jury's verdict on request (i.e., a judgment notwithstanding the verdict, or JNOV). In a non-jury trial, the court will issue a **judgment**. This may occur immediately at the end of the trial or weeks or even months later. A judgment is the relief awarded by the court after a final determination of the rights and obligations of the parties before the court.

Appeal

All appeals from district court cases involving claims arising under the patent laws must be brought in the United States Court of Appeals for the Federal Circuit (the Federal Circuit) in the District of Columbia. The Federal Circuit was established to bring about uniformity in application of the patent laws. Prior to 1982, there was considerable business risk for a plaintiff in a patent litigation suit, because of the inconsistent application of patent law and the lack of technical knowledge by appeals judges. To avoid inconsistent standards throughout the country, the Federal Circuit was created, including judges skilled in the sciences and intellectual property law.

Either party to a patent lawsuit may appeal the final determination of the district court to the Federal Circuit. (If the trial was conducted by a magistrate, the parties also may consent to an appeal to a judge of the district court). In the instance of an appeal to the Federal Circuit, a three-member panel of judges will review the trial court record to determine if so serious a legal error occurred that the outcome should be disturbed. If the parties are not satisfied with the Federal Circuit determination, the only other recourse is by petition of certiorari to the U.S. Supreme Court. However, if the U.S. Supreme Court refuses to hear the case, the determination of the Federal Circuit is the final determination in the case.

Rules regarding appellate procedure are provided in the Federal Rules of Appellate Procedure and the Rules of the Supreme Court of the United

LEGAL TERMS

judgment
  The relief awarded by the court after a final determination of the rights and obligations of the parties before the court.

States. The Notice of Appeal must be filed with the clerk of the district court within 30 days after the date of entry of the judgment or order. However, if the United States is a party to the lawsuit, the appeal may be filed within 60 days of entry of the judgment. Figure 12-8 is an example of the Notice of Appeal from the issuance of a preliminary injunction.

NID⟩R

The National Institute for Dispute Resolution is an example of a private organization that specializes in arbitration and mediation.

Alternative Dispute Resolution

As indicated in chapter 6, many disputes regarding intellectual property rights are resolved privately through informal procedures known as *arbitration* and *mediation*. Arbitration is the referral of a dispute to one or more impartial persons, usually for final and binding determination. Mediation is an alternative to arbitration in which the parties submit their dispute to an impartial mediator who assists the parties in reaching a settlement.

NOTICE OF APPEAL

IN THE UNITED STATES DISTRICT COURT
NORTHERN DISTRICT OF CALIFORNIA

EFFECTSCO, a New York corporation,	) No._____
	)
	)
Plaintiff,	) NOTICE OF
	) APPEAL
v.	)
	)
	)
SPECIALFX, INC., a California corporation,	)
Defendant.	)
	)

Notice is hereby given that the above-named defendant, SPECIALFX, Inc., hereby appeals to the United States Court of Appeals for the Federal Circuit from the Order of the Honorable Wilma Weston, entered on December 10, 1992, granting plaintiff's motion for a preliminary injunction which prohibits defendants from selling its *In-a-Fog* special effects fog-making apparatus.

By:_____
    Attorney for Defendant, SPECIALFX, Inc.

Dated:_____

FIGURE 12-8
Sample Notice of Appeal

Disputes regarding patent ownership or infringement involve technical and scientific issues. Therefore, the parties may desire to have the matter decided by a person versed in the subject matter art. In addition, the expense of patent litigation disfavors smaller entities. Finally, patent litigation is often a burden on the court system, requiring lengthy trials and extensive expert opinions. For these reasons, arbitration of patent disputes is encouraged. In addition, interference proceedings can also be arbitrated.[22]

The American Arbitration Association has established special Patent Arbitration Rules and has gathered a national panel of patent arbitrators. Arbitration can be initiated by an agreement or by submission of the parties. The following example is an arbitration clause prepared by the American Arbitration Association, which could be included in an agreement relating to patent rights (i.e., a license agreement, professional services agreement, manufacturing agreement, etc.).

EXAMPLE: Patent Arbitration Clause

Any controversy or claim arising out of or relating to this contract or the breach thereof, including any dispute relating to patent validity or infringement arising under this contract, shall be settled by arbitration in accordance with the Patent Arbitration Rules of the American Arbitration Association, and judgment upon the award rendered by Arbitrator(s) may be entered in any court having jurisdiction thereof.

If the parties do not have such an agreement but still wish to submit the matter to arbitration, the following language, provided by the American Arbitration, will provide for submission of a patent dispute.

EXAMPLE: Agreement to Submit Patent Dispute to Arbitration

We, the undersigned, hereby submit to arbitration under the Patent Arbitration Rules of the American Arbitration Association the following controversy [cite briefly the matter in dispute, including specific reference to any existing patent validity or infringement dispute arbitrable under 35 U.S.C. § 294(a)]. We further agree that the above controversy be submitted to (one) (three) Arbitrator(s) selected from the national panel of Arbitrators of the AAA. We further agree that we will faithfully observe this agreement and the Rules and that we will abide by and perform any award and that a judgment of a Court having jurisdiction may be entered upon the award.

Even though a patent dispute is arbitrated, the parties may still resort to the courts to compel arbitration, appoint an arbitrator, compel attendance of witnesses, or to vacate, confirm, modify, or correct an arbitration award. International arbitration disputes are often resolved through the International Chamber of Commerce in Stockholm or the London Court of Arbitration in England.

Litigation Checklists

The following checklists are for plaintiffs and defendants involved in a patent infringement lawsuit.

Patent Infringement Dispute: Plaintiff's Checklist

- **Interview the Client.** The following information should be obtained:
  - ☐ Patent owner's name, address, and business form (i.e., corporation, partnership, etc.), as well as name and address of patent applicant (i.e., inventor).
  - ☐ Information about all patents or transfers regarding the invention (i.e., assignments or other documents proving the chain of title).
  - ☐ Has patent been issued or has application been filed?
  - ☐ Patent owner's use of notice (e.g., "patent pending").
  - ☐ Extent of sale, manufacture, and distribution of the invention.
  - ☐ Owner's knowledge and discovery of the infringement.
  - ☐ Any license agreements for use, sale, or manufacture of invention.
  - ☐ Any undisclosed information that is likely to affect litigation (any skeletons in the closet)?
- **Acquire Evidence of the Infringement.** It is impossible to make a case for patent infringement without direct proof of the infringing activity.
  - ☐ If possible, purchase or acquire the infringing invention or witness the infringing device.
  - ☐ Trace the chain of distribution of the infringing invention (locate manufacturer, distributor, and retailers of infringing invention, as this may lead to other defendants).
  - ☐ Review dates of infringement.
- **Obtain Information about all Infringing Parties.** The patent owner should have researched the infringement to determine the names of the infringing parties.
  - ☐ Determine name, address, and business form of all infringing parties (databases such as LEXIS®, Dialog®, or Westlaw® may provide information regarding business form (i.e., corporation or partnership), and agent for service).
  - ☐ Set up computer index (directory of all persons involved in litigation, facts, relationships, and caselaw).
  - ☐ Investigate whether infringing party has been sued for patent infringement previously.
  - ☐ Review previous patent searches and, if necessary, order patent search regarding infringing product or process.
- **Review Legal Claims and Possible Defenses Regarding Infringement.** An infringer should not be confronted without first reviewing all possible

claims and defenses. Untimely contact may tip off the infringer and result in the destruction of evidence. In the case of mobile infringers such as t-shirt vendors, it may result in relocation. In addition, a confrontation may become heated and emotional, possibly leading to hostility resulting in additional causes of action. For example, a patent owner improperly takes infringing materials, assaults a vendor, or slanders the infringer.

- ☐ Determine if additional claims, such as trade secrecy, trademark, contract, antitrust, or other contract, tort, or related claims, can be made as a result of the infringing activity.
- ☐ List *all* possible patent and equitable defenses and review the list with the client.
- ☐ Perform legal research and review caselaw and statutes regarding infringement issues and possible defenses (including issues of invalidity, misuse, etc.).

- ■ **Confront the Infringer: Prepare Cease and Desist Letter**. The cease and desist letter is a summary of the patent owner's charges and a request that the recipient of the letter halt all infringing activity. (Not a legal precedent to bringing infringement litigation.)
  - ☐ Consider whether the cease and desist letter will trigger destruction of evidence or the liquidation or transfer of assets. If so, proceed with ex parte temporary restraining order or consider filing suit and securing a writ of seizure.
  - ☐ Consider whether the cease and desist letter will trigger a declaratory action. Discuss with the client.

- ■ **Attempt Settlement of the Dispute**. A settlement is a written agreement in which the parties formally resolve the infringement dispute.
  - ☐ Determine sums that will compensate the plaintiff for all damages (including attorney fees and related costs).
  - ☐ Review state law regarding required language for settlement agreements.
  - ☐ Consider what nonmonetary remedies are sought (e.g., does the plaintiff want the infringing invention?).

- ■ **Consider Alternative Dispute Resolution**. If the parties cannot resolve their dispute among themselves, it is still possible to avoid litigation if the parties agree to alternative dispute resolution such as mediation or arbitration. In addition, the parties may wish to stay any litigation during a reexamination of the patent by the Patent and Trademark Office.
  - ☐ Will the parties stay litigation during a reexamination procedure?
  - ☐ Is there an agreement between the parties compelling arbitration or mediation?
  - ☐ Will both parties submit to mediation or patent arbitration? If so, where?
  - ☐ Locate patent arbitration rules and procedures from arbitrating entity (e.g., American Arbitration Association).

- ■ **File the Lawsuit.**
  - ☐ Review the Federal Rules of Civil Procedure and obtain local court rules.
  - ☐ Obtain civil cover sheet and summons from federal clerk.
  - ☐ Determine venue.

- □ Assist in preparation of complaint.
- □ Arrange for filing of complaint, issuance of summons, and preparation of civil cover sheet.
- □ Coordinate service of process.

■ **Discovery**. Coordination of discovery requires preparation of a discovery plan. Many attorneys begin the procedure with interrogatories to determine names and addresses of relevant parties. This is often followed by depositions and requests for production of documents. Finally, requests for admissions are used to confirm or deny relevant information.

- □ Consider whether protective orders are required.
- □ Calendar all discovery received and propounded for appropriate deadlines.
- □ Summarize and index depositions, interrogatory responses, and documents for use at trial.
- □ Prepare pretrial motions.

■ **Trial.**

- □ Prepare lists of witnesses (and expert witnesses).
- □ Review evidence for purposes of pretrial motions to limit admission or scope of evidence (e.g., motions in limine).
- □ Prepare trial notebook.
- □ Assist in preparation of jury instructions.

Patent Infringement Dispute: Defendant's Checklist

■ **Interview the Client.** The following information should be obtained:

- □ Plaintiff's name, address, and business form (i.e., corporation, partnership, etc.).
- □ All patents or transfers regarding plaintiff's or defendant's invention (i.e., licenses, manufacturing agreements, or assignments).
- □ Defendant's use, sale, manufacture, or distribution of the allegedly infringing invention (how widely has it been disseminated?).
- □ Defendant's intent or knowledge of the alleged infringement.
- □ Does defendant have insurance that covers this type of dispute?

■ **Review the Plaintiff's Invention and Title to the Invention.**

- □ Review dates of infringement.
- □ Acquire copies of plaintiff's patent and file wrapper history.
- □ Perform patent search for plaintiff's invention and perform search of prior art.
- □ If possible, acquire plaintiff's invention.

■ **Obtain Information about all Parties.**

- □ Determine name, address, and business form of all possible parties to lawsuit, including other potential defendants (databases such as LEXIS®, Dialog®, or Westlaw® may provide information regarding business form (i.e., corporation or partnership), and agent for service).
- □ Set up computer index (directory of all persons involved in litigation, facts, relationships, and caselaw).

- **Review Legal Claims and Possible Defenses Regarding Infringement.**
  - ☐ List *all* possible patent and equitable defenses and review the list with the client.
  - ☐ Perform legal research and review caselaw and statutes regarding infringement issues.
  - ☐ Are there any counterclaims that the defendant may wish to file?
- **Responding to Cease and Desist Letter.**
  - ☐ Review and respond to the accuracy of the allegations in the letter.
  - ☐ Consider whether defendant should cease activity pending resolution of the dispute.
  - ☐ Consider whether defendant should file an action for declaratory relief.
- **Attempt Settlement of the Dispute.** A settlement is a written agreement in which the parties formally resolve the infringement dispute.
- **Consider Alternative Dispute Resolution.**
  - ☐ Is there an agreement between the parties compelling arbitration or mediation?
  - ☐ Will both parties submit to mediation or patent arbitration?
- **Respond to the Complaint.**
  - ☐ Calendar response—20 days from service.
  - ☐ Review Federal Rules of Civil Procedure and obtain local court rules.
  - ☐ Determine whether venue or jurisdiction is improper.
  - ☐ Assist in preparation of answer.
  - ☐ If appropriate, prepare counterclaim.
- **Discovery.** Coordination of discovery requires preparation of a discovery plan. Many attorneys begin the procedure with interrogatories to determine names and addresses of relevant parties. This is often followed by depositions and requests for production of documents. Finally, requests for admissions are used to confirm or deny relevant information.
  - ☐ Calendar all discovery received and propounded for appropriate deadlines.
  - ☐ Summarize and index depositions, interrogatory responses, and documents for use at trial.
  - ☐ Determine need, if any, for protective orders.
- **Trial.**
  - ☐ Prepare lists of witnesses (and expert witnesses).
  - ☐ Review evidence regarding pretrial motions (e.g., motions in limine).
  - ☐ Prepare trial notebook.
  - ☐ Assist in preparation of jury instructions.

SUMMARY

12.1 A patent search is initiated to determine the patentability of an invention or to assess facts in patent litigation or licensing. Patent searches can be performed independently or with the aid of professional searchers or computer online database services.

12.2 The patent application includes a carefully drafted set of specifications as well as a declaration, drawings, fees, and other supporting statements. Processing of the application may take up to two years. Maintenance fees must be paid during the life of the patent and patent notice must be included on the invention.

12.3 Patents may be infringed literally or under the doctrine of equivalents. A willful infringement may result in damages up to triple the award. A U.S. patent is presumed valid and the defendant has the greater burden of proof in proving invalidity.

12.4 Prior to filing a patent infringement suit, the plaintiff must determine issues of jurisdiction and venue and must determine whether to send the alleged infringer a cease and desist letter. A complaint for patent infringement includes a request for injunctive relief and also may include additional claims for trademark, trade dress, or copyright infringement. Patent disputes may also be resolved by alternative dispute resolution procedures such as arbitration.

NOTES

1. 35 U.S.C. § 112 (patent specifications).
2. 37 C.F.R. § 1.78 (cross-references).
3. 37 C.F.R. § 1.73 (summary of invention).
4. 35 U.S.C. § 113; 37 C.R.F. §§ 1.53, 1.84 (patent drawings).
5. 35 U.S.C. § 115, 37 C.F.R. §§ 1.51-1.68, 1.75 (applicant's oath).
6. 35 U.S.C. §§ 119, 365 (foreign priority).
7. 37 C.F.R. § 1.34 (power of attorney).
8. 37 C.F.R. § 1.9 (small entity exceptions).
9. 35 U.S.C. § 261; 37 C.F.R. §§ 1.332, 1.334 (patent assignments).
10. MPEP § 708.02 (Petition to Make Special).
11. 35 U.S.C. § 251 (reissuance).
12. 35 U.S.C. § 41; 37 C.F.R. §§ 1.20, 1.362, 1.378 (patent maintenance fees).
13. 35 U.S.C. §§ 287, 292 (patent notice).
14. 35 U.S.C. § 271(b) (inducing patent infringement).
15. 35 U.S.C. § 271(c) (contributory infringement).
16. 35 U.S.C. § 286 (patent infringement statute of limitations).
17. 35 U.S.C. § 282 (presumption of patent validity).
18. 35 U.S.C. § 284 (damages for patent infringement); 35 U.S.C. § 289 (damages for design patent infringement).
19. 35 U.S.C. § 285 (attorney fees).
20. 28 U.S.C. §§ 1391(b), 1400; Fed. R. Civ. P. 12(b)(3) (patent venue).
21. Fed. R. Civ. P. 26 (federal discovery).
22. 35 U.S.C. § 294; 9 U.S.C. § 135(d) (patent arbitration).

QUESTIONS FOR REVIEW AND DISCUSSION

1. Where can a listing of patent attorneys and patent agents be obtained?
2. Besides the Patent and Trademark Office, where can patent records or abstracts be found?
3. What book is used as a guide for the examination of patents?
4. What is the purpose of the background section of the patent specifications?
5. Why is the independent claim more important than the dependent claims?
6. What is the purpose of the patent applicant's declaration?
7. What three parties may qualify for small entity status?
8. What is the advantage of including the assignment with the patent application?
9. Under what conditions can the processing of a patent application be accelerated?
10. What is the difference between a reissuance and a reexamination?
11. Which party has the greater burden of proof in proving patent invalidity?
12. What is the advantage of patent arbitration over litigation?

ACTIVITIES

1. Review the background for the low-headroom popcorn popper, which is meant to be fixed underneath a kitchen cabinet. Imagine that this device has a unique casing that features a rounded fiberglass shell and stainless steel trim. Would it be patent infringement for another company to copy the design for use on a low-headroom toaster oven? If it is not patent infringement, what other claims of infringement could be made?
2. Review the factual summary in the Commentary to this chapter. If SpecialFX decides to litigate, what claims would be made in the complaint? What remedies would be sought by SpecialFX? What defenses would be presented by Effectsco?
3. Review the facts regarding the Black & Decker lawsuit. Did either party prevail in the appeal? Why?

PROJECT

Locate patentable objects (e.g., a stapler, power drill, toaster) and find the patent number on those objects. Order copies of these patents from the Patent and Trademark Office, or research the patents in an online database or at the Patent Deposit Library in your state. Analyze the patents and prepare a report memorandum detailing ownership, expiration date, and dates when maintenance fees are due.

FOR MORE INFORMATION

Obtaining Copies of Patents

Provide patent number and appropriate fee—$3.00 for utility and design patents; $12.00 for color plant patents. Available from:
Commissioner of Patents and Trademarks, Washington, DC 20231

Patent Online Search Companies

Mead Data Central LEXIS/NEXIS, 9393 Springboro Pike, P.O. Box 933, Dayton, OH 45401.

Dialog Information Services, Inc., 3460 Hillview Avenue, Palo Alto, CA 94304

IFI/Plenum Data Corporation, 302 Swann Ave., Alexandria, VA 22301.

Prentice Hall Legal & Financial Services, 300 Franklin Center, 29100 Northwestern Highway, Southfield, MI 48034-1095.

Patent Applications

D. Pressman, *Patent It Yourself* (Nolo Press 1985). User-friendly, one-volume guide with step-by-step guidance for preparing an application and obtaining a patent.

J. Sheldon, *How to Write a Patent Application* (Practising Law Institute 1992). One-volume treatise with detailed analysis of all types of patent applications, as well as applicable references from C.F.R., U.S.C., and MPEP.

Kramer & Brufsky, *Patent Law Practice Forms* (Clark Boardman Callaghan 1991). A multivolume treatise that includes all of the forms and rules used for patent applications, prosecution and litigation.

Manual of Classification. A looseleaf book containing the classes and subclasses of inventions in the Patent and Trademark Office. Available from the Superintendent of Documents, U.S. Government Printing Office, Washington, DC 20402 (also available on many database services).

Classification Definitions. Contains the changes in classification of patents as well as definitions of new and revised classes and subclasses. Available from the Patent and Trademark Office, Washington, DC 20231.

Manual of Patent Examining Procedure. Also known as the MPEP. A looseleaf reference work used by patent examiners. Available from the Superintendent of Documents, U.S. Government Printing Office, Washington, DC 20402.

Horwitz, *Patent Office Rules and Practice* (Matthew Bender 1959). Nine-volume treatise (forms volumes are available separately) that includes complete copy of the MPEP, all statutes and regulations, PTO Notices, and rules.

Deposit Accounts

To establish a Patent and Trademark Office deposit account, call 703-308-0902.

Official Gazette

Published weekly, the *Official Gazette* comes in two parts, one for trademarks and one for patents. Sold by subscription and by single copy. Provides current information about patents granted during the publication period, as well as changes in patent law. Available from:

Superintendent of Documents, U.S. Government Printing Office, Washington, DC 20402.

Patent Litigation

Kramer & Brufsky, *Patent Law Practice Forms* (Clark Boardman Callaghan 1991). Multivolume treatise that includes all of the forms and rules used for patent litigation.

R. A. White, *Patent Litigation: Procedure and Tactics* (Matthew Bender 1971). One-volume treatise; part of the Matthew Bender Patent Law and Practice Series

Chisum, *Patent Law Digest* (Matthew Bender 1992). Paperbound summaries of patent decisions of the Federal Circuit.

Chernoff, *Federal Circuit Patent Case Digests* (Clark Boardman Callaghan 1990). One loose-leaf volume; summary of Federal Circuit patent decisions.

Patent Arbitration

T. L. Creel, ed., *Guide to Patent Arbitration* (BNA Books 1987). One-volume text dealing with patent arbitration.

APPENDIX A

Table of Contents Copyright Office Application Forms, Circulars, Regulations, and Announcements (Revised September 21, 1992)

Application Forms

FORM CA: For supplementary registration to correct or amplify information given in the copyright record of an earlier registration

FORM SE: For registration of each individual issue of a serial

FORM SE/GROUP: and SHORT FORM SE Specialized SE forms for use when certain requirements are met

FORM GR/CP: An adjunct application to be used for registration of a group of contributions to periodicals

FORM PA: For published and unpublished works of the performing arts (musical and dramatic works, pantomimes and dramatic works, motion pictures, and other audiovisual works)

FORM RE: For claims to renewal of copyright in works copyright under the law in effect through December 31, 1977 (1909 Copyright Act)

FORM SR: For published and unpublished sound recordings

FORM TX: For published and unpublished nondramatic literary works

FORM VA: For published and unpublished works of the visual arts (pictorial, graphic, and sculptural works)

FORM G/DN: For group registration of daily newspapers

Circulars

Sl-9 General Announcement
1 Copyright Basics
1b Limitations on the Information Furnished by the Copyright Office
1e The Certification Space of the Application Form
2 Publications on Copyright
2b Selected Bibliographies on Copyright
3 Copyright Notice
SL-4 Copyright Fees Increase
5 How to Open and Maintain a Deposit Account in the Copyright Office
6 Obtaining Copies of Copyright Office Records and Deposits
7b "Best Edition" of Published Copyrighted Works for the Collections of the Library of Congress
7c The Effects of Not Replying Within 120 Days to Copyright Office Correspondence
7d Mandatory Deposit of Copies or Phonorecords for the Library of Congress
8 Supplementary Copyright Registration
9 Works-Made-for-Hire Under the 1976 Copyright Act
12 Recordation of Transfers & Other Documents
13 Trademarks
14 Copyright Registration for Derivative Works
15 Renewal of Copyright
15a Duration of Copyright
15t Extension of Copyright Terms
21 Reproduction of Copyrighted Works by Educators and Librarians
22 How to Investigate the Copyright Status of a Work
23 The Copyright Card Catalog and the Online Files of the Copyright Office

530

Announcements

APPENDIX B

Copyright Search Report: Stephen King's *The Shining*

©Thomson & Thomson

The bestselling author of more than 30 novels of horror and fantasy, Stephen King. Photo by Tabitha King.

INVOICE <u>10000</u>

Copyright Research Report

Client Name: XYZ Productions

Attention: Mr. John Jones

Date Received: 4/10/90

Date Mailed: 4/11/90

Property Searched: **THE SHINING**

For/By: Novel

Analyst: Jerry L. Robb/bjm

Scope of Search: Full

Service: ___x___ Reg. _____ Expedited

Thomson & Thomson

COPYRIGHT RESEARCH GROUP, 500 E Street, SW, Suite 970, Washington, DC 20024-2710
Telephone: (202) 546-8046 (800) 356-8630 FAX: (202) 546-8069 Telex: 6974942 (CPYRGHT)

SAMPLE REPORT

April 10, 1990

Mr. John Jones
XYZ Productions
123 Main Street
Anywhere, USA

Copyright Report - THE SHINING

Dear Mr. Jones:

A search of the records of the Copyright Office, the card indices of the Library of Congress and the records and files of this office reveals that the **novel** by Stephen King entitled **THE SHINING** was published by Doubleday and Company and copyrighted in the name of the author as of a publication date of January 28, 1977 under entry No. A: 824323.

We have examined a copy of the novel and find that it carries the following copyright notice: Copyright © 1977 by Stephen King.

An excerpt from the novel, also entitled **THE SHINING**, was published in <u>Reflections</u> magazine, issue of June 1977. No record of copyright registration for the story or the magazine in which it appeared is found. The Library of Congress does not have a copy of the magazine, so that we have not been able to determine whether the excerpt carried a separate copyright notice.

According to the book "Stephen King: The Art of Darkness", the original draft for the novel entitled **THE SHINING** included a prologue entitled "Before The Play" and an epilogue entitled "After The Play", both of which were deleted from the final version of the novel. The prologue to the book entitled "Before The Play" was published in <u>Whispers</u> magazine, issue of August 1982. This prologue carries the notice "Copyright © 1982 by Stephen King", but we do not find that it has been separately registered for copyright. No record of publication or copyright registration for the epilogue entitled "After The Play" is found.

The novel was republished in paperback by New American Library in 1980, and is currently in print.

The novel has been variously published abroad, including China, Budapest, Stockholm, Italy and Spain.

Copyright Report - THE SHINING

Derivative Works

A **motion picture** in approximately 146 minutes running time entitled **THE SHINING**, based on the novel by Stephen King, was produced and directed by Stanley Kubrick and released in 1980 by Warner Bros. According to the copyright application, the motion picture was created in 1980, published May 23, 1980 and registered for copyright in the name of Warner Bros. Inc., July 31, 1980 under entry No. PA: 77-409. The application author for the motion picture, additional dramatic action and dialogue, audio, visual and cinematographic material was given as Hawk Films Ltd., employer for hire. Pre-existing material was given as the screenplay and previously released music. Copyright is claimed on the motion picture, additional dramatic action and dialogue, audio, visual and cinematographic material.

The motion picture was released in Great Britain by Columbia-EMI-Warner in October 1980.

The picture is currently listed as available for television export through Warner Bros.-TV International. It is available in video format through Warner Home Video (one version in English and one with Spanish subtitles). It premiered over the Showtime network January 5, 1986; on Cinemax January 13, 1986 and on the Movie Channel January 16, 1986.

The **screenplay** for the motion picture, also entitled **THE SHINING**, based on the novel of the same title, was created in 1978 and registered for copyright as an unpublished work in the name of Warner Bros. Inc., May 23, 1980 under entry No. PAU: 205-059. Copyright is claimed on new dialogue, dramatic action, plot and character development.

A **work** entitled **THE SHINING**, based on the novel by Stephen King, was created in 1978 by Bob Radliff and registered for copyright as an unpublished work in the name of Bob Radliff, March 13, 1980 under entry No. PAU: 181-461. Copyright is claimed on the words and music depicting situations described in the book.

Recorded Instruments

By instrument dated **October 7, 1976**, recorded October 25, 1976 in Vol. 1604, pages 48-50, Stephen King and Doubleday and Company, Inc. assigned to Producers Group, forever, the motion

Copyright Report - THE SHINING

picture and television rights in the literary and/or dramatic work entitled **THE SHINING**, and all parts thereof, and all motion picture and television rights and the copyright thereof, together with the right to make and exploit a motion picture and television production based thereon, subject to the terms and conditions of an agreement dated August 1, 1976 between the Producers Group and Stephen King.

By instrument dated **May 31, 1978**, recorded June 5, 1978 in Vol. 1665, page 104, Stephen King and Doubleday and Company, by P.D. Knecht, attorney-in-fact, assigned to Warner Brothers, Inc. the sole and exclusive motion picture, television and allied rights in and to **THE SHINING**, subject to the terms and conditions of an agreement between King and assignee's predecessor, the Producers Circle Co. dated August 1, 1976 and December 9, 1976.

By instrument dated **December 31, 1983**, recorded December 29, 1983 in Vol. 2041, pages 432-445, Warner Bros. Inc. and Warner Bros. Television Distribution, Inc. mortgaged and assigned for security to Bank of America National Trust and Savings Association all its right, title and interest in the copyright in numerous listed motion pictures, including **THE SHINING**.

In addition, the following documents have been recorded in connection with the paperback edition of the novel:

By instrument dated **December 28, 1983**, recorded January 3, 1984 in Vol. 2042, pages 4-36, The New American Library, Inc. assigned to New American Library all its right, title and interest in the copyrights and copyright licenses which were owned by it in numerous books including **THE SHINING**.

By instrument dated as of **December 28, 1983**, recorded January 30, 1984 in Vol. 2045, pages 825-870, NAL Acquisition Company granted to Manufacturers Hanover Trust Co. a continuing lien and security interest in the copyrights and all its right, title and interest in the contracts relating to numerous books including **THE SHINING**.

By instrument dated **March 31, 1985, April 30, 1985, May 3, 1985**, recorded July 5, 1985 in Vol. 2122, pages 62-74, New American Library and Manufacturers Hanover Trust Company filed a Third Amendment to the above Copyright Security Agreement, pursuant to a Financing Agreement between any NAL Acquisition Company and Manufacturers Trust Company dated as of December 28, 1983, amended March 1, 1985, adding copyrights acquired by the company from time to time. The attached schedule contained the work entitled **THE SHINING** by Stephen King. It was further noted

Copyright Report - THE SHINING

in the Amendment that NAL Acquisition Company had changed its
name to New American Library by Amendment No. 1 to the amended
and restated NAL Acquisition Company, Ltd. Partnership Agreement
dated as of January 31, 1984.

By instrument dated **December 3, 1986**, recorded February 2,
1987, in Vol. 2214, pages 1-134, New American Library assigned to
NAL Penguin Inc. all its right, title and interest, including the
copyright, renewals and extensions thereof, in connection with
the book entitled **THE SHINING** and 5,113 others.
No further document affecting any right, title or interest
in the novel or motion picture based thereon is found of record
in the Copyright Office.

Newspaper and Trade Notices

Variety, issue of May 28, 1980, reported that following the
New York and Los Angeles preliminary breaks of Warner Brothers'
THE SHINING on May 23, producer-director Stanley Kubrick ordered
the snipping of a brief epilogue, in which Shelley Duvall
is visited in the hospital by her expired husband's former employer.

Variety, issue of November 26, 1980, reported from Rio De
Janeiro that **THE SHINING** would be shown there with three prints
in a Portuguese version and one in the original.

The Hollywood Reporter, issue of October 1, 1981, reported
that June E. Pritchard had filed a $75 million lawsuit in
Superior Court against Stephen King, Warner Bros. and Doubleday &
Co., claiming that nightmarish incidents of her life were stolen
as material for the novel and film entitled **THE SHINING**. She
said that incidents in the book had been told by her in
confidence to a psychiatric social worker while she was under
therapy at County's-UCLA Medical Center in Torrance from 1972-
1978, and that the social worker shared the material with King.

Variety, issue of July 11, 1984 reported that the Motion
Picture Association of America had granted an "R" rating for the
motion picture entitled TERROR IN THE AISLES, following changes
in the final section of the film, which consisted of clips from
five motion pictures, including **THE SHINING**.

Copyright Report - THE SHINING

Biographical Information

A biographical sketch of Stephen King is included in
"Contemporary Authors, New Revision Series, Vol. 1." His address
was given on an unrelated copyright application last year as:
c/o of Adele Leone Agency Inc., 26 Nantucket Place, Scarsdale,
New York, 10583.

Sincerely yours,

Jerry L. Robb

JLR/blm/bjm

Enclosure

APPENDIX C

Code of Federal Regulations

CODE OF FEDERAL REGULATIONS
Title 37—Patents, Trademarks, and Copyrights;
Revised as of July 1, 1991
CHAPTER II—COPYRIGHT OFFICE,
LIBRARY OF CONGRESS
PART 201—GENERAL PROVISIONS
§ 201.4 Recordation of transfers and
certain other documents.

37 CFR 201.4

(a) General. (1) This section prescribes conditions for the recordation of transfers of copyright ownership and other documents pertaining to a copyright under section 205 of Title 17 of the United States Code, as amended by Pub. L. 94-553. The filing or recordation of the following documents is not within the provisions of this section:

(i) Certain contracts entered into by cable systems located outside of the 48 contiguous States (17 U.S.C. 111(e); see 37 CFR 201.12);

(ii) Notices of identity and signal carriage complement, and statements of account, of cable systems (17 U.S.C. 111(d); see 37 CFR 201.11; 201.17);

(iii) Original, signed notices of intention to obtain compulsory license to make and distribute phonorecords of nondramatic musical works (17 U.S.C. 115(b); see 37 CFR 201.18);

(iv) License agreements, and terms and rates of royalty payments, voluntarily negotiated between one or more public broadcasting entities and certain owners of copyright (17 U.S.C. 118; see 37 CFR 201.9);

(v) Notices of termination (17 U.S.C. 203, 304(c); see 37 CFR 201.10); and

(vi) Statements regarding the identity of authors of anonymous and pseudonymous works, and statements relating to the death of authors (17 U.S.C. 302).

(2) A "transfer of copyright ownership" has the meaning set forth in section 101 of Title 17 of the United States Code, as amended by Pub. L. 94-553. A document shall be considered to "pertain to a copyright" if it has a direct or indirect relationship to the existence, scope, duration, or identification of a copyright, or to the ownership, division, allocation, licensing, transfer, or exercise of rights under a copyright. That relationship may be past, present, future, or potential.

(3) For purposes of this section:

(i) A "sworn certification" is an affidavit under the official seal of any officer authorized to administer oaths within the United States, or if the original is located outside of the United States, under the official seal of any diplomatic or consular officer of the United States or of a person authorized to administer oaths whose authority is proved by the certificate of such an officer, or a statement in accordance with section 1746 of Title 28 of the United States Code; and

(ii) An "official certification" is a certification, by the appropriate Government official, that the original of the document is on file in a public office and that the reproduction is a true copy or the original.

(b) Forms. The Copyright Office does not provide forms for the use of persons recording documents.

(c) Recordable documents. Any transfer of copyright ownership (including any instruments of conveyance, or note or memorandum of the transfer), or any other document pertaining to a copyright, may be recorded in the Copyright Office if it is accompanied by the fee set forth in paragraph (d) of this section, and if the requirements of this paragraph with respect to signatures, completeness, and legibility are met.

(1) To be recordable, the document must bear the actual signature or signatures of the person or persons who executed it. Alternatively, the document may be recorded if it is a legible photocopy or other legible facsimile reproduction of the signed document, accompanied by a sworn certification or an official certification that the reproduction is a true copy of the signed document. Any sworn certification accompanying a reproduction shall be signed by at least one of the parties to the signed document, or by an authorized representative of that person.

(2) To be recordable, the document must be complete by its own terms. (i) A document that contains a reference to any schedule, appendix, exhibit, addendum, or other material as being attached to the document or made a part of it shall be recordable only if the attachment is also submitted for recordation with the document or if the reference is deleted by the parties to the document. If a document has been submitted for recordation and has been returned by the Copyright Office at the request of the sender for deletion of the reference to an attachment, the document will be recorded only if the deletion is signed or initialed by the persons who executed the document or by their authorized representatives. In exceptional cases a document containing a reference to an attachment will be recorded without the attached material and without deletion of the reference if the person seeking recordation submits a written request specifically asserting that: (A) The attachment is completely unavailable for recordation; and (B) the attachment is not essential to the identification of the subject matter of the document; and (C) it would be impossible or wholly impracticable to have the parties to the document sign or initial a deletion of the reference. In such exceptional cases, the Copyright Office records of the document will be annotated to show that recordation was made in response to a specific request under this paragraph.

(ii) If a document otherwise recordable under this indicates on its face that it is a self-contained part of a larger instrument (for example: if it is designated "Attachment A" or "Exhibit B"), the Copyright Office will raise the question of completeness, but will record the document if the person requesting recordation asserts that the document is sufficiently complete as it stands.

(iii) When the document submitted for recordation merely identifies or incorporates by reference another document, or certain terms of another document, the Copyright Office will raise no question of completeness, and will not require recordation of the other document.

(3) To be recordable, the document must be legible and capable of being reproduced in legible microform copies.

(d) Fee. For a document consisting of six pages or less covering no more than one title, the basic recording fee is $10. An additional charge of 50 cents is made for each page over six and each title over one. For these purposes:

(1) A fee is required for each separate transfer or other document, even if two or more documents appear on the same page;

(2) The term "title" generally denotes "appellation" or "denomination" rather than "registration," "work," or "copyright"; and

(3) In determining the number of pages in a document, each side of a leaf bearing textual matter is regarded as a "page."

(e) Recordation. The date of recordation is the date when a proper document under paragraph (c) of this section and a proper fee under paragraph (d) of this section are all received in the Copyright Office. After recordation the document is returned to the sender with a certificate of record.

SOURCE: 43 FR 35044, Aug. 8, 1978, as amended at 53 FR 123, Jan. 5, 1988

Title 37—Patents, Trademarks, and Copyrights; Revised as of July 1, 1991
CHAPTER II—COPYRIGHT OFFICE, LIBRARY OF CONGRESS
PART 202—REGISTRATION OF CLAIMS TO COPYRIGHT
§ 202.19 Deposit of published copies or phonorecords for the Library of Congress.
37 CFR 202.19

(a) General. This section prescribes rules pertaining to the deposit of copies and phonorecords of published works for the Library of Congress under section 407 of title 17 of the United States Code, as amended by Pub. L. 94-553. The provisions of this section are not applicable to the deposit of copies and phonorecords for purposes of copyright registration under section 408 of title 17, except as expressly adopted in § 202.20 of these regulations.

(b) Definitions. For the purposes of this section:

(1)(i) The "best edition" of a work is the edition, published in the United States at any time before the date of deposit, that the Library of Congress determines to be most suitable for its purposes.

(ii) Criteria for selection of the "best edition" from among two or more published editions of the same version of the same work are set forth in the statement entitled "Best Edition of Published Copyrighted Works for the Collections of the Library of Congress" (hereafter referred to as the "Best Edition Statement") in effect at the time of deposit. Copies of the Best Edition Statement are available upon request made to the Deposits and Acquisitions Division of the Copyright Office.

(iii) Where no specific criteria for the selection of the "best edition" are established in the Best Edition Statement, that edition which, in the judgment of the Library of Congress, represents the highest quality for its purposes shall be considered the "best edition". In such cases:

(A) When the Copyright Office is aware that two or more editions of a work have been published it will consult with other appropriate officials of the Library of Congress to obtain instructions as to the "best edition" and (except in cases for which special relief is granted) will require deposit of that edition; and

(B) When a potential depositor is uncertain which of two or more published editions comprises the "best edition", inquiry should be made to the Deposits and Acquisitions Division of the Copyright Office.

(iv) Where differences between two or more "editions" of a work represent variations in copyrightable content, each edition is considered a separate version, and hence a different work, for the purpose of this section, and criteria of "best edition" based on such differences do not apply.

(2) A "complete" copy includes all elements comprising the unit of publication of the best edition of the work, including elements that, if considered separately, would not be copyrightable subject matter or would otherwise be exempt from mandatory deposit requirements under paragraph (c) of this section. In the case of sound recordings, a "complete" phonorecord includes the phonorecord, together with any printed or other visually perceptible material published with such phonorecord (such as textual or pictorial matter appearing on record sleeves or album covers, or embodied in leaflets or booklets included in a sleeve, album, or other container). In the case of a musical composition published in copies only, or in both copies and phonorecords:

(i) If the only publication of copies in the United States took place by the rental, lease, or lending a full score and parts, a full score is a "complete" copy; and

(ii) If the only publication of copies in the United States took place by the rental, lease, or lending of a conductor's score and parts, a conductor's score is a "complete" copy.

In the case of a motion picture, a copy is "complete" if the reproduction of all of the visual and aural elements comprising the copyrightable subject matter in the work is clean, undamaged, undeteriorated, and free of splices, and if the copy itself and its physical housing are free of any defects that would interfere with the performance of the work or that would cause mechanical, visual, or audible defects or distortions.

(3) The terms "copies," "collective work," "device," "fixed," "literary work," "machine," "motion picture," "phonorecord," "publication," "sound recording," and "useful article," and their variant forms, have the meanings given to them in section 101 of title 17.

(4) "Title 17" means title 17 of the United States Code, as amended by Pub. L. 94-553.

(c) Exemptions from deposit requirements. The following categories of material are exempt from the deposit requirements of section 407(a) of title 17:

(1) Diagrams and models illustrating scientific or technical works or formulating scientific or technical information in linear or three-dimensional form, such as an architectural or engineering blueprint, plan, or design, a mechanical drawing, or an anatomical model.

(2) Greeting cards, picture postcards, and stationery.

(3) Lectures, sermons, speeches, and addresses when published individually and not as a collection of the works of one or more authors.

(4) Literary, dramatic, and musical works published only as embodied in phonorecords. This category does not exempt the owner of copyright, or of the exclusive right of publication, in a sound recording resulting from the fixation of such works in a phonorecord from the applicable deposit requirements for the sound recording.

(5) Automated databases available only online in the United States but not including automated databases distributed only in the form of machine-readable copies (such as magnetic tape or disks, punch cards, or the like) from which the work cannot ordinarily be visually perceived except with the aid of a machine or device, and computerized information works in the nature of statistical compendia, serials, and reference works. Also works published in a form requiring the use of a machine or device for purposes of optical enlargement (such as film, filmstrips, slide films and works published in any variety or microform), and works published in visually perceptible form but used in connection with optical scanning devices, are not within this category and are subject to the applicable deposit requirements.

(6) Three-dimensional sculptural works, and any works published only as reproduced in or on jewelry, dolls, toys, games, plaques, floor coverings, wallpaper and similar commercial wall coverings, textiles and other fabrics, packaging material, or any useful article. Globes, relief models, and similar cartographic representations of area are not within this category and are subject to the applicable deposit requirements.

(7) Prints, labels, and other advertising matter, including catalogs, published in connection with the rental lease, lending, licensing, or sale of articles of merchandise, works of authorship, or services.

(8) Tests, and answer material for tests when published separately from other literary works.

(9) Works first published as individual contributions to collective works. This category does not exempt the owner of copyright, or of the exclusive right of publication, in the collective work as a whole, from the applicable deposit requirements for the collective work.

(10) Works first published outside the United States and later published in the United States without change in copyrightable content, if:

(i) Registration for the work was made under 17 U.S.C. 408 before the work was published in the United States; or

(ii) Registration for the work was made under 17 U.S.C. 408 after the work was published in the United States but before a demand for deposit is made under 17 U.S.C. 407(d).

(11) Works published only as embodied in a soundtrack that is an integral part of a motion picture. This category does not exempt the owner of copyright, or of the exclusive right of publication, in the motion picture, from the applicable deposit requirements for the motion picture.

(12) Motion pictures that consist of television transmission programs and that have been published, if at all, only by reason of a license or other grant to a nonprofit institution of the right to make a fixation of such programs directly from a transmission to the public, with or without the right to make further uses of such fixations.

(d) Nature of required deposit. (1) Subject to the provisions of paragraph (d)(2) of this section, the deposit required to satisfy the provisions of section 407(a) of title 17 shall consist of:

(i) In the case of published works other than sound recordings, two complete copies of the best edition; and

(ii) In the case of published sound recordings, two complete phonorecords of the best edition.

(2) In the case of certain published works not exempt from deposit requirements under paragraph (c) of this section, the following special provisions shall apply:

(i) In the case of published three-dimensional cartographic representations of area, such as globes and relief models, the deposit of one complete copy of the best edition of the work will suffice in lieu of the two copies required by paragraph (d)(1) of this section.

(ii) In the case of published motion pictures, the deposit of one complete copy of the best edition of the work will suffice in lieu of the two copies required by paragraph (d)(1) of this section. Any deposit of a published motion picture must be accompanied by a separate description of its contents, such as a continuity, pressbook, or synopsis. The Library of Congress may, at its sole discretion, enter into an agreement permitting the return of copies of published motion pictures to the depositor under certain conditions and establishing certain rights and obligations of the Library with respect to such copies. In the event of termination of such an agreement by the Library it shall not be subject to reinstatement, nor shall the depositor or any successor in interest of the depositor be entitled to any similar or subsequent agreement with the Library, unless at the

sole discretion of the Library it would be in the best interests of the Library to reinstate the agreement or enter into a new agreement.

(iii) In the case of any published work deposited in the form of a hologram, the deposit shall be accompanied by: (A) Two sets of precise instructions for displaying the image fixed in the hologram; and (B) two sets of identifying material in compliance with § 202.21 of these regulations and clearly showing the displayed image.

(iv) In any case where an individual author is the owner of copyright in a published pictorial or graphic work and (A) less than five copies of the work have been published, or (B) the work has been published and sold or offered for sale in a limited edition consisting of no more than three hundred numbered copies, the deposit of one complete copy of the best edition of the work or, alternatively, the deposit of photographs or other identifying material in compliance with § 202.21 of these regulations, will suffice in lieu of the two copies required by paragraph (d)(1) of this section.

(v) In the case of a musical composition published in copies only, or in both copies and phonorecords, if the only publication of copies in the United States took place by rental, lease, or lending, the deposit of one complete copy of the best edition will suffice in lieu of the two copies required by paragraph (d)(1) of this section.

(vi) In the case of published multimedia kits, that include literary works, audiovisual works, sound recordings, or any combination of such works, the deposit of one complete copy of the best edition will suffice in lieu of the two copies required by paragraph (d)(1) of this section.

(vii) In the case of published computer programs and published computerized information works, such as statistical compendia, serials, and reference works that are not copy-protected, the deposit of one complete copy.

SOURCE: 51 FR 6403, Feb. 24, 1986, as amended at 54 FR 42299, Oct. 16, 1989

AUTHORITY: Sec. 702, 90 Stat. 2541, 17 U.S.C. 702; sections 202.3, 202.19, 202.20, 202.21 and 202.22 are also issued under 17 U.S.C. 407 and 408.

Title 37—Patents, Trademarks, and Copyrights; Revised as of July 1, 1991
CHAPTER II—COPYRIGHT OFFICE, LIBRARY OF CONGRESS
PART 202—REGISTRATION OF CLAIMS TO COPYRIGHT
§ 202.20 Deposit of copies and phonorecords for copyright registration.
37 CFR 202.20

(a) General. This section prescribes rules pertaining to the deposit of copies and phonorecords of published and unpublished works for the purpose of copyright registration under section 408 of title 17 of the United States Code, as amended by Pub. L. 94-553. The provisions of this section are not applicable to the deposit of copies and phonorecords for the Library of Congress under section 407 of title 17, except as expressly adopted in § 202.19 of these regulations.

(b) Definitions. For the purposes of this section:

(1) The best edition of a work has the meaning set forth in § 202.19(b)(1) of these regulations.

(2) A complete copy or phonorecord means the following:

(i) Unpublished works. Subject to the requirements of paragraph (b)(2)(vi) of this section, a "complete" copy or phonorecord of an unpublished work is a copy or phonorecord representing the entire copyrightable content of the work for which registration is sought;

(ii) Published works. Subject to the requirements of paragraphs (b)(2)(iii) through (vi) of this section, a "complete" copy or phonorecord of a published work includes all elements comprising the applicable unit of publication of the work, including elements that, if considered separately, would not be copyrightable subject matter. However, even where certain physically separable elements included in the applicable unit of publication are missing from the deposit, a copy or phonorecord will be considered "complete" for purposes of registration where:

(A) The copy or phonorecord deposited contains all parts of the work for which copyright registration is sought; and

(B) The removal of the missing elements did not physically damage the copy or phonorecord or garble its contents; and

(C) The work is exempt from the mandatory deposit requirements under section 407 of title 17 of the United States Code and § 202.19(c) of these regulations, or the copy deposited consists entirely of a container, wrapper, or holder, such as an envelope, sleeve, jacket, slipcase, box, bag, folder, binder, or other receptacle acceptable for deposit under paragraph (c)(2) of this section;

(iii) Contributions to collective works. In the case of a published contribution to a collective work, a "complete" copy or phonorecord is the entire collective work including the contribution or, in the case of a newspaper, the entire section including the contribution;

(iv) Sound recordings. In the case of published sound recordings, a "complete" phonorecord has the meaning set forth in § 202.19(b)(2) of these regulations;

(v) Musical scores. In the case of a musical composition published in copies only, or in both copies and phonorecords:

(A) If the only publication of copies took place by the rental, lease, or lending of a full score and parts, a full score is a "complete" copy; and

(B) If the only publication of copies took place by the rental, lease, or lending of a conductor's score and parts, a conductor's score is a "complete" copy;

(vi) Motion pictures. In the case of a published or unpublished motion picture, a copy is "complete" if the reproduction of all of the visual and aural elements comprising the copyrightable subject matter in the work is clean, undamaged, undeteriorated, and free of splices, and if the copy itself and its physical housing are free of any defects that would interfere with the performance of the work or that would cause mechanical, visual, or audible defects or distortions.

(3) The terms copy, collective work, device, fixed, literary work, machine, motion picture, phonorecord, publication, sound recording, transmission program, and useful article, and their variant forms, have the meanings given to them in section 101 of title 17.

(4) A secure test is a nonmarketed test administered under supervision at specified centers on specific dates, all copies of which are accounted for and either destroyed or returned to restricted locked storage following each administration. For these purposes a test is not marketed if copies are not sold but it is distributed and used in such a manner that ownership and control of copies remain with the test sponsor or publisher.

(5) Title 17 means title 17 of the United States Code, as amended by Pub. L. 94-553.

(6) For the purposes of determining the applicable deposit requirements under this § 202.20 only, the following shall be considered as unpublished motion pictures: motion pictures that consist of television transmission programs and that have been published, if at all, only by reason of a license or other grant to a nonprofit institution of the right to make a fixation of such programs directly from a transmission to the public, with or without the right to make further uses of such fixations.

(c) Nature of required deposit. (1) Subject to the provisons of paragraph (c)(2) of this section, the deposit required to accompany an application for registration of claim to copyright under section 408 of title 17 shall consist of:

(i) In the case of unpublished works, one complete copy or phonorecord.

(ii) In the case of works first published in the United States before January 1, 1978, two complete copies or phonorecords of the work as first published.

(iii) In the case of works first published in the United States on or after January 1, 1978, two complete copies or phonorecords of the best edition.

(iv) In the case of works first published outside of the United States, whenever published, one complete copy or phonorecord of the work as first published. For the purposes of this section, any works simultaneously first published within and outside of the United States shall be considered to be first published in the United States.

(2) In the case of certain works, the special provisions set forth in this clause shall apply. In any case where this clause specifies that one copy or phonorecord may be submitted, that copy or phonorecord shall represent the best edition, or the work as first published, as set forth in paragraph (c)(1) of this section.

(i) General. In the following cases the deposit of one complete copy or phonorecord will suffice in lieu of two copies or phonorecords:

(A) Published three-dimensional cartographic representations of area, such as globes and relief models;

(B) Published diagrams illustrating scientific or technical works or formulating scientific or technical information in linear or other two-dimensional form, such as an architectural or engineering blueprint, or a mechanical drawing;

(C) Published greeting cards, picture postcards, and stationery;

(D) Lectures, sermons, speeches, and addresses published individually and not as a collection of the works of one or more authors;

(E) Musical compositions published in copies only, or in both copies and phonorecords, if the only publication of copies took place by rental, lease, or lending;

(F) Published multimedia kits or any part thereof;

(G) Works exempted from the requirement of depositing identifying material under paragraph (c)(2)(xi)(B)(5) of this section;

(H) Literary, dramatic, and musical works published only as embodied in phonorecords, although this category does not exempt the owner of copyright in a sound recording;

(I) Choreographic works, pantomimes, literary, dramatic, and musical works published only as embodied in motion pictures;

(J) Published works in the form of two-dimensional games, decals, fabric patches or emblems, calendars, instructions for needle work, needle work and craft kits; and

(K) Works reproduced on three-dimensional containers such as boxes, cases, and cartons.

(ii) Motion pictures. In the case of published or unpublished motion pictures, the deposit of one complete copy will suffice. The deposit of a copy or copies for any published or unpublished motion picture must be accompanied by a separate description of its contents, such as a continuity, pressbook, or synopsis. In any case where the deposit copy or copies required for registration of a motion picture cannot be viewed for examining purposes on equipment in the Examining Division of the Copyright Office, the description accompanying the deposit must comply with § 202.21(h) of these regulations. The Library of Congress may, at its sole discretion, enter into an agreement permitting the return of copies of published motion pictures to the depositor under certain conditions and establishing certain rights and obligations of the Library of Congress with respect to such copies. In the event of termination of such an agreement by the Library, it shall not be subject to reinstatement, nor shall the depositor or any successor in interest of the depositor be entitled to any similar or subsequent agreement with the Library, unless at the sole discretion of the Library it would be in the best interests of the Library to reinstate the agreement or enter into a new agreement. In the case of unpublished motion pictures (including television transmission programs that have been fixed and transmitted to the public, but have not been published), the deposit of identifying material in compliance with § 202.21 of these regulations may be made and will suffice in lieu of an actual copy. In the case of colorized versions of motion pictures made from pre-existing black and white motion pictures, in addition to the deposit of one complete copy of the colorized motion picture and the separate description of its contents as specified above, the deposit shall consist of one complete print of the black and white version of the motion picture from which the colorized version was prepared. If special relief from this requirement is requested and granted, the claimant shall make a good faith effort to deposit the best available, near-archival quality black and white print, as a condition of any grant of special relief.

(iii) Holograms. In the case of any work deposited in the form of a three-dimensional hologram, the copy or copies shall be accompanied by:

(A) Precise instructions for displaying the image fixed in the hologram, and

(B) Photographs or other identifying material complying with § 202.21 of these regulations and clearly showing the displayed image.

The number of sets of instructions and identifying material shall be the same as the number of copies required. In the case of a work in the form of a two-dimensional hologram, the image of which is visible without the use of a machine or device, one actual copy of the work shall be deposited.

(iv) Certain pictorial and graphic works. In the case of any unpublished pictorial or graphic work, deposit of identifying material in compliance with § 202.21 of these regulations may be made and will suffice in lieu of deposit of an actual copy. In the case of a published pictorial or graphic work, deposit of one complete copy, or of identifying material in compliance with § 202.21 of these regulations, may be made and will suffice in lieu of deposit of two actual copies where an individual author is the owner of copyright, and either:

(A) Less than five copies of the work have been published; or

(B) The work has been published and sold or offered for sale in a limited edition consisting of no more than 300 numbered copies.

(v) Commercial prints and labels. In the case of prints, labels, and other advertising matter, including catalogs, published in connection with the rental, lease, lending, licensing, or sale of articles of merchandise, works of authorship, or services, the deposit of one complete copy will suffice in lieu of two copies. Where the print or label is published in a larger work, such as a newspaper or other periodical, one copy of the entire page or pages upon which it appears may be submitted in lieu of the entire larger work. In the case of prints or labels physically inseparable from a three-dimensional object, identifying material complying with § 202.21 of these regulations must be submitted rather than an actual copy or copies except under the conditions of paragraph (c)(2)(xi)(B)(4) of this section.

(vi) Tests. In the case of tests, and answer material for tests, published separately from other literary works, the deposit of one complete copy will suffice in lieu of two copies. In the case of any secure test the Copyright Office will return the deposit to the applicant promptly after examination: Provided, That sufficient portions, description, or the like are retained so as to constitute a sufficient archival record of the deposit.

(vii) Computer programs and databases embodied in machine-readable copies. In cases where a computer program, database, compilation, statistical compendium or the like, if unpublished is fixed, or if published is published only in the form of machine-readable copies (such as magnetic tape or disks, punched cards, semiconductor chip products, or the like) from which the work cannot ordinarily be perceived except with the aid of a machine or device, the deposit shall consist of:

(A) For published or unpublished computer programs, one copy of identifying portions of the program, reproduced in a form visually perceptible without the aid of a machine or device, either on paper or in microform. For these purposes "identifying portions" shall mean one of the following:

(1) The first and last 25 pages or equivalent units of the source code if reproduced on paper, or at least the first and last 25 pages or equivalent units of the source code if reproduced in microform, together with the page or equivalent unit containing the copyright notice, if any. If the program is 50 pages or less, the required deposit will be the entire source code. In the case of revised versions of computer programs, if the revisions occur throughout the entire program, the deposit of the page containing the copyright notice and the first and last 25 pages of source code will suffice; if the revisions do not occur in the first and last 25 pages, the deposit should consist of the page containing the copyright notice and any 50 pages of source code representative of the revised material; or

(2) Where the program contains trade secret material, the page or equivalent unit containing the copyright notice, if any, plus one of the following: the first and last 25 pages or equivalent units of source code with portions of the source code containing trade secrets blocked-out, provided that the blocked-out portions are proportionately less than the material remaining, and the deposit reveals an appreciable amount of original computer code; or the first and last 10 pages or equivalent units of source code alone with no blocked-out portions; or the first and last 25 pages of object code, together with any 10 or more consecutive pages of source code with no blocked-out portions; or for programs consisting of or less than 25 pages or equivalent units, source code with the trade secret portions blocked-out, provided that the blocked-out portions are proportionately less than the material remaining, and the remaining portion reveals an appreciable amount of original computer code. If the copyright claim is in a revision not contained in the first and last 25 pages, the deposit shall consist of either 20 pages of source code representative of the revised material with no blocked-out portions, or any 50 pages of source code representative of the revised material with portions of the source code containing trade secrets blocked-out, provided that the blocked-out portions are proportionately less than the material remaining and the deposit reveals an appreciable amount of original computer code. Whatever method is used to block out trade secret material, at least an appreciable amount of original computer code must remain visible.

(B) Where registration of a program containing trade secrets is made on the basis of an object code deposit the Copyright Office will make registration under its rule of doubt and warn that no determination has been made concerning the existence of copyrightable authorship.

(C) Where the application to claim copyright in a computer program includes a specific claim in related computer screen displays, the deposit, in addition to the identifying portions specified in paragraph (c)(2)(vii)(A) of this section, shall consist of:

(1) Visual reproductions of the copyrightable expression in the form of printouts, photographs, or drawings no smaller than 3x3 inches and no larger than 9x12 inches; or

(2) If the authorship in the work is predominantly audiovisual, a one-half inch VHS format videotape reproducing the copyrightable expression, except that printouts, photographs, or drawings no smaller than 3x3 inches and no larger than 9x12 inches must be deposited in lieu of videotape where the computer screen material simply constitutes a demonstration of the functioning of the computer program.

(D) For published and unpublished automated databases, compilations, statistical compendia, and the like, so fixed or published, one copy of identifying portions of the work, reproduced in a form visually perceptible without the aid of a machine or device, either on paper or in microform. For these purposes:

(1)   Identifying portions shall generally mean either the first and last 25 or equivalent units of the work if reproduced on paper or in microform.

(2)   Datafile and file shall mean a group of data records pertaining to a common subject matter regardless of their size or the number of data items in them.

(3)   In the case of individual registration of a revised version of the works identified in this paragraph (c)(2)(vii)(D), the identifying portions deposited shall contain 50 representative pages or data records which have been added or modified.

(4)   If the work is an automated database comprising multiple separate or distinct data files, "identifying portions" shall instead consist of 50 complete data records from each data file or the entire data file, whichever is less, and the descriptive statement required by paragraph (c)(2)(vii)(D)(5).

(5)   In the case of group registration for revised or updated versions of a database, the claimant shall deposit identifying portions that contain 50 representative pages or equivalent units, or representative data records which have been marked to disclose (or do in fact disclose solely) the new material added on one representative publication date if published, or on one representative creation date, if unpublished, and shall also deposit a brief typed or printed descriptive statement containing the notice of copyright information required under "(6)" or "(7)" immediately below, if the work bears a notice, and;

(i)   The title of the database;

(ii)   A subtitle, date of creation or publication, or other information, to distinguish any separate or distinct data files for cataloging purposes;

(iii)   The name and address of the copyright claimant;

(iv)   For each separate file, its name and content, including its subject, the origin(s) of the data, and the approximate number of data records it contains; and

(v)   In the case of revised or updated versions of an automated database, information as to the nature and frequency of changes in the database and some identification of the location within the database or the separate data files of the revisions.

(vi)   For a copyright notice embodied in machine-readable form, the statement shall describe exactly the visually perceptible content of the notice which appears in or with the database, and the manner and frequency with which it is displayed (e.g., at user's terminal only at sign-on, or continuously on terminal display, or on printouts, etc.).

(vii)   If a visually perceptible copyright notice is placed on any copies of the work (or on magnetic tape reels or containers therefor), a sample of such notice must also accompany the statement.

(viii)   Machine-readable copies of works other than computer programs and databases. Where a literary, musical, pictorial, graphic, or audiovisual work, or a sound recording, except for literary works which are computer programs, databases, compilations, statistical compendia or the like, if unpublished has been fixed or, if published, has been published only in machine-readable form, the deposit must consist of identifying material. The type of identifying material submitted should generally be appropriate to the type of work embodied in machine-readable form, but in all cases should be that which best represents the copyrightable content of the work. In all cases the identifying material must include the title of the work. A synopsis may also be requested in addition to the other deposit materials as appropriate in the discretion of the Copyright Office. In the case of any published work subject to this section, the identifying material must include a representation of the copyright notice, if one exists. Identifying material requirements for certain types of works are specified below. In the case of the types of works listed below, the requirements specified shall apply except that, in any case where the specific requirements are not appropriate for a given work the form of the identifying material required will be determined by the Copyright Office in consultation with the applicant, but the Copyright Office will make the final determination of the acceptability of the identifying material.

(A)   For pictorial or graphic works, the deposit shall consist of identifying material in compliance with § 202.21 of these regulations;

(B)   For audiovisual works, the deposit shall consist of either a videotape of the work depicting representative portions of the copyrightable content, or a series of photographs or drawings, depicting representative portions of the work, plus in all cases a separate synopsis of the work;

(C)   For musical compositions, the deposit shall consist of a transcription of the entire work such as a score, or a reproduction of the entire work on an audio-cassette or other phonorecord;

(D)   For sound recordings, the deposit shall consist of a reproduction of the entire work on an audiocassette or other phonorecord;

(E)   For literary works, the deposit shall consist of a transcription of representative portions of the work including the first and last 25 pages or equivalent units, and five or more pages indicative of the remainder.

(ix)   Copies containing both visually-perceptible and machine-readable material. Where a published literary work is embodied in copies containing both visually perceptible and machine-readable material, the deposit shall consist of the visually perceptible material and identifying portions of the machine-readable material.

(x)   Works reproduced in or on sheetlike materials. In the case of any unpublished work that is fixed, or any published work that is published, only in the form of a two-dimensional reproduction on sheetlike materials such as textiles and other fabrics, wallpaper and similar commercial wall coverings, carpeting, floor tile, and similar commercial floor coverings, and wrapping paper and similar packaging material, the deposit shall consist of one copy in the form of an actual swatch or piece of such material sufficient to show all elements of the work in which copyright is claimed and the copyright notice appearing on the work, if any. If the work consists of a repeated pictorial or graphic design, the complete design and at least part of one repetition must be shown. If the sheetlike material in or on which a published work has been reproduced has been embodied in or attached to a three-dimensional object, such as furniture, or any other three-dimensional manufactured article, and the work has been published only in that form, the deposit must consist of identifying material complying with § 202.21 of these regulations instead of a copy. If the sheet-like material in or on which a published work has been reproduced has been embodied in or attached to a two-dimensional object such as wearing apparel, bed linen, or a similar item, and the work has been published only in that form, the deposit must consist of identifying material complying with § 202.21 of these regulations instead of a copy unless the copy can be folded for storage in a form that does not exceed four inches in thickness.

(xi)　Works reproduced in or on three-dimensional objects. (A) In the following cases the deposit must consist of identifying material complying with § 210.21 of these regulations instead of a copy or copies:

(1)　Any three-dimensional sculptural work, including any illustration or formulation of artistic expression or information in three-dimensional form. Examples of such works include statues, carvings, ceramics, moldings, constructions, models, and maquettes; and

(2)　Any two-dimensional or three-dimensional work that, if unpublished, has been fixed, or, if published, has been published only in or on jewelry, dolls, toys, games, except as provided in paragraph (c)(2)(xi)(B)(3) below, or any three-dimensional useful article.

(B)　In the following cases the requirements of paragraph (c)(2)(xi)(A) of this section for the deposit of identifying material shall not apply:

(1)　Three-dimensional cartographic representations of area, such as globes and relief models;

(2)　Works that have been fixed or published in or on a useful article that comprises one of the elements of the unit of publication of an educational or instructional kit which also includes a literary or audio-visual work, a sound recording, or any combination of such works;

(3)　Published games consisting of multiple parts that are packaged and published in a box or similar container with flat sides and with dimensions of no more than 12x24x6 inches;

(4)　Works reproduced on three-dimensional containers or holders such as boxes, cases, cartons, where the container or holder can be readily opened out, unfolded,

slit at the corners, or in some other way made adaptable for flat storage, and the copy, when flattened, does not exceed 96 inches in any dimension; or

(5)　Any three-dimensional sculptural work that, if unpublished, has been fixed, or, if published, has been published only in the form of jewelry cast in base metal which does not exceed four inches in any dimension.

(xii)　Soundtracks. For separate registration of an unpublished work that is fixed, or a published work that is published, only as embodied in a soundtrack that is an integral part of a motion picture, the deposit of identifying material in compliance with § 202.21 of these regulations will suffice in lieu of an actual copy of the motion picture.

(xiii)　Oversize deposits. In any case where the deposit otherwise required by this section exceeds 96 inches in any dimension, identifying material complying with § 202.21 of these regulations must be submitted instead of an actual copy or copies.

(xiv)　Pictorial advertising material. In the case of published pictorial advertising material, except for advertising material published in connection with motion pictures, the deposit of either one copy as published or prepublication material consisting of camera-ready copy is acceptable.

(xv)　Contributions to collective works. In the case of published contributions to collective works, the deposit of either one complete copy of the best edition of the entire collective work, the complete section containing the contribution if published in a newspaper, the entire page containing the contribution, the contribution cut from the paper in which it appeared, or a photocopy of the contribution itself as it was published in the collective work, will suffice in lieu of two complete copies of the entire collective work.

(xvi)　Phonorecords. In any case where the deposit phonorecord or phonorecords submitted for registration of a claim to copyright is inaudible on audio playback devices in the Examining Division of the Copyright Office, the Office will seek an appropriate deposit in accordance with paragraph (d) of this section.

(xvii)　Group registration of serials. For group registration of related serials, as specified in § 202.3(b)(5), the deposit must consist of one complete copy of the best edition of each issue included in the group registration. In addition, two complimentary subscriptions to any serial for which group registration is sought must be entered and maintained in the name of the Library of Congress, and the copies must be submitted regularly and promptly after publication.

(d)　Special relief. (1) In any case the Register of Copyrights may, after consultation with other appropriate officials of the Library of Congress and upon such conditions as the Register may determine after such consultation:

(i)　Permit the deposit of one copy or phonorecord, or alternative identifying material, in lieu of the one or two copies or phonorecords otherwise required by paragraph (c)(1) of this section;

(ii) Permit the deposit of incomplete copies or phonorecords, or copies or phonorecords other than those normally comprising the best edition; or

(iii) Permit the deposit of an actual copy or copies, in lieu of the identifying material otherwise required by this section; or

(iv) Permit the deposit of identifying material which does not comply with § 202.21 of these regulations.

(2) Any decision as to whether to grant such special relief, and the conditions under which special relief is to be granted, shall be made by the Register of Copyrights after consultation with other appropriate officials of the Library of Congress, and shall be based upon the acquisition policies of the Library of Congress then in force and the archival and examining requirements of the Copyright Office.

(3) Requests for special relief under this paragraph may be combined with requests for special relief under § 202.19(e) of these regulations. Whether so combined or made solely under this paragraph, such requests shall be made in writing to the Chief, Examining Division of the Copyright Office, shall be signed by or on behalf of the person signing the application for registration, and shall set forth specific reasons why the request should be granted.

(4) The Register of Copyrights may, after consultation with other appropriate officials of the Library of Congress, terminate any ongoing or continuous grant of special relief. Notice of termination shall be given in writing and shall be sent to the individual person or organization to whom the grant of special relief had been given, at the last address shown in the records of the Copyright Office. A notice of termination may be given at any time, but it shall state a specific date of termination that is at least 30 days later than the date the notice is mailed. Termination shall not affect the validity of any deposit or registration made earlier under the grant of special relief.

(e) Use of copies and phonorecords deposited for the Library of Congress. Copies and phonorecords deposited for the Library of Congress under section 407 of title 17 and § 202.19 of these regulations may be used to satisfy the deposit provisions of this section if they are accompanied by an application for registration of claim to copyright in the work represented by the deposit, and either a registration fee or a deposit account number on the application.

SOURCE: [51 FR 6405, Feb. 24, 1986, as amended at 53 FR 29890, Aug. 9, 1988; 54 FR 13176, 13181, Mar. 31, 1989; 54 FR 21059, May 16, 1989; 55 FR 50557, Dec. 7, 1990]

AUTHORITY: Sec. 702, 90 Stat. 2541, 17 U.S.C. 702; § 202.3, 202.19, 202.20, 202.21, and 202.22 are also issued under 17 U.S.C. 407 and 408.

Title 37—Patents, Trademarks, and Copyrights; Revised as of July 1, 1991
CHAPTER II—COPYRIGHT OFFICE, LIBRARY OF CONGRESS
PART 202—REGISTRATION OF CLAIMS TO COPYRIGHT
§ 202.21 Deposit of identifying material instead of copies.
37 CFR 202.21

(a) General. Subject to the specific provisions of paragraphs (f) and (g) of this section, and to §§ 202.19(e)(1)(iv) and 202.20(d)(1)(iv), in any case where the deposit of identifying material is permitted or required under § 202.19 or § 202.20 of these regulations for published or unpublished works, the material shall consist of photographic prints, transparencies, photostats, drawings, or similar two-dimensional reproductions or renderings of the work, in a form visually perceivable without the aid of a machine or device. In the case of pictorial or graphic works, such material should reproduce the actual colors employed in the work. In all other cases, such material may be in black and white or may consist of a reproduction of the actual colors.

(b) Completeness; number of sets. As many pieces of identifying material as are necessary to show the entire copyrightable content in the ordinary case, but in no case less than an adequate representation of such content, of the work for which deposit is being made, or for which registration is being sought shall be submitted. Except in cases falling under the provisions of § 202.19(d)(2)(iii) or § 202.20(c)(2)(iii) with respect to holograms, only one set of such complete identifying material is required.

(c) Size. Photographic transparencies must be at least 35mm in size and, if such transparencies are 3x3 inches or less, must be fixed in cardboard, plastic, or similar mounts to facilitate identification, handling, and storage. The Copyright Office prefers that transparencies larger than 3x3 inches be mounted in a way that facilitates their handling and preservation, and reserves the right to require such mounting in particular cases. All types of identifying material other than photographic transparencies must be not less than 3x3 inches and not more than 9x12 inches, but preferably 8x10 inches. Except in the case of transparencies, the image of the work must be either lifesize or larger, or if less than lifesize must be large enough to show clearly the entire copyrightable content of the work.

(d) Title and dimensions. At least one piece of identifying material must, on its front, back, or mount, indicate the title of the work; and the indication of an exact measurement of one or dimensions of the work is preferred.

(e) Copyright notice. In the case of works published with notice of copyright, the notice and its position on the work must be clearly shown on at least one piece of identifying material. Where necessary because of the size or position of the notice, a separate drawing or similar reproduction shall be submitted. Such reproduction shall be no smaller than 3x3 inches and no larger than 9x12 inches, and shall show the exact appearance and content of the notice, and its specific position on the work.

(f) For separate registration of an unpublished work that is fixed, or a published work that is published, only as embodied in a soundtrack that is an integral part of a motion picture, identifying material deposited in lieu of an actual copy of the motion picture shall consist of:

(1) A transcription of the entire work, or a reproduction of the entire work on a phonorecord; and

(2) Photographs or other reproductions from the motion picture showing the title of the motion picture, the soundtrack credits, and the copyright notice for the soundtrack, if any. The provisions of paragraphs (b), (c), (d), and (e) of this section do not apply to identifying material deposited under this paragraph (f).

(g) (1) In the case of unpublished motion pictures (including transmission programs that have been fixed and transmittted to the public, but have not been published), identifying material deposited in lieu of an actual copy shall consist of either:

(i) An audio cassette or other phonorecord reproducing the entire soundtrack or other sound portion of the motion picture, and description of the motion picture; or

(ii) A set consisting of one frame enlargement or similar visual reproduction from each 10-minute segment of the motion picture, and a description of the motion picture.

(2) In either case the "description" may be a continuity, a pressbook, or a synopsis but in all cases it must include:

(i) The title or continuing title of the work, and the episode title, if any;

(ii) The nature and general content of the program;

(iii) The date when the work was first fixed and whether or not fixation was simultaneous with first transmission;

(iv) The date of first transmission, if any;

(v) the running time; and

(vi) The credits appearing on the work, if any.

(3) The provisions of paragraphs (b), (c), (d), and (e) of this section do not apply to identifying material submitted under this paragraph (g).

(h) In the case where the deposit copy or copies of a motion picture cannot be viewed for examining purposes on equipment in the Examining Division of the Copyright Office, the "description" required by § 202.20(c)(2)(ii) of these regulations may be a continuity, a press-book, a synopsis, or a final shooting script

but in all cases must be sufficient to indicate the copyrightable material in the work and include

(1) The continuing title of the work and the episode title, if any;

(2) The nature and general content of the program and of its dialogue or narration, if any;

(3) The running time; and

(4) All credits appearing on the work including the copyright notice, if any. The provisions of paragraphs (b), (c), and (d) of this section do not apply to identifying material submitted under this paragraph (h).

SOURCE: 51 FR 6409, Feb. 24, 1986

AUTHORITY: Sec. 702, 90 Stat. 2541, 17 U.S.C. 702; sections 202.3, 202.19, 202.20, 202.21 and 202.22 are also issued under 17 U.S.C. 407 and 408.

Title 37—Patents, Trademarks, and Copyrights; Revised as of July 1, 1991
CHAPTER II—COPYRIGHT OFFICE, LIBRARY OF CONGRESS
PART 202—REGISTRATION OF CLAIMS TO COPYRIGHT
§ 202.22 Acquisition and deposit of unpublished television transmission programs.
37 CFR 202.22

(a) General. This section prescribes rules pertaining to the acquisition of copies of unpublished television transmission programs by the Library of Congress under section 407(e) of Title 17 of the United States Code, as amended by Pub. L. 94-553. It also prescribes rules pertaining to the use of such copies in the registration of claims to copyright, under section 408(b)(2).

(b) Definitions. For purposes of this section:

(1) The terms copies, fixed, publication, and transmission program and their variant forms, have the meanings given to them in section 101 of Title 17. The term network station has the meaning given it in section 111(f) of Title 17.

(2) Title 17 means Title of the United States Code, as amended by Pub. L. 94-553.

(c) Off-the-air copying. (1) Library of Congress employees acting under the general authority of the Librarian of Congress may make a fixation of an unpublished television transmission program directly from a transmission to the public in the United States, in accordance with section 407(e)(1) and (4) of Title 17 of the United States Code. The choice of programs selected for fixation shall be based on the Library of Congress acquistion policies in effect at the time of fixation. Specific notice of an intent to copy a transmission program off-the-air will ordinarily not be given. In general, the Library of Congress will seek to copy off-the-air substantial portion of the programming transmitted by noncommercial educational broadcast stations as defined in section 397 of Title 47 of the United States Code, and will copy off-the-air selected programming transmitted by commercial broadcast stations, both network and independent.

(2)   Upon written request addressed to the Chief, Motion Picture, Broadcasting and Recorded Sound Division by a broadcast station or other owner of the right of transmission, the Library of Congress will inform the requestor whether a particular transmission program has been copied off-the-air by the Library.

(3)   The Library of Congress will not knowingly copy off-the-air any unfixed or published television transmission program under the copying authority of section 407(e) of Title 17 of the United States Code.

(4)   The Library of Congress is entitled under this paragraph (c) to presume that a television program transmitted to the public in the United States by a noncommercial educational broadcast station as defined in section 397 of Title 47 of the United States Code has been fixed but not published.

(5)   The presumption established by paragraph (c)(4) of this section may be overcome by written declaration and submission of appropriate documentary evidence to the Chief, Motion Picture, Broadcasting and Recorded Sound Division, either before or after off-the-air copying of the particular transmission program by the Library of Congress. Such written submission shall contain:

(i)   The identification, by title and time of broadcast, of the transmission program in question;

(ii)   A brief statement declaring either that the program was not fixed or that it was published at the time of transmission;

(iii)   If it is declared that the program was published at the time of transmission, a brief statement of the facts of publication, including the date and place thereof, the method of publication, the name of the owner of the right of first publication, and whether the work was published in the United States with notice of copyright; and

(iv)   The actual handwritten signature of an officer or other duly authorized agent of the organization which transmitted the program in question.

(6)   A declaration that the program was unfixed at the time of transmission shall be accepted by the Library of Congress, unless the Library can cite evidence to the contrary, and the off-the-air copy will either be

(i)   Erased; or

(ii)   Retained, if requested by the owner of copyright or of any exclusive right, to satisfy the deposit provision of section 408 of Title 17 of the United States Code.

(7)   If it is declared that the program was published at the time of transmission, the Library of Congress is entitled under this section to retain the copy to satisfy the deposit requirement of section 407(a) of title 17 of the United States Code.

(8)   The Library of Congress in making fixations of unpublished transmission programs transmitted by commercial broadcast stations shall not do so without notifying the transmitting organization or its agent that such activity is taking place. In the case of network stations, the notification will be sent to the particular network. In the case of any other commercial broadcasting station, the notification will be sent to the particular broadcast station that has transmitted, or will transmit, the program. Such notice shall, if possible, be given by the Library of Congress prior to the time of broadcast. In every case, the Library of Congress shall transmit such notice no later than fourteen days after such fixation has occurred. Such notice shall contain:

(i)   The identification, by title and time of broadcast, of the transmission program in question;

(ii)   A brief statement asserting the Library of Congress' belief that the transmission program has been, or will be by the date of transmission, fixed and is unpublished, together with language converting the notice to a demand for deposit under section 407(a) and (b) of title 17 of the United States Code, if the transmission program has been published in the United States.

(9)   The notice required by paragraph (c)(8) of this section shall not cover more than one transmission program except that the notice may cover up to thirteen episodes of one title if such episodes are generally scheduled to be broadcast at the same time period on a regular basis, or may cover all the episodes comprising the title if they are scheduled to be broadcast within a period of not more than two months.

(d)   Demands for deposit of a television transmission program.

(1)   The Register of Copyrights may make a written demand upon the owner of the right of transmission in the United States to deposit a copy of a specific transmission program for the benefit of the Library of Congress under the authority of section 407(e)(2) of Title 17 of the United States Code.

(2)   The Register of Copyrights is entitled to presume, unless clear evidence to the contrary is proffered, that the transmitting organization is the owner of the United States transmission right.

(3)   Notices of demand shall be in writing and shall contain:

(i)   The identification, by title and time of broadcast, of the work in question;

(ii)   An explanation of the optional forms of compliance, including transfer of ownership of a copy to the Library, lending a copy to the Library for reproduction, or selling a copy to the Library at a price not to exceed the cost of reproducing and supplying the copy;

(iii)   A ninety-day deadline by which time either compliance or a request for an extension of a request to adjust the scope of the demand or the method for fulfilling it shall have been received by the Register of Copyrights;

(iv)   A brief description of the controls which are placed on the copies' use;

(v) A statement concerning the Register's perception of the publication status of the program, together with language converting this demand to a demand for a deposit, under 17 U.S.C. 407 (a) and (c), if the recipient takes the position that the work is published; and

(vi) A statement that a compliance copy must be made and retained if the notice is received prior to transmission.

(4) With respect to paragraph (d)(3)(ii) of this section, the sale of a copy in compliance with a demand of this nature shall be at a price not to exceed the cost to the Library of reproducing and supplying the copy. The notice of demand should therefore inform the recipient of that cost and set that cost, plus reasonable shipping charges, as the maximum price for such a sale.

(5) Copies transferred, lent, or sold under paragraph (d) of this section shall be of sound physical condition as described in Appendix A to this section.

(6) Special relief. In the case of any demand made under paragraph (d) of this section the Register of Copyrights may, after consultation with other appropriate officials of the Library of Congress and upon such conditions as the Register may determine after such consultation,

(i) Extend the time period provided in subparagraph (d)(3)(iii);

(ii) Make adjustments in the scope of the demand; or

(iii) Make adjustments in the method of fulfilling the demand. Any decision as to whether to allow such extension or adjustments shall be made by the Register of Copyrights after consultation with other appropriate officials of the Library of Congress and shall be made as reasonably warranted by the circumstances. Requests for special relief under paragraph (d) of this section shall be made in writing to the Chief, Acquisitions and Processing Division of the Copyright Office, shall be signed by or on behalf of the owner of the right of transmission in the United States and shall set forth the specific reasons why the request shall be granted.

(e) Disposition and use of copies. (1) All copies acquired under this section shall be maintained by the Motion Picture, Broadcasting and Recorded Sound Division of the Library of Congress. The Library may make one archival copy of a program which it has fixed under the provisions of section 407(e)(1) of Title 17 of the United States Code and paragraph (c) of this section.

(2) All copies acquired or made under this section, except copies of transmission programs consisting of a regularly scheduled newscast or on-the-spot coverage of news events, shall be subject to the restrictions concerning copying and access found in Library of Congress Regulation 818-17, Policies Governing the Use and Availability of Motion Pictures and Other Audiovisual Works in the Collections of the Library of Congress, or its successors. Copies of transmission programs consisting of regularly scheduled newscasts or on-the-spot coverage of news events are subject to the provisions of the "American Television and Radio Archives Act" (section 170 of Title 2 of the United States Code) and such regulations as the Librarian of Congress shall prescribe.

(f) Registration of claims to copyright. (1) Copies fixed by the Library of Congress under the provisions of paragraph (c) of this section may be used as the deposit for copyright registration provided that:

(i) The application and fee, in a form acceptable for registration, is received by the Copyright Office not later than ninety days after transmission of the program, and

(ii) Correspondence received by the Copyright Office in the envelope containing the application and fee states that a fixation of the instant work was made by the Library of Congress and requests that the copy so fixed be used to satisfy the registration deposit provisions.

(2) Copies transferred, lent, or sold to the Library of Congress under the provisions of a paragraph (d) of this section may be used as the deposit for copyright registration purposes only when the application and fee, in a form acceptable for registration, accompany, in the same container, the copy lent, transferred, or sold, and there is an explanation that the copy is intended to satisfy both the demand issued under section 407(e)(2) of Title 17 of the United States Code and the registration deposit provisions.

(g) Agreements modifying the terms of this section. (1) The Library of Congress may, at its sole discretion, enter into an agreement whereby the provision of copies of unpublished television transmission programs on terms different from those contained in this section is authorized.

(2) Any such agreement may be terminated without notice by the Library of Congress.

SOURCE: [48 FR 37208, Aug. 17, 1983, as amended at 56 FR 7815, Feb. 26, 1991]

AUTHORITY: (17 U.S.C. 407, 408, 702)

Title 37—Patents, Trademarks, and Copyrights; Revised as of July 1, 1991
CHAPTER II—COPYRIGHT OFFICE, LIBRARY OF CONGRESS
PART 202—REGISTRATION OF CLAIMS TO COPYRIGHT
§ 202.23 Full-term retention of copyright deposits.
37 CFR 202.23

(a) General. (1) This section prescribes conditions under which a request for full term retention, under the control of the Copyright Office, of copyright deposits (copies, phonorecords, or identifying material) of published works may be made and granted or denied pursuant to section 704(e) of Title 17 of the United States

Code. Only copies, phonorecords, or identifying material deposited in connection with registration of a claim to copyright under Title 17 of the United States Code are within the provisions of this section. Only the depositor or the copyright owner of record of the work identified by the copyright deposit, or a duly authorized agent of the depositor or copyright owner may request full term retention. A fee for this service is fixed by this section pursuant to section 708(a)(11) of Title 17 of the United States Code.

(2) For purposes of this section, "under the control of the Copyright Office" shall mean within the confines of Copyright Office buildings and under the control of Copyright Office employees, including retention in a Federal records center, but does not include transfer to the Library of Congress collections.

(3) For purposes of this section, "full term retention" means retention for a period of 75 years from the date of publication of the work identified by the particular copyright deposit which is retained.

(4) For purposes of this section, "copyright deposit" or its plural means the copy, phonorecord, or identifying material submitted to the Copyright Office in connection with a published work that is subsequently registered and made part of the records of the Office.

(b) Form and content of request for full term retention—(1) Forms. The Copyright Office does not provide printed forms for the use of persons requesting full term retention of copyright deposits.

(2) Requests for full term retention must be made in writing, addressed to the Chief, Records Management Division of the Copyright Office, and shall: (i) Be signed by or on behalf of the depositor or the copyright owner of record, and (ii) clearly indicate that full term retention is desired.

(3) The request for full term retention must adequately identify the particular copyright deposit to be retained, preferably by including the title used in the registration application, the name of the depositor or copyright owner of record, the publication date, and, if registration was completed earlier, the registration number.

(c) Conditions under which requests will be granted or denied—(1) General. A request that meets the requirements of subsection (b) will generally be granted if the copyright deposit for which full term retention is requested has been continuously in the custody of the Copyright Office and the Library of Congress has not, by the date of the request, selected the copyright deposit for its collections.

(2) Time of request. The request for full term retention of a particular copyright deposit may be made at the time of deposit or at any time thereafter; however, the request will be granted only if at least one copy, phonorecord, or set of identifying material is in the custody of the Copyright Office at the time of the request. Where the request is made concurrent with the initial deposit of the work for registration, the requestor must submit one copy or phonorecord more than the number specified in § 202.20 of 37 CFR for the particular work.

(3) One deposit retained. The Copyright Office will retain no more than one copy, phonorecord, or set of identifying material for a given registered work.

(4) Denial of request for full term retention. The Copyright Office reserves the right to deny the request for full term retention where: (i) The excessive size, fragility, or weight of the deposit would, in the sole discretion of the Register of Copyrights, constitute an unreasonable storage burden. The request may nevertheless be granted if, within 60 calendar days of the original denial of the request, the requestor pays the reasonable administrative costs, as fixed in the particular case by the Register of Copyrights, of preparing acceptable identifying materials for retention in lieu of the actual copyright deposit;

(ii) The Library of Congress has selected for its collections the single copyright deposit, or both, if two copies or phonorecords were deposited; or

(iii) Retention would result in a health or safety hazard, in the sole judgment of the Register of Copyrights. The request may nevertheless be granted if, within 60 calendar days of the original denial of the request, the requestor pays the reasonable administrative costs, as fixed in the particular case by the Register of Copyrights, of preparing acceptable identifying materials for retention in lieu of the actual copyright deposit.

(d) Form of copyright deposit. If full term retention is granted, the Copyright Office will retain under its control the particular copyright deposit used to make registration for the work. Any deposit made on or after September 19, 1978 shall satisfy the requirements of 37 CFR 202.20 and 202.21.

(e) Fee for full term retention. (1) Pursuant to section 708(a)(11) of Title 17 of the United States Code, the Register of Copyrights has fixed the fee for full term retention at $135.00 for each copyright deposit granted full term retention.

(2) A check or money order in the amount of $135.00 payable to the Register of Copyrights, must be received in the Copyright Office within 60 calendar days from the date of mailing of the Copyright Office's notification to the requestor that full term retention has been granted for a particular copyright deposit.

(3) The Copyright Office will issue a receipt acknowledging payment of the fee and identifying the copyright deposit for which full term retention has been granted.

(f) Selection by Library of Congress—(1) General. All published copyright deposits are available for selection by the Library of Congress until the Copyright Office has formally granted a request for full term retention. Unless the requestor has deposited the additional copy or phonorecord specified by paragraph (c)(2) of this section, the Copyright Office will not process a request for full term retention submitted concurrent with a copyright registration application and deposit, until the Library of Congress has had a reasonable amount of time to make its selection determination.

(2) A request for full term retention made at the time of deposit of a published work does not affect the right of the Library to select one or both of the copyright deposits.

(3) If one copyright deposit is selected, the second deposit, if any, will be used for full term retention.

(4) If both copyright deposits are selected, or, in the case where the single deposit made is selected, full term retention will be granted only if the additional copy or phonorecord specified by paragraph (c)(2) of this section was deposited.

(g) Termination of full term storage. Full term storage will cease 75 years after the date of publication of the work identified by the copyright deposit retained, and the copyright deposit will be disposed of in accordance with section 704, paragraphs (b) through (d), of Title 17 of the United States Code.

SOURCE: 48 FR 32777, July 19, 1983

AUTHORITY: Sec. 702, 90 Stat. 2541, 17 U.S.C. 702; sections 202.3, 202.19, 202.20, 202.21 and 202.22 are also issued under 17 U.S.C. 407 and 408.

APPENDIX D

Copyright Forms

FORM TX

For a Literary Work
UNITED STATES COPYRIGHT OFFICE

REGISTRATION NUMBER

TX	TXU

EFFECTIVE DATE OF REGISTRATION

Month	Day	Year

DO NOT WRITE ABOVE THIS LINE. IF YOU NEED MORE SPACE, USE A SEPARATE CONTINUATION SHEET.

1

TITLE OF THIS WORK ▼

PREVIOUS OR ALTERNATIVE TITLES ▼

PUBLICATION AS A CONTRIBUTION If this work was published as a contribution to a periodical, serial, or collection, give information about the collective work in which the contribution appeared. **Title of Collective Work ▼**

If published in a periodical or serial give: **Volume ▼**   **Number ▼**   **Issue Date ▼**   **On Pages ▼**

2

a

NAME OF AUTHOR ▼

DATES OF BIRTH AND DEATH
Year Born ▼   Year Died ▼

Was this contribution to the work a "work made for hire"?
☐ Yes
☐ No

AUTHOR'S NATIONALITY OR DOMICILE
Name of Country
OR { Citizen of ▶_____
Domiciled in ▶_____

WAS THIS AUTHOR'S CONTRIBUTION TO THE WORK
Anonymous?   ☐ Yes ☐ No
Pseudonymous? ☐ Yes ☐ No

If the answer to either of these questions is "Yes," see detailed instructions.

NATURE OF AUTHORSHIP Briefly describe nature of the material created by this author in which copyright is claimed. ▼

NOTE

Under the law, the "author" of a "work made for hire" is generally the employer, not the employee (see instructions). For any part of this work that was "made for hire" check "Yes" in the space provided, give the employer (or other person for whom the work was prepared) as "Author" of that part, and leave the space for dates of birth and death blank.

b

NAME OF AUTHOR ▼

DATES OF BIRTH AND DEATH
Year Born ▼   Year Died ▼

Was this contribution to the work a "work made for hire"?
☐ Yes
☐ No

AUTHOR'S NATIONALITY OR DOMICILE
Name of country
OR { Citizen of ▶_____
Domiciled in ▶_____

WAS THIS AUTHOR'S CONTRIBUTION TO THE WORK
Anonymous?   ☐ Yes ☐ No
Pseudonymous? ☐ Yes ☐ No

If the answer to either of these questions is "Yes," see detailed instructions.

NATURE OF AUTHORSHIP Briefly describe nature of the material created by this author in which copyright is claimed. ▼

c

NAME OF AUTHOR ▼

DATES OF BIRTH AND DEATH
Year Born ▼   Year Died ▼

Was this contribution to the work a "work made for hire"?
☐ Yes
☐ No

AUTHOR'S NATIONALITY OR DOMICILE
Name of Country
OR { Citizen of ▶_____
Domiciled in ▶_____

WAS THIS AUTHOR'S CONTRIBUTION TO THE WORK
Anonymous?   ☐ Yes ☐ No
Pseudonymous? ☐ Yes ☐ No

If the answer to either of these questions is "Yes," see detailed instructions.

NATURE OF AUTHORSHIP Briefly describe nature of the material created by this author in which copyright is claimed. ▼

3

a

YEAR IN WHICH CREATION OF THIS WORK WAS COMPLETED This information must be given in all cases. ◀ Year

b

DATE AND NATION OF FIRST PUBLICATION OF THIS PARTICULAR WORK
Complete this information Month ▶_____ Day ▶_____ Year ▶_____
ONLY if this work has been published.   ◀ Nation

4

See instructions before completing this space.

COPYRIGHT CLAIMANT(S) Name and address must be given even if the claimant is the same as the author given in space 2.▼

TRANSFER If the claimant(s) named here in space 4 are different from the author(s) named in space 2, give a brief statement of how the claimant(s) obtained ownership of the copyright.▼

DO NOT WRITE HERE OFFICE USE ONLY

APPLICATION RECEIVED

ONE DEPOSIT RECEIVED

TWO DEPOSITS RECEIVED

REMITTANCE NUMBER AND DATE

MORE ON BACK ▶
• Complete all applicable spaces (numbers 5-11) on the reverse side of this page.
• See detailed instructions.
• Sign the form at line 10.

DO NOT WRITE HERE
Page 1 of_____pages

EXAMINED BY

FORM TX

CHECKED BY

☐ CORRESPONDENCE
Yes

FOR
COPYRIGHT
OFFICE
USE
ONLY

DO NOT WRITE ABOVE THIS LINE. IF YOU NEED MORE SPACE, USE A SEPARATE CONTINUATION SHEET.

PREVIOUS REGISTRATION Has registration for this work, or for an earlier version of this work, already been made in the Copyright Office?

☐ Yes   ☐ No   If your answer is "Yes," why is another registration being sought? (Check appropriate box) ▼

a. ☐ This is the first published edition of a work previously registered in unpublished form.

b. ☐ This is the first application submitted by this author as copyright claimant.

c. ☐ This is a changed version of the work, as shown by space 6 on this application.

If your answer is "Yes," give: **Previous Registration Number** ▼   **Year of Registration** ▼

5

DERIVATIVE WORK OR COMPILATION   Complete both space 6a & 6b for a derivative work; complete only 6b for a compilation.

a. **Preexisting Material**   Identify any preexisting work or works that this work is based on or incorporates. ▼

b. **Material Added to This Work**   Give a brief, general statement of the material that has been added to this work and in which copyright is claimed. ▼

6

See instructions
before completing
this space.

—space deleted—

7

REPRODUCTION FOR USE OF BLIND OR PHYSICALLY HANDICAPPED INDIVIDUALS   A signature on this form at space 10, and a check in one of the boxes here in space 8, constitutes a non-exclusive grant of permission to the Library of Congress to reproduce and distribute solely for the blind and physically handicapped and under the conditions and limitations prescribed by the regulations of the Copyright Office: (1) copies of the work identified in space 1 of this application in Braille (or similar tactile symbols); or (2) phonorecords embodying a fixation of a reading of that work; or (3) both.

a ☐ Copies and Phonorecords   b ☐ Copies Only   c ☐ Phonorecords Only

8

See instructions.

DEPOSIT ACCOUNT   If the registration fee is to be charged to a Deposit Account established in the Copyright Office, give name and number of Account.
Name ▼   **Account Number** ▼

CORRESPONDENCE   Give name and address to which correspondence about this application should be sent.   Name/Address/Apt/City/State/Zip ▼

Area Code & Telephone Number ▶

9

Be sure to
give your
daytime phone
◀ number.

CERTIFICATION*   I, the undersigned, hereby certify that I am the

Check one ▶

☐ author
☐ other copyright claimant
☐ owner of exclusive right(s)
☐ authorized agent of

of the work identified in this application and that the statements made by me in this application are correct to the best of my knowledge.

Name of author or other copyright claimant, or owner of exclusive right(s) ▲

Typed or printed name and date ▼ If this application gives a date of publication in space 3, do not sign and submit it before that date.

_____ date ▶ _____

Handwritten signature (X) ▼

10

**MAIL
CERTIFI-
CATE TO**

Name ▼

Number/Street/Apartment Number ▼

City/State/ZIP ▼

**Certificate
will be
mailed in
window
envelope**

YOU MUST:
• Complete all necessary spaces
• Sign your application in space 10

SEND ALL 3 ELEMENTS
IN THE SAME PACKAGE:
1. Application form
2. Nonrefundable $20 filing fee
   in check or money order
   payable to *Register of Copyrights*
3. Deposit material
   MAIL TO:
Register of Copyrights
Library of Congress
Washington, D.C. 20559

Copyright fees are ad-
justed at 5-year inter-
vals, based on in-
creases or decreases in
the Consumer Price In-
dex. The next adjust-
ment is due in 1995.
Contact the Copyright
Office in January 1995
for the new fee sched-
ule.

11

* 17 U.S.C. § 506(e)   Any person who knowingly makes a false representation of a material fact in the application for copyright registration provided for by section 409, or in any written statement filed in connection with the application, shall be fined not more than $2,500.

June 1992—100,000

☆U.S. GOVERNMENT PRINTING OFFICE: 1992-312-432/60,004

⊘ Filling Out Application Form TX

Detach and read these instructions before completing this form. Make sure all applicable spaces have been filled in before you return this form.

BASIC INFORMATION

When to Use This Form: Use Form TX for registration of published or unpublished non-dramatic literary works, excluding periodicals or serial issues. This class includes a wide variety of works: fiction, non-fiction, poetry, textbooks, reference works, directories, catalogs, advertising copy, compilations of information, and computer programs. For periodicals and serials, use Form SE.

Deposit to Accompany Application: An application for copyright registration must be accompanied by a deposit consisting of copies or phonorecords representing the entire work for which registration is to be made. The following are the general deposit requirements as set forth in the statute:

Unpublished Work: Deposit one complete copy (or phonorecord).

Published Work: Deposit two complete copies or one phonorecord of the best edition.

Work First Published Outside the United States: Deposit one complete copy (or phonorecord) of the first foreign edition.

Contribution to a Collective Work: Deposit one complete copy (or phonorecord) of the best edition of the collective work.

The Copyright Notice: For works first published on or after March 1, 1989, the law provides that a copyright notice in a specified form "may be placed on all publicly distributed copies from which the work can be visually perceived." Use of the copyright notice is the responsibility of the copyright owner and does not require advance permission from the Copyright Office. The required form of the notice for copies generally consists of three elements: (1) the symbol "©", or the word "Copyright," or the abbreviation "Copr."; (2) the year of first publication; and (3) the name of the owner of copyright. For example: "© 1989 Jane Cole." The notice is to be affixed to the copies "in such manner and location as to give reasonable notice of the claim of copyright." Works first published prior to March 1, 1989, **must** carry the notice or risk loss of copyright protection.

For information about notice requirements for works published before March 1, 1989, or other copyright information, write: Information Section, LM-401, Copyright Office, Library of Congress, Washington, D.C. 20559.

PRIVACY ACT ADVISORY STATEMENT Required by the Privacy Act of 1974 (Public Law 93-579)	PRINCIPAL USES OF REQUESTED INFORMATION
	• Establishment and maintenance of a public record
	• Examination of the application for compliance with legal requirements
AUTHORITY FOR REQUESTING THIS INFORMATION	OTHER ROUTINE USES
• Title 17, U.S.C., Secs. 409 and 410	• Public inspection and copying
FURNISHING THE REQUESTED INFORMATION IS	• Preparation of public indexes
• Voluntary	• Preparation of public catalogs of copyright registrations
BUT IF THE INFORMATION IS NOT FURNISHED	• Preparation of search reports upon request
• It may be necessary to delay or refuse registration	NOTE
• You may not be entitled to certain relief, remedies, and benefits provided in chapters 4 and 5 of title 17, U.S.C	• No other advisory statement will be given you in connection with this application
	• Please keep this statement and refer to it if we communicate with you regarding this application

LINE-BY-LINE INSTRUCTIONS

1 SPACE 1: Title

Title of This Work: Every work submitted for copyright registration must be given a title to identify that particular work. If the copies or phonorecords of the work bear a title (or an identifying phrase that could serve as a title), transcribe that wording *completely* and *exactly* on the application. Indexing of the registration and future identification of the work will depend on the information you give here.

Previous or Alternative Titles: Complete this space if there are any additional titles for the work under which someone searching for the registration might be likely to look, or under which a document pertaining to the work might be recorded.

Publication as a Contribution: If the work being registered is a contribution to a periodical, serial, or collection, give the title of the contribution in the "Title of this Work" space. Then, in the line headed "Publication as a Contribution," give information about the collective work in which the contribution appeared.

2 SPACE 2: Author(s)

General Instructions: After reading these instructions, decide who are the "authors" of this work for copyright purposes. Then, unless the work is a "collective work," give the requested information about every "author" who contributed any appreciable amount of copyrightable matter to this version of the work. If you need further space, request Continuation sheets. In the case of a collective work, such as an anthology, collection of essays, or encyclopedia, give information about the author of the collective work as a whole.

Name of Author: The fullest form of the author's name should be given. Unless the work was "made for hire," the individual who actually created the work is its "author." In the case of a work made for hire, the statute provides that "the employer or other person for whom the work was prepared is considered the author."

What is a "Work Made for Hire"? A "work made for hire" is defined as: (1) "a work prepared by an employee within the scope of his or her employment"; or (2) "a work specially ordered or commissioned for use as a contribution to a collective work, as a part of a motion picture or other audiovisual work, as a translation, as a supplementary work, as a compilation, as an instructional text, as a test, as answer material for a test, or as an atlas, if the parties expressly agree in a written instrument signed by them that the work shall be considered a work made for hire." If you have checked "Yes" to indicate that the work was "made for hire," you must give the full legal name of the employer (or other person for whom the work was prepared). You may also include the name of the employee along with the name of the employer (for example: "Elster Publishing Co., employer for hire of John Ferguson").

"Anonymous" or "Pseudonymous" Work: An author's contribution to a work is "anonymous" if that author is not identified on the copies or phonorecords of the work. An author's contribution to a work is "pseudonymous" if that author is identified on the copies or phonorecords under a fictitious name. If the work is "anonymous" you may: (1) leave the line blank; or (2) state "anonymous" on the line; or (3) reveal the author's identity. If the work is "pseudonymous" you may: (1) leave the line blank; or (2) give the pseudonym and identify it as such (for example: "Huntley Haverstock, pseudonym"); or (3) reveal the author's name, making clear which is the real name and which is the pseudonym (for example: "Judith Barton, whose pseudonym is Madeline Elster"). However, the citizenship or domicile of the author **must** be given in all cases.

Dates of Birth and Death: If the author is dead, the statute requires that the year of death be included in the application unless the work is anonymous or pseudonymous. The author's birth date is optional, but is useful as a form of identification. Leave this space blank if the author's contribution was a "work made for hire."

Author's Nationality or Domicile: Give the country of which the author is a citizen, or the country in which the author is domiciled. Nationality or domicile **must** be given in all cases.

Nature of Authorship: After the words "Nature of Authorship" give a brief general statement of the nature of this particular author's contribution to the work. Examples: "Entire text"; "Coauthor of entire text"; "Chapters 11-14"; "Editorial revisions"; "Compilation and English translation"; "New text."

3 SPACE 3: Creation and Publication

General Instructions: Do not confuse "creation" with "publication." Every application for copyright registration must state "the year in which creation of the work was completed." Give the date and nation of first publication only if the work has been published.

Creation: Under the statute, a work is "created" when it is fixed in a copy or phonorecord for the first time. Where a work has been prepared over a period of time, the part of the work existing in fixed form on a particular date constitutes the created work on that date. The date you give here should be the year in which the author completed the particular version for which registration is now being sought, even if other versions exist or if further changes or additions are planned.

Publication: The statute defines "publication" as "the distribution of copies or phonorecords of a work to the public by sale or other transfer of ownership, or by rental, lease, or lending"; a work is also "published" if there has been an "offering to distribute copies or phonorecords to a group of persons for purposes of further distribution, public performance, or public display." Give the full date (month, day, year) when, and the country where, publication first occurred. If first publication took place simultaneously in the United States and other countries, it is sufficient to state "U.S.A."

4 SPACE 4: Claimant(s)

Name(s) and Address(es) of Copyright Claimant(s): Give the name(s) and address(es) of the copyright claimant(s) in this work even if the claimant is the same as the author. Copyright in a work belongs initially to the author of the work (including, in the case of a work made for hire, the employer or other person for whom the work was prepared). The copyright claimant is either the author of the work or a person or organization to whom the copyright initially belonging to the author has been transferred.

Transfer: The statute provides that, if the copyright claimant is not the author, the application for registration must contain "a brief statement of how the claimant obtained ownership of the copyright." If any copyright claimant named in space 4 is not an author named in space 2, give a brief statement explaining how the claimant(s) obtained ownership of the copyright. Examples: "By written contract"; "Transfer of all rights by author"; "Assignment"; "By will." Do not attach transfer documents or other attachments or riders.

5 SPACE 5: Previous Registration

General Instructions: The questions in space 5 are intended to find out whether an earlier registration has been made for this work and, if so, whether there is any basis for a new registration. As a general rule, only one basic copyright registration can be made for the same version of a particular work.

Same Version: If this version is substantially the same as the work covered by a previous registration, a second registration is not generally possible unless: (1) the work has been registered in unpublished form and a second registration is now being sought to cover this first published edition; or (2) someone other than the author is identified as copyright claimant in the earlier registration, and the author is now seeking registration in his or her own name. If either of these two exceptions apply, check the appropriate box and give the earlier registration number and date. Otherwise, do not submit Form TX; instead, write the Copyright Office for information about supplementary registration or recordation of transfers of copyright ownership.

Changed Version: If the work has been changed, and you are now seeking registration to cover the additions or revisions, check the last box in space 5, give the earlier registration number and date, and complete both parts of space 6 in accordance with the instructions below.

Previous Registration Number and Date: If more than one previous registration has been made for the work, give the number and date of the latest registration.

6 SPACE 6: Derivative Work or Compilation

General Instructions: Complete space 6 if this work is a "changed version," "compilation," or "derivative work," and if it incorporates one or more earlier works that have already been published or registered for copyright, or that have fallen into the public domain. A "compilation" is defined as "a work formed by the collection and assembling of preexisting materials or of data that are selected, coordinated, or arranged in such a way that the resulting work as a whole constitutes an original work of authorship." A "derivative work" is "a work based on one or more preexisting works." Examples of derivative works include translations, fictionalizations, abridgments, condensations, or "any other form in which a work may be recast, transformed, or adapted." Derivative works also include works "consisting of editorial revisions, annotations, or other modifications" if these changes, as a whole, represent an original work of authorship.

Preexisting Material (space 6a): For derivative works, complete this space and space 6b. In space 6a identify the preexisting work that has been recast, transformed, or adapted. An example of preexisting material might be: "Russian version of Goncharov's 'Oblomov'." Do not complete space 6a for compilations.

Material Added to This Work (space 6b): Give a brief, general statement of the new material covered by the copyright claim for which registration is sought. **Derivative work** examples include: "Foreword, editing, critical annotations"; "Translation"; "Chapters 11-17." If the work is a **compilation**, describe both the compilation itself and the material that has been compiled. Example: "Compilation of certain 1917 Speeches by Woodrow Wilson." A work may be both a derivative work and compilation, in which case a sample statement might be: "Compilation and additional new material."

7 SPACE 7: Manufacturing Provisions

Due to the expiration of the Manufacturing Clause of the copyright law on June 30, 1986, this space has been deleted.

8 SPACE 8: Reproduction for Use of Blind or Physically Handicapped Individuals

General Instructions: One of the major programs of the Library of Congress is to provide Braille editions and special recordings of works for the exclusive use of the blind and physically handicapped. In an effort to simplify and speed up the copyright licensing procedures that are a necessary part of this program, section 710 of the copyright statute provides for the establishment of a voluntary licensing system to be tied in with copyright registration. Copyright Office regulations provide that you may grant a license for such reproduction and distribution solely for the use of persons who are certified by competent authority as unable to read normal printed material as a result of physical limitations. The license is entirely voluntary, nonexclusive, and may be terminated upon 90 days notice.

How to Grant the License: If you wish to grant it, check one of the three boxes in space 8. Your check in one of these boxes, together with your signature in space 10, will mean that the Library of Congress can proceed to reproduce and distribute under the license without further paperwork. For further information, write for Circular R63.

9,10,11 SPACE 9, 10, 11: Fee, Correspondence, Certification, Return Address

Fee: Copyright fees are adjusted at 5-year intervals, based on increases or decreases in the Consumer Price Index. The next adjustment is due in 1995. Contact the Copyright Office in January 1995 for the new fee schedule.
Deposit Account: If you maintain a Deposit Account in the Copyright Office, identify it in space 9. Otherwise leave the space blank and send the fee of $20 with your application and deposit.

Correspondence (space 9): This space should contain the name, address, area code, and telephone number of the person to be consulted if correspondence about this application becomes necessary.

Certification (space 10): The application can not be accepted unless it bears the date and the **handwritten signature** of the author or other copyright claimant, or of the owner of exclusive right(s), or of the duly authorized agent of author, claimant, or owner of exclusive right(s).

Address for Return of Certificate (space 11): The address box must be completed legibly since the certificate will be returned in a window envelope.

FORM PA

UNITED STATES COPYRIGHT OFFICE

REGISTRATION NUMBER

PA   PAU

EFFECTIVE DATE OF REGISTRATION

_____
Month   Day   Year

DO NOT WRITE ABOVE THIS LINE. IF YOU NEED MORE SPACE, USE A SEPARATE CONTINUATION SHEET.

1

TITLE OF THIS WORK ▼

PREVIOUS OR ALTERNATIVE TITLES ▼

NATURE OF THIS WORK ▼ See instructions

2

a

NAME OF AUTHOR ▼

DATES OF BIRTH AND DEATH
Year Born ▼   Year Died ▼

Was this contribution to the work a "work made for hire"?
☐ Yes
☐ No

AUTHOR'S NATIONALITY OR DOMICILE
Name of Country
OR { Citizen of ▶ _____
Domiciled in ▶ _____

WAS THIS AUTHOR'S CONTRIBUTION TO THE WORK
Anonymous? ☐ Yes ☐ No
Pseudonymous? ☐ Yes ☐ No

If the answer to either of these questions is "Yes," see detailed instructions

NATURE OF AUTHORSHIP   Briefly describe nature of the material created by this author in which copyright is claimed. ▼

NOTE

Under the law, the "author" of a "work made for hire" is generally the employer, not the employee (see instructions). For any part of this work that was "made for hire" check "Yes" in the space provided, give the employer (or other person for whom the work was prepared) as "Author" of that part, and leave the space for dates of birth and death blank

b

NAME OF AUTHOR ▼

DATES OF BIRTH AND DEATH
Year Born ▼   Year Died ▼

Was this contribution to the work a "work made for hire"?
☐ Yes
☐ No

AUTHOR'S NATIONALITY OR DOMICILE
Name of country
OR { Citizen of ▶ _____
Domiciled in ▶ _____

WAS THIS AUTHOR'S CONTRIBUTION TO THE WORK
Anonymous? ☐ Yes ☐ No
Pseudonymous? ☐ Yes ☐ No

If the answer to either of these questions is "Yes," see detailed instructions

NATURE OF AUTHORSHIP   Briefly describe nature of the material created by this author in which copyright is claimed. ▼

c

NAME OF AUTHOR ▼

DATES OF BIRTH AND DEATH
Year Born ▼   Year Died ▼

Was this contribution to the work a "work made for hire"?
☐ Yes
☐ No

AUTHOR'S NATIONALITY OR DOMICILE
Name of Country
OR { Citizen of ▶ _____
Domiciled in ▶ _____

WAS THIS AUTHOR'S CONTRIBUTION TO THE WORK
Anonymous? ☐ Yes ☐ No
Pseudonymous? ☐ Yes ☐ No

If the answer to either of these questions is "Yes," see detailed instructions

NATURE OF AUTHORSHIP   Briefly describe nature of the material created by this author in which copyright is claimed. ▼

3

a   **YEAR IN WHICH CREATION OF THIS WORK WAS COMPLETED**   This information must be given in all cases.   ◀ Year

b   **DATE AND NATION OF FIRST PUBLICATION OF THIS PARTICULAR WORK**   Complete this information ONLY if this work has been published. Month ▶ _____ Day ▶ _____ Year ▶ _____ ◀ Nation

4

See instructions before completing this space

COPYRIGHT CLAIMANT(S) Name and address must be given even if the claimant is the same as the author given in space 2.▼

TRANSFER If the claimant(s) named here in space 4 are different from the author(s) named in space 2, give a brief statement of how the claimant(s) obtained ownership of the copyright.▼

DO NOT WRITE HERE OFFICE USE ONLY

APPLICATION RECEIVED

ONE DEPOSIT RECEIVED

TWO DEPOSITS RECEIVED

REMITTANCE NUMBER AND DATE

MORE ON BACK ▶   • Complete all applicable spaces (numbers 5 9) on the reverse side of this page
    • See detailed instructions   • Sign the form at line 8.

DO NOT WRITE HERE
Page 1 of _____ pages

EXAMINED BY _____

FORM PA

CHECKED BY _____

☐ CORRESPONDENCE
Yes

FOR
COPYRIGHT
OFFICE
USE
ONLY

DO NOT WRITE ABOVE THIS LINE. IF YOU NEED MORE SPACE, USE A SEPARATE CONTINUATION SHEET.

PREVIOUS REGISTRATION Has registration for this work, or for an earlier version of this work, already been made in the Copyright Office?

Yes   No   If your answer is "Yes," why is another registration being sought? (Check appropriate box) ▼

a. ☐ This is the first published edition of a work previously registered in unpublished form.

b. ☐ This is the first application submitted by this author as copyright claimant.

c. ☐ This is a changed version of the work, as shown by space 6 on this application.

If your answer is "Yes," give: **Previous Registration Number** ▼ _____   **Year of Registration** ▼ _____

5

DERIVATIVE WORK OR COMPILATION   Complete both space 6a & 6b for a derivative work; complete only 6b for a compilation.
a. Preexisting Material   Identify any preexisting work or works that this work is based on or incorporates. ▼

_____

_____

b.   Material Added to This Work   Give a brief, general statement of the material that has been added to this work and in which copyright is claimed. ▼

_____

_____

6

See instructions
before completing
this space.

DEPOSIT ACCOUNT   If the registration fee is to be charged to a Deposit Account established in the Copyright Office, give name and number of Account.
Name ▼   **Account Number** ▼

_____   _____

7

CORRESPONDENCE   Give name and address to which correspondence about this application should be sent.   Name/Address/Apt/City/State/Zip ▼

_____

_____

_____

Be sure to
give your
daytime phone
number ◄

Area Code & Telephone Number ▶ _____

CERTIFICATION*   I, the undersigned, hereby certify that I am the

Check only one ▼

☐ author

☐ other copyright claimant

☐ owner of exclusive right(s)

☐ authorized agent of _____
                    Name of author or other copyright claimant, or owner of exclusive right(s) ▲

8

of the work identified in this application and that the statements made
by me in this application are correct to the best of my knowledge.

Typed or printed name and date ▼ If this application gives a date of publication in space 3, do not sign and submit it before that date.

_____   date ▶ _____

☞ **Handwritten signature (X)** ▼

_____

**MAIL
CERTIFI-
CATE TO**

Name ▼ _____

Number/Street/Apartment Number ▼ _____

City/State/ZIP ▼ _____

**Certificate
will be
mailed in
window
envelope**

YOU MUST:
• Complete all necessary spaces
• Sign your application in space 8
**SEND ALL 3 ELEMENTS
IN THE SAME PACKAGE:**
1. Application form
2. Nonrefundable $20 filing fee
   in check or money order
   payable to *Register of Copyrights*
3. Deposit material
MAIL TO:
Register of Copyrights
Library of Congress
Washington, D.C. 20559

9

* 17 U.S.C. § 506(e) Any person who knowingly makes a false representation of a material fact in the application for copyright registration provided for by section 409, or in any written statement filed in connection with the application, shall be fined not more than $2,500.

▲ February 1991—200,000

☆U.S. GOVERNMENT PRINTING OFFICE: 1991- 282-170/20,011

✒️Filling Out Application Form PA

Detach and read these instructions before completing this form. Make sure all applicable spaces have been filled in before you return this form.

BASIC INFORMATION

When to Use This Form: Use Form PA for registration of published or unpublished works of the performing arts. This class includes works prepared for the purpose of being "performed" directly before an audience or indirectly "by means of any device or process." Works of the performing arts include: (1) musical works, including any accompanying words; (2) dramatic works, including any accompanying music; (3) pantomimes and choreographic works; and (4) motion pictures and other audiovisual works.

Deposit to Accompany Application: An application for copyright registration must be accompanied by a deposit consisting of copies or phonorecords representing the entire work for which registration is to be made. The following are the general deposit requirements as set forth in the statute:

Unpublished Work: Deposit one complete copy (or phonorecord).

Published Work: Deposit two complete copies or one phonorecord of the best edition.

Work First Published Outside the United States: Deposit one complete copy (or phonorecord) of the first foreign edition.

Contribution to a Collective Work: Deposit one complete copy (or phonorecord) of the best edition of the collective work.

Motion Pictures: Deposit *both* of the following: (1) a separate written description of the contents of the motion picture; and (2) for a published work, one complete copy of the best edition of the motion picture; or, for an unpublished work, one complete copy of the motion picture or identifying material. Identifying material may be either an audiorecording of the entire soundtrack or one frame enlargement or similar visual print from each 10-minute segment.

The Copyright Notice: For works first published on or after March 1, 1989, the law provides that a copyright notice in a specified form "may be placed on all publicly distributed copies from which the work can be visually perceived." Use of the copyright notice is the responsibility of the copyright owner and does not require advance permission from the Copyright Office. The required form of the notice for copies generally consists of three elements: (1) the symbol "©", or the word "Copyright," or the abbreviation "Copr."; (2) the year of first publication; and (3) the name of the owner of copyright. For example: "© 1989 Jane Cole." The notice is to be affixed to the copies "in such manner and location as to give reasonable notice of the claim of copyright." Works first published prior to March 1, 1989, **must** carry the notice or risk loss of copyright protection.

For information about notice requirements for works published before March 1, 1989, or other copyright information, write: Information Section, LM-401, Copyright Office, Library of Congress, Washington, D.C. 20559.

PRIVACY ACT ADVISORY STATEMENT Required by the Privacy Act of 1974 (P.L. 93-579)

The authority for requesting this information is title 17, U.S.C., secs. 409 and 410. Furnishing the requested information is voluntary. But if the information is not furnished, it may be necessary to delay or refuse registration and you may not be entitled to certain relief, remedies, and benefits provided in chapters 4 and 5 of title 17, U.S.C.

The principal uses of the requested information are the establishment and maintenance of a public record and the examination of the application for compliance with legal requirements.

Other routine uses include public inspection and copying, preparation of public indexes, preparation of public catalogs of copyright registrations, and preparation of search reports upon request. NOTE: No other advisory statement will be given in connection with this application. Please keep this statement and refer to it if we communicate with you regarding this application.

LINE-BY-LINE INSTRUCTIONS

1 SPACE 1: Title

Title of This Work: Every work submitted for copyright registration must be given a title to identify that particular work. If the copies or phonorecords of the work bear a title (or an identifying phrase that could serve as a title), transcribe that wording *completely* and *exactly* on the application. Indexing of the registration and future identification of the work will depend on the information you give here. If the work you are registering is an entire "collective work" (such as a collection of plays or songs), give the overall title of the collection. If you are registering one or more individual contributions to a collective work, give the title of each contribution, followed by the title of the collection. Example: "'A Song for Elinda' in *Old and New Ballads for Old and New People.*"

Previous or Alternative Titles: Complete this space if there are any additional titles for the work under which someone searching for the registration might be likely to look, or under which a document pertaining to the work might be recorded.

Nature of This Work: Briefly describe the general nature or character of the work being registered for copyright. Examples: "Music"; "Song Lyrics"; "Words and Music"; "Drama"; "Musical Play"; "Choreography"; "Pantomime"; "Motion Picture"; "Audiovisual Work."

2 SPACE 2: Author(s)

General Instructions: After reading these instructions, decide who are the "authors" of this work for copyright purposes. Then, unless the work is a "collective work," give the requested information about every "author" who contributed any appreciable amount of copyrightable matter to this version of the work. If you need further space, request additional Continuation Sheets. In the case of a collective work, such as a songbook or a collection of plays, give information about the author of the collective work as a whole.

Name of Author: The fullest form of the author's name should be given. Unless the work was "made for hire," the individual who actually created the work is its "author." In the case of a work made for hire, the statute provides

that "the employer or other person for whom the work was prepared is considered the author."

What is a "Work Made for Hire"? A "work made for hire" is defined as: (1) "a work prepared by an employee within the scope of his or her employment"; or (2) "a work specially ordered or commissioned for use as a contribution to a collective work, as a part of a motion picture or other audiovisual work, as a translation, as a supplementary work, as a compilation, as an instructional text, as a test, as answer material for a test, or as an atlas, if the parties expressly agree in a written instrument signed by them that the work shall be considered a work made for hire." If you have checked "Yes" to indicate that the work was "made for hire," you must give the full legal name of the employer (or other person for whom the work was prepared). You may also include the name of the employee along with the name of the employer (for example: "Elster Music Co., employer for hire of John Ferguson").

"Anonymous" or "Pseudonymous" Work: An author's contribution to a work is "anonymous" if that author is not identified on the copies or phonorecords of the work. An author's contribution to a work is "pseudonymous" if that author is identified on the copies or phonorecords under a fictitious name. If the work is "anonymous" you may: (1) leave the line blank; or (2) state "anonymous" on the line; or (3) reveal the author's identity. If the work is "pseudonymous" you may: (1) leave the line blank; or (2) give the pseudonym and identify it as such (for example: "Huntley Haverstock, pseudonym"); or (3) reveal the author's name, making clear which is the real name and which is the pseudonym (for example: "Judith Barton, whose pseudonym is Madeline Elster"). However, the citizenship or domicile of the author **must** be given in all cases.

Dates of Birth and Death: If the author is dead, the statute requires that the year of death be included in the application unless the work is anonymous or pseudonymous. The author's birth date is optional, but is useful as a form of identification. Leave this space blank if the author's contribution was a "work made for hire."

Author's Nationality or Domicile: Give the country of which the author is a citizen, or the country in which the author is domiciled. Nationality or domicile **must** be given in all cases.

Nature of Authorship: Give a brief general statement of the nature of this particular author's contribution to the work. Examples: "Words"; "Co-Author of Music"; "Words and Music"; "Arrangement"; "Co-Author of Book and Lyrics"; "Dramatization"; "Screen Play"; "Compilation and English Translation"; "Editorial Revisions."

3 SPACE 3: Creation and Publication

General Instructions: Do not confuse "creation" with "publication." Every application for copyright registration must state "the year in which creation of the work was completed." Give the date and nation of first publication only if the work has been published.

Creation: Under the statute, a work is "created" when it is fixed in a copy or phonorecord for the first time. Where a work has been prepared over a period of time, the part of the work existing in fixed form on a particular date constitutes the created work on that date. The date you give here should be the year in which the author completed the particular version for which registration is now being sought, even if other versions exist or if further changes or additions are planned.

Publication: The statute defines "publication" as "the distribution of copies or phonorecords of a work to the public by sale or other transfer of ownership, or by rental, lease, or lending"; a work is also "published" if there has been an "offering to distribute copies or phonorecords to a group of persons for purposes of further distribution, public performance, or public display." Give the full date (month, day, year) when, and the country where, publication first occurred. If first publication took place simultaneously in the United States and other countries, it is sufficient to state "U.S.A."

4 SPACE 4: Claimant(s)

Name(s) and Address(es) of Copyright Claimant(s): Give the name(s) and address(es) of the copyright claimant(s) in this work even if the claimant is the same as the author. Copyright in a work belongs initially to the author of the work (including, in the case of a work made for hire, the employer or other person for whom the work was prepared). The copyright claimant is either the author of the work or a person or organization to whom the copyright initially belonging to the author has been transferred.

Transfer: The statute provides that, if the copyright claimant is not the author, the application for registration must contain "a brief statement of how the claimant obtained ownership of the copyright." If any copyright claimant named in space 4 is not an author named in space 2, give a brief statement explaining how the claimant(s) obtained ownership of the copyright. Examples: "By written contract"; "Transfer of all rights by author"; "Assignment"; "By will." Do not attach transfer documents or other attachments or riders.

5 SPACE 5: Previous Registration

General Instructions: The questions in space 5 are intended to find out whether an earlier registration has been made for this work and, if so, whether there is any basis for a new registration. As a general rule, only one basic copyright registration can be made for the same version of a particular work.

Same Version: If this version is substantially the same as the work covered by a previous registration, a second registration is not generally possible unless: (1) the work has been registered in unpublished form and a second registration is now being sought to cover this first published edition; or (2) someone other than the author is identified as copyright claimant in the earlier registration, and the author is now seeking registration in his or her own name. If either of these two exceptions apply, check the appropriate box and give the

earlier registration number and date. Otherwise, do not submit Form PA; instead, write the Copyright Office for information about supplementary registration or recordation of transfers of copyright ownership.

Changed Version: If the work has been changed, and you are now seeking registration to cover the additions or revisions, check the last box in space 5, give the earlier registration number and date, and complete both parts of space 6 in accordance with the instructions below.

Previous Registration Number and Date: If more than one previous registration has been made for the work, give the number and date of the latest registration.

6 SPACE 6: Derivative Work or Compilation

General Instructions: Complete space 6 if this work is a "changed version," "compilation," or "derivative work," and if it incorporates one or more earlier works that have already been published or registered for copyright, or that have fallen into the public domain. A "compilation" is defined as "a work formed by the collection and assembling of preexisting materials or of data that are selected, coordinated, or arranged in such a way that the resulting work as a whole constitutes an original work of authorship." A "derivative work" is "a work based on one or more preexisting works." Examples of derivative works include musical arrangements, dramatizations, translations, abridgments, condensations, motion picture versions,or "any other form in which a work may be recast, transformed, or adapted." Derivative works also include works "consisting of editorial revisions, annotations, or other modifications" if these changes, as a whole, represent an original work of authorship.

Preexisting Material (space 6a): Complete this space **and** space 6b for derivative works. In this space identify the preexisting work that has been recast, transformed, or adapted. For example, the preexisting material might be: "French version of Hugo's 'Le Roi s'amuse'." Do not complete this space for compilations.

Material Added to This Work (space 6b): Give a brief, general statement of the **additional** new material covered by the copyright claim for which registration is sought. In the case of a derivative work, identify this new material. Examples: "Arrangement for piano and orchestra"; "Dramatization for television"; "New film version"; "Revisions throughout; Act III completely new." If the work is a compilation, give a brief, general statement describing both the material that has been compiled **and** the compilation itself. Example: "Compilation of 19th Century Military Songs."

7,8,9 SPACE 7, 8, 9: Fee, Correspondence, Certification, Return Address

Deposit Account: If you maintain a Deposit Account in the Copyright Office, identify it in space 7. Otherwise leave the space blank and send the fee of $20 with your application and deposit.

Correspondence (space 7): This space should contain the name, address, area code, and telephone number of the person to be consulted if correspondence about this application becomes necessary.

Certification (space 8): The application cannot be accepted unless it bears the date and the **handwritten signature** of the author or other copyright claimant, or of the owner of exclusive right(s), or of the duly authorized agent of the author, claimant, or owner of exclusive right(s).

Address for Return of Certificate (space 9): The address box must be completed legibly since the certificate will be returned in a window envelope.

MORE INFORMATION

How To Register a Recorded Work: If the musical or dramatic work that you are registering has been recorded (as a tape, disk, or cassette), you may choose either copyright application Form PA or Form SR, Performing Arts or Sound Recordings, depending on the purpose of the registration.

Form PA should be used to register the underlying musical composition or dramatic work. Form SR has been developed specifically to register a "sound recording" as defined by the Copyright Act—a work resulting from the "fixation of a series of sounds," separate and distinct from the underlying musical or dramatic work. Form SR should be used when the copyright claim is limited to the sound recording itself. (In one instance, Form SR may also be used to file for a copyright registration for both kinds of works—see (4) below.) Therefore:

(1) File Form PA if you are seeking to register the musical or dramatic work, not the "sound recording," even though what you deposit for copyright purposes may be in the form of a phonorecord.

(2) File Form PA if you are seeking to register the audio portion of an audiovisual work, such as a motion picture soundtrack; these are considered integral parts of the audiovisual work.

(3) File Form SR if you are seeking to register the "sound recording" itself, that is, the work that results from the fixation of a series of musical, spoken, or other sounds, but not the underlying musical or dramatic work.

(4) File Form SR if you are the copyright claimant for both the underlying musical or dramatic work and the sound recording, *and* you prefer to register both on the same form.

(5) File both forms PA and SR if the copyright claimant for the underlying work and sound recording differ, or you prefer to have separate registration for them.

"Copies" and "Phonorecords":

To register for copyright, you are required to deposit "copies" or "phonorecords." These are defined as follows:

Musical compositions may be embodied (fixed) in "copies," objects from which a work can be read or visually perceived, directly or with the aid of a machine or device, such as manuscripts, books, sheet music, film, and videotape. They may also be fixed in "phonorecords," objects embodying fixations of sounds, such as tapes and phonograph disks, commonly known as phonograph records. For example, a song (the work to be registered) can be reproduced in sheet music ("copies") or phonograph records ("phonorecords"), or both.

FORM VA
For a Work of the Visual Arts
UNITED STATES COPYRIGHT OFFICE

REGISTRATION NUMBER

_____

VA   VAU

EFFECTIVE DATE OF REGISTRATION

_____

Month   Day   Year

DO NOT WRITE ABOVE THIS LINE. IF YOU NEED MORE SPACE, USE A SEPARATE CONTINUATION SHEET.

1

TITLE OF THIS WORK ▼   **NATURE OF THIS WORK ▼** See instructions

PREVIOUS OR ALTERNATIVE TITLES ▼

PUBLICATION AS A CONTRIBUTION If this work was published as a contribution to a periodical, serial, or collection, give information about the collective work in which the contribution appeared.   **Title of Collective Work ▼**

If published in a periodical or serial give: **Volume ▼**   **Number ▼**   **Issue Date ▼**   **On Pages ▼**

2 **a**

NAME OF AUTHOR ▼   **DATES OF BIRTH AND DEATH**
Year Born ▼ Year Died ▼

Was this contribution to the work a "work made for hire"?   **AUTHOR'S NATIONALITY OR DOMICILE**
Name of Country
☐ Yes
☐ No   OR { Citizen of ▶_____
              Domiciled in▶_____

WAS THIS AUTHOR'S CONTRIBUTION TO THE WORK
Anonymous?   ☐ Yes ☐ No
Pseudonymous? ☐ Yes ☐ No
If the answer to either of these questions is "Yes," see detailed instructions.

NATURE OF AUTHORSHIP Check appropriate box(es). **See instructions**
☐ 3-Dimensional sculpture   ☐ Map   ☐ Technical drawing
☐ 2-Dimensional artwork   ☐ Photograph   ☐ Text
☐ Reproduction of work of art   ☐ Jewelry design   ☐ Architectural work
☐ Design on sheetlike material

NOTE

Under the law, the "author" of a "work made for hire" is generally the employer, not the employee (see instructions). For any part of this work that was "made for hire" check "Yes" in the space provided, give the employer (or other person for whom the work was prepared) as "Author" of that part, and leave the space for dates of birth and death blank.

b

NAME OF AUTHOR ▼   **DATES OF BIRTH AND DEATH**
Year Born ▼ Year Died ▼

Was this contribution to the work a "work made for hire"?   **AUTHOR'S NATIONALITY OR DOMICILE**
Name of Country
☐ Yes
☐ No   OR { Citizen of ▶_____
              Domiciled in▶_____

WAS THIS AUTHOR'S CONTRIBUTION TO THE WORK
Anonymous?   ☐ Yes ☐ No
Pseudonymous? ☐ Yes ☐ No
If the answer to either of these questions is "Yes," see detailed instructions.

NATURE OF AUTHORSHIP Check appropriate box(es). **See instructions**
☐ 3-Dimensional sculpture   ☐ Map   ☐ Technical drawing
☐ 2-Dimensional artwork   ☐ Photograph   ☐ Text
☐ Reproduction of work of art   ☐ Jewelry design   ☐ Architectural work
☐ Design on sheetlike material

3 **a**

YEAR IN WHICH CREATION OF THIS WORK WAS COMPLETED This information must be given ◀ Year in all cases.

b **DATE AND NATION OF FIRST PUBLICATION OF THIS PARTICULAR WORK**
Complete this information ONLY if this work has been published.   Month ▶_____ Day▶_____ Year▶_____   ◀ Nation

4

See instructions before completing this space.

COPYRIGHT CLAIMANT(S) Name and address must be given even if the claimant is the same as the author given in space 2. ▼

TRANSFER If the claimant(s) named here in space 4 are different from the author(s) named in space 2, give a brief statement of how the claimant(s) obtained ownership of the copyright. ▼

APPLICATION RECEIVED

ONE DEPOSIT RECEIVED

TWO DEPOSITS RECEIVED

REMITTANCE NUMBER AND DATE

DO NOT WRITE HERE
OFFICE USE ONLY

MORE ON BACK ▶   • Complete all applicable spaces (numbers 5-9) on the reverse side of this page.
• See detailed instructions.   • Sign the form at line 8.

DO NOT WRITE HERE

Page 1 of _____ pages

EXAMINED BY		FORM VA
CHECKED BY		
☐	CORRESPONDENCE Yes	FOR COPYRIGHT OFFICE USE ONLY

DO NOT WRITE ABOVE THIS LINE. IF YOU NEED MORE SPACE, USE A SEPARATE CONTINUATION SHEET.

PREVIOUS REGISTRATION Has registration for this work, or for an earlier version of this work, already been made in the Copyright Office?

☐ **Yes** ☐ **No** If your answer is "Yes," why is another registration being sought? (Check appropriate box) ▼

a. ☐ This is the first published edition of a work previously registered in unpublished form.

b. ☐ This is the first application submitted by this author as copyright claimant.

c. ☐ This is a changed version of the work, as shown by space 6 on this application.

If your answer is "Yes," give: **Previous Registration Number** ▼   **Year of Registration** ▼

5

DERIVATIVE WORK OR COMPILATION Complete both space 6a & 6b for a derivative work; complete only 6b for a compilation.

a. **Preexisting Material** Identify any preexisting work or works that this work is based on or incorporates. ▼

b. **Material Added to This Work** Give a brief, general statement of the material that has been added to this work and in which copyright is claimed. ▼

6

See instructions
before completing
this space.

DEPOSIT ACCOUNT If the registration fee is to be charged to a Deposit Account established in the Copyright Office, give name and number of Account.

Name ▼   **Account Number** ▼

7

CORRESPONDENCE Give name and address to which correspondence about this application should be sent.   Name/Address/Apt/City/State/Zip ▼

Area Code & Telephone Number▶

Be sure to
give your
daytime phone
◀ number

CERTIFICATION* I, the undersigned, hereby certify that I am the

Check only one ▼

☐ author

☐ other copyright claimant

☐ owner of exclusive right(s)

☐ authorized agent of _____

Name of author or other copyright claimant, or owner of exclusive right(s) ▲

8

of the work identified in this application and that the statements made
by me in this application are correct to the best of my knowledge.

Typed or printed name and date ▼ If this application gives a date of publication in space 3, do not sign and submit it before that date.

_____ date▶ _____

☞ **Handwritten signature (X)** ▼

9

MAIL CERTIFI- CATE TO	Name ▼
Certificate will be mailed in window envelope	Number/Street/Apartment Number ▼
	City/State/ZIP ▼

YOU MUST:
• Complete all necessary spaces
• Sign your application in space 8

**SEND ALL 3 ELEMENTS
IN THE SAME PACKAGE:**
1. Application form
2. Nonrefundable $20 filing fee in check or money order payable to *Register of Copyrights*
3. Deposit material

MAIL TO:
Register of Copyrights
Library of Congress
Washington, D.C. 20559

The Copyright Office
has the authority to ad-
just fees at 5-year intervals, based on changes
in the Consumer Price
Index. The next adjust-
ment is due in 1995.
Please contact the
Copyright Office after
July 1995 to determine
the actual fee schedule.

*17 U.S.C. § 506(e): Any person who knowingly makes a false representation of a material fact in the application for copyright registration provided for by section 409, or in any written statement filed in connection with the application, shall be fined not more than $2,500.

July 1992—100,000

☆U.S. GOVERNMENT PRINTING OFFICE: 1992-312-432/60,009

⊘Filling Out Application Form VA

Detach and read these instructions before completing this form.
Make sure all applicable spaces have been filled in before you return this form.

BASIC INFORMATION

When to Use This Form: Use Form VA for copyright registration of published or unpublished works of the visual arts. This category consists of "pictorial, graphic, or sculptural works," including two-dimensional and three-dimensional works of fine, graphic, and applied art, photographs, prints and art reproductions, maps, globes, charts, technical drawings, diagrams, and models.

What Does Copyright Protect? Copyright in a work of the visual arts protects those pictorial, graphic, or sculptural elements that, either alone or in combination, represent an "original work of authorship." The statute declares: "In no case does copyright protection for an original work of authorship extend to any idea, procedure, process, system, method of operation, concept, principle, or discovery, regardless of the form in which it is described, explained, illustrated, or embodied in such work."

Works of Artistic Craftsmanship and Designs: "Works of artistic craftsmanship" are registrable on Form VA, but the statute makes clear that protection extends to "their form" and not to "their mechanical or utilitarian aspects." The "design of a useful article" is considered copyrightable "only if, and only to the extent that, such design incorporates pictorial, graphic, or sculptural features that can be identified separately from, and are capable of existing independently of, the utilitarian aspects of the article."

Labels and Advertisements: Works prepared for use in connection with the sale or advertisement of goods and services are registrable if they contain "original work of authorship." Use Form VA if the copyrightable material in the work you are registering is mainly pictorial or graphic; use Form TX if it consists mainly of text. **NOTE:** Words and short phrases such as names, titles, and slogans cannot be protected by copyright, and the same is true of standard symbols, emblems, and other commonly used graphic designs that are in the public domain. When used commercially, material of that sort can sometimes be protected under state laws of unfair competition or under the Federal trademark laws. For information about trademark registration, write to the Commissioner of Patents and Trademarks, Washington, D.C. 20231.

Architectural Works: Copyright protection extends to the design of buildings created for the use of human beings. Architectural works created on or after December 1, 1990, or that on December 1, 1990, were unconstructed and embodied only in unpublished plans or drawings are eligible. Request Circular 41 for more information.

Deposit to Accompany Application: An application for copyright registration must be accompanied by a deposit consisting of copies representing the entire work for which registration is to be made.

Unpublished Work: Deposit one complete copy.

Published Work: Deposit two complete copies of the best edition.

Work First Published Outside the United States: Deposit one complete copy of the first foreign edition.

Contribution to a Collective Work: Deposit one complete copy of the best edition of the collective work.

The Copyright Notice: For works first published on or after March 1, 1989, the law provides that a copyright notice in a specified form "may be placed on all publicly distributed copies from which the work can be visually perceived." Use of the copyright notice is the responsibility of the copyright owner and does not require advance permission from the Copyright Office. The required form of the notice for copies generally consists of three elements: (1) the symbol "©", or the word "Copyright," or the abbreviation "Copr."; (2) the year of first publication; and (3) the name of the owner of copyright. For example: "© 1991 Jane Cole." The notice is to be affixed to the copies "in such manner and location as to give reasonable notice of the claim of copyright." Works first published prior to March 1, 1989, **must** carry the notice or risk loss of copyright protection.

For information about notice requirements for works published before March 1, 1989, or other copyright information, write: Information Section, LM-401, Copyright Office, Library of Congress, Washington, D.C. 20559.

LINE-BY-LINE INSTRUCTIONS

Please type or print using dark ink.

1 SPACE 1: Title

Title of This Work: Every work submitted for copyright registration must be given a title to identify that particular work. If the copies of the work bear a title (or an identifying phrase that could serve as a title), transcribe that wording *completely* and *exactly* on the application. Indexing of the registration and future identification of the work will depend on the information you give here. For an architectural work that has been constructed, add the date of construction after the title; if unconstructed at this time, add "not yet constructed."

Previous or Alternative Titles: Complete this space if there are any additional titles for the work under which someone searching for the registration might be likely to look, or under which a document pertaining to the work might be recorded.

Publication as a Contribution: If the work being registered is a contribution to a periodical, serial, or collection, give the title of the contribution in the "Title of This Work" space. Then, in the line headed "Publication as a Contribution," give information about the collective work in which the contribution appeared.

Nature of This Work: Briefly describe the general nature or character of the pictorial, graphic, or sculptural work being registered for copyright. Examples: "Oil Painting"; "Charcoal Drawing"; "Etching"; "Sculpture"; "Map"; "Photograph"; "Scale Model"; "Lithographic Print"; "Jewelry Design"; "Fabric Design."

2 SPACE 2: Author(s)

General Instruction: After reading these instructions, decide who are the "authors" of this work for copyright purposes. Then, unless the work is a "collective work," give the requested information about every "author" who contributed any appreciable amount of copyrightable matter to this version of the work. If you need further space, request Continuation Sheets. In the case of a collective work, such as a catalog of paintings or collection of cartoons by various authors, give information about the author of the collective work as a whole.

Name of Author: The fullest form of the author's name should be given. Unless the work was "made for hire," the individual who actually created the work is its "author." In the case of a work made for hire, the statute provides that "the employer or other person for whom the work was prepared is considered the author."

What is a "Work Made for Hire"? A "work made for hire" is defined as: (1) "a work prepared by an employee within the scope of his or her employment"; or (2) "a work specially ordered or commissioned for use as a contribution to a collective work, as a part of a motion picture or other audiovisual work, as a translation, as a supplementary work, as a compilation, as an instructional text, as a test, as answer material for a test, or as an atlas, if the parties expressly agree in a written instrument signed by them that the work shall be considered a work made for hire." If you have checked "Yes" to indicate that the work was "made for hire," you must give the full legal name of the employer (or other person for whom the work was prepared). You may also include the name of the employee along with the name of the employer (for example: "Elster Publishing Co., employer for hire of John Ferguson").

"Anonymous" or "Pseudonymous" Work: An author's contribution to a work is "anonymous" if that author is not identified on the copies or phonorecords of the work. An author's contribution to a work is "pseudonymous" if that author is identified on the copies or phonorecords under a fictitious name. If the work is "anonymous" you may: (1) leave the line blank; or (2) state "anonymous" on the line; or (3) reveal the author's identity. If the work is "pseudonymous" you may: (1) leave the line blank; or (2) give the pseudonym and identify it as such (for example: "Huntley Haverstock, pseudonym"); or (3) reveal the author's name, making clear which is the real name and which is the pseudonym (for example: "Henry Leek, whose pseudonym is Priam Farrel"). However, the citizenship or domicile of the author **must** be given in all cases.

Dates of Birth and Death: If the author is dead, the statute requires that the year of death be included in the application unless the work is anonymous or pseudonymous. The author's birth date is optional, but is useful as a form of identification. Leave this space blank if the author's contribution was a "work made for hire."

Author's Nationality or Domicile: Give the country of which the author is a citizen or the country in which the author is domiciled. Nationality or domicile **must** be given in all cases.

Nature of Authorship: Catagories of pictorial, graphic and sculptural authorship are listed below. Check the box(es) that best describe(s) each author's contribution to the work.

3-Dimensional sculptures: fine art sculptures. toys, dolls, scale models, and sculptural designs applied to useful articles.

2-Dimensional artwork: watercolor and oil paintings; pen and ink drawings; logo illustrations; greeting cards; collages; stencils; patterns; computer graphics; graphics appearing in screen displays; artwork appearing on posters, calendars, games, commercial prints and labels and packaging, as well as 2-dimensional artwork applied to useful articles.

Reproductions of works of art: reproductions of preexisting artwork made by, for example, lithography, photoengraving, or etching.

Maps: cartographic representations of an area such as state and county maps, atlases, marine charts, relief maps and globes.

Photographs: pictorial photographic prints and slides and holograms.

Jewelry designs: 3-dimensional designs applied to rings, pendants, earrings, necklaces and the like.

Designs on sheetlike materials: designs reproduced on textiles, lace and other fabrics; wallpaper; carpeting; floor tile; wrapping paper and clothing.

Technical drawings: diagrams illustrating scientific or technical information in linear form such as architectural blueprints or mechanical drawings.

Text: textual material that accompanies pictorial, graphic or sculptural works such as comic strips, greeting cards, games rules, commercial prints or labels, and maps.

Architectural works: designs of buildings, including the overall form as well as the arrangement and composition of spaces and elements of the design. NOTE: Any registration for the underlying architectural plans must be applied for on a separate Form VA, checking the box "Technical drawing."

3 SPACE 3: Creation and Publication

General Instructions: Do not confuse "creation" with "publication." Every application for copyright registration must state "the year in which creation of the work was completed." Give the date and nation of first publication only if the work has been published.

Creation: Under the statute, a work is "created" when it is fixed in a copy or phonorecord for the first time. Where a work has been prepared over a period of time, the part of the work existing in fixed form on a particular date constitutes the created work on that date. The date you give here should be the year in which the author completed the particular version for which registration is now being sought, even if other versions exist or if further changes or additions are planned.

Publication: The statute defines "publication" as "the distribution of copies or phonorecords of a work to the public by sale or other transfer of ownership, or by rental, lease, or lending"; a work is also "published" if there has been an "offering to distribute copies or phonorecords to a group of persons for purposes of further distribution, public performance, or public display." Give the full date (month, day, year) when, and the country where, publication first occurred. If first publication took place simultaneously in the United States and other countries, it is sufficient to state "U.S.A."

4 SPACE 4: Claimant(s)

Names(s) and Address(es) of Copyright Claimant(s): Give the name(s) and address(es) of the copyright claimant(s) in this work even if the claimant is the same as the author. Copyright in a work belongs initially to the author of the work (including, in the case of a work made for hire, the employer or other person for whom the work was prepared). The copyright claimant is either the author of the work or a person or organization to whom the copyright initially belonging to the author has been transferred.

Transfer: The statute provides that, if the copyright claimant is not the author, the application for registration must contain "a brief statement of how the claimant obtained ownership of the copyright." If any copyright claimant named in space 4 is not an author named in space 2, give a brief statement explaining how the claimant(s) obtained ownership of the copyright. Examples: "By written contract"; "Transfer of all rights by author"; "Assignment"; "By will". Do not attach transfer documents or other attachments or riders.

5 SPACE 5: Previous Registration

General Instructions: The questions in space 5 are intended to find out whether an earlier registration has been made for this work and, if so, whether there is any basis for a new registration. As a rule, only one basic copyright registration can be made for the same version of a particular work.

Same Version: If this version is substantially the same as the work covered by a previous registration, a second registration is not generally possible unless: (1) the work has been registered in unpublished form and a second registration is now being sought to cover this first published edition; or (2) someone other than the author is identified as a copyright claimant in the earlier registration, and the author is now seeking registration in his or her own name. If either of these two exceptions apply, check the appropriate box and give the earlier registration number and date. Otherwise, do not submit Form VA; instead, write the Copyright Office for information about supplementary registration or recordation of transfers of copyright ownership.

Changed Version: If the work has been changed, and you are now seeking registration to cover the additions or revisions, check the last box in space 5, give the earlier registration number and date, and complete both parts of space 6 in accordance with the instruction below.

Previous Registration Number and Date: If more than one previous registration has been made for the work, give the number and date of the latest registration.

6 SPACE 6: Derivative Work or Compilation

General Instructions: Complete space 6 if this work is a "changed version," "compilation," or "derivative work," and if it incorporates one or more earlier works that have already been published or registered for copyright, or that have fallen into the public domain. A "compilation" is defined as "a work formed by the collection and assembling of preexisting materials or of data that are selected, coordinated, or arranged in such a way that the resulting work as a whole constitutes an original work of authorship." A "derivative work" is "a work based on one or more preexisting works." Examples of derivative works include reproductions of works of art, sculptures based on drawings, lithographs based on paintings, maps based on previously published sources, or "any other form in which a work may be recast, transformed, or adapted." Derivative works also include works "consisting of editorial revisions, annotations, or other modifications" if these changes, as a whole, represent an original work of authorship.

Preexisting Material (space 6a): Complete this space **and** space 6b for derivative works. In this space identify the preexisting work that has been recast, transformed, or adapted. Examples of preexisting material might be "Grunewald Altarpiece" or "19th century quilt design." Do not complete this space for compilations.

Material Added to This Work (space 6b): Give a brief, general statement of the **additional** new material covered by the copyright claim for which registration is sought. In the case of a derivative work, identify this new material. Examples: "Adaptation of design and additional artistic work"; "Reproduction of painting by photolithography"; "Additional cartographic material"; "Compilation of photographs." If the work is a compilation, give a brief, general statement describing both the material that has been compiled and the compilation itself. Example: "Compilation of 19th century political cartoons."

7,8,9 SPACE 7,8,9: Fee, Correspondence, Certification, Return Address

Fee: The Copyright Office has the authority to adjust fees at 5-year intervals, based on changes in the Consumer Price Index. The next adjustment is due in 1995. Please contact the Copyright Office after July 1995 to determine the actual fee schedule.

Deposit Account: If you maintain a Deposit Account in the Copyright Office, identify it in space 7. Otherwise leave the space blank and send the fee of $20 with your application and deposit.

Correspondence (space 7): This space should contain the name, address, area code, and telephone number of the person to be consulted if correspondence about this application becomes necessary.

Certification (space 8): The application cannot be accepted unless it bears the date and the **handwritten signature** of the author or other copyright claimant, or of the owner of exclusive right(s), or of the duly authorized agent of the author, claimant, or owner of exclusive right(s).

Address for Return of Certificate (space 9): The address box must be completed legibly since the certificate will be returned in a window envelope.

FORM SR
UNITED STATES COPYRIGHT OFFICE

REGISTRATION NUMBER

_____

SR   SRU

EFFECTIVE DATE OF REGISTRATION

_____

Month   Day   Year

DO NOT WRITE ABOVE THIS LINE. IF YOU NEED MORE SPACE, USE A SEPARATE CONTINUATION SHEET.

1

TITLE OF THIS WORK ▼

_____

PREVIOUS OR ALTERNATIVE TITLES ▼

_____

NATURE OF MATERIAL RECORDED ▼ See instructions

☐ Musical   ☐ Musical-Dramatic
☐ Dramatic   ☐ Literary
☐ Other _____

2

a

NAME OF AUTHOR ▼

DATES OF BIRTH AND DEATH
Year Born ▼   Year Died ▼

Was this contribution to the work a "work made for hire"?
☐ Yes
☐ No

AUTHOR'S NATIONALITY OR DOMICILE
Name of Country
OR { Citizen of ▶ _____
     Domiciled in ▶ _____

WAS THIS AUTHOR'S CONTRIBUTION TO THE WORK
Anonymous?   ☐ Yes ☐ No
Pseudonymous? ☐ Yes ☐ No

If the answer to either of these questions is "Yes," see detailed instructions

NATURE OF AUTHORSHIP Briefly describe nature of the material created by this author in which copyright is claimed. ▼

NOTE
Under the law, the "author" of a "work made for hire" is generally the employer, not the employee (see instructions). For any part of this work that was "made for hire" check "Yes" in the space provided, give the employer (or other person for whom the work was prepared) as "Author" of that part, and leave the space for dates of birth and death blank

b

NAME OF AUTHOR ▼

DATES OF BIRTH AND DEATH
Year Born ▼   Year Died ▼

Was this contribution to the work a "work made for hire"?
☐ Yes
☐ No

AUTHOR'S NATIONALITY OR DOMICILE
Name of country
OR { Citizen of ▶ _____
     Domiciled in ▶ _____

WAS THIS AUTHOR'S CONTRIBUTION TO THE WORK
Anonymous?   ☐ Yes ☐ No
Pseudonymous? ☐ Yes ☐ No

If the answer to either of these questions is "Yes," see detailed instructions

NATURE OF AUTHORSHIP Briefly describe nature of the material created by this author in which copyright is claimed. ▼

c

NAME OF AUTHOR ▼

DATES OF BIRTH AND DEATH
Year Born ▼   Year Died ▼

Was this contribution to the work a "work made for hire"?
☐ Yes
☐ No

AUTHOR'S NATIONALITY OR DOMICILE
Name of Country
OR { Citizen of ▶ _____
     Domiciled in ▶ _____

WAS THIS AUTHOR'S CONTRIBUTION TO THE WORK
Anonymous?   ☐ Yes ☐ No
Pseudonymous? ☐ Yes ☐ No

If the answer to either of these questions is "Yes," see detailed instructions

NATURE OF AUTHORSHIP Briefly describe nature of the material created by this author in which copyright is claimed. ▼

3

a **YEAR IN WHICH CREATION OF THIS WORK WAS COMPLETED** This information must be given in all cases.
◀ Year

b **DATE AND NATION OF FIRST PUBLICATION OF THIS PARTICULAR WORK**
Complete this information Month ▶ _____ Day ▶ _____ Year ▶ _____
ONLY if this work has been published.
◀ Nation

4

COPYRIGHT CLAIMANT(S) Name and address must be given even if the claimant is the same as the author given in space 2.▼

See instructions before completing this space

TRANSFER If the claimant(s) named here in space 4 are different from the author(s) named in space 2, give a brief statement of how the claimant(s) obtained ownership of the copyright.▼

DO NOT WRITE HERE
OFFICE USE ONLY

APPLICATION RECEIVED

ONE DEPOSIT RECEIVED

TWO DEPOSITS RECEIVED

REMITTANCE NUMBER AND DATE

MORE ON BACK ▶ • Complete all applicable spaces (numbers 5-9) on the reverse side of this page
• See detailed instructions   • Sign the form at line 8.

DO NOT WRITE HERE
Page 1 of _____ pages

EXAMINED BY

FORM SR

CHECKED BY

☐ CORRESPONDENCE
Yes

☐ DEPOSIT ACCOUNT
FUNDS USED

FOR
COPYRIGHT
OFFICE
USE
ONLY

DO NOT WRITE ABOVE THIS LINE. IF YOU NEED MORE SPACE, USE A SEPARATE CONTINUATION SHEET.

PREVIOUS REGISTRATION Has registration for this work, or for an earlier version of this work, already been made in the Copyright Office?

☐ **Yes** ☐ **No** If your answer is "Yes," why is another registration being sought? (Check appropriate box) ▼

a. ☐ This is the first published edition of a work previously registered in unpublished form.

b. ☐ This is the first application submitted by this author as copyright claimant.

c. ☐ This is a changed version of the work, as shown by space 6 on this application.

If your answer is "Yes," give: **Previous Registration Number ▼**   **Year of Registration ▼**

5

DERIVATIVE WORK OR COMPILATION   Complete both space 6a & 6b for a derivative work; complete only 6b for a compilation.

a.   Preexisting Material   Identify any preexisting work or works that this work is based on or incorporates. ▼

b.   Material Added to This Work   Give a brief, general statement of the material that has been added to this work and in which copyright is claimed.▼

6

See instructions
before completing
this space.

DEPOSIT ACCOUNT   If the registration fee is to be charged to a Deposit Account established in the Copyright Office, give name and number of Account.
Name ▼   **Account Number ▼**

7

CORRESPONDENCE   Give name and address to which correspondence about this application should be sent.   Name/Address/Apt/City/State/Zip ▼

Area Code & Telephone Number ▶

Be sure to
give your
daytime phone
◀ number.

CERTIFICATION*   I, the undersigned, hereby certify that I am the
Check one ▼

☐ author

☐ other copyright claimant

☐ owner of exclusive right(s)

☐ authorized agent of
                      Name of author or other copyright claimant, or owner of exclusive right(s) ▲

of the work identified in this application and that the statements made
by me in this application are correct to the best of my knowledge.

8

Typed or printed name and date ▼ If this application gives a date of publication in space 3, do not sign and submit it before that date.

                                                                date ▶

                  Handwritten signature (X) ▼

**MAIL
CERTIFI-
CATE TO**

**Certificate
will be
mailed in
window
envelope**

Name ▼

Number/Street/Apartment Number ▼

City/State/ZIP ▼

9

YOU MUST
• Complete all necessary spaces
• Sign your application in space 8
SEND ALL 3 ELEMENTS
IN THE SAME PACKAGE
1. Application form
2. Nonrefundable $20 filing fee
   in check or money order
   payable to *Register of Copyrights*
3. Deposit material
MAIL TO
Register of Copyrights
Library of Congress
Washington, D.C. 20559

* 17 U.S.C. § 506(e) Any person who knowingly makes a false representation of a material fact in the application for copyright registration provided for by section 409 or in any written statement filed in connection with the application, shall be fined not more than $2,500.

May 1991—75,000

S. GOVERNMENT PRINTING OFFICE:1991-282-170/20,017

⦿Filling Out Application Form SR

Detach and read these instructions before completing this form. Make sure all applicable spaces have been filled in before you return this form.

BASIC INFORMATION

When to Use This Form: Use Form SR for copyright registration of published or unpublished sound recordings. It should be used where the copyright claim is limited to the sound recording itself, and it may also be used where the same copyright claimant is seeking simultaneous registration of the underlying musical, dramatic, or literary work embodied in the phonorecord.

With one exception, "sound recordings" are works that result from the fixation of a series of musical, spoken, or other sounds. The exception is for the audio portions of audiovisual works, such as a motion picture soundtrack or an audio cassette accompanying a filmstrip; these are considered a part of the audiovisual work as a whole.

Deposit to Accompany Application: An application for copyright registration of a sound recording must be accompanied by a deposit consisting of phonorecords representing the entire work for which registration is to be made.

Unpublished Work: Deposit one complete phonorecord.

Published Work: Deposit two complete phonorecords of the best edition, together with "any printed or other visually perceptible material" published with the phonorecords.

Work First Published Outside the United States: Deposit one complete phonorecord of the first foreign edition.

Contribution to a Collective Work: Deposit one complete phonorecord of the best edition of the collective work.

The Copyright Notice: For sound recordings first published on or after March 1, 1989, the law provides that a copyright notice in a specified form "may be placed on all publicly distributed phonorecords of the sound recording." Use of the copyright notice is the responsibility of the copyright owner and does not require advance permission from the Copyright Office. The required form of the notice for phonorecords of sound recordings consists of three elements: (1) the symbol "℗" (the Letter "P" in a circle); (2) the year of first publication of the sound recording; and (3) the name of the owner of copyright. For example: "℗ 1989 XYZ Record Co." The notice is to be "placed on the surface of the phonorecord, or on the label or container, in such manner and location as to give reasonable notice of the claim of copyright." Works first published prior to March 1, 1989, **must** carry the notice or risk loss of copyright protection.

For information about notice requirements for works published before March 1, 1989, or other copyright information, write: Information Section, LM-401, Copyright Office, Library of Congress, Washington, D.C. 20559.

LINE-BY-LINE INSTRUCTIONS

1 SPACE 1: Title

Title of This Work: Every work submitted for copyright registration must be given a title to identify that particular work. If the phonorecords or any accompanying printed material bear a title (or an identifying phrase that could serve as a title), transcribe that wording completely and exactly on the application. Indexing of the registration and future identification of the work may depend on the information you give here.

Nature of Material Recorded: Indicate the general type or character of the works or other material embodied in the recording. The box marked "Literary" should be checked for nondramatic spoken material of all sorts, including narration, interviews, panel discussions, and training material. If the material recorded is not musical, dramatic, or literary in nature, check "Other" and briefly describe the type of sounds fixed in the recording. For example: "Sound Effects"; "Bird Calls"; "Crowd Noises."

Previous or Alternative Titles: Complete this space if there are any additional titles for the work under which someone searching for the registration might be likely to look, or under which a document pertaining to the work might be recorded.

2 SPACE 2: Author(s)

General Instructions: After reading these instructions, decide who are the "authors" of this work for copyright purposes. Then, unless the work is a "collective work," give the requested information about every "author" who contributed any appreciable amount of copyrightable matter to this version of the work. If you need further space, request additional Continuation Sheets. In the case of a collective work, such as a collection of previously published or registered sound recordings, give information about the author of the collective work as a whole. If you are submitting this Form SR to cover the recorded musical, dramatic, or literary work as well as the sound recording itself, it is important for space 2 to include full information about the various authors of all of the material covered by the copyright claim, making clear the nature of each author's contribution.

Name of Author: The fullest form of the author's name should be given. Unless the work was "made for hire," the individual who actually created the work is its "author." In the case of a work made for hire, the statute provides that "the employer or other person for whom the work was prepared is considered the author."

What is a "Work Made for Hire"? A "work made for hire" is defined as: (1) "a work prepared by an employee within the scope of his or her employment"; or (2) "a work specially ordered or commissioned for use as a contribution to a collective work, as a part of a motion picture or other audiovisual work, as a translation, as a supplementary work, as a compilation, as an instructional text, as a test, as answer material for a test, or as an atlas, if the parties expressly agree in a written instrument signed by them that the work shall be considered a work made for hire." If you have checked "Yes" to indicate that the work was "made for hire," you must give the full legal name of the employer (or other person for whom the work was prepared). You may also include the name of the employee along with the name of the employer (for example: "Elster Record Co., employer for hire of John Ferguson").

"Anonymous" or "Pseudonymous" Work: An author's contribution to a work is "anonymous" if that author is not identified on the copies or phonorecords of the work. An author's contribution to a work is "pseudonymous" if that author is identified on the copies or phonorecords under a fictitious name. If the work is "anonymous" you may: (1) leave the line blank; or (2) state "anonymous" on the line; or (3) reveal the author's identity. If the work is "pseudonymous" you may: (1) leave the line blank; or (2) give the pseudonym and identify it as such (for example: "Huntley Haverstock, pseudonym"); or (3) reveal the author's name, making clear which is the real name and which is the pseudonym (for example: "Judith Barton, whose pseudonym is Madeline Elster"). However, the citizenship or domicile of the author **must** be given in all cases.

Dates of Birth and Death: If the author is dead, the statute requires that the year of death be included in the application unless the work is anonymous or pseudonymous. The author's birth date is optional, but is useful as a form of identification. Leave this space blank if the author's contribution was a "work made for hire."

Author's Nationality or Domicile: Give the country of which the author is a citizen, or the country in which the author is domiciled. Nationality or domicile **must** be given in all cases.

Nature of Authorship: Give a brief general statement of the nature of this particular author's contribution to the work. If you are submitting this Form SR to cover both the sound recording and the underlying musical, dramatic, or literary work, make sure that the precise nature of each author's contribution is reflected here. Examples where the authorship pertains to the recording: "Sound Recording"; "Performance and Recording"; "Compilation and Remixing of Sounds." Examples where the authorship pertains to both the recording and the underlying work: "Words, Music, Performance, Recording"; "Arrangement of Music and Recording"; "Compilation of Poems and Reading."

3 SPACE 3: Creation and Publication

General Instructions: Do not confuse "creation" with "publication." Every application for copyright registration must state "the year in which creation of the work was completed." Give the date and nation of first publication only if the work has been published.

Creation: Under the statute, a work is "created" when it is fixed in a copy or phonorecord for the first time. Where a work has been prepared over a period of time, the part of the work existing in fixed form on a particular date constitutes the created work on that date. The date you give here should be the year in which the author completed the particular version for which registration is now being sought, even if other versions exist or if further changes or additions are planned.

Publication: The statute defines "publication" as "the distribution of copies or phonorecords of a work to the public by sale or other transfer of ownership, or by rental, lease, or lending"; a work is also "published" if there has been an "offering to distribute copies or phonorecords to a group of persons for purposes of further distribution, public performance, or public display." Give the full date (month, day, year) when, and the country where, publication first occurred. If first publication took place simultaneously in the United States and other countries, it is sufficient to state "U.S.A."

4 SPACE 4: Claimant(s)

Name(s) and Address(es) of Copyright Claimant(s): Give the name(s) and address(es) of the copyright claimant(s) in this work even if the claimant is the same as the author. Copyright in a work belongs initially to the author of the work (including, in the case of a work made for hire, the employer or other person for whom the work was prepared). The copyright claimant is either the author of the work or a person or organization to whom the copyright initially belonging to the author has been transferred.

Transfer: The statute provides that, if the copyright claimant is not the author, the application for registration must contain "a brief statement of how the claimant obtained ownership of the copyright." If any copyright claimant named in space 4 is not an author named in space 2, give a brief statement explaining how the claimant(s) obtained ownership of the copyright. Examples: "By written contract"; "Transfer of all rights by author"; "Assignment"; "By will." Do not attach transfer documents or other attachments or riders.

5 SPACE 5: Previous Registration

General Instructions: The questions in space 5 are intended to find out whether an earlier registration has been made for this work and, if so, whether there is any basis for a new registration. As a rule, only one basic copyright registration can be made for the same version of a particular work.

Same Version: If this version is substantially the same as the work covered by a previous registration, a second registration is not generally possible unless: (1) the work has been registered in unpublished form and a second registration is now being sought to cover this first published edition; or (2) someone other than the author is identified as copyright claimant in the earlier registration, and the author is now seeking registration in his or her own name. If either of these two exceptions apply, check the appropriate box and give the earlier registration number and date. Otherwise, do not submit Form SR; instead, write the Copyright Office for information about supplementary registration or recordation of transfers of copyright ownership.

Changed Version: If the work has been changed, and you are now seeking registration to cover the additions or revisions, check the last box in space 5, give the earlier registration number and date, and complete both parts of space 6 in accordance with the instructions below.

Previous Registration Number and Date: If more than one previous registration has been made for the work, give the number and date of the latest registration.

6 SPACE 6: Derivative Work or Compilation

General Instructions: Complete space 6 if this work is a "changed version," "compilation," or "derivative work," and if it incorporates one or more earlier works that have already been published or registered for copyright, or that have fallen into the public domain, or sound recordings that were fixed before February 15, 1972. A "compilation" is defined as "a work formed by the collection and assembling of preexisting materials or of data that are selected, coordinated, or arranged in such a way that the resulting work as a whole constitutes an original work of authorship." A "derivative work" is "a work based on one or more preexisting works." Examples of derivative works include recordings reissued with substantial editorial revisions or abridgments of the recorded sounds, and recordings republished with new recorded material, or "any other form in which a work may be recast, transformed, or adapted." Derivative works also include works "consisting of editorial revisions, annotations, or other modifications" if these changes, as a whole, represent an original work of authorship.

Preexisting Material (space 6a): Complete this space **and** space 6b for derivative works. In this space identify the preexisting work that has been recast, transformed, or adapted. For example, the preexisting material might be: "1970 recording by Sperryville Symphony of Bach Double Concerto." Do not complete this space for compilations.

Material Added to This Work (space 6b): Give a brief, general statement of the **additional** new material covered by the copyright claim for which registration is sought. In the case of a derivative work, identify this new material. Examples: "Recorded performances on bands 1 and 3"; "Remixed sounds from original multitrack sound sources"; "New words, arrangement, and additional sounds." If the work is a compilation, give a brief, general statement describing both the material that has been compiled **and** the compilation itself. Example: "Compilation of 1938 Recordings by various swing bands."

7,8,9 SPACE 7, 8, 9: Fee, Correspondence, Certification, Return Address

Deposit Account: If you maintain a Deposit Account in the Copyright Office, identify it in space 7. Otherwise leave the space blank and send the fee of $20 with your application and deposit.

Correspondence (space 7): This space should contain the name, address, area code, and telephone number of the person to be consulted if correspondence about this application becomes necessary.

Certification (space 8): The application cannot be accepted unless it bears the date and the **handwritten signature** of the author or other copyright claimant, or of the owner of exclusive right(s), or of the duly authorized agent of the author, claimant, or owner of exclusive right(s).

Address for Return of Certificate (space 9): The address box must be completed legibly since the certificate will be returned in a window envelope.

MORE INFORMATION

"Works": "Works" are the basic subject matter of copyright; they are what authors create and copyright protects. The statute draws a sharp distinction between the "work" and "any material object in which the work is embodied."

"Copies" and "Phonorecords": These are the two types of material objects in which "works" are embodied. In general, **copies** are objects from which a work can be read or visually perceived, directly or with the aid of a machine or device, such as manuscripts, books, sheet music, film, and videotape. **Phonorecords** are objects embodying fixations of sounds, such as audio tapes and phonograph disks. For example, a song (the "work") can be reproduced in sheet music ("copies") or phonograph disks ("phonorecords"), or both.

"Sound Recordings": These are "works," not "copies" or "phonorecords." "Sound recordings" are "works that result from the fixation of a series of musical, spoken, or other sounds, but not including the sounds accompanying a motion picture or other audiovisual work." Example: When a record company issues a new release, the release will typically involve two distinct "works": the "musical work" that has been recorded, and the "sound recording" as a separate work in itself. The material objects that the record company sends out are "phonorecords": physical reproductions of both the "musical work" and the "sound recording."

Should You File More Than One Application? If your work consists of a recorded musical, dramatic, or literary work, and both that "work," and the sound recording as a separate "work," are eligible for registration, the application form you should file depends on the following:

File Only Form SR if: The copyright claimant is the same for both the musical, dramatic, or literary work and for the sound recording, and you are seeking a single registration to cover both of these "works."

File Only Form PA (or Form TX) if: You are seeking to register only the musical, dramatic, or literary work, not the sound recording. Form PA is appropriate for works of the performing arts; Form TX is for nondramatic literary works.

Separate Applications Should Be Filed on Form PA (or Form TX) and on Form SR if: (1) The copyright claimant for the musical, dramatic, or literary work is different from the copyright claimant for the sound recording; or (2) You prefer to have separate registrations for the musical, dramatic, or literary work and for the sound recording.

FORM SE
UNITED STATES COPYRIGHT OFFICE

REGISTRATION NUMBER

U

EFFECTIVE DATE OF REGISTRATION

| Month | Day | Year |

DO NOT WRITE ABOVE THIS LINE. IF YOU NEED MORE SPACE, USE A SEPARATE CONTINUATION SHEET.

1 TITLE OF THIS SERIAL ▼

Volume ▼   Number ▼   Date on Copies ▼   Frequency of Publication ▼

PREVIOUS OR ALTERNATIVE TITLES ▼

2 a NAME OF AUTHOR ▼

DATES OF BIRTH AND DEATH
Year Born ▼   Year Died ▼

Was this contribution to the work a "work made for hire"?
☐ Yes
☐ No

AUTHOR'S NATIONALITY OR DOMICILE
Name of Country
OR { Citizen of ▶
Domiciled in ▶

WAS THIS AUTHOR'S CONTRIBUTION TO THE WORK
Anonymous? ☐ Yes ☐ No
Pseudonymous? ☐ Yes ☐ No
If the answer to either of these questions is "Yes," see detailed instructions.

NATURE OF AUTHORSHIP   Briefly describe nature of the material created by this author in which copyright is claimed. ▼
☐ Collective Work   Other:

NOTE

Under the law, the "author" of a "work made for hire" is generally the employer, not the employee (see instructions) For any part of this work that was "made for hire" check "Yes" in the space provided, give the employer (or other person for whom the work was prepared) as "Author" of that part, and leave the space for dates of birth and death blank

b NAME OF AUTHOR ▼

DATES OF BIRTH AND DEATH
Year Born ▼   Year Died ▼

Was this contribution to the work a "work made for hire"?
☐ Yes
☐ No

AUTHOR'S NATIONALITY OR DOMICILE
Name of country
OR { Citizen of ▶
Domiciled in ▶

WAS THIS AUTHOR'S CONTRIBUTION TO THE WORK
Anonymous? ☐ Yes ☐ No
Pseudonymous? ☐ Yes ☐ No
If the answer to either of these questions is "Yes," see detailed instructions.

NATURE OF AUTHORSHIP   Briefly describe nature of the material created by this author in which copyright is claimed. ▼
☐ Collective Work   Other:

c NAME OF AUTHOR ▼

DATES OF BIRTH AND DEATH
Year Born ▼   Year Died ▼

Was this contribution to the work a "work made for hire"?
☐ Yes
☐ No

AUTHOR'S NATIONALITY OR DOMICILE
Name of Country
OR { Citizen of ▶
Domiciled in ▶

WAS THIS AUTHOR'S CONTRIBUTION TO THE WORK
Anonymous? ☐ Yes ☐ No
Pseudonymous? ☐ Yes ☐ No
If the answer to either of these questions is "Yes," see detailed instructions.

NATURE OF AUTHORSHIP   Briefly describe nature of the material created by this author in which copyright is claimed. ▼
☐ Collective Work   Other:

3 a YEAR IN WHICH CREATION OF THIS ISSUE WAS COMPLETED   This information must be given in all cases.
◀ Year

b DATE AND NATION OF FIRST PUBLICATION OF THIS PARTICULAR ISSUE
Complete this information ONLY if this work has been published.
Month ▶   Day ▶   Year ▶   ◀ Nation

4 COPYRIGHT CLAIMANT(S) Name and address must be given even if the claimant is the same as the author given in space 2.▼

See instructions before completing this space.

TRANSFER If the claimant(s) named here in space 4 are different from the author(s) named in space 2, give a brief statement of how the claimant(s) obtained ownership of the copyright.▼

DO NOT WRITE HERE
OFFICE USE ONLY

APPLICATION RECEIVED

ONE DEPOSIT RECEIVED

TWO DEPOSITS RECEIVED

REMITTANCE NUMBER AND DATE

MORE ON BACK ▶
• Complete all applicable spaces (numbers 5-11) on the reverse side of this page
• See detailed instructions.   • Sign the form at line 10

DO NOT WRITE HERE
Page 1 of_____pages

EXAMINED BY _____

CHECKED BY _____

☐ CORRESPONDENCE
Yes

FORM SE

FOR
COPYRIGHT
OFFICE
USE
ONLY

DO NOT WRITE ABOVE THIS LINE. IF YOU NEED MORE SPACE, USE A SEPARATE CONTINUATION SHEET.

PREVIOUS REGISTRATION   Has registration for this issue, or for an earlier version of this particular issue, already been made in the Copyright Office?

☐ **Yes** ☐ **No** If your answer is "Yes," why is another registration being sought? (Check appropriate box) ▼

a. ☐ This is the first published version of an issue previously registered in unpublished form.

b. ☐ This is the first application submitted by this author as copyright claimant.

c. ☐ This is a changed version of this issue, as shown by space 6 on this application.

If your answer is "Yes," give: **Previous Registration Number ▼** _____   **Year of Registration ▼** _____

5

DERIVATIVE WORK OR COMPILATION   Complete both space 6a & 6b for a derivative work; complete only 6b for a compilation.

a. **Preexisting Material**   Identify any preexisting work or works that this work is based on or incorporates. ▼

b. **Material Added to This Work**   Give a brief, general statement of the material that has been added to this work and in which copyright is claimed. ▼

See instructions
before completing
this space

6

—space deleted—

7

REPRODUCTION FOR USE OF BLIND OR PHYSICALLY HANDICAPPED INDIVIDUALS   A signature on this form at space 10, and a check in one of the boxes here in space 8, constitutes a non-exclusive grant of permission to the Library of Congress to reproduce and distribute solely for the blind and physically handicapped and under the conditions and limitations prescribed by the regulations of the Copyright Office: (1) copies of the work identified in space 1 of this application in Braille (or similar tactile symbols); or (2) phonorecords embodying a fixation of a reading of that work; or (3) both.

a ☐ Copies and Phonorecords   **b** ☐ Copies Only   **c** ☐ Phonorecords Only

See instructions

8

DEPOSIT ACCOUNT   If the registration fee is to be charged to a Deposit Account established in the Copyright Office, give name and number of Account.
Name ▼ _____   **Account Number ▼** _____

CORRESPONDENCE   Give name and address to which correspondence about this application should be sent.   Name Address Apt City State Zip ▼

Area Code & Telephone Number ▶ _____

Be sure to
give your
daytime phone
◀ number

9

CERTIFICATION* I, the undersigned, hereby certify that I am the

Check one ▶

☐ author
☐ other copyright claimant
☐ owner of exclusive right(s)
☐ authorized agent of _____

Name of author or other copyright claimant, or owner of exclusive right(s) ▲

of the work identified in this application and that the statements made by me in this application are correct to the best of my knowledge.

Typed or printed name and date ▼ If this application gives a date of publication in space 3, do not sign and submit it before that date.

_____ **date ▶** _____

☞ **Handwritten signature (X) ▼**

10

MAIL CERTIFI-CATE TO

Name ▼ _____

Number Street Apartment Number ▼ _____

City State ZIP ▼ _____

Certificate will be mailed in window envelope

YOU MUST
· Complete all necessary spaces
· Sign your application in space 10
SEND ALL 3 ELEMENTS IN THE SAME PACKAGE
1. Application form
2. Nonrefundable $20 filing fee in check or money order payable to *Register of Copyrights*
3. Deposit material
MAIL TO:
Register of Copyrights
Library of Congress
Washington, D.C. 20559

11

* 17 U.S.C. § 506(e): Any person who knowingly makes a false representation of a material fact in the application for copyright registration provided for by section 409, or in any written statement filed in connection with the application, shall be fined not more than $2,500.

▲ February 1991—50,000   ✰U.S. GOVERNMENT PRINTING OFFICE: 1991- 282-170/20,013

⊘Filling Out Application Form SE

Detach and read these instructions before completing this form. Make sure all applicable spaces have been filled in before you return this form.

BASIC INFORMATION

When To Use This Form: Use a separate Form SE for registration of each individual issue of a serial, Class SE. A serial is defined as a work issued or intended to be issued in successive parts bearing numerical or chronological designations and intended to be continued indefinitely. This class includes a variety of works: periodicals; newspapers; annuals; the journals, proceedings, transactions, etc., of societies. Do not use Form SE to register an individual contribution to a serial. Request Form TX for such contributions.

Deposit to Accompany Application: An application for copyright registration must be accompanied by a deposit consisting of copies or phonorecords representing the entire work for which registration is to be made. The following are the general deposit requirements as set forth in the statute:

Unpublished Work: Deposit one complete copy (or phonorecord).

Published Work: Deposit two complete copies (or phonorecords) of the best edition.

Work First Published Outside the United States: Deposit one complete copy (or phonorecord) of the first foreign edition.

Mailing Requirements: It is important that you send the application, the deposit copy or copies, and the $20 fee together in the same envelope or package. The Copyright Office cannot process them unless they are received together. Send to: *Register of Copyrights, Library of Congress, Washington, D.C. 20559.*

The Copyright Notice: For works first published on or after March 1, 1989, the law provides that a copyright notice in a specified form "may be placed on all publicly distributed copies from which the work can be visually perceived." Use of the copyright notice is the responsibility of the copyright owner and does not require advance permission from the Copyright Office. The required form of the notice for copies generally consists of three elements: (1) the symbol "©", or the word "Copyright," or the abbreviation "Copr."; (2) the year of first publication; and (3) the name of the owner of copyright. For example: "© 1989 Jane Cole." The notice is to be affixed to the copies "in such manner and location as to give reasonable notice of the claim of copyright." Works first published prior to March 1, 1989, **must** carry the notice or risk loss of copyright protection.

For information about notice requirements for works published before March 1, 1989, or other copyright information, write: Information Section, LM-401, Copyright Office, Library of Congress, Washington, D.C. 20559.

PRIVACY ACT ADVISORY STATEMENT Required by the Privacy Act of 1974 (P.L. 93-579)
The authority for requesting this information is title 17, U.S.C., secs. 409 and 410. Furnishing the requested information is voluntary. But if the information is not furnished, it may be necessary to delay or refuse registration and you may not be entitled to certain relief, remedies, and benefits provided in chapters 4 and 5 of title 17, U.S.C.
The principal uses of the requested information are the establishment and maintenance of a public record and the examination of the application for compliance with legal requirements.
Other routine uses include public inspection and copying, preparation of public indexes, preparation of public catalogs of copyright registrations, and preparation of search reports upon request.
NOTE: No other advisory statement will be given in connection with this application. Please keep this statement and refer to it if we communicate with you regarding this application.

LINE-BY-LINE INSTRUCTIONS

1 SPACE 1: Title

Title of This Serial: Every work submitted for copyright registration must be given a title to identify that particular work. If the copies or phonorecords of the work bear a title (or an identifying phrase that could serve as a title), copy that wording *completely* and *exactly* on the application. Give the volume and number of the periodical issue for which you are seeking registration. The "Date on copies" in space 1 should be the date appearing on the actual copies (for example: "June 1981," "Winter 1981"). Indexing of the registration and future identification of the work will depend on the information you give here.

Previous or Alternative Titles: Complete this space only if there are any additional titles for the serial under which someone searching for the registration might be likely to look, or under which a document pertaining to the work might be recorded.

2 SPACE 2: Author(s)

General Instructions: After reading these instructions, decide who are the "authors" of this work for copyright purposes. In the case of a serial issue, the organization which directs the creation of the serial issue as a whole is generally considered the author of the "collective work" (see "Nature of Authorship") whether it employs a staff or uses the efforts of volunteers. Where, however, an individual is independently responsible for the serial issue, name that person as author of the "collective work."

Name of Author: The fullest form of the author's name should be given. In the case of a "work made for hire," the statute provides that "the employer or other person for whom the work was prepared is considered the author." If this issue is a "work made for hire," the author's name will be the full legal name of the hiring organization, corporation, or individual. The title of the periodical should not ordinarily be listed as "author" because the title itself does not usually correspond to a legal entity capable of authorship. When an individual creates an issue of a serial independently and not as an "employee" of an organization or corporation, that individual should be listed as the "author."

Author's Nationality or Domicile: Give the country of which the author is a citizen, or the country in which the author is domiciled. Nationality or domicile **must** be given in all cases. The citizenship of an organization formed under United States Federal or state law should be stated as "U.S.A."

What is a "Work Made for Hire"? A "work made for hire" is defined as: (1) "a work prepared by an employee within the scope of his or her employment"; or (2) "a work specially ordered or commissioned for use as a contribution to a collective work, as a part of a motion picture or other audiovisual work, as a translation, as a supplementary work, as a compilation, as an instructional text, as a test, as answer material for a test, or as an atlas, if the parties expressly agree in a written instrument signed by them that the work shall be considered a work made for hire." An organization that uses the efforts of volunteers in the creation of a "collective work" (see "Nature of Authorship") may also be considered the author of a "work made for hire" even though those volunteers were not specifically paid by the organization. In the case of a "work made for hire," give the full legal name of the employer and check "Yes" to indicate that the work was made for hire. You may also include the name of the employee along with the name of the employer (for example: "Elster Publishing Co., employer for hire of John Ferguson").

"Anonymous" or "Pseudonymous" Work: Leave this space **blank** if the serial is a "work made for hire." An author's contribution to a work is "anonymous" if that author is not identified on the copies or phonorecords of the work. An author's contribution to a work is "pseudonymous" if that author is identified on the copies or phonorecords under a fictitious name. If the work is "anonymous" you may: (1) leave the line blank; or (2) state "anonymous" on the line; or (3) reveal the author's identity. If the work is "pseudonymous" you may: (1) leave the line blank; or (2) give the pseudonym and identify it as such (for example: "Huntley Haverstock, pseudonym"); or (3) reveal the author's name, making clear which is the real name and which is the pseudonym (for example: "Judith Barton, whose pseudonym is Madeline Elster"). However, the citizenship or domicile of the author **must** be given in all cases.

Dates of Birth and Death: Leave this space blank if the author's contribution was a "work made for hire." If the author is dead, the statute requires that the year of death be included in the application unless the work is anonymous or pseudonymous. The author's birth date is optional, but is useful as a form of identification.

Nature of Authorship: Give a brief statement of the nature of the particular author's contribution to the work. If an organization directed, controlled, and supervised the creation of the serial issue as a whole, check the box "collective work." The term "collective work" means that the author is responsible for compilation and editorial revision, and may also be responsible for certain individual contributions to the serial issue. Further examples of "Authorship" which may apply both to organizational and to individual authors are "Entire text"; "Entire text and/or illustrations"; "Editorial revision, compilation, plus additional new material."

3 SPACE 3: Creation and Publication

General Instructions: Do not confuse "creation" with "publication." Every application for copyright registration must state "the year in which creation of the work was completed." Give the date and nation of first publication only if the work has been published.

Creation: Under the statute, a work is "created" when it is fixed in a copy or phonorecord for the first time. Where a work has been prepared over a period of time, the part of the work existing in fixed form on a particular date constitutes the created work on that date. The date you give here should be the year in which this particular issue was completed.

Publication: The statute defines "publication" as "the distribution of copies or phonorecords of a work to the public by sale or other transfer of ownership, or by rental, lease, or lending"; a work is also "published" if there has been an "offering to distribute copies or phonorecords to a group of persons for purposes of further distribution, public performance, or public display." Give the full date (month, day, year) when, and the country where, publication of this particular issue first occurred. If first publication took place simultaneously in the United States and other countries, it is sufficient to state "U.S.A."

4 SPACE 4: Claimant(s)

Name(s) and Address(es) of Copyright Claimant(s): This space must be completed. Give the name(s) and address(es) of the copyright claimant(s) of this work even if the claimant is the same as the author named in space 2. Copyright in a work belongs initially to the author of the work (including, in the case of a work made for hire, the employer or other person for whom the work was prepared). The copyright claimant is either the author of the work or a person or organization to whom the copyright initially belonging to the author has been transferred.

Transfer: The statute provides that, if the copyright claimant is not the author, the application for registration must contain "a brief statement of how the claimant obtained ownership of the copyright." A transfer of copyright ownership (other than one brought about by operation of law) must be in writing. If any copyright claimant named in space 4 is not an author named in space 2, give a brief, general statement describing the means by which that claimant obtained ownership of the copyright from the original author. Examples: "By written contract"; "Written transfer of all rights by author"; "Assignment"; "Inherited by will." Do not attach the actual document of transfer or other attachments or riders.

5 SPACE 5: Previous Registration

General Instructions: This space applies only rarely to serials. Complete space 5 if this particular issue has been registered earlier or if it contains a substantial amount of material that has been previously registered. Do not complete this space if the previous registrations are simply those made for earlier issues.

Previous Registration:
a. Check this box if this issue has been registered in unpublished form and a second registration is now sought to cover the first published edition.
b. Check this box if someone other than the author is identified as copyright claimant in the earlier registration and the author is now seeking registration in his or her own name. If the work in question is a contribution to a collective work, as opposed to the issue as a whole, file Form TX, not Form SE.
c. Check this box (and complete space 6) if this particular issue, or a substantial portion of the material in it, has been previously registered and you are now seeking registration for the additions and revisions which appear in this issue for the first time.

Previous Registration Number and Date: Complete this line if you checked one of the boxes above. If more than one previous registration has been made for the issue or for material in it, give only the number and year date for the latest registration.

6 SPACE 6: Derivative Work or Compilation

General Instructions: Complete space 6 if this issue is a "changed version," "compilation," or "derivative work," which incorporates one or more earlier works that have already been published or registered for copyright, or that have fallen into the public domain. Do not complete space 6 for an issue consisting of entirely new material appearing for the first time, such as a new issue of a continuing serial. A "compilation" is defined as "a work formed by the collection and assembling of preexisting materials or of data that are selected, coordinated, or arranged in such a way that the resulting work as a whole constitutes an original work of authorship." A "derivative work" is "a work based on one or more preexisting works." Examples of derivative works include translations, fictionalizations, abridgments, condensations, or "any other form in which a work may be recast, transformed, or adapted." Derivative works also include works "consisting of editorial revisions, annotations, or other modifications" if these changes, as a whole, represent an original work of authorship.

Preexisting Material (space 6a): For derivative works, complete this space and space 6b. In space 6a identify the preexisting work that has been recast, transformed, adapted, or updated. Example: "1978 Morgan Co. Sales Catalog." Do not complete space 6a for compilations.

Material Added to This Work (space 6b): Give a brief, general statement of the new material covered by the copyright claim for which registration is sought. **Derivative work** examples include: "Editorial revisions and additions to the Catalog"; "Translation"; "Additional material." If a periodical issue is a **compilation**, describe both the compilation itself and the material that has been compiled. Examples: "Compilation of previously published journal articles"; "Compilation of previously published data." An issue may be both a derivative work and a compilation, in which case a sample statement might be: "Compilation of [describe] and additional new material."

7 SPACE 7: Manufacturing Provisions

Due to the expiration of the Manufacturing Clause of the copyright law on June 30, 1986, this space has been deleted.

8 SPACE 8: Reproduction for Use of Blind or Physically Handicapped Individuals

General Instructions: One of the major programs of the Library of Congress is to provide Braille editions and special recordings of works for the exclusive use of the blind and physically handicapped. In an effort to simplify and speed up the copyright licensing procedures that are a necessary part of this program, section 710 of the copyright statute provides for the establishment of a voluntary licensing system to be tied in with copyright registration. Copyright Office regulations provide that you may grant a license for such reproduction and distribution solely for the use of persons who are certified by competent authority as unable to read normal printed material as a result of physical limitations. The license is entirely voluntary, nonexclusive, and may be terminated upon 90 days notice.

How to Grant the License: If you wish to grant it, check one of the three boxes in space 8. Your check in one of these boxes, together with your signature in space 10, will mean that the Library of Congress can proceed to reproduce and distribute under the license without further paperwork. For further information, write for Circular 63.

9,10,11 SPACE 9, 10, 11: Fee, Correspondence, Certification, Return Address

Deposit Account: If you maintain a Deposit Account in the Copyright Office, identify it in space 9. Otherwise leave the space blank and send the fee of $20 with your application and deposit.

Correspondence (space 9): This space should contain the name, address, area code, and telephone number of the person to be consulted if correspondence about this application becomes necessary.

Certification (space 10): The application cannot be accepted unless it bears the date and the **handwritten signature** of the author or other copyright claimant, or of the owner of exclusive right(s), or of the duly authorized agent of the author, claimant, or owner of exclusive right(s).

Address for Return of Certificate (space 11): The address box must be completed legibly since the certificate will be returned in a window envelope.

SHORT FORM SE

For a Serial
UNITED STATES COPYRIGHT OFFICE

REGISTRATION NUMBER

EFFECTIVE DATE OF REGISTRATION
(Assigned by Copyright Office)

Month	Day	Year

APPLICATION RECEIVED

ONE DEPOSIT RECEIVED

TWO DEPOSITS RECEIVED

EXAMINED BY

CORRESPONDENCE ☐

DO NOT WRITE ABOVE THIS LINE.

1 TITLE OF THIS SERIAL AS IT APPEARS ON THE COPY

Volume▼   Number▼   Date on Copies▼   ISSN▼

2 NAME AND ADDRESS OF THE AUTHOR AND COPYRIGHT CLAIMANT IN THIS COLLECTIVE WORK MADE FOR HIRE

3 DATE OF PUBLICATION OF THIS PARTICULAR ISSUE
Month▼   Day▼   Year▼

YEAR IN WHICH CREATION OF
THIS ISSUE WAS COMPLETED
(IF EARLIER THAN THE YEAR OF
PUBLICATION):
Year▼

CERTIFICATION*: I, the undersigned, hereby certify that I am the copyright claimant or the authorized agent of the copyright claimant of the work identified in this application, that all the conditions specified in the instructions on the back of this form are met, and that the statements made by me in this application are correct to the best of my knowledge.

Handwritten signature (X) _____

Typed or printed name of signer _____

PERSON TO CONTACT FOR CORRESPONDENCE ABOUT THIS CLAIM

Name ▶ _____
Daytime telephone number ▶ _____
Address (if other than given below) ▶ _____

DEPOSIT ACCOUNT

Account number ▶ _____
Name of account ▶ _____

MAIL CERTIFICATE TO

Name▼

Number/Street/Apartment Number▼

Certificate will be mailed in window envelope

City/State/ZIP▼

YOU MUST:
• Complete all necessary spaces
• Sign your application

SEND ALL 3 ELEMENTS
IN THE SAME PACKAGE:
1. Application form
2. Nonrefundable $20 filing fee in check or money order payable to *Register of Copyrights*
3. Deposit material

MAIL TO
Register of Copyrights
Library of Congress
Washington, D.C. 20559

Copyright fees are adjusted at 5-year intervals, based on increases or decreases in the Consumer Price Index. The next adjustment is due in 1995. Contact the Copyright Office in January 1995 for the new fee schedule.

*17 U.S.C. §506(e): Any person who knowingly makes a false representation of a material fact in the application for copyright registration provided for by section 409, or in any written statement filed in connection with the application, shall be fined not more than $2,500.

June 1992—50,000

☆U.S. GOVERNMENT PRINTING OFFICE: 1992—312-432/60,001

⊘Filling Out Short Form SE

BASIC INFORMATION

Read these instructions before completing this form. Make sure all applicable spaces have been filled in before you return this form.

When to Use This Form: All the following conditions must be met in order to use this form. If any one of the conditions does not apply, you must use Form SE. Incorrect use of this form will result in a delay in your registration.

The claim must be in a collective work.
The work must be essentially an all-new collective work or issue.
The author must be a citizen or domiciliary of the United States.
The work must be a work made for hire.
The author(s) and claimant(s) must be the same person(s) or organization(s).
The work must be first published in the United States.

Deposit to Accompany Application: An application for registration of a copyright claim in a serial issue first published in the United States must be accompanied by a deposit consisting of two copies (or phonorecords) of the best edition.

Fee: The filing fee of $20.00 must be sent for each issue to be registered. Do not send cash or currency.

Copyright fees are adjusted at 5-year intervals, based on increases or decreases in the Consumer Price Index. The next adjustment is due in 1995. Contact the Copyright Office in January 1995 for the new fee schedule.

Mailing Requirements: It is important that you send the application, the deposit copies, and the $20.00 fee together in the same envelope or package. Send to: Register of Copyrights, Library of Congress, Washington, D.C. 20559.

Reproduction for Use of Blind or Physically Handicapped Individuals: A signature on this form and a check in one of these boxes constitutes a nonexclusive grant of permission to the Library of Congress to reproduce and distribute solely for the blind and physically handicapped under the conditions and limitations prescribed by the regulations of the Copyright Office: (1) copies of the work identified in space 1 of this application in Braille (or similar tactile symbols); or (2) phonorecords embodying a fixation of a reading of that work; or (3) both.

☐ Copies only   ☐ Phonorecords only   ☐ Copies and phonorecords

Collective Work: The term "collective work" refers to a work, such as a serial issue, in which a number of contributions are assembled into a collective whole. A claim in the "collective work" extends to all copyrightable authorship created by employees of the author, as well as any independent contributions in which the claimant has acquired ownership of the copyright.

Publication: The statute defines "publication" as "The distribution of copies or phonorecords of a work to the public by sale or other transfer of ownership, or by rental, lease, or lending;" a work is also "published" if there has been an "offering to distribute copies or phonorecords to a group of persons for purposes of further distribution, public performance, or public display."

Creation: A work is "created" when it is fixed in a copy (or phonorecord) for the first time.

Work Made for Hire: A "work made for hire" is defined as: (1) a work prepared by an employee within the scope of his or her employment; or (2) a work specially ordered or commissioned for certain uses (including use as a contribution to a collective work), if the parties expressly agree in a written instrument signed by them that the work shall be considered a work made for hire. The employer is the author of a work made for hire.

The Copyright Notice: For works first published on or after March 1, 1989, the law provides that a copyright notice in a specified form "may be placed on all publicly distributed copies from which the work can be visually perceived." Use of the copyright notice is the responsibility of the copyright owner and does not require advance permission from the Copyright Office. The required form of the notice for copies generally consists of three elements: (1) the symbol "©", or the word "Copyright," or the abbreviation "Copr."; (2) the year of first publication; and (3) the name of the owner of copyright. For example: "©1992 Jane Cole." The notice is to be affixed to the copies "in such manner and location as to give reasonable notice of the claim of copyright." Works first published prior to March 1, 1989, **must** carry the notice or risk loss of copyright protection.

For information about notice requirements for works published before March 1, 1989, or other copyright information, write: Information Section, LM-401, Copyright Office, Library of Congress, Washington, D.C. 20559.

PRIVACY ACT ADVISORY STATEMENT Required by the Privacy Act of 1974 (P.L. 93-579)
The authority for requesting this information is title 17 U.S.C.,secs. 409 and 410. Furnishing the requested information is voluntary. But if the information is not furnished, it may be necessary to delay or refuse registration and you may not be entitled to certain relief, remedies, and benefits provided in chapters 4 and 5 of title 17, U.S.C.

The principal uses of the requested information are the establishment and maintenance of a public record and the examination of the application for compliance with legal requirements.

Other routine uses include public inspection and copying, preparation of public indexes, preparation of public catalogs of copyright registrations, and preparation of search reports upon request.

NOTE: No other advisory statement will be given in connection with this application. Please keep this statement and refer to it if we communicate with you regarding this application.

SPACE-BY-SPACE INSTRUCTIONS

1 SPACE 1: Title

Every work submitted for copyright registration must be given a title to identify that particular work. Give the complete title of the periodical, including the volume, number, issue date, or other indicia printed on the copies. If possible, give the International Standard Serial Number (ISSN).

2 SPACE 2: Author and Copyright Claimant

Give the fullest form of the author and claimant's name. If there are joint authors and owners, give the names of all the author/owners. (It is assumed that the authors and claimants are the same, that the work is made for hire, and that the claim is in the collective work).

3 SPACE 3: Date of Publication of This Particular Work

Give the exact date on which publication of this issue first took place. The full date, including month, day, and year must be given.

Year in Which Creation of This Issue Was Completed: Give the year in which this serial issue was fixed in a copy or phonorecord for the first time. If no year is given, it is assumed that the issue was created in the same year in which it was published. The date must be the same as or no later than the publication date.

Certification: The application cannot be accepted unless it bears the handwritten signature of the copyright claimant or the duly authorized agent of the copyright claimant.

Person to Contact for Correspondence About This Claim: Give the name and telephone number, including area code, of the person to whom any correspondence concerning this claim should be addressed. Give the address only if it is different from the address for mailing of the certificate.

Deposit Account: If the filing fee is to be charged against a Deposit Account in the Copyright Office, give the name and number of the account in this space. Otherwise, leave the space blank and forward the $20.00 filing fee with your application and deposit.

Mailing Address of Certificate: This address must be complete and legible since the certificate will be mailed in a window envelope.

FORM SE/GROUP

UNITED STATES COPYRIGHT OFFICE

REGISTRATION NUMBER

EFFECTIVE DATE OF REGISTRATION
(Assigned by Copyright Office)

Month	Day	Year

APPLICATION RECEIVED

ONE DEPOSIT RECEIVED

EXAMINED BY   CORRESPONDENCE

DO NOT WRITE ABOVE THIS LINE.

1

List in order of publication

No previous registration under identical title ☐

TITLE ▼   ISSN▼

Volume▼	Number▼	Issue date on copies▼	Month, day and year of publication ▼
1.			
2.			
3.			
4.			
5.			
6.			
7.			
8.			
9.			
10.			
11.			
12.			
13.			
14.			

2

NAME AND ADDRESS OF THE AUTHOR/COPYRIGHT CLAIMANT IN THESE COLLECTIVE WORKS MADE FOR HIRE

FOR NON-U.S. WORKS: Author's citizenship ▼   Domicile ▼   Nation of publication ▼

CERTIFICATION*:   I, the undersigned, hereby certify that I am the copyright claimant or the authorized agent of the copyright claimant of the works identified in this application, that all the conditions specified in the instructions on the back of this form are met, that I have deposited two complimentary subscription copies with the Library of Congress, and that the statements made by me in this application are correct to the best of my knowledge.

Signature (X) _____   Typed or printed name _____

PERSON TO CONTACT FOR CORRESPONDENCE ABOUT THIS CLAIM

Name▶ _____

Daytime telephone number▶ _____

Address (if other than given below) ▶ _____

DEPOSIT ACCOUNT

Account number▶ _____

Name of account▶ _____

MAIL CERTIFI-CATE TO

Name▼

Number/Street/Apartment Number▼

Certificate will be mailed in window envelope

City/State/ZIP▼

REPRODUCTION FOR USE OF BLIND OR PHYSICALLY HANDICAPPED INDIVIDUALS

a ☐ Copies and Phonorecords

b ☐ Copies Only

c ☐ Phonorecords Only

MAIL TO
Register of Copyrights
Library of Congress
Washington, D.C. 20559

*17 U.S.C. §506(e): Any person who knowingly makes a false representation of a material fact in the application for copyright registration provided for by section 409, or in any written statement filed in connection with the application, shall be fined not more than $2,500.

November 1990—30,000

☆ U.S. GOVERNMENT PRINTING OFFICE: 1990–282-170/20,008

✐Form SE/GROUP

BASIC INFORMATION

Read these instructions before completing this form.
Make sure all applicable spaces have been filled in
before you return this form.

When to Use This Form:
All the following conditions must be met in order to use this form. If any one of the conditions does not apply, you must register the issues separately using Form SE or Short Form SE.

1. You must have given a complimentary subscription for two copies of the serial to the Library of Congress, confirmed by letter to the General Counsel, Copyright Office. Subscription copies must be mailed **separately** to:
   Library of Congress
   Group Periodicals Registration
   Washington, D.C. 20540
2. The claim must be in the collective works.
3. The works must be essentially all new collective works or issues.
4. Each issue must be a work made for hire.
5. The author(s) and claimant(s) must be the same person(s) or organization(s) for all of the issues.
6. Each issue must have been created no more than one year prior to publication.
7. All issues in the group must have been published within the same calendar year.

Which Issues May Be Included in a Group Registration:
You may register two or more issues of a serial published at intervals of one week or longer under the same continuing title, provided that the issues were published within a 90-day period during the same calendar year.

Deposit to Accompany Application:
Send one copy of each issue included in the group registration with the application and fee.

Fee:
A nonrefundable filing fee of $10.00 FOR EACH ISSUE LISTED ON FORM SE/GROUP must be sent with the application or charged to an active deposit account in the Copyright Office. There is a minimum fee of $20.00 for Form SE/Group. Special handling is not available for Form SE/Group.

Mailing Instructions:
Send the application, deposit copies, and fee together in the same package to: Register of Copyrights, Library of Congress, Washington, D.C. 20559.

International Standard Serial Number (ISSN):
ISSN is an internationally accepted code for the identification of serial publications. If a published serial has not been assigned an ISSN, application forms and additional information may be obtained from National Serials Data Program, Library of Congress, Washington, D.C. 20540. Do not contact the Copyright Office for ISSNs.

Collective Work:
The term "collective work" refers to a work, such as a serial issue, in which a number of contributions are assembled into a collective whole. A claim in the "collective work" extends to all copyrightable authorship created by employees of the author, as well as any independent contributions in which the claimant has acquired ownership of the copyright.

Publication:
The statute defines "publication" as "The distribution of copies or phonorecords of a work to the public by sale or other transfer of ownership, or by rental, lease, or lending;" a work is also "published" if there has been an "offering to distribute copies or phonorecords to a group of persons for purposes of further distribution, public performance, or public display."

Creation:
A work is "created" when it is fixed in a copy (or phonorecord) for the first time. For a serial, the year in which the collective work was completed is the creation date.

Work Made for Hire:
A "work made for hire" is defined as: (1) a work prepared by an employee within the scope of his or her employment; or (2) a work specially ordered or commissioned for certain uses (including use as a contribution to a collective work), if the parties expressly agree in a written instrument signed by them that the work shall be considered a work made for hire. The employer is the author of a work made for hire.

The Copyright Notice:
For works first published on or after March 1, 1989, the law provides that a copyright notice in a specified form "may be placed on all publicly distributed copies from which the work can be visually perceived." Use of the copyright notice is the responsibility of the copyright owner and does not require advance permission from the Copyright Office. The required form of the notice for copies generally consists of three elements: (1) the symbol "©", or the word "Copyright," or the abbreviation "Copr."; (2) the year of first publication; and (3) the name of the owner of copyright. For example: "©1990 Jane Cole." The notice is to be affixed to the copies "in such manner and location as to give reasonable notice of the claim of copyright." Works first published prior to March 1, 1989, **must** carry the notice or risk loss of copyright protection.

For information about notice requirements for works published before March 1, 1989, or other copyright information, write: Information Section, LM-401, Copyright Office, Library of Congress, Washington, D.C. 20559.

SPACE-BY-SPACE INSTRUCTIONS

1 SPACE 1: Title and Date of Publication

Give the complete title of the serial, followed by the International Standard Serial Number (ISSN), if available. List the issues in the order of publication. For each issue, give the volume, number, and issue date appearing on the copies, followed by the complete date of publication, including month, day, and year. If you have not previously registered this **identical title** under Section 408 of the Copyright Act, please indicate by checking the box.

2 SPACE 2: Author and Copyright Claimant

Give the fullest form of the author and claimant's name and mailing address. If there are joint authors and claimants, give the names and addresses of all the author/claimants. If the work is not of U.S. origin, add the citizenship or domicile of the author/claimant, or the nation of publication.

Certification:
The application cannot be accepted unless it bears the handwritten signature of the copyright claimant or the duly authorized agent of the copyright claimant.

Person to Contact for Correspondence About This Claim:
Give the name and telephone number, including area code, of the person to whom any correspondence concerning this claim should be addressed. Give the address only if it is different from the address for mailing of the certificate.

Deposit Account:
If the filing fee is to be charged against a deposit account in the Copyright Office, give the name and number of the account in this space. Otherwise, leave the space blank and forward the filing fee with your application and deposit.

Mailing Address of Certificate:
This address must be complete and legible since the certificate will be mailed in a window envelope.

Reproduction for Use of Blind or Physically Handicapped Individuals:
A signature on this form and a check in one of these boxes constitutes a nonexclusive grant of permission to the Library of Congress to reproduce and distribute solely for the blind and physically handicapped under the conditions and limitations prescribed by the regulations of the Copyright Office: (1) copies of the work identified in space 1 of this application in Braille (or similar tactile symbols); or (2) phonorecords embodying a fixation of a reading of that work; or (3) both.

 **FORM CA**

UNITED STATES COPYRIGHT OFFICE

REGISTRATION NUMBER

| TX | TXU | PA | PAU | VA | VAU | SR | SRU | RE |

Effective Date of Supplementary Registration

. . . .
(Month)   (Day)   (Year)

DO NOT WRITE ABOVE THIS LINE. FOR COPYRIGHT OFFICE USE ONLY

A
Basic
Instructions

TITLE OF WORK:

REGISTRATION NUMBER OF THE BASIC REGISTRATION: **YEAR OF BASIC REGISTRATION:**

NAME(S) OF AUTHOR(S):   **NAME(S) OF COPYRIGHT CLAIMANT(S):**

B
Correction

LOCATION AND NATURE OF INCORRECT INFORMATION IN BASIC REGISTRATION:
Line Number: . . . .   Line Heading or Description . . . .

INCORRECT INFORMATION AS IT APPEARS IN BASIC REGISTRATION:

CORRECTED INFORMATION:

EXPLANATION OF CORRECTION: (Optional)

C
Amplification

LOCATION AND NATURE OF INFORMATION IN BASIC REGISTRATION TO BE AMPLIFIED:
Line Number: . . . .   Line Heading or Description . . . .

AMPLIFIED INFORMATION:

EXPLANATION OF AMPLIFIED INFORMATION: (Optional)

EXAMINED BY: ....

CHECKED BY: ....

FORM CA RECEIVED:

CORRESPONDENCE:
☐ YES

REMITTANCE NUMBER AND DATE:

REFERENCE TO THIS REGISTRATION
ADDED TO BASIC REGISTRATION:
☐ YES   ☐ NO

DEPOSIT ACCOUNT FUNDS USED: ☐

FOR
COPYRIGHT
OFFICE
USE
ONLY

DO NOT WRITE ABOVE THIS LINE. FOR COPYRIGHT OFFICE USE ONLY

CONTINUATION OF: (Check which) ☐ PART B OR ☐ PART C

D

Continuation

DEPOSIT ACCOUNT: If the registration fee is to be charged to a Deposit Account established in the Copyright Office, give the name and number of Account:

Name . . . . Account Number . . . .

CORRESPONDENCE: Give name and address to which correspondence should be sent:

Name . . . . Apt. No. . . . .

Address . . . .
           (Number and Street)   (City)   (State)   (ZIP Code)

Daytime telephone number (. . . . .) . . . .

E

Deposit
Account and
Mailing
Instructions

CERTIFICATION* I, the undersigned, hereby certify that I am the: (Check one)

☐ author ☐ other copyright claimant ☐ owner of exclusive right(s) ☐ authorized agent of: . . . .
                        (Name of author or other copyright claimant, or
                        owner of exclusive right(s))

of the work identified in this application and that the statements made by me in this application are correct to the best of my knowledge.

Handwritten signature: (X) . . . .

Typed or printed name: . . . .

Date: . . . .

*17USC §506(e): FALSE REPRESENTATION—Any person who knowingly makes a false representation of a material fact in the application for copyright registration provided for by section 409, or in any written statement filed in connection with the application, shall be fined not more than $2,500.

F

Certification
(Application
must be
signed)

**MAIL
CERTIFICATE
TO**

(Certificate will
be mailed in
window envelope)

. . . .
            (Name)

. . . .
     (Number, Street and Apartment Number)

. . . .
     (City)   (State)   (ZIP Code)

G

Address for
Return of
Certificate

November 1991—25,000

☆U.S. GOVERNMENT PRINTING OFFICE: 1991-312-432/40,009

FORM CA

UNITED STATES COPYRIGHT OFFICE
LIBRARY OF CONGRESS
WASHINGTON, D.C. 20559

Application for
Supplementary Copyright Registration
*To Correct or Amplify Information Given in the
Copyright Office Record of an Earlier Registration*

What is "Supplementary Copyright Registration?"
Supplementary registration is a special type of copyright registration provided for in section 408(d) of the copyright law.

Purpose of Supplementary Registration. As a rule, only one basic copyright registration can be made for the same work. To take care of cases where information in the basic registration turns out to be incorrect or incomplete, the law provides for "the filing of an application for supplementary registration, to correct an error in a copyright registration or to amplify the information given in a registration."

Earlier Registration Necessary. Supplementary registration can be made only if a basic copyright registration for the same work has already been completed.

Who May File. Once basic registration has been made for a work, any author or other copyright claimant, or owner of any exclusive right in the work, who wishes to correct or amplify the information given in the basic registration, may submit Form CA.

Please Note:
- Do not use Form CA to correct errors in statements on the copies or phonorecords of the work in question, or to reflect changes in the content of the work. If the work has been changed substantially, you should consider making an entirely new registration for the revised version to cover the additions or revisions.
- Do not use Form CA as a substitute for renewal registration. For works originally copyrighted between January 1, 1950 and December 31, 1977, registration of a renewal claim within strict time limits is necessary to extend the first 28-year copyright term to the full term of 75 years. This cannot be done by filing Form CA.
- Do not use Form CA as a substitute for recording a transfer of copyright or other document pertaining to rights under a copyright. Recording a document under section 205 of the statute gives all persons constructive notice of the facts stated in the document and may have other important consequences in cases of infringement or conflicting transfers. Supplementary registration does not have that legal effect.

How to Apply for Supplementary Registration:

First: Study the information on this page to make sure that filing an application on Form CA is the best procedure to follow in your case.

Second: Turn this page over and read through the specific instructions for filling out Form CA. Make sure, before starting to complete the form, that you have all of the detailed information about the basic registration you will need.

Third: Complete all applicable spaces on this form, following the line-by-line instructions on the back of this page. Use typewriter, or print the information in dark ink.

Fourth: Detach this sheet and send your completed Form CA to: Register of Copyrights, Library of Congress, Washington, D.C. 20559. Unless you have a Deposit Account in the Copyright Office, your application must be accompanied by a nonrefundable filing fee in the form of a check or money order for $20 payable to: *Register of Copyrights.* Do not send copies, phonorecords, or supporting documents with your application, since they cannot be made part of the record of a supplementary registration.

What Happens When a Supplementary Registration is Made?

When a supplementary registration is completed, the Copyright Office will assign it a new registration number in the appropriate registration category, and issue a certificate of supplementary registration under that number. The basic registration will not be expunged or cancelled, and the two registrations will both stand in the Copyright Office records. The supplementary registration will have the effect of calling the public's attention to a possible error or omission in the basic registration, and of placing the correct facts or the additional information on official record.

INSTRUCTIONS
For Completing FORM CA (Supplementary Registration)

PART A: BASIC INSTRUCTIONS

- *General Instructions:* The information in this part identifies the basic registration to be corrected or amplified. Each item must agree exactly with the information as it already appears in the basic registration, that is, the registration you wish to correct (even if the purpose of filing Form CA is to change one of these items).
- *Title of Work:* Give the title as it appears in the basic registration, including previous or alternative titles if they appear.
- *Registration Number:* This is a series of numerical digits, preceded by one or more letters. The registration number appears in the upper right-hand corner of the certificate of registration.
- *Registration Date:* Give the year when the basic registration was completed.
- *Name(s) of Author(s) and Name(s) of Copyright Claimant(s):* Give all of the names as they appear in the basic registration.

PART B: CORRECTION

- *General Instructions:* Complete this part **only** if information in the basic registration was incorrect at the time that basic registration was made. Leave this part blank and complete Part C, instead, if your purpose is to add, update, or clarify information rather than to rectify an actual error.
- *Location and Nature of Incorrect Information:* Give the line number and the heading or description of the space in the basic registration where the error occurs (for example: "Line number 3 . . . Citizenship of author").
- *Incorrect Information as it Appears in Basic Registration:* Transcribe the erroneous statement exactly as it appears in the basic registration.
- *Corrected Information:* Give the statement as it should have appeared.
- *Explanation of Correction (Optional):* If you wish, you may add an explanation of the error or its correction.

PART C: AMPLIFICATION

- *General Instructions:* Complete this part if you want to provide any of the following: (1) additional information that could have been given but was omitted at the time of basic registration; (2) changes in facts, such as changes of title or address of claimant, that have occurred since the basic registration; or (3) explanations clarifying information in the basic registration.
- *Location and Nature of Information to be Amplified:* Give the line number and the heading or description of the space in the basic registration where the information to be amplified appears.
- *Amplified Information:* Give a statement of the added, updated, or explanatory information as clearly and succinctly as possible.
- *Explanation of Amplification (Optional):* If you wish, you may add an explanation of the amplification.

PARTS D, E, F, G: CONTINUATION, FEE, MAILING INSTRUCTIONS AND CERTIFICATION

- *Continuation (Part D):* Use this space if you do not have enough room in Parts B or C.
- *Deposit Account and Mailing Instructions (Part E):* If you maintain a Deposit Account in the Copyright Office, identify it in Part E. Otherwise, you will need to send the nonrefundable filing fee of $20 with your form. The space headed "Correspondence" should contain the name and address of the person to be consulted if correspondence about the form becomes necessary.
- *Certification (Part F):* The application is not acceptable unless it bears the handwritten signature of the author, or other copyright claimant, or of the owner of exclusive right(s), or of the duly authorized agent of such author, claimant, or owner.
- *Address for Return of Certificate (Part G):* The address box must be completed legibly, since the certificate will be returned in a window envelope.

PRIVACY ACT ADVISORY STATEMENT
Required by the Privacy Act of 1974 (Public Law 93-579)

AUTHORITY FOR REQUESTING THIS INFORMATION:
· Title 17, U.S.C., Sec. 408 (d)

FURNISHING THE REQUESTED INFORMATION IS:
· Voluntary

BUT IF THE INFORMATION IS NOT PROVIDED:
· It may be necessary to delay or refuse supplementary registration

PRINCIPAL USES OF REQUESTED INFORMATION:
· Establishment and maintenance of a public record
· Evaluation for compliance with legal requirements

OTHER ROUTINE USES:
· Public inspection and copying
· Preparation of public indexes

· Preparation of public catalogs of copyright registrations
· Preparation of search reports upon request

NOTE:
· No other Advisory Statement will be given you in connection with the application
· Please retain this statement and refer to it if we communicate with you regarding this application

ADJUNCT APPLICATION
*for Copyright Registration for a
Group of Contributions to Periodicals*

 **FORM GR/CP**

UNITED STATES COPYRIGHT OFFICE

REGISTRATION NUMBER		
TX	PA	VA

EFFECTIVE DATE OF REGISTRATION

. . . .
(Month)   (Day)   (Year)

FORM GR/CP RECEIVED

Page _____ of _____ pages

- Use this adjunct form only if you are making a single registration for a group of contributions to periodicals, and you are also filing a basic application on Form TX, Form PA, or Form VA. Follow the instructions, attached.

- Number each line in Part B consecutively. Use additional Forms GR/CP if you need more space.

- Submit this adjunct form with the basic application form. Clip (do not tape or staple) and fold all sheets together before submitting them.

DO NOT WRITE ABOVE THIS LINE. FOR COPYRIGHT OFFICE USE ONLY

A

Identification
of
Application

IDENTIFICATION OF BASIC APPLICATION:
● This application for copyright registration for a group of contributions to periodicals is submitted as an adjunct to an application filed on: (Check which)

☐ Form TX   ☐ Form PA   ☐ Form VA

IDENTIFICATION OF AUTHOR AND CLAIMANT: (Give the name of the author and the name of the copyright claimant in all of the contributions listed in Part B of this form. The names should be the same as the names given in spaces 2 and 4 of the basic application.)
Name of Author: . . . .
Name of Copyright Claimant: . . . .

B

Registration
for Group of
Contributions

COPYRIGHT REGISTRATION FOR A GROUP OF CONTRIBUTIONS TO PERIODICALS: (To make a single registration for a group of works by the same individual author, all first published as contributions to periodicals within a 12-month period (see instructions), give full information about each contribution. If more space in needed, use additional Forms GR/CP.)

☐ Title of Contribution: . . . .
Title of Periodical: . . . . Vol. . . . . No. . . . . Issue Date . . . . Pages . . . . . .
Date of First Publication: . . . . Nation of First Publication . . . .
(Month)   (Day)   (Year)   (Country)

☐ Title of Contribution: . . . .
Title of Periodical: . . . . Vol. . . . . No. . . . . Issue Date . . . . Pages . . . . . .
Date of First Publication: . . . . Nation of First Publication . . . .
(Month)   (Day)   (Year)   (Country)

☐ Title of Contribution: . . . .
Title of Periodical: . . . . Vol. . . . . No. . . . . Issue Date . . . . Pages . . . . . .
Date of First Publication: . . . . Nation of First Publication . . . .
(Month)   (Day)   (Year)   (Country)

☐ Title of Contribution: . . . .
Title of Periodical: . . . . Vol. . . . . No. . . . . Issue Date . . . . Pages . . . . . .
Date of First Publication: . . . . Nation of First Publication . . . .
(Month)   (Day)   (Year)   (Country)

☐ Title of Contribution: . . . .
Title of Periodical: . . . . Vol. . . . . No. . . . . Issue Date . . . . Pages . . . . . .
Date of First Publication: . . . . Nation of First Publication . . . .
(Month)   (Day)   (Year)   (Country)

☐ Title of Contribution: . . . .
Title of Periodical: . . . . Vol. . . . . No. . . . . Issue Date . . . . Pages . . . . . .
Date of First Publication: . . . . Nation of First Publication . . . .
(Month)   (Day)   (Year)   (Country)

☐ Title of Contribution: . . . .
Title of Periodical: . . . . Vol. . . . . No. . . . . Issue Date . . . . Pages . . . . . .
Date of First Publication: . . . . Nation of First Publication . . . .
(Month)   (Day)   (Year)   (Country)

FOR
COPYRIGHT
OFFICE USE
ONLY

DO NOT WRITE ABOVE THIS LINE. FOR COPYRIGHT OFFICE USE ONLY

☐ Title of Contribution: ....
Title of Periodical: .... Vol. ..... No. ..... Issue Date .... Pages ......
Date of First Publication: .... Nation of First Publication ....
(Month)   (Day)   (Year)   (Country)

B
Continued

☐ Title of Contribution: ....
Title of Periodical: .... Vol. ..... No. ..... Issue Date .... Pages ......
Date of First Publication: .... Nation of First Publication ....
(Month)   (Day)   (Year)   (Country)

☐ Title of Contribution: ....
Title of Periodical: .... Vol. ..... No. ..... Issue Date .... Pages ......
Date of First Publication: .... Nation of First Publication ....
(Month)   (Day)   (Year)   (Country)

☐ Title of Contribution: ....
Title of Periodical: .... Vol. ..... No. ..... Issue Date .... Pages ......
Date of First Publication: .... Nation of First Publication ....
(Month)   (Day)   (Year)   (Country)

☐ Title of Contribution: ....
Title of Periodical: .... Vol. ..... No. ..... Issue Date .... Pages ......
Date of First Publication: .... Nation of First Publication ....
(Month)   (Day)   (Year)   (Country)

☐ Title of Contribution: ....
Title of Periodical: .... Vol. ..... No. ..... Issue Date .... Pages ......
Date of First Publication: .... Nation of First Publication ....
(Month)   (Day)   (Year)   (Country)

☐ Title of Contribution: ....
Title of Periodical: .... Vol. ..... No. ..... Issue Date .... Pages ......
Date of First Publication: .... Nation of First Publication ....
(Month)   (Day)   (Year)   (Country)

☐ Title of Contribution: ....
Title of Periodical: .... Vol. ..... No. ..... Issue Date .... Pages ......
Date of First Publication: .... Nation of First Publication ....
(Month)   (Day)   (Year)   (Country)

☐ Title of Contribution: ....
Title of Periodical: .... Vol. ..... No. ..... Issue Date .... Pages ......
Date of First Publication: .... Nation of First Publication ....
(Month)   (Day)   (Year)   (Country)

☐ Title of Contribution: ....
Title of Periodical: .... Vol. ..... No. ..... Issue Date .... Pages ......
Date of First Publication: .... Nation of First Publication ....
(Month)   (Day)   (Year)   (Country)

☐ Title of Contribution: ....
Title of Periodical: .... Vol. ..... No. ..... Issue Date .... Pages ......
Date of First Publication: .... Nation of First Publication ....
(Month)   (Day)   (Year)   (Country)

☐ Title of Contribution: ....
Title of Periodical: .... Vol. ..... No. ..... Issue Date .... Pages ......
Date of First Publication: .... Nation of First Publication ....
(Month)   (Day)   (Year)   (Country)

▲ October 1991—25,000   U.S. GOVERNMENT PRINTING OFFICE: 1991: 312-432/40,008

THIS FORM:

- Can be used solely as an adjunct to a basic application for copyright registration.

- Is not acceptable unless submitted together with Form TX, Form PA, or Form VA.

- Is acceptable only if the group of works listed on it all qualify for a single copyright registration under 17 U.S.C. § 408 (c)(2).

 **FORM GR/CP**

UNITED STATES COPYRIGHT OFFICE
LIBRARY OF CONGRESS
WASHINGTON, D.C. 20559

ADJUNCT APPLICATION
for Copyright Registration for a
Group of Contributions to Periodicals

WHEN TO USE FORM GR/CP: Form GR/CP is the appropriate adjunct application form to use when you are submitting a basic application on Form TX, Form PA, or Form VA, for a group of works that qualify for a single registration under section 408(c)(2) of the copyright statute.

WHEN DOES A GROUP OF WORKS QUALIFY FOR A SINGLE REGISTRATION UNDER 17 U.S.C. §408 (c)(2)?

For all works first published on or after March 1, 1989, a single copyright registration for a group of works can be made if **all** of the following conditions are met:

(1) All of the works are by the same author, who is an individual (not an employer for hire); and

(2) All of the works were first published as contribution to periodicals (including newspapers) within a 12-month period; and

(3) All of the works have the same copyright claimant; and

(4) One copy of the entire periodical issue or newspaper section in which each contribution was first published must be deposited with the application; and

(5) The application must identify each contribution separately, including the periodical containing it and the date of its first publication.

Note: For contributions that were first published prior to March 1, 1989, in addition to the conditions listed above, each contribution as first published must have borne a separate copyright notice, and the name of the owner of copyright in the work (or an abbreviation or alternative designation of the owner) must have been the same in each notice.

How to Apply for Group Registration:

First: Study the information on this page to make sure that all of the works you want to register together as a group qualify for a single registration.

Second: Turn this page over and read through the detailed instructions for group registration. Decide which form you should use for the basic registration (Form TX for nondramatic literary works; or Form PA for musical, dramatic, and other works of the performing arts; or Form VA for pictorial and graphic works). Be sure that you have all of the information you need before you start filling out both the basic and the adjunct application forms.

Third: Complete the basic application form, following the detailed instructions accompanying it **and the special instructions on the reverse of this page.**

Fourth: Complete the adjunct application on Form GR/CP and mail it, together with the basic application form and the required copy of each contribution, to: Register of Copyrights, Library of Congress, Washington, D.C. 20559. Unless you have a Deposit Account in the Copyright Office, your application and copies must be accompanied by a check or money order for $20, payable to: *Register of Copyrights.*

PROCEDURE FOR GROUP REGISTRATION

TWO APPLICATION FORMS MUST BE FILED

When you apply for a single registration to cover a group of contributions to periodicals, you must submit two application forms:

(1) A basic application on either Form TX, or Form PA, or Form VA. It must contain all of the information required for copyright registration except the titles and information concerning publication of the contributions.

(2) An adjunct application on Form GR/CP. The purpose of this form is to provide separate identification for each of the contributions and to give information about their first publication, as required by the statute.

WHICH BASIC APPLICATION FORM TO USE

The basic application form you choose to submit should be determined by the nature of the contributions you are registering. As long as they meet the statutory qualifications for group registration (outlined on the reverse of this page), the contributions can be registered together even if they are entirely different in nature, type, or content. However, you must choose which of three forms is generally the most appropriate on which to submit your basic application:

Form TX: for nondramatic literary works consisting primarily of text. Examples are fiction, verse, articles, news stories, features, essays, reviews, editorials, columns, quizzes, puzzles, and advertising copy.

Form PA: for works of the performing arts. Examples are music, drama, choreography, and pantomimes.

Form VA: for works of the visual arts. Examples are photographs, drawings, paintings, prints, art reproductions, cartoons, comic strips, charts, diagrams, maps, pictorial ornamentation, and pictorial or graphic material published as advertising.

If your contributions differ in nature, choose the form most suitable for the majority of them.

REGISTRATION FEE FOR GROUP REGISTRATION

The fee for registration of a group of contributions to periodicals is $20, no matter how many contributions are listed Form GR/CP. Unless you maintain a Deposit Account in the Copyright Office, the registration fee must accompany your application forms and copies. Make your remittance payable to: *Register of Copyrights.*

WHAT COPIES SHOULD BE DEPOSITED FOR GROUP REGISTRATION?

The application forms you file for group registration must be accompanied by one complete copy of each contribution listed in Form GR/CP, exactly as the contribution was first published in a periodical. The deposit must consist of the entire issue of the periodical containing the contribution; or, if the contribution was first published in a newspaper, the deposit should consist of the entire section in which the contribution appeared. Tear sheets or proof copies are not acceptable for deposit.

COPYRIGHT NOTICE REQUIREMENTS

For published works, the law provides that a copyright notice in a specified form "may be placed on all publicly distributed copies from which the work can be visually perceived." The required form of the notice generally consists of three elements: (1) the symbol "©", or the word "Copyright", or the abbreviation "Copr."; (2) the year of first publication of the work; and (3) the name of the owner of copyright in the work, or an abbreviation or alternative form of the name. For example: "© 1991 Samuel Craig".

Works published prior to March 1, 1989, **must** carry a notice of copyright or risk loss of copyright protection. Furthermore, among the conditions for group registration of contributions to periodicals for works first **published prior to March 1, 1989,** the statute establishes two requirements involving the copyright notice:

(1) Each of the contributions as first published must have borne a separate copyright notice; and

(2) "The name of the owner of copyright in the work, or an abbreviation by which the name can be recognized, or a generally known alternative designation of the owner" must have been the same in each notice.

Works first published after March 1, 1989, need not meet the two above requirements.

> **NOTE:** The advantage of group registration is that it allows any number of works published within a 12-month period to be registered "on the basis of a single deposit, application, and registration fee." On the other hand, group registration may also have disadvantages under certain circumstances. If infringement of a published work begins before the work has been registered, the copyright owner can still obtain the ordinary remedies for copyright infringement (including injunctions, actual damages and profits, and impounding and disposition of infringing articles). However, in that situation--where the copyright in a published work is infringed before registration is made--the owner cannot obtain special remedies (statutory damages and attorney's fees) unless registration was made within 3 months after first publication of the work.

HOW TO FILL OUT THE BASIC APPLICATION FORM WHEN APPLYING FOR GROUP REGISTRATION

In general, the instructions for filling out the basic application (Form TX, Form PA, or Form VA) apply to group registrations. In addition, please observe the following specific instructions:

Space 1 (Title): Do not give information concerning any of the contributions in space 1 of the basic application. Instead, in the block headed "Title of this Work," state: "See Form GR/CP, attached." Leave the other blocks in space 1 blank.

Space 2 (Author): Give the name and other information concerning the author of all of the contributions listed in Form GR/CP. To qualify for group registration, all of the contributions must have been written by the same individual author.

Space 3 (Creation and Publication): In the block calling for the year of creation, give the year of creation of the last of the contributions to be completed. Leave the block calling for the date and nation of first publication blank.

Space 4 (Claimant): Give all of the requested information, which must be the same for all of the contributions listed on Form GR/CP.

Other Spaces: Complete all of the applicable spaces, and be sure that the form is signed in the certification space.

HOW TO FILL OUT FORM GR/CP

Part A: IDENTIFICATION OF APPLICATION

• **Identification of Basic Application:** Indicate, by checking one of the boxes, which of the basic application forms (Form TX, or Form PA, or Form VA) you are filing for registration.

• **Identification of Author and Claimant:** Give the name of the individual author exactly as it appears in line 2 of the basic application, and give the name of the copyright claimant exactly as it appears in line 4. These must be the same for all of the contributions listed in Part B of Form GR/CP.

PART B: REGISTRATION FOR GROUP OF CONTRIBUTIONS

• **General Instructions:** Under the statute, a group of contributions to periodicals will qualify for a single registration only if the application "identifies each work separately, including the periodical containing it and its date of first publication." Part B of the Form GR/CP provides lines enough to list 19 separate contributions; if you need more space, use additional Forms GR/CP. If possible, list the contributions in the order of their publication, giving the earliest first. Number each line consecutively.

• **Important:** All of the contributions listed on Form GR/CP must have been published within a single 12-month period. This does not mean that all of the contributions must have been published during the same calendar year, but it does mean that, to be grouped in a single application, the earliest and latest contributions must not have been published more than 12 months apart. Example: Contributions published on April 1, 1978, July 1, 1978, and March 1, 1979, could be grouped together, but a contribution published on April 15, 1979, could not be registered with them as part of the group.

• **Title of Contribution:** Each contribution must be given a title that is capable of identifying that particular work and of distinguishing it from others. If the contribution as published in the periodical bears a title (or an identifying phrase that could serve as a title), transcribe its wording completely and exactly.

• **Identification of Periodical:** Give the over-all title of the periodical in which the contribution was first published, together with the volume and issue number (if any) and the issue date.

• **Pages:** Give the number of the page of the periodical issue on which the contribution appeared. If the contribution covered more than one page, give the inclusive pages, if possible.

• **First Publication:** The statute defines "publication" as "the distribution of copies or phonorecords of a work to the public by sale or other transfer of ownership, or by rental, lease, or lending;" a work is also "published" if there has been an "offering to distribute copies or phonorecords to a group of persons for purposes of further distribution, public performance, or public display." Give the full date (month, day, and year) when and the country where, publication of the periodical issue containing the contribution first occurred. If first publication took place simultaneously in the United States and other countries, it is sufficient to state "U.S.A."

FORM RE
UNITED STATES COPYRIGHT OFFICE

REGISTRATION NUMBER

EFFECTIVE DATE OF RENEWAL REGISTRATION
. . . .
(Month)   (Day)   (Year)

DO NOT WRITE ABOVE THIS LINE. FOR COPYRIGHT OFFICE USE ONLY

1 Renewal Claimant(s)	**RENEWAL CLAIMANT(S), ADDRESS(ES), AND STATEMENT OF CLAIM:** (See Instructions)

1   Name . . . .
    Address . . . .
    Claiming as . . . .
                                            (Use appropriate statement from instructions)

2   Name . . . .
    Address . . . .
    Claiming as . . . .
                                              (Use appropriate statement from instructions)

3   Name . . . .
    Address . . . .
    Claiming as . . . .
                                              (Use appropriate statement from instructions)

2
 Work
 Renewed

TITLE OF WORK IN WHICH RENEWAL IS CLAIMED:

RENEWABLE MATTER:

CONTRIBUTION TO PERIODICAL OR COMPOSITE WORK:
Title of periodical or composite work: . . . .
If a periodical or other serial, give: Vol. . . . . No. . . . . Issue Date . . . .

3
 Author(s)

AUTHOR(S) OF RENEWABLE MATTER:

4
 Facts of
 Original
 Registration

ORIGINAL REGISTRATION NUMBER:
. . . .

ORIGINAL COPYRIGHT CLAIMANT:

ORIGINAL DATE OF COPYRIGHT:
● If the original registration for this work was made in published form, give:
DATE OF PUBLICATION: . . . .
                 (Month)   (Day)   (Year)   **} OR {** ● If the original registration for this work was made in unpublished form, give:
DATE OF REGISTRATION: . . . .
                 (Month)   (Day)   (Year)

	EXAMINED BY:	RENEWAL APPLICATION RECEIVED:	FOR COPYRIGHT OFFICE USE ONLY
	CHECKED BY:		
	CORRESPONDENCE: ☐ YES	REMITTANCE NUMBER AND DATE:	
	DEPOSIT ACCOUNT FUNDS USED: ☐		

DO NOT WRITE ABOVE THIS LINE. FOR COPYRIGHT OFFICE USE ONLY

RENEWAL FOR GROUP OF WORKS BY SAME AUTHOR: To make a single registration for a group of works by the same individual author published as contributions to periodicals (see instructions), give full information about each contribution. If more space is needed, request continuation sheet (Form RE/CON).

5 Renewal for Group of Works

1
Title of Contribution: ....
Title of Periodical: .... Vol. .... No. .... Issue Date ....
Date of Publication: .... Registration Number: ....
          (Month)   (Day)   (Year)

2
Title of Contribution: ....
Title of Periodical: .... Vol. .... No. .... Issue Date ....
Date of Publication: .... Registration Number: ....
          (Month)   (Day)   (Year)

3
Title of Contribution: ....
Title of Periodical: .... Vol. .... No. .... Issue Date ....
Date of Publication: .... Registration Number: ....
          (Month)   (Day)   (Year)

4
Title of Contribution: ....
Title of Periodical: .... Vol. .... No. .... Issue Date ....
Date of Publication: .... Registration Number: ....
          (Month)   (Day)   (Year)

5
Title of Contribution: ....
Title of Periodical: .... Vol. .... No. .... Issue Date ....
Date of Publication: .... Registration Number: ....
          (Month)   (Day)   (Year)

6
Title of Contribution: ....
Title of Periodical: .... Vol. .... No. .... Issue Date ....
Date of Publication: .... Registration Number: ....
          (Month)   (Day)   (Year)

DEPOSIT ACCOUNT: If the registration fee is to be charged to a Deposit Account established in the Copyright Office, give name and number of Account.

Name :..
Account Number: ....

CORRESPONDENCE: Give name and address to which correspondence about this application should be sent:
Name: ....
Address: ....
                                        (Apt.)
        (City)   (State)   (ZIP)

6 Fee and Correspondence

CERTIFICATION* I, the undersigned, hereby certify that I am the: (Check one)
☐ renewal claimant   ☐ duly authorized agent of: ....
                                     (Name of renewal claimant)

of the work identified in this application and that the statements made by me in this application are correct to the best of my knowledge.

Handwritten signature: (X) ....

Typed or printed name: ....

Date: ....

***17U.S.C. §506(e): FALSE REPRESENTATION**—Any person who knowingly makes a false representation of a material fact in the application for copyright registration provided for by section 409, or in any written statement filed in connection with the application, shall be fined not more than $2,500.

7 Certification (Application must be signed)

	MAIL CERTIFICATE TO	**8**
.... (Name)		Address for Return of Certificate
.... (Number, Street and Apartment Number)	(Certificate will be mailed in window envelope)	
.... (City) (State) (ZIP Code)		

APPLICATION FOR
Renewal Registration

 **FORM RE**

UNITED STATES COPYRIGHT OFFICE
LIBRARY OF CONGRESS
WASHINGTON, D.C. 20559

HOW TO REGISTER A RENEWAL CLAIM:

● **First:** Study the information on this page and make sure you know the answers to two questions:
　　(1) What are the renewal time limits in your case?
　　(2) Who can claim the renewal?

● **Second:** Turn this page over and read through the specific instructions for filling out Form RE. Make sure, before starting to complete the form, that the copyright is now eligible for renewal, that you are authorized to file a renewal claim, and that you have all of the information about the copyright you will need.

● **Third:** Complete all applicable spaces on Form RE, following the line-by-line instructions on the back of this page. Use typewriter, or print the information in dark ink.

● **Fourth:** Detach this sheet and send your completed Form RE to: Register of Copyrights, Library of Congress, Washington, D.C. 20559. Unless you have a Deposit Account in the Copyright Office, your application must be accompanied by a check or money order for $12, payable to: *Register of Copyrights*. Do not send copies, phonorecords, or supporting documents with your renewal application.

WHAT IS RENEWAL OF COPYRIGHT? For works originally copyrighted between January 1, 1950 and December 31, 1977, the statute now in effect provides for a first term of copyright protection lasting for 28 years, with the possibility of renewal for a second term of 47 years. If a valid renewal registration is made for a work, its total copyright term is 75 years (a first term of 28 years, plus a renewal term of 47 years). Example: For a work copyrighted in 1960, the first term will expire in 1988, but if renewed at the proper time the copyright will last through the end of 2035.

SOME BASIC POINTS ABOUT RENEWAL:
　(1) There are strict time limits and deadlines for renewing a copyright.
　(2) Only certain persons who fall into specific categories named in the law can claim renewal.
　(3) The present copyright law does away with renewal requirements for works first copyrighted after 1977. However, copyrights that were already in their first copyright term on January 1, 1978 (that is, works originally copyrighted between January 1, 1950 and December 31, 1977) **still have to be renewed** in order to be protected for a second term.

TIME LIMITS FOR RENEWAL REGISTRATION: The present copyright statute provides that, in order to renew a copyright, the renewal application and fee must be received in the Copyright Office "within one year prior to the expiration of the copyright." It also provides that all terms of copyright will run through the end of the year in which they would otherwise expire. Since all copyright terms will expire on December 31st of their last year, all periods for renewal registration will run from December 31st of the 27th year of the copyright, and will end on December 31st of the following year.

To determine the time limits for renewal in your case:
　(1) First, find out the date of original copyright for the work. (In the case of works originally registered in unpublished form, the date of copyright is the date of registration; for published works, copyright begins on the date of first publication.)
　(2) Then add 28 years to the year the work was originally copyrighted.
Your answer will be the calendar year during which the copyright will be eligible for renewal, and December 31st of that year will be the renewal deadline. Example: A work originally copyrighted on April 19, 1963, will be eligible for renewal between December 31, 1990, and December 31, 1991.

WHO MAY CLAIM RENEWAL: Renewal copyright may be claimed only by those persons specified in the law. Except in the case of four specific types of works, the law gives the right to claim renewal to the individual author of the work, regardless of who owned the copyright during the original term. If the author is dead, the statute gives the right to claim renewal to certain of the author's beneficiaries (widow and children, executors, or next of kin, depending on the circumstances). The present owner (proprietor) of the copyright is entitled to claim renewal only in four specified cases, as explained in more detail on the reverse of this page.

CAUTION: Renewal registration is possible only if an acceptable application and fee are **received** in the Copyright Office during the renewal period and before the renewal deadline. If an acceptable application and fee are not received before the renewal deadline, the work falls into the public domain and the copyright cannot be renewed. The Copyright Office has no discretion to extend the renewal time limits.

INSTRUCTIONS FOR COMPLETING FORM RE

SPACE 1: RENEWAL CLAIM(S)
● **General Instructions:** In order for this application to result in a valid renewal, space 1 must identify one or more of the persons who are entitled to renew the copyright under the statute. Give the full name and address of each claimant, with a statement of the basis of each claim, using the wording given in these instructions.
● **Persons Entitled to Renew:**
A. The following persons may claim renewal in all types of works except those enumerated in Paragraph B, below:
1. The author, if living. State the claim as: *the author*
2. The widow, widower, and/or children of the author, if the author is not living. State the claim as:
the widow (widower) of the author . . . .
(Name of author)
and/or the child (children) of the deceased author . . . .
(Name of author)
3. The author's executor(s), if the author left a will and if there is no surviving widow, widower, or child. State the claim as: *the executor(s) of the author* . . . .
(Name of author)

4. The next of kin of the author, if the author left no will and if there is no surviving widow, widower, or child. State the claim as: *the next of kin of the deceased author* . . . . *there being no will.*
(Name of author)
B. In the case of the following four types of works, the proprietor (owner of the copyright at the time of renewal registration) may claim renewal:
1. Posthumous work (a work as to which no copyright assignment or other contract for exploitation has occurred during the author's lifetime). State the claim as: *proprietor of copyright in a posthumous work.*
2. Periodical, cyclopedic, or other composite work. State the claim as: *proprietor of copyright in a composite work.*
3. "Work copyrighted by a corporate body otherwise than as assignee or licensee of the individual author." State the claim as: *proprietor of copyright in a work copyrighted by a corporate body otherwise than as assignee or licensee of the individual author.* (This type of claim is considered appropriate in relatively few cases.)
4. Work copyrighted by an employer for whom such work was made for hire. State the claim as: *proprietor of copyright in a work made for hire.*

SPACE 2: WORK RENEWED
● **General Instructions:** This space is to identify the particular work being renewed. The information given here should agree with that appearing in the certificate of original registration.
● **Title:** Give the full title of the work, together with any subtitles or descriptive wording included with the title in the original registration. In the case of a musical composition, give the specific instrumentation of the work.
● **Renewable Matter:** Copyright in a new version of a previous work (such as an arrangement, translation, dramatization, compilation, or work republished with new matter) covers only the additions, changes, or other new material appearing for the first time in that version. If this work was a new version, state in general the new matter upon which copyright was claimed.

● **Contribution to Periodical, Serial, or other Composite Work:** Separate renewal registration is possible for a work published as a contribution to a periodical, serial, or other composite work, whether the contribution was copyrighted independently or as part of the larger work in which it appeared. Each contribution published in a separate issue ordinarily requires a separate renewal registration. However, the law provides an alternative, permitting groups of periodical contributions by the same individual author to be combined under a single renewal application and fee in certain cases.
If this renewal application covers a single contribution, give all of the requested information in space 2. If you are seeking to renew a group of contributions, include a reference such as "See page 5" in space 2 and give the requested information about all of the contributions in space 5.

SPACE 3: AUTHOR(S)
● **General Instructions:** The copyright secured in a new version of a work is independent of any copyright protection in material published earlier. The only "authors" of a new version are those who contributed copyrightable matter to it. Thus, for renewal purposes, the person

who wrote the original version on which the new work is based cannot be regarded as an "author" of the new version, unless that person also contributed to the new matter.
● **Authors of Renewable Matter:** Give the full names of all authors who contributed copyrightable matter to this particular version of the work.

SPACE 4: FACTS OF ORIGINAL REGISTRATION
● **General Instructions:** Each item in space 4 should agree with the information appearing in the original registration for the work. If the work being renewed is a single contribution to a periodical or composite work that was not separately registered, give information about the particular issue in which the contribution appeared. You may leave this space blank if you are completing space 5.
● **Original Registration Number:** Give the full registration number, which is a series of numerical digits, preceded by one or more letters.

The registration number appears in the upper right hand corner of the certificate of registration.
● **Original Copyright Claimant:** Give the name in which ownership of the copyright was claimed in the original registration.
● **Date of Publication or Registration:** Give only one date. If the original registration gave a publication date, it should be transcribed here; otherwise the registration was for an unpublished work, and the date of registration should be given.

SPACE 5: GROUP RENEWALS
● **General Instructions:** A single renewal registration can be made for a group of works if **all** of the following statutory conditions are met: (1) all of the works were written by the same author, who is named in space 3 and who is or was an individual (not an employer for hire); (2) all of the works were first published as contributions to periodicals (including newspapers) and were copyrighted on their first publication; (3) the renewal claimant or claimants, and the basis of claim or claims, as stated in space 1, is the same for all of the works; (4) the renewal application and fee are "received not more than 28 or less than 27 years after the 31st day of December of the calendar year in which all of the works were first published"; and (5) the renewal application identifies each work separately, including the periodical

containing it and the date of first publication.
Time Limits for Group Renewals: To be renewed as a group, all of the contributions must have been first published during the same calendar year. For example, suppose six contributions by the same author were published on April 1, 1963, July 1, 1963, November 1, 1963, February 1, 1964, July 1, 1964, and March 1, 1965. The three 1963 copyrights can be combined and renewed at any time during 1991, and the two 1964 copyrights can be renewed as a group during 1992, but the 1965 copyright must be renewed by itself, in 1993.
Identification of Each Work: Give all of the requested information for each contribution. The registration number should be that for the contribution itself if it was separately registered, and the registration number for the periodical issue if it was not.

SPACES 6, 7, AND 8:
FEE, MAILING INSTRUCTIONS, AND CERTIFICATION
● **Deposit Account and Mailing Instructions (Space 6):**
If you maintain a Deposit Account in the Copyright Office, identify it in space 6. Otherwise, you will need to send the renewal registration fee of $12 with your form. The space headed "Correspondence" should contain the name and address of the person to be consulted if

correspondence about the form becomes necessary.
● **Certification (Space 7):** The renewal application is not acceptable unless it bears the handwritten signature of the renewal claimant or the duly authorized agent of the renewal claimant.
● **Address for Return of Certificate (Space 8):** The address box must be completed legibly, since the certificate will be returned in a window envelope.

CONTINUATION SHEET
FOR APPLICATION FORMS

- This Continuation Sheet is used in conjunction with Basic Forms PA, SE, SR, TX, and VA **only**. Indicate which basic form you are continuing in the space in the upper right-hand corner.

- If at all possible, try to fit the information called for into the spaces provided on the basic form.

- If you do not have space enough for all the information you need to give on the basic form, use this continuation sheet and submit it with the basic form.

- If you submit this continuation sheet, clip (do not tape or staple) it to the basic form and fold the two together before submitting them.

- **Part A** of this sheet is intended to identify the basic application.
  Part B is a continuation of Space 2.
  Part C (on the reverse side of this sheet) is for the continuation of Spaces 1, 4, or 6. The other spaces on the basic form call for specific items of information and should not need continuation.

DO NOT WRITE ABOVE THIS LINE. FOR COPYRIGHT OFFICE USE ONLY

FORM ____ /CON
UNITED STATES COPYRIGHT OFFICE

REGISTRATION NUMBER

PA PAU SE SEG SEU SR SRU TX TXU VA VAU

EFFECTIVE DATE OF REGISTRATION

(Month)   (Day)   (Year)

CONTINUATION SHEET RECEIVED

Page _____ of _____ pages

A
Identification of Application

IDENTIFICATION OF CONTINUATION SHEET: This sheet is a continuation of the application for copyright registration on the basic form submitted for the following work:
- TITLE: (Give the title as given under the heading "Title of this Work" in Space 1 of the basic form.)

- NAMES(S) AND ADDRESS(ES) OF COPYRIGHT CLAIMANT(S) : (Give the name and address of at least one copyright claimant as given in Space 4 of the basic form.)

B
Continuation of Space 2

d

NAME OF AUTHOR ▼	DATES OF BIRTH AND DEATH
	Year Born ▼ Year Died ▼

Was this contribution to the work a "work made for hire"?
☐ Yes
☐ No

AUTHOR'S NATIONALITY OR DOMICILE
Name of Country
OR { Citizen of ▶ _____
Domiciled in ▶ _____

WAS THIS AUTHOR'S CONTRIBUTION TO THE WORK
Anonymous? ☐ Yes ☐ No
Pseudonymous? ☐ Yes ☐ No
If the answer to either of these questions is "Yes" see detailed instructions.

NATURE OF AUTHORSHIP Briefly describe nature of the material created by the author in which copyright is claimed. ▼

e

NAME OF AUTHOR ▼	DATES OF BIRTH AND DEATH
	Year Born ▼ Year Died ▼

Was this contribution to the work a "work made for hire"?
☐ Yes
☐ No

AUTHOR'S NATIONALITY OR DOMICILE
Name of Country
OR { Citizen of ▶ _____
Domiciled in ▶ _____

WAS THIS AUTHOR'S CONTRIBUTION TO THE WORK
Anonymous? ☐ Yes ☐ No
Pseudonymous? ☐ Yes ☐ No
If the answer to either of these questions is "Yes" see detailed instructions.

NATURE OF AUTHORSHIP Briefly describe nature of the material created by the author in which copyright is claimed. ▼

f

NAME OF AUTHOR ▼	DATES OF BIRTH AND DEATH
	Year Born ▼ Year Died ▼

Was this contribution to the work a "work made for hire"?
☐ Yes
☐ No

AUTHOR'S NATIONALITY OR DOMICILE
Name of Country
OR { Citizen of ▶ _____
Domiciled in ▶ _____

WAS THIS AUTHOR'S CONTRIBUTION TO THE WORK
Anonymous? ☐ Yes ☐ No
Pseudonymous? ☐ Yes ☐ No
If the answer to either of these questions is "Yes" see detailed instructions.

NATURE OF AUTHORSHIP Briefly describe nature of the material created by the author in which copyright is claimed. ▼

Use the reverse side of this sheet if you need more space for continuation of Spaces 1, 4, or 6 of the basic form.

CONTINUATION OF (Check which): ☐ **Space 1**   ☐ **Space 4**   ☐ **Space 6**

C

**Continuation
of other
Spaces**

November 1991—50,000

☆U.S. GOVERNMENT PRINTING OFFICE: 1991-312-432/40,010

APPENDIX E

Trade Secrets

THE UNIFORM TRADE SECRETS ACT

§ 1. Definitions

As used in this Act, unless the context requires otherwise:

(1) "Improper means" includes theft, bribery, misrepresentation, breach or inducement of a breach of a duty to maintain secrecy, or espionage through electronic or other means. Reverse engineering or independent derivation alone shall not be considered improper means.

(2) "Misappropriation" means:

(i) Acquisition of a trade secret of another by a person who knows or has reason to know that the trade secret was acquired by improper means; or

(ii) Disclosure or use of a trade secret of another without express or implied consent by a person who:

(A) Used improper means to acquire knowledge of the trade secret; or

(B) At the time of disclosure or use, knew or had reason to know that his or her knowledge of the trade secret was:

(I) Derived from or through a person who had utilized improper means to acquire it;

(II) Acquired under circumstances giving rise to a duty to maintain its secrecy or limit its use; or

(III) Derived from or through a person who owed a duty to the person seeking relief to maintain its secrecy or limit its use; or

(C) Before a material change of his or her position, knew or had reason to know that it was a trade secret and that knowledge of it had been acquired by accident or mistake.

(3) "Person" means a natural person, corporation, business trust, estate, trust, partnership, association, joint venture, government, governmental subdivision or agency, or any other legal or commercial entity.

(4) "Trade secret" means information, including a formula, pattern, compilation, program, device, method, technique, or process that:

(i) Derives independent economic value, actual or potential, from not being generally known to the public or to other persons who can obtain economic value from its disclosure or use; and

(ii) Is the subject of efforts that are reasonable under the circumstances to maintain its secrecy.

§ 2. Injunctive Relief

(a) Actual or threatened misappropriation may be enjoined. Upon application to the court, an injunction shall be terminated when the trade secret has ceased to exist, but the injunction may be continued for an additional period of time in order to eliminate commercial advantage that otherwise would be derived from the misappropriation.

(b) In exceptional circumstances, an injunction may condition future use upon payment of a reasonable circumstances include, but are not limited to, a material and prejudicial change of position prior to acquiring knowledge or reason to know of misappropriation that renders a prohibitive injunction inequitable.

(c) In appropriate circumstances, affirmative acts to protect a trade secret may be compelled by court order.

§ 3. Damages

(a) Except to the extent that a material and prejudicial change of position prior to acquiring knowledge or reason to know of misappropriation renders a monetary recovery inequitable, a complainant is entitled to recover damages for misappropriation. Damages can include both the actual loss caused by misappropriation and the unjust enrichment caused by misappropriation that is not taken into account in computing actual loss. In lieu of damages measured by any other methods, the damages caused by misappropriation may be measured by imposition of liability for a reasonable royalty for a misappropriator's unauthorized disclosure or use of a trade secret.

(b) If willful and malicious misappropriation exists, the court may award exemplary damages in an amount not exceeding twice any award made under subdivision (a) or (b).

§ 4. Attorney Fees

If (i) a claim of misappropriation is made in bad faith, (ii) a motion to terminate an injunction is made or resisted in bad faith, or (iii) willful and malicious misappropriation exists, the court may award reasonable attorney's fees to the prevailing party.

§ 5. Preservation of Secrecy

In an action under this Act, a court shall preserve the secrecy of an alleged trade secret by reasonable means, which may include granting protective orders in connection with discovery proceedings, holding in-camera hearings, sealing the records of the action, and ordering any person involved in the litigation not to disclose an alleged trade secret without prior court approval.

§ 6. Statute of Limitations

An action for misappropriation must be brought within three years after the misappropriation is discovered or by the exercise of reasonable diligence should have been discovered. For the purposes of this section, a continuing misappropriation constitutes a single claim.

§ 7. Effect of Title on Other Statutes or Remedies

(a) Except as provided in subsection (b), this Act displaces conflicting tort, restitutionary, and other law of this State providing civil remedies for misappropriation of a trade secret.

(b) This Act does not affect

(1) contractual remedies, whether or not based upon misappropriation of a trade secret,

(2) other civil remedies that are not based upon misappropriation of a trade secret; or

(3) criminal remedies, whether or not based upon misappropriation of a trade secret.

§ 8. Uniformity of Application and Construction

This Act shall be applied and construed to effectuate its general purpose to make uniform the law with respect to the subject of this Act among states enacting it.

§ 9. Short Title

This act may be cited as the Uniform Trade Secrets Act.

§ 10. Severability

If any provision of this Act or its application to any person or circumstances is held invalid, the invalidity does not affect other provisions or applications of the title which can be given effect without the invalid provision or application, and to this end the provisions of this Act are severable.

§ 11. Time of Taking Effect

This Act takes effect on _____ and does not apply to misappropriation occurring prior to the effective date. With respect to a continuing misappropriation that began prior to the effective date, the Act also does not apply to continuing misappropriation that occurs after the effective date.

States That Have Adopted Some Version of the Uniform Trade Secrets Act

	Statute Adopted or Based upon UTSA
Alabama*	Ala. Code. § 8-27-1 *et seq.*
Alaska	Alaska Stat. § 45.50.910 *et seq.*
Arkansas	Ark. Code Ann. § 4-75-601 *et seq.*
California	Cal. Civ. Code § 3426 *et seq.*
Colorado	Colo. Rev. Stat § 7-74-101
Connecticut	Conn. Gen. Stat. § 35-50 *et seq.*
Delaware	Del. Code Ann. tit. 6, § 2001 *et seq.*
District of Columbia	D.C. Code Ann. § 48-501 *et seq.*
Florida	Fla. Stat. Ann. § 688.001 *et seq.*
Hawaii	Haw. Rev. Stat. § 482B-1 *et seq.*
Idaho	Idaho Code § 48-801 *et seq.*
Illinois	Ill. Ann. Stat. ch. 140, paras. 351-59
Indiana	Ind. Code. Ann. § 24-3-1
Kansas	Kan. Stat. Ann. § 60-3320 *et seq.*
Louisiana	La. Rev. Stat. Ann. § 51:1431 *et seq.*
Maine	Me. Rev. Stat. Ann. tit. 10, § 1541 *et seq.*
Maryland	Md. Com. Law Code Ann. § 11-1201 *et seq.*
Minnesota	Minn. Stat. Ann. § 325C.01 *et seq.*
Montana	Mont. Code Ann. § 30-14-401 *et seq.*
Nebraska	Neb. Rev. Stat. § 87-501 *et seq.*
Nevada	Nev. Rev. Stat. § 600A.010 *et seq.*
New Mexico	N.M. Stat. Ann. § 57-3A-1 *et seq.*
North Carolina*	N.C. Gen. Stat. § 66-152 *et seq.*
North Dakota	N.D. Cent. Code § 47-25.1-01 *et seq.*
Oklahoma	Okla. Gen. Laws § 6-41-1
Oregon	Or. Rev. Stat. § 646-461 *et seq.*
Rhode Island	R.I. Gen. Laws § 6-41-1 *et seq.*
South Dakota	S.D. Codified Laws § 37-29-1 *et seq.*
Utah	Utah Code Ann. § 13-24-1 *et seq.*
Virginia	Va. Code Ann. § 59.1-336 *et seq.*
Washington	Wash. Rev. Code. Ann. § 19.108.010 *et seq.*
West Virginia	W. Va. Code. § 47-22-1 *et seq.*
Wisconsin	Wis. Stat. Ann. § 134.90

*Although they have adopted portions of the UTSA, Alabama and North Carolina are considered to be "major departures" from the UTSA because Alabama narrows trade secret protection and North Carolina broadens it.

APPENDIX F

Trademarks

DECLARATION OF USE OF A MARK UNDER SECTION 8 OF THE TRADEMARK ACT OF 1946, AS AMENDED	MARK (Identify the mark)	
	REGISTRATION NO.	DATE OF REGISTRATION:

TO THE ASSISTANT SECRETARY AND COMMISSIONER OF PATENTS AND TRADEMARKS:

REGISTRANT'S NAME:[1]

REGISTRANT'S CURRENT MAILING ADDRESS: _____
_____
_____

GOODS AND/OR SERVICES AND USE IN COMMERCE STATEMENT:

The mark shown in Registration No. _____ owned by the above-identified registrant is in use in

_____ commerce on or in connection with all of the goods and/or services identified in the
(type of)[2]

registration, (*except* for the following)[3] _____

_____ ;

as evidenced by the attached specimen(s)[4] showing the mark as currently used.

DECLARATION

The undersigned being hereby warned that willful false statements and the like so made are punishable by fine or imprisonment, or both, under 18 U.S.C. 1001, and that such willful false statements may jeopardize the validity of this document, declares that he/she is properly authorized to execute this document on behalf of the registrant; he/she believes the registrant to be the owner of the above identified registration; the trademark/service mark is in use in commerce; and all statements made of his/her own knowledge are true and all statements made on information and belief are believed to be true.

_____   _____
Date   Signature

_____   _____
Telephone Number   Print or Type Name and Position
                                                           [if applicable][5]

PTO Form 1583 (Rev. 1/93)   U.S. DEPARTMENT OF COMMERCE/Patent and Trademark Office
OMB No. 0651-0009 (Exp. 6/30/95)

PTO Form 1583

FOOTNOTES

1. The present owner of the registration must file this form between the 5th and 6th year after the date of registration. If ownership of the registration has changed since the registration date, provide supporting documentation if available or a verified explanation. The present owner should refer to itself as the registrant.

2. "Type of Commerce" must be specified as "interstate," "territorial," "foreign," or such other commerce as may lawfully be regulated by Congress. Foreign registrants must specify commerce which Congress may regulate, using wording such as "foreign commerce between the U.S. and a foreign country."

3. List only those goods and/or services for which registrant is no longer using the mark. You should fill in this blank only if you are no longer using the mark on all the goods or services in the registration.

4. A specimen showing current use of the registered mark for at least one product or service in each class of the registration must be submitted with this form. Examples of specimens are tags or labels for goods, and advertisements for services.

5. If the present owner is an individual, the individual should sign the declaration.

   If the present owner is a partnership, the declaration should be signed by a General Partner.

   If the present owner is a corporation or similar juristic entity, the declaration should be signed by an officer of the corporation/entity. Please print or type the officer title of the person signing the declaration.

NOTE: If the registration is owned by more than one party, as joint owners, each owner must sign this declaration.

FEES

For each declaration under Section 8, the required fee is $100.00 per international class. Please be aware that our fees may change. Changes, if any, are normally effective October 1 of each year. If this declaration is intended to cover less than the total number of classes in the registration, please specify the classes for which the declaration is submitted. The declaration, with appropriate fee(s), should be sent to:

Commissioner of Patents & Trademarks
Washington, D.C. 20231

MAILING INSTRUCTION BOX

You can ensure timely filing of this form by following the procedure described in 37 CFR 1.10 as follows: (1) on or before the due date for filing this form, deposit the completed form with the U.S. Post Office using the "Express Mail Post Office to Addressee" Service; (2) include a certificate of "Express Mail" under 37 CFR 1.10. Papers properly mailed under 37 CFR 1.10 are considered received by the PTO on the date that they are deposited with the Post Office.

When placing the certificate directly on the correspondence, use the following language:

Certificate of Express Mail Under 37 CFR 1.10

"Express Mail" mailing label number: _____
Date of Deposit: _____
I hereby certify that this paper and fee is being deposited with the United States Postal Service "Express Mail Post Office to Addressee" service under 37 CFR 1.10 on the date indicated above and is addressed to the Commissioner of Patents and Trademarks, Washington, D.C. 20231.

_____   _____
(Typed or printed name of person mailing   (Signature of person mailing paper & fee)
paper & fee)

This form is estimated to take 15 minutes to complete. Time will vary depending upon the needs of the individual case. Any comments on the amount of time you require to complete this form should be sent to the Office of Management and Organization, U.S. Patent and Trademark Office, U.S. Department of Commerce, Washington, D.C. 20231, and to the Office of Information and Regulatory Affairs, Office of Management and Budget, Washington, D.C. 20503. **DO NOT SEND FORMS TO EITHER OF THESE ADDRESSES.**

PTO Form 1583 *continued*

COMBINED DECLARATION OF USE AND INCONTESTABILITY UNDER SECTIONS 8 & 15[1] OF THE TRADEMARK ACT OF 1946, AS AMENDED	MARK (Identify the mark)	
	REGISTRATION NO.	DATE OF REGISTRATION:

TO THE ASSISTANT SECRETARY AND COMMISSIONER OF PATENTS AND TRADEMARKS:

REGISTRANT'S NAME:[2]

REGISTRANT'S CURRENT MAILING ADDRESS: _____

_____

_____

GOODS AND/OR SERVICES AND USE IN COMMERCE STATEMENT:

The mark shown in Registration No. _____, owned by the above-identified registrant, has been in

continuous use in _____ commerce for five consecutive years from the date of registration or the

(type of)[3]

date of publication under §12(c)[4] to the present, on or in connection with all of the goods and/or services

identified in the registration, (*except* for the following)[5] _____

_____;

as evidenced by the attached specimen(s)[6] showing the mark as currently used. There has been no final

decision adverse to registrant's claim of ownership of such mark for such goods or services, or to registrant's

right to register the same or to keep the same on the register; and there is no proceeding involving said

rights pending and not disposed of either in the Patent and Trademark Office or in the courts.

DECLARATION

The undersigned being hereby warned that willful false statements and the like so made are punishable by fine or imprisonment, or both, under 18 U.S.C. 1001, and that such willful false statements may jeopardize the validity of this document, declares that he/she is properly authorized to execute this document on behalf of the registrant; he/she believes the registrant to be the owner of the above identified registration; the trademark/service mark is in use in commerce; and all statements made of his/her own knowledge are true and all statements made on information and belief are believed to be true.

_____
Date

_____
Signature

_____
Telephone Number

_____
Print or Type Name and Position
[if applicable][7]

PTO-FB-TM (Combined 8 & 15) (Rev. 1/93)   U.S. DEPARTMENT OF COMMERCE/Patent and Trademark Office
OMB No. 0651-0009 (Exp. 6/30/95)

PTO Form PTO-FB-TM

FOOTNOTES

1. If you do not have five years of continuous use, you should file a Section 8 affidavit only. Please see PTO Form #1583.

2. The present owner of the registration must file this form between the 5th and 6th year after registration. If ownership of the registration has changed since the registration date, provide supporting documentation if available or a verified explanation. The present owner should refer to itself as the registrant.

3. "Type of Commerce" must be specified as "interstate," "territorial," "foreign," or such other commerce as may lawfully be regulated by Congress. Foreign registrants must specify commerce which Congress may regulate, using wording such as "foreign commerce between the U.S. and a foreign country."

4. This combined form is only appropriate when the five year period of continuous use, which is required for Section 15, (1) occurs between the 5th and 6th year after registration, or (2) after publication under §12(c) as is required for Section 8.

5. List only those goods and/or services for which registrant is no longer using the mark. You should fill in this blank only if you are no longer using the mark on all the goods or services in the registration.

6. A specimen showing current use of the registered mark for at least one product or service in each class of the registration must be submitted with this form. Examples of specimens are tags or labels for goods, and advertisements for services.

7. If the present owner is an individual, the individual should sign the declaration.

   If the present owner is a partnership, the declaration should be signed by a General Partner.

   If the present owner is a corporation or similar juristic entity, the declaration should be signed by an officer of the corporation/entity. Please print or type the officer title of the person signing the declaration.

NOTE: If the registration is owned by more than one party, as joint owners, each owner must sign this declaration.

FEES

For each declaration under Sections 8 & 15, the required fee is $200.00 per international class. Please be aware that our fees may change. Changes, if any, are normally effective October 1 of each year. If this declaration is intended to cover less than the total number of classes in the registration, please specify the classes for which the declaration is submitted. The declaration, with appropriate fee(s), should be sent to:

Commissioner of Patents & Trademarks
Washington, D.C. 20231

MAILING INSTRUCTION BOX

You can ensure timely filing of this form by following the procedure described in 37 CFR 1.10 as follows: (1) on or before the due date for filing this form, deposit the completed form with the U.S. Post Office using the "Express Mail Post Office to Addressee" Service; (2) include a certificate of "Express Mail" under 37 CFR 1.10. Papers properly mailed under 37 CFR 1.10 are considered received by the PTO on the date that they are deposited with the Post Office.

When placing the certificate directly on the correspondence, use the following language:

Certificate of Express Mail Under 37 CFR 1.10

"Express Mail" mailing label number: _____
Date of Deposit: _____
I hereby certify that this paper and fee is being deposited with the United States Postal Service "Express Mail Post Office to Addressee" service under 37 CFR 1.10 on the date indicated above and is addressed to the Commissioner of Patents and Trademarks, Washington, D.C. 20231.

_____   _____
(Typed or printed name of person mailing   (Signature of person mailing paper & fee)
paper & fee)

This form is estimated to take 15 minutes to complete. Time will vary depending upon the needs of the individual case. Any comments on the amount of time you require to complete this form should be sent to the Office of Management and Organization, U.S. Patent and Trademark Office, U.S. Department of Commerce, Washington, D.C. 20231, and to the Office of Information and Regulatory Affairs, Office of Management and Budget, Washington, D.C. 20503. **DO NOT SEND FORMS TO EITHER OF THESE ADDRESSES.**

PTO Form PTO-FB-TM *continued*

DECLARATION OF INCONTESTABILITY OF A MARK UNDER SECTION 15 OF THE TRADEMARK ACT OF 1946 AS AMENDED	MARK (Identify the mark)	
	REGISTRATION NO.	DATE OF REGISTRATION:

TO THE ASSISTANT SECRETARY AND COMMISSIONER OF PATENTS AND TRADEMARKS:

REGISTRANT'S NAME:[1]

REGISTRANT'S CURRENT MAILING ADDRESS: _____

_____

_____

GOODS AND/OR SERVICES AND USE IN COMMERCE STATEMENT:

The mark shown in Registration No. _____ owned by the above-identified registrant has been in

continuous use in _____ commerce for five consecutive years from _____ to the present
        (type of)[2]   (date)

on or in connection with all the goods and/or services identified in the registration, (*except* for the following)[3]

_____

_____.

There has been no final decision adverse to registrant's claim of ownership of such mark for such goods or

services, or to registrant's right to register the same or to keep the same on the register; and there is no

proceeding involving said rights pending and not disposed of either in the Patent and Trademark Office or in

the courts.

DECLARATION

The undersigned being hereby warned that willful false statements and the like so made are punishable
by fine or imprisonment, or both, under 18 U.S.C. 1001, and that such willful false statements may
jeopardize the validity of this document, declares that he/she is properly authorized to execute this
document on behalf of the registrant; he/she believes the registrant to be the owner of the above
identified registration; the trademark/service mark is in use in commerce; and all statements made of
his/her own knowledge are true and all statements made on information and belief are believed to be
true.

_____   _____
Date   Signature

_____   _____
Telephone Number   Print or Type Name and Position
                                      [if applicable][4]

PTO Form 4.16 (Rev. 1/93)   U.S. DEPARTMENT OF COMMERCE/Patent and Trademark Offic
OMB No. 0651-0009 (Exp. 6/30/95)

FOOTNOTES

1. The present owner of the registration must file this form. If ownership of the registration has changed since the registration date, provide supporting documentation if available or a verified explanation. If the present owner is a successor to the original registrant, then the present owner should refer to itself as the registrant.

2. "Type of Commerce" must be specified as "interstate," "territorial," "foreign," or such other commerce as may lawfully be regulated by Congress. Foreign registrants must specify commerce which Congress may regulate, using wording such as "foreign commerce between the U.S. and a foreign country."

3. List only those goods and/or services for which registrant is no longer using the mark. You should fill in this blank **only** if you are no longer using the mark on all the goods or services in the registration.

4. If the present owner is an individual, the individual should sign the declaration.

    If the present owner is a partnership, the declaration should be signed by a General Partner.

    If the present owner is a corporation or similar juristic entity, the declaration should be signed by an officer of the corporation/entity. Please print or type the officer title of the person signing the declaration.

NOTE: If the registration is owned by more than one party, as joint owners, each owner must sign this declaration.

FEES

For each declaration under Section 15, the required fee is $100.00 per international class. Please be aware that our fees may change. Changes, if any, are normally effective October 1 of each year. If this declaration is intended to cover less than the total number of classes in the registration, please specify the classes for which the declaration is submitted. The declaration, with appropriate fee(s), should be sent to:

Commissioner of Patents & Trademarks
Washington, D.C. 20231

MAILING INSTRUCTION BOX

You can ensure timely filing of this form by following the procedure described in 37 CFR 1.10 as follows: (1) on or before the due date for filing this form, deposit the completed form with the U.S. Post Office using the "Express Mail Post Office to Addressee" Service; (2) include a certificate of "Express Mail" under 37 CFR 1.10. Papers properly mailed under 37 CFR 1.10 are considered received by the PTO on the date that they are deposited with the Post Office.

When placing the certificate directly on the correspondence, use the following language:

Certificate of Express Mail Under 37 CFR 1.10

"Express Mail" mailing label number: _____
Date of Deposit: _____
I hereby certify that this paper and fee is being deposited with the United States Postal Service "Express Mail Post Office to Addressee" service under 37 CFR 1.10 on the date indicated above and is addressed to the Commissioner of Patents and Trademarks, Washington, D.C. 20231.

_____   _____
(Typed or printed name of person mailing   (Signature of person mailing paper & fee)
paper & fee)

This form is estimated to take 15 minutes to complete. Time will vary depending upon the needs of the individual case. Any comments on the amount of time you require to complete this form should be sent to the Office of Management and Organization, U.S. Patent and Trademark Office, U.S. Department of Commerce, Washington, D.C. 20231, and to the Office of Information and Regulatory Affairs, Office of Management and Budget, Washington, D.C. 20503. **DO NOT SEND FORMS TO EITHER OF THESE ADDRESSES.**

PTO Form 4.16 *continued*

<table>
<tr><td>APPLICATION FOR RENEWAL OF REGISTRATION OF A MARK UNDER SECTION 9 OF THE TRADEMARK ACT OF 1946, AS AMENDED</td><td colspan="2">MARK (Identify the mark)</td></tr>
<tr><td></td><td>REGISTRATION NO.</td><td>DATE OF REGISTRATION:</td></tr>
</table>

TO THE ASSISTANT SECRETARY AND COMMISSIONER OF PATENTS AND TRADEMARKS:

REGISTRANT'S NAME:[1]

REGISTRANT'S CURRENT MAILING ADDRESS: _____

GOODS AND/OR SERVICES AND USE IN COMMERCE STATEMENT:

The mark shown in Registration No. _____ owned by the above-identified registrant is still in use

in _____ commerce on or in connection with all of the goods and/or services identified in the
(type of)[2]

registration, (*except* for the following)[3] _____

_____ ;

as evidenced by the attached specimen(s)[4] showing the mark as currently used.

DECLARATION

The undersigned being hereby warned that willful false statements and the like so made are punishable by fine or imprisonment, or both, under 18 U.S.C. 1001, and that such willful false statements may jeopardize the validity of this document, declares that he/she is properly authorized to execute this document on behalf of the registrant; he/she believes the registrant to be the owner of the above identified registration; the trademark/service mark is in use in commerce; and all statements made of his/her own knowledge are true and all statements made on information and belief are believed to be true.

_____   _____
Date   Signature

_____   _____
Telephone Number   Print or Type Name and Position
                                                  [if applicable][5]

FOOTNOTES

1. The present owner of the registration must file this form between the 5th and 6th year after the date of registration. If ownership of the registration has changed since the registration date, provide supporting documentation if available or a verified explanation. The present owner should refer to itself as the registrant.

2. "Type of Commerce" must be specified as "interstate," "territorial," "foreign," or such other commerce as may lawfully be regulated by Congress. Foreign registrants must specify commerce which Congress may regulate, using wording such as "foreign commerce between the U.S. and a foreign country."

3. List only those goods and/or services for which registrant is no longer using the mark. You should fill in this blank **only** if you are no longer using the mark on all the goods or services in the registration.

4. A specimen showing current use of the registered mark for at least one product or service in each class of the registration must be submitted with this form. Examples of specimens are tags or labels for goods, and advertisements for services.

5. If the present owner is an individual, the individual should sign the declaration.

   If the present owner is a partnership, the declaration should be signed by a General Partner.

   If the present owner is a corporation or similar juristic entity, the declaration should be signed by an officer of the corporation/entity. Please print or type the officer title of the person signing the declaration.

NOTE: If the registration is owned by more than one party, as joint owners, each owner must sign this declaration.

FEES

For each declaration under Section 8, the required fee is $100.00 per international class. Please be aware that our fees may change. Changes, if any, are normally effective October 1 of each year. If this declaration is intended to cover less than the total number of classes in the registration, please specify the classes for which the declaration is submitted. The declaration, with appropriate fee(s), should be sent to:

Commissioner of Patents & Trademarks
Washington, D.C. 20231

MAILING INSTRUCTION BOX

You can ensure timely filing of this form by following the procedure described in 37 CFR 1.10 as follows: (1) on or before the due date for filing this form, deposit the completed form with the U.S. Post Office using the "Express Mail Post Office to Addressee" Service; (2) include a certificate of "Express Mail" under 37 CFR 1.10. Papers properly mailed under 37 CFR 1.10 are considered received by the PTO on the date that they are deposited with the Post Office.

When placing the certificate directly on the correspondence, use the following language:

Certificate of Express Mail Under 37 CFR 1.10

"Express Mail" mailing label number: _____
Date of Deposit: _____
I hereby certify that this paper and fee is being deposited with the United States Postal Service "Express Mail Post Office to Addressee" service under 37 CFR 1.10 on the date indicated above and is addressed to the Commissioner of Patents and Trademarks, Washington, D.C. 20231.

_____   _____
(Typed or printed name of person mailing   (Signature of person mailing paper & fee)
paper & fee)

This form is estimated to take 15 minutes to complete. Time will vary depending upon the needs of the individual case. Any comments on the amount of time you require to complete this form should be sent to the Office of Management and Organization, U.S. Patent and Trademark Office, U.S. Department of Commerce, Washington, D.C. 20231, and to the Office of Information and Regulatory Affairs, Office of Management and Budget, Washington, D.C. 20503. **DO NOT SEND FORMS TO EITHER OF THESE ADDRESSES.**

PTO Form 4.13a *continued*

COLLECTIVE MEMBERSHIP MARK APPLICATION, PRINCIPAL REGISTER, WITH DECLARATION	MARK (Word(s) and/or Design)	CLASS NO. 200

TO THE ASSISTANT SECRETARY AND COMMISSIONER OF PATENTS AND TRADEMARKS:

APPLICANT'S NAME:

APPLICANT'S BUSINESS ADDRESS: _____
(Display address exactly as it
should appear on registration)

APPLICANT'S ENTITY TYPE: (Check one and supply requested information)

	Individual - Citizen of (Country):
	Partnership - State where organized (Country, if appropriate): _____ Names and Citizenship (Country) of General Partners:_____
	Corporation - State (Country, if appropriate) of Incorporation:
	Other (Specify Nature of Entity and Domicile):

Applicant requests registration of the collective membership mark shown in the accompanying drawing in the United States Patent and Trademark Office on the Principal Register established by the Act of July 5, 1946 (15 U.S.C. 1051 et. seq., as amended.) to indicate membership in a(n): _____

(Specify the type or nature of the organization, for example, a social club, labor union, political society, or an association of real estate brokers.)

BASIS FOR APPLICATION: (Check boxes which apply, but never both the first AND second boxes, and supply requested information related to each box checked)

[ ] Applicant is exercising legitimate control over the use of the mark in commerce by its members to indicate membership. (15 U.S.C. 1051(a) and 1054 as amended.) Three specimens showing the mark as used by the members in commerce are submitted with this application.

• Date of first use of the mark by members in commerce which the U.S. Congress may regulate (for example, interstate or between the U.S. and a specified foreign country): _____
• Specify the type of commerce: _____
(for example, interstate or between the U.S. and a specified foreign country)
• Date of first use anywhere (the same as or before use in commerce date): _____
• Specify manner or method of using mark to indicate membership: _____

(for example, mark is applied to membership cards, certificates, window decals)

[ ] Applicant has a bona fide intention to exercise legitimate control over the use of the mark in commerce by its members to indicate membership. (15 U.S.C. 1051(b) and 1054, as amended.)
• Specify intended manner or method of using mark to indicate membership: _____

(for example, mark will be applied to membership cards, certificates, window decals)

[ ] Applicant has a bona fide intention to exercise legitimate control over the use of the mark in commerce by its members to indicate membership, and asserts a claim of priority based upon a foreign application in accordance with 15 U.S.C. 1126(d), as amended.
• Country of foreign filing: _____   • Date of foreign filing: _____

[ ] Applicant has a bona fide intention to exercise legitimate control over the use of the mark in commerce by its members to indicate membership and, accompanying this application, submits a certification or certified copy of a foreign registration in accordance with 15 U.S.C. 1126(e), as amended.
• Country of registration: _____   • Registration number: _____

NOTE: Declaration, on Reverse Side, MUST be Signed

PTO FORM 4.8
OMB 0651-0009 (Exp. 6/30/92)   U.S. DEPARTMENT OF COMMERCE/Patent and Trademark Office

PTO Form 4.8 (Collective Membership Mark)

Applicant controls (or, if the application is being filed under 15 U.S.C. 1051(b), applicant intends to control) the use of the mark by the members in the following manner: _____

_____

NOTE: If applicant's bylaws or other written provisions specify the manner of control, or intended manner of control, it will be sufficient to state such bylaws or other written provisions.

DECLARATION

The undersigned being hereby warned that willful statements and the like so made are punishable by fine or imprisonment, or both, under 18 U.S.C. 1001, and that such willful false statements may jeopardize the validity of the application or any resulting registration, declares that he/she is properly authorized to execute this application on behalf of the applicant; he/she believes the applicant to be the owner of the membership mark sought to be registered, or, if the application is being filed under 15 U.S.C. 1051(b), he/she believes applicant is entitled to exercise legitimate control over use of the mark in commerce; to the best of his/her knowledge and belief no other person, firm, corporation, or association has the right to use the above identified mark in commerce, either in the identical form thereof or in such near resemblance thereto as to be likely, when used on or in connection with the goods/services of such other person, to cause confusion, or to cause mistake, or to deceive; and that all statements made of his/her own knowledge are true and that all statements made on information and belief are believed to be true.

_____   _____
Date   Signature

_____   _____
Telephone Number   Print or Type Name and Position

INSTRUCTIONS AND INFORMATION FOR APPLICANT

TO RECEIVE A FILING DATE, THE APPLICATION **MUST** BE COMPLETED AND SIGNED BY THE APPLICANT AND SUBMITTED ALONG WITH:

1. The prescribed **FEE ($210.00)** for each class of goods/services listed in the application;
2. A **DRAWING PAGE** displaying the mark in conformance with 37 CFR 2.52;
3. If the application is based on use of the mark in commerce, **THREE (3) SPECIMENS** (evidence) of the mark as used by members in commerce. All three specimens may be the same.
4. An **APPLICATION WITH DECLARATION** (this form) - The application must be signed in order for the application to receive a filing date. Only the following person may sign the declaration, depending on the applicant's legal entity: (a) the individual applicant; (b) an officer of the corporate applicant; (c) one general partner of a partnership applicant; (d) all joint applicants.

SEND APPLICATION FORM, DRAWING PAGE, FEE, AND SPECIMENS (IF APPROPRIATE) TO:

U.S. DEPARTMENT OF COMMERCE
Patent and Trademark Office
Washington, D.C. 20231

Additional information concerning the requirements for filing an application is available in a booklet entitled **Basic Facts About Trademarks**, which may be obtained by writing to the above address or by calling: (703) 305-HELP.

This form is estimated to take an average of 1 hour to complete, including time required for reading and understanding instructions, gathering necessary information, recordkeeping, and actually providing the information. Any comments on this form, including the amount of time required to complete this form, should be sent to the Office of Management and Organization, U.S. Patent and Trademark Office, U.S. Department of Commerce, Washington, D.C. 20231, and to Paperwork Reduction Project 0651-0009, Office of Information and Regulatory Affairs, Office of Management and Budget, Washington, D.C. 20503. Do NOT send completed forms to either of these addresses.

<table>
<tr>
<td>COLLECTIVE TRADEMARK/SERVICE MARK APPLICATION, PRINCIPAL REGISTER, WITH DECLARATION</td>
<td>MARK (Word(s) and/or Design)</td>
<td>CLASS NO. (If known)</td>
</tr>
</table>

TO THE ASSISTANT SECRETARY AND COMMISSIONER OF PATENTS AND TRADEMARKS:

APPLICANT'S NAME:

APPLICANT'S BUSINESS ADDRESS: _____
(Display address exactly as it
should appear on registration) _____

APPLICANT'S ENTITY TYPE: (**Check one** and supply requested information)

	Individual - Citizen of (Country):
	Partnership - State where organized (Country, if appropriate): _____ Names and Citizenship (Country) of General Partners: _____
	Corporation - State (Country, if appropriate) of Incorporation: _____
	Other (Specify Nature of Entity and Domicile): _____

Applicant requests registration of the collective mark shown in the accompanying drawing in the United States Patent and Trademark Office on the Principal Register established by the Act of July 5, 1946 (15 U.S.C. 1051 et. seq., as amended.) for the following goods/services (**SPECIFIC GOODS AND/OR SERVICES MUST BE INSERTED HERE**): _____

BASIS FOR APPLICATION: (Check boxes which apply, **but never both the first AND second boxes**, and supply requested information related to each box checked)

[ ]	Applicant is exercising legitimate control over the use of the mark in commerce by its members on or in connection with the above-identified goods/services. (15 U.S.C. 1051(a) and 1054 as amended.) Three specimens showing the mark as used by the members in commerce are submitted with this application. •Date of first use of the mark by a member in commerce which the U.S. Congress may regulate (for example, interstate or between the U.S. and a specified foreign country): _____ •Specify the type of commerce: _____ (for example, interstate or between the U.S. and a specified foreign country) •Date of first use anywhere (the same as or before use in commerce date): _____ •Specify manner or method of using mark on or in connection with the goods/services: _____ (for example, trademark is applied to labels, service mark is used in advertisements)
[ ]	Applicant has a bona fide intention to exercise legitimate control over the use of the mark in commerce by its members on or in connection with the above-identified goods/services. (15 U.S.C. 1051(b) and 1054, as amended.) •Specify intended manner or method of using mark on or in connection with the goods/services: _____ (for example, mark will be applied to labels, mark will be used in advertisements)
[ ]	Applicant has a bona fide intention to exercise legitimate control over the use of the mark in commerce by its members on or in connection with the above-identified goods/services and asserts a claim of priority based upon a foreign application in accordance with 15 U.S.C. 1126(d), as amended. • Country of foreign filing: _____ • Date of foreign filing: _____
[ ]	Applicant has a bona fide intention to exercise legitimate control over the use of the mark in commerce by its members on or in connection with the above-identified goods/services and, accompanying this application, submits a certification or certified copy of a foreign registration in accordance with 15 U.S.C. 1126(e), as amended. • Country of registration: _____ • Registration number: _____

NOTE: **Declaration, on Reverse Side, MUST be Signed**

PTO FORM 4.8
OMB 0651-0009 (Exp. 6/30/92)

U.S. DEPARTMENT OF COMMERCE/Patent and Trademark Office

PTO Form 4.8 (Collective Trademark)

Applicant controls (or, if the application is being filed under 15 U.S.C. 1051(b), applicant intends to control) the use of the mark by the members in the following manner: _____

_____

_____

NOTE: If applicant's bylaws or other written provisions specify the manner of control, or intended manner of control, it will be sufficient to state such bylaws or other written provisions.

DECLARATION

The undersigned being hereby warned that willful statements and the like so made are punishable by fine or imprisonment, or both, under 18 U.S.C. 1001, and that such willful false statements may jeopardize the validity of the application or any resulting registration, declares that he/she is properly authorized to execute this application on behalf of the applicant; he/she believes the applicant to be the owner of the trademark/service mark sought to be registered, or, if the application is being filed under 15 U.S.C. 1051(b), he/she believes applicant is entitled to exercise legitimate control over use of the mark in commerce; to the best of his/her knowledge and belief no other person, firm, corporation, or association has the right to use the above identified mark in commerce, either in the identical form thereof or in such near resemblance thereto as to be likely, when used on or in connection with the goods/services of such other person, to cause confusion, or to cause mistake, or to deceive; and that all statements made of his/her own knowledge are true and that all statements made on information and belief are believed to be true.

_____   _____
Date   Signature

_____   _____
Telephone Number   Print or Type Name and Position

INSTRUCTIONS AND INFORMATION FOR APPLICANT

TO RECEIVE A FILING DATE, THE APPLICATION **MUST** BE COMPLETED AND SIGNED BY THE APPLICANT AND SUBMITTED ALONG WITH:

1. The prescribed **FEE ($210.00)** for each class of goods/services listed in the application;
2. A **DRAWING PAGE** displaying the mark in conformance with 37 CFR 2.52;
3. If the application is based on use of the mark in commerce, **THREE (3) SPECIMENS** (evidence) of the mark as used by members in commerce for each class of goods and services. All three specimens may be the same.
4. An **APPLICATION WITH DECLARATION** (this form) - The application must be signed in order for the application to receive a filing date. Only the following person may sign the declaration, depending on the applicant's legal entity: (a) the individual applicant; (b) an officer of the corporate applicant; (c) one general partner of a partnership applicant; (d) all joint applicants.

SEND APPLICATION FORM, DRAWING PAGE, FEE, AND SPECIMENS (IF APPROPRIATE) TO:

U.S. DEPARTMENT OF COMMERCE
Patent and Trademark Office
Washington, D.C. 20231

Additional information concerning the requirements for filing an application is available in a booklet entitled **Basic Facts About Trademarks**, which may be obtained by writing to the above address or by calling (703) 305-HELP.

This form is estimated to take an average of 1 hour to complete, including time required for reading and understanding instructions, gathering necessary information, recordkeeping, and actually providing the information. Any comments on this form, including the amount of time required to complete this form, should be sent to the Office of Management and Organization, U.S. Patent and Trademark Office, U.S. Department of Commerce, Washington, D.C. 20231, and to Paperwork Reduction Project 0651-0009, Office of Information and Regulatory Affairs, Office of Management and Budget, Washington, D.C. 20503. Do NOT send completed forms to either of these addresses.

PTO Form 4.8 *continued*

CERTIFICATION MARK APPLICATION, PRINCIPAL REGISTER, WITH DECLARATION	MARK (Word(s) and/or Design)
	CLASS [ ] A. Goods [ ] B. Services

TO THE ASSISTANT SECRETARY AND COMMISSIONER OF PATENTS AND TRADEMARKS:

APPLICANT'S NAME:

APPLICANT'S BUSINESS ADDRESS: _____
(Display address exactly as it
should appear on registration) _____

APPLICANT'S ENTITY TYPE: (Check one and supply requested information)

	Individual - Citizen of (Country):
	Partnership - State where organized (Country, if appropriate): _____ Names and Citizenship (Country) of General Partners: _____
	Corporation - State (Country, if appropriate) of Incorporation: _____
	Other (Specify Nature of Entity and Domicile):

Applicant requests registration of the certification mark shown in the accompanying drawing in the United States Patent and Trademark Office on the Principal Register established by the Act of July 5, 1946 (15 U.S.C. 1051 et. seq., as amended.) for the following goods/services (SPECIFIC GOODS AND/OR SERVICES MUST BE INSERTED HERE): _____

The certification mark, as used (or, if filing under 15 U.S.C. 1051(b), intended to be used) by authorized persons, certifies (or, if filing under 15 U.S.C. 1051(b), is intended to certify): _____

(for example, a particular regional origin of the goods, a characteristic of the goods or services, that labor was performed by a particular group)

BASIS FOR APPLICATION: (Check boxes which apply, but never both the first AND second boxes, and supply requested information related to each box checked)

[ ]	Applicant is exercising legitimate control over the use of the certification mark in commerce on or in connection with the above-identified goods/services. (15 U.S.C. 1051(a) and 1054, as amended.) Three specimens showing the mark as used by authorized persons in commerce are submitted with this application. •Date of first use of the mark by authorized person in commerce which the U.S. Congress may regulate (for example, interstate or between the U.S. and a specified foreign country): _____ •Specify the type of commerce: _____ (for example, interstate or between the U.S. and a specified foreign country) •Date of first use anywhere by an authorized person (the same as or before use in commerce date): _____ •Specify manner of using mark on or in connection with the goods/services: _____ (for example, mark is applied to labels for goods or mark is used on advertisements for services)
[ ]	Applicant has a bona fide intention to exercise legitimate control over the use of the certification mark in commerce on or in connection with the above-identified goods/services. (15 U.S.C. 1051(b) and 1054, as amended.) •Specify intended manner of using mark on or in connection with the goods/services: _____ (for example, mark will be applied to labels for goods or mark will be used on advertisements for services)
[ ]	Applicant has a bona fide intention to exercise legitimate control over the use of the certification mark in commerce on or in connection with the above-identified goods/services, and asserts a claim of priority based upon a foreign application in accordance with 15 U.S.C. 1126(d), as amended. • Country of foreign filing: _____ • Date of foreign filing: _____
[ ]	Applicant has a bona fide intention to exercise legitimate control over the use of the certification mark in commerce on or in connection with the above-identified goods/services and, accompanying this application, submits a certification or certified copy of a foreign registration in accordance with 15 U.S.C. 1126(e), as amended. • Country of registration: _____ • Registration number: _____

PTO FORM 4.9   U.S. DEPARTMENT OF COMMERCE/Patent and Trademark Office
OMB 0651-0009 (Exp. 6/30/92)

PTO Form 4.9

Applicant is not engaged (or, if filing under 15 U.S.C. 1051(b), will not engage) in the production or marketing of the goods or services to which the mark is applied.

The applicant must also provide a copy of the standards the applicant uses to determine whether goods or services will be certified. If the applicant files based on prior use in commerce, this should be provided with this application. In an application filed based on an intent to use in commerce, this should be provided with the Amendment to Allege Use or Statement or Use.

DECLARATION

The undersigned being hereby warned that willful false statements and the like so made are punishable by fine or imprisonment, or both, under 18 U.S.C. 1001, and that such willful false statements may jeopardize the validity of the application or any resulting registration, declares that he/she is properly authorized to execute this application on behalf of the applicant; he/she believes the applicant to be the owner of the mark sought to be registered, or, if the application is being filed under 15 U.S. 1051(b), he/she believes applicant is entitled to exercise legitimate control over use of the mark in commerce; to the best of his/her knowledge and belief no other person, firm, corporation, or association has the right to use the above identified mark in commerce, either in the identical form thereof or in such near resemblance thereto as to be likely, when used on or in connection with the goods/services of such other person, to cause confusion, or to cause mistake, or to deceive; and that all statements made of his/her own knowledge are true and that all statements made on information and belief are believed to be true.

Date	Signature
Telephone Number	Print or Type Name and Position

INSTRUCTIONS AND INFORMATION FOR APPLICANT

TO RECEIVE A FILING DATE, THE APPLICATION MUST BE COMPLETED AND SIGNED BY THE APPLICANT AND SUBMITTED ALONG WITH:

1. The prescribed **FEE ($210.00)** for each class of goods/services listed in the application;
2. A **DRAWING PAGE** displaying the mark in conformance with 37 CFR 2.52;
3. If the application is based on use of the mark in commerce, **THREE (3) SPECIMENS** (evidence) of the mark as used by authorized persons in commerce. All three specimens may be the same and may be in the nature of: (a) labels showing the mark which are placed on the goods; (b) photographs of the mark as it appears on the goods, (c) brochures or advertisements showing the mark as used in connection with the services.
4. An **APPLICATION WITH DECLARATION** (this form) - The application must be signed in order for the application to receive a filing date. Only the following person may sign the declaration, depending on the applicant's legal entity: (a) the individual applicant; (b) an officer of the corporate applicant; (c) one general partner of a partnership applicant; (d) all joint applicants.

SEND APPLICATION FORM, DRAWING PAGE, FEE, AND SPECIMENS (IF APPROPRIATE) TO:

U.S. DEPARTMENT OF COMMERCE
Patent and Trademark Office
Washington, D.C. 20231

Additional information concerning the requirements for filing an application is available in a booklet entitled **Basic Facts About Trademarks**, which may be obtained by writing to the above address or by calling: (703) 305-HELP.

This form is estimated to take an average of 1 hour to complete, including time required for reading and understanding instructions, gathering necessary information recordkeeping, and actually providing the information. Any comments on this form, including the amount of time required to complete this form, should be sent to the Office of Management and Organization, U.S. Patent and Trademark Office, U.S. Department of Commerce, Washington, D.C. 20231, and to Paperwork Reduction Project 0651-0009, Office of Information and Regulatory Affairs, Office of Management and Budget, Washington, D.C. 20503. Do NOT send completed forms to either of these addresses.

| **AMENDMENT TO ALLEGE USE UNDER 37 CFR 2.76, WITH DECLARATION** | MARK (Identify the mark) |
| | SERIAL NO. |

TO THE ASSISTANT SECRETARY AND COMMISSIONER OF PATENTS AND TRADEMARKS:

APPLICANT NAME:

Applicant requests registration of the above-identified trademark/service mark in the United States Patent and Trademark Office on the Principal Register established by the Act of July 5, 1946
(15 U.S.C. 1051 et. seq., as amended). Three specimens showing the mark as used in commerce are submitted with this amendment.

☐ Check here if Request to Divide under 37 CFR 2.87 is being submitted with this amendment.

Applicant is using the mark in commerce on or in connection with the following goods/services:

_____

(NOTE: Goods/services listed above may not be broader than the goods/services identified in the application as filed)

Date of first use of mark anywhere: _____

Date of first use of mark in commerce
which the U.S. Congress may regulate: _____

Specify type of commerce: (e.g., interstate, between the U.S. and a specified foreign country) _____

Specify manner or mode of use of mark on or in connection with the goods/services: (e.g., trademark is applied to labels, service mark is used in advertisements) _____

The undersigned being hereby warned that willful false statements and the like so made are punishable by fine or imprisonment, or both, under 18 U.S.C. 1001, and that such willful false statements may jeopardize the validity of the application or any resulting registration, declares that he/she is properly authorized to execute this Amendment to Allege Use on behalf of the applicant; he/she believes the applicant to be the owner of the trademark/service mark sought to be registered; the trademark/ service mark is now in use in commerce; and all statements made of his/her own knowledge are true and all statements made on information and belief are believed to be true.

_____ _____
Date   Signature

_____ _____
Telephone Number   Print or Type Name and Position

PTO Form 1579 (REV. 6-92)
OMB No. 0651-0009
Exp. 6-30-95

U.S. DEPARTMENT OF COMMERCE/Patent and Trademark Office

INSTRUCTIONS AND INFORMATION FOR APPLICANT

In an application based upon a bona fide intention to use a mark in commerce, applicant must use its mark in commerce before a registration will be issued. After use begins, the applicant must submit, along with evidence of use (specimens) and the prescribed fee(s), **either:**

> (1) an Amendment to Allege Use under 37 CFR 2.76, or
> (2) a Statement of Use under 37 CFR 2.88.

The difference between these two filings is the timing of the filing. Applicant may file an Amendment to Allege Use before approval of the mark for publication for opposition in the **Official Gazette**, or, if a final refusal has been issued, prior to the expiration of the six month response period. Otherwise, applicant must file a Statement of Use after the Office issues a Notice of Allowance. The Notice of Allowance will issue after the opposition period is completed if no successful opposition is filed. Neither Amendment to Allege Use or Statement of Use papers will be accepted by the Office during the period of time between approval of the mark for publication for opposition in the **Official Gazette** and the issuance of the Notice of Allowance.

Applicant may call (703) 305-8747 to determine whether the mark has been approved for publication for opposition in the **Official Gazette.**

Before filing an Amendment to Allege Use or a Statement of Use, applicant must use the mark in commerce on or in connection with **all** of the goods/services for which applicant will seek registration, **unless** applicant submits with the papers, a request to divide out from the application the goods or services to which the Amendment to Allege Use or Statement of Use pertains. (See: 37 CFR 2.87, Dividing an application)

Applicant **must** submit with an Amendment to Allege Use or a Statement of Use:

> (1) the appropriate fee of $100 per class of goods/services listed in the Amendment to Allege Use or the Statement of Use, and

> (2) three (3) specimens or facsimiles of the mark as used in commerce for each class of goods/services asserted (e.g., photograph of mark as it appears on goods, label containing mark which is placed on goods, or brochure or advertisement showing mark as used in connection with services).

Cautions/Notes concerning completion of this Amendment to Allege Use form:

> (1) The goods/services identified in the Amendment to Allege Use must be within the scope of the goods/services identified in the application as filed. Applicant may delete goods/services. Deleted goods/services may not be reinstated in the application at a later time.

> (2) Applicant may list dates of use for only one item in each class of goods/services identified in the Amendment to Allege Use. However, applicant must have used the mark in commerce on all the goods/services in the class.

> (3) Only the following person may sign the verification of the Amendment to Allege Use, depending on the applicant's legal entity: (a) the individual applicant; (b) an officer of corporate applicant; (c) one general partner of partnership applicant; (d) all joint applicants.

MAIL COMPLETED FORM TO:

**COMMISSIONER OF PATENTS AND TRADEMARKS
WASHINGTON, D.C. 20231**

This form is estimated to take 15 minutes to complete including time required for reading and understanding instructions, gathering necessary information, record keeping and actually providing the information. Any comments on the amount of time you require to complete this form should be sent to the Office of Management and Organization, U.S. Patent and Trademark Office, U.S. Department of Commerce, Washington D.C., 20231, and to the Office of Information and Regulatory Affairs, Office of Management and Budget, Washington, D.C. 20503. Do not send completed from to OMB.

<table>
<tr><td>

**STATEMENT OF USE
UNDER 37 CFR 2.88, WITH
DECLARATION**

</td><td>

MARK (Identify the mark)

SERIAL NO.

</td></tr>
</table>

TO THE ASSISTANT SECRETARY AND COMMISSIONER OF PATENTS AND TRADEMARKS:

APPLICANT NAME:

NOTICE OF ALLOWANCE ISSUE DATE:

Applicant requests registration of the above-identified trademark/service mark in the United States Patent and Trademark Office on the Principal Register established by the Act of July 5, 1946
(15 U.S.C. 1051 et. seq., as amended). Three (3) specimens showing the mark as used in commerce are submitted with this statement.

☐   Check here only if a Request to Divide under 37 CFR 2.87 is being submitted with this Statement.

Applicant is using the mark in commerce on or in connection with the following goods/services: (Check One)

☐   Those goods/services identified in the Notice of Allowance in this application.

☐   Those goods/services identified in the Notice of Allowance in this application except: (Identify goods/services to be deleted from application) _____

_____

_____

Date of first use of mark anywhere: _____

Date of first use of mark in commerce
which the U.S. Congress may regulate: _____

Specify type of commerce: (e.g., interstate, between the U.S. and a specified foreign country) _____

_____

Specify manner or mode of use of mark on or in connection with the goods/services: (e.g., trademark is applied to labels, service mark is used in advertisements) _____

_____

The undersigned being hereby warned that willful false statements and the like so made are punishable by fine or imprisonment, or both, under 18 U.S.C. 1001, and that such willful false statements may jeopardize the validity of the application or any resulting registration, declares that he/she is properly authorized to execute this Statement of Use on behalf of the applicant; he/she believes the applicant to be the owner of the trademark/service mark sought to be registered; the trademark/ service mark is now in use in commerce; and all statements made of his/her own knowledge are true and all statements made on information and belief are believed to be true.

_____   _____
Date   Signature

_____   _____
Telephone Number   Print or Type Name and Position

PTO Form 1580 (REV. 6-92)
OMB No. 0651-0009
Exp. 6-30-95

U.S. DEPARTMENT OF COMMERCE/Patent and Trademark Office

PTO Form 1580

INSTRUCTIONS AND INFORMATION FOR APPLICANT

In an application based upon a bona fide intention to use a mark in commerce, applicant must use its mark in commerce before a registration will be issued. After use begins, the applicant must submit, along with evidence of use (specimens) and the prescribed fee(s), **either:**

(1) an Amendment to Allege Use under 37 CFR 2.76, or
(2) a Statement of Use under 37 CFR 2.88.

The difference between these two filings is the timing of the filing. Applicant may file an Amendment to Allege Use before approval of the mark for publication for opposition in the **Official Gazette**, or, if a final refusal has been issued, prior to the expiration of the six month response period. Otherwise, applicant must file a Statement of Use after the Office issues a Notice of Allowance. The Notice of Allowance will issue after the opposition period is completed if no successful opposition is filed. Neither Amendment to Allege Use or Statement of Use papers will be accepted by the Office during the period of time between approval of the mark for publication for opposition in the **Official Gazette** and the issuance of the Notice of Allowance.

Applicant may call (703) 305-8747 to determine whether the mark has been approved for publication for opposition in the **Official Gazette**.

Before filing an Amendment to Allege Use or a Statement of Use, applicant must use the mark in commerce on or in connection with **all** of the goods/services for which applicant will seek registration, **unless** applicant submits with the papers, a request to divide out from the application the goods or services to which the Amendment to Allege Use or Statement of Use pertains. (See: 37 CFR 2.87, Dividing an application)

Applicant **must** submit with an Amendment to Allege Use or a Statement of Use:

(1) the appropriate fee of $100 per class of goods/services listed in the Amendment to Allege Use or the Statement of Use, and

(2) three (3) specimens or facsimiles of the mark as used in commerce for each class of goods/services asserted (e.g., photograph of mark as it appears on goods, label containing mark which is placed on goods, or brochure or advertisement showing mark as used in connection with services).

Cautions/Notes concerning completion of this Statement of Use form:

(1) The goods/services identified in the Statement of Use must be identical to the goods/services identified in the Notice of Allowance. Applicant may delete goods/services. Deleted goods/services may not be reinstated in the application at a later time.

(2) Applicant may list dates of use for only one item in each class of goods/services identified in the Statement of Use. However, applicant must have used the mark in commerce on all the goods/services in the class. Applicant must identify the particular item to which the dates apply.

(3) Only the following person may sign the verification of the Statement of Use, depending on the applicant's legal entity: (a) the individual applicant; (b) an officer of corporate applicant; (c) one general partner of partnership applicant; (d) all joint applicants.

MAIL COMPLETED FORM TO:

COMMISSIONER OF PATENTS AND TRADEMARKS
BOX ITU
WASHINGTON D.C. 20231

This form is estimated to take 15 minutes to complete including time required for reading and understanding instructions, gathering necessary information, record keeping and actually providing the information. Any comments on the amount of time you require to complete this form should be sent to the Office of Management and Organization, U.S. Patent and Trademark Office, U.S. Department of Commerce, Washington D.C., 20231, and to the Office of Information and Regulatory Affairs, Office of Management and Budget, Washington, D.C. 20503. Do not send completed form to OMB.

PTO Form 1580 *continued*

<table>
<tr>
<td>

REQUEST FOR EXTENSION OF TIME UNDER 37 CFR 2.89 TO FILE A STATEMENT OF USE, WITH DECLARATION

</td>
<td>

MARK (Identify the mark)

SERIAL NO.

</td>
</tr>
</table>

TO THE ASSISTANT SECRETARY AND COMMISSIONER OF PATENTS AND TRADEMARKS:

APPLICANT NAME:

NOTICE OF ALLOWANCE MAILING DATE:

Applicant requests a six-month extension of time to file the Statement of Use under 37 CFR 2.88 in this application.

☐   Check here if a Request to Divide under 37 CFR 2.87 is being submitted with this request.

Applicant has a continued bona fide intention to use the mark in commerce in connection with the following goods/services: (Check one below)

☐   Those goods/services identified in the Notice of Allowance in this application.

☐   Those goods/services identified in the Notice of Allowance in this application except: (Identify goods/services to be **deleted** from application) _____

_____

This is the _____ request for an Extension of Time following mailing of the Notice of Allowance.
      (Specify: First - Fifth)

If this is not the first request for an Extension of Time, check one box below. If the first box is checked, explain the circumstance(s) of the non-use in the space provided:

☐   Applicant has not used the mark in commerce yet on all goods/services specified in the Notice of Allowance; however, applicant has made the following ongoing efforts to use the mark in commerce on or in connection with each of the goods/services specified above:

_____

_____

If additional space is needed, please attach a separate sheet to this form

☐   Applicant believes that it has made valid use of the mark in commerce, as evidenced by the Statement of Use submitted with this request; however, if the Statement of Use does not meet minimum requirements under 37 CFR 2.88(e), applicant will need additional time in which to file a new statement.

The undersigned being hereby warned that willful false statements and the like so made are punishable by fine or imprisonment, or both, under 18 U.S.C. 1001, and that such willful false statements may jeopardize the validity of the application or any resulting registration, declares that he/she is properly authorized to execute this Request for Extension of Time to File a Statement of Use on behalf of the applicant; he/she believes the applicant to be entitled to use the trademark/service mark sought to be registered; and all statements made of his/her own knowledge are true and all statements made on information and belief are believed to be true.

_____   _____
Date   Signature

_____   _____
Telephone Number   Print or Type Name and Position

PTO Form 1581 (REV. 6-92)   U.S. DEPARTMENT OF COMMERCE/Patent and Trademark Office
OMB No. 0651 - 0009
Exp. 6-30-95

PTO Form 1581

INSTRUCTIONS AND INFORMATION FOR APPLICANT

Applicant must file a Statement of Use within six months after the mailing of the Notice of Allowance in an application based upon a bona fide intention to use a mark in commerce, UNLESS, within that same period, applicant submits a request for a six-month extension of time to file the Statement of Use. The request **must**:

(1) be in writing,
(2) include applicant's verified statement of continued bona fide intention to use the mark in commerce,
(3) specify the goods/services to which the request pertains as they are identified in the Notice of Allowance, and
(4) include a fee of $100 for each class of goods/services.

Applicant may request four further six-month extensions of time. No extension may extend beyond 36 months from the issue date of the Notice of Allowance. Each request must be filed within the previously granted six-month extension period and must include, in addition to the above requirements, a showing of **GOOD CAUSE**. This good cause showing must include:

(1) applicant's statement that the mark has not been used in commerce yet on all the goods or services specified in the Notice of Allowance with which applicant has a continued bona fide intention to use the mark in commerce, **and**

(2) applicant's statement of ongoing efforts to make such use, which may include the following: (a) product or service research or development, (b) market research,
(c) promotional activities, (d) steps to acquire distributors, (e) steps to obtain required governmental approval, or (f) similar specified activity .

Applicant may submit one additional six-month extension request during the existing period in which applicant files the Statement of Use, unless the granting of this request would extend beyond 36 months from the issue date of the Notice of Allowance. As a showing of good cause, applicant should state its belief that applicant has made valid use of the mark in commerce, as evidenced by the submitted Statement of Use, but that if the Statement is found by the PTO to be defective, applicant will need additional time in which to file a new statement of use.

 Only the following person may sign the verification of the Request for Extentsion of Time, depending on the applicant's legal entity: (a) the individual applicant; (b) an officer of corporate applicant; (c) one general partner of partnership applicant; (d) all joint applicants.

MAIL COMPLETED FORM TO:

**COMMISSIONER OF PATENTS & TRADEMARKS
BOX ITU
WASHINGTON, D.C. 20231**

This form is estimated to take 15 minutes to complete including time required for reading and understanding instructions, gathering necessary information, record keeping and actually providing the information. Any comments on the amount of time you require to complete this form should be sent to the Office of Management and Organization, U.S. Patent and Trademark Office, U.S. Department of Commerce, Washington D.C., 20231, andto the Office of Information and Regulatory Affairs, Office of Management and Budget, Washington, D.C. 20503. Do not send completed form to OMB

PTO Form 1581 *continued*

FORM PTO-1594
1-31-92

RECORDATION FORM COVER SHEET
TRADEMARKS ONLY

U.S. DEPARTMENT OF COMMERCE
Patent and Trademark Office

Tab settings ⇨ ⇨ ⇨ ▼   ▼   ▼   ▼   ▼   ▼   ▼

To the Honorable Commissioner of Patents and Trademarks: Please record the attached original documents or copy thereof.

1. Name of conveying party(ies):

☐ Individual(s)   ☐ Association
☐ General Partnership   ☐ Limited Partnership
☐ Corporation-State
☐ Other _____

Additional name(s) of conveying party(ies) attached? ☐ Yes ☐ No

2. Name and address of receiving party(ies):

Name: _____

Internal Address: _____

Street Address: _____

City: _____ State: ____ ZIP: _____

☐ Individual(s) citizenship _____
☐ Association _____
☐ General Partnership _____
☐ Limited Partnership _____
☐ Corporation-State _____
☐ Other _____

If assignee is not domiciled in the United States, a domestic representative designation is attached: ☐ Yes ☐ No

(Designations must be a separate document from Assignment)

Additional name(s) & address(es) attached?   ☐ Yes ☐ No

3. Nature of conveyance:

☐ Assignment   ☐ Merger
☐ Security Agreement ☐ Change of Name
☐ Other _____

Execution Date: _____

4. Application number(s) or registration number(s):

A. Trademark Application No.(s)

B. Trademark registration No.(s)

Additional numbers attached? ☐ Yes ☐ No

5. Name and address of party to whom correspondence concerning document should be mailed:

Name: _____

Internal Address: _____

_____

_____

Street Address: _____

_____

City: _____ State: ____ ZIP: _____

6. Total number of applications and registrations involved: ....

7. Total fee (37 CFR 3.41): .... $ _____

☐ Enclosed

☐ Authorized to be charged to deposit account

8. Deposit account number:

_____

(Attach duplicate copy of this page if paying by deposit account)

DO NOT USE THIS SPACE

9. Statement and signature.
To the best of my knowledge and belief, the foregoing information is true and correct and any attached copy is a true copy of the original document.

_____   _____   _____
Name of Person Signing   Signature   Date

Total number of pages comprising cover sheet:

OMB No. 0651-0011 (exp. 4/94)

- Do not detach this portion -

Mail documents to be recorded with required cover sheet information to:

Commissioner of Patents and Trademarks
Box Assignments
Washington, D.C. 20231

Public burden reporting for this sample cover sheet is estimated to average about 30 minutes per document to be recorded, including time for reviewing the document and gathering the data needed, and completing and reviewing the sample cover sheet. Send comments regarding this burden estimate to the U.S. Patent and Trademark Office, Office of information Systems, PK2-1000C, Washington, D.C. 20231, and to the Office of Management and Budget, Paperwork Reduction Project (0651-0011), Washington, D.C. 20503.

PTO Form 1594

GUIDELINES FOR COMPLETING TRADEMARKS COVER SHEETS

Cover Sheet information must be submitted with each document to be recorded. If the document to be recorded concerns both patents and trademarks, separate patent and trademark cover sheets, including any attached pages for continuing information, must accompany the document. All pages of the cover sheet should be numbered consecutively, for example, if both a patent and trademark cover sheet is used, and information is continued on one additional page for both patents and trademarks, the pages of the cover sheet would be numbered from 1 to 4.

Item 1. Name of Conveying Party(ies).

Enter the full name of the party(ies) conveying the interest. If there is more than one conveying party, enter a check mark in the "Yes" box to indicate that additional information is attached. The name of the second and any subsequent conveying party(ies) should be placed on an attached page clearly identified as a continuation of the information in Item 1. Enter a check mark in the "No" box, if no information is contained on an attached page.

Item 2. Name and Address of Receiving Party(ies).

Enter the name and full address of the first party receiving the interest. If there is more than one party receiving the interest, enter a check mark in the "Yes" to indicate that additional information is attached. An entity type must be indicated for each receiving party, and the citizenship of individuals must be indicated. If the receiving party is an assignee not domiciled in the United States, a designation of domestic representative is required. A designation of domestic representative must be contained in a document separate from the assignment document. Place a check mark in appropriate box to indicate whether or not a designation of domestic representative is attached. Enter a check mark in the "No" box, if no information is contained on an attached page.

Item 3. Nature of Conveyance.

Place a check mark in the appropriate box describing the nature of the conveying assignment document. If the "Other" box is checked, specify the nature of the conveyance. Enter the execution date of the document. It is preferable to use the name of the month, or an abbreviation of that name, in order that confusion over dates is minimized.

Item 4. Application Number(s) or Registration number(s).

Indicate the application number(s) including series code and serial number, and/or registration number(s) against which the document is to be recorded. Enter a check mark in the appropriate box: "Yes" or "No" if additional numbers appear on attached pages. Be sure to identify numbers included on attached pages as the continuation of Item 4.

Item 5. Name and Address of Party to whom correspondence concerning the document should be mailed.

Enter the name and full address of the party to whom correspondence is to be mailed.

Item 6. Total Applications and Registration Involved.

Enter the total number of applications and trademarks identified for recordation. Be sure to include all applications and registrations identified on the cover sheet and on additional pages.

Item 7. Total Fee Enclosed.

Enter the total fee enclosed or authorized to be charged. A fee is required for each application and registration against which the document is recorded.

Item 8. Deposit Account Number.

Enter the deposit account number to authorize charges. Attach a duplicate copy of cover sheet to be used for the deposit charge account transaction.

Item 9. Statement and Signature.

Enter the name of the person submitting the document. The submitter must sign and date the cover sheet, confirming that to the best of the persons knowledge and belief, the information contained on the cover sheet is correct and that any copy of the document is a true copy of the original document. Enter the total number of pages contained in the cover sheet package, including any attached pages containing information continued from Items on the cover sheet.

PTO Form 1594 *continued*

State Unfair Competition, Trademark, and Dilution Statutes			
	Unfair Competition Statute	Trademark Statute	Dilution Statute
Alabama	Ala. Code § 8-19-1 *et seq.*	Ala. Code § 8-12-6 *et seq.*	Ala. Code § 8-12-17
Alaska	Alaska Stat. § 45.50.471 *et seq.*	Alaska Stat. § 45.50.010 *et seq.*	X
Arizona	Ariz. Rev. Stat. Ann. § 44-1521 *et seq.*	Ariz. Rev. Stat. Ann. § 44-1441 *et seq.*	X
Arkansas	Ark. Code Ann. § 70-901 *et seq.*	Ark. Code Ann. § 4-71-101 *et seq.*	Ark. Code Ann. § 4-7-113
California	Cal. Bus. & Prof. Code § 17200 *et seq.*	Cal. Bus. & Prof. Code § 14200 *et seq.*	Cal. Bus. & Prof. Code § 14330
Colorado	Colo. Rev. Stat. § 6-1-101 *et seq.*	Colo. Rev. Stat § 7-70-102 *et seq.*	X
Connecticut	Conn. Gen. Stat. § 42-110(a) *et seq.*	Conn. Gen. Stat. 621a, § 35-11a *et seq.*	Conn. Gen. Stat. 621a, § 35-11i(c)
Delaware	Del. Code Ann. tit. 6, § 2511 *et seq.*	Del. Code Ann. tit. 6, § 3301 *et seq.*	Del. Code Ann. tit. 6, § 3313
District of Columbia	D.C. Code Ann. § 28-3904 *et seq.*	Trademarks registrable under the Lanham Act, 15 U.S.C. § 1051 *et seq.*	X
Florida	Fla. Stat. Ann. § 501.201 *et seq.*	Fla. Stat. Ann. § 495.011 *et seq.*	Fla. Stat. Ann. § 495.151
Georgia	Ga. Code Ann. § 10-1-390 *et seq.*	Ga. Code Ann. § 10-1-440 *et seq.*	Ga. Code Ann. § 10-1-451(b)
Hawaii	Haw. Rev. Stat. § 480-1 *et seq.*	Haw. Rev. Stat. § 482 *et seq.*	X
Idaho	Idaho Code § 48-601 *et seq.*	Idaho Code § 48-501 *et seq.*	Idaho Code § 48-512
Illinois	Ill. Ann. Stat. ch. 121 1/2, para 261 *et seq.*	Ill. Rev. Stat. ch. 140, para. 8-22	Ill. Rev. Stat. ch. 140, para. 22
Indiana	Ind. Code § 24-5-0.5-1 *et seq.*	Ind. Code § 24-2-1-1 *et seq.*	X
Iowa	Iowa Code § 714.16	Iowa Code § 548 *et seq.*	Iowa Code § 548.11(2)
Kansas	Kan. Stat. Ann. § 50-623 *et seq.*	Kan. Stat. Ann. § 81-111 *et seq.*	X
Kentucky	Ky. Rev. Stat. Ann. § 367.110 *et seq.*	Ky. Rev. Stat. Ann. § 365.560 *et seq.*	X
Louisiana	La. Rev. Stat. Ann. § 51-1401 *et seq.*	La. Rev. Stat. Ann. § 51-211 *et seq.*	La. Rev. Stat. Ann. § 51-223.1
Maine	Me. Rev. Stat. Ann. tit. 5, § 206 *et seq.*	Me. Rev. Stat. Ann. tit. 10, § 1521 *et seq.*	Me. Rev. Stat. Ann. tit. 10, § 1530 *et seq.*
Maryland	Md. Com. Law Code Ann. § 13-101 *et seq.*	Md. Ann. Code art. 41, § 3-101 *et seq.*	X

	State Unfair Competition, Trademark, and Dilution Statutes (Continued)		
	Unfair Competition Statute	Trademark Statute	Dilution Statute
Massachusetts	Mass. Gen. Laws Ann. ch. 93A, § 1 *et seq.*	Mass. Ann. Laws ch. 110B, § 1 *et seq.*	Mass. Ann. Laws ch. 110B, § 12
Michigan	Mich. Comp. Laws § 445.901 *et seq.*	Mich. Comp. Laws § 429.31 *et seq.*	X
Minnesota	Minn. Stat. Ann. § 325F.68 *et seq.*	Minn. Stat. Ann. § 333.001 *et seq.*	X
Mississippi	Miss. Code Ann. § 75-24-1 *et seq.*	Miss. Code Ann. § 75-25-1 *et seq.*	X
Missouri	Mo. Rev. Stat. § 407.010 *et seq.*	Mo. Rev. Stat. § 417.005 *et seq.*	Mo. Rev. Stat. § 417.061(1)
Montana	Mont. Code. Ann. § 30-14-101 *et seq.*	Mont. Code. Ann. § 30-13-301 *et seq.*	Mont. Code. Ann. § 30-13-3334
Nebraska	Neb. Rev. Stat. § 59-1601 *et seq.*	Neb. Rev. Stat. § 87-101 *et seq.*	Neb. Rev. Stat. § 87-122
Nevada	Nev. Rev. Stat. § 598-360 *et seq.*	Nev. Rev. Stat. § 600.240 *et seq.*	X
New Hampshire	N.H. Rev. Stat. Ann. § 358-A:1 *et seq.*	N.H. Rev. Stat. Ann. § 350-A *et seq.*	N.H. Rev. Stat. Ann. § 350-A:12
New Jersey	N.J. Rev. Stat. Ann. § 56:8-1 *et seq.*	N.J. Rev. Stat. Ann. § 56:3-13.1 *et seq.*	X
New Mexico	N.M. Stat. Ann. § 57-12-1 *et seq.*	N.M. Stat. Ann. § 57-3-1 *et seq.*	N.M. Stat. Ann. § 57-3-10
New York	N.Y. Gen. Bus. Law § 349 *et seq.*	N.Y. Gen. Bus. Law § 360 *et seq.*	N.Y. Gen. Bus. Law § 368-d
North Carolina	N.C. Gen. Stat. § 75-1 *et seq.*	N.C. Gen. Stat. § 80-1 *et seq.*	X
North Dakota	N.D. Cent. Code § 51-15-01 *et seq.*	N.D. Cent. Code § 47-22	X
Ohio	Ohio Rev. Code Ann. § 1345.01 *et seq.*	Ohio Rev. Code Ann. § 1329.54 *et seq.*	X
Oklahoma	Okla. Stat. Ann. tit. 15, § 751 *et seq.*	Okla. Stat. Ann. tit. 78, § 21 *et seq.*	X
Oregon	Or. Rev. Stat. § 646.605 *et seq.*	Or. Rev. Stat. § 647.005 *et seq.*	Or. Rev. Stat. § 647.107
Pennsylvania	Pa. Stat. Ann. tit. 73, § 201-1 *et seq.*	54 Pa. Cons. Stat. Ann. § 1101 *et seq.*	54 Pa. Cons. Stat. Ann. § 1124
Rhode Island	R.I. Gen. Laws § 6-13.1-1 *et seq.*	R.I. Gen. Laws § 6-2-1 *et seq.*	R.I. Gen. Laws § 6-2-12
South Carolina	S.C. Code Ann. § 39-5-10 *et seq.*	S.C. Code Ann. § 39-15-120 *et seq.*	X

	State Unfair Competition, Trademark, and Dilution Statutes (Continued)		
	Unfair Competition Statute	Trademark Statute	Dilution Statute
South Dakota	S.D. Codified Laws § 37-24-1 *et seq.*	S.D. Codified Laws § 37-6 *et seq.*	X
Tennessee	Tenn. Code Ann. § 47-18-101 et seq.	Tenn. Code Ann. § 47-25-501 *et seq.*	Tenn. Code Ann. § 47-25-512
Texas	Tex. Bus. & Com. Code § 17.41 *et seq.*	Tex. Bus. & Com. Code § 16.01 *et seq.*	Tex. Bus. & Com. Code § 16.29
Utah	Utah Code Ann. § 13-11 1 et seq.	Utah Code Ann. § 70-3-1 *et seq.*	X
Vermont	Vt. Stat. Ann. tit. 9, § 2541 *et seq.*	Vt. Stat. Ann. tit. 9, § 2521 *et seq.*	X
Virginia	Va. Code Ann. § 59.1-196 *et seq.*	Va. Code Ann. § 59.1-77 *et seq.*	X
Washington	Wash. Rev. Code § 19.86.010 *et seq.*	Wash. Rev. Code § 19.77.010 *et seq.*	Wash. Rev. Code § 19.77
West Virginia	W. Va. Code § 46A-6-101 *et seq.*	W. Va. Code § 47-2-1 *et seq.*	X
Wisconsin	Wis. Stat. § 100.20 *et seq.*	Wis. Stat. § 132.01 *et seq.*	X
Wyoming	Wyo. Stat. § 40-12-101 *et seq.*	Wyo. Stat. § 40-1-101 *et seq.*	X

State Trademark Registration Addresses	
	Where to File State Trademark Application
Alabama	Secretary of State Lands & Trademark Division Room 528, State Office Building Montgomery, AL 36130-7701
Alaska	Department of Commerce & Economic Development Corporations Section P.O. Box D Juneau, AK 99811
Arizona	Office of the Secretary of State 1700 W. Washington Phoenix, AZ 85007-2808
Arkansas	Secretary of State State Capitol Little Rock, AR 72201-1094
California	Secretary of State Trademark Unit 1230 "J" Street Sacramento, CA 95814
Colorado	Secretary of State Corporations Office, Suite 200 1560 Broadway Denver, CO 80202
Connecticut	Secretary of State Division of Corporations & Trademarks, Attn.: Trademarks 30 Trinity Street Hartford, CT 06106
Delaware	Department of State Division of Corporations Att: Trademark Filings John G. Townsend Building P.O. Box 898 Dover, DE 19903
Florida	Corporate Records Bureau, Division of Corporations Department of State P.O. Box 6327 Tallahassee, FL 32301
Georgia	Secretary of State State of Georgia 306 West Floyd Towers 2 Martin Luther King Drive Atlanta, GA 30334

State Trademark Registration Addresses (Continued)	
	Where to File State Trademark Application
Hawaii	Department of Commerce & Consumer Affairs Business Registration Division 1010 Richards Street Honolulu, HI 96813
Idaho	Secretary of State Room 203 Statehouse Boise, ID 83720
Illinois	Secretary of State Index Department, Trademark Division 111 East Monroe Springfield, IL 62756
Indiana	Secretary of State Trademark Division Room 155, State House Indianapolis, IN 46204
Iowa	Secretary of State Corporate Division Hoover Building Des Moines, IA 50319
Kansas	Secretary of State State Capitol 2d Floor Topeka, KS 66612-1594
Kentucky	Secretary of State Frankfort, KY 40601
Louisiana	Secretary of State Corporations Division P.O. Box 94125 Baton Rouge, LA 70804-9125
Maine	Secretary of State State of Maine, Trademarks Division of Public Administration State House, Station 101 Augusta, ME 04333
Maryland	Secretary of State State House Annapolis, MD 21401

State Trademark Registration Addresses (Continued)	
	Where to File State Trademark Application
Massachusetts	Secretary of State Room 1711 One Ashburton Place Boston, MA 02108
Michigan	Michigan Department of Commerce Corporations & Securities Bureau Securities Division P.O. Box 30222 Lansing, MI 48909
Minnesota	Secretary of State Corporation Division 180 State Office Building St. Paul, MN 55155
Mississippi	Secretary of State P.O. Box 1350 Jackson, MS 39215
Missouri	Secretary of State P.O. Box 778 Jefferson City, MO 65101
Montana	Secretary of State Montana State Capitol Helena, MT 59620
Nebraska	Secretary of State State Capitol Building Lincoln, NE 68509
Nevada	Secretary of State Capitol Complex Carson City, NV 89710
New Hampshire	Corporate Division Secretary of State State House Annex Concord, NH 03301
New Jersey	Secretary of State State House CN-300 West State Street Trenton, NJ 08625
New Mexico	Secretary of State Lamy Building 4901 Old Santa Fe Trail Santa Fe, NM 87503

	State Trademark Registration Addresses **(Continued)**
	Where to File State Trademark Application
New York	Secretary of State Department of State Miscellaneous Records 162 Washington Avenue Albany, NY 12231
North Carolina	Trademark Division Secretary of State 300 North Salisbury Street Raleigh, NC 27611
North Dakota	Secretary of State State Capitol 600 East Boulevard Avenue Bismarck, ND 58505
Ohio	Secretary of State Corporations Department 30 East Broad Street, 14th Floor Columbus, OH 43266-0418
Oklahoma	Secretary of State State of Oklahoma 101 State Capitol Building Oklahoma City, OK 73105
Oregon	Director/Corporation Division Secretary of State 158 12th Street NE Salem, OR 97310-0210
Pennsylvania	Department of State Corporation Bureau 308 North Office Building Harrisburg, PA 17120
Puerto Rico	Secretary of State P.O. Box 3271 San Juan, PR 00904
Rhode Island	Secretary of State Trademarks Division 100 North Main Street Providence, RI 02903
South Carolina	Secretary of State P.O. Box 11350 Columbia, SC 29211

State Trademark Registration Addresses (Continued)	
	Where to File State Trademark Application
South Dakota	Secretary of State State Capitol Building 500 East Capitol Pierre, SD 57501
Tennessee	Secretary of State Suite 500 James K. Polk Building Nashville, TN 37219
Texas	Secretary of State Corporate Section, Trademark Office P.O. Box 13697, Capitol Station Austin, TX 78711-3697
Utah	Division of Corporations & Commercial Code Herbert M. Wells Building 160 East 300 South Salt Lake City, UT 84111
Vermont	Secretary of State Corporations Division State Office Building Montpelier, VT 05602
Virginia	State Corporation Commission Division of Securities & Retail Franchises 1220 Bank Street Richmond, VA 23209
Washington	Corporations Division Secretary of State Republic Bldg.—2d Floor 505 Union Avenue SE Olympia, WA 98504
West Virginia	Secretary of State Corporations Division State Capitol Charleston, WV 25305
Wisconsin	Secretary of State Trademark Records P.O. Box 7848 Madison, WI 53707-7848
Wyoming	Secretary of State Corporation Division Capitol Building Cheyenne, WY 82002

APPENDIX G

Patent Directory Libraries Offering CASSIS

Listing of Patent Directory Libraries Offering CASSIS—Classification and Search Support Information System	
	Name of Library
Alabama	Auburn University Library Birmingham Public Library
Alaska	Anchorage Municipal Library
Arizona	Tempe: Noble Library, Arizona State University
Arkansas	Little Rock: Arkansas State Library
California	Los Angeles Public Library Sacramento: California State Library San Diego Public Library Sunnyvale: Patent Information Clearinghouse
Colorado	Denver Public Library
Connecticut	New Haven: Science Park Library
Delaware	Newark: University of Delaware Library
District of Columbia	Washington: Howard University Library
Florida	Fort Lauderdale: Broward County Main Library Miami-Dade Public Library
Georgia	Atlanta: Price Gilbert Memorial Library, Georgia Institute of Technology
Idaho	Moscow: University of Idaho Library
Illinois	Chicago Public Library Springfield: Illinois State Library
Indiana	Indianapolis-Marion County Public Library
Louisiana	Baton Rouge: Troy H. Middleton Library, Louisiana State University
Maryland	College Park: Engineering and Physical Sciences Library, University of Maryland
Massachusetts	Amherst: Physical Sciences Library, University of Massachusetts Boston Public Library
Michigan	Ann Arbor: Engineering Transportation Library, University of Michigan Detroit Public Library
Minnesota	Minneapolis Public Library & Information Center
Missouri	Kansas City: Linda Hall Library St. Louis Public Library
Montana	Butte: Montana College of Mineral Science and Technology Library
Nebraska	Lincoln: Engineering Library, University of Nebraska-Lincoln
Nevada	Reno: University of Nevada Library

	Listing of Patent Directory Libraries Offering CASSIS— Classification and Search Support Information System (Continued)
	Name of Library
New Hampshire	Durham: University of New Hampshire Library
New Jersey	Newark Public Library
New Mexico	Albuquerque: University of New Mexico Library
New York	Albany: New York State Library Buffalo and Erie County Public Library New York Public Library (The Research Libraries)
North Carolina	Raleigh: D.H. Hill Library, North Carolina State University
Ohio	Cincinnati & Hamilton County Public Library Cleveland Public Library Columbus: Ohio State University Libraries Toledo/Lucas County Public Library
Oklahoma	Stillwater: Oklahoma State University Library
Oregon	Salem: Oregon State Library
Pennsylvania	Philadelphia: Free Library Pittsburgh: Carnegie Library of Pittsburgh University Park: Pattee Library, Pennsylvania State University
Rhode Island	Providence Public Library
South Carolina	Charleston: Medical University of South Carolina Library
Tennessee	Memphis & Shelby County Public Library Nashville: Vanderbilt University Library
Texas	Austin: McKinney Engineering Library, University of Texas at Austin College Station: Sterling C. Evans Library, Texas A&M University Dallas Public Library Houston: The Fondren Library, Rice University
Utah	Salt Lake City: Marriott Library, University of Utah
Virginia	Richmond: Virginia Commonwealth University Library
Washington	Seattle: Engineering Library, University of Washington
Wisconsin	Madison: Kurt F. Wendt Library, University of Wisconsin-Madison Milwaukee Public Library

GLOSSARY

abandonment of trademark   Loss of trademark rights resulting from nonuse of the mark; demonstrated by sufficient evidence that the owner intends to discontinue use of the mark. May also occur when a mark has lost its distinctiveness or through the owner's misuse of trademark rights.

abstract   Summary of the invention that enables the reader to determine the character of the patentable subject matter.

access   The reasonable opportunity of the defendant to view or hear the copyrighted work.

actual damages   The plaintiff's provable monetary damages resulting from the infringing acts.

Amendment to Allege Use   Amendment to an intent-to-use application indicating use of a mark in commerce; the amendment can only be filed before approval of the mark for publication (or, if there is a rejection, within six months of the response period).

answer   Written response to the complaint, in which the defendant admits or denies the complaint's allegations and provides a list of defenses.

arbitrary mark   Word or image that has a common meaning that does not describe or suggest the goods or services with which it is associated.

arbitration   Referral of a dispute to one or more impartial persons for final or advisory determination.

architectural work   The design of a building as embodied in any tangible medium of expression, including a building, architectural plans, or drawings; it includes the overall form as well as the arrangement and composition of spaces and elements in the design, but does not include individual standard features.

article of manufacture   A single object without movable parts or an object whose movable parts are incidental to its function.

audiovisual works   Works that consist of a series of related images which are intrinsically intended to be shown by the use of machines or devices, such as projectors, viewers, or electronic equipment, together with accompanying sounds, if any, regardless of the nature of the material objects, such as films or tapes, in which the works are embodied.

author   Person or entity that creates a copyrightable work or expression, whether literary, musical, or otherwise; or, under certain circumstances, the person or entity that commissions the work or pays for the work under an employment agreement.

authorization of agent   Inventor's or patent owner's authorization of representation by a patent agent.

automated database   A body of facts, data, or other information assembled into an organized format suitable for use in a computer and comprising one or more files.

basic registration   The primary copyright record made for each version of a particular work.

best edition   The edition, published in the United States at any time before the date of deposit, that the Library of Congress determines to be most suitable for its purposes.

best mode   Requirement that the inventor disclose the principal and preferred method of embodying the invention.

cable system   Facility that receives television broadcast signals and makes secondary transmissions of such signals by wires, cables, or other channels of communication to subscribing members of the public.

cancellation proceeding   Administrative action brought before the Trademark Trial and Appeal Board to cancel a federal registration of a mark; must be based upon one of the statutory grounds provided in the Lanham Act and the party bringing the action must prove that it would be damaged.

cease and desist letter   Correspondence from the owner of a proprietary work that informs the allegedly infringing party of the validity and ownership of the proprietary work, the nature of the infringement, and remedies available to the owner; requests the cessation of all infringing activity.

certification mark   Mark indicating that third-party goods or services meet certain standards, such as regional origin, material, mode of manufacture, quality, or accuracy, or that the work or labor was performed by a member of a certain organization.

choreography   Composition and arrangement of dance movements.

civil cover sheet   Form required at the time of filing of the complaint for court use in maintaining certain statistical records.

claims   Portion of patent that defines the novel and nonobvious elements of the invention or discovery; protection under patent law extends only to matter within the scope of the claims.

clean room   Method of developing proprietary material in which an isolated development team is monitored; the purpose is to provide evidence that similarities in works or products are due to legitimate considerations and not copying.

clear and convincing proof   Evidence that is highly probable and free from serious doubt.

coin-operated phonorecord player   Machine or device employed solely for the performance of non-dramatic musical works by means of phonorecords and upon insertion of coins or currency (or their equivalent). To qualify for compulsory license, such a device must meet the requirements of 17 U.S.C. § 116.

collaboration agreement   Contract in which joint authors specify the rights, obligations, percentage of copyright ownership and revenues attributable to each author.

collateral estoppel   When a plaintiff is restricted because of facts that were determined in a previous action.

collective mark   Mark used by members of a collective group or organization to signify membership or source of the group's goods or services.

collective work   A work, such as a periodical issue, anthology, or encyclopedia, in which a number of contributions, constituting separate and independent works in themselves, are assembled into a collective whole.

commerce   For federal trademark registration purposes, any commerce lawfully regulated by the United States. For state trademark registration purposes, generally any commerce occurring within the state of registration.

common law   A system of legal rules derived from the precedents and principles established by court decisions.

common law copyright   A system of protection based upon the precedents and principles established by court decisions; affected unpublished, unregistered works created before January 1, 1978; applied by state courts or federal courts interpreting state law.

compilation   A work formed by the collection and assembling of preexisting materials or of data that are selected, coordinated, or arranged in such a way that the resulting work as a whole constitutes an original work of authorship. The term *compilation* includes collective works.

complaint   Initial document filed in a lawsuit; sets forth the basis of the plaintiff's claims and requests certain remedies.

complete copy   All elements comprising the unit of publication of the best edition of the work, including elements that, if considered separately, would not be copyrightable subject matter or would otherwise be exempt from mandatory deposit requirements.

compulsory copyright license   System established by statute that permits the use of copyrighted works under certain circumstances and provided that certain fixed fees are paid.

computer program   A set of statements or instructions to be used directly or indirectly in a computer to bring about a certain result.

concurrent use   When more than one person is entitled to use a similar mark; results from a determination by either the Commissioner of the Patent and Trademark Office or by a court of competent jurisdiction.

concurrent use proceeding   An administrative proceeding when the user of a trademark desires to federally register a trademark concurrently with another person already using the mark in a geographic area; provided that the junior user did not know (or had no reason to know) of the senior user's use of the trademark.

confidentiality agreement (also known as nondisclosure agreement)   Contract that restricts the disclosure of trade secrets.

continuation application   Second patent application filed after an earlier filed application has been disallowed (but not yet abandoned); a method of resubmitting the application with new claims or further evidence in support of patentability.

continuation in part application   A second subsequent patent application containing new material not previously disclosed in an earlier filed application; a method of supplementing an earlier patent application with new matter to cover improvements.

contributory copyright infringer (also called vicarious infringer)   One who, with knowledge or reason to know of infringing activity of another, induces, causes or materially contributes to the infringement of a copyright; or one who has the right and ability to supervise the infringing activities and also has a direct financial interest in such activities.

copy   Tangible object (other than phonorecords) in which a work is fixed by any method now known or later developed, and from which the work can be perceived, reproduced, or otherwise communicated, either directly or with the aid of a machine or device. The term *copies* includes the material object (other than a phonorecord) in which the work is first fixed.

copyright   The legal right to exclude others, for a limited time, from copying, selling, performing, displaying, or making derivative versions of a work of authorship.

counterclaim   Claim for relief usually asserted by the defendant against an opposing party, usually the plaintiff.

counterfeiting   Extreme form of trademark infringement in which an identical or indistinguishable trademark is used on goods or services for which the original mark is still being used.

covenant not to compete   Contract provision that restrains a person from engaging in a business, trade, or profession for a period of time; may not be enforceable in some states.

created   When a work of authorship is fixed in a copy or phonorecord for the first time. If a work is prepared over a period of time, the portion of it that has been fixed at any particular time constitutes the work as of that time; if the work has been prepared in different versions, each version constitutes a separate work.

date of invention   Either the date the invention was conceived (providing that the applicant diligently reduced the invention to practice) or the actual date of reduction to practice.

declaratory relief action   Request that the court sort out the rights and legal obligations of the parties in the midst of an actual controversy.

deposition   Oral or written testimony of a party or witness, given under oath.

derivative work A work based upon one or more preexisting works, such as a translation, musical arrangement, dramatization, fictionalization, motion picture version, sound recording, art reproduction, abridgment, condensation, or any other form in which a work may be recast, transformed, or adapted. A work consisting of editorial revisions, annotations, elaborations, or other modifications that, as a whole, represent an original work of authorship is also a derivative work.

design patent Legal protection granted for a new, original, and ornamental design for an article of manufacture; protects only the aesthetic appearance of an article, not its structure or utilitarian features.

device Anything that serves to differentiate goods or services.

dilution The adverse effect of use of a similar mark on the reputation of a distinctive mark, even though the use may not confuse consumers as to the source of the goods or services; occurs when the defendant's use weakens or reduces the distinctive quality of the mark. A claim of dilution is available only under state laws sometimes known as *antidilution* statutes.

disclaimer Statement that a trademark owner asserts no exclusive right in a specific portion of a mark, apart from its use within the mark.

display publicly To show a copy of a copyrighted work, either directly or by means of a film, slide, television image, or any other device or process where the public is gathered *or* the work is transmitted or otherwise communicated to the public; in the case of a motion picture or other audiovisual work, the nonsequential showing of individual images.

diversity The right to file a lawsuit based upon nonfederal claims in federal court; parties must be from different states and the matter in controversy must be more than $50,000.

divisional application Application made for an independent invention that has grown out of an earlier application; a method of dividing an original application that contains two or more inventions. Trademark applications may also be divided (*see* 37 C.F.R. § 2.87).

doctrine of equivalents Right of patent owner to prevent sale, use, or manufacture of a discovery or invention if it employs substantially the same means to achieve substantially the same results in substantially the same way as that claimed.

dramatic works Narrative presentations (and any accompanying music) that generally use dialogue and stage directions as the basis for a theatrical exhibition.

drawing (trademark) A substantially exact representation of the mark as used (or, in the case of intent-to-use applications, as intended to be used). A drawing is required for all federal trademark applications and for many state trademark applications.

ephemeral recordings Copies or phonorecords of works, made for purposes of later transmission.

estoppel Defense to infringement in which the defendant prevents the plaintiff from contradicting behavior upon which the defendant has justifiably relied. To assert successfully an estoppel defense, the plaintiff must know the facts of the defendant's conduct and the defendant must have a justifiable belief that such infringing conduct is permitted.

evaluation agreement Contract by which one party promises to submit an idea and the other party promises to evaluate the idea. After the evaluation, the evaluator will either enter into an agreement to exploit the idea or promise not to use or disclose the idea.

exclusive jurisdiction A court's sole authority to hear a certain type of case.

exclusive license Agreement to restrict the grant of proprietary rights to one person.

exhaustion doctrine Once a patented product (or product resulting from a patented process) is sold or licensed, the patent owner loses some or all patent rights as to the resale of that particular article.

experimental use doctrine Rule excusing an inventor from the one year bar, provided that the alleged sale or public use was primarily for the purpose of perfecting or testing the invention.

extended renewal term An extension of the renewal term from 28 to 47 years for works registered under the Copyrights Act of 1909 that were in their renewal term on January 1, 1978, or that were renewed after January 1, 1978.

fair use   Right to use copyrighted material for limited purposes and without authorization from the author; determined by a federal court after it weighs several factors, including the nature of the copyrighted work, the purpose and character of the use, the amount and substantiality of the portion borrowed, and the effect of the use on the market for the copyrighted material.

fanciful mark   Term that is coined or made up for trademark purposes; generally a word or combination of letters that has no dictionary meaning.

fiduciary relationship   A special relationship of trust, confidence, or responsibility between persons.

file wrapper estoppel (also called prosecution history estoppel)   Affirmative defense used in patent infringement litigation that precludes patent owner from asserting rights that were disclaimed during the patent application process.

first sale doctrine   In copyright law, the legal doctrine upholding the right of the owner of a lawfully made copy or phonorecord to sell or otherwise dispose of possession of that copy or phonorecord, without the authority of the copyright owner. The doctrine includes the right of the owner of a lawfully made copy to display that copy publicly, either directly or by the projection of no more than one image at a time, to viewers present at the place where the copy is located without authorization from the copyright owner.

fixed   Embodiment of a work in a tangible medium of expression by or under the authority of the author, which is sufficiently permanent or stable to permit it to be perceived, reproduced, or otherwise communicated for a period of more than transitory duration; in the case of sounds, images, or both that are being transmitted, a work is "fixed" if a fixation of the work is being made simultaneously with its transmission.

generic term   Term that describes an entire group or class of goods.

genericide   Process by which trademark rights are lost because consumers have begun to think of the trademark as the descriptive name for the goods.

good will   Tendency or likelihood of a consumer to repurchase goods or services based upon the name or source of the goods or services.

hallmark   Graphic icon (rather than a word or group of words) that functions to identify the source for various products or services from one company.

house mark   Mark that functions to identify the source for various products or services from one company.

improper means   The illegal acquisition of trade secrets through theft, bribery, misrepresentation, breach, or inducement of a breach of a duty to maintain secrecy, or espionage through electronic or other means.

incontestable   Trademark that is immune from challenge except on certain grounds specified in § 33(b) of the Lanham Act; provides conclusive evidence of the registrant's exclusive right to use the registered mark in commerce in connection with the specified goods or services.

information disclosure statement (IDS)   Pertinent information regarding an application provided to the Patent and Trademark Office; includes prior art, any related patents, and printed publications by the inventor.

infringement   Violation of any exclusive right granted under intellectual property law.

injunction   Court order directing the defendant to stop certain activities.

intellectual property   Any product of the human mind that is protected under law.

intellectual property audit   A review and analysis of a company's intellectual property portfolio.

intent-to-use application   Application for federal trademark registration based upon the trademark owner's bona fide intention to use the mark in commerce.

inter partes proceeding Formal administrative hearing involving more than one party.

interference proceeding Administrative hearing before the Trademark Trial and Appeal Board, brought when two trademark applications are pending that conflict, or when a pending application conflicts with a registered mark that is not incontestable; permitted only under extraordinary circumstances. See *patent interference*.

International Schedule of Classes of Goods and Services A system for classifying goods and services, applicable to federal trademark applications filed on or after September 1, 1973.

interrogatories Written questions that must be answered under oath.

joint ownership agreement Contract detailing the conditions, obligations, and ownership interest of the joint creators of an invention.

joint work Work prepared by two or more authors with the intention that their contributions will be merged into inseparable or interdependent parts of a unitary whole.

judgment Relief awarded by the court after a final determination of the rights and obligations of the parties before the court.

junior user A party that adopts and uses a trademark similar to a mark previously adopted and used by a senior user.

jurisdiction A court's authority to hear a certain type of case.

jury instructions Explanations of the legal rules that the jury members are instructed by the judge to use in reaching a verdict.

laches Defense to infringement in which the defendant argues that the plaintiff's delay in bringing the lawsuit is so unreasonable that the plaintiff should be barred from proceeding.

license A contract that grants rights or permission to do something, subject to certain conditions.

literary works Works, other than audiovisual works, expressed in words, numbers, or other verbal or numerical symbols or indicia, regardless of the nature of the material objects, such as books, periodicals, manuscripts, phonorecords, film, tapes, disks, or cards, in which they are embodied.

logo Graphic symbols that function as a mark.

machine Device such as an engine or apparatus that accomplishes a result by the interaction of its parts.

magistrate An officer of the court who may exercise some of the authority of a federal district court judge, including the authority to conduct a jury or nonjury trial.

mechanical rights Rights to prepare and distribute phonorecords of a nondramatic musical work under a compulsory license.

mediation An alternative to arbitration in which the parties submit their dispute to an impartial mediator, who assists the parties in reaching a settlement.

misappropriation of trade secret Improper acquisition of a trade secret by a person who has reason to know that the trade secret was obtained by improper means, or the disclosure or use of a trade secret without consent by a person who either had a duty to maintain secrecy or who used improper means to acquire the secret.

moral rights Rights that protect the professional honor and reputation of an artist by guaranteeing the right to claim or disclaim authorship of a work and the right to prevent, in certain cases, distortion, mutilation, or other modification of the work.

motion Request for an order of the court.

motion for preliminary injunction Request that the court issue an order directing the defendant to stop certain activities.

motion for summary judgment Request that the court order a judgment without having a trial, because there is no genuine issue as to any material fact(s).

motion in limine Request made to the court, usually prior to the trial, that certain information not be presented to the jury.

motion picture Audiovisual works consisting of a series of related images that, when shown in succession, impart an impression of motion, together with accompanying sounds, if any.

multimedia work Work that combines authorship in two or more media.

multiple file database Collection of separate and distinct groups of data records.

musical work A composition incorporating melody, rhythm, and harmonic elements (and accompanying lyrics, if any).

new matter New subject matter that does not conform to and is not supported by the original patent application; material that cannot be added to the patent application by amendment.

nondisclosure agreement See *confidentiality agreement.*

nonobviousness Requirement that, to acquire a U.S. patent, the subject matter of the patent application be sufficiently different from what has been used or described before so that it would not have been obvious to a person having ordinary skill in the area of technology related to the invention.

novelty Statutory requirement that an invention must differ in some way from the publicly known or existing knowledge in the field.

novelty search See *patent search.*

on sale bar (also called one year grace period or one year bar) Doctrine that prevents an inventor from acquiring patent protection if the application is filed more than one year after the earliest date of sale or offer of sale or public use of the invention in the United States.

one year bar See *on sale bar.*

one year grace period See *on sale bar.*

opposition proceeding Action brought before the Trademark Trial and Appeal Board to prevent the federal registration of a mark; must be based upon one of the statutory grounds provided in the Lanham Act and the party bringing the action must prove that it would be damaged.

option agreement Agreement whereby one party pays the other for the opportunity to later exploit an idea or work.

owner of copyright Person or persons holding title to copyright; either the author or any party to whom the author has licensed or transferred a right under copyright.

pantomime Form of theater expressed by gestures but without words.

patent The legal right, for a limited term, to exclude others from using, selling, or making an invention or discovery as described in the patent claims.

patent agent A nonattorney licensed by the Patent and Trademark Office to prepare and prosecute patent applications.

patent attorney An attorney licensed by the Patent and Trademark Office to prepare and prosecute applications and perform other legal tasks.

patent interference (also called interference proceeding) Proceeding instituted in the Patent and Trademark Office to determine any question of priority of invention between two or more parties claiming the same patentable invention.

patent misuse Defense in patent infringement that prevents a patent owner who has abused patent law from enforcing patent rights.

patent search (also called novelty search) Noncomprehensive prior art search intended to help the inventor determine whether to file a patent application.

pendency period Time between filing of the patent application and issuance of a patent (usually 18 months or more).

pendent jurisdiction Authority of the federal courts to hear a matter normally within the jurisdiction of state courts. Pendent jurisdiction exists when the state law matter is combined with a claim that is within the authority of the federal courts.

perform publicly To recite, render, play, dance, or act a work, either directly or by means of any device or process, where the public is gathered *or* the work is transmitted or otherwise communicated to the public; in the case of a motion picture or other audiovisual work, to show its images in any sequence or to make the sounds accompanying it audible.

performing rights society An association or corporation that licenses the public performance of nondramatic musical works on behalf of the copyright owners, such as the American Society of Composers, Authors and Publishers (ASCAP); Broadcast Music, Inc. (BMI); or the Society of European Authors and Composers, Inc. (SESAC).

permanent injunction Durable injunction issued after a final judgment on the merits of the case; permanently restrains the defendant from engaging in the infringing activity.

Petition to Cancel Initial pleading filed by the petitioner in a cancellation proceeding.

Petition to Make Special Request to accelerate processing of a patent application.

phonorecords Material objects in which sounds, other than those accompanying a motion picture or other audiovisual work, are fixed by any method now known or later developed, and from which the sounds can be perceived, reproduced, or otherwise communicated, either directly or with the aid of a machine or device. The term *phonorecords* includes the material object in which the sounds are first fixed.

pictorial, graphic, and sculptural works
Two-dimensional and three-dimensional works of fine, graphic, and applied art, photographs, prints and art reproductions, maps, globes, charts, diagrams, models, and technical drawings, including architectural plans. Such works include works of artistic craftsmanship insofar as their form but not their mechanical or utilitarian aspects are concerned. The design of a useful article is considered a pictorial, graphic, or sculptural work only if, and only to the extent that, such design incorporates pictorial, graphic, or sculptural features that can be identified separately from, and are capable of existing independently of, the utilitarian aspects of the article.

plant patent Legal protection granted to the person who first appreciates the distinctive qualities of a plant and reproduces it by means other than seeds.

power of attorney Inventor's or patent owner's authorization of representation by a patent attorney.

preemption Authority of the federal government to preclude the states from exercising powers granted to the federal government by the Constitution.

preliminary injunction Injunction granted after a noticed hearing at which the parties have an opportunity to present evidence, including the likelihood of the plaintiff's success on the merits, the balancing of hardships, the public interest, and the irreparability of the harm to be suffered if the injunction is not granted; lasts until a final judgment has been rendered.

preponderance of the evidence Proof that produces the belief that the facts are more likely true than not.

presumption An inference as to the truth or validity of an allegation. A presumption shifts the burden to the other party to disprove or show, with sufficient evidence, the falsity or invalidity of the allegation.

primary transmission A transmission made to the public by a facility whose signals are received and further transmitted by a secondary transmission service, regardless of where or when the performance or display was first transmitted.

prior art Publicly known or existing knowledge in the field of the invention or discovery which is available prior to, or at the time of, the invention.

priority of invention U.S. patent policy awarding a patent to the first person to invent over persons who subsequently invent the same patentable concept.

process Method of accomplishing a result through a series of steps involving physical or chemical interactions.

prosecution Process by which an inventor or patent practitioner guides the application through the Patent and Trademark Office.

prosecution history estoppel See *file wrapper estoppel*.

public domain Material that is not protected under copyright law and is free for use by the public.

publication Distribution of copies or phonorecords of a work to the public by sale or other transfer of ownership, or by rental, lease, or lending; the offering to distribute copies or phonorecords to a group of persons for purposes of further distribution, public performance, or public display.

reduction to practice Contemplation of the actual and complete use of the invention for its intended purpose (e.g., the physical prototyping and successful testing of the invention). The act of preparing and filing a patent application is considered a *constructive reduction to practice.*

reexamination Review by the Patent and Trademark Office of the patentability of one or more claims of an in-force patent, based upon substantial new evidence of prior art not previously considered.

reissue patent Patent granted to correct errors made in a patent that is in effect (i.e., an in-force patent) and that, as the result of such error, is rendered wholly or partially inoperative or invalid. Errors resulting from fraud or deceptive intent cannot be corrected by means of a reissue patent.

renewal term For works registered under the Copyright Act of 1909, it is a 28-year period following the initial 28-year term of copyright protection; renewal must have been made during the 28th year following first publication.

repair doctrine Right of an authorized licensor of a patented device to repair and replace unpatented components.

request for admission Request for a party to the lawsuit to admit the truthfulness of a fact or statement.

request for production of documents Method by which a party to a lawsuit may obtain documents or other physical evidence from another party.

request to divide out Statement included in an Amendment to Allege Use or a Statement of Use, asking to separate from the application certain goods for which the trademark has not been used.

reverse doctrine of equivalents Affirmative defense used in patent infringement when the allegedly infringing device performs the same function in a substantially different way.

reverse engineering Disassembly and examination of products that are available to the public.

rule of doubt Legal doctrine declaring that a work is registered even though a reasonable doubt exists at the Copyright Office as to whether the requirements of the Copyright Act have been met or whether the deposit materials constitute protectible subject matter under copyright law.

secondary meaning Demonstration that the consuming public associates a descriptive mark with a single source; usually proved by advertising, promotion, and sales.

secondary transmission The further transmitting of a primary transmission simultaneously with the primary broadcast; also, a nonsimultaneous transmission of a primary broadcast by a cable system not located within the United States.

Section 8 affidavit Declaration of continued use of a federally registered trademark filed between the fifth and sixth year following registration. Failure to file in this time period will result in the registration being cancelled and may result in loss of trademark rights.

Section 9 affidavit Declaration seeking renewal of a federal trademark registration; must be filed within six months of the expiration of the term of trademark registration, or within three months thereafter, in which event the applicant must also pay a late filing fee.

Section 15 affidavit Declaration of five years of continuous use of a federally registered trademark on the Principal Register; if filed and accepted by the Patent and Trademark Office, the mark becomes incontestable.

Section 44 application Application for federal trademark registration by the foreign owner of a mark registered in a foreign country, provided that country is a party to an international convention or treaty of which the United States is a member.

secure test A nonmarketed test administered under supervision at specified centers on specified dates, all copies of which are accounted for and either destroyed or returned to restricted locked storage following each administration. A test is *nonmarketed* if copies are not sold and the test is distributed and used in such a manner that ownership and control of copies remain with the test sponsor or publisher.

senior user   The first party to adopt and use a particular mark in connection with its goods or services.

serial   Work, such as a newspaper, magazine, newsletter, or journal, issued or intended to be issued in successive parts bearing numerical or chronological designations and intended to be continued indefinitely.

service mark   Mark used in the sale or advertising of services to identify and distinguish services performed for the benefit of others.

settlement   Agreement between the parties in which the dispute is formally resolved.

shop right   Power of an employer to claim the non-exclusive right to use in its business an invention made by an employee using company time, facilities, or materials.

shrinkwrap agreement   A license between the manufacturer of a computer software program and a consumer, which grants certain legal rights and warranties in exchange for the right to use the program; usually triggered by the opening of the plastic shrinkwrap containing the computer software program diskettes or by return of the software registration or warranty card.

single file database   Database that consists of data records pertaining to a single common subject matter.

sound recordings   Works that result from the fixation of a series of musical, spoken, or other sounds, but not including the sounds accompanying a motion picture or other audiovisual work, regardless of the nature of the material objects, such as disks, tapes, or other phonorecords, in which they are embodied.

specification   Patent application disclosure by the inventor; drafted so that an individual skilled in the art to which the invention pertains could, by reading the patent, make and use the invention without the necessity of further experiment.

Statement of Use   Declaration indicating use of a mark in commerce; the declaration can be filed only after a Notice of Allowance has been issued.

statute of limitations   Time limit during which the plaintiff must file a lawsuit. In copyright, it is three years from the date when the infringing activity occurred (or when the copyright owner could have reasonably known that the infringing activity occurred).

statutory damages   An award of damages prescribed by statute and not contingent upon proof of the plaintiff's loss or the defendant's profits.

substantial similarity   Two works have similarities that can result only from copying, rather than from coincidence, common source derivation, or independent creation.

summons   Document served with the complaint, which explains that the defendant has been sued and has a certain time limit within which to respond.

suppression   Concealment or acts of delay in introducing an invention, which can result in loss of the inventor's claim of priority of invention.

synchronization right   The right to record music in timed relation to visual images and to reproduce, perform, and distribute the musical work in connection with an audiovisual work.

temporary restraining order (TRO)
Injunction, often granted ex parte, that is of short duration and remains in effect only until the court has an opportunity to schedule a hearing for and rule on a motion for a preliminary injunction.

tenancy in common   A legal form of co-ownership of property that grants to each co-owner an independent right to use or license the property, subject to a duty of accounting to the other co-owners for any profits; upon a co-owner's death, that co-owner's share goes to his or her beneficiaries or heirs, but not to other co-owners.

tie-in   See *tying*.

trade dress   The total image and overall appearance of a product or service.

trade name   Name of a business or company; generally not protectible as a trademark unless used to identify and distinguish goods or services.

trade secret   Any formula, pattern, device, or compilation of information that is used in a business, that is the subject of reasonable efforts to preserve confidentiality, and that gives the owner of the secret an opportunity to obtain an advantage over competitors who do not know or use it.

trademark Any word, symbol, design, device, slogan, or combination that identifies and distinguishes goods.

trademark infringement Use of a substantially similar mark by a junior user that creates a likelihood of consumer confusion.

trademark license Agreement granting limited trademark rights.

transfer of copyright ownership An assignment, mortgage, exclusive license, transfer by will or intestate succession or any other change in the ownership of any or all of the exclusive rights in a copyright, whether or not it is limited in time or place of effect, but not including a nonexclusive license.

transmit To communicate a copyrighted work by any device or process whereby images or sounds are received beyond the place from which they are sent.

tying (also called tie-in) Business practice by which the purchase of a patented item is tied to a second, nonpatented item; an unjustified tying arrangement is patent misuse.

unclean hands Defense asserted when the plaintiff has committed a serious act of wrongdoing in regard to the lawsuit or the activity precipitating the lawsuit.

unfair competition A collection of common law principles that protect against unfair business practices.

use in commerce Use of a trademark by placing it on goods or containers, tags or labels, displays associated with the goods (or, if otherwise impracticable, on documents associated with the goods) and selling or transporting the goods in commerce regulated by the United States.

    Also, use of a service mark when the mark is used or displayed in the sale or advertising of services and the services are rendered in commerce regulated by the United States.

useful article An article having an intrinsic utilitarian function that is not merely to portray the appearance of the article or to convey information. An article that is normally a part of a useful article is considered a useful article.

usefulness An invention must have a use or purpose and must work (i.e., be capable of performing its intended purpose).

utility patents Legal protection granted for inventions or discoveries that are categorized as machines, processes, compositions, articles of manufacture, or new uses of any of these.

vicarious infringer See *contributory infringer.*

visually perceptible copy A copy that can be visually observed when it is embodied in a material object, either directly or with the aid of a machine or device.

voir dire Process by which the judge and attorneys for the parties question potential jurors.

work made for hire (1) a work prepared by an employee within the scope of his or her employment; or (2) a work specially ordered or commissioned for use as a contribution to a collective work, as a part of a motion picture or other audiovisual work, as a translation, as a supplementary work, as a compilation, as an instructional text, as a test, as answer material for a test, or as an atlas, if the parties expressly agree in a written instrument signed by them that the work shall be considered a work made for hire.

work of authorship Creation of intellectual or artistic effort fixed or embodied in a perceptible form and meeting the statutory standards of copyright protection.

work of visual art Under the Copyright Act of 1976, either (1) a painting, drawing, print, or sculpture, existing in a single copy, in a limited edition of 200 copies or fewer that are signed and consecutively numbered by the author, or, in the case of a sculpture, in multiple cast, carved, or fabricated sculptures of 200 or fewer that are consecutively numbered by the author and bear the signature or other identifying mark of the author; or (2) a still photographic image produced for exhibition purposes only, existing in a single copy that is signed by the author, or in a limited edition of 200 copies or fewer that are signed and consecutively numbered by the author.

writ of seizure Order of the court directing the federal marshal to seize and hold infringing merchandise; granted only upon payment of a bond of not less than twice the value of the infringing articles.

INDEX

NOTE: Italicized page numbers refer to non-text material.